Music Finders
Series Editor: David Daniels

Designed with working musicians, conductors, program directors, and librarians in mind, these practical reference books put the music you need at your fingertips: title, publisher, duration, instrumentation, and appendixes for cross-referencing are all provided in these carefully researched volumes. Using the orchestral repertoire as a starting point, this series will also encompass chamber music, ballet, opera, thematic music, and repertoire of individual instruments.

The Music Finders series is based on the Scarecrow titles *Orchestral Music: A Handbook* by David Daniels (2005) and *Orchestral Pops: A Handbook* by Lucy Manning (2008).

Chamber Orchestra and Ensemble Repertoire: A Catalog of Modern Music, by Dirk Meyer. 2011.

Chamber Orchestra and Ensemble Repertoire

A Catalog of Modern Music

Dirk Meyer

The Scarecrow Press, Inc.
Lanham, Maryland • Toronto • Plymouth, UK
2011

SCARECROW PRESS, INC.

Published in the United States of America
by Scarecrow Press, Inc.
A wholly owned subsidary of The Rowman & Littlefield Publishing Group, Inc.
4501 Forbes Boulevard, Suite 200, Lanham, Maryland 20706
www.scarecrowpress.com

Estover Road
Plymouth PL6 7PY
United Kingdom

British Library Cataloguing in Publication Information Available

Library of Congress Cataloging-in-Publication Data
Meyer, Dirk, 1977–
  Chamber orchestra and ensemble repertoire : a catalog of modern music / Dirk Meyer.
    p. cm. — (Music finders)
  Includes bibliographical references.
  ISBN 978-0-8108-7731-3 (cloth : alk. paper)
1. Chamber orchestra music–20th century–Bibliography. 2. Chamber orchestra music–21st century–Bibliography. 3. Instrumental ensembles–20th century–Bibliography. 4. Instrumental ensembles–21st century–Bibliography. 5. Chamber music–20th century–Bibliography. 6. Chamber music–21st century–Bibliography. I. Title.
  ML128.O5M49 2011
  016.78430263–dc22   2010043229

♾™ The paper used in this publication meets the minimum requirements of American National Standard for Information Sciences—Permanence of Paper for Printed Library Materials, ANSI/NISO Z39.48-1992.
Manufactured in the United States of America.

To my parents,

Astrid & Peter

CONTENTS

FOREWORD

This book is the first in the Scarecrow Press series of *Music Finders*, intended to assist the user in finding the right music at the right time for the right purpose. It is appropriate to begin this series with a book like Dirk Meyer's—a book that is firmly anchored in the music of our own time.

The twentieth century saw a loosening of the boundaries between music for chamber ensemble on the one hand and for small orchestra on the other. In part this may have been because the increasing complexity of rhythm and texture in the last century made the presence of a conductor increasingly necessary.

So it is well that *Chamber Orchestra and Ensemble Repertoire: A Catalog of Modern Music* leaves behind such arbitrary distinctions. Dirk Meyer has produced a reference work that will prove invaluable to contemporary music ensembles as well as chamber orchestras.

David Daniels

PREFACE

Some years ago, while acquiring my graduate degrees, I founded a chamber orchestra. My friends used to call it the *DLO* (Dirk's Little Orchestra). My goal was to promote modern music by performing the music of the twentieth and twenty-first centuries and commissioning new works from young composers.

Soon it became clear that the biggest challenge that I would encounter with the *DLO* was to research repertoire. There was no source available that would provide all the performance information needed: What is the instrumentation? How long is the piece? Who is the publisher? The fact that my needs were very specific—with a very limited instrumentation, sometimes even representing an odd combination of instruments—did not make it any easier. That was how the idea for this catalog was born.

Today, just like during my college years, there is no reference book for chamber orchestra music available. To my knowledge the only such attempt that has ever been made is Cecilia Saltonstall's *Catalog of Music for Small Orchestra*, first published in 1947 and revised in 1981.[1] Unfortunately this work has long been out of print and it does not provide the reader with all the useful appendices that make a reference book valuable.

This catalog attempts to fill this gap. It provides all the performance information necessary for almost four thousand titles. It is divided into three categories: chamber orchestra, ensemble and string orchestra. Much like David Daniels's book *Orchestral Music*,[2] it includes an extended appendix that will allow the user to research the compositions according to certain criteria such as instrumentation or duration. And since this is a catalog for modern music, I also included a listing of twenty-first century repertoire.

The majority of the information included in this catalog was collected from publishers' websites and catalogs. Unfortunately those sources are not always reliable and so, when available, I checked the scores or parts to verify the given information. Nevertheless, this is not the case for all listings. While I have tried to verify the information as thoroughly and comprehensively as possible, there will be some inaccuracies. My goal is to continuously improve this catalog, and I appreciate any comments or corrections that the user might have.

In recent years more and more major orchestras have programmed repertoire for chamber orchestra—for financial as well as esthetic reasons. At the same time we have seen a growth of New Music ensembles, especially in university and conservatory circles. My hope is that this catalog will help to facilitate the work of conductors, librarians, and administrators, and make a whole new world of exciting instrumental repertoire more accessible.

Terms & Criteria

The terms "chamber orchestra" and "ensemble" are very broad and can include all sorts of different groups and sizes. In the following, the term "ensemble" will be used for smaller groups of about seven to fifteen players. Anything larger will be referred to as "chamber orchestra." The term "string orchestra" refers to any group that consists of only string players. Any combination of violins, violas, celli and double basses may be used and no specific size limitations apply.

The amount of available repertoire for any size orchestra or ensemble is overwhelming. So for the purposes of this catalog I have limited the repertoire included by the following criteria:

---

[1] Saltonstall, *Catalog of Music for Small Orchestra* (Washington, DC: Music Library Assn., 1947) and Saltonstall, *A New Catalog of Music for Small Orchestra* (Stratham, 1981).
[2] Daniels, *Orchestral Music: A Handbook*, fourth edition (Lanham, MD: The Scarecrow Press, 2005).

- Only compositions written around 1900 and later are included.
- The minimum size for ensembles is seven players.
- The maximum size for chamber orchestras can obviously vary greatly depending on the number of string players used, but the largest pieces included in this catalog can be performed with an orchestra of about 45 players.
- No compositions for band are included.
- Choir works and chamber operas or oratorios are not included.
- Works that are written entirely for electronics (no actual instrumentalists involved) are not included.
- All compositions must be available through a publishing house or directly through the composer.

Often times I did not include a composition in this catalog if it is already listed in Daniels's above mentioned book. Of course this is not to say that there will be no duplicates, but it illuminates the fact that this catalog should be seen in addition to his book.

Instrumentation Formula

This catalog uses the same instrumentation formula as David Daniels's *Orchestral Music: A Handbook*[3] (fourth edition). It is arranged in the following order:
    Flutes, Oboes, Clarinets, Bassoons — Horns, Trumpets, Trombones, Tuba — Saxophones — Auxiliary Instruments — Percussion — Harp — Piano — Strings (with the string count given in brackets where necessary)

Additional instruments and other comments are given in brackets. A dot (.) separates one player from another, a slash (/) indicates doubling. Example:

    1[1/pic] 2[1.2/eh] 2[1.bcl] 1 — 1 0 1[btbn] 0 — ssx/asx — accordion — 1perc — hpsd — str[1.1.1.1.1]

This composition calls for:
1 Flute (doubling on Piccolo)
2 Oboes (the second doubling on English Horn)
2 Clarinets (the second playing bass clarinet throughout)
1 Bassoon
1 Horn
no Trumpets
1 Bass Trombone
no Tuba
1 Saxophone (one player doubling soprano and alto saxophones)
1 Accordion
1 Percussionist
1 Harpsichord
Strings (1 First Violin, 1 Second Violin, 1 Viola, 1 Cello, 1 Bass)

A list of percussion instruments is provided whenever available.

---

[3] Daniels, *Orchestral Music: A Handbook*, fourth edition (Lanham, MD: The Scarecrow Press, 2005).

Duration, Movements and Date of Composition

The duration of the piece is given in minutes. Obviously the duration of a work depends on many factors and the given value is an approximation. Wherever known, I have included the durations of the different movements. If the movements have distinctive titles (as opposed to just tempo indications), these are listed too. The date of the composition is given in brackets after the title, wherever available.

Publishers

The compositions included in this catalog are all published and readily available. The publisher is listed at the bottom of each entry. A complete list of publishers can be found in the appendix.

Verein für Musikalische Privataufführungen

In 1918 Arnold Schönberg founded the *Verein für Musikalische Privataufführungen* (Society for Private Musical Performances) in Vienna. During the three years of its existence, the members of this society produced a large amount of arrangements of major symphonic works. While most of these arrangements were transcriptions for one or two pianos or for other small chamber groups, a total of twenty-two arrangements were created for larger ensembles. Most of these titles are unknown to the larger public but would make a wonderful addition to any chamber orchestra concert. A listing with all available information about these arrangements can be found in the appendix (see page 399). I hope that their inclusion in this catalog will help to promote these one-of-a-kind compositions.

Acknowledgements

This catalog was first started during my time at Michigan State University. Back then my teachers Leon Gregorian and Raphael Jimenez, as well as my old friend and mentor Kevin Rhodes, were extremely helpful and supportive of this endeavor.

In recent years many other people have been critical in the completion of this book, and I am grateful to all of them! A special mention needs to be extended to Justin Vibbard, Principal Librarian of the Sarasota Orchestra. Not only was his assistance crucial for creating a functional database that I could work with, he was also always available whenever I needed advice on the world of music publishers and bibliography.

Obviously this catalog is designed after David Daniels's *Orchestral Music: A Handbook*. Not only do I owe a debt of gratitude to him for letting me venture into a different area of orchestral repertoire following his example. I am also grateful for his support during the creation of this catalog. His help and advice were crucial for the completion of my work.

Finally I would like to thank my wife, Jennifer, for her support and endurance of many long days in front of the computer, which usually resulted in a less than desirable state of mind on my part.

ABBREVIATIONS

/	One player doubles on two instruments	kybd	Keyboard
4hand	4 Hands (Piano, etc.)	lg	large
A	Alto Voice	mand	Mandolin
ad lib	ad libitum (optional)	marac	Maracas
afl	Alto Flute	marim	Marimba
amp	amplified	Mz	Mezzo-Soprano Voice
asx	Alto Saxophone	ob	Oboe
atbn	Alto Trombone	ob d'am	Oboe d'amore
B	Bass Voice	obdac	Oboe da Caccia
Bar	Baritone Voice	opt	optional
basset hn	Basset Horn	org	Organ
bassx	Bass Saxophone	ped bd	Pedal Bass Drum
bcl	Bass Clarinet	perc	Percussion
bd	Bass Drum	pic	Piccolo Flute
bfl	Bass Flute	pic tpt	Piccolo Trumpet
bgtr	Bass Guitar	pf	Piano
bn	Bassoon	prepf	Prepared Piano
bsx	Baritone Saxophone	rec	Recorder (Flute)
btbn	Bass Trombone	S	Soprano Voice
btpt	Bass Trumpet	sandblk	Sandblock (Percussion)
cast	Castanets	sd	Snare Drum
cbcl	Contrabass Clarinet	set	Drum Set, Drum Kit
cbn	Contra Bassoon	sizzle cym	Sizzle Cymbal
cbtbn	Contrabass Trombone	sm	small
cbtu	Contrabass Tuba	ssx	Soprano Saxophone
cel	Celesta	str	Strings
cimb	Cimbalom	str 4t	String Quartet
cl	Clarinet	str 5t	String Quintet
crot	Crotales	sus	suspended
crt	Cornet	sx	Saxophone
CT	Counter Tenor Voice	synth	Synthesizer
cym	Cymbals (pair of crash cymbals)	T	Tenor Voice
db	Double Bass	tambn	Tambourine
dr	Drum	tbn	Trombone
Ebcl	E-flat Clarinet	td	Tenor Drum
eh	English Horn	templeblk	Templeblock
elec	electric (i.e., guitar)	tmp	Timpani
elec bgtr	Electric Bass Guitar	tpt	Trumpet
elec gtr	Electric Guitar	tri	Triangle
elec org	Electric Organ	tsx	Tenor Saxophone
elec pf	Electric Piano	ttbn	Tenor Trombone
euph	Euphonium	tu	Tuba
field dr	Field Drum	va	Viola
fl	Flute	vc	Violoncello
flug	Flugel Horn	vib	Vibraphone
glsp	Glockenspiel	vn	Violin
gtr	Guitar	w/	with
ham org	Hammond Organ	w/o	without
harm	Harmonium	wag tu	Wagner Tuba
hi-hat	Hi-Hat Cymbal	woodblk	Woodblock
hn	French Horn	xyl	Xylophone
hpsd	Harpsichord		

ALPHABETICAL LISTING BY COMPOSER

A

Aa, Michel van der (1970-)

Above; For Ensemble and Soundtrack (1999)   16'
1 1 1 1 — 0 1 0 0 — tape — 1perc — str[1.1.1.1.1]
Soundtrack can be purchased.
Donemus

Attach; For Ensemble and Soundtrack (1999)   17'
0 1 2[1.bcl] 1 — 0 1 0 0 — tape — 2perc — str[1.1.1.1.1]
Donemus

Here trilogy; For Soprano, Chamber Orchestra and Soundtrack (2001-2003)   50'
solo S
0 0 2 1 — 0 1 1 0 — soundtrack — 2perc — str[6.6.6.4.2]
See individual listings for detailed information.
Contents - Here [enclosed]; Here [in circles]; Here [to be found]
mvt durations: 17' 15' 18'
Donemus

Here [enclosed] (2003)   17'
0 0 1 1 — 0 1 1 0 — laptop, "theatrical object" — 1perc — str[6.6.6.4.2]
Donemus

Here [in circles] (2002)   15'
solo S
0 0 2[1.bcl] 0 — 0 1 0 0 — tape — 1perc — str[1.1.1.1.1]
Donemus

Here [to be found] (2001)   18'
solo S
0 0 1 1 — 0 1 1 0 — laptop — 1perc — str[6.6.6.4.2]
Donemus

Imprint; For Baroque Orchestra (2005)   14'
solo vn
0 2 0 0 — 0 0 0 0 — portative organ — hpsd — str[4.4.3.2.1]
Portative organ to be played by solo violinist. Period instruments (415 Hz tuning) or modern instruments played in a baroque way.
Boosey & Hawkes

Abels, Michael (1962-)

Delights & Dances (2007)   12'
solo str 4t
str
Subito

Frederick's Fables (1993-1994)   37'
solo narrator
2[1.2/pic] 2[1.2/eh] 2[1.2/bcl] 2 — 2 2 2 0 — tmp+2 — hp — cel — str
Based on the stories of Leo Lionni
Contents - 1. Frederick; 2. The Greentail Mouse; 3. Theodore & the Talking Mushroom; 4. Alexander & the Wind-Up Mouse
mvt durations: 7' 10' 9' 11'
Subito

More Seasons (1999)   12'
2[1.2/pic] 2 0 2 — 2 2 0 0 — tmp — hpsd — str
Early baroque themes served in a late 20th-century puree.
Subito

Abendroth, Walter (1896-1973)

Concerto for Orchestra, op.14 (1935)   19'
2 2 2 2 — 4 2 0 0 — tmp+1 — str
perc: cym, sd, td, tri
Sikorski

Divertimento für Kammerorchester, op.24 (1949)   16'
1 1 1 1 — 1 1 1 0 — 2perc — str
Sikorski

Konzertante Phantasie für Orchester, op.23 (1948)   16'
1 2 0 2 — 0 3 2 0 — tmp+1 — hpsd — str
perc: tri
Sikorski

Sinfonietta, op.32 (1959)   19'
1 2 1 2 — 1 2 2 0 — tmp+1 — str
Contents - 1. Comodo; 2. Adagio; 3. Moderato
mvt durations: 5' 8' 6'
Sikorski

Abrahamsen, Hans   (1952-)

Aarhus Ragtime (1990)   3'
  1[1/pic] 1 1 1 — 1 1 1 0 — 1perc — pf —
  str[1.1.1.1.1]
  Hansen

Foam (1970)   14'
  2 1 1 1 — 1 1 1 0 — 4perc — hp — pf —
  str[2.2.3.3.2]
  Hansen

Märchenbilder (1984)   14'
  1 1 1 1 — 1 1 1 0 — 1perc — pf — str[1.1.1.1.1]
  Hansen

Stratifications (1975)   8'
  2 2 2 1 — 2 2 1 0 — 2perc — pf — str
  Hansen

Absil, Jean   (1893-1974)

Deux Danses Rituelles   7'
  2[1.2/pic] 1 2 2 — 3 0 0 0 — 2perc — hp — cel
  — str
  Chester Novello

Introduction et Valses (1964)   13'
  2[1.2/pic] 1 2 1 — 3 2 1 0 — tmp+1 — hp — str
  Chester Novello

Petite Suite, op.20 (1936)   12'
  1 1 1 1 — 2 0 0 0 — tmp+1 — str
  Contents - 1. Marche; 2. Conte; 3. Carrousel
  Bosworth; Fleisher; Schirmer

Sérénade (1965)
  2[1.2/pic] 2 2 2 — 2 2 0 0 — tmp+2 — hp — cel
  — str
  Chester Novello

Triptique   10'
  2[1.2/pic] 1 2 2 — 3 0 0 0 — tmp+1 — cel — str
  Chester Novello

Acker, Dieter   (1940-2006)

Texturae II (1972)   21'
  solo pf
  1[1/afl/pic] 1[1/eh] 1[1/bcl] 1 — 1 0 0 0 — 2perc
  — str[4.0.2.2.1]
  Breitkopf

Adamo, Mark   (1962-)

Alcott Music: Suite from "Little   20'
Women" (2007)
  1perc — hp — pf/cel — str
  perc: chimes, glsp, ratchet sd, sm sus cym, sm tam-tam, tmp,vib
  Schirmer

Overture to Lysistrata (2005)   4'
  2[1.2/pic] 2[1.eh] 2[1.2/asx] 2 — 2 2 0 0 —
  tmp+2 — str
  Schirmer

Adams, John   (1947-)

Chairman Dances; Foxtrot for   12'
Orchestra (1985)
  2[1/pic.2/pic] 2 2[1.2/bcl] 2 — 4 2 2 1 — tmp+3
  — hp — pf — str
  perc: ped bd, cym, sus cym, sizzle cym, hi-hat, sd, tri, tambn, glsp,
  xyl, vib, crot, belltree, claves, cast, sandblks, 2 woodblks
  AMP; Schirmer

Chamber Symphony (1992)   22'
  1[pic] 1 2[Ebcl.bcl] 2[1.cbn] — 1 1 1 0 — 1perc
  — kybd — str[1.0.1.1.1]
  perc: claves, conga, cowbell, hi-hat, sd, ped bd, woodblk, 2 bongos,
  3 tom-tom, roto toms, tambn, timbale, dr set
  Keyboard sampler = Yamaha SY-77/SY-99 or Kurzweil
  K2000/2500. Complete technical specification on
  www.earbox.com/tech-guide/ep/ja-cs-eq.htm
  Contents - 1. Mongrel Airs; 2. Aria with walking bass; 3.
  Roadrunner   · great music, very hard
  mvt durations: 8' 8' 6'   · different
  Boosey & Hawkes

Christian Zeal and Activity (1973)   10'
  1 0 1 1 — 0 0 0 0 — recorded tape — hp — str
  Tape may also be prepared by performing organization.
  Boosey & Hawkes

Shaker Loops (1978)   25'
  str
  Arranged for String Orchestra in 1983.
  AMP
  - in the Chairman dances sound world
  - harder than it sounds?

Addison, John   (1920-1998)

Concerto for Trumpet and Strings   18'
  solo tpt
  1perc — str
  Schirmer (E.C.)

Adès, Thomas (1971-)

Chamber Symphony, op.2 (1990)   13'
1[pic/afl] 1 2[basset hn.bcl] 0 — 1 1 1 0 — 2perc
— pf — str[1.1.1.1.1]
perc: tri, cowbell, woodblk, sd, hit-hat, guiro, 3 tam-tam, 2 sm finger
drum, wood chimes, flexatone, bell tree, shell chimes, marim, crot
Tpt doubles on wine bottle, pf doubles on accordion.
Faber

Concerto Conciso, op.18 (1997)   8'
solo pf
0 0 1 0 — 0 1 1 1 — bsx — 1perc — str[3.0.0.0.1]
perc: tmp, crot, roto toms, tuned templeblks, 2 wood dr, log dr, wood
chimes, hi-hat, tam-tam, anvil, ped bd
All strings and clarinet need amplification, bass requires a
contact microphone.
Faber

Living Toys, op.9 (1993)   17'
1[1/pic] 1[1/eh] 1[Ebcl/bcl] 1[1/cbn] — 1 1[1/pic tpt]
1 0 — 1perc — pf — str[1.1.1.1.1]
perc: 3 gong, 2 tmp, 2 crot, talking drum, tri, 2 sus cym, sus sheet of
paper, 2 cowbell, 2 templeblks, guiro, cast, small sd, field dr, ped bd,
vibraslap
Ob doubles on sopranino rec. Hn doubles on whip.
Faber

The Origin of the Harp, op.13   9'
(1994)
0 0 3[1.2/bcl.3/bcl] 0 — 0 0 0 0 — 1perc —
str[0.0.3.3.0]
perc: 3 sus cym, szl cym, 2 windchimes, bd, 2 pair of marimba
mallets with small rattles attached, 7 gong, marim, 2 ped rototom,
tmp, marimbula, pf
Third vc doubles on rainstick.
Faber

Adler, Samuel (1928-)

Beyond the Pale; A Portrait of a   14'
Klezmer for Clarinet and String
Orchestra (2007)
solo cl
str
Presser

City By The Lake; A Portrait of   7'
Rochester, NY (1968)
2[1.2/pic] 2 2 2 — 2 2 3 1 — tmp+1 — hp — str
Schirmer

Concertino for Strings (1956)   10'
str
Schirmer

Concerto for Guitar and Orchestra   21'
(1994)
solo gtr
2 2 2 2 — 2 2 0 0 — tmp+1 — str
Presser

Concerto for Horn and Orchestra   20'
(2002)
solo hn
2 2 2 2 — 2 2 0 0 — tmp+1 — str
Presser

Concerto No.2 for Piano and   22'
Orchestra (1997)
solo pf
2 2 2 2 — 2 2 2 1 — tmp+2 — str
Presser

Elegy for String Orchestra (1962)   8'
str
Presser

Show An Affirming Flame; A Poem   5'
for Orchestra ("September 1, 1939"
by W. H. Auden) (2001)
2[1.2/pic] 2 2 2 — 2 2 0 0 — tmp+1 — str
Presser

Time In Tempest Everywhere; For   17'
Soprano, Oboe and Chamber
Orchestra (1993)
solo S, ob
2 1 2 2 — 2 0 0 0 — 1perc — pf — str
After poems by W. H. Auden.
Presser

Adolphe, Bruce (1955-)

Marita and Her Heart's Desire; A   22'
Chamber Music Fairy Tale for
Family Audiences (1993)
1[1/pic] 1 1 1 — 0 0 1 0 — female narrator with
multiple voices — 1perc — hp — str[1.1.1.1.1]
MMB

Three Pieces; For Kids in the   12'
Audience and Chamber Orchestra
(1988)
2 2 2 2 — 2 2 0 0 — kids in the audience — str
Live performance includes rehearsal with audience.
Movements may be performed separately.
Contents - 1. Ta Woop; 2. Rainbow; 3. T-D-T (Texture-
Dynamics-Timbre)
MMB

Aguila, Miguel del   (1957-)

Concerto for Clarinet (2003)   20'
solo cl
1 1 1 1 — 1 1 1 1 — 2perc — pf — str[1.0.1.1.1]
perc: I: tambn, military dr, tmp, bd, tri, sus cym, cym, tam-tam II:
glsp, xyl, 2 tom-tom, pea whistle, 2 marac, chimes, 4 templeblks
Version for full strings is available too.
Peer

Concerto for Piano (1997)   25'
solo pf
2[1.2/pic] 2[1.2/eh] 2[1.2/bcl] 2[1.2/cbn] — 2 2 2
1 — 2perc — str
Peer

Conga for Orchestra, op.44 (1994)   11'
2[1.2/pic] 2 2 2 — 3 2 2 1 — tmp+4 — hp — pf
— str
perc: tri, xyl, glass wind chimes, cowbells, bird whistle, jazz bell,
woodblk, bd, congas, timbales, hi-hat, 2 tom-tom, whip, tam-tam,
marac, sus cym, glsp, 2 police whistles, wind machine, cym, chimes,
military dr
Orchestral version of his "Conga Line in Hell." Possible with
3 percussionists with authorized omissions.
Peer

A Conga Line in Hell, op.40 (1993)   11'
1 0 1 0 — 0 0 0 0 — 1perc — hp — pf —
str[0.0.0.8.0]
Peer

A Conga Line in Hell, op.43 (1994)   11'
1 1 1 1 — 1 1 1 1 — 1perc — hp — pf —
str[1.1.1.1.1]
Version for ensemble.
Peer

Hexen (1987)   12'
solo bn
str
Peer

Salon Buenos Aires; Orchestral   21'
Version (2010)
2 2 2 2 — 2 2 1 0 — tmp+2 — hp — pf/cel — str
perc: glsp, vib, xyl, lg sus cym, sm sus cym, marac, bd, wind
machine, tri, tam-tam, cym, cowbell, timbales, reco-reco, agogo,
samba whistle
Contents - 1. Samba; 2. Tango to Dream (Tango para
soñar); 3. Obsessed Milonga (Milonga obsesionada)
mvt durations: 5' 11' 5'
Peer

Toccata, op.28 (1988)   7'
1[1/pic] 1 1 1 — 2 1 1 1 — 6perc — pf — str
perc: I: 3 tmp, reco-reco II: 2 bongos, conga, sus cym III: agogo
bells, bd, 2 tom-tom, templeblks IV: chimes, 2 bottles, hi-hat, tri, sd
V: xyl, marac, tam-tam, siren VI: glsp, woodblk, tambn, cym
Peer

Aitken, Robert   (1939-)

Spiral (1975)   16'
2 2 2 2 — 2 2 0 0 — 1perc — str
Peer

Albéniz, Isaac   (1860-1909)

Iberia: Evocatión (1906)   7'
2[1.2/afl] 2 2[1.2/bcl] 2 — 2 2 0 0 — 1perc — str
Orchestrated by Jesús Rueda (2005).
Tritó

Iberia: Lavapiés (1908)   7'
2 2 2 2 — 2 2 0 0 — 1perc — str
Orchestrated by Jesús Rueda (2005).
Tritó

Iberia: Triana (1907)   6'
2 2 2[1.2/bcl] 2 — 2 2 0 0 — tmp+1 — str
Orchestrated by Jesús Rueda (2005).
Tritó

Albert, Stephen   (1941-1992)

Distant Hills; Chamber Version   31'
(1989)
solo S, T
1 1 1 1 — 1 0 0 0 — pf — str[1.1.1.1.1]
Extra strings may be added.
Contents - 1. Sun's Heat; 2. Flower of the Mountain
Schirmer

Flower of the Mountain: From   16'
"Distant Hills" (1985)
solo S
1 1 1 1 — 1 0 0 0 — pf — str[1.1.1.1.1]
Extra strings may be added.
Schirmer

Flower of the Mountain: From   16'
"Distant Hills." Version for full
Orchestra (1985)
solo S
2[1.2/pic] 2[1.2/eh] 2 2 — 2 2 0 0 — tmp+1 — hp
— pf — str
Schirmer

Into Eclipse; Chamber with voice   30'
version. (1981)
solo T
1[pic] 0 1[Ebcl] 0 — 1 1 0 0 — 2perc — hp — pf
— str[1.1.1.1.1]
Schirmer

TreeStone (1983) 45'
  solo S, T
  1 0 1 0 — 1 1 0 0 — 1perc — hp — pf —
  str[1.1.1.1.1]
  Schirmer

Albin, Roger (1920-2001)

Chantefables pour les enfants 10'
sages; Pour Soprano et 20
musiciens
  solo S
  1 1 2 2 — 1 1 1 0 — tmp+3 — hp — pf/cel —
  str[1.1.1.1.1]
  After texts by Robert Desnos.
  Rideau Rouge

Albright, William Hugh (1944-1998)

Gothic Suite; For Organ, Strings 16'
and Percussion (1973)
  solo org
  1perc — str
  Strings without db.
  Contents - 1. Masque; 2. Cakewalk; 3. Tarantella Demente
  UE

Alexandrov, Anatoly (1888-1982)

Classic Suite in B-flat major, op.32 18'
(1926)
  3 2 2 2 — 2 1 0 0 — tmp+1 — str
  Schirmer

Alfvén, Hugo (1872-1960)

Elegi; För liten orkester, ur 4'
orkestersviten Gustav II Adolf
(1938)
  0 1 2 1 — 0 0 0 0 — str
  Fleisher; Gehrmans

Alizade, Akshin (1937-)

Symphony No.4 (1998) 13'
  1 1 1 1 — 1 0 0 0 — 1perc — str[5.5.4.3.2]
  Schirmer

Ali-Zadeh, Franghiz (1947-)

Crossing II (1993) 15'
  1 1 0 1 — 1 0 1 0 — 1perc — hp — str[1.0.1.1.1]
  perc: vib -EF music. PP
  Schirmer - extended technique

Dilogie II for Nine Players (1989) 14'
  1 1 1 1 — 1 0 0 0 — str[1.1.1.1.0]
  Schirmer

Mirage for Ud and Chamber 10'
Ensemble (1998)
  solo Ud
  1 1 1 0 — 0 0 0 0 — mand — tmp+2 — hp —
  str[1.0.1.1.1]
  Schirmer

Silk Road; Concerto for Percussion 25'
and Chamber Orchestra (1999)
  solo perc
  1 1 1 1 — 1 0 1 0 — str
  Schirmer

Sturm und Drang for Chamber 13'
Orchestra (1998)
  1 1 1 1 — 1 0 0 0 — 1perc — str[5.5.4.3.2]
  Schirmer

Almand, Claude (1915-1957)

Chorale for Chamber Orchestra 5'
  1 1 2 0 — 2 0 0 0 — str
  Fleisher

Alnar, Hasan Ferit (1906-1978)

Zwei Türkische Orchesterstücke; 15'
Improvisation und zwei Tänze
(1935)
  2 2 2 2 — 2 2 0 0 — 1perc — str
  UE

Alonso-Crespo, Eduardo (1956-)

Concerto for Bassoon (1996) 24'
  solo bn
  2 1 2 0 — 2 0 0 0 — tmp+3 — pf — str
  Subito

Sinfonietta for Strings (1996) 10'
str
Subito

Yubarta: Overture (1989) 5'
2 2 2 2 — 2 2 1 0 — tmp+2 — hp — str
Subito

Alwyn, William (1905-1985)

Concerto Grosso No.1 in Bb (1943) 11'
1 1 0 0 — 2 1 0 0 — tmp+1 — str
Lengnick

Elizabethan Dances for Orchestra 16'
(1958)
2 2 2 2 — 4 3 3 0 — tmp+1 — hp — cel — str
Lengnick

Sinfonietta for String Orchestra 26'
(1970)
str
Lengnick

Amram, David (1930-)

Shakespearean Concerto 22'
0 1 0 0 — 2 0 0 0 — str
Peters

Amrhein, Karen Amanda (1970-)

Event Horizon; For Clarinet and 15'
Orchestra (2002)
solo cl
1 1 1 1 — 2 0 0 1[euph] — 1perc — pf — str
perc: marim
Contents - 1. Prelude; 2. Night; 3. Event Horizon
Happy Lemon

Amy, Gilbert (1936-)

7 Sites; For 14 players (1975) 20'
1 0 1 0 — 1 1 0 0 — 2perc — hp — pf —
str[1.1.2.2.0]
UE

D'Après "Ecrits Sur Toiles"; Pour 16'
Orchestre de Chambre (1984)
2[1/afl.2/pic] 2[1.2/eh] 2 2 — 2 0 0 0 —
str[6.6.4.4.2]
Amphion

Echos 13; For Horn, Trombone,
Harp, Piano and 9 Instruments
(1976)
solo hn, tbn, hp, pf
2 0 2[1.bcl] 1 — 0 0 0 0 — str[1.0.1.1.1]
UE

Écrits Sur Toiles; Pour Ensemble 17'
de Chambre & Voix récitée (1983)
solo narrator
1[1/pic] 0 1 0 — 1 0 0 0 — pf/cel — str[1.0.1.1.0]
After letters by Rainer Maria Rilke.
Amphion

Jeux et formes; For Oboe and 28'
Chamber Ensemble (1971)
solo ob
1 1 2 1 — 1 2 2 0 — 1perc — hp — pf/cel —
str[1.1.1.1.0]
perc: marim
UE

Shin'anim Sha'ananim (1979) 15'
solo Mz, cl, vc
3 0 3 0 — 0 1 0 0 — 2perc — hp — pf/cel —
str[0.0.0.4.2]
UE

La Variation Ajoutée; Pour 17 18'
Instruments & Bande
Électroacoustique (1984)
2[1/pic.2/afl] 1[1/eh] 2 1 — 1 0 1 1 — tape —
2perc — hp — pf — str[1.0.1.1.1]
Revised in 1986. String should be amplified if possible.
Amphion

Anderson, Allen (1951-)

Charrette (1984) 13'
1[1/pic] 1 1[1/bcl] 0 — 0 0 0 0 — 1perc — pf —
str[1.0.1.1.1]
Schirmer

Anderson, Julian (1967-)

Alhambra Fantasy (2000) 15'
1[1/pic] 1 1[1/bcl] 1[1/cbn] — 1 1 1 0 — 2perc —
hp — pf/cel — str[1.1.1.1.1]
perc: sd, whip, sleigh bells, cym, 2 anvil, 2 cowbells, 4 congas, 3
gong, 2 tam-tam, table, vib, cast, Chinese cym, almglocken, td, bd,
metal dustbin, 2 rin, chimes
Faber

Book of Hours; In two parts (2004)   22'
2[1.2/pic/afl] 1 2[1/Ebcl.2/bcl] 1[1/bcn] — 1 1[1/pic
tpt] 1 0 — sample trigger keyboard, 1 or 2
computers, mixing desk, 6 loudspeakers — 2perc —
hp — 2pf[pf/cel.synth] — str[1.1.1.1.1]
perc: chimes, marim, 2 glsp, lg tam-tam, 2 tri, crot, bd, 15 thai tuned
gongs, lg sus cym, lg sd
Fl 1 also plays: extra fl tuned down 1/4 tone and extra pic
tuned down 1/4 tone.
Cl 1 also plays: B-flat cl tuned down 1/4 tone.
Cel requires extended range to low G.
Faber

Khorovod (1994)   12'
1[1/pic] 1 1 1[1/cbn] — 1 1 1 0 — 2perc — pf/cel
— str[1.1.1.1.1]
perc: whip, guiro, chimes, crot, marac, sleigh bells, vib, 5 templeblks,
4 sus cym, Chinese cym, hi-hat, sd, ped bd, marim, vibraslap, 2 tri,
bd, bongos, 3 congas, 2 tumbas, 2 tom-tom, anvil, tam-tam, referees
whistle
Faber

Tiramisu (1994)   10'
1[1/pic/afl] 0 1[1/bcl] 1 — 1 0 0 0 — 1perc — hp
— str[1.0.1.1.1]
perc: crot, marim, whip, ped bd, 2 tri, 5 templeblks, sus cym, chimes,
vib, woodchimes
Faber

Anderson, T.J.   (1928-)

Chamber Symphony (1968)   14'
1 1 1 1 — 1 1 1 0 — tmp+1 — hp — cel —
str[1.1.1.1.1]
ACA

André, Mark   (1964-)

Fatal (1995)   27'
0 0 1[bcl] 0 — 0 0 0 1 — cimb — 2perc — hp —
2pf[prepf.hpsd] — str[0.0.0.0.1]
Durand

...Das O...: From ...22,1... (2003)   23'
0 0 2 2 — 0 0 2 0 — 2 S, 2 A, electronics —
4perc — 2hp — 2pf — str[0.0.0.2.2]
Durand

Angerer, Paul   (1927-)

Musica Fera (1956)   18'
2 2 2 2 — 3 3 2 1 — tmp+1 — str
UE

Sinfonia (1945)   17'
1 1 0 2 — 1 2 0 0 — tmp — org — str
UE

Antheil, George   (1900-1959)

Archipelago "Rhumba" (1935)   6'
2[1.2/pic] 2 2 2 — 4 3 2 1 — 4perc — hp — pf —
str
Schirmer

Dreams (1934)   25'
1[1/pic] 1 2 1 — 2 2 1 0 — 1perc — pf — str
Schirmer

A Jazz Symphony (1925)   13'
1 0 3 0 — 0 3 3 0 — 1perc — pf — str
Arranged for orchestra in 1955.
Weintraub

Lithuanian Night (1919)   4'
str
Schirmer

Music to a World's Fair Film (1939)   11'
1[1/pic] 1 1 1 — 1 2 1 0 — narrator[opt] — 1perc
— pf — str
Schirmer

Serenade (1948)   15'
str
Weintraub

Serenade II (1949)   21'
2 1 1 1 — 2 1 1 0 — 1perc — pf — str[6.6.4.4.2]
Schirmer

Suite for Orchestra (1926)   8'
2[1.2/pic] 2 2 0 — 3 0 0 1 — str
Schirmer

Water Music for 4th of July Evening
(1942)
str
Schirmer

Antoniou, Theodore   (1935-)

Cheironomiës - Gesten.   *999'*
Conductor's Improvisation;
Klangskizze in Modellen für variable
Besetzung (1971)
    2 0 1 0 — 0 0 1 0 — 2perc — pf — str[1.1.1.1.1]
    Can be performed with variable instrumentation: 8 or more
    instruments or voices of choice. Use the study score as
    performance material.
Bärenreiter

Concertino for Piano, Strings and   *11'*
Percussion, op.16b (1962)
    solo pf
    1perc — str
Bärenreiter

Concerto for Violin and Orchestra,   *20'*
op.28 (1965)
    solo vn
    1 1 1 1 — 1 1 1 1 — 3perc — hp — cel — str
Bärenreiter

Events I (1967/68)   *20'*
    solo vn, pf
    2[1.2/pic] 2 2 2 — 4 2 3 1 — 3perc — hp — hpsd
    — str
Bärenreiter

Events III; Music for Orchestra,   *12'*
Tape and Slide-Projection (1969)
    1 1 1 1 — 0 0 0 0 — tape, slide projection —
    2perc — pf — str
    Requires a slide (dia) projector.
Bärenreiter

Jeux for Violoncello and String   *13'*
Orchestra, op.22 (1963)
    solo vc
    str
Bärenreiter

Katharsis; After the poem by Toula
S. Tolia with illustrations by Kostas
Andreou
    solo fl
    0 1 2 0 — 0 0 2 1 — tape, slide and movie
    projection — 2perc — 2pf[pf.elec org] — str[0.0.0.1.2]
    Media projection ad lib.
Bärenreiter

Kinesis ABCD for two String   *15'*
Groups, op.31 (1966)
    str[6.6.6.4.2]
    Each string group requires (3.3.3.2.1)
Bärenreiter

Op Ouvertüre für Orchester und   *15'*
drei Lautsprechergruppen
(Tonband) (1966)
    1 1 2[1.bcl] 0 — 2 2 2 1 — tape — 3perc — 2pf
    — str
    Requires three groups of speakers.
Bärenreiter

Aperghis, Georges   (1945-)

Ascoltare stanca; Pour 18   *10'*
Instrumentistes (1972)
    1[1/pic] 2 0 0 — 2 0 0 0 — 2pf[pf.hpsd] —
    str[3.3.2.2.1]
Salabert

B.W.V. (1973)   *17'*
    solo S, Mz, CT, T, 2 Bar
    2[rec.rec] 0 4[1.2.bcl.bcl] 0 — 0 0 4 0 — 2perc —
    3pf[pf.hpsd.org] — str[0.0.1.1.4]
Salabert

Babil (1996)   *15'*
    solo cl
    1[1/pic] 1 1 1[1/cbn] — 1 1 1 1 — 1perc — pf —
    str[1.1.1.1.1]
    perc: marim
Durand

Concerto Grosso; Pour Trois   *50'*
Chanteurs, Actrice, 19
Instrumentistes et band magnétique
(1972)
    solo Mz, Bar, B
    0 0 3 2 — 0 0 3 1 — actress — 4perc — pf —
    str[0.0.0.4.1]
Amphion

Dark Side (2003)   *30'*
    solo Mz
    2 2[1.2/eh] 2 2 — 2 1 0 1 — 3perc — pf —
    str[2.1.2.2.1]
Durand

Il Gigante Golia; Texte d'un petit   *10'*
motet sarde pour Soprano et
orchestre de 16 musiciens (1975)
    solo S
    1 2[1.2/eh] 2[1.2/bcl] 1 — 1 1 1 0 — 2perc — pf
    — str[1.0.1.1.1]
Salabert

Heysel; Pour 18 Instrumentistes   *5'*
(2002)
    1 1 2 1 — 1 1 1 0 — 2perc — 2pf — str[1.1.1.2.1]
Durand

In extremis; Pour 8 Instrumentistes 15'
(1998)
   1 0 0 0 — 1 0 0 1 — 1perc — pf — str[0.0.1.1.1]
Durand

Parenthèses; Pour Percussion Solo 17'
et 16 Instrumentistes (1977)
   solo perc
   2 0 2 1 — 1 1 1 0 — 2perc — hp — pf —
str[1.0.1.1.1]
Salabert

Pièce pour douze, op.99 (1991) 13'
   0 2 1 2 — 2 0 0 1 — 2perc — pf — str[0.0.0.0.1]
Durand

Le Reste du temps (2003) 15'
   solo vc, cimb
   0 0 2 1 — 1 0 0 0 — 1perc — pf — str[1.0.1.1.0]
Durand

Ritournelles (1992) 12'
   solo 2 Bar
   1[pic] 0 1[bcl] 0 — 0 0 0 0 — mand, gtr — tmp —
hp — pf — str[0.0.0.1.1]
Durand

Variations pour quatorze 13'
instruments (1973)
   1 1 1 1 — 1 0 0 0 — gtr — 1perc — hp — pf —
str[1.1.1.1.1]
Salabert

Von Zeit zu Zeit; Pour 16 20'
Instrumentistes (1971)
   1 1 2 1 — 1 1 2 1 — 1perc — ham org —
str[1.0.1.1.1]
Amphion

Apostel, Hans Erich (1901-1972)

Adagio, op.11 (1937) 22'
   2hp — 2pf[pf.cel] — str
   Second movement from his "Symphony op.11."
UE

Five Austrian Miniatures (1959) 12'
   2[1.2/pic] 2 2 2 — 2 2 1 0 — tmp+1 — str
UE

Kammersymphonie (Chamber 30'
Symphony), op.41 (1968)
   1 1 1 1 — 1 0 0 0 — 1perc — str[1.1.1.1.1]
UE

Variations on Three Folksongs, 14'
op.23 (1956)
   1 1 2 2 — 2 1 0 0 — tmp+1 — str
   Contents - 1. Spinn, spinn; 2. Bald gras ich am Neckar; 3.
Der Tirolerbua
UE

Arbeau, Pierre (1897-1972)

Paysage d'Auvergne; Danse
paysanne pour orchestre
   1 1 1 1 — 1 0 0 0 — tmp — harm[opt] — str
Durand

Poème slave
   1 1 1 1 — 1 0 0 0 — 1perc —harm[opt] — str
Durand

Polichinelle
   1 1 1 1 — 2 0 0 0 — tmp+1 — str
Durand

Ardevol, José (1911-1981)

Concerto Grosso No.1 15'
   1 1 0 1 — 0 2 0 0 — pf — str
Peer

Concerto Grosso No.2 20'
   0 2 2 2 — 0 2 1 0 — pf — str[1.1.0.1.0]
Peer

Musica para Pequena Orquesta. Himno 25'
(Music for Small Orchestra. Hymn)
   0 0 0 0 — 2 0 0 0 — tmp+1 — hp —
2pf[pf/cel.hpsd] — str
   perc: xyl, dr, bombo, tri, cym, tam-tam, woodblk
Peer

Argento, Dominick (1927-)

The Boor: Overture to the opera 6'
(1957)
   1 1 2[1.bcl] 1 — 2 1 1 0 — 1perc — pf — str
   perc: sd, tri, xyl
Boosey & Hawkes

The Dream of Valentino: Dances 6'
from Valentino
   2[1.pic] 2[1.eh] 2 2[1.cbn] — 3 2 1 1 — tmp+2 —
2pf[pf.synth] — str
   perc: bd, belltree, cast, claves, marac, tambn, tam-tam, tri
   Recommended synthesizer: Yamaha DX7
Boosey & Hawkes

Royal Invitation; Homage to the   23'
Queen of Tonga (1964)
    1 2 0 2 — 2 0 0 0 — str
   Boosey & Hawkes

Valse Triste (1996)   2'
    hp — str[1.1.2.2.1]
   Boosey & Hawkes

Armstrong, Craig   (1959-)

Slow Movement (1994)   12'
    str
   Chester Novello

Arnell, Richard   (1917-2009)

Classical Variations in C (1939)   12'
    str
   AMP

Sonata for Chamber Orchestra,   6'
op.18
    1 1 1 1 — 2 0 0 0 — str
   Presser

Arnold, Malcolm   (1921-2006)

Concerto for 28 Players, op.105   22'
(1970)
    1 2 0 1 — 2 0 0 0 — str[6.6.4.4.2]
   Faber

Concerto for Clarinet and Orchestra   18'
No.2, op.115 (1974)
    solo cl
    2[1.pic] 2 0 2 — 2 0 0 0 — tmp/perc — str
    perc: bd, sd, woodblk, cowbell, sus cym
   Faber

Concerto for Guitar and Chamber   22'
Orchestra (1959)
    solo gtr
    1 0 1 0 — 1 0 0 0 — str
   Paterson

Concerto for Organ and Orchestra   13'
(1954)
    solo org
    0 0 0 0 — 0 3 0 0 — tmp — str
   Chester Novello

Serenade for Small Orchestra   14'
(1950)
    2 2 2 2 — 2 2 0 0 — tmp — str
   Lengnick

Sinfonietta No.1, op.48 (1954)   12'
    0 2 0 0 — 2 0 0 0 — str
   Paterson

Sinfonietta No.2, op.65 (1958)   13'
    2 0 0 0 — 2 0 0 0 — str
   Paterson

Sinfonietta No.3 (1964)   15'
    2 2 0 2 — 2 0 0 0 — str
   Paterson

Symphonic Study "Machines,"   6'
op.30 (1951)
    0 0 0 0 — 4 3 3 1 — tmp+2 — str
    perc: xyl, sd, cym, bd, tam-tam
   Faber

Symphony for Strings (1946)   24'
    str
   Lengnick

Trevelyan Suite, op.96 (1967)   8'
    3 2 2 0 — 2 0 0 0 — str[0.0.0.1.0]
   Faber

Variations on a Ukranian Folk Song,   15'
op.9a (1993)
    str
    Arrangement of his Piano Variations, op.9.
   Lengnick

Arutiunian, Alexander   (1920-)

Sinfonietta (1966)   — 60's balkan music   20'
    str   - folky
   Schirmer   - difficult

Asia, Daniel   (1953-)

B for J   5'
    1 0 1 0 — 0 0 1 0 — 1perc — elec org — str
    perc: vib
   Presser

Rivalries   14'
    1 1 1 1 — 1 1 1 0 — ssx — tmp+4 — pf — str
   Presser

Songs from the Page of Swords 25'
   solo Bar, ob
   1 0 2 1 — 1 0 0 0 — 1perc — pf — str[1.1.1.1.1]
Presser

Symphony No.4 25'
   2 2 2 2 — 4 2 2 0 — tmp+3 — hp — pf/cel — str
Presser

Three Movements for Trumpet and 12'
Orchestra
   solo tpt
   1perc — hp — pf/cel/elec org — str
Presser

V'shamru; For Baritone (Cantor) 7'
and Chamber Orchestra
   solo Bar
   1 1 1 1 — 1 0 0 0 — hp — org — str
Presser

Ast, Max   (1875-1964)

Es ist alles wie ein wunderbarer 4'
Garten
   solo medium voice
   2 2 2 2 — 2 0 0 0 — hp — str
UE

Atterberg, Kurt   (1887-1974)

Barocco-Suite No.5, op.23 16'
   1 2[1.eh] 1 0 — 0 0 0 0 — str[3.0.0.1.1]
   Also possible with strings (1.1.1.1.1).
Breitkopf

Concerto for Cello in C minor, op.21 35'
   solo vc
   2 2 2 2 — 2 2 2 0 — tmp — str
Breitkopf

Concerto for Horn in A minor, op.28 23'
   solo hn
   2perc — pf — str
Breitkopf

Concerto for Violin in E minor, op.7 35'
   solo vn
   2 2 2 2 — 2 2 1 0 — tmp — str
Breitkopf

De Fåvitska Jungfrurna; The wise 18'
and the foolish virgins. Rhapsody
on old Swedish folksongs (1947)
   2 2 2 2 — 3 0 0 0 — str
Fleisher

Suite No.2 (1915) 10'
   1 0 1 0 — 0 0 0 0 — str
Nordiska

Suite No.7, op.29 30'
   str
Breitkopf

Suite pastorale in modo antico 20'
   solo 2vn, va
   str
   New version of Suite No.8. Also possible with soli: 3vn or
   2vn and 1vc.
Breitkopf

Symphony No.4 in G minor, op.14 22'
   2[1.2/pic] 2 2 2 — 4 2 2 1 — tmp — str
Breitkopf

Eine Värmlandsrhapsodie, op.36 9'
(1934)
   2 2 2 2 — 2 2 0 0 — 1perc — hp — str
UE

Aubert, Louis   (1877-1968)

Caprice (1924) 7'
   solo vn
   2 2 2 2 — 2 2 0 0 — tmp — hp — str
Durand

La Lettre (1900) 3'
   2 2 2 2 — 2 0 0 0 — hp — str
Durand

La Mauvaise Prière (1932) 3'
   solo voice
   1 0 1 0 — 0 2 1 0 — 1perc — str[2.0.0.1.1]
Durand

Le Nez de Martin (1943) 8'
   solo voice
   2 2 2 2 — 2 0 3 0 — tmp+1 — hp — str
Durand

Sérénade (1906) 3'
   solo voice
   2 2 2 2 — 4 2 0 0 — tmp+1 — hp — str
Durand

Sérénade mélancolique (1923)   2'
　　solo voice
　　2 2 2 2 — 2 0 0 0 — hp — str
　　Durand

Silence (1908)   4'
　　solo voice
　　2 2 2 2 — 2 2 0 0 — tmp — hp — str
　　Durand

Le sommeil de colombes   2'
　　solo voice
　　2 2 2 2 — 4 0 0 0 — hp — cel — str
　　Durand

Visage penché (1907)   3'
　　solo voice
　　2 2 2 2 — 2 0 0 0 — hp — str
　　Durand

Auerbach, Lera   (1973-)

Concerto for Violin No.1, op.56   28'
(2000)
　　solo vn
　　2[1.2/pic] 2[1.2/eh] 2[1.2/bcl] 2[1.2/cbn] — 4 0 0
　　0 — 1perc — hp — 2pf[cel.pf] — str
　　perc: tmp, tri, whistle, flexatone, templeblk, tambn, bd, cym, crot,
　　chimes, tam-tam, glsp, xyl, vib, musical saw
　　Sikorski

Concerto for Violin No.2, op.77   14'
(2004)
　　solo vn
　　2[1.2/pic] 2[1.2/eh] 2[1.2/bcl] 2[1.2/cbn] — 2 2 0
　　0 — 1perc — pf — str
　　perc: tmp, tri, flexatone, templeblk, bd, gong, vib
　　Sikorski

Dialogues on Stabat Mater (2005)   39'
　　solo vn, va, vib
　　str
　　Sikorski

Fragile Solitudes; Shadowbox for   30'
String Quartet and Orchestra (2008)
　　solo str 4t
　　2[1/pic.1/afl] 2[1.eh] 2[1.bcl] 2[1.2/cbn] — 0 0 0 0
　　— cel — str
　　At least one db with C-extension needed.
　　Sikorski

Serenade for a Melancholic Sea,   10'
op.68 (2002)
　　solo vn, vc, pf
　　str
　　Sikorski

Suite Concertante, op.60 (2001)   30'
　　solo vn, pf
　　str
　　Sikorski

Auric, Georges   (1899-1983)

Ecossaise (1952)
　　2 2 2 2 — 2 2 0 0 — tmp+1 — hp — str
　　Excerpt from "La Guirlande de Campra."
　　Salabert

La fontaine de jouvence   7'
　　1 1 1 1 — 0 1 0 0 — 1perc — pf (or cel) —
　　str[2.0.2.2.1]
　　Eschig

Imaginées VI (1976)   12'
　　solo ob
　　1 0 1 0 — 0 0 0 0 — pf — str[1.1.1.2.1]
　　Salabert

La Peintre et son Modèle; Ballet in   15'
one act (1950)
　　2 2 2 2 — 2 2 1 0 — tmp+1 — pf — str
　　Salabert

Avshalomov, Jacob   (1919-)

Cues from "The Little Clay Cart"   12'
(1954)
　　2[1.2/pic] 1 2 0 — 0 0 0 0 — banjo — 4perc —
　　hp — str
　　Fleisher

Evocations for Clarinet and   21'
Chamber Orchestra
　　solo cl
　　1 0 0 0 — 0 0 0 0 — tmp+3 — str
　　Schirmer (E.C.)

B

Babbitt, Milton (1916-)

All Set (1957)   8'
0 0 0 0 — 0 1 1 0 — 2sx[asx.tsx] — 1perc — pf
— str[0.0.0.0.1]
perc: dr, vib
AMP

Composition for 12 Instruments   7'
(1948)
1 1 1 1 — 1 1 0 0 — hp — cel — str[1.0.1.1.1]
AMP

Correspondences for String   11'
Orchestra and Tape (1967)
tape — str
AMP

Bacewicz, Grażyna (1909-1969)

Contradizione (1966)   16'
1 1 1 1 — 1 1 0 0 — 2perc — hp — cel —
str[1.1.1.1.1]
PWM

Simfonietta (1935)   12'
str
PWM

Symphoniette (1929)   8'
str
PWM

Symphony for String Orchestra   27'
(1946)
str
PWM

Bachelet, Alfred (1864-1944)

Poème
solo vc
2 2 2 2 — 2 0 0 0 — tmp — hp — str
Durand

Bäck, Sven-Erik (1919-1994)

Chamber Symphony (1955)   13'
1[1/pic] 0 1 1 — 1 1 1 0 — tmp+1 —
str[0.0.3.2.1]
Nordiska

Fantasia on "Dies Sind Die Heiligen   13'
Zehn Gebot" (1957)
1[1/pic] 1 1 1 — 2 1 1 0 — tmp — pf — str
Nordiska

Four Motets   21'
2 2 2 2 — 4 2 2 0 — tmp+1 — hp — str
Nordiska

Four Motets for Strings (1984)   16'
str
Nordiska

A Game Around A Game (1959)   15'
tmp+4 — 2pf[pf.cel] — str
Nordiska

Movimento I (1965)   17'
1[1/pic] 0 1 0 — 0 1 1 0 — tmp+1 — 2hp —
pf/cel — str[0.0.3.2.1]
Nordiska

Sinfonia per archi (1951)   20'
str
Nordiska

String Symphony (1986)   26'
str
Nordiska

Sumerkei   15'
str
Nordiska

Bacon, Ernst (1898-1990)

Remembering Ansel Adams
solo cl
tmp+1 — str
perc: bongo
Fleisher

Bacri, Nicolas   (1961-)

Capriccio notturno; In Memoriam   17'
Carl Nielsen, op.20 (1987)
    solo cl
    1[1/pic/afl] 1[1/eh] 1[1/bcl] 1 — 2 1 1 0 — 2perc
    — hp — pf/cel — str[1.0.2.3.1]
    Also possible with str (4.0.8.6.3).
Durand

Concerto; Épisodes pour trompette   13'
et orchestre, op.39 (1992)
    solo tpt
    2[1.2/pic] 1 1 0 — 2 0 0 0 — tmp+1[opt] —
    str[6.6.4.4.2]
Durand

Concerto for Flute and Orchestra,   17'
op.63 (1999)
    solo fl
    2 2 2 2 — 2 0 0 0 — tmp+1 — str
Salabert

Folia; Chaconne symphonique pour   8'
orchestre, op.30. In Memoriam
Benjamin Britten (1990)
    2[1.2/pic] 2 2 2 — 2 2 0 0 — tmp+1[opt] —
    str[8.8.6.4.2]
Durand

Notturni; Concerto da camera quasi   13'
una sinfonia piccola, op.14 (1986)
    solo S
    1 0 1 0 — 0 0 0 0 — gtr — 1perc — pf —
    str[1.0.0.1.0]
Durand

Symphony No.4; Symphonie   14'
Classique Sturm und Drang, op.49
(1995)
    2 2 2 2 — 2 0 0 0 — tmp — str
    Fl, Cl, Bn and tmp are opt.
Durand

Symphony No.5; Concerto pour   29'
orchestre, op.55 (1997)
    2[1/pic.2/pic] 2 2 2[1.2/cbn] — 2 2 0 0 — tmp+2
    — pf[opt] — str[8.8.6.4.2]
Durand

Baggiani, Guido   (1932-)

Double (1984)   14'
    2 3 3 2 — 2 0 0 0 — str[0.0.0.0.2]
Salabert

Memoria (1983)   12'
    1 1 2 1 — 1 1 2 1 — electronics — 1perc — pf —
    str[2.1.1.1.1]
    perc: marim
Salabert

Bainbridge, Simon   (1952-)

For Miles (1994)   11'
    solo tpt
    0 1[1/eh] 2 0 — 0 0 0 0 — str[0.0.2.1.1]
    Bass requires C extension.
Novello

Landscape and Memory (1995)   16'
    2[1/pic.2/pic/afl] 1[eh] 2[1.2/bcl] 1 — 1 1 1 0 —
    1perc — hp — pf — str[4.0.2.2.1]
Novello

Baird, Tadeusz   (1928-1981)

Four Novelettes (1967)   12'
    2 1 2 1 — 1 1 1 0 — tmp+3 — hp — 2pf[pf.cel] —
    str[1.1.2.2.1]
PWM; Hansen

Overture in Old Style (1950)   7'
    2 2 0 2 — 2 0 0 0 — 1perc — str
PWM

String Quartet; (Arranged for String   18'
Orchestra) (1957)
    str
Hansen

Baker, David   (1931-)

Concerto for Cello (1975)   15'
    solo vc
    1 1 1 1 — 2 0 0 0 — tmp+1 — str
    Strings without celli.
AMP

Bales, Richard   (1915-1998)

Primavera   5'
1 1 2 1 — 2 2 1 0 — tmp+1 — str
perc: cym, glsp
Fleisher

Ballif, Claude   (1924-2004)

Alma redemptoris mater, op.7   14'
(1952)
solo 2S, A, CT, T, B
2[1.2/pic] 1 0 1 — 0 0 0 0 — hp — harm —
str[0.0.1.1.0]
Excerpt No.1 from his "Quatre Antiennes à la Sainte
Vierge."
Durand

Deuxième concert symphonique   25'
"Haut les Rêves!"; En homage à
Gaston Bachelard, op.49, No.2
(1984)
solo vn
2[1.2/pic] 2 1 1 — 2 0 0 0 — str[7.0.2.2.1]
Durand

Imaginaire No.1, op.41, No.1 (1963)   13'
1 0 1 0 — 0 1 1 0 — hp — str[1.0.0.1.0]
Durand

Imaginaire No.3, op.41, No.3 (1969)   30'
0 0 1 1 — 1 0 0 0 — str[0.0.2.1.1]
Durand

La musique d'Erich Zahn (1964)   14'
1[1/pic] 1[1/eh] 1[1/bcl] 2 — 1 0 2 0 — 1perc —
hp — str[1.1.1.1.1]
Durand

Quatre antiennes à la Sainte   67'
Vierge, op.7 (1952)
solo 2 S, A, CT, T, Bar
3[1/pic.2/bfl.3/bfl] 2[1/ob d'am.2/eh] 0 1[1/cbn] — 1
1 1 0 — 3perc — hp — 3pf[cel.cel.harm] —
str[0.0.1.1.0]
Contents - 1. Alma Redemtoris Mater; 2. Ave regina
caelorum; 3. Regina caeli; 4. Salve regina
mvt durations: 14' 19' 14' 20'
Durand

Suite Dracoula (1990)   20'
1[1/pic] 1[1/eh] 0 0 — 1 0 1 0 — ssx/asx — 2
accordion — 1perc — hpsd — str[1.1.1.1.1]
Durand

Le Taille-Lyre, op.64, No.1 (1990)   11'
1 0 1 0 — 0 0 1 0 — accordion — pf —
str[0.0.1.1.0]
Durand

Balogh, Ernö   (1897-1989)

Pastorale and Capriccio, op.21   6'
1 0 1 0 — 0 0 0 0 — pf — str
Fleisher

Baltakas, Vykintas   (1972-)

about to drink dense clouds (2003)   7'
solo female narrator
1[1/pic] 1 2[1.Ebcl] 0 — 0 0 0 1 — 1perc — pf —
str[1.0.1.0.1]
UE

Banfield, Raffaello de   (1922-2008)

Liebeslied (Love Song) (1968)   5'
solo S
2 2 2 2 — 2 2 0 0 — tmp+1 — hp — str
Salabert

Serale (1968)   5'
solo S
2 1 2 2 — 2 0 2 1 — 1perc — hp — org — str
Salabert

Der Tod der Geliebten (The Death   8'
of the Beloved) (1969)
solo S
2 2 2 2 — 2 2 0 0 — 1perc — hp — str
Salabert

Banks, Don   (1923-1980)

Elizabethan Miniatures (1962)   6'
1 0 0 0 — 0 0 0 0 — lute[or hp or gtr], va da
gamba[or vc] — str
Schott

Equation I and II (1969)   13'
0 0 0 0 — 0 1 0 0 — tsx — gtr — 3perc — hp —
pf — str[1.0.1.1.1]
perc: bongo, tri, woodblk, 3 Chinese templeblks, cym, jazz kit (sd,
bd, 2 tom-tom, 3 cym, hi-hat), vib, glsp
Schott

Sonata da Camera; In Memoriam   15'
Matyas Seiber (1961)
   1 0 2[1.bcl] 0 — 0 0 0 0 — 1perc — pf —
   str[1.0.1.1.0]
   perc: 2 tmp, xyl, 3 cym, gong
Schott

Bantock, Granville   (1868-1946)

Celtic Symphony (1940)   20'
   hp — str
Novello

Four Landscapes from the Chinese   10'
(1936)
   2 1 2 1 — 0 0 0 0 — tmp — hp — str
Novello

Hamabdil; Hebrew melody for   4'
Violoncello with Accompaniment of
Strings, Kettledrum and Harp
(1919)
   solo vc
   tmp — hp — str
Fleisher

The Helena Variations   18'
   3[1.2.pic] 2 2 2 — 4 2 3 1 — tmp+2 — str
Breitkopf

Pierrot of the Minute; Comedy   10'
Overture
   3[1.2.pic] 1 2 1 — 3 2 1 0 — tmp+1 — hp — str
Breitkopf

Russian Scenes (1902)   26'
   2 2 2 2 — 2 2 3 0 — tmp+1 — 2hp — str
Bosworth

Sapphic Poem (1908)
   solo vc
   2 2 2 2 — 2 1 0 0 — tmp+1 — str
   perc: tri
Novello

Barati, George   (1913-1996)

Chamber Concerto (1952)   23'
   1 1 1 1 — 0 0 0 0 — str
   All woodwinds are optional.
Fleisher; CFE

Barber, Samuel   (1910-1981)

Adagio for Strings (1938)   8'
   str
Schirmer

Capricorn Concerto (1944)   14'
   solo fl, ob, tpt
   str
Schirmer; Luck's

Concerto for Violin, op.14 (1939)   23'
   solo vn
   2[1.2/pic] 2 2 2 — 2 2 0 0 — tmp[/sd] — pf — str
   mvt durations: 10' 9' 4'
Schirmer

Essay No.1, op.12 (1937)   8'
   2 2 2 2 — 4 3 3 1 — tmp — pf — str
Schirmer

Knoxville: Summer of 1915, op.24   16'
(1947)
   solo S
   1[1/pic] 1[1/eh] 1 1 — 2 1 0 0 — 1perc — hp —
   str
   perc: tri
Schirmer; Luck's

Medea: Ballet Suite, op.23 (1947)   27'
   2[1.2/pic] 2[1.2/eh] 2 2 — 2 2 2 0 — tmp+3 — hp
   — pf — str
   perc: bd, cym, sus cym, sd, tom-tom, xyl
   Contents - 1. Parados; 2. Choros. Medea and Jason; 3. The
   Young Princess. Jason; 4. Choros; 5. Medea; 6. Kantikos
   Agonias; 7. Exodos
   mvt durations: 3' 5' 3' 3' 7' 3' 3'
Schirmer

Serenade, op.1 (1928)   10'
   str
Schirmer

Barclay, Robert Lenard   (1918-1980)

Nocturne and Scherzo (1947)   11'
   2 2 2 2 — 0 0 0 0 — tmp — hp — str
   mvt durations: 6' 5'
Fleisher

Symphony in One Movement   15'
(1950)
   2 2 2 2 — 4 2 0 0 — tmp — str
   Hn 3 & 4 optional.
Boosey & Hawkes

Barlow, Fred   (1881-1951)

Cinq Enfantines   4'
2 1 2 1 — 2 2 0 0 — tmp+1 — hp — cel — str
Orchestrated by Roger Ellis.
Eschig

Lune de miel
1 1 1 1 — 2 0 0 0 — hp — str
Durand

Barlow, Wayne   (1912-1996)

The Winter's Passed (1940)   5'
solo ob
str
Fischer (C.); Luck's

Barnett, Carol   (1949-)

Sumervar (1988)   6'
2[1.pic] 2 1 2 — 2 0 0 0 — str
Fleisher

Barraud, Henry   (1900-1997)

Concerto da Camera (1934)   18'
1 1 1 1 — 2 1 1 0 — 1perc — hp — cel — str
UE

Images pour un Poète Maudit; Pour   20'
25 musiciens (1954)
1 0 1 1 — 0 1 0 0 — tmp+1 — hp — 2pf[pf.cel] —
str[5.4.3.2.2]
Salabert

Barreau, Gisèle   (1948-)

Piano-piano (1981)   17'
2 1 2 1 — 1 1 1 0 — 3perc — 2pf — str[1.1.1.1.1]
Salabert

Bartel, Hans-Christian   (1932-)

Concerto (1967)   25'
2 2 2 2 — 3 3 2 1 — tmp+1 — pf — str
Breitkopf

Concerto for Small Orchestra and   22'
Solo Viola (1963)
solo va
1 1 2 1 — 1 1 0 0 — tmp+1 — str
Breitkopf

Bartholomée, Pierre   (1937-)

Fancy as a Ground (1980)   20'
0 1 1 1 — 1 1 1 0 — tmp+1 — hp — 2pf[pf.cel] —
str[1.1.2.1.1]
UE

Bartók, Béla   (1881-1945)

Bartók Suite   7'
1 1 2 1 — 2 2 1 0 — 1perc — str
perc: tri, tmp, cym, woodblk, sd, bd
Arranged by T. Serly.
Peer

Concerto for Piano No.1 (1926)   24'
solo pf
2[1.2/pic] 2[1.2/eh] 2[1.2/bcl] 2 — 4 2 3 0 —
tmp+3 — str
perc: bd, cym, sus cym, sd, sd without snares, tam-tam, tri
mvt durations: 9' 8' 7'
Boosey & Hawkes

Dance Suite (1923)   17'
2[1/pic.2/pic] 2[1.2/eh] 2[1.2/bcl] 2[1.2/cbn] — 4 2
2 1 — tmp+3 — hp — 2pf[cel.pf] — str
Celesta also helps cover piano 4-hand.
Boosey & Hawkes

Divertimento (1940)   26'
str
mvt durations: 9' 11' 7'
Boosey & Hawkes

Five Songs, op.15 (1916)   17'
solo medium voice
2 2 2 2 — 3 0 0 0 — pf — str
Edited by Zoltán Kodály.
UE

Hungarian Folksongs (1917)   9'
2 2 2 2 — 2 2 2 1 — 1perc — hp — str
Composer's arrangements of 15 Hungarian folk songs.
Boosey & Hawkes

Music for Strings, Percussion and 27'
Celesta (1936)
tmp+3 — hp — 2pf[cel.pf] — str
perc: bd, cym, sd, sd w/o snares, tam-tam, xyl
Requires double string orchestra.
mvt durations: 7' 7' 7' 6'
Boosey & Hawkes

Rhapsody No.1 (1928) 11'
solo vn
2[1.2/pic] 2 2[1.2/bcl] 2 — 2 2 1 1 — cimb (or hp
& pf) — 1perc — hp — pf — str
perc: tri
Contents - 1. Lassu; 2. Friss
mvt durations: 5' 6'
Boosey & Hawkes

Rhapsody No.2 (1928) 11'
solo vn
2[1.2/pic] 2[1.2/eh] 2[1.2/bcl] 2 — 2 2 1 1 —
tmp+2 — hp — pf/cel — str
perc: bd, cym, sus cym, sd, tri
Contents - 1. Lassu; 2. Friss
mvt durations: 5' 6'
Boosey & Hawkes

Rumanian Folk Dances (1915) 7'
2[1/pic.2] 0 2 2 — 2 0 0 0 — str
Contents - 1. Jocul Cu Bata; 2. Braul; 3.Pe Loc; 4.
Buciumeana; 5. Poarga Romaneasca; 6. Maruntel; 7.
Maruntel
mvt durations: 1'30" 0'30" 1'20" 2' 0'30" 0'15" 0'45"
Boosey & Hawkes; Luck's; Kalmus

Rumanian Folk Dances (1915) 7'
str
Arrangement for string orchestra by A. Willner.
Boosey & Hawkes; Luck's

Suite, op.14 (1916) 9'
2[1/pic.2/pic] 2 1 2 — 2 0 0 0 — pf[opt] — str
Arranged for small orchestra by Antal Dorati.
UE

Suite No.2, op.4 (1907) 35'
2[1.2/pic] 2[1.2/eh] 2[1/Ebcl.2/bcl] 2[1.2/cbn] — 3
2 0 0 — tmp+1 — 2hp — str
perc: gong, cym, tgl, bd, tambn
Revised in 1920 and 1943.
Boosey & Hawkes

Suite Paysanne Hongroise (1917) 13'
solo fl
str
Boosey & Hawkes

Three Village Scenes (1926) 12'
solo four or eight female voices
1[1/pic] 1[1/eh] 2[1/Ebcl.2/asx] 1 — 1 1 1 0 —
ssx — 1perc — hp — pf — str[1.1.1.1.1]
Boosey & Hawkes

Two Portraits, op.5 (1910) 13'
2[1.2/pic] 2[1.2/eh] 2[1/Ebcl.2/Ebcl/bcl] 2 — 4 2 2
1 — tmp+1 — 2hp — str
perc: bd, cym, tam-tam, tri, sd
Boosey & Hawkes

Two Village Scenes; (Slovak 3'
Folksongs) (1924)
solo S
1 1 2 1 — 1 0 0 0 — 1perc — hp — pf — str
Edited by Antal Dorati.
UE

Bates, Mason (1977-)

Icarian Rhapsody (2001) 12'
str
Holab

Music from Underground Spaces 14'
(2008)
2[1.2/pic] 2[1.2/eh] 2[1.2/bcl] 2[1.2/cbn] — 4 3 3
1 — electronics (1 performer) — 3perc — hp — pf —
str
perc: I: marim, hi-hat, cym, bowed crot II: vib, 3 tam-tam III: 3 sus
cym, glsp, bd, xyl, tmp, log dr
Contents - 1.Tunnels; 2. Infernos; 3. Crystalline Cities; 4.
Tectonic Plates
Holab

Omnivorous Furniture (2004) 16'
1[1/pic] 1 1[1/Ebcl] 1[1/cbn] — 1 1 1[btbn] 0 —
electronics — 1perc — hp — pf — str[1.1.1.1.1]
perc: xyl, marim, vib, sus cym, cym, sizzle cym, finger cym, 2 tri, 2
tam-tams, 3 Chinese gongs, bowed crot, bd
Holab

Rusty Air in Carolina (2006) 13'
2[1.2/pic] 2[1.2/eh] 2[1.2/bcl] 2[1.2/cbn] — 4 3 3
1 — electronics — 3perc — hp — pf — str
perc: I: marim, hi-hat, cym, bowed crot II: vib, 3 tam-tam III: 3 sus
cym, glsp, bd, xyl, tmp, log dr
Contents - 1. Nan's Porch; 2. Katydid Country; 3. Southern
Midnight; 4. Locusts Singing in the Heat of Dawn
Holab

Sounds for His Animation; Concerto 15'
for Synthesizer and Chamber
Orchestra (1998)
solo synth
1 1 2[1.2/Ebcl] 2[1.cbn] — 2 1 1 1 — 1perc —
str[1.1.1.1.1]
Holab

White Lies For Lomax (2008) 7'
3[1.2/pic.pic] 2 2[1.Ebcl] 2 — 4 3 3 1 — CD —
tmp+3 — hp — pf/cel — str
Holab

Bauer, Marion   (1882-1955)

Concertino (1940)   9'
  0 1 1 0 — 0 0 0 0 — str
  Boosey & Hawkes

Baumann, Herbert   (1925-)

Nordic Impressions; Suite for String   8'
Orchestra (1959)
  str
  Sikorski

Baur, Jürg   (1918-2010)

Abbreviaturen (1969)   14'
  str[7.0.3.2.1]
  Breitkopf

Carmen Variations; Theme,   20'
Variations and Finale on a Theme
from Bizet's "Carmen" (1947)
  2 2 2 2 — 3 2 3 0 — tmp+2 — hp — str
  Breitkopf

Concertino (1959)   15'
  solo fl, ob, cl
  tmp — str
  Breitkopf

Concerto da camera; Auf der Suche   17'
nach der verlorenen Zeit (1975)
  solo rec
  1[1/pic] 2[1.eh] 0 2 — 2 1 1 0 — gtr[opt] —
  tmp+2 — hp — str
  Breitkopf

Concerto for Viola (1952)   20'
  solo va
  1 1 2 2 — 2 1 1 0 — tmp+3 — hp — str
  Breitkopf

Concerto for Violin No.2; In form of   28'
a ballad (1978)
  solo vn
  2 2 2 2 — 4 2 3 0 — tmp+3 — hp — str
  Breitkopf

Frammenti; Erinnerungen an   22'
Schubert (1996)
  2[1.2/pic] 2[1.2/eh] 2 2 — 2 2 3 0 — tmp+2 — hp
  — str
  Breitkopf

Fresken (1985)   15'
  str
  Breitkopf

Sentieri musicali; Auf Mozarts   20'
Spuren. Sinfonietta (1990)
  2[1.2/pic] 2[1.2/eh] 2 2 — 2 2 3 0 — tmp+2 — hp
  — str
  Breitkopf

Sentimento del tempo (1980)   27'
  solo ob, cl, bn
  0 0 0 0 — 2 2 2 0 — tmp+3 — hp — str
  Breitkopf

Triton-Sinfonietta; Drei Grotesken   11'
(1974)
  1 1 1 1 — 2 1 1 0 — tmp+3 — str
  Breitkopf; Schirmer

Bavicchi, John   (1922-)

Canto I, op.96 (1987)   11'
  str
  BKJ

Concertante, op.44 (1961)   15'
  0 1 0 1 — 0 0 0 0 — str
  BKJ

Concerto for Clarinet and String   20'
Orchestra, op.11 (1954)
  solo cl
  str
  Oxford

Fantasia on Korean Folk Tunes,   8'
op.53 (1966)
  2 1 3[1.2.bcl] 1 — 2 2 3 1 — tmp+1 — str
  BKJ

Fantasy, op.36 (1959)   10'
  1 1 1 1 — 1 0 0 0 — hp — str
  BKJ

Farewell & Hail, op.28 (1957)   11'
  solo S
  0 0 0 0 — 0 1 0 0 — str
  Poem by Norma Farber.
  BKJ

Fireworks, op.48 (1962)   20'
  1 0 1 0 — 1 0 0 0 — Bar[opt] — tmp/perc — pf —
  str
  BKJ

Four Songs, op.6 (1952)   14'
  solo contralto
  2 1 2[1.bcl] 0 — 2 0 0 0 — str
  Contents - 1. To Lorna; 2. In Memoriam; 3. Lament; 4. The
  Search
  BKJ

Music for Small Orchestra, op.81   8'
(1981)
  2 2 2 2 — 2 2 0 0 — tmp — str
  BKJ

There is sweet music here, op.93   15'
(1985)
  solo S
  2 2 2 2 — 2 2 1 0 — tmp — str
  BKJ

Bawden, Rupert   (1958-)

The Angel and the Ship of Souls   18'
(1983)
  1 1 1[1/bcl] 1 — 1 1 1 0 — 1perc — pf —
  str[1.0.1.1.1]
  Novello

The Donkey Dances (1995)   15'
  1[1/pic] 1[1/eh] 1[1/bcl] 0 — 0 0 0 0 — accordion
  — hp — pf — str[1.0.1.1.1]
  Novello

Ultima Scena (1989)   17'
  2[1/pic/afl.pic] 0 1[1/Ebcl/bcl/cbcl] 0 — 0 0 0 0 —
  hp — pf — str[1.1.1.1.0]
  Novello

Wanderjahr (1990)   18'
  1[1/pic] 0 1 0 — 0 0 0 0 — pf — str[1.1.1.1.0]
  Novello

Bajoras, Feliksas   (1934-)

Präludium und Toccata für   6'
Streichorchester (1966)
  str
  Schirmer

Bazelaire, Paul   (1886-1958)

Aria, op.112
  solo vc
  2 0 0 0 — 0 0 0 0 — 2hp — str
  Durand

Beck, Jeremy   (1960-)

Sparks and Flame (Ash) (1997)   5'
  1 0 1 1 — 2 0 0 0 — pf — str
  Fleisher

Becker, Günther   (1924-2007)

Concerto (1974)   15'
  solo ob
  2[1.2/pic] 2[1.2/eh] 2 2 — 4 2 2 0 — live
  electronics — 1perc — pf — str
  Breitkopf

Correspondences I (1966)   14'
  solo cl (cl/Ebcl/asx)
  2[1.2/pic] 2[1.eh] 1 1 — 2 2 2 0 — 2tmp+4 — str
  Breitkopf

Correspondences II (1968)   11'
  gtr — hp — hpsd — str[1.1.1.1.0]
  Breitkopf

Game for Nine (1962)   9'
  1 0 2[1.bcl] 0 — 0 0 0 0 — gtr — 2perc —
  str[1.0.1.1.0]
  Breitkopf

Un poco giocoso; Concertante   20'
Scenes (1983)
  solo tu
  1[1/pic] 1 1 — 1 1 1 0 — 1perc — hp — pf —
  str[1.0.1.1.1]
  Breitkopf

Becker, John J.   (1886-1961)

When the Willow Nods: Second   15'
Suite in one Movement from Stage
Work No.5-b
  1 1 1 1 — 1 1 0 0 — tmp+1 — pf — str
  perc: gong
  Fleisher

Bedford, David   (1937-)

Piece for Mo (1963)   9'
  accordion — 2perc — str[3.0.0.1.1]
  UE

Symphony for 12 Musicians (1981)   23'
  1 2 0 1 — 1 0 0 0 — 2perc — str[1.1.1.1.1]
  UE
  Played by London Sinfonietta

That White and Radiant Legend   15'
(1966)
   solo S, narrator
   1 1 1 1 — 0 0 0 0 — str[1.0.1.1.1]
UE

The Transfiguration: A Meditation   12'
(1988)
   2 2 0 0 — 0 0 0 0 — 3perc — pf — str[4.4.2.2.2]
UE

This One For You (1965)   11'
   2 2 2 2 — 2 2 0 0 — str
UE

Trona For 12 (1967)   10'
   1 1 1 1 — 0 2 2 0 — str[1.1.1.1.0]
UE

The Valley Sleeper, the Children,   18'
the Snakes and the Giant (1982)
   2 2 2 2 — 2 2 0 0 — 1perc — str
UE

With 100 Kazoos; For Chamber   18'
Ensemble and 100 kazoos (1971)
   1 1 2 0 — 1 1 1 0 — 100 kazoos played by the
   audience — str
UE

Bedford, Herbert   (1867-1945)

The Lonely Dancer of Gedār;   4'
Oriental Dance for Small Orchestra,
op.36 (1926)
   1 1 0 1 — 1 0 0 0 — tmp+1 — str
Fleisher

Beltrami, Marco   (1966-)

Iskios; City of Shadows   14'
   1[1/pic/afl] 1[1/eh] 2[1.2/bcl] 1 — 1 1 1 0 — 1perc
   — pf — str[1.1.1.1.1]
   perc: vib, glsp, chimes, 2 tmp, marac, tri, sizzle cym, 2 sus cym, 2
   tam-tam, 2 tom-tom, timbales, brake dr, bd, conga
Peer

Ben-Haim, Paul   (1897-1984)

Chorale Prelude by J. S. Bach   4'
   1 2[1.2/eh] 0 1 — 1 1 1 0 — 1perc — hp — cel —
   str
   perc: glsp
Presser

Concerto for Violin and Orchestra   22'
   solo vn
   2[1.2/pic] 2[1.2/eh] 2 2 — 2 2 0 0 — tmp+1 — hp
   — cel — str
Presser

Kabbalat shabbat; (Friday Evening   40'
Service)
   1 1[eh] 0 0 — 0 1 0 0 — hp — str[1.1.1.1.1]
Presser

Lift Up Your Heads; Motet (1961)   10'
   solo S
   1 1 1 0 — 0 0 0 0 — hp — hpsd — str[1.0.1.1.0]
Presser

Melodies from the East   15'
   solo low voice
   2 1[eh] 1 1 — 2 2 0 0 — hp — str
Presser

Myrtle Blossoms from Eden   15'
   solo S or Contralto or Bar
   2 2 2 2 — 2 2 0 0 — tmp+1 — hp — str
Presser

Benjamin, Arthur   (1893-1960)

Ballade (1947)   12'
   str
Boosey & Hawkes

Caribbean Dance; A New Jamaican   3'
Rumba (1946)
   2 1 2 1 — 2 2 1 0 — tmp+2 — 2pf[pf.cel] — str
   perc: glsp, xyl, tri, marac, sd
   Cel, xyl and glsp ad lib.
Boosey & Hawkes

From San Domingo (1945)   3'
   1 1 2 1 — 2 1 0 0 — tsx — tmp+1 — pf — str
   perc: cym, templeblks, tri, xyl
Boosey & Hawkes

Light Music Suite (1935)   14'
   2[1.2/pic] 1 1 1 — 2 2 1 0 — tmp+1 — 2pf[cel.pf]
   — str
   perc: bd, cym, sd, tambn, tri
Boosey & Hawkes

Overture to an Italian Comedy   6'
(1937)
   2[1.2/pic] 2 2 2 — 4 2 3 0 — tmp+3 — hp — pf
   — str
   perc: bd, glsp, sd, tambn, tri
   Hn 3&4, all tbn and glsp are opt.
Boosey & Hawkes

Sonatina for Chamber Orchestra   11'
(1940)
  2[1.pic] 1 1 0 — 0 0 0 0 — hp[or pf] — str
Boosey & Hawkes

Two Jamaican Pieces (1938)   5'
  1 1 2[1.2(opt)] 1 — 2 1 0 0 — asx[opt] —
  tmp[opt]+1perc — pf — str
  perc: glsp, marac, xyl
  Contents - 1. Jamaican Song; 2. Jamaican Rumba
Boosey & Hawkes

Waltz and Hyde Park Gallop: From   8'
the film "An Ideal Husband" (1947)
  2 2 2 2 — 4 2 3 1 — tmp+1 — hp — str
  perc: sd, tri, tambn
Boosey & Hawkes

Benjamin, George   (1960-)

At First Light (1982)   20'
  1[1/pic/afl] 1 1[1/bcl] 1[1/cbn] — 1 1[1/pic tpt] 1 0
  — 1perc — pf/cel — str[1.1.1.1.1]
  perc: 4 sus cym, 2 tri, 2 crot, gong, vib, guiro, marac, whip,
  templeblk, ping-pong ball, flat bottomed drinking glass, lg
  newspaper, tam-tam, sd
Faber

Fanfare for Aquarius (1983)   1'
  1[pic] 1 1 1 — 1 1 1 0 — 1perc — hp — pf —
  str[1.1.1.1.1]
  perc: crot, tambn, 2 bongo, whip, cym
Faber

Olicantus (2002)   4'
  2 0 1[1/bcl.bcl] 0 — 2 0 0 0 — 2perc — hp — cel
  — str[1.1.1.1.1]
  perc: vib, chimes
Faber

Three Inventions for Chamber   15'
Orchestra (1995)
  2[1/pic.2/pic/afl] 1[1/eh] 3[1.2/bcl.bcl/cbcl] 1[1/cbn]
  — 2 1[1/pic tpt/flug] 1[1/euph] 0 — 2perc — hp —
  pf/cel — str[2.1.2.2.2]
  perc: 2 vib, glsp, 5 cym, crot, 3 bongos, washing board, 2 mini sd, 2
  bd, 4 bongos, 2 tam-tam
  Vn 2 doubles on va.
Faber

Bennett, Richard Rodney   (1936-)

A Book of Hours (1991)   16'
  1 1 1 1 — 1 0 0 0 — hp — str[1.1.1.1.1]
Novello

Calendar; For Chamber Ensemble   10'
(1960)
  1[1/pic] 0 1 1 — 0 1 1 0 — tmp+3 — pf —
  str[1.0.1.1.0]
EMI

Commedia III (1973)   17'
  1[1/pic] 1[1/eh] 1 0 — 1 1 0 0 — 2perc — pf/cel
  — str[1.0.0.1.0]
Novello

Concerto for Guitar and Chamber   20'
Ensemble (1970)
  solo gtr
  1 1 1 0 — 1 1 0 0 — 2perc — cel — str[1.0.1.1.0]
UE

Country Dances; Book 1 (2001)   12'
  2[1.2/pic] 2 2 2 — 2 2 0 0 — tmp+1 — hp — str
Novello

Dream Dancing (1986)   16'
  1 1[1/eh] 1[1/bcl] 1 — 1 1 0 0 — hp —
  2pf[pf/cel.amp hpsd] — str[1.0.1.1.1]
Novello

Metamorphoses (1980)   13'
  str[2.2.2.2.0]
Novello

Music for Strings (1977)   17'
  str[6.4.2.2.1]
  Also possible with (8.6.4.4.2).
Novello

Nocturnes (1963)   12'
  1 1 1 1 — 1 0 0 0 — hp — str
Belwin

Reflections on a 16th-Century Tune   15'
(1999)
  str
Novello

Reflections on a Theme of William   15'
Walton; For 11 Solo Strings (1985)
  str[3.3.2.2.1]
Novello

Serenade for Small Orchestra   14'
(1977)
  2[1.2/pic] 2 2 1 — 2 2 1 0 — tmp+3 — pf — str
Novello

Sinfonietta (1984)   10'
  2[1.2/pic] 2 2 2 — 2 2 0 0 — tmp+1 — pf — str
Novello

Suite: From "The Aviary" and from
"The Insect World" (1965)   9'
    solo medium voice (opt)
    1 1 1 1 — 2 1 1 0 — 1perc — hp[or pf] — str
UE

Suite Française for Small Orchestra
(1970)   7'
    2[1.2/pic] 1 2 1 — 2 1 1 0 — tmp+2 — hp — str
    perc: glsp, xyl
EMI

Benson, Warren   (1924-2005)

Aeolian Song   5'
    solo asx
    1[1/pic] 1 1 1 — 1 0 0 0 — 1perc — str
    perc: bells
    Second movement of his "Concertino" set for chamber
    orchestra.
Presser

Shadow Wood; Six Poems of
Tennessee Williams (1992)   20'
    2[1.2/pic] 1 3[1.2.3/bcl] 1 — 1 1 1 0 — 4perc —
    hp — str[0.0.0.0.1]
Presser

Bentzon, Jørgen   (1897-1951)

Sinfonia Buffo, op.35 (1939)   5'
    0 0 0 0 — 0 1 0 0 — 1perc — pf — str
Hansen

Sinfonietta, op.41 (1941)   14'
    str
Hansen

Bentzon, Niels Viggo   (1919-2000)

Brillantes Concertino: No.5 from
"Divertimento for Mozart" (1956)   3'
    solo pf
    2 2 2 2 — 2 2 0 0 — tmp — str
    For more information see: Mozart, Wolfgang Amadeus.
UE

Chamber Concerto for 11
Instruments, op.52 (1948)   18'
    0 0 1 1 — 0 2 0 0 — tmp+2 — 3pf —
    str[0.0.0.0.1]
Hansen

Concerto per archi, op.114 (1957)   16'
    str
Hansen

Copenhagen Concerto, op.167
(1964)   18'
    str
Hansen

Copenhagen Concerto No.2,
op.168 (1964)   18'
    str
Hansen

Copenhagen Concerto No.3,
op.169 (1964)   12'
    str
Hansen

Divertimento, op.19 (1942)   20'
    str
Hansen

Lille Suite, op.60 (1950)   20'
    str
Hansen

Mini-Symphony, op.231 (1968)   13'
    2 2 2 2 — 2 1 1 0 — tmp+1 — str
Hansen

Overture for Chamber Orchestra,
op.14 (1942)   10'
    1 2 0 0 — 1 0 0 0 — 1perc — pf — str
Hansen

Prelude and Rondo, op.56 (1949)   9'
    2 2 2 2 — 2 0 0 0 — str
Hansen

Pupitre 14, op.339 (1974)   15'
    1 1 1 1 — 1 0 0 0 — gtr — 1perc — hp — pf —
    str
Hansen

Sinfonia, op.402 (1977)   25'
    2 2 2 2 — 2 2 1 0 — tmp — str
Hansen

Sinfonia da Camera, op.139 (1962)   20'
    1 1 1 1 — 1 1 1 1 — tmp+2 — pf — str[1.1.1.1.1]
Hansen

Sonata for 12 Instruments, op.257
(1970)   12'
    1 1 1 1 — 1 1 1 0 — pf — str[1.0.1.1.1]
Hansen

Symphony No.6, op.66 (1950)   30'
2[1.2/pic] 2 2 2 — 2 0 0 0 — tmp — str
Hansen

Symphony No.11, op.158 (1964)   18'
2 2 2 2 — 2 0 0 0 — tmp+1 — str
Hansen

Two Monkton-Blues, op.127 (1960)   7'
0 0 3[1.2/bcl.Ebcl] 0 — 4 1 1 1 — 2perc — pf —
str[0.0.0.0.1]
Hansen

Berg, Alban   (1885-1935)

Five Orchestra Songs, op.4 (1912)   10'
solo medium voice
1 1 1 1 — 1 0 0 0 — 2pf[pf.harm] — str
Arranged by Diderik Wagenaar.
Contents - 1. Seele, wie bist du schöner; 2. Sahst du nach
dem Gewitterregen; 3. Über die Grenzen des All; 4. Nichts
ist gekommen; 5. Hier ist Friede
UE

Bergman, Erik   (1911-2006)

Silence and Eruptions, op.91 (1979)   25'
1 1 1 1 — 0 0 0 0 — 1perc — pf — str[1.1.1.1.0]
Novello

Tutti e soli, op.113 (1990)   22'
1[1/pic] 0 1 1[1/cbn] — 0 0 0 0 — 1perc —
str[6.5.4.3.2]
Novello

Bergsma, William   (1921-1994)

Symphony for Chamber Orchestra   14'
(1942)
1[1/pic] 0 1 0 — 2 1 0 0 — tmp+1 — pf — str
perc: bd
Fleisher

Berio, Luciano   (1925-2003)

Air: From "Opera" (1969)   7'
solo S
2 1 2 2 — 3 0 0 0 — 2sx[asx.tsx] — 3perc —
3pf[2pf.elec org] — str[0.0.1.1.1]
UE

Calmo (1989)   20'
solo Mz —> Mezzo
2[1/pic.afl] 0 4[Ebcl.2.3.bcl] 1 — 1 2 1 0 — asx —
1perc — hp — str[0.0.3.3.2]
UE

Chemins II; (su Sequenza VI)   12'
(1967)
1 0 1 0 — 0 0 1 0 — 2perc — hp — elec org —
str[0.0.1.1.0]
UE

Chemins IIb (1970)   11'
2[1.2/pic] 1 2 2[1.cbn] — 2 3 2 1 — 2sx[asx.tsx]
— elec gtr — 3perc — 2pf[pf.elec org] —
str[1.0.6.4.3]
UE

Chemins IV; (su Sequenza VII)   10'
(1975)
solo ob (or ssx)
str[3.0.3.3.2]
UE

Chemins V; (su Sequenza XI)   20'
(1992)
solo gtr
3 0 2[1.bcl] 1 — 1 2 1 0 — tsx — accordion —
1perc — 2hp — str[12.0.8.4.3]
perc: marim
UE

Concertino (1949)   11'
solo vn, cl, hp, cel
str
UE

Corale; (su Sequenza VIII) (1981)   15'
solo vn
0 0 0 0 — 2 0 0 0 — str(min)[6.6.4.4.3]
UE

E vó: Sicilian Lullaby from "Opera"   4'
(1972)
solo S
1 1 3 0 — 0 1 1 0 — 1perc — 2pf[pf.elec org] —
str[1.0.1.1.1]
UE

Folk Songs (1964)   23'
   solo Mz
   1[1/pic] 0 1 0 — 0 0 0 0 — 2perc — hp[or gtr] —
   str[0.0.1.1.0]
   Arrangements of Folk Songs from different countries.
   Version for Mz and 7 instruments.
   Contents - 1. Black is the Colour (USA); 2. I wonder as I
   wander (USA); 3. Loosin Yelav (Armenia); 4. Rossignolet du
   Bois (France); 5. A la Femminisca (Sicily); 6. La Donna
   Ideale (Italy); 7. Ballo (Italy); 8. Motettu de Tristura
   (Sardinia); 9. Malorous qu'o un Fenno (Auvergne, France)
   UE

Folk Songs (1964)   23'
   solo Mz
   2[1/pic.2] 1 3[1.2.bcl] 1 — 1 1 1 0 — 2perc — hp
   — str
   Arrangements of Folk Songs from different countries.
   Version for Mz and orchestra (1973).
   Contents - 1. Black is the Colour (USA); 2. I wonder as I
   wander (USA); 3. Loosin Yelav (Armenia); 4. Rossignolet du
   Bois (France); 5. A la Femminisca (Sicily); 6. La Donna
   Ideale (Italy); 7. Ballo (Italy); 8. Motettu de Tristura
   (Sardinia); 9. Malorous qu'o un Fenno (Auvergne, France)
   UE

Kol od; (Chemins VI) (1996)   20'
   3[pic.2.3] 1 4[Ebcl.2.3.bcl] 1 — 2 2 1 1 —
   2sx[ssx.asx] — accordion — cel — str[4.0.3.3.2]
   UE

"points on the curve to find..."   16'
   (1974)
   solo pf
   3 2[1.eh] 3 2 — 2 2 1 1 — 1[asx/tsx] — cel —
   str[0.0.1.2.1]
   UE

Re-Call (1995)   4'
   2[1.pic] 1 4[Ebcl.2.3.bcl] 1 — 2 3 2 1 —
   str[2.0.2.2.1]
   UE

Requies (1984)   17'
   2[1.pic] 2[1.eh] 3[Ebcl.2.bcl] 2 — 2 2 1 0 — 1perc
   — hp — cel — str[8.8.6.5.3]
   perc: marim
   Also possible with strings (8.8.4.4.3).
   UE

Ritorno Degli Snovidenia (The   19'
return of the dreams) (1977)
   solo vc
   3 2 3[1.2.bcl] 2 — 2 2 2 1 — asx — pf —
   str[3.0.3.3.2]
   UE

Tempi Concertati (1959)   16'
   solo fl
   1[pic] 2[1.eh] 3[1.2.bcl] 1 — 1 1 1 0 — 2perc —
   2hp — 2pf[pf.pf/cel] — str[1.0.2.2.1]
   UE

Variazione sull'aria di Papageno: 3'
No.2 from "Divertimento for Mozart"
(1956)
   0 0 2[basset hn] 0 — 0 0 0 0 — str
   For more information see: Mozart, Wolfgang Amadeus.
   Schott

Berkeley, Lennox   (1903-1989)

Antiphon (1973)   13'
   str
   Chester Novello

Diversions for Eight Instruments,   18'
op.63 (1964)
   0 1 1 1 — 1 0 0 0 — pf — str[1.0.1.1.0]
   Chester Novello

Divertimento in Bb, op.18 (1943)   17'
   2 2 2 2 — 2 2 1 0 — tmp — str
   Chester Novello

Nocturne, op.25 (1946)   11'
   2 2 2 2 — 2 0 0 0 — tmp — hp — str
   Chester Novello

Partita, op.66 (1965)   12'
   1 1 2 1 — 2 1 1 0 — tmp+1 — str
   Chester Novello

Serenade for Strings (1939)   14'
   str
   Chester Novello

Sinfonietta, op.34 (1950)   13'
   2 2 2 2 — 2 0 0 0 — tmp — str
   Chester Novello

Suite for Strings (1974)   11'
   str
   Chester Novello

Variations on an Elizabethan
Theme; (Sellinger's Round) (1953)
   str
   Chester Novello

Windsor Variations, op.75 (1969)   12'
   1[1/pic] 2 0 2 — 2 0 0 0 — str
   Chester Novello

Berlin, David   (1943-)

Structures for Chamber Orchestra   8'
(1975)
   1[1/pic] 1 1 1 — 1 1 2 0 — 1perc — str
Fleisher

Bermel, Derek   (1967-)

Continental Divide (1996)   10'
   1[1/pic] 1[1/eh] 1[1/bcl] 1[1/cbn] — 1 1 1 1 —
elec gtr, elec bgtr (covered by db player) — 1perc —
pf/cel — str[1.1.1.1.1]
   perc: xyl, sd, cym, gongs, hi-hat, woodblk, tambn, whip, flexatone,
ratchet
Peer; Faber

Hot Zone (1996)   6'
   1 1 1 1 — 1 1 1 0 — 2sx[asx.tsx] — 2 singers —
1perc — 2pf[pf.kybd] — str[0.0.0.1.1]
   Db doubles on elec bgtr.
Faber

Natural Selection (2000)   15'
   1[1/pic] 1[1/eh] 1 1[1/cbn] — 1 1[1/flug] 1 0 —
1perc — hp — pf — str[1.1.1.1.1]
   perc: drum kit, 5 templeblks, 3 tom-tom, sd, ride cym, hi-hat, bd,
gong, sus cym, tri, cowbell, cast, ratchet, flexatone, anvil, vib, xyl,
glsp, chimes
Faber

Tag Rag (2003)   4'
   2[1.pic] 2 2[1/Ebcl.bcl] 2[1.cbn] — 2 2 2 1 — asx
— elec gtr — 2perc — pf — str
   perc: bd, field dr, sd, xyl, sm and lg woodblks, conga, tri, sus cym
Peer

Three Rivers (2001)   13'
   1[1/pic] 0 2[1/Ebcl.2/bcl] 1 — 0 1 1 0 — 2perc —
kybd — str[1.0.0.1.1]
   perc: I: drum set II: vib, xyl, woodblk, metal sticks, sd, whistle, ratchet
Peer; Faber

Turning Variations (2006)   18'
   2[1.2/pic] 2[1.2/eh] 2[1.2/Eblc] 2[1.2/cbn] — 2 2 2
1 — tmp+2 — hp — str
   perc: glsp, crot, xyl, flexatone, gongs, tri, sleigh bells, sus cym,
Chinese cym, cym, tam-tam, vibraslap, ratchet, latin cowbell, cast,
woodblk, cabasa, lion's roar, tam-tam, sd, timbale, 4 toms, conga,
bd, sm bd
Peer

Berners, Lord   (1883-1950)

Adagio, Variations and Hornpipe: 5'
From "The Triumph of Neptune"
(1926)
   str
Chester Novello

For a Statesman: No.1 of "Three   3'
Small Funeral Marches" (1916)
   1[1/pic] 1 2 1 — 2 2 1 0 — tmp+1 — str
Chester Novello

L'Uomo dai Baffi (1918)   11'
   1 1 1 1 — 0 0 0 0 — pf — str[1.1.1.1.1]
Chester Novello

Bernstein, Leonard   (1918-1990)

1600 Pennsylvania Avenue: Suite   18'
for Orchestra (1976)
   2 2 2 2 — 2 2 2 1 — tmp+3 — harm — str
   perc: xyl, vib, glsp, sus cym, cym, tri, guiro, woodblk, 3 templeblks,
tambn, 3 high dr, sd, td, bd
   Suite from the musical. Arranged by Harmon.
Boosey & Hawkes

Arias and Barcarolles (1988)   31'
   solo Mz, Bar
   2perc — str
   perc: xyl, glsp, vib, small cym, sm sd, lg sd, chimes, sm bd, tamb,
tri, crot, sm tam-tam, police whistle, sm woodblk, lg woodblk, sm sus
cym, td
   Orchestrated with the assistance of Bright Sheng.
Boosey & Hawkes

Clarinet Sonata (1942)   11'
   solo cl
   tmp/perc — pf — str
   perc: tmp, tri, glsp, woodblk, xyl
   Arr. by Sid Ramin.
Boosey & Hawkes

Facsimile (1946)   19'
   2[1.2/pic] 2 2[1.2/Ebcl] 2 — 4 3[1.2.crt] 2 1 —
tmp+2 — pf — str
   perc: tri, sd, cym, sus cym, woodblk, bd, glsp
Boosey & Hawkes

Fancy Free: Three Dance   7'
Variations (1944)
   2[1.2/pic] 2 2 2 — 4 3 3 1 — tmp+3 — pf — str
   perc: bd, sus cym, sd, tri
   Contents - 1. Galop; 2. Waltz; 3. Danzon
   mvt durations: 1' 3' 3'
Boosey & Hawkes

Halil; Nocturne for Solo Flute and   *16'*
Small Orchestra (1981)
  solo fl
  2[pic.afl] 0 0 0 — 0 0 0 0 — tmp+5 — hp — str
  <small>perc: bd, cym, 2 sus cym, 4 sd, 4 tom-tom, 2 tri, 2 gongs, tam-tam,
  glsp, xyl, vib, chimes, 4 woodblks, whip</small>
  Boosey & Hawkes

Mass: Meditation No.1 (1971)   *5'*
  solo vn
  1 0 0 0 — 0 0 0 0 — tmp/perc — hp — org — str
  <small>perc: tmp, vib, xyl, marim, glsp, sus cym</small>
  Chamber version.
  Boosey & Hawkes

Mass: Two Meditations (1971)   *8'*
  2perc — hp — 2pf[org.pf] — str
  <small>perc: sus cym, cym, glsp, marim, vib, xyl, 4 templeblks, 2 sd</small>
  Boosey & Hawkes

On the Town: Three Dance   *10'*
Episodes (1945)
  1[1/pic] 1[1/eh] 3[1/Ebcl.2.3/bcl] 0 — 2 3 3 1 —
  asx — tmp+2 — pf — str
  <small>perc: sus cym, sd, bd, tri, set, woodblk, xyl</small>
  Sx part can be covered by cl 2.
  Contents - 1. The Great Lover; 2. Lonely Town (Pas de
  deux); 3. Times Square 1944
  <small>mvt durations: 2' 3' 5'</small>
  Boosey & Hawkes

Prelude, Fugue and Riffs; For Solo   *9'*
Clarinet and Orchestra (1949)
  solo cl
  0 0 1 0 — 2 3 3 1 — 3perc — pf — str
  <small>perc: sd, bd, 4 tom-tom, cym, sus cym, hi-hat, xyl, vib, woodblk</small>
  Arr. by Luas Foss in 1998.
  Boosey & Hawkes

Serenade; After Plato's   *31'*
"Symposium" (1954)
  solo vn
  tmp+5 — hp — str
  <small>perc: tambn, xyl, glsp, sus cym, chimes, tri, sd, td, 2 Chinese blocks,
  2bd</small>
  Contents - 1. Phaedras-Pausanias; 2. Aristophanes; 3.
  Eryximachus; 4. Agathon; 5. Socrates-Alcibiades
  <small>mvt durations: 7' 4' 2' 8'10'</small>
  Boosey & Hawkes

Besch, Otto   (1885-1966)

Divertimento (1941)   *12'*
  2[1.2/pic] 1 2 2 — 2 2 0 0 — tmp — str
  Boosey & Hawkes

Beydts, Louis   (1895-1953)

À travers Paris; Images
Symphoniques (1958)
  1 1 1 1 — 1 1 0 0 — 1perc — hp — pf — str
  Salabert

Chansons pour les oiseaux   *8'*
  solo voice
  1 1 0 1 — 0 0 0 0 — hp — str
  Durand

Hue!; Croquis parisien pour petit   *4'*
orchestre (1958)
  1 1 1 1 — 1 1 1 0 — 1perc — pf — str
  Salabert

Le Voyage de Tchong-Li (1932)
  1 1 0 1 — 0 0 0 0 — 1perc — 3pf[pf.cel.hpsd] —
  str
  Salabert

Beyer, Frank Michael   (1928-2008)

Architettura per musica (1989)   *16'*
  1 1 1 1 — 1 1 1 0 — 1perc — hp — str[1.1.1.1.1]
  Boosey & Hawkes

Canto di giorno; For Cello and   *20'*
Orchestra (1998/99)
  solo vc
  1[1/pic] 2[1.eh] 2[1.bcl] 1 — 1 1 1 0 — 2perc —
  hp — str[8.6.4.4.3]
  <small>perc: vib, marim, chimes</small>
  Boosey & Hawkes

Canzona di Ombra; For Solo Oboe   *8'*
and Strings (1986)
  solo ob
  str[4.4.3.2.1]
  Boosey & Hawkes

Concerto for Oboe and String   *18'*
Orchestra (1986)
  solo ob
  str
  Boosey & Hawkes

Concerto for Viola and Orchestra   *25'*
(2003)
  solo va
  1 2[1.eh] 2[1.bcl] 1 — 1 1 1 1 — 3perc — hp —
  str
  <small>perc: vib, marim, 6 sus cym, chimes, 3 tam-tam, bd, 6 gongs</small>
  Boosey & Hawkes

Deutsche Tänze (German Dances)   *12'*
(1982)
   solo vc, db
   1[1/pic] 2 1 2 — 1 1 0 0 — str
Boosey & Hawkes

Griechenland; For Three Groups of   *21'*
Strings (1981)
   str[12.10.8.6.4]
Boosey & Hawkes

Liturgia (1996)   *20'*
   str
Boosey & Hawkes

Meridian; Concerto for Flute and   *20'*
String Ensemble (2004)
   solo fl
   str[4.4.3.2.1]
Boosey & Hawkes

Musik der Frühe; Concerto for Violin   *27'*
and Orchestra (1993)
   solo vn
   2[1.2/pic] 2 2[1.2/bcl] 2[1.2/cbn] — 2 2 1 1 —
   tmp+3 — hp — pf — str
   perc: 4 woodblks, 4 bongos, 4 tom-tom, 5 sus cym, bd, 2 tam-tam,
   chimes, vib, cowbell
Boosey & Hawkes

Musikalisches Opfer; Ricercare a 3,   *35'*
Fuga canonica & 9 Kanons (1985)
   1 2[1.2/eh] 2[1.2/bcl] 1 — 1 1 0 0 — hp —
   str(min)[1.0.1.1.1]
   Arrangement of J. S. Bach's "Musical Offering." For
   performance together with the arrangement of Bach's
   "Ricercare a 6" by Anton Webern.
Boosey & Hawkes

Passionato con Arietta (2005)   *15'*
   str[4.4.3.2.1]
Boosey & Hawkes

Ricercare I (1957)   *20'*
   2 0 3[1.2.bcl] 0 — 0 0 0 0 — hp — str
Boosey & Hawkes

Streicherfantasien; On a motif by   *14'*
Johann Sebastian Bach (1977)
   str[7.6.5.4.3]
Boosey & Hawkes

Versi (1968)   *11'*
   str[4.4.3.3.1]
Boosey & Hawkes

Beyer, Johanna   (1888-1944)

Fragment for Chamber Orchestra   *7'*
(1937)
   1 1 1 1 — 1 0 0 0 — 1perc — pf — str
Fleisher

Beynon, Jared   (1949-)

Unicorn (1974)   *11'*
   1[afl] 0 1[bcl] 0 — 0 0 0 0 — 2perc — cel — str
Fleisher

Bialas, Günter   (1907-1995)

Concerto for Violoncello and   *16'*
Orchestra (1960)
   solo vc
   3[1.2.pic] 2 2 2 — 2 2 2 1 — tmp+2 — hp — str
Bärenreiter

Concerto for Violoncello and   *20'*
Orchestra No.2 (1992)
   solo vc
   2[1.2/pic] 1 1 1 — 1 1 1 1 — tmp+1 — pf — str
Bärenreiter

Concerto lirico for Piano and   *21'*
Orchestra (1967)
   solo pf
   2[1.2/pic] 2 2 2 — 4 3 3 1 — tmp+3 — hp — str
Bärenreiter

Music in Two Movements for Harp   *18'*
and String Orchestra (1966)
   solo hp
   str
Bärenreiter

Sinfonia Piccola (1960)   *15'*
   1[1/pic] 1 1 0 — 0 0 0 0 — str
Bärenreiter

Trauermusik (1994)   *16'*
   solo va
   2 1 1 1 — 2 1 1 1 — tmp+2 — hp — str
Bärenreiter

Der Weg nach Eisenstadt; Haydn   *16'*
Phantasies for Small Orchestra
(1980)
   1[1/pic] 2 0 2 — 2 0 0 0 — tmp — str
Bärenreiter

Biersack, Anton   (1907-1982)

Bagatellen   *17'*
2[1.2/pic] 2 2 2 — 0 1 0 0 — tmp+1 — str
perc: sd
Schott

Biggs, John   (1932-)

Concerto for Cello and Chamber   *22'*
Orchestra (1996)
solo vc
0 2 0 2 — 2 0 0 0 — str
Fleisher; Consort

Binkerd, Gordon   (1916-2003)

Movement for Orchestra (1964)   *11'*
2 2 2 2 — 2 2 0 0 — tmp — str
Boosey & Hawkes

Symphony No.3 (1959)   *12'*
3[1.2.pic] 2 2 2 — 3 3 3 1 — tmp — str
Boosey & Hawkes

Two Meditations for Strings (1981)   *5'*
str
Boosey & Hawkes

Birkenkötter, Jörg   (1963-)

Four Pieces for Ensemble (1996)   *14'*
1[1/pic] 1[1/eh] 2[1.2/bcl] 1 — 1 1 1 0 — 2perc —
pf — str[1.1.1.1.1]
Breitkopf

Halt! (1995)   *16'*
1[1/pic] 1 2[1.2/bcl] 1 — 1 1 1 0 — 2perc — pf —
str[1.1.1.1.1]
Breitkopf

Klänge Schatten (1989)   *23'*
1[1/pic] 1[1/eh] 1[1/bcl] 1[1/cbn] — 1 1 1 0 —
3perc — hp — pf/cel — str[1.0.1.1.1]
Breitkopf

Schwebende Form (1999)   *17'*
1[1/pic] 0 1[1/bcl] 0 — 0 0 0 0 — 1perc — pf —
str[1.0.1.1.0]
Breitkopf

Birtwistle, Sir Harrison   (1934-)

An die Musik (1988)   *5'*
solo S
1 1 1 1 — 0 0 0 0 — 1perc — str[1.1.1.1.1]
UE

Carmen Arcadiae Perpetuum   *12'*
(1978)
1[1/pic] 1 1[1/bcl] 1[1/cbn] — 1 1 1 0 — 1perc —
pf — str[1.1.1.1.1]
perc: marim
Also possible with strings (6.6.4.4.2).
UE

Endless Parade (1987)   *18'*
solo tpt
1perc — str[14.0.4.4.2]
perc: vib
UE

Four Poems by Jaan Kaplinski   *9'*
(1991)
solo S
1 1 1 1 — 1 1 0 0 — hp — pf — str[1.1.1.1.1]
UE

Prologue (1971)   *8'*
solo T
0 0 0 1 — 1 2 1 0 — str[1.0.0.0.1]
UE

Secret Theatre (1984)   *28'*
1[1/pic] 1 1 1[1/cbn] — 1 1 1 0 — 1perc — pf —
str[1.1.1.1.1]
UE

Silbury Air (1977)   *15'*
1[1/pic/afl] 1[1/eh] 1[1/bcl] 1 — 1 1 1 0 — 1perc
— hp — pf — str[1.1.1.1.1]
UE

Songs by Myself (1984)   *10'*
solo S
1[1/afl] 0 0 0 — 0 0 0 0 — 1perc — pf —
str[1.0.1.1.1]
perc: vib
UE

Three Movements with Fanfares   *14'*
(1964)
1 1 1 1 — 2 2 2 0 — 1perc — hp — str
UE

Tragoedia (1965)   *13'*
1 1 1 1 — 1 0 0 0 — hp — str[1.1.1.1.0]
Fl, ob, cl, bn and hn double on claves.
UE

Words Overheard (1985)   8'
    solo S
    1 1 0 1 — 0 0 0 0 — str[12.0.4.4.2]
UE

Bittner, Julius   **(1874-1939)**

Der Musikant: Serenade (1911)   4'
    1 1 2 1 — 2 0 0 0 — str
Fleisher

Bjelinski, Bruno   **(1909-1992)**

Concerto for Flute and Strings   15'
(1955)
    solo fl
    str
UE

Mediterranian Sinfonietta   18'
    3[1.2.pic] 2 2 2 — 2 2 0 0 — tmp+1 — str
Breitkopf

Pinocchio; Ballet in 4 acts (1960)
    2 2 2 2 — 2 2 0 0 — tmp+2 — pf — str
    Also available: Suite No.1 (15') and Suite No.2 (15'). Both
    suites have the same instrumentation as the full ballet.
Breitkopf

Serenade (1957)   16'
    0 0 0 0 — 0 1 0 0 — 1perc — pf — str
UE

Blacher, Boris   **(1903-1975)**

Alla Marcia (1934)   6'
    2[1.2/pic] 2 2 2 — 4 3 3 1 — tmp+1 — str
Boosey & Hawkes

Collage (1968)   17'
    2[1.pic] 2[1.eh] 2[1.bcl] 2[1.cbn] — 1 1 1 1 —
    tmp+2 — hp — 2pf[pf.cel] — str
    String section includes solo string quartet.
Boosey & Hawkes

Concertante Musik (1937)   11'
    2[1.2/pic] 2 2 2 — 4 2 3 1 — tmp — str
Boosey & Hawkes

Concerto for Cello (1964)   22'
    solo vc
    1 1 1 1 — 1 1 1 0 — str
Boosey & Hawkes; Bote & Bock

Concerto for High Trumpet and   10'
String Orchestra (1970)
    solo pic tpt
    str
Boosey & Hawkes

Concerto for Piano No.1, op.28   19'
(1947)
    solo pf
    1 1 1 1 — 2 1 1 0 — str
Boosey & Hawkes; Bote & Bock

Concerto for Piano No.2; In variable   19'
Metres (1952)
    solo pf
    1[1/pic] 0 1 1 — 1 1 0 0 — 1perc — str
Boosey & Hawkes

Concerto for String Orchestra   20'
(1940)
    str
Boosey & Hawkes

Concerto for Viola (1954)   20'
    solo va
    1 1 1 1 — 1 1 1 0 — str
Boosey & Hawkes

Concerto for Violin (1948)   18'
    solo vn
    1 1 1 1 — 2 1 1 0 — str
Boosey & Hawkes

Demeter: Suite (1963)   22'
    2 2[1.eh] 2[1.bcl] 2[1.cbn] — 1 1 1 0 — 1perc —
    pf — str
Boosey & Hawkes

Dialog (1950)   20'
    solo fl, vn, pf
    str
UE

Divertimento (1935)   10'
    str
Boosey & Hawkes

Feste im Süden: Suite (1935)   24'
    2[1.2/pic] 2 2 2 — 2 2 2 0 — glass harmonica[opt]
    — tmp+1 — str
Boosey & Hawkes

Fürstin Tarakanowa: Suite (1940)   16'
    3[1.2.3/pic] 2 2 2 — 4 3 3 1 — tmp+1 — str
Boosey & Hawkes

Hommage à Mozart;	7'
Metamorphoses on a group of	
Mozart themes for Orchestra (1956)	
1 2 0 2 — 2 2 0 0 — tmp — str	
Boosey & Hawkes	

Kleine Marschmusik (1932)	6'
2 2 2 2 — 2 2 2 0 — tmp — str	
Boosey & Hawkes	

Lysistrata: Suite from the ballet	11'
(1950)	
3[1.2.3/pic] 2 2 2 — 4 3 3 1 — tmp+1 — str	
Boosey & Hawkes	

Musica giocosa (1959)	7'
2 2 2 2 — 4 2 3 1 — tmp — str	
Boosey & Hawkes	

Orchester-Capriccio über ein	10'
Volkslied (1933)	
2 2 2 2 — 2 2 2 0 — tmp — str	
Boosey & Hawkes	

Parergon zum "Eugen Onegin"	13'
(1966)	
solo S	
1 1 1 1 — 2 0 0 0 — str	
UE	

Partita (1945)	18'
1perc — str	
Boosey & Hawkes	

Pentagramm (1974)	22'
str	
Boosey & Hawkes	

Rondo (1938)	10'
3[1.2.pic] 2 2 2 — 4 2 3 1 — tmp — str	
Boosey & Hawkes	

Studie im Pianissimo (1953)	14'
2[1.2/pic] 2 2 2 — 4 3 3 1 — str	
Boosey & Hawkes	

Symphony (1938)	25'
3[1.2.3/pic] 2 2 2 — 4 2 3 1 — tmp — str	
Boosey & Hawkes late romantic stylings. Fine	

but unispired(?)

Two Inventions (1954)	12'
2 2 2 2 — 4 2 0 0 — tmp+1 — str	
Boosey & Hawkes; Bote & Bock	

Variations on a Theme of Muzio	19'
Clementi (1961)	
solo pf	
2 2 2 2 — 4 2 3 1 — tmp+1 — hp — cel — str	
Boosey & Hawkes	

Black, Stanley (1913-2002)

A Costume Comedy Overture	4'
(1955)	
2 2 2 2 — 2 2 0 0 — tmp — str	
Boosey & Hawkes	

Percussion Fantasy	6'
2 2 2 2 — 2 2 0 0 — tmp+1 — str	
Boosey & Hawkes	

Blackford, Richard (1954-)

Music for Carlow (1987)	6'
str	
Based on two Irish airs: "Follow me up to Carlow" and	
"Eileen aroon."	
Novello	

Blake, David (1936-)

Chamber Symphony (1966)	25'
1[1/pic] 1[1/eh] 1 1 — 2 1 0 0 — 1perc — str	
Novello	

Nocturne (1994)	14'
str	
Novello	

Scherzo and Two Dances (1981)	7'
1[1/pic] 0 2[1/Ebcl.2/bcl/ssx] 0 — 0 0 0 0 — pf —	
str[1.0.1.1.0]	
Novello	

Seasonal Variants (1985)	18'
1[1/pic] 0 2[1.2/bcl] 0 — 0 0 0 0 — pf —	
str[1.0.1.1.0]	
Novello	

Sonata alla Marchia (1978)	12'
0 2 0 0 — 2 0 0 0 — str	
Novello	

Blech, Leo (1871-1958)

Six Children's Songs 9'
solo high voice
2 2 2 2 — 2 1 0 0 — 1perc — hp — str
From op.21, 24, 25 and 27.
Contents - 1. Ein kleines Lied; 2. Heimkehr vom Feste; 3.
Nur eine kleine Geige; 4. Tintenheinz und
Plätscherlottchen; 5. Veilchen; 6. Wiegenlied im Herbst
UE

Bleyle, Karl (1880-1969)

Bacchanten-Overture, op.52 5'
2 2 2 2 — 3 2 0 1 — tmp+1 — hp — str
Breitkopf

Reineke Fuchs; Overture, op.23 7'
3 2 2 2 — 3 3 1 0 — tmp+1 — hp — str
Breitkopf

Schneewittchensuite, op.50 15'
2[1.2/pic] 2 2 2 — 3 2 0 1 — tmp — hp — str
Breitkopf

Bliss, Arthur (1891-1975)

Music for Strings (1935) 23'
str
Novello

Two Contrasts for String Orchestra 11'
(1970)
str
Novello

Bloch, Ernest (1880-1959)

Four Episodes (1929) 14'
1 1 1 1 — 1 0 0 0 — pf — str
Contents - 1. Humoresque Macabre; 2. Obsession; 3. Calm;
4. Chinese
Fleisher; Birchard

Blomdahl, Karl-Birger (1916-1968)

Adagio from "Vaknatten": Incidental 6'
music from the play (1945)
1 1 0 0 — 2 0 0 0 — str
Nordiska

Concerto grosso (1944) 20'
1[1/pic] 0 1 1 — 1 0 0 0 — str
Nordiska

Game for Eight; Choreographic Suite 25'
for Chamber Orchestra (1962)
1[1/pic] 1[1/eh] 1[1/bcl/asx] 1[1/cbn] — 1 1 2 0 —
tmp+4 — hp — 2pf[4hand.4hand/cel] — str[2.0.2.2.2]
perc: xyl, vib, glsp, sd, marching dr, basque dr, bd, tri, cym, tam-tam,
templeblk, woodblk, cenc, marac, guiro, claves, whip
Schott

Preludio and Allegro (1948) 6'
str
Nordiska

Blumer, Theodor (1881-1964)

Lyrisches Intermezzo (1939) 6'
1 1 2 1 — 2 2 1 0 — tmp+1 — hp[opt] —cel[opt]
— str
Fleisher; Zimmermann

Vagabund; Scherzo for Orchestra 5'
(1955)
2 2 2 2 — 2 2 1 0 — tmp+1 — str
Sikorski

Boccadoro, Carlo (1963-)

Adagio 9'
1 1 1 1 — 1 0 0 0 — str[1.1.1.1.1]
Presser

Ae Fond Kiss; For 7 Instruments 15'
1 0 1 0 — 0 0 0 0 — pf — str[1.1.1.1.0]
Presser

Mouvement for Orchestra 9'
2 2 2 2 — 2 2 0 0 — tmp — hp — str
Presser

Boelter, Karl (1952-)

Concerto for Violin and Orchestra 22'
(1999)
solo vn
2[1/pic.2] 2 2 2 — 4 3 3 1 — tmp+1 — hp — str
Boelter

Dharma (2001) 12'
1 1 1 1 — 2 1 0 0 — tmp+1 — pf — str
Boelter

Images from Goldsmith (2001)   18'
   solo hn
   0 0 2 2 — 0 0 0 0 — str
   Contents - 1. These Rocks by Custom Turn to Beds of
   Down; 2. Sprightly Land of Mirth and Social Ease; 3. I see
   the Lords of Human Kind Pass By; 4. Where the Broad
   Ocean Leans Against the Land
   mvt durations: 5' 3' 4' 6'
   Boelter

Boivin, Philippe   (1954-)

Concerto for Alto and Orchestra   15'
(1986)
   solo va
   2[1.2/pic] 2[1.2/eh] 2[1.2/Ebcl] 2 — 2 1 1 0 —
   str[8.8.6.6.4]
   Salabert

Bolcom, William   (1938-)

Commedia for (Almost) 18th   10'
Century Orchestra (1971)
   solo 2vn, vc
   1[1/pic] 2 1[1/Ebcl] 2 — 4 0 0 0 — tmp[opt] — pf
   — str
   Hn 3 and 4 are optional.
   Marks

Concertante for Violin, Flute and   18'
Oboe (1961)
   solo vn, fl, ob
   1 1 3 2 — 2 1 0 0 — hp — str
   Marks

Concerto for Violin and Orchestra in   23'
D (1983) Not bad! worth a full listen
   solo vn
   2 2 2 2 — 2 2 2 1 — tmp+2 — hp — pf/cel — str
   Marks

Concerto Serenade for Violin and   17'
String Orchestra (1964)
   solo vn
   str
   Marks

Medusa; A Monodrama for dramatic   25'
soprano and String Orchestra
(2003)
   solo S
   str
   Marks

Octet   20'
   1 0 1 1 — 0 0 0 0 — pf — str[1.0.1.1.1]
   Presser

Open House   35'
   solo T
   1 2 1 2 — 2 0 0 0 — 1perc — kybd — str
   Presser

Orphée Sérénade (1984)   20'
   solo pf
   1[1/pic] 1 1[1/Ebcl] 1 — 1 0 0 0 — pf —
   str(min)[1.1.1.1.1]
   Marks

A Seattle Overture; Seattle on a   6'
beautiful day (2005)
   2[1.2/pic] 2[1.eh] 3[1.2.bcl] 2[1.2/cbn] — 2 3 1
   — tmp+3 — hp — pf — str
   Marks

Session I   8'
   1[1/pic] 1[1/eh] 0 1 — 0 0 1 0 — 1perc —
   str[0.0.1.1.0]
   Presser

Session IV   8'
   0 0 1 0 — 0 0 1 0 — tape — 2perc — hp — pf —
   str[0.0.2.1.0]
   Tape to be prepared by the performers.
   Presser

Spring Concertino (1987)   10'
   solo ob
   2 1[1/eh] 2 2 — 1 0 0 0 — hp — str
   Marks

Summer Divertimento (1973)   25'
   2 0 1[1/Ebcl] 1 — 0 1 0 0 — 1perc — 2pf[hpsd.pf]
   — str[3.0.2.2.2]
   Marks

Symphony No.1 (1957)   18'
   2[1.2/pic] 1 1 1 — 4 2 1 0 — tmp+1 — pf — str
   Marks

Symphony No.3 (1979)   35'
   1[1/pic/afl] 2[1.2/eh] 1[1/Ebcl/bcl] 2 — 2 0 0 0 —
   pf/cel/elec pf — str[6.4.4.3.1]
   Marks

Bon, André   (1946-)

Ode; Pour orchestre "Mozart"   13'
(1979)
   2 2 2 2 — 2 0 0 0 — tmp — str[6.6.4.4.2]
Amphion

Ode II; Pour orchestre de chambre   15'
(1985)
   2 2 0 1 — 2 0 0 0 — tmp[opt] — str[4.3.2.2.1]
Amphion

Travelling (1989)   13'
   1 1 1 1 — 1 0 0 0 — hp — str[1.1.1.1.1]
Amphion

Bond, Victoria   (1945-)

Concertino (1980)   10'
   1 2 1 2 — 2 0 0 0 — tmp+1 — str
Subito

Journal (1981)   8'
   1 2 1 2 — 2 2 0 0 — tmp+1 — str
Subito; Fleisher

Bondon, Jacques   (1927-2008)

Chant et Danse (1974)   7'
   solo tbn
   1 1 1 1 — 1 1 1 0 — 1perc — str
Eschig

Symphonie latine (1973)   18'
   2 2 2 2 — 2 2 1 0 — tmp+1 — str
Eschig

Trois images concertantes (1982)   18'
   solo bn
   2 2 2 2 — 2 2 2 0 — 1perc — str
Eschig

Bonnet, Antoine   (1958-)

D'une Source Oubliée I (1987)   15'
   2 0 2 0 — 1 0 1 0 — 2perc — pf — str[1.0.1.3.1]
Salabert

La terre habitable I; Les eaux   13'
étroites (1998)
   1[1/afl] 1[1/eh] 2[1.bcl] 1 — 1 1 1 1 — 2perc — pf
   — str[1.1.2.2.1]
   perc: vib, marim
   Cycle of five pieces after texts by Julien Gracq.
Amphion

La terre habitable II; Aubrac (1995)   9'
   0 1[eh] 0 1 — 0 1 0 0 — 2perc — pf —
   str[1.0.1.1.0]
   Revised version (1996). Cycle of five pieces after texts by
   Julien Gracq.
Amphion

La terre habitable III; Les hautes   3'
terres du Sertalejo (1996)
   1 1 2[1.bcl] 1 — 1 1 1 1 — 2perc — pf —
   str[1.1.2.2.1]
   Cycle of five pieces after texts by Julien Gracq.
Amphion

La terre habitable IV; La presqu'île   12'
(1996)
   1 0 2[1.bcl] 0 — 1 0 1 1 — 2perc — pf —
   str[1.0.1.1.1]
   Cycle of five pieces after texts by Julien Gracq.
Amphion

La terre habitable V; Liberté grande   9'
(1997)
   1[1/afl] 1[1/eh] 2[1.bcl] 1 — 1 1 1 1 — 2perc — pf
   — str[1.1.2.2.1]
   Cycle of five pieces after texts by Julien Gracq.
Amphion; Salabert

Trajectoires (1988)   42'
   2[1/pic.2/afl] 0 2[1/Ebcl.2/bcl] 0 — 2 1 1 0 —
   4perc — pf — str[3.0.3.6.2]
Amphion

Boone, Charles   (1939-)

Fields / Singing (1976)   15'
   solo S
   2 1 0 0 — 0 1 2 0 — 2perc — pf — str[2.0.1.2.1]
Salabert

Linea Meridiana (1975)   13'
   solo S, A, CT
   1 0 1 0 — 0 0 0 0 — 1perc — hp — 2pf[pf.ham
   org] — str[0.0.1.1.0]
Salabert

San Zeno / Verona (1976)   *10'*
  1 1 1 1[1/cbn] — 0 0 0 0 — 2perc — 2pf[pf.org] —
  str[1.1.1.1.1]
  Salabert

Second Landscape (1973)   *14'*
  1 1 1 1[1/cbn] — 0 2 0 0 — 2perc — pf —
  str[1.1.1.1.2]
  Version with strings (6.6.4.4.2) is also available.
  Salabert

Trace (1983)   *20'*
  solo fl
  1 1 1 0 — 0 1 0 0 — 1perc — pf/org —
  str[1.0.1.1.1]
  Salabert

Borges, Joaquin   (1954-)

Suite Sofia (1993)   *22'*
  str
  Unión

Borkovec, Pavel   (1894-1972)

Sinfonietta da Camera (1947)   *22'*
  2[1.2/pic] 1 1 1 — 2 1 0 0 — 1perc — pf —
  str[6.6.6.4.2]
  perc: tri, sd
  Schott

Bose, Hans-Jürgen von   (1953-)

Concertino Per il H. W. H. (1991)   *3'*
  1 1 1 1 — 1 1 1 0 — tmp+1 — pf/synth —
  str[1.1.1.1.1]
  perc: tom-tom, sd, xyl
  Schott

Musik für ein Haus voll Zeit (1978)   *14'*
  2[1/pic.2/afl] 1[1/ob d'am] 3[1/Ebcl.2.bcl] 1[1/cbn] —
  1 1 1 0 — 3perc — 2hp[amp hp.hp] —
  2pf[pf/cel.hpsd/elec org] — str[4.0.3.3.1]
  perc: tmp, tom-tom, gong, glsp, chimes, crot, cym, tam-tam, bd,
  flexatone, marac, 2 lotos fl, paper, glsp
  Strings amplified.
  Schott

Prozess (1988)   *12'*
  1[1/pic/afl] 1[1/eh] 2 1[cbn] — 1 1 1 0 — tmp+2 —
  pf — str[1.1.1.1.1]
  perc: cym, chimes, bongos, tom-tom, 2 sd, bd, glsp, xyl, marim
  Schott

Scene (1991)   *23'*
  1[1/pic/afl] 1 1[1/Ebcl/bcl] 1[1/cbn] — 1 1[1/pic tpt]
  1 1 — 1[ssx/bsx/bassx] — tmp+2 — hp —
  2pf[pf/synth.synth] — str[1.1.2.2.2]
  perc: 3 tri, chimes, 4 cym, metal plate, hi-hat, tam-tam, 5 bongos, 5
  gong, tom-tom, sd, bd, marac, woodblk, claves, hyoshigi, glsp, xyl,
  vib, marim
  Schott

Travesties in a Sad Landscape   *12'*
(1978)
  1[1/pic/afl] 1[1/eh] 1[1/bcl] 1[cbn] — 1 1 1 0 —
  accordion — tmp+1 — 2pf[pf/cel.hamorg] —
  str[2.0.1.1.1]
  perc: chimes, flexatone, lotos fl, vib
  Schott

Bossi, Marco Enrico   (1861-1925)

Siciliana e Giga (stile antico) per   *6'*
Orchestra, op.73
  2[1.pic] 1 1 1 — 1 0 0 0 — tmp — str
  Fleisher

Boßler, Kurt   (1911-1976)

Metamorphosen (1973/74)   *8'*
  solo 2 tpt
  tmp+1 — str
  Bärenreiter

Boucourechliev, André   (1925-1997)

Le Chevelure de Bérénice (1988)   *20'*
  1 1 1 1 — 1 1 1 0 — 1perc — str[7.0.2.2.1]
  Salabert

Concerto for Piano and Orchestra   *21'*
(1975)
  solo pf
  2[1.2/pic] 0 2 2 — 2 2 1 0 — 2perc — str
  Salabert

Lit de Neige (1984)   *20'*
  solo S
  2 1 2 1 — 1 1 1 0 — 3perc — hp — pf/cel —
  str[1.1.1.1.1]
  Salabert

Boulez, Pierre   (1925-)

His music is hella hard for all involved (rewarding

Dérive 2; (Work in progress) He dead)   22' the)
(1988/2001)
    0 1[eh] 1 1 — 1 0 0 0 — 2perc — hp — pf —
    str[1.0.1.1.0]   *Great piece. Variable length.*
    perc: marim, vib   *Super difficult.*
UE

Domaines (1969)   29'
    solo cl
    1 1 1[bcl] 1 — 1 1 4[atbn.2ttbn.btbn] 0 — asx —
    elec gtr — 1perc — hp — str[1.1.2.2.1]
    perc: marim
UE

Mémoriale: (...explosante-   7'
fixe...Originel) (1985)
    solo fl
    0 0 0 0 — 2 0 0 0 — str[3.0.2.1.0]
UE

Originel: From "...explosante-   7'
fixe..." (1993)
    solo (midi) fl
    2 2[1.2/eh] 3[1.2.bcl] 2 — 2 2 2 1 — electronics
    — str[3.0.2.2.1]
    Orchestra version of his "Mémoriale."
UE

Transitoire V: From "...explosante-   15'
fixe..." (1993)
    solo (midi) fl
    2 2 3[1.2.bcl] 2 — 2 2 2 1 — electronics —
    str[3.0.2.2.1]
UE

Transitoire VII: From "...explosante-   13'
fixe..." (1991)
    solo (midi) fl
    2 2 3[1.2.bcl] 2 — 2 2 2 1 — electronics —
    str[3.0.2.2.1]
UE

Bousch, François   (1946-)

Spirales Insolites (1982)   17'
    2 0 2[1.2/bcl] 0 — 1 0 0 0 — 1perc — hp — synth
    — str[1.1.1.1.1]
    Salabert

Boutry, Roger   (1932-)

Sérénade   14'
    solo asx
    1 1 1 1 — 1 1 1 1 — pf — str
    Salabert

Boyle, Rory   (1951-)

Moel Bryn Divisions (1985)   10'
    str
    Chester Novello

Night Pictures (1986)   12'
    1[1/pic/afl] 1 1 — 1 1 1 0 — 1perc — pf —
    str[1.1.1.1.1]
    Chester Novello

Brandmüller, Theo   (1948-)

Ach, trauriger Mond; Klage um   14'
Federico Garcia Lorca (1977)
    solo perc
    str
    Boosey & Hawkes

Carillon joyeux (1994)   10'
    str[6.5.4.4.1]
    Breitkopf

Concerto for Organ (1981)   25'
    solo org
    0 0 0 0 — 0 3 0 0 — 2perc — str
    Boosey & Hawkes

Missa Morgenstern (1978)   17'
    1[1/pic] 0 1[bcl] 0 — 0 0 0 0 — tmp+2 — pf —
    str[1.0.1.1.0]
    Breitkopf

Reminiszenzen (1976)   15'
    3[1.2/pic.rec] 2 2 2 — 2 2 3 0 — tmp+2 — str
    Boosey & Hawkes

Si j'etais Domenico...;   25'
Phantasmagorie für Streicher mit
konzertierendem Cembalo (1984)
    solo hpsd
    str
    Breitkopf

Venezianische Schatten (1981)   8'
    1[1/pic] 1[eh] 1 1[1/cbn] — 2 1 0 0 — 2perc — str
    Boosey & Hawkes

Brant, Henry   (1913-2008)

Lyric Piece (1933)   *5'*
1 1 1 1 — 1 1 1 0 — str
Fleisher

Prelude and Fugue (1935)   *5'*
0 0 0 0 — 2 2 2 1 — str
Fleisher

A Requiem in Summer; In Memory   *10'*
of my Father
2 2 2 2 — 0 0 0 0 — str
Strings without db.
Fleisher

Brauel, Henning   (1940-)

Les Fenêtres Simultanées (1975)   *11'*
1 1 1 1 — 2 1 1 0 — str[7.0.3.2.1]
Schott

Braun, Peter Michael   (1936-)

Problems and Solutions (1974)   *18'*
str
Boosey & Hawkes

Quanta (1958)   *31'*
1[1/pic] 1[1/eh] 1 1[cbn] — 0 0 0 0 — 1perc — hp
— str[1.0.1.1.1]
perc: marim
Schirmer

Terms (1963)   *20'*
0 0 1 1 — 0 1 0 0 — 2perc — hp — 2pf[pf.org] —
str[1.0.0.1.0]
Schirmer

Braun, Yehezkel   (1922-)

Apartment To Let   *19'*
1[1/pic] 1 1 1 — 1 0 0 0 — narrator — str
Text by Lea Goldberg.
Presser

Concerto for Clarinet and Chamber   *22'*
Orchestra
solo cl
2 0 0 2 — 2 0 0 0 — str
Presser

Emek Hayarden (The Yordan   *24'*
Valley): Ballet Suite
1 0 1 1 — 1 1 1 0 — 1perc — pf — str[0.0.0.0.1]
Presser

Et Laetitia Cordis   *23'*
solo fl
0 2 0 2 — 2 2 0 0 — 1perc — str
Presser

Illuminations to the Book of Ruth   *18'*
2[1.2/pic] 1[1/eh] 0 1 — 2 1 1 0 — 4perc — hp —
hpsd — str
Presser

Serenade for Chamber Orchestra   *12'*
1 1 1 1 — 1 0 0 0 — str
Presser

Serenade II   *21'*
1[1/pic] 1 1 1 — 1 0 0 0 — str
Presser

Braunfels, Walter   (1882-1954)

Abschied vom Walde (1913)   *5'*
solo T
2 2 2 2 — 4 1 0 0 — tmp — hp — str
Finale from his opera "Die Vögel."
UE

Divertimento, op.42 (1929)   *20'*
2[1.2/pic] 2 2 2 — 1 2 0 0 — 2sx — tmp — hp —
str
UE

Bräutigam, Helmut   (1914-1942)

Concerto for Flute, Oboe and   *25'*
Bassoon
solo fl, ob, bn
0 0 0 0 — 2 0 0 0 — str
Breitkopf

Festliche Musik (1939)   *7'*
2 2 0 0 — 0 2 0 0 — str
Breitkopf

Music for Orchestra, Wk.8   *24'*
2 2 2 2 — 4 2 0 0 — tmp+1 — str
Breitkopf

Tänzerische Suite   *28'*
2 2 2 2 — 2 2 0 0 — tmp+1 — str
Breitkopf

Bresgen, Cesar (1913-1988)

Concerto for Horn (1963)   16'
solo hn
1[1/pic] 0 1 1 — 0 1 0 0 — tmp+1 — str
perc: sd
Breitkopf

Concerto for Trombone (1980)   19'
solo atbn
2 2 2 2 — 3 2 0 0 — tmp+1 — hp — cel — str
Breitkopf

Double Concerto (1979)   23'
solo 2vc
1[1/pic] 1 2[1.2/bcl] 0 — 2 1 1 0 — tmp+1 — str
Breitkopf

Elenka (1980)   22'
solo balalaika, hp
1[1/pic] 1 2 1 — 2 1 1 0 — tmp+1 — str
Breitkopf

Intrada (1965)   7'
2[1.2/pic] 2 2 2 — 4 2 3 0 — tmp+1 — str
Breitkopf

Bridge, Frank (1879-1941)

Norse Legend (1905)   5'
1 1 2 1 — 2 2 1 0 — tmp+1 — hp — str
Boosey & Hawkes

Rosemary (1906)   2'
str
Also possible with tmp-hp-str.
Boosey & Hawkes

There Is A Willow Grows Aslant A   10'
Brook (1928)
1 1 2 1 — 1 0 0 0 — hp — str
Fleisher

Two Entr'actes (1926)   7'
1 1 2 1 — 2 2 1 0 — tmp — hp — str
Boosey & Hawkes

Two Intermezzi: From the incidental   10'
music to the play "Threads" (1921)
1 1 2 1 — 2 2 1 0 — tmp+1 — str
perc: tri
Boosey & Hawkes

Two Old English Songs (1916)   10'
str
Db is optional.
Contents - 1. Sally in our Alley; 2. Cherry Ripe
Boosey & Hawkes

Vignettes de danse (1925)   10'
1[1/pic] 1 2 1 — 2 2 1 0 — tmp+1 — hp — str
perc: cym, tri, cast[opt], sd[opt], tambn
Boosey & Hawkes

Britten, Benjamin (1913-1976)

Concerto for Piano No.1; Original   34'
version, op.13 (1938)
solo pf
2[1/pic.2/pic] 2[1.2/eh] 2 2 — 4 2 3 1 — tmp+2 —
hp — str
Contents - 1. Toccata; 2. Waltz; 3. Impromptu; 4. March
mvt durations: 12' 5' 8' 9'
Boosey & Hawkes

Concerto for Violin and Viola;   25'
Double Concerto (1932)
solo vn, va
2[1.2/pic] 2 2 2 — 2 2 0 0 — tmp+1 — str
perc: cym
mvt durations: 7' 7' 8'
Oxford

Concerto for Violin No.1, op.15   31'
(1939)
solo vn
3[1.2/pic.3/pic] 2[1.2/eh] 2 2 — 4 3 3 1 — tmp+2
— hp — str
perc: sd, cym, glsp, bd, td, tri
Boosey & Hawkes

Death in Venice: Suite, op.88a   27'
(1973)
2[1.2/pic] 2 2[1.2/bcl] 2 — 2 2 2 1 —
tmp[tmp/crot]+4perc — hp — pf — str[6.4.3.3.2]
perc: tuned dr, cym, bell, 2 glsp, vib, 2 gong, xyl, sus cym, 2 tam-
tam, marim, 3 tom-tom, 3 Chinese dr
Compiled by Steuart Bedford in 1984.
Faber

Gloriana: The Courtly Dances   10'
(1953)
2 2 2 2 — 4 2 3 1 — tmp+2 — str
perc: td, sd, tambn, cym, bd, tri
Contents - 1. March; 2. Coranto; 3. Pavane; 4. Morris
Dance; 5. Lavolta; 6. Reprise of the March
Boosey & Hawkes

Irish Reel (1936)   3'
1[1/pic] 1 1 1 — 1 0 0 0 — tmp — hp — str
Faber

Johnson Over Jordan: Suite (1939)　　18'
　1[1/pic] 1 2[1/Ebdl.2/bcl/asx] 1 — 0 2 1 0 —
　tmp+1 — pf — str
　perc: sus cym, cym, bd, tam-tam, td, sd
Faber

Lachrymae, op.48a (1948)　　15'
　solo va
　str
　Arranged by the composer in 1976.
Boosey & Hawkes

Matinées musicales, op.24; Second　　16'
Suite of Five Movements from
Rossini (1941)
　2[1.2/pic] 2 2 2 — 2 2 3 0 — tmp+2 — hp[or pf] —
　cel[or pf] — str
　perc: sd, tambn, bd, cym, sus cym, tri, td, woodblk
　Contents - 1. March; 2. Nocturne; 3. Waltz; 4. Pantomime;
　5. Moto Perpetuo (Solfeggi e Gorgheggi)
　mvt durations: 3' 4' 2' 4' 3'
Boosey & Hawkes; Luck's

Men of Goodwill; Variations on a　　8'
Christmas Carol (God rest ye,
merry Gentlemen) (1947)
　3[1.2.pic] 2 2 2 — 4 2 3 1 — tmp+2 — hp — str
　perc: cym, sus cym, sd, td, bd, xyl
Faber

Overture Paul Bunyan (1978)　　5'
　2[1.pic] 1 3[1.2.bcl] 1 — 2 2 2 1 — tmp+2 —
　hp[opt] — pf[opt] — str
　perc: bd, sd, cym, tambn, tri, td
Faber

Peter Grimes: Four Sea Interludes,　　16'
op.33a (1945)
　2[1/pic.2/pic] 2 2[1.2/Ebcl] 3[1.2.cbn] — 4 3 3 1 —
　tmp+2 — hp — str
　perc: chimes, xyl, sd, tambn, cym, gong, bd
　Contents - 1. Dawn; 2. Sunday Morning; 3. Moonlight; 4.
　Storm
　mvt durations: 3' 4' 4' 5'
Boelke

Peter Grimes: Passacaglia, op.33b　　7'
(1945)
　2[1.2/pic] 2 2 3[1.2/cbn] — 4 3 3 1 — tmp+3 — hp
　— cel — str
　perc: sd, gong, cym, tam-tam, bd, td, tambn
Boosey & Hawkes

Phaedra; Cantata for Mezzo-　　15'
Soprano and Small Orchestra,
op.93 (1975)
　solo Mz
　tmp+2 — hpsd — str
　perc: chimes, cym, tam-tam, td, bd, sus cym
Faber

Plymouth Town (1931)　　25'
　1 1 2 2 — 2 1 1 0 — tmp+1 — str
　perc: bd, cym
Faber

Prelude and Fugue, op.29 (1943)　　9'
　str[5.5.3.3.2]
Boosey & Hawkes

Quatre Chansons Françaises　　15'
(1928)
　solo S
　2 1 3[1.2.bcl] 2 — 4 0 0 0 — 1perc — hp — pf —
　str
　perc: sus cym
Faber

Simple Symphony, op.4 (1934)　　16'
　str
　Contents - 1. Boisterous Bourée; 2. Playful Pizzicato; 3.
　Sentimental Sarabande; 4. Frolicsome Finale
　mvt durations: 3' 3' 7' 3'　*Neo classical/Baroque*
Oxford

Sinfonietta, op.1 (1932)　　15'
　1 1 1 1 — 1 0 0 0 — str(min)[1.1.1.1.1]
Boosey & Hawkes　*More musically interesting than Op.4*
　　　　　　　　Popular conductor piece
Sinfonietta, op.1 (1932)　　15'
　1 1 1 1 — 2 0 0 0 — str
　Version for small orchestra arranged by the composer in
　1936.
Boosey & Hawkes

Soirées musicales, op.9; Suite of　　11'
Five Movements from Rossini
(1936)
　2[1/pic.2/pic] 2 2 2 — 4 2 3 0 — tmp+3 — hp[or
　pf] — str
　Payable with: 1 1 1 0 - 0 1 1 0 - 1perc - hp(or pf) - str
　Contents - 1. March; 2. Canzonetta; 3. Tirolese; 4. Bolero;
　5. Tarantella
　mvt durations: 1' 3' 2' 2' 2'
Boosey & Hawkes

Suite on English Folk Tunes, op.90　　14'
(1974)
　2[1.2/pic] 2[1.2/eh] 2 2 — 2 2 0 0 — tmp+2 — hp
　— str
　perc: sd, bd, tabor, tri, tamburo
Faber

Symphony for Cello and Orchestra,　　35'
op.68 (1963)
　solo vc
　2[1.2/pic] 2 2[1.2/bcl] 2[1.cbn] — 2 2 1 1 — tmp+2
　— str
　perc: bd, cym, tambn, whip, gong, sd, td, vib, tam-tam
　mvt durations: 13' 4' 10' 8'
Boosey & Hawkes

Temporal Variations (1936)   *15'*
  solo ob
  str
Faber

Variations on "Sellenger's Round";   *13'*
Aldeburgh Variations (1953)
  str
  Composite work written by Britten, Berkeley, Oldham,
  Searle, Tippet, Walton.
Boosey & Hawkes

Variations on a Theme of Frank   *25'*
Bridge, op.10 (1937)
  str
Boosey & Hawkes

The Young Person's Guide to the   *17'*
Orchestra, op.34; Variations and
Fugue on a Theme of Purcell
(1946)
  3[1.2.pic] 2 2 2 — 4 2 3 1 — speaker[opt] —
  tmp+5 — hp — str
  perc: xyl, tri, sd, cym, bd, tambn, gong, whip, cast, Chinese block
  Omissions, authorized by the composer, make a
  performance with 4 percussionists possible.
Boosey & Hawkes

Brizzi, Aldo   (1960-)

Le Erbe Nella Thule (1985)   *24'*
  solo S
  1 0 0 0 — 1 0 0 0 — 1perc — hp — str[1.1.1.1.0]
Salabert

Brødsgaard, Anders   (1955-)

Ghostorchestra (1993)   *20'*
  1 1 0 0 — 0 1 0 0 — electronics — hp — pf —
  str[1.0.1.1.0]
Hansen

Magam (2002)   *8'*
  1[1/pic] 1 1 1 — 1 0 0 0 — 1perc — pf —
  str[1.1.1.1.1]
  perc: marim
Hansen

Procession II (1986)   *25'*
  1 1 2 0 — 1 1 1 0 — 1 — 3perc — pf —
  str[1.1.3.2.1]
Hansen

Brott, Alexander   (1915-2005)

Three Astral Visions (1959)   *29'*
  str
Boosey & Hawkes

Brouk, Joanna   (1949-)

Lalinia electra; Part 1
  2 2[1.eh] 2 2 — 2 1 0 0 — cel — str
Fleisher

Brouwer, Léo   (1939-)

Concerto for Guitar No.1 (1972)   *26'*
  solo gtr
  1 1 1 1 — 1 1 0 0 — 3perc — cel — str
Eschig

Concerto for Guitar No.4; Concierto   *34'*
de Toronto (1987)
  solo gtr
  1[1/pic] 0 2[1.2/Ebcl] 0 — 1 1 0 0 — 2perc — pf
  — str
EDY

Retrats catalans (1983)   *18'*
  solo gtr
  2 0 0 0 — 0 0 0 0 — tmp+1 — pf — str[4.3.2.2.1]
Eschig

Brown, Earle   (1926-2002)

Available Forms I (1961)   *7'*
  1 1 3[1.bcl.Ebcl] 0 — 1 1 1 0 — 2perc — hp — pf
  — str[1.1.1.1.1]
  Variable duration: 7'-15'.
AMP

Centering (1973)   *20'*
  solo vn
  1 0 1 1 — 1 1 1 0 — pf — str[1.0.1.1.0]
Peters

Event: Synergy II; For instrumental
Ensemble and two conductors
(1968)
  2 3[1.2.eh] 4[1.2.3.bcl] 2 — 0 0 0 0 —
  str[4.0.2.2.0]
  Two conductors needed. Variable duration.
  Other possible instrumentations: 12(1.eh)1(bcl)1 - 0000 -
  str(1.1.1.1.0) or 11(eh)21 - 0000 - str(1.1.1.1.0).
Peters

Module 3 (1969)   10'
　　1 1 2 1 — 1 2 1 0 — 3perc — hp — pf — str
　　Variable duration (ca.10-15).
　Peters

Modules 1 & 2 (1966)   10'
　　2 2[1.eh] 2[1.bcl] 2[1.cbn] — 2 2 2 1 — str
　　Variable duration (ca.10-20). Movements can be performed
　　separately.
　Peters

Novara (1962)   6'
　　1 0 1[bcl] 0 — 0 1 0 0 — pf — str[1.1.1.1.0]
　　Variable duration (ca.6-12).
　Peters

Sign Sounds (1972)   15'
　　1 0 2 1 — 0 1 1 0 — 4perc — hp — 2pf[pf.cel] —
　　str[1.1.1.1.1]
　　Variable duration (ca.15-18).
　Peters

Brown, James Francis   (1969-)

Sinfonietta (2000)   19'
　　1 1 1 1 — 1 0 0 0 — str[2.2.2.2.1]
　Faber

Brunner, Adolf   (1901-1992)

Partita for Piano and Orchestra   17'
(1938/39)
　　solo pf
　　2 2 2 2 — 2 2 0 0 — tmp+1 — str
　Bärenreiter

Bruns, Victor   (1904-1996)

Concerto, op.61   17'
　　solo eh
　　1 1 1 1 — 2 0 0 0 — 1perc — str
　Breitkopf

Concerto for Bassoon, op.41   20'
　　solo bn
　　1 1 1 1 — 2 2 0 0 — 1perc — str
　Breitkopf

Concerto for Cello, op.29   32'
　　solo vc
　　2 2 2 2 — 4 2 3 1 — tmp+1 — str
　Breitkopf

Concerto for Clarinet, op.76   25'
　　solo cl
　　1 1 1 1 — 2 0 0 0 — tmp+1 — str
　Breitkopf

Concerto for Doublebass, op.73   18'
　　solo db
　　str
　Breitkopf

Concerto for Flute, op.51   17'
　　solo fl
　　1 1 1 1 — 2 0 0 0 — tmp+1 — str
　Breitkopf

Concerto for Flute and English   20'
Horn, op.74
　　solo fl, eh
　　1perc — str
　Breitkopf

Concerto for Horn, op.63   20'
　　solo hn
　　1 1 2 1 — 0 0 0 0 — tmp+1 — str
　Breitkopf

Concerto for Trumpet, op.50   16'
　　solo tpt
　　1 1 1 1 — 3 0 1 0 — tmp+1 — str
　Breitkopf

Concerto for Viola, op.69   25'
　　solo va
　　1 1 1 1 — 2 0 0 0 — tmp+1 — str
　Breitkopf

Concerto for Violin, op.36   25'
　　solo vn
　　2 2 2 2 — 4 2 3 1 — tmp+1 — str
　Breitkopf

Concerto for Violin, op.53   24'
　　solo vn
　　1 1 1 1 — 2 0 0 0 — 1perc — str
　Breitkopf

Das Edelfräulein als Bäuerin: 17'
Orchestersuite, op.69
　　2 2 2 2 — 4 2 3 0 — 1perc — hp — str
　Breitkopf

Minna von Barnhelm: Overture,   6'
op.39
　　2 1 2 2 — 2 2 0 0 — 1perc — cel — str
　Breitkopf

Sinfonietta, op.23   26'
  2 2 1 — 3 2 0 0 — tmp — str
Breitkopf

Symphony No.6; Sinfonia breve,   25'
op.67
  3 2 2 2 — 4 3 0 0 — tmp+1 — str
Breitkopf

Brust, Herbert   (1900-1968)

Kurische Nehrung, op.36   12'
  1 1[1/eh] 2 0 — 1 1 1 0 — 1perc — 2pf[pf.harm]
  — str
Boosey & Hawkes

Ostpreußische Fischertänze, op.34   13'
  1 1 1 0 — 0 1 1 0 — tmp+1 — pf — str
Boosey & Hawkes

Bruun, Peter   (1968-)

Bag Den Kan Fredens Ranker Gro   7'
(Behind it grow the branches of
peace) (1999)
  1[afl] 1[eh] 1 1 — 1 0 0 0 — str[1.0.1.1.0]
Hansen

Himmel og Jord (Heaven and Earth)   8'
(1996)
  1 0 1 0 — 0 0 0 0 — gtr — 1perc — cel —
  str[0.0.1.0.1]
Hansen

Tre Små Stykker (2004)   10'
  1 1 1 0 — 0 2 1 0 — 1perc — pf — str[3.2.1.1.1]
Hansen

Twelve to Remember, Twelve to   13'
Come (2001)
  solo tbn
  1[1/pic/afl] 1[1/eh] 1[1/Ebcl] 1 — 1 0 1 0 — elec
  gtr, accordion — 1perc — hp — pf — str[1.1.1.1.1]
Hansen

Bryars, Gavin   (1943-)

Aus den Letzten Tagen (1991)   15'
  0 0 1[1/bcl] 0 — 0 0 0 0 — 2perc — kybd —
  str[1.1.0.1.0]
  perc: marim, vib
  Kybd = Korg M1
Schott

Four Elements (1990)   30'
  0 0 1[bcl] 0 — 1 1[flug] 1 1 — asx — taped
  voice[or A] — 2perc — 2pf[pf.kybd] — str[0.0.0.0.1]
  perc: vib, marim, chimes, sus cym, sizzle cym, antique cym, tam-
  tam, Japanese temple bell, water gong, marktree, cast, bd
Schott

Buck, Ole   (1945-)

Aquarelles (1983)   9'
  1 0 1 0 — 0 0 0 0 — gtr — 1perc — pf —
  str[1.0.0.1.0]
Hansen

Chamber Music I (1979)   10'
  1 1 1 1 — 1 1 0 0 — str[1.1.1.1.0]
Hansen

Chamber Music II (1982)   10'
  1 1 1 1 — 1 0 0 0 — str[1.1.1.1.0]
Hansen

Flower Ornament Music (2002)   18'
  1[1/afl] 1[1/eh] 1[1/bcl] 1 — 1 1 1 0 — 3perc — hp
  — pf — str[1.1.1.1.1]
Hansen

Landscapes I (1992)   20'
  1 0 1 0 — 0 1 0 0 — hp — pf — str[1.0.1.1.0]
Hansen

Landscapes II (1994)   20'
  1 0 1 0 — 0 1 0 0 — hp — pf — str[1.0.1.1.0]
Hansen

Landscapes III   21'
  1 0 1 1 — 0 1 0 0 — hp — pf — str[1.0.1.1.0]
Hansen

Landscapes IV (1995)   7'
  1 0 1 1 — 0 1 0 0 — hp — pf — str[1.0.1.1.0]
Hansen

Overture (1966)   7'
  2 2 2 2 — 2 2 0 0 — tmp — str
Hansen

Pastorals (1975)   16'
  2 2 2 1 — 1 2 0 0 — 1perc — str
Hansen

Preludes I - V (1967)   7'
  1 1 1 1 — 1 1 1 0 — 1perc — pf — str
Hansen

A Tree (1996)   *12'*
1 1 1 1 — 1 1 0 0 — 1perc — pf — str[1.1.1.1.1]
Hansen

Burgan, Patrick   (1960-)

Oiseau d'éternité; Five Poems for   *15'*
Soprano, Mezzo-Soprano and
Baritone
solo S, Mz, Bar
1 0 0 1 — 1 1 0 0 — asx — hp — str[1.0.0.0.0]
Presser

Burgon, Geoffrey   (1941-2010)

Brideshead Variations (1981)   *18'*
1[1/pic] 1[1/eh] 0 1 — 1 1 0 0 — hp — str
Chester Novello

The Chronicles of Narnia Suite   *14'*
(1991)
1[1/pic] 1 0 1 — 1 1 0 0 — 1perc — str
Chester Novello

Goldberg's Dream (Running   *20'*
Figures); Ballet (1975)
1[1/pic] 1 1 0 — 1 1 1 0 — 1perc —
3pf[pf.harm.hpsd] — str[1.0.1.1.0]
Chester Novello

Suite from Bleak House (1991)   *12'*
1 0 1 1 — 1 1[1/crt] 0 0 — hp[opt] — str
Chester Novello

Suite from Martin Chuzzlewit   *24'*
(1994)
1[1/pic] 1[1/eh] 1[1/bcl] 1 — 1 0 0 0 — tmp/perc
— str
Chester Novello

Burkhard, Willy   (1900-1955)

Canzona, op.76 (1945)   *9'*
solo 2 fl
str
Bärenreiter

Concertino, op.94 (1954)   *14'*
solo 2 fl, hpsd
str
Bärenreiter

Concerto for Viola and Orchestra,   *20'*
op.93 (1953)
solo va
2[1.2/pic] 2 3[1.2.bcl] 2 — 3 2 2 0 — tmp+2 — str
Bärenreiter

Concerto for Violin, op.69 (1943)   *20'*
solo vn
0 0 1 1 — 2 0 0 0 — hp — str
UE

Kleine konzertante Suite   *16'*
(Kaleidoskop) für Orchester, op.79
(1946)
2[1/pic.2] 2 2 2 — 2 2 1 0 — tmp+2 — hp — str
Bärenreiter

Serenade, op.77 (1945)   *25'*
1 0 1 1 — 1 0 0 0 — hp — str[1.0.1.0.1]
Boosey & Hawkes

Toccata, op.55 (1939)   *12'*
str
Boosey & Hawkes

Toccata for Chamber Orchestra,   *23'*
op.86 (1951)
1[1/pic] 0 1 1 — 0 1 0 0 — tmp+2 — str
Bärenreiter

Burt, Francis   (1926-)

Blind Visions (1995)   *17'*
solo ob
0 0 0 0 — 0 2[1/pic tpt.2/pic tpt] 2[1/atbn.2] 0 —
cimb — 3perc — str[8.6.4.4.2]
UE

Echoes (1989)   *10'*
1 0 1 0 — 1 1 0 0 — 1perc — pf — str[1.0.1.1.0]
UE

The Skull; Cantata for Tenor and   *10'*
Orchestra (1955)
solo T
1 1 1 1 — 1 1 1 0 — str
UE

Busch, Adolf   (1891-1952)

Concerto for Violin   *25'*
solo vn
2 2 2 2 — 2 2 0 0 — tmp — str
Breitkopf

Divertimento, op.30   19'
  1 1 1 1 — 2 1 0 0 — tmp — str
Breitkopf

Variations on a Theme by W. A.   20'
Mozart
  2 2 2 2 — 3 2 0 0 — tmp — str
Breitkopf

Bush, Alan   (1900-1995)

Partita Concertante, op.63 (1965)   14'
  2 1 2 1 — 2 2 1 0 — tmp+1 — str
Novello

Busoni, Ferruccio   (1866-1924)

Berceuse élégiaque (1907)   9'
  2 1 2[1.bcl] 2 — 2 0 0 0 — tmp[tmp/gong] — hp
  — pf/cel — str[6.6.4.4.2]
Arrangement of Busoni's "Berceuse No.7" by John Adams
(1989). See also "Verein für Musikalische
Privataufführungen" (Appendix p.399) for Erwin Stein's
arrangement.
Boosey & Hawkes

Concert Piece in D major;   21'
Concertino Part I, op.31a (Busoni
Verz. 236)
  solo pf
  2 2 2 2 — 4 2 3 0 — tmp — str
Breitkopf

Concertante Suite from W. A.   11'
Mozart's Opera "Idomeneo"
(Busoni Verz. B85)
  2 2 2 2 — 2 2 3 0 — tmp — str
Breitkopf

Indian Fantasia, op.44 (Busoni   28'
Verz. 264)
  solo pf
  2[1.2/pic] 2[1.2/eh] 2 2 — 3 2 0 0 — tmp+4 — hp
  — str
Breitkopf

Lustspiel Overture, op.38 (Busoni   8'
Verz. 245)
  3[1.2.pic] 2 2 2 — 4 2 0 0 — tmp+1 — str
Breitkopf

Romanza e Scherzoso in F minor;   10'
Concertino Part II, op.54 (Busoni
Verz. 290)
  solo pf
  2[1.2/pic] 2 2 2 — 4 2 3 0 — tmp+1[opt] — str
  perc: glsp
Breitkopf

Rondo concertante (Busoni Verz.   9'
B87)
  solo pf
  1 0 2 2 — 2 2 0 0 — tmp — str
  Based on the Finale of Mozart's K.482
Breitkopf

Tanzwalzer, op.53 (Busoni Verz.   13'
288)
  2[1.2/pic] 2 2 2 — 4 2 3 0 — tmp+2 — str
Breitkopf

Büsser, Henri   (1872-1973)

Dors là-bas petit Baya; Berceuse   3'
d'Afrique
  solo voice
  1 1 1 1 — 1 0 0 0 — hp — str
Eschig

Soupir, op.109, No.3   3'
  solo voice
  1 1 1 1 — 1 0 0 0 — str
Eschig

Butting, Max   (1888-1976)

Sinfonietta mit Banjo; 1.   18'
Rundfunkmusik, op.37 (1929)
  2 1 2 3 — 1 3 3 0 — 1 — banjo — 1perc —
  str[1.0.1.1.1]
UE

C

Cage, John   (1912-1992)

Cheap Imitation; Version for 24   35'
Players
 3[1.2/pic.2/afl] 2[1.2/eh] 2[1.2/bcl] 1 — 1 1 1 1 —
 asx — gtr — 2perc — hp — 2pf[pf.cel] —
 str[1.1.1.1.1]
 perc: chimes, glsp, marim
Peters

Concerto for Prepared Piano and   22'
Chamber Orchestra very cool piece!
 solo prepared pf
 1[1/pic] 2[1.eh] 2 1 — 1 1 2 1 — 4perc — hp —
 pf/cel — str[1.1.1.1.1]
Peters

Fourteen   15'
 solo pf
 2[1/pic.bfl] 0 2[1.bcl] 0 — 1 1 0 0 — 2perc —
 str[1.1.1.1.1]
Peters

Quartets I-VIII; For an Orchestra of   40'
24 Instruments
 1 2 1 2 — 2 0 0 0 — str[5.4.3.3.1]
 Also available: "Quartets I-VIII. For an Orchestra of 41
 Instruments": 2222 - 2200 - str (8.7.6.5.3).
Peters

The Seasons; Ballet in One Act   15'
 2[1.2/pic] 2[1.2/eh] 2[1/Ebcl.2/bcl] 2 — 2 2 2 0 —
 tmp+1 — hp — pf/cel — str[8.6.4.3.2]
 perc: glsp, xyl, cym, tam-tam, bd
Peters

Sixteen Dances Also worth a listen   53'
 1 0 0 0 — 0 1 0 0 — 4perc — pf — str[1.0.0.1.0]
Peters

Ten   30'
 1 1 1 0 — 0 0 1 0 — 1perc — pf — str[1.1.1.1.0]
Peters

Thirteen   30'
 1 1 1 1 — 0 1 1 0 — tmp+2 — str[1.1.1.1.0]
 perc: 2 xyl
Peters

Twenty Three —> could pair well w/   23'
 str[13.0.5.5.0]   Metamorphosen
Peters

Campo, Frank   (1927-)

Partita for Two Chamber   14'
Orchestras, op.45
 1 1 2[1.bcl] 1 — 1 0 0 0 — 2perc — str
 Groups are: 102(1.bcl)0-0000-1perc-str and 0101-1000-
 1perc-str
Fleisher

Campos-Parsi, Héctor   (1922-1998)

Divertimento del Sur
 1 0 1 0 — 0 0 0 0 — str
Peer

Capanna, Robert   (1952-)

Concerto for Chamber Orchestra
(1974)
 1[1/afl] 1[1/eh] 1 1 — 1 1 1 0 — 1perc — hp — pf
 — str
Fleisher

Carter, Elliott   (1908-)

Concerto for Clarinet (1996)   18'
 solo cl
 1 2[1.2/eh] 0 1 — 1 1 1 1 — 3perc — hp — pf —
 str[1.1.1.1.1]
 perc: glsp, 4 bongos, 3 tom-tom, 3 sus cym, wood dr, tam-tam, xyl, 2
 metal blocks, templeblk, 2 sd, vib, woodblk, cencerros, bd
Boosey & Hawkes

Concerto for Flute (2008)   13'
 solo fl
 1[1/pic] 1[1/eh] 2[1.2/bcl] 1[1/cbn] — 2 1 1 0 —
 1perc — hp — pf — str(min)[2.2.2.2.2]
 perc: marim, xyl, vib, log dr, 5 templeblks, 2 woodblks, sd, 4 bongos,
 4 tom-tom, 2 cym, tam-tam, shaker, almglocke, bd, pipe
Boosey & Hawkes

46

Concerto for Oboe, Concertino   25'
Group and Orchestra (1987)
    solo ob
    1[1/afl/pic] 0 1[1/bcl] 0 — 1 0 1 0 —— 1perc —
    str[10.8.2.6.4]
    Concertino group: 4 va, 1 perc (4 tmp, vib, glsp, 2
    metal blks, 2 woodblks, 4 templeblks, 2 cowbells, 4
    bongo, 2 tom-tom, sus cym, guiro)
    perc: marim, xyl, bd, tam-tam, military dr, 2 sd, 2 sus cym
    Also possible with strings (8.6.0.4.2).
Boosey & Hawkes

Dialogues; For Piano and large   14'
Ensemble (2003)
    solo pf
    1[1/pic] 1[1/eh] 1 1[1/cbn] — 2 1 1 0 —
    str(min)[2.2.2.2.2]
Boosey & Hawkes

The Minotaur: Suite from the Ballet   25'
(1947)
    2[1.2/pic] 2[1.2/eh] 2[1.2/bcl] 2 — 4 2 2 0 —
    tmp+1 — pf — str
AMP

A Mirror on Which to Dwell; For   20'
Soprano and Ensemble (1975)
    solo S
    1[1/pic, afl] 1[1/eh] 1[1/Ebcl/bcl] 0 — 0 0 0 0 —
    1perc — pf — str[1.0.1.1.1]
AMP

Pastoral   9'
    solo eh
    1perc — str
Presser

Penthode; For five groups of four   18'
instrumentalists (1985)
    1[1/pic/afl] 1[1/eh] 2[1/Ebcl.bcl/cbcl] 1 — 1 2 1 1
    — 3perc — hp — pf — str[1.1.1.1.1]
    perc: marim, 3 templeblks, 2 woodblk, sd, sus cym, wood dr, gavel,
    vib, crot, tgl, guiro, military dr, gong, tam-tam, claves,
    whip, 4 bongos, small sd, 3 tom-tom, bd, cowbell
Boosey & Hawkes

Réflexions (2004)   10'
    2[1/pic/afl.2/pic] 2[1.eh] 2[1/Ebcl.2/bcl/cbcl]
    2[1.2/cbn] — 2 2 2 0 — 3perc — hp — pf —
    str[2.1.2.2.1]
    perc: 4 bongos, 4 woodblks, bd, gong, 3 sus cym, 3 sd, xylorimba, 4
    tom-tom, tam-tam, stones, 2 log dr, tri, vib, glsp, 4 templeblks,
    cowbell, almglocke, hammer, guiro, claves
Boosey & Hawkes

Sound Fields (2007)   4'
    str[9.6.6.6.4]
Boosey & Hawkes

Symphony No.1 (1942)   25'
    2 2 2[1.2/Ebcl] 2 — 2 2 1 0 — tmp — str
AMP

Syringa (1978)   20'
    solo Mz, db, gtr
    1 1[eh] 1[bcl] 0 — 0 0 1 0 — 1perc — pf —
    str[1.0.1.1.1]
AMP

Three Poems of Robert Frost   6'
(1975)
    solo medium voice
    1 1 2 1 — 0 0 0 0 — gtr — pf — str[1.1.1.1.1]
AMP

Variations for Orchestra (1955)   24'
    2[1.2/pic] 2 2 2 — 4 2 3 1 — tmp+1 — hp — str
AMP

Casella, Alfredo   (1883-1947)

Concerto Romano, op.43 (1926)   30'
    solo org
    0 0 0 0 — 0 3 3 0 — tmp — str
UE

Divertimento Per Fulvia: Suite from   15'
"La camera dei disegni," op.64
(1940)
    2 1 2 1 — 2 1 0 0 — 1perc — cel — str
UE

Serenata, op.46b (1930)   22'
    2 1 2 2 — 2 1 1 0 — tmp+1 — str
    Contents - 1. Marchia; 2. Notturno; 3. Gavotta; 4. Cavatina;
    5. Finale
UE

Casken, John   (1949-)

Amarantos (1978)   16'
    1[1/afl] 1 1[1/bcl] 0 — 1 1 0 0 — 1perc — pf —
    str[0.0.1.1.0]
    perc: 2 bongo, bd, tam-tam, marac
Schott

Vaganza (1985)   27'
    1[1/afl/pic] 1[1/eh] 1[1/Ebcl/bcl/ssx] 1[1/cbn] — 1 1
    1 0 — 1perc — hp — org — str[1.1.1.1.1]
    perc: bell tree, 2 bongo, 2 gong, sus cym, ped bd, sd, whip, guiro,
    ratchet, tam-tam, 3 woodblks, xyl
Schott

Cassadó, Gaspar (1897-1966)

Concerto for Cello 20'
solo vc
2 2 2 2 — 2 2 0 0 — 1perc — hp — str
UE

Cassuto, Alvaro (1938-)

Song of Loneliness (1972) 13'
1 1 1 1 — 1 1 0 0 — 1perc — pf — str[1.0.1.1.1]
Also possible with strings (1.1.1.1.1).
Schirmer

Castelnuovo-Tedesco, Mario (1895-1968)

Concerto for 2 Guitars and Orchestra, op.201 26'
solo 2 gtr
2 1 2 1 — 2 1 0 0 — tmp+3 — str
Presser

Concerto for Piano in G Major, op.46 (1927) 28'
solo pf
2 2 2 2 — 2 2 0 0 — tmp+2 — str
UE

Figures 14'
solo hpsd, vn, va, vc
2 1 2 1 — 2 1 1 0 — 1perc — hp — str
Presser

Three Sephardic Songs 9'
solo medium voice
1 1 1 1 — 1 0 0 0 — 1perc — str
Presser

Castro, José Maria (1892-1964)

Concerto Grosso 12'
2 2 2 2 — 2 1 0 0 — str
Peer

Cerha, Friedrich (1926-)

1. Keintate (1982) 50'
solo medium voice (Chansonnier)
0 0 2 0 — 2 0 0 0 — accordion — 1perc — str[1.1.1.1.1]
UE

2. Keintate (1985) 57'
solo medium voice (Chansonnier)
0 0 2 0 — 2 0 0 0 — accordion — str[1.1.1.1.1]
UE

Concertino; For Violin, Accordion and Chamber Orchestra (1994) 17'
solo vn, accordion
1 0 1 0 — 1 1 0 0 — asx — 1perc — str(min)[1.1.1.1.1]
UE

In Memoriam Ernst Klein (1985) 16'
solo medium voice (Chansonnier)
0 0 2 0 — 2 0 0 0 — accordion — 1perc — str[1.1.1.1.1]
UE

Jahrlang ins Ungewisse Hinab (1996) 27'
1[1/pic] 0 2[1.bcl] 1[1/cbn] — 2 2 2 0 — accordion, S — 4perc — hp — 2pf[pf.org] — str[1.1.1.1.1]
UE

Lichtenberg-Splitter (1997) 25'
solo Bar
1[1/pic/afl] 1 2[1.bcl] 0 — 1 1 1 0 — 1[ssx/asx] — 1perc — 2pf[pf.org] — str[1.0.1.1.1]
UE

Phantasiestück in C.'s Manier (1989) 12'
solo vc
1[1/pic] 1 2 1 — 2 1 1 0 — ssx — 2perc — org — str(min)[1.1.1.1.1]
UE

Quellen (1992) 13'
0 0 1 0 — 1 0 1 0 — ssx — gtr, accordion — 3perc — org — str[1.1.0.0.0]
UE

Scherzino (2000) 2'
2 1 2 1 — 1 1 1 0 — 1perc — str[1.1.1.1.1]
UE

Sinfonie (1975) 12'
2 2 2 2 — 2 1 1 1 — str
UE

Chapple, Brian (1945-)

Little Symphony (1982) 12'
1[1/pic] 2[1.2/eh] 0 2 — 2 0 0 0 — str
Chester Novello

Venus Fly Trap (1979)   20'
  1[1/pic] 1 1[1/Ebcl] 1 — 1 1 1 0 — pf —
  str[1.1.1.1.1]
Chester Novello

Chávez, Carlos   (1899-1978)

Cantos de México (1933)   4'
  1 1 1 0 — 0 1 0 0 — gtr — 8perc — hp —
  str[2.0.0.0.0]
Carlanita

Discovery (1969)   20'
  1[1/pic] 2[1.eh] 1 1 — 2 1 0 0 — tmp — str
Schirmer

Energia; For Nine Instruments   5'
(1925)
  2[1.pic] 0 0 1 — 1 1 1[btbn] 0 — str[0.0.1.1.1]
EMI

Sarabande: From "The Daughter of   5'
Colchis"
  str
EMI

Sinfonía (1915)   30'
  .2 2 2 3 — 4 3 3 1 — tmp — str
Carlanita

Sinfonía de Antígona; Symphony   11'
No.1 (Chamber Version) (1933)
  1[pic] 2[1.eh] 1 0 — 0 1 0 0 — 2perc — hp —
  no str
Schirmer

Sinfonía India; (Symphony No.2)   11'
(1935)
  2 1 3 1 — 2 2 1 0 — 4perc — hp — str
  Reduced orchestration.
Schirmer

Sinfonía No.5 (1953)   21'
  str
Kalmus

Sonante (1974)   10'
  str
Carlanita

Suite for Double Quartet   23'
  1 1 1 1 — 0 0 0 0 — str[1.1.1.1.0]
EMI

Chen, Qigang   (1951-)

Extase   17'
  solo ob
  2 1 2 2 — 2 2 0 0 — 2perc — str
Presser

Extase II   17'
  solo ob
  1 1 1 1 — 1 1 0 0 — 1perc — hp — pf —
  str[1.1.1.1.1]
Presser

Luminères de Guang-Ling   15'
  2 1 1 1 — 2 0 0 0 — 2perc — hp — pf —
  str[3.0.1.1.1]
Presser

Un Pétale de Lumière   16'
  solo fl
  2 2 2 2 — 2 2 0 0 — 2perc — str
Presser

Chen, Yi   (1953-)

Sparkle; Octet   10'
  1[1/pic] 0 1 0 — 0 0 0 0 — 2perc — pf —
  str[1.0.0.1.1]
Presser

Cheslock, Louis   (1899-1981)

Theme and Variations (1934)   10'
  1 0 0 0 — 1 0 0 0 — 2pf[4hand] — str
Fleisher

Chou, Wen-Chung   (1923-)

Landscapes   8'
  2 2 0 0 — 2 0 2 0 — tmp+1 — hp — str
Peters

Two Miniatures from T'ang (1957)   5'
  2 0 1 0 — 1 0 0 0 — 1perc — hp — pf — str
  Strings without db.
Fleisher

Yu ko   5'
  1[afl] 1[eh] 1[bcl] 0 — 0 0 2 0 — 2perc — pf —
  str[1.0.0.0.0]
Peters

Christensen, Bernhard   (1906-2004)

Skolen på Hovedet (1933)
   0 0 0 0 — 0 2 1 0 — 3[asx.asx.tsx] — gtr — 1perc
   — pf — str[0.0.0.0.1]
Hansen

Clarke, Henry   (1907-1992)

Saraband for the Golden Goose
(1957)
   1 1 1 1 — 1 1 1 0 — str
Fleisher

Clarke, James   (1971-)

Self Portrait (1991)
   1 0 1 0 — 1 1 1 0 — 3[asx.tsx.bsx] — elec gtr,
   elec bgtr — 1perc — kybd — str[1.1.0.1.0]
Fleisher

Cohn, James   (1928-)

Homage (1959)   *7'*
   1[1/pic] 1 1 1 — 1 1 1 0 — asx — tmp+3 — str
Fleisher

The Little Circus, op.51 (1974)   *6'*
   1[1/pic] 0 2 1[1/cbn] — 2 2 2 1 — tmp+1 —
   str[5.4.3.2.1]
Boosey & Hawkes

Sinfonietta in F (1955)   *14'*
   1[1/pic] 1 2 1 — 2 0 0 0 — tmp+1 — str
   perc: glsp
Fleisher

Symphony No.3 in G, op.27 (1955)   *21'*
   1 1 1 1 — 1 1 1 0 — 1 — tmp+1 — str
Boosey & Hawkes

Symphony No.4 in A, op.29 (1956)   *16'*
   1 1 1 1 — 1 1 0 0 — 1 — tmp+1 — str
Boosey & Hawkes

Symphony No.5 in B-flat, op.32   *23'*
(1959)
   1 1 1 1 — 1 1 1 0 — 1 — tmp+1 — str
Boosey & Hawkes

Variations on The Wayfaring   *11'*
Stranger (1960)
   1 1 1 1 — 1 1 1 0 — sx — tmp+1 — str
Boosey & Hawkes

Coleman, Linda Robbins   (1954-)

For A Beautiful Land (1996)   *12'*
   2[1.2/pic] 2 2 2 — 2 0 0 0 — tmp+2 — str
   perc: 2 cym, sus cym, sd, glsp, gong, tri
Coleman

Colgrass, Michael   (1932-)

Rhapsodic Fantasy (1964)   *8'*
   solo perc
   1[1/pic] 1 1 1 — 1 1 1 0 — tmp+3 — hp — cel —
   str
MCA

Consoli, Marc-Antonio   (1941-)

Odefonia (1978)   *24'*
   2[1.2/pic] 2[1.2/eh] 2[1.2/bcl] 2 — 2 2 1 0 — 3perc
   — str[0.0.0.4.2]
Margun

Converse, Frederick Shepherd   (1871-1940)

Indian Serenade, op.14, No.2
   2 2 2 2 — 3 0 0 0 — hp — str
Fleisher

Three Old Fashioned Dances for
Chamber Orchestra, op.102 (1938)
   1[1/pic] 1 1 1 — 2 2 1 0 — tmp+1 — hp[or pf] —
   str
   perc: tri
Fleisher

Conyngham, Barry   (1944-)

Concerto for Double Bass;   *17'*
Shadows of Noh (1979)
   solo db
   2 2 3 2 — 2 2 2 0 — 2perc — pf —
   str(min)[2.2.2.1.1]
   The wind and brass count can be extended ad lib.
UE

Dwellings (1982)   25'
    1 1 1 0 — 1 1 0 0 — gtr — 1perc — hp — pf —
    str[1.0.1.1.1]
UE

Glimpses of Bennelong (1987)   15'
    1 2 0 0 — 2 0 0 0 — str
UE

Coolidge, Peggy Stuart   (1913-1981)

Pioneer Dances   12'
    1 1 2 1 — 1 2 1 0 — tmp+1 — str
    perc: sd, bd, xyl, tambn, chimes, vib, cym
Peer

Rhapsody for Harp   9'
    solo hp
    3 1 2 1 — 2 2 1 0 — 2perc — str
    perc: tmp, chimes, sd, sus cym, bd
Peer

Cooper, Paul   (1926-1996)

Double Concerto (1985)   19'
    solo vn, va
    2 2 2 2 — 2 2 0 0 — tmp+2 — hp — cel — str
Schirmer

Love Songs and Dances;   14'
Concertante for 21 Players (1987)
    1[1/pic/afl] 1[1/eh] 1[1/bcl] 1 — 1 1 1 0 — 1perc
    — hp — str[4.3.2.2.1]
Schirmer

Symphony No.3; "Lamentations"   20'
(1971)
    str
Schirmer

Copland, Aaron   (1900-1990)

Appalachian Spring: Suite (full   24'
Orchestra version) (1944)
    2[1.2/pic] 2 2 2 — 2 2 2 0 — tmp+2 — hp — pf —
    str
    perc: bd, sus cym, sd, tabor, tri, glsp, xyl, woodblk, claves
Boosey & Hawkes

Appalachian Spring: Suite (original 24'
version) (1944)
    1 0 1 1 — 0 0 0 0 — pf — str[2.2.2.2.1]
Boosey & Hawkes

Billy the Kid: Prairie Night &   5'
Celebration Dance (1938)
    1[1/pic] 1 2 1 — 1 2 2 0 — tmp+2 — pf — str
    perc: xyl, bd, sd
Boosey & Hawkes

Billy the Kid: Waltz (Billy and his 4'
Sweetheart) (1938)
    1 1 2 1 — 1 2 1 0 — hp[or pf] — str
Boosey & Hawkes; Luck's

The City: Incidental music for the 22'
documentary film (1939)
    1[1/pic] 1[1/eh] 3[1.2.bcl/asx] 1 — 2 2 1 0 —
    1perc — pf — str
    perc: bd, tmp, bell, sus cym
Boosey & Hawkes

Concerto for Clarinet (1948)   18'
    solo cl
    hp — pf — str
    mvt durations: 10' 8'
Boosey & Hawkes

Dance Panels; Ballet in Seven   26'
Sections (1959)
    2[1/opt afl.2/pic] 1 2 1 — 2 2 1 0 — 2perc — str
    perc: sd, sus cym, xyl, tri, field dr, glsp, bd, cym, woodblk, templeblks
Boosey & Hawkes

Down a Country Lane (1962)   3'
    2 1 2 1 — 2 1 1 0 — str
Boosey & Hawkes

Eight Poems of Emily Dickinson   21'
(1958-70)
    solo medium voice
    1[1/pic] 1 2[1.Ebcl] 1 — 1 1 1 0 — hp —
    str[8.6.4.3.2]
    Contents - 1. Nature, the Gentlest Mother; 2. There Came a
    Wind Like a Bugle; 3. The World Feels Dusty; 4. Heart, We
    Will Forget Him; 5. Dear March, Come In!; 6. Sleep Is
    Supposed to Be; 7. Going to Heaven!; 8. The Chariot
    mvt durations: 4' 2' 2' 2' 2' 3' 3' 3'
Boosey & Hawkes

John Henry (1940)   4'
    2[1.2/pic] 2 2 — 2 2 1 0 — tmp+2 — pf[opt] —
    str
    perc: tri, anvil, bd, sd, sand paper
    Possible with winds: 1 1 2 1.
Boosey & Hawkes

Letter from Home (1944)   6'
    2 2[1.2(opt)] 3[1.2.bcl(opt)] 2[1.2(opt)] — 2 2 2 0
    — tmp+2 — hp[opt] — pf[opt] — str
    perc: glsp, sus cym, tri, bd
VAAP

Music for Movies (1942)   16'
1[1/pic] 1 1 1 — 1 2 1 0 — 1perc — pf[or hp] —
str
perc: glsp, xyl, sus cym, tri, bd, sd
Music from the movies *The City*, *Of Mice and Men* and *Our Town*.
Contents - 1. New England Countryside; 2. Barley Wagons;
3. Sunday Traffic; 4. Grovers Corners; 5. Threshing
Machines
mvt durations: 5' 2' 3' 3' 3'
Boosey & Hawkes

Music for the Theatre (1925)   21'
1[1/pic] 1[1/eh] 1[1/Ebcl] 1 — 0 2 1 0 — 1perc —
pf — str
perc: xyl, glsp, woodblk, sus cym, bd, sd
Contents - 1. Prologue; 2. Dance; 3. Interlude; 4. Burlesque;
5. Epilogue
mvt durations: 6' 3' 5' 3' 4'
Boosey & Hawkes

Old American Songs; First Set (1950)   14'
solo medium voice
1[1/pic] 1 2 1 — 1 1 1 0 — hp — str
Contents - 1. Boatmen's Dance; 2. The Dodger; 3. Long
Time Ago; 4. Simple Gifts; 5. I Bought Me a Cat
mvt durations: 4' 2' 3' 2' 3'
Boosey & Hawkes

Old American Songs; Second Set   13'
(1952)
solo medium voice
1[1/pic] 1 2 1 — 2 1 1 0 — hp — str
Contents - 1. The Little Horses; 2. Zion's Walls; 3. Golden
Willow Tree; 4. At the River; 5. Ching-a-Ring Chaw
mvt durations: 3' 2' 4' 2' 2'
Boosey & Hawkes

Orchestral Variations (1957)   14'
2[1/pic, 2/pic] 2[1.eh] 2[1.2/bcl] 2 — 4 2 3 1 —
tmp+3 — hp — str
perc: bd, bongos, crot, chimes, congas, cowbell, cym, glsp, sd, tam-
tam, td, woodblk, xyl, sus cym
Boosey & Hawkes

An Outdoor Overture (1938)   10'
3[1.2.pic] 2 2 2 — 4 2 3 0 — tmp+3 —
2pf[pf.cel(opt)] — str
perc: xyl, sd, cym, tri, bd
Boosey & Hawkes

Prairie Journal (1937)   13'
2[1.2/pic] 2 2 1 — 2 3[1.2.3(opt)] 2 1 —
3[asx/cl.asx/cl.tsx/bcl] — tmp+1 — hp — pf/cel — str
perc: vib, xyl, tri, bd
Originally titled "Music for Radio." Retitled 1968.
Boosey & Hawkes

Quiet City (1940)   10'
solo tpt, eh (or ob)
str
Boosey & Hawkes

Rodeo (1942)   24'
2[1.2/pic] 2[1.2/eh] 2[1.2/bcl] 2[1.2/cbn] — 4 3 3 1
— tmp+2 — hp[opt] — pf — str
perc: sd, woodblk, tri, cym, cym, bd, rattle, xyl, glsp
Arranged for reduced orchestra by Jonathan McPhee
(1999).
Boosey & Hawkes

Symphony No.1: Prelude (1924)   6'
1 1 1 1 — 1 1 0 0 — hp — str
Arranged by the composer (1934).
Boosey & Hawkes

Three Latin American Sketches   11'
(1959-72)
1[1/pic] 1 1 1 — 0 1 0 0 — 1perc — 2pf[1.2(opt)]
— str
perc: claves, woodblk, xyl, rattle, whip, tri, congas, sus cym
Contents - 1. Estribilo; 2. Paisaje Mexicano; 3. Danza de
Jalisco
mvt durations: 3' 4' 4'
Boosey & Hawkes

Two Pieces (1928)   11'
str
Boosey & Hawkes

Cordero, Roque   (1917-2008)

Dodecaconcerto   30'
1 1[eh] 1 1 — 1 1 1 0 — asx — 1perc —
str[1.0.1.1.0]
perc: 5 templeblks, 5 tam-tam, 2 sus cym, sd, woodblk
Peer

Ocho Miniaturas   11'
1 1 1 1 — 1 1 1 0 — str
Peer

Permutaciones 7   9'
0 0 1 0 — 0 1 0 0 — tmp — pf — str[1.0.1.0.1]
Peer

Corigliano, John   (1938-)

The Cloisters (1965)   13'
solo voice
2 2 2 2 — 2 2 0 0 — tmp+1 — str
Schirmer

Conjurer; Concerto for   35'
Percussionist and String Orchestra
(2007)
solo perc
str
Contents - 1. Wood; 2. Metal; 3. Skin
Schirmer

Creations: Two Scenes from   27'
Genesis (1972)
    2[1.2/pic] 2[1.2/eh] 2[1.2/bcl] 2[1.2/cbn] — 2 1 1 0
    — narrator — tmp+1 — hp — pf — str
Schirmer

Elegy (1965)   7'
    2[1.2/pic] 2 2 2 — 2 1 1[btbn] 0 — tmp+1 — pf —
    str
Schirmer

Gazebo Dances (1974)   16'
    2[1.2/pic] 2 2 2 — 4 3 3 1 — tmp+3 — pf — str
    perc: xyl, sd, td, bd, sus cym, cym, tri, tambn, handbell
Schirmer

Poem in October (1970)   17'
    solo T
    1 1 1 0 — 1 0 0 0 — hpsd — str
    Alternate orchestration: solo T - 1110 - 0000 - hpsd - str
    (1.1.1.1.0).
Schirmer

The Red Violin: Suite for Violin and   25'
Orchestra (1999)
    solo vn
    tmp+3 — hp — str
Schirmer

Symphony No.2 for String really great music   35'
Orchestra (2000)   maybe way too hard
    str (min)[6.5.4.4.2]   score online
Schirmer   need good solo players

2001 Pulitzer Winner (handwritten, left margin)

Troubadours; Variations for Guitar   23'
and Chamber Orchestra (1993)
    solo gtr
    2[1.2/pic] 1 2 0 — 0 0 0 0 — offstage:
    ob.ob/eh.2bn.2hn — 2perc — pf[opt] — str
    (min)[6.6.4.4.2]
Schirmer

Voyage; For String Orchestra   8'
(1976)
    str
Schirmer

Voyage; For Flute and String   8'
Orchestra (1983)
    solo fl
    str
Schirmer

Cotton, Jeffery   (1957-)

Concerto for Clarinet, Strings and   27'
Harp (2003)
    solo cl
    hp — str
Cotton

Symphony for Strings (2004)   30'
    str
Cotton

Cowell, Henry   (1897-1965)

Air and Scherzo (1963)   8'
    solo asx
    2 1 2 1 — 0 0 0 0 — str
    Arranged by the composer from the original alto sax and
    piano version (1961).
AMP

American Melting Pot Set (1940)   18'
    1 1 1 1 — 2 1 1 1 — 1perc — str
    Contents - 1. Chorale (Teutonic-American); 2. Air (Afro-
    American); 3. Satire (Franco-American); 4. Alapria (Oriental-
    American); 5. Slavic Dance (Slavic-American); 6. Rhumba
    With Added Eighth (Latin-American); 7. Square Dance
    (Celtic-American).
Fleisher

Carol (1965)   9'
    2 2 2 2 — 2 2 0 0 — hp[or pf] — str
AMP

Concerto No.1 for Koto and   24'
Orchestra (1961)
    solo koto
    2[1.pic] 2 2 2 — 2 2 2 0 — tmp+2 — hp — str
AMP

Ensemble; Revised Version of   19'
String Quintet and Thundersticks
(1956)
    str
AMP

Exultation
    str
AMP

Hymn and Fuguing Tune No.2   5'
(1944)
    str
AMP

Hymn and Fuguing Tune No.3 7'
(1944)
    2 2 2 2 — 4 2 2 1 — tmp+1 — str
perc: chimes, xyl
Two hn are optional.
AMP

Hymn and Fuguing Tune No.5 6'
(1945)
    str
AMP

Hymn and Fuguing Tune No.10 8'
(1955)
    solo ob
    str
AMP

Hymn, Chorale and Fuguing Tune 8'
No.8 (1947)
    str
AMP

Movement (1934) 4'
    str
AMP

Old American Country Set (1939) 12'
    2 2 2 2 — 2 2 1 1 — banjo — 1perc — str
AMP

Ongaku (1957) 14'
    2 2[1.2/eh] 2 2 — 2 2 0 0 — tmp+1 — hp — cel
    — str
AMP

Polyphonica; For 12 Instruments or 4'
Chamber Orchestra (1930)
    1 1 1 1 — 1 1 1 0 — str[1.1.1.1.1]
Chamber Orchestra version to be performed with full
strings.
AMP

Saturday Night at the Firehouse 4'
(1948)
    1 1 2 1 — 2 2 0 0 — 1perc — str
AMP

Sinfonietta (1928) 14'
    1 1 1 1 — 1 1 1 0 — str[2.2.1.1.1]
AMP

Symphonic Set, op.17 (1939) 14'
    2 2 3[1.2.bcl/tsx] 2 — 2 2 2 1 — tmp+1 — str
perc: chimes, xyl, cym, bd, sd
Boosey & Hawkes

Symphony No.10 (1953) 23'
    2 2[1.2/eh] 2[1.2/bcl] 2 — 2 2 0 0 — tmp — str
AMP

Symphony No.16; Icelandic (1962) 22'
    2 2 2 2 — 2 2 2 1 — tmp+2 — hp — str
AMP

Symphony No.17; Lancaster (1962) 22'
    2 2 2 2 — 4 2 2 1 — tmp+2 — str
AMP

Symphony No.7 (1952) 24'
    2 1[1/eh] 2[1.2/bcl] 1 — 2 1 1 0 — tmp+1 — pf —
    str
perc: xyl
AMP

Symphony No.9 (1953) 22'
    2 2 2 2 — 2 2 2 0 — tmp+1 — hp[or pf] — str
AMP

Teheran Movement (1957) 5'
    1 1 1 1 — 0 1 0 0 — str
Fleisher

Cowie, Edward (1943-)

Leonardo (1982) 25'
    2[1/pic.2/afl] 2[1.2/eh] 2[1/Ebcl.2/bcl] 2 — 2 0 0 0
    — str
Schott

Crawford Seeger, Ruth (1901-1953)

Music for Small Orchestra (1926) 10'
    1 0 1 1 — 0 0 0 0 — pf — str[2.2.0.2.0]
A-R Editions

Rissolty-Rossolty 3'
    1 1 2 1 — 2 2 1 0 — tmp — str
Presser

Three Songs 9'
    solo contralto, ob, perc, pf
    0 0 1 1 — 1 1 1 0 — str
Can be done with or without the orchestral parts (soli only).
Text by Carl Sandburg.
Presser

Creston, Paul (1906-1985)

Out of the Cradle Endlessly   15'
Rocking; After the poem by Walt
Whitman (1934)
   2 1 2[1.bcl] 1 — 1 1 1 1 — tmp+1 — hp —
   2pf[cel.org(opt)] — str
Fleisher

Cruft, Adrian (1921-1987)

Partita, op.7 (1951)   15'
   2[1.2/pic] 2 2 2 — 2 1 0 0 — tmp — str
Fleisher

Crumb, David (1962-)

Variations   20'
   solo vc
   2[1/pic.2/afl] 1[1/eh] 1[1/Ebcl] 1 — 1 0 0 0 —
   2perc — hp — pf — str[1.1.1.1.1]
Presser

Csonka, Paul (1905-1995)

Prisma Sinfonico (Symphonic   6'
Prism)
   2 2 2 2 — 2 2 1 0 — tmp — str
Peer

Czernowin, Chaya (1957-)

Afatsim (1996)   10'
   1[bfl] 1 1[bcl] 0 — 0 0 0 0 — tmp+1 — pf —
   str[1.0.1.1.1]
   perc: gong, 2 bend cym, marim
   5-string db required.
Schott

Winter Songs I-III (2003)
   1[amp bfl] 0 1[bcl] 0 — 0 0 1[btbn] 1 — 3perc —
   str[0.0.1.1.1]
   Can be performed separately. No.1 does not use
   percussion.
   Contents - 1. Pending Light; 2. Stones; 3. Roots
   mvt durations: 14' 16' 18'
Schott

D

Dalby, Martin (1942-)

Aleph (1975)   17'
   2 0 0 0 — 1 1 1 0 — 1perc — str[0.0.0.0.2]
   perc: cym
Novello

Cancionero Para Una Mariposa   17'
(1971)
   1 0 0 2 — 0 0 2 0 — str[0.0.0.2.0]
Novello

Chamber Symphony; O Bella e   22'
Vaga Aurora (1982)
   1[1/pic] 0 2[1/bcl.2/bcl] 0 — 1 1 0 0 — 1perc —
   hp — str[1.0.1.1.1]
Novello

De Patre Ex Filio (1988)   12'
   0 0 1 1 — 1 0 0 0 — str[1.1.1.1.1]
Novello

Man Walking; Serenade for Octet   18'
(1981)
   0 1 0 1 — 1 0 0 0 — str[1.1.1.1.1]
Novello

Nozze di Primavera (1984)   13'
   2 2 2 2 — 2 2 0 0 — tmp — str
Novello

Dale, Benjamin (1885-1943)

A Holiday Tune (1925)
   1 1 2 1 — 2 0 0 0 — str
Fleisher; Augener

Prunella (1923)
   1 1 2 1 — 2 0 0 0 — str
Fleisher; Augener

D'Alessandro, Raffaele (1911-1959)

Concerto Grosso, op.57 (1947)   12'
   str
Boosey & Hawkes

Dallapiccola, Luigi   (1904-1975)

Piccola Musica Notturna (1954)   7'
2 2 2 2 — 2 2 0 0 — tmp+2 — hp — cel — str
perc: xyl, cym, sm cym, sm tam-tam, lg tam-tam, tamburo, bd, chimes
Version for ensemble is also available: 1110 - 0000 - hp - cel - str[1.0.1.1.0]
Schott

Danielpour, Richard   (1956-)

Adagietto for String Orchestra   10'
(2005)
str
AMP

Apparitions (2003)   28'
tmp+3 — hp — pf/cel — str
Orchestration of his String Quartet No.4 (Apparitions).
AMP

First Light; Concerto for Chamber   13'
Orchestra in One Movement (1988)
1 1[1/eh] 1 1 — 2 1 1 0 — tmp+2 — hp — pf — str
perc: 3 sus cym, xyl, glsp, chimes, 2 sd, vib, low gong, tom-tom
Chamber Orchestra version.
AMP

First Light (1988)   13'
2 2[1.2/eh] 2 2 — 4[(3&4opt)] 2 2 0 — tmp+2 — hp —amp pf — str
AMP

Metamorphosis; Piano Concerto   28'
No.1 (1990)
solo pf
2[1.2/pic] 2[1.2/eh] 2[1.2/bcl] 2 — 2 2 2 0 — tmp+3 — hp — str
AMP

Nocturne (2000)   3'
str
AMP

Sonnets to Orpheus; Book 1 (1992)   28'
solo S
1 0 1 0 — 1 0 0 0 — pf/cel — str[1.1.1.1.1]
After texts by Rainer Maria Rilke.
AMP

Sonnets to Orpheus; Book 2 (1994)   25'
solo Bar
1 0 1 0 — 1 0 0 0 — 1perc — pf — str[1.1.1.1.1]
After texts by Rainer Maria Rilke.
AMP

Souvenirs (2008)   15'
2[1.2/pic] 2[1.2/eh] 2[1.2/bcl] 2 — 2 2 2 0 — tmp — str
AMP

Swan Song (2003)   8'
str
String Orchestra setting of the 3rd movement of his String Quartet No.4 (Apparitions).
AMP

Washington Speaks (2005)   7'
solo narrator
2 2 2 3[1.2.cbn] — 4 2 3 0 — tmp+2 — str
With texts by George Washington.
AMP

Daniels, Mabel W.   (1878-1971)

Deep Forest; Prelude for Little Symphony   6'
Orchestra, op.34, No.1 (1932)
1 1 1 1 — 1 1 0 0 — tmp+1 — str
perc: chimes, cym
Fleisher; Fischer (J.)

Daugherty, Michael   (1954-)

Dead Elvis (1993)   9'
solo bn
0 0 1 0 — 0 1 1 0 — 1perc — str[1.0.0.0.1]
perc: lg brake dr, lg and sm bongo, lg cowbell, crot, lg ride cym
Peer

Ghost Ranch (2005)   6'
0 0 0 0 — 4 0 0 0 — tmp — str
Boosey & Hawkes

Jackie's Song (1995)   7'
solo vc
1[1/pic] 0 1[bcl] 0 — 0 0 0 0 — 1perc — pf — str[1.0.0.0.0]
perc: bongos, lg and sm tri, cast, chimes, tambn, crot, sd
Peer

Mxyzptlk: From "Metropolis   7'
Symphony" (1989)
solo 2 fl [1.2/pic]
0 2 2 2 — 2 2 1 0 — 1perc — synth — str
perc: 2 gong, 3 tri, 3 woodblks, sus cym
Faber; Peer

Oh, Lois!: From "Metropolis   5'
Symphony" (1989)
2[1/pic.2] 2 2 2 — 4 3 3[1.2.btbn] 0 — tmp+2 — synth — str
perc: 2 tri, 2 gong, 2 bd, 2 flexatone, 2 whip
Faber

Pachelbel's Key; For Youth   5'
Orchestra (2002)
    2 2 2 2 — 4[3&4 opt] 2 2 1 — tmp — str
Boosey & Hawkes

Snap! (1987)   7'
    1[1/pic] 1 2[1/Ebcl.bcl] 0 — 1 1 1[btbn] 0 — 3perc
    — synth — str[1.1.1.1.1]
    perc: 2 cym, xyl, vib, glsp, tri
    Also possible with small string section.
Faber; Peer

Strut (1989)   6'
    str
Boosey & Hawkes

Sunset Strip (1999)   15'
    2[1.pic] 2 2[1.bcl] 2 — 2 2 0 0 — 1perc — pf —
    str
    perc: 2 latin cowbells, 3 agogo bells, 2 cym, tri, wind chimes, 2
    bongos, marac, claves, vibraslap, whip, tambn, bell tree
Boosey & Hawkes

Tell My Fortune (2004)   28'
    2[1.2/pic/afl] 2[1.eh] 2[1.bcl] 2[1.cbn] — 2 2 0 0 —
    2perc — pf — str
    Contents - 1. Palm; 2. Crystal; 3. Card
Boosey & Hawkes

Davico, Vincenzo   (1889-1969)

Poemetti Pastorali (1924)   9'
    1 1 1 1 — 1 0 0 0 — hp — pf — str[1.1.1.1.1]
Fleisher; Eschig

David, Johann Nepomuk   (1895-1977)

Chaconne, Wk71 (1972)   13'
    2 2 2 2 — 4 2 3 0 — tmp+1 — str
Breitkopf

Concerto for Flute (1936)   36'
    solo fl
    0 2 2 2 — 2 0 0 0 — tmp+1 — str
Breitkopf

Concerto for Organ, Wk61 (1965)   23'
    solo org
    2 0 0 0 — 0 0 3 0 — tmp+1 — hp — str
Breitkopf

Concerto for Violin and Cello, Wk68   19'
(1969)
    solo vn, vc
    1 0 1 0 — 1 0 0 0 — tmp+1 — hp — str[0.0.2.0.1]
Breitkopf

Concerto for Violin No.1, Wk45   32'
(1952)
    solo vn
    1 1 1 1 — 1 0 0 0 — tmp+1 — hp — str
    String section without violins.
Breitkopf

Concerto for Violin No.2, Wk50   20'
(1957)
    solo vn
    str
Breitkopf

Concerto for Violin No.3, Wk56   24'
(1961)
    solo vn
    2[1.pic] 1 2[1.bcl] 1 — 2 1 1 0 — tmp+4 — str
Breitkopf

Concerto No.1, Wk40/1 (1950)   22'
    str
Breitkopf

Concerto No.2, Wk40/2 (1951)   15'
    str
Breitkopf

Concerto No.3 (1974)   16'
    str
Breitkopf

Kume, kum, Geselle min;   20'
Divertimento nach alten
Volksliedern, Wk24 (1939)
    1 1 1 1 — 1 0 0 0 — tmp+1 — hp — cel — str
Breitkopf

Magische Quadrate; Symphonische   33'
Phantasie, Wk52 (1959)
    2[1.pic] 1 1 1 — 2 1 1 0 — sx — tmp+3 — hp —
    str
Breitkopf

Partita No.2, Wk27 (1940)   27'
    2[1.2/pic] 2[1.2/eh] 2[1.bcl] 2[1.cbn] — 2 2 2 0 —
    tmp — str
Breitkopf

Sinfonia breve, Wk47 (1955)   20'
    1 1 3[1.2.bcl] 1 — 4 0 0 0 — tmp+2 — str
Breitkopf

Sinfonia per archi, Wk54 (1959)   18'
    str
Breitkopf

Sinfonia preclassica super nomen   20'
H-A-S-E, Wk44 (1953)
   2 0 0 0 — 2 0 0 0 — str
Breitkopf

Symphonic Variations on a Theme   16'
by H. Schütz, Wk29b (1942)
   2[1.2/pic] 2 2 2 — 0 2 2 0 — tmp+2 — str
Breitkopf

Symphony No.1 in A minor, Wk18   36'
(1937)
   2 2 2 2 — 4 2 0 0 — tmp+1 — hp — str
Breitkopf

Symphony No.3, Wk28 (1941)   38'
   2 2 2 2 — 4 2 0 0 — tmp — str
Breitkopf

Symphony No.7, Wk49 (1957)   30'
   2 2 2 2 — 4 2 0 0 — tmp+1 — str
Breitkopf

Symphony No.8, Wk59 (1965)   25'
   1 1 1 1 — 2 0 0 0 — tmp+1 — hp — str
Breitkopf

Variations on a Theme by J. S.   18'
Bach, Wk29a (1942)
   1 2 0 1 — 2 0 0 0 — tmp+1 — str
   perc: glsp
Breitkopf

Davis, Anthony   (1951-)

Litany of Sins (1991)   30'
   1 1 1 1 — 1 0 0 0 — hp — str[1.1.1.1.1]
   Can be done with full strings.
Schirmer

Notes from the Underground   9'
(1988)
   2[1.2/pic] 2 2 2 — 2 2 2 1 — 4perc — pf — str
Schirmer

Undine (1986)   20'
   1[1/pic] 0 1[1/cbcl] 1 — 0 0 0 0 — 1perc — pf —
   str[1.0.0.1.0]
Schirmer

Wayang II (1982)   9'
   1 0 0 0 — 0 0 1 0 — 2perc — pf — str[1.0.0.1.1]
Schirmer

Wayang IV (1981)   20'
   1 0 1 0 — 0 0 1 0 — 3perc — pf — str[1.0.0.1.0]
Schirmer

Davis, John David   (1867-1942)

The Embroidered Pannier; An Old
Dance (1934)
   1[opt] 0 1[opt] 1[opt] — 1[opt] 0 0 0 — str
Fleisher; Augener

Davison, John   (1930-1999)

Symphony No.6   8'
   0 2 0 0 — 2 0 0 0 — str
Fleisher

Dazzi, Gualtiero   (1960-)

Sable; In Memoriam Edmond Jabès   13'
(1991)
   1 0 1 0 — 1 0 0 0 — 1perc — str[1.0.1.1.0]
Chester Novello

De Brant, Cyr   (1896-1999)

A Song of Yesteryear: Sarabande   2'
   1 1 1 1 — 1 0 0 0 — str
Fleisher

Dean, Brett   (1961-)

Carlo; Music for Strings and   21'
sampler (1997)
   sampler — str[4.4.3.3.1]
Boosey & Hawkes

Etüdenfest (2000)   10'
   solo pf
   str[5.4.3.3.1]
Boosey & Hawkes

Short Stories; Five Interludes for   12'
String Orchestra (2005)
   str
   Contents - 1. Devotional; 2. Premonitions; 3. Embers; 4.
   Komarov's Last Words; 5. Arietta
Boosey & Hawkes

Testament; Music for Orchestra,   14'
after "Testament: Music for twelve
Violas" (2008)
  2[1/pic.2/pic] 2 2 2 — 2 2 0 0 — tmp[tmp/sus
  cym] — str
  All string players need an additional bow without any rosin
  on the hairs.
  Boosey & Hawkes

Debussy, Claude   (1862-1918)

Coquetterie Posthume   7'
  solo S
  1 0 1 0 — 1 0 0 0 — 1perc — pf — str[1.0.0.1.0]
  Arranged by Costin Miereanu.
  Salabert

Deux Arabesques   7'
  1 0 1 0 — 0 0 0 0 — hp — str[1.1.1.1.0]
  Arranged by Kenneth Hesketh.
  Schott

Lindaraja (1901)   6'
  2 2 2 2 — 2 1 0 0 — tmp+2 — hp — str
  Edited by Bill Hopkins (1975).
  UE

Musique   3'
  solo S
  1 0 2 0 — 0 0 0 0 — 1perc — cel — str[1.0.0.1.0]
  Arranged by Costin Miereanu.
  Salabert

Petite suite   13'
  1 1 1 1 — 1 1 0 0 — tmp+1 — hp — hpsd —
  str(min)[1.1.1.1.1]
  Orchestrated by David Walter.
  Durand

La plus que lente; Valse pour   4'
orchestre (1912)
  1 0 1 0 — 0 0 0 0 — cimb — pf — str
  Durand

Trois Poèmes de Stephane   10'
Mallarme
  solo S
  2 0 2[1.2/bcl] 0 — 0 0 0 0 — pf — str[1.1.1.1.0]
  Arranged by Colin Matthews.
  Faber

Degen, Helmut   (1911-1995)

Chamber Symphony; (Symphony   21'
No.2) (1947)
  2[1.2/pic] 1 0 1 — 2 1 0 0 — str
  Schott

Kleine Weihnachtsmusik (1942)
  1 1 0 0 — 0 0 0 0 — str
  Fleisher; Tonger

Del Tredici, David   (1937-)

1980 Politzer winner

Acrostic Song (1987)   4'
  1 0 1 0 — 0 1 0 0 — 1perc — pf — str[1.1.1.1.1]
  perc: chimes
  Boosey & Hawkes

Haddock's Eyes (1985)   20'
  solo S (amp)
  1[1/pic] 0 1 0 — 1 1 0 0 — pf — str[1.1.1.1.1]
  Boosey & Hawkes

Syzygy (1966)   24'
  solo S, hn
  2[1/pic.pic/afl] 2[1.2/eh] 2[1.2/bcl] 2[1.2/cbn] —
  2[1.2(opt)] 2 0 0 — 2perc — str[1.1.2.1.1]
  perc: chimes
  Text by James Joyce.
  Boosey & Hawkes

Vintage Alice; Fantascene on a   28'
Mad Tea-Party for Soprano Solo,
Folk Group and Chamber Orchestra
(1972)
  solo S (amp)
  1[1/pic] 1 1[Ebcl] 1 — 2 1 1 0 —tmp+1 —
  str(min)[1.1.1.1.1]
  Folk Group: 2 ssx, mand, tenor banjo, accordion
  perc: cym, whip
  Boosey & Hawkes

Delás, José Luis de   (1928-)

Cinco Sellos (1972)   9'
  1 0 2[1.bcl] 0 — 0 1 0 0 — tape — 1perc — pf —
  str[1.0.0.1.1]
  Breitkopf

Concetti; Musica para Gesualdo di   15'
Venosa (1974)
  2[1/pic.afl] 1 2[1.bcl] 1 — 1 1 1 0 — gtr — 2perc
  — hp — 2pf[pf.hpsd/cel] — str[1.1.2.1.2]
  Breitkopf

Conjuntos (1975)   15'
  1[1/afl] 1 1 0 — 1 0 0 0 — tape — 1perc — hp —
  pf — str
Breitkopf

Denkbild - Kurze Schatten (1977)   14'
  1 0 1[1/bcl] 0 — 1 0 0 0 — gtr — 1perc —
  str[0.0.1.1.0]
Breitkopf

Eilanden (1967)   14'
  0 0 1 0 — 0 0 0 0 — tape, gtr — 1perc — hp —
  2pf[hpsd.harm] — str[1.1.1.0.0]
Breitkopf

Imago (1965)   14'
  2[1.afl] 0 2[1.bcl] 0 — 0 0 0 0 — 2perc — hp —
  2pf[pf.cel] — str[1.0.1.1.0]
Breitkopf

Delius, Frederick   (1862-1934)

Air and Dance (1915)   5'
  solo fl
  str(min)[4.4.3.3.2]
  Arranged by Eric Fenby.
Boosey & Hawkes

Fennimore and Gerda: Intermezzo   5'
(1910)
  2 2[1.eh] 2 2 — 2 1 0 0 — str
Boosey & Hawkes

Five Little Pieces (1923)   7'
  1 1 2 1 — 2 1 0 0 — tmp[opt] — str
  Arranged by Eric Fenby.
Boosey & Hawkes

Hassan: Intermezzo and Serenade   4'
(1923)
  1 2[1.eh] 1 1 — 2 1 0 0 — tmp — hp — str
  Arranged by Thomas Beecham. Serenade only uses: hp-str
Boosey & Hawkes

Irmelin: Prelude (1892)   5'
  2 3[1.2(opt).eh(opt)] 3[1.2.bcl(opt)] 2 — 2 0 0 0 —
  hp — str
Boosey & Hawkes

Petite Suite No.1 (1889)   14'
  3[1.2.pic] 2 2 2 — 4 2 0 0 — tmp+1 — hp — str
  perc: cym, sd
Boosey & Hawkes

Petite Suite No.2 (1890)   10'
  2 2 2 2 — 2 0 0 0 — str
Boosey & Hawkes

A Song Before Sunrise (1918)   6'
  2 1 2 2 — 2 0 0 0 — tmp — str
Kalmus; Augener

Two Pieces for Small Orchestra   12'
(1912)
  1 1 2 2 — 2 0 0 0 — str
  Contents - 1. On Hearing the First Cuckoo in Spring; 2.
  Summer Night on the River
Kalmus

Denhoff, Michael   (1955-)

Einsamkeit; In Memoriam W.   12'
Buchebner (1982)
  1[1/pic] 1 1 — 1 1 1 0 — 1perc — hp —
  str(min)[1.1.1.1.1]
  perc: tam-tam
Breitkopf

Melancolia; Annäherungen an einen   21'
Kupferstich von A. Dürer (1980)
  2[1.afl] 2[1.eh] 2[1.bcl] 1[cbn] — 0 0 0 0 — 1perc
  — hp — pf — str[0.0.4.4.2]
Breitkopf

O Orpheus singt; Five lyric pieces   16'
(1977)
  0 0 1 1 — 1 0 0 0 — str[1.1.1.1.1]
Breitkopf

Denisov, Edison   (1929-1996)

Aquarell (1975)   10'
  str[7.7.4.4.2]
Breitkopf

Chamber Symphony (1982)   21'
  1 1 1 1 — 1 1 1 0 — 1perc — pf — str[1.0.1.1.0]
  perc: vib
VAAP

Chamber Symphony No.2 (1994)   20'
  1 1 1 1 — 1 1 1 0 — 1perc — kybd —
  str[1.1.1.1.1]
Boosey & Hawkes

Concerto for Flute and Harp   27'
  solo fl, hp
  0 2 0 0 — 2 0 0 0 — str
Presser

Epitaph (1983)   6'
1 1 1 1 — 1 1 1 0 — 1perc — pf — str[1.1.1.1.1]
perc: 5 bongos, 4 tom-tom, tri, sus cym
Boosey & Hawkes; Ricordi

Es ist genug; Variations on a   14'
Theme by J. S. Bach (1986)
solo va
1 1 0 0 — 0 0 0 0 — cel — str[1.1.1.1.1]
Possible with full strings.
Breitkopf

Femme et Oiseaux (1996)   15'
1 1 1 1 — 0 0 0 0 — pf — str[1.1.1.1.0]
Boosey & Hawkes; VAAP

Fünf Geschichten vom Herrn   13'
Keuner (Five Stories of Mr. Keuner)
(1966)
solo T
0 0 1[1/Ebcl] 0 — 0 1 1 0 — asx — 1perc — pf —
str[0.0.0.0.1]
Contents - 1. Weise am Weisen ist die Haltung; 2. Der
Zweckdiener; 3. Form und Stoff; 4. Das Wiedersehen; 5.
Wenn die Haifische Menschen wären
UE

Happy End; For two Violins, Cello,   7'
Double Bass and String Orchestra
(1985)
solo 2 vn, vc, db
str
Boosey & Hawkes

Hommage à Pierre (1985)   10'
2 0 2 0 — 1 0 0 0 — 1perc — hp — pf — str
perc: vib
Strings without db.
Fleisher; Leduc

Die Sonne der Inkas; Cantata   18'
(1964)
solo S, 3 narrators
1 1 1 0 — 1 1 0 0 — tmp+1 — 2pf —
str[1.0.0.1.0]
UE

Dennison, Sam   (1926-)

Adagio for Solo Horn and Chamber   6'
Symphony
solo hn
2 2 2 2 — 0 0 0 0 — tmp — str
Kalmus

Dessau, Paul   (1894-1979)

Alice Helps the Romance (1929)   8'
1[1/pic] 1 1[1/asx] 0 — 0 1 1 0 — banjo[opt] —
1perc — pf — str
perc: tmp, tri, gun, cym, sd, bd
Music to Walt Disney's short film of the same title.
Schott

Alice in the Wooly West (1926)   7'
1[1/pic] 1 1 0 — 0 1 1 0 — 2perc — pf —
str[5.0.0.1.1]
perc: tmp, tri, sd, bd with cym, whistle, whip
Music to Walt Disney's short film of the same title.
Schott

Alice the Firefighter (1926)   7'
1[1/pic] 1[opt] 1 0 — 0 1 1 0 — 2perc — pf —
str[1.0.0.1.1]
perc: tmp, glsp, xyl, chimes, tri, sleigh bells, sd, bd with cym, gun,
guiro
Music to Walt Disney's short film of the same title.
Schott

Alice's Monkey Business (1928)   8'
1[1/pic] 1 1 0 — 0 1 1 0 — 1perc — pf —
str[1.0.0.1.1]
perc: tmp, tri, gun, bd with cym
Music to Walt Disney's short film of the same title.
Schott

Musik für 15 Streichinstrumente   11'
(1979)
str[5.4.3.2.1]
Boosey & Hawkes

Sonatine; For Small Orchestra and   7'
Obbligato Piano (1975)
1[1/pic] 1 1 1 — 2 2 2 0 — tmp+1 — pf — str
Boosey & Hawkes

Diamond, David   (1915-2005)

Concerto for Small Orchestra   15'
1 1 1 1 — 2 1 0 0 — tmp — str
Peer

Elegies   18'
1 1[eh] 0 0 — 0 0 0 0 — str
Contents - 1. In Memory of William Faulkner; 2. In Memory
of Edward Estlin Cummings
Peer

Heroic Piece   11'
1[1/pic] 2[1.eh] 1 1 — 2 1 1 1 — 1perc — str
perc: sus cym
Peer

Hommage à Satie; À Mémoire for   7'
Chamber Orchestra (1934)
  2 1 1 1 — 2 0 0 0 — tmp+1 — hp — str
perc: cym
Fleisher

Music for Chamber Orchestra   17'
  2[1/pic.2/afl] 1[1/eh] 1[1/Ebcl] 1 — 2 1 1 0 —
tmp+1 — hp — pf — str
Peer

Rounds for String Orchestra (1944)   12'
  str
Boosey & Hawkes

Dickinson, Peter   (1934-)

Juilliard Dances (1959)   12'
  1 0 1 1 — 0 1 1 0 — 1perc — 2pf[pf.cel] —
str[0.0.0.1.0]
Novello

Diehl, Paula   (1925-)

Insiders (1992)   6'
  0 1[eh] 0 1 — 0 1 1 0 — 1perc — pf — str
Fleisher

Right of Way (1994)   18'
  0 3[1.2.eh] 2[1.bcl] 0 — 0 0 0 0 — 2perc — str
Fleisher

Dillon, James   (1950-)

...Once Upon A Time   10'
  1[afl/pic] 1[1/eh] 1 1 — 1 1 1 0 — str[0.0.0.0.1]
Peters

Überschreiten   24'
  1 1 2[1.bcl] 1[1/cbn] — 1 1 1 1 — 1perc — pf/ham
org — str[1.1.1.1.1]
Part 1 of a "German" triptych.
Peters

Vernal Showers   14'
  solo vn
  1[1/pic/afl] 1 0 0 — 0 0 0 0 — gtr, mand — 1perc
— hp — hpsd — str[0.0.1.1.1]
Peters

Windows and Canopies   22'
  2[1/pic.2/afl] 2[1.2/eh] 0 1[1/cbn] — 2 0 0 0 —
1perc — str[7.0.2.2.1]
Peters

Zone (...de azul)   7'
  0 0 1 0 — 1 1 1 0 — pf — str[1.0.1.1.0]
Peters

Dittrich, Paul-Heinz   (1930-)

Abwärts wend ich mich (1989)   60'
  2 1 3 1 — 2 2 2 0 — 3perc — pf — str
After texts by Novalis.
Breitkopf

Concert Avec Plusieurs Instruments   16'
No.1 (1976)
  1 1 0 0 — 1 0 0 0 — hpsd — str[1.0.1.1.1]
Breitkopf

Concerto for Oboe (1976)   14'
  solo ob
  2 0 2 0 — 2 1 1 0 — 2perc — elec pf —
str[2.2.2.2.2]
UE

Dobbins, Lori   (1958-)

Music for Chamber Orchestra   12'
(1987)
  1 1 1 1 — 2 1 1[btbn] 0 — 2perc — hp — pf —
str[1.0.1.1.1]
GunMar

Döhl, Friedhelm   (1936-)

Ikaros; Ballet nach einem Gedicht   8'
von E. Lindgren (1978)
  2[1.2/pic] 2[1.2/eh] 2 2[1.2/cbn] — 2 2 2 0 —
3perc — str
Breitkopf

Medeas Lied (1991)   7'
  1 0 1 0 — 0 0 0 0 — 1perc — pf — str[1.0.1.1.0]
Breitkopf

Octet, (Varianti) (1961)   12'
  1 1 1 1 — 0 0 0 0 — str[1.1.1.1.0]
Breitkopf

Passion (1984)   16'
  2[1/pic.2/pic] 1 2 2[1.2/cbn] — 2 3 2 0 — 3perc —
str
Breitkopf

Dohnanyi, Ernest von   (1877-1960)

Concert Piece in D, op.12 (1904)   22'
  solo vc
  2[1.2/pic] 2 2 2 — 2 2 0 0 — tmp — str
Kalmus

The Veil of Pierette: Pierrot's   6'
complaint of love, op.18, No.1
(1910)
  1 2 2 2 — 4 0 0 0 — tmp — str
Kalmus; Luck's

The Veil of Pierette: Waltz, op.18,   2'
No.2 (1910)
  2 2[1.eh] 2 2 — 2 0 0 0 — str
Kalmus; Luck's

The Veil of Pierette: Jolly Funeral   3'
March, op.18, No.3 (1910)
  1 1 2 3[1.2.cbn] — 4 2 3 0 — tmp — str
Kalmus; Luck's

The Veil of Pierette: Wedding   6'
Waltz, op.18, No.4 (1910)
  2 2 2 2 — 4 2 3 0 — tmp+2 — str
  perc: tri, cym, sd
Kalmus; Luck's

The Veil of Pierette: Menuett, op.18,   2'
No.5 (1910)
  2 1 2 2 — 2 0 0 0 — str
Kalmus; Luck's

The Veil of Pierette: Pierette's   7'
dance of madness, op.18, No.6
(1910)
  2 2 3[1.2.Ebcl] 3[1.2.cbn] — 4 2 3 1 — tmp+1 —
  hp — str
  perc: tam-tam
Kalmus; Luck's

Donato, Anthony   (1909-1990)

Mission San José de Aguaya   5'
  2 2 2 2 — 0 0 0 0 — str
Fleisher

Serenade for Small Orchestra   13'
(1961)
  1[1/pic] 1 1 1 — 1 1 1 0 — tmp+1 — hp — str
Fleisher

Donovan, Richard   (1891-1970)

Symphony for Chamber Orchestra   25'
(1937)
  1 1 1 1 — 0 1 0 0 — tmp+1 — str
Fleisher

Druckman, Jacob   (1928-1996)

Nor Spell, Nor Charm (1990)   15'
  1[1/afl] 2 2[1.2/bcl] 2 — 2 0 0 0 — pf/synth — str
Boosey & Hawkes

Dubois, Pierre-Max   (1930-1995)

Analogie; Suite for Orchestra (1981)   13'
  2 1 1 1 — 2 1 1 1 — tmp+1 — str
Presser

Concerto for Flute and Chamber   15'
Orchestra
  solo fl
  0 0 1 1 — 1 0 0 0 — tmp — str
Presser

Concerto for Horn and Chamber   16'
Orchestra
  solo hn
  1 1 1 1 — 0 1 0 0 — tmp — str
Presser

Queue Leu Leu; File de Danses   20'
(1989)
  2 1 2 1 — 2 1 1 0 — tmp+1 — pf — str
Presser

Sérieux s'abstenir (1983)   11'
  1 1 2 1 — 1 1 1 1 — sx — gtr, accordion —
  tmp+1 — pf — str
Presser

Trois Sérénades   10'
  0 1 1 1 — 0 0 0 0 — asx — 2perc — str
Presser

Duddell, Joe   (1972-)

Alberti Addict (2000)   14'
  1 1[eh] 1[bcl] 1 — 2 2 1 0 — bgtr — 2perc — hp
  — pf — str[2.0.2.1.1]
  perc: sd, ped bd, bongo, cym, woodblk, marim, vib, crot
Schott

Dukas, Paul (1865-1935)

Villanelle (1906)   6'
solo hn
2[1.2/pic] 2 2 2 — 2 2 0 0 — tmp+2 — str
perc: tri, glsp
Orchestrated by Donald G. Miller.
Kalmus

Duparc, Henri (1848-1933)

Aux étoiles (1910)   3'
2 2 2 2 — 2 0 0 0 — str
Salabert

Danse Lente (1910)   6'
2 2 2 2 — 4 2 0 0 — tmp — str
Orchestrated by G. Samazeuilh.
Salabert

E

Earls, Paul (1934-1999)

And On The Seventh Day (1955)   7'
1 1 1 1 — 1 0 0 0 — str
Fleisher

Eaton, John (1935-)

Adagio and Allegro (1960)   8'
1 1 0 0 — 0 0 0 0 — str
Malcom

Eben, Petr (1929-2007)

Concerto for Organ No.2   24'
solo org
0 0 0 0 — 2 2 2 0 — tmp+1 — str
Presser

Eberhard, Dennis (1943-2005)

Endgame (1987)   27'
0 0 1 1 — 1 0 0 0 — str[1.1.1.1.1]
Margun

Eckhardt-Gramatté, Sophie Carmen (1899-1974)

Triple Concerto (1949)   23'
solo cl, bn, tpt
tmp+1 — str
UE

Eder, Helmut (1916-2005)

Concerto for Oboe and Orchestra, op.35 (1962)   11'
solo ob
2[1.2/pic] 0 0 1 — 1 1 1 0 — asx — 2perc — hpsd — str
Bärenreiter

Symphony III for String Orchestra, op.29 (1959)
str
Bärenreiter

64

EDLUND   EINEM

Edlund, Lars   (1922-)

Tracce (1972)   22'
  1 1 1 1 — 0 0 0 0 — tmp+1 — hpsd — str
Nordiska

Edwards, Ross   (1943-)

Yarrageh; Nocturne (1989)   15'
  solo perc
  0 0 0 0 — 2 2 3 0 — pf/cel — str
UE

Einem, Gottfried von   (1918-1996)

Bruckner Dialog, op.39 (1971)   15'
  3[1.2.pic] 2 2 2 — 4 3 3 1 — tmp — str
Boosey & Hawkes

Capriccio, op.2 (1943)   8'
  3[1.2.3/pic] 2 2 2 — 4 3 3 1 — tmp — str
Boosey & Hawkes

Concertino Carintico, op.86 (1989)   13'
  str[4.3.2.2.1]
Boosey & Hawkes

Concerto for Orchestra, op.4 (1943)   21'
  3[1.2.3/pic] 2 2 2 — 4 3 3 1 — tmp — str
Boosey & Hawkes

Concerto for Organ, op.62 (1981)   30'
  solo org
  0 0 0 0 — 0 0 3 0 — tmp+5 — str
UE

*Die Frau des Pontiphar (Pontiphar's
Wife)* (1947)
  1 0 1 0 — 1 1 0 0 — 1perc — hp — str[0.0.1.0.1]
UE

Introduktion - Wandlungen: No.1   6'
*from "Divertimento for Mozart,"
op.21*
  2 2 2 2 — 2 2 0 0 — tmp — str
  For more information see: Mozart, Wolfgang Amadeus.
UE

Kammergesänge, op.32 (1964)   11'
  solo medium voice
  0 2 0 1 — 2 2 0 0 — str
UE

Medusa, op.24; Ballet in three   30'
*scenes to a scenario by M. Gale
Hoffman* (1957)
  3[1.2.3/pic] 2 2 2 — 4 3 3 1 — tmp+1 — hp — str
Boosey & Hawkes

Medusa, op.24a: Three Movements   16'
for Orchestra (1957)
  3[1.2.3/pic] 2 2 2 — 4 3 3 1 — tmp+1 — hp — str
Boosey & Hawkes

Münchner Symphonie, op.70 (1983)   22'
  2[1.2/pic] 2 2 2 — 2 2 2 0 — tmp+1 — str
  perc: tri, tambn, sd, td, bd, sus cym
Boosey & Hawkes

Nachtstück, op.29 (1960)   13'
  3[1.2.pic] 2 2 2 — 4 3 3 1 — tmp — str
Boosey & Hawkes

Philadelphia Symphony, op.28   18'
(1961)
  3[1.2.pic] 2 2 2 — 4 3 3 1 — tmp — str
Boosey & Hawkes

Prinz Chocolat; Musical fairytale in   35'
5 episodes, op.66 (1983)
  solo narrator
  1 1 1 1 — 1 1 0 0 — tmp+1 — str
UE

Prinzessin Turandot, op.1; Ballet in   50'
*two scenes to a scenario by Luigi
Malipiero* (1943)
  3[1.2.3/pic] 2 2 2 — 4 3 3 1 — tmp+1 — hp — str
Boosey & Hawkes

Rondo vom goldenen Kalb; Three   45'
*Nocturnes to scenes by Tatjana
Gsovsky, op.13* (1950)
  2[1.2/pic] 2 2 2 — 4 3 3 1 — tmp — str
Boosey & Hawkes

Steinbeis-Serenade; Variations,   13'
op.61 (1981)
  0 1 1 1 — 1 1 0 0 — pf — str[1.0.0.1.0]
UE

Symphonische Szenen, op.22   26'
(1956)
  3[1.2.3/pic] 2 2 2 — 4 3 3 1 — tmp — str
Boosey & Hawkes

Symphony No.4, op.80 (1986)   35'
  2 2 2 2 — 2 2 2 1 — tmp+1 — hp — str
UE

Tanz-Rondo, op.27 (1959)   *14'*
  3[1.2.3/pic] 2 2 2 — 4 3 3 1 — tmp — hp — str
  Boosey & Hawkes

Turandot, op.1a; Four Episodes for   *20'*
Orchestra (1954)
  3[1.2.3/pic] 2 2 2 — 4 3 3 1 — tmp+1 — hp — str
  Boosey & Hawkes

Wiener Symphonie, op.49 (1976)   *32'*
  3[1.2.pic] 2 2 2 — 4 3 3 1 — tmp — str
  Boosey & Hawkes

Einfeldt, Dieter   **(1935-)**

Apokalypse   *21'*
  0 0 1 1 — 0 1 1 0 — 1perc — str[1.0.0.0.1]
  Peer

Mobiles   *16'*
  1 0 1 0 — 0 0 0 0 — 1perc — pf — str[1.0.1.1.1]
  perc: sd, tambn, 4 templeblks, 3 bongos, tri, whip, sus cym, ratchet,
  guiro, claves, woodblk
  Peer

Sinfonia da Camera   *17'*
  1[1/pic(opt)] 0 1 0 — 0 0 1 0 — 2perc — pf —
  str[1.0.1.1.0]
  Peer

Eisler, Hanns   **(1898-1962)**

Five Pieces for Orchestra: From the   *15'*
music to the film "The 400 Million"
(1938)
  1 1 1 1 — 1 1 1 0 — 1perc — str
  Breitkopf

Grapes of Wrath - Death;
Alternative music to the film of the
same name (1942)
  1 1 2 2 — 2 3 2 1 — 1perc — str
  Breitkopf

Suite for Orchestra No.2: From the   *12'*
music to the film "Niemandsland,"
op.24 (1931)
  0 0 3 0 — 0 2 1 1 — 2 — banjo — 1perc — pf —
  str[0.0.0.1.1]
  Breitkopf

Suite for Orchestra No.3: From the   *12'*
music to the film "Kuhle Wampe,"
op.26 (1931)
  0 0 3 0 — 0 2 1 1 — 2 — banjo — 1perc — pf —
  str[0.0.0.1.1]
  Breitkopf

Suite for Orchestra No.5: From the   *20'*
music to the film "Dans les Rues,"
op.34 (1933)
  0 0 3 0 — 0 3 1 1 — 2 — banjo — 1perc — pf —
  str[0.0.0.1.1]
  Breitkopf

Suite for Orchestra No.6: From the   *14'*
music to the film "Le Grand Jeu,"
op.40 (1933)
  0 0 3 0 — 0 3 1 1 — 2 — banjo — 1perc — pf —
  str[0.0.0.1.1]
  Breitkopf

Suite No.1: From the movie "Opus   *15'*
III," op.23 (1930)
  2 1 2 1 — 0 2 1 1 — 2sx[asx.tsx] — banjo —
  2perc — pf — str
  Potpourri über russische Volkslieder (Unterhaltungsmusik
  Nr.2) can be performed separately (8 minutes).
  Contents - 1. Präludium in Form einer Passacaglia; 2.
  Intermezzo (Unterhaltungsmusik Nr.1); 3. Potpourri über
  russische Volkslieder (Unterhaltungsmusik Nr.2); 4. Die
  Hörfleißübung
  UE

Three Pieces for Orchestra: From   *14'*
the music to the film "The 400
Million" (1938)
  1 1 1 1 — 1 1 1 0 — 1perc — str
  Breitkopf

Eitler, Esteban   **(1913-1960)**

Divertimento 1950 (1950)
  2 2 2 2 — 2 2 1 0 — str
  Fleisher

Ekimovsky, Viktor   **(1947-)**

Brandenburg Concerto for Flute,   *12'*
Oboe, Violin, Strings and
Harpsichord (1979)
  1 1 0 0 — 0 0 0 0 — hpsd — str (min)[3.0.2.1.1]
  Sikorski

Ekström, Lars (1956-)

Järnnatten (The Lonely Night) 14'
(1987)
1 2 1 3[1.2.cbn] — 1 2 2 0 — 1perc — pf — str
Nordiska

Elgar, Edward (1857-1934)

Chanson de Matin, op.15, No.2 3'
(1899)
1 1 2 1 — 2 0 0 0 — hp[opt] — str
Luck's; Novello

Chanson de Nuit, op.15, No.1 4'
(1899)
1 1 2 1 — 2 0 0 0 — hp — str
Luck's; Novello

Dream Children, op.43 (1902) 7'
2 2 2 2 — 4 0 0 0 — tmp — hp — str
Kalmus

Falstaff: Two Interludes (1913) 7'
3[1.2.pic] 2 2 2 — 2 0 0 0 — tmp+1 — hp — str
Kalmus

Grania and Diarmid: There are 3'
seven that pull the thread, op.42
(1901)
solo voice
1 0 1 1 — 1 0 0 0 — hp — str
Kalmus

May Song (1901) 4'
1 1 2 1 — 2 2[crt.crt] 1 0 — tmp+1 — str
perc: tri
Kalmus

Minuet, op.21 (1897) 4'
1 1 2 1 — 2 0 0 0 — tmp[opt] — str
Kalmus

Salut d'Amour, op.12 (1889) 4'
1 2 2 2 — 2 0 0 0 — str
Kalmus; Luck's

Serenade in E minor, op.20 (1892) 12'
str
mvt durations: 6' 3' 3'
Breitkopf

Serenade Lyrique (1899) 3'
2 2 2 2 — 2 0 0 0 — tmp — hp — str
Kalmus

Sospiri, op.70 (1914) 6'
hp[or pf] — org [or harm, opt] — str
Breitkopf; Kalmus; Luck's

Elias, Alfonso de (1902-1984)

El Jardín Encantado; Tríptico
Sinfonico
2 2 2 2 — 2 0 0 0 — tmp — str
Contents - 1. En El Jardín; 2. Contemplación; 3. La Fuente Maravillosa
Fleisher

Suite para orquesta de cámara
0 1 0 1 — 0 1 0 0 — pf — str
Fleisher

Engelmann, Hans Ulrich (1921-)

Capricciosi (1968) 10'
1 1 1 1 — 1 1 1 1 — tmp+1 — hp — pf — str
Breitkopf

Ciacona (1993) 11'
1 0 1[bcl] 0 — 0 0 0 0 — 1perc — pf — str[1.0.1.1.0]
perc: vib
Breitkopf

Concerto for Cello (1948) 12'
solo vc
str
Breitkopf

Ezra Pound Music (1959) 9'
1[1/pic] 2[1.eh] 0 1 — 0 0 1 0 — 4perc — str[0.0.0.4.4]
Breitkopf

Impromptu (1949) 6'
1[1/pic] 1 1 1 — 4 3 3 1 — tmp+3 — pf — str
Breitkopf

Kaleidoskop (1941) 10'
1 1 1 1 — 0 3 3 0 — 1 — tmp+2 — str
Breitkopf

Nocturnos, op.18 (1958) 15'
solo S
1 0 0 0 — 0 1 1 0 — ssx — elec gtr — 3perc — hp — hpsd — str[1.1.1.1.0]
Contents - 1. Noce de Luna; 2. Pantomime
Breitkopf

Partita (1953)   12'
  0 0 0 0 — 0 3 0 0 — tmp+3 — str
Breitkopf

Shadows; Scenes for Orchestra (1964)   12'
  1 1 1 1 — 1 1 1 0 — mand — 3perc — hp — pf — str
Breitkopf

Sinfonia da Camera (1981)   14'
  1 1 1 1 — 1 0 0 0 — pf — str[1.1.1.1.0]
Breitkopf

Strukturen; Den Taten der neuen Bildhauer (1954)   9'
  1 1 1 1 — 1 1 1 0 — tmp+4 — hp — pf — str
  Strings without db.
Breitkopf

Trias (1962)   18'
  solo pf
  1 1 1 1 — 1 1 1 1 — tape — 3perc — str
Breitkopf

Eötvös, Peter   (1944-)

Chinese Opera (1986)   35'
  2 2[1.2/eh] 3[1.2.3/bcl] 2 — 2 2 2 1 — 3perc — hp — synth — str[2.0.2.2.1]
  Recommended synth is Yamaha DX-7.
Salabert

Eppert, Carl   (1882-1961)

A Little Symphony; Symphony No.2 (1933)   18'
  2[1.2/pic] 1 2 2 — 2 2 0 0 — tmp+1 — hp — str
Fleisher

Erb, Donald   (1927-2008)

Chamber Concerto   11'
  solo pf
  2[1.pic] 2 0 1 — 2 1 1 0 — str
Presser

Erbse, Heimo   (1924-2005)

Allegro - Lento - Allegro: No.3 from "Divertimento for Mozart" (1956)   2'
  2 2 4[1.2.basset hn.basset hn] 3[1.2.cbn] — 2 2 0 0 — tmp — no str
  For more information see: Mozart, Wolfgang Amadeus.
UE

Capriccio, op.4 (1952)   13'
  1perc — pf — str
Boosey & Hawkes

Concerto for Piano, op.22 (1965)   21'
  solo pf
  2[1.2/pic] 2[1.2/eh] 2 2[1.2/cbn] — 4 2 3 0 — tmp+1 — str
Boosey & Hawkes

For String and Wind Players (1970)   19'
  0 1 1 1 — 1 0 0 0 — str[1.1.1.1.1]
Schirmer

Erdmann, Dietrich   (1917-2009)

Concert Piece   6'
  0 0 0 0 — 2 0 0 0 — asx — 2perc — str
Breitkopf

Concerto (1986)   23'
  solo vc
  1 1 1 1 — 1 0 0 0 — 1perc — str[1.0.1.1.1]
Breitkopf

Concerto (1988)   18'
  solo vn
  1 1 1 1 — 1 0 0 0 — 1perc — str
Breitkopf

Concerto for Mandolin (1979)   23'
  solo mand
  2 0 2 0 — 2 0 0 0 — tmp+1 — str
Breitkopf

Concerto for Piano (1950)   23'
  solo pf
  2[1.2/pic] 2 2 2 — 2 3 3 0 — tmp+1 — str
Breitkopf

Divertimento (1953)   23'
  str
Breitkopf

Epitaph (1987)   *12'*
   0 0 2[1.bcl] 0 — 0 0 0 0 — mand, gtr —
str[1.0.1.1.0]
Breitkopf

Musica Multicolore (1981)   *15'*
   0 1 1 1 — 1 0 0 0 — 1perc — str[1.0.1.1.1]
Breitkopf

Nuancen (1978)   *13'*
   1 0 1 0 — 0 0 0 0 — 1perc — str[1.0.1.1.1]
Breitkopf

Serenità notturna (1984)   *15'*
   str
Breitkopf

Erdmann, Eduard   (1896-1958)

Ständchen, op.16 (1930)   *15'*
   2 2 2 2 — 2 1 1 0 — 1perc — hp — str
UE

Erickson, Robert   (1917-1997)

Concerto for Piano and 7   *20'*
Instruments
   solo pf
   1 1 1 0 — 0 1 1 0 — 1perc — str[0.0.0.0.1]
Presser

Essl, Karl-Heinz   (1960-)

Et Consumimur Igni (1960)   *16'*
   0 0 0 0 — 2 2 2 0 — 3perc — str[3.0.3.3.0]
Breitkopf

O Tiempo Tus Piramides (1989)   *20'*
   1 1 1 1 — 1 1 1 0 — 2perc — str[3.3.3.2.1]
UE

Etler, Alvin   (1913-1973)

Elegy for Small Orchestra (1959)   *4'*
   1 1 2 2 — 2 0 0 0 — str
AMP; Fleisher

Music for Chamber Orchestra   *15'*
   1 1 1 1 — 2 1 1 0 — 1perc — str
  perc: sd
Fleisher

Ettinger, Max   (1874-1951)

An den Wassern Babylons; Songs   *15'*
of Babylonian Jews for Small
Orchestra
   1 1 1 0 — 0 2 1 0 — tmp+1 — str
Fleisher

F

Falla, Manuel de (1876-1946)

El Amor Brujo; (First Version) 34'
(1915)
    solo Mz
    1[1/pic] 1 0 0 — 1 1 0 0 — 1perc — pf —
    str[2.2.2.2.1]
      perc: chimes
    Chester Novello

El Amor Brujo; (Second Version) 23'
(1925)
    solo Mz
    2[1.2/pic] 1[1/eh] 2 1 — 2 2 0 0 — tmp+1 — pf —
    str
    Chester Novello

El Amor Brujo: Chanson du Feu 3'
Follet
    solo medium voice
    1 0 2 0 — 2 0 0 0 — pf — str
    Chester Novello

El Amor Brujo: Récit du Pécheur et 8'
Pantomime
    solo Mz
    2[1.pic] 1 2 1 — 2 2 0 0 — tmp — pf — str
    Chester Novello

El Amor Brujo: Ritual Fire Dance 5'
    2[1.2/pic] 1 2 1 — 2 2 0 0 — tmp — pf — str
    Chester Novello

El Corregidor y la Molinera (1917) 43'
    solo Mz
    1[1/pic] 1 1 1 — 1 1 0 0 — pf — str
    Chester Novello

Fuego Fatuo (1919) 45'
    2[1.2/pic] 1[1/eh] 2 2 — 2 2 3 0 — tmp+1 — hp —
    2pf[4hand] — str
    Suite taken from the unfinished opera based on the music of
    Chopin. Arranged by Antonio Ros Marba.
    Chester Novello

Noches en los Jardines de España 23'
(Nights in the Gardens of Spain)
(1915)
    solo pf
    2[1.2/pic] 3[1.2.eh] 2 2 — 2 2 0 0 — tmp+1 — hp
    — str
    Version for chamber orchestra.
    Chester Novello

Seven Popular Spanish Songs 11'
(1915)
    solo medium voice
    2 2[1.eh] 3[1.2.bcl] 2 — 2 0 0 0 — tmp+1 — hp —
    str
    Orchestrated by Ernesto Halffter (1945).
    Eschig

Seven Popular Spanish Songs 11'
(1915)
    2 2[1.eh] 3 3 — 2 2 2 1 — tmp+2 — str
    Orchestrated by Luciano Berio (1978).
    Chester Novello; Eschig

El Sombrero des Tres Picos: Suite 11'
No.1 (1919)
    2[1.2/pic] 2[1.2/eh] 2 2 — 2 2 0 0 — tmp+1 — hp
    — pf — str
      perc: sus cym, glsp, xyl
    Contents - 1. Introduction; 2. Afternoon; 3. Dance of the
    Miller's Wife (Fandango); 4. The Corregidor; 5. The Grapes
    Chester Novello; Kalmus; Luck's

Farago, Marcel (1924-)

Divertimento for Chamber 10'
Orchestra, op.18
    1[1/pic] 1 1 1 — 1 1 1 0 — tmp+1 — hp — str
    Fleisher

Farkas, Ferenc (1905-2000)

Concertino for Harp and Orchestra 15'
(1937)
    solo hp
    1 1 2 1 — 2 1 0 0 — tmp — str
    UE

Concertino for Harpsichord and 16'
String Orchestra (1949)
    solo hpsd
    str
    UE

Kalender (1955) 18'
    solo S, T
    1 1 1 1 — 1 0 0 0 — hp — str[1.1.1.1.1]
    UE

Two Hungarian Dances (1949) 10'
    2 1 2 1 — 2 2 1 0 — tmp+1 — hp — str
    EMI

Fauré, Gabriel   (1845-1924)

Ballade, op.19   15'
  solo pf
  2 2 2 2 — 2 0 0 0 — str
Kalmus; Leduc; Luck's

Concerto for Violin in D minor   24'
  solo vn
  2 2 2 2 — 4 2 3 1 — tmp — str
  Edited by Pietro Spada.
Presser

Fantasie, op.111 (1919)   18'
  solo pf
  2 2 2 2 — 4 1 0 0 — tmp — hp — str
Durand

L'Horizon chimérique, op.118   7'
(1921)
  solo voice
  2 2 2 2 — 2 0 3 0 — 1perc — hp — str
Durand

Masques et Bergamasques, op.112 14'
(1919)
  2 2 2 2 — 2 2 0 0 — tmp — hp — str
Durand

Romance, op.28   6'
  2 1 2 2 — 1 0 0 0 — hp — str
  Orchestrated by P. Gaubert.
Leduc

Symphony in F major   12'
  2 2 2 2 — 4 0 0 0 — str
Presser

Faust, George   (1937-)

Adagio for Small Orchestra (1966) 6'
  2 2 2 2 — 2 0 0 0 — hp — str
Fleisher

Felder, David   (1953-)

Coleccion Nocturna (1984)   18'
  solo cl/bcl, pf
  2 2 2 2 — 2 2 2 0 — tape — 1perc — hp — str
Presser

Gone Grey (2004)   15'
  electronics[opt] — str
Presser

Journal (1990)   11'
  1[1/pic/afl] 1[1/eh] 1[1/bcl] 0 — 1 1 1 0 — 1perc
  — hp — pf/cel — str
Presser

Passageways IIA (1991)   4'
  1[1/pic] 1 1 0 — 0 0 1[btbn] 0 — 1perc — pf —
  str[1.0.0.1.0]
Presser

Three Lines from Twenty Poems   9'
(1987)
  1 1[1/eh] 2[1.2/bcl] 1[1/cbn] — 1 1 2[1.btbn] 1 —
  2perc — hp — pf — str
Presser

Feldman, Morton   (1926-1987)

For Frank O'Hara (1973)   13'
  1[1/pic/afl] 0 1 0 — 0 0 0 0 — 2perc — pf —
  str[1.0.0.1.0] *EFM*
  perc: glsp, xyl, vib, chimes, gong, cym, 2 sd, bd, tri, tmp
UE

For Samuel Beckett; For 23 players 55'
(1987)
  2 2 2 2 — 2 2 2 1 — 1perc — hp — pf —
  str[1.1.1.1.1]
  perc: vib
UE

Madame Press Died Last Week at   4'
Ninety (1970)
  2 0 0 0 — 1 1 1 1[or bcl] — 1perc — cel —
  str[0.0.0.2.2]
  perc: glsp
UE

Samuel Beckett, Words & Music   42'
(1987)
  2[1/pic.2] 0 0 0 — 0 0 0 0 — 1perc — pf —
  str[1.0.1.1.0]
  perc: vib
UE

The Turfan Fragments (1980)   17'
  2 2 2 2 — 2 2 2 0 — str[0.0.6.4.4]
UE

Voice and Instruments 1 (1972)   15'
  solo S
  2 1 2 1 — 1 1 1 0 — tmp — hp — cel — str
UE

Fenby, Eric   (1906-1997)

Rossini on Ilkla Moor; Overture   8'
(1938)
  2[1.2/pic] 2 2 2 — 2 2 1 0 — tmp+1 — str
  perc: cym, bd
Boosey & Hawkes

Fennelly, Brian   (1937-)

Sigol for Strings (2007)   14'
  str
ACA

Fenney, William   (1891-1957)

Romance in Early Spring
  2 2 2 2 — 2 0 0 0 — tmp — str
Fleisher

Ferguson, Howard   (1908-1999)

Concerto for Piano and String   25'
Orchestra, op.12 (1951)
  solo pf
  str
Boosey & Hawkes

Four Diversions on Ulster Airs, op.7   12'
(1942)
  2[1.2/pic] 2 1 2 — 4 2 3 0 — tmp+1 — str
  perc: cym, sd
  Possible with 2 2 2 2 - 2 2 0 0 - tmp+1 - str
Boosey & Hawkes

Overture for an Occasion, op.16   8'
(1953)
  2[1.2/pic] 2 2 2 — 4 2 3 0 — tmp+1 — str
  perc: cym, bd, sd, tambn
Boosey & Hawkes

Serenade (1933)   22'
  0 0 1 1 — 1 0 0 0 — str
Boosey & Hawkes

Ferrari, Luc   (1929-2005)

Entrée; For 15 Instruments   25'
  1 1 2 1 — 0 1 1 0 — 2perc — 2pf[pf.cel] —
  str[1.0.1.1.1]
Presser

Flashes; For 14 Instruments   16'
  1[pic] 1 1 1 — 1 1 1 0 — 2perc — str[1.1.1.1.1]
Presser

Ficher, Jacobo   (1896-1978)

Dos Poemas; De El Jardino de R.   8'
Tagore, op.10, No.16
  1 1 1 1 — 2 0 0 0 — str
Fleisher

Seis Fabulas (Six Fables)   20'
  2 2 2 2 — 2 2 0 0 — tmp[tmp/tri] — str
Peer

Filippi, Amedeo De   (1898-1990)

Raftsman's Dance (1939)   3'
  1 1 2 1 — 2 2 1 0 — tmp+1 — pf — str
Fleisher

Fine, Irving   (1914-1962)

Serious Song; A Lament for String   10'
Orchestra (1955)
  str
Boosey & Hawkes

Finke, Fidelio   (1891-1968)

Eight Bagatelles   15'
  2 2 2 2 — 2 2 3 0 — tmp+1 — str
Breitkopf

Festliche Musik   8'
  2 1 1 2 — 1 2 2 0 — tmp+1 — str
Breitkopf

Finnissy, Michael   (1946-)

Câtana (1984)   16'
  1 1 1 0 — 0 0 0 0 — 1perc — hp — pf —
  str[1.0.1.1.0]
Presser

Folk-Song Set (1970)   13'
   solo voice
   0 1[eh] 1 0 — 0 1[flug] 0 0 — 1perc —
   str[1.1.1.1.1]
   <small>Alternate instrumentation: 1010 - 0000 - pf - str(1.0.1.1.0)-
   voice</small>
UE

From the Revelations of St. John   7'
the Divine (1965)
   solo S
   1 0 0 0 — 0 0 0 0 — str[1.1.2.2.0]
UE

Finzi, Gerald   (1901-1956)

Introit (1925)   8'
   solo vn
   1 2[1.eh] 2 1 — 2 1 0 0 — str
Kalmus

Love's Labour's Lost: Three   6'
Soliloquies, op.28 (1955)
   1 1 1 1 — 1 0 0 0 — str
Boosey & Hawkes

Love's Labour's Lost: Suite, op.28b   23'
(1955)
   2 1 2 1 — 2 1 0 0 — tmp+1 — str
   <small>perc: cym, tri, bd, sd, tambn</small>
Boosey & Hawkes

Prelude, op.25 (1920s)   5'
   str
Boosey & Hawkes

Romance, op.11 (1928)   8'
   str
Boosey & Hawkes

A Severn Rhapsody, op.3 (1923)   6'
   1 1[1/eh] 1[1/bcl] 0 — 1 0 0 0 — str
Kalmus

Firsova, Elena   (1950-)

Autumn Music, op.39 (1988)   11'
   1 2 0 2 — 2 0 0 0 — str[8.6.4.4.2]
Boosey & Hawkes; Fleisher

Chamber Concerto No.1; For Flute   12'
and Strings, op.19 (1978)
   solo fl
   str
Boosey & Hawkes

Chamber Concerto No.2, op.26;   12'
Concerto for Cello No.2 (1982)
   solo vc
   1 1 1 1 — 1 1 1 0 — 1perc — hp — cel —
   str[4.2.4.3.1]
   <small>perc: chimes, glsp, vib</small>
Boosey & Hawkes

Chamber Concerto No.3; For Piano   15'
and Orchestra, op.33 (1985)
   solo pf
   1[1/pic] 0 0 0 — 4 1 1 0 — 1perc — str[6.4.4.4.1]
   <small>perc: sus cym, gong, tam-tam, glsp, vib, chimes</small>
Boosey & Hawkes

Chamber Concerto No.4; For Horn   13'
and 13 Performers, op.37 (1987)
   solo hn
   1 1 1 1 — 0 1 1 0 — 1perc — cel — str[1.1.1.1.1]
   <small>perc: 3 bongos, 3 tom-tom, glsp, Indian jingles</small>
Boosey & Hawkes

Chamber Concerto No.5; For Cello
and Small Orchestra (1996)
   solo vc
   hp — cel — str
Boosey & Hawkes

Chamber Concerto No.6; The   18'
Temple of Mnemosyne, op.80
(1996)
   solo pf
   1 1 2[1.bcl] 1 — 1 0 0 0 — 3perc — str[3.0.3.2.1]
   <small>perc: tam-tam, tri, 2 sus cym, gong, crot, vib, chimes, glass bells</small>
Boosey & Hawkes

Concerto for Cello, op.10 (1973)   18'
   solo vc
   2 1 1 1 — 3 1 0 0 — 1perc — hp — cel — str
Boosey & Hawkes

Mnemosyne (1995)
   1 1 2 1 — 1 0 0 0 — 1perc — hp — cel —
   str[3.0.2.2.1]
Sikorski

Music for Twelve (1986)   12'
   1 1 1 1 — 1 1 0 0 — hp — cel — str[1.1.1.1.0]
VAAP

Postlude; For Harp and Orchestra,   5'
op.18 (1977)
   solo hp
   1perc — cel — str
   <small>perc: chimes, glsp</small>
Boosey & Hawkes

Fitelberg, Jerzy (1903-1951)

Suite No.3 (1930)   23'
  2 1 2 2 — 0 2 2 0 — 1perc — pf — str
  Strings without vc or db.
UE

Fletcher, Horace Grant (1913-2002)

Two Orchestral Pieces for Small   13'
Orchestra (1956)
  2 2 2 2 — 2 2 1 0 — tmp — str
  Contents - 1. Sumare; 2. Wintare
Fleisher

Foerster, Josef Bohuslav (1859-1951)

Ballata, op.92 (1911)   8'
  solo vn
  2 2 2 2 — 4 2 0 0 — tmp — hp — str
UE

Fómina, Silvia (1962-)

Permanenza; Für   15'
mikropolyphonisches, im Raum
verteiltes Orchester (1994)
  2 0 3 0 — 1 0 1 0 — tape — str[5.0.3.3.2]
  Ensemble spread throughout the room.
UE

Fontyn, Jacqueline (1930-)

Nonetto (1969)   12'
  1 1 1 1 — 1 0 0 0 — str[1.0.1.1.1]
Limelette; Fleisher

Forst, Rudolf (1900-1973)

Divertimento for Chamber   16'
Orchestra
  1[1/pic] 1[1/eh] 2 1 — 1 1 0 0 — str
  Contents - 1. Vocalise; 2. Tempo di Valse; 3. Pastorale; 4.
  Toccata
Fleisher

Fortner, Wolfgang (1907-1987)

Suite for Orchestra; After music by   20'
Jan Pieters Sweelinck (1930)
  0 0 0 2 — 0 2 0 0 — 3[2asx(or 2eh).tsx] — 3tmp
  — str[0.0.8.8.6]
Schott

Foss, Lukas (1922-2009)

His oboe concerto is great

Concerto for Percussion and   30'
Chamber Orchestra (1974)
  solo perc
  1[1/pic] 1 1[1/ssx] 1 — 1 2 2 1 — elec gtr —
  3perc — 2pf[pf.elec org] — str[3.2.2.2.1]
  Version No.1.
Salabert

Concerto for Percussion and   45'
Chamber Orchestra (1974)
  solo perc
  1 1 1 1 — 1 2 2 1 — str[3.2.2.2.1]
  Extended version (Version No.2).
Salabert

Measure for Measure (1984)   10'
  solo T
  1 2 0 2 — 0 2 2 0 — 2tmp — hp — str
  Version for T and orchestra of "Symphonie de Rossi."
Salabert

Orpheus (1974)   21'
  solo gtr
  0 2 0 0 — 0 0 0 0 — 1perc — 2hp — pf — str
Salabert

Symphonie de Rossi; Suite   9'
Salomon Rossi (1975)
  1 3 0 2 — 0 2 2 0 — 2tmp — hp — str
Salabert

Foulds, John (1880-1939)

Keltic Suite, op.29 (1911)   15'
  2[1.2/pic] 2 2 2 — 2 2 3 1 — tmp+1 — hp — str
  perc: tri, cym, sd
Boosey & Hawkes

Music-Pictures (Group IV), op.55   10'
(1917)
  str
Boosey & Hawkes

Frackenpohl, Arthur (1924-)

Divertimento in F (1952) 14'
  1 0 1 0 — 1 1 1 0 — str
Fleisher

Françaix, Jean (1912-1997)

85 Measures et un Da Capo (1991) 3'
  2 0 0 1 — 0 2 1 0 — 2sx[asx.tsx] — 1perc —
str[3.0.1.1.0]
perc: sd
Schott

Onze Variations sur un Thème de 10'
Haydn (1982)
  0 2 2 2 — 2 1 0 0 — str[0.0.0.0.1]
Requires 5 string db.
Schott

Sérénade (1934) 10'
  1 1 1 1 — 1 1 1 0 — str[1.1.1.1.1]
Schott

Franceschini, Romulus (1929-1994)

White Spirituals 18'
solo voice
1[1/pic] 1 2[1.bcl] 1 — 2 1 1 0 — str
Contents - 1. Green Fields; 2. Invitation; 3. Royal
Proclamation; 4. Dunlap's Creek; 5. Amazing Grace; 6.
Davisson's Retirement; 7. Sawyers Exit; 8. Missionary's
Farewell; 9. We'll Shout and Give Him Glory
Kalmus

Franco, Johan (1908-1988)

Sinfonia (1932) 8'
  1 1 1 1 — 1 1 1 0 — asx — tmp+1 — str
Fleisher

Frank, Gabriela Lena (1972-)

Elegía Andina (2000) 11'
  2 2 2 2 — 2 2 0 0 — tmp+1 — str
Schirmer

Manchay Tiempo (Time of Fear) 13'
(2005)
  1perc — hp — pf — str
Schirmer

→ I bet I can get something free

Franke, Bernd (1959-)

Konform - Kontraform (1988) 12'
  0 2[1.eh] 0 0 — 0 0 1 0 — 1perc — pf —
str[0.0.1.1.1]
Breitkopf

Frankel, Benjamin (1906-1973)

Bagatelles "Cinque Pezzi Notturni" 11'
(1959)
  1 1 1 1 — 1 0 0 0 — hp — str[1.1.1.1.1]
Novello

Catalogue of Incidents (1965) 20'
  0 1[1/eh] 2 1 — 1 0 0 0 — tmp+1 — hp —
str[1.0.1.1.1]
Novello

Franze, Juan Pedro (1922-)

Lamento quechua, op.6 (1952) 4'
  1 1 0 1 — 2 0 0 0 — 3perc — hp — str
Fleisher

Frazelle, Kenneth (1955-)

Concerto for Chamber Orchestra 27'
(2002)
  2 2 2 2 — 2 2 0 0 — tmp+2 — str
Subito

The Four Winds; (After Mozart) 25'
(2000)
solo fl, ob, bn, hn
  2 2 2 2 — 2 2 0 0 — tmp+1 — str
Subito

Laconic Variations (1997) 11'
  2 2 2 2 — 2 2 0 0 — tmp+1 — str
Subito

Freyhan, Michael (1940-)

Toy Symphony (1962) 7'
  2 0 2 0 — 0 2 0 0 — toys — 1perc — str
Chester Novello

Fricker, Peter Racine   (1920-1990)

Fantasie: No.4 from "Divertimento   3'
for Mozart" (1956)
   2 2 2 2 — 2 2 0 0 — tmp — str
For more information see: Mozart, Wolfgang Amadeus.
UE

Frounberg, Ivar   (1950-)

En Vue de Roesnaes (1981)   7'
   0 1 2 0 — 0 1 0 0 — 2perc — 2pf[pf.cel] —
str[0.0.1.0.0]
Hansen

Fuchs, Kenneth   (1956-)

Face of the Night; (After a Painting   22'
by Robert Motherwell)
   0 1[1/eh] 0 0 — 0 0 0 0 — 2perc — hp —
str[1.0.1.1.0]
Presser

Out of the Dark; (After Three   14'
Paintings by Helen Frankenthaler)
   1 1 1 1 — 1 0 0 0 — str[1.1.1.1.0]
Can be done with strings (3.3.2.2.0).
Presser

Fujiie, Keiko   (1963-)

Beber, op.31 (1994)   10'
   2[1.2/pic] 2 2[1/Ebcl.2/bcl] 2 — 2 2 0 0 — 3perc
— str
perc: I=glsp, vib, sistrum, marim, sm Chinese gong, wooden board,
binzasara II=antique cym, chinese gong, sus cym, bd, steel dr, vib
III=4timp, glass wind bell, bd
Boosey & Hawkes

Fuleihan, Anis   (1900-1970)

Divertimento   9'
   0 2 1 1 — 1 1 0 0 — str
Peer

Divertimento No.2 (1941)
   0 1 0 1 — 1 1 0 0 — str
Fleisher

Fundal, Karsten   (1966-)

Hoquetus (1984)   10'
   1 1 1 1 — 1 0 0 0 — str[1.1.1.1.0]
Hansen

Oscillation (2000)   13'
   1 1 1 1 — 1 1 1 0 — 1perc — pf — str
Hansen

Zoom; Figure and Ground Study III   5'
(1997)
   1 0 1 1 — 0 1 0 0 — 1perc — pf — str[1.0.1.1.0]
Hansen

Furrer, Beat   (1954-)

Gaspra (1988)   17'
   1 0 1 0 — 0 0 0 0 — 1perc — pf — str[1.0.1.1.0]
UE

Illuminations (1985)   20'
   solo S
   1 0 2 0 — 0 0 2 0 — 2perc — pf — str[0.0.0.2.1]
Strings (vc and db) may be extended in numbers.
UE

In der Stille des Hauses wohnt ein   12'
Ton (In the silence of the house
there lives a sound) (1987)
   1 0 2 0 — 0 1 2 1 — 2perc — pf — str[1.0.1.2.1]
UE

Narcissus-Fragment; For 2   19'
Narrators and 26 Players (1993)
   solo 2 narrators
   2 0 2 1 — 2 2 2 1 — 1 — 3perc — hp — pf —
str[2.0.2.2.2]
UE

Nuun (1996)   17'
   solo 2 pf
   2[1.2/pic] 1 3[1.2.bcl] 1[1/cbn] — 2 2 2 0 —
ssx/tsx — 3perc — str[2.0.2.2.2]
UE

Studie 2; A un moment de terre   17'
perdue (1990)
   1 0 2 0 — 0 1 2 1 — tsx — 2perc — pf —
str[1.0.1.1.1]
UE

Fussell, Charles   (1938-)

*Aria of the Blessed Virgin after
Henry Purcell* (1968)
    1 2[1.eh] 0 0 — 0 1 0 0 — mand — hpsd —
    str[0.0.2.2.1]
    Schirmer

Füssl, Karl Heinz   (1924-1992)

Concerto Rapsodico (1957)   7'
    solo A or Mz
    0 0 2 0 — 1 1 1 0 — 1perc — hp — pf — str
    UE

Dialogue in Praise of the Owl and   16'
the Cuckoo (1947)
    solo T
    1 0 1 0 — 0 0 1 0 — gtr — hp — str[1.0.0.0.1]
    UE

Refrains, op.13 (1972)   22'
    solo pf
    2 2 2 2 — 2 2 0 1 — tmp+1 — str
    UE

Szenen, op.6 (1964)   23'
    str
    Boosey & Hawkes

G

Gál, Hans   (1890-1987)

Ballet Suite "Scaramussio," op.36   25'
(1929)
    2 2 2 2 — 2 2 1 0 — tmp+1 — str
    perc: tri, cym, tambn, sd, glsp
    Schott

Concerto for Cello, op.67   32'
    solo vc
    2[1.2/pic] 2 2 2 — 2 2 0 0 — tmp — str
    Breitkopf

Concerto for Piano, op.57   34'
    solo pf
    2[1.2/pic] 2 2 2 — 2 2 1 0 — tmp — str
    Breitkopf

Concerto for Violin, op.39   25'
    solo vn
    1 2 2 2 — 2 1 1 0 — tmp — str
    Breitkopf

Idyllikon; Four Movements for Small   29'
Orchestra, op.79 (1959)
    2[1.2/pic] 2[1.2/eh] 2 2 — 2 0 0 0 — tmp — str
    Boosey & Hawkes

Musik, op.73   20'
    str
    Breitkopf

Symphony No.2, op.53   47'
    2[1.2/pic] 2[1.2/eh] 2[1.2/bcl] 2 — 3 2 3 0 —
    tmp+1 — hp — str
    Breitkopf

Zauberspiegel-Suite; Weihnachtsmusik.   20'
Musik zu einem Märchenspiel, op.38
(Magic Mirror Suite; Christmas music.
Music to a fairytale play) (1930)
    1 1 1 1 — 1 1 1 0 — 1perc — pf — str
    UE

Ganne, Louis   (1862-1923)

Deux Airs de Ballet: Pasquinade
(1897)
  2[1.pic] 0 2 0 — 0 0 0 0 — str
  Includes only one of the two airs, the Pasquinade.
  Enoch & Cie; Fleisher

Garcia Leoz, Jesus   (1904-1953)

Sonatina (1945)
  3[1.2.pic] 2 2 2 — 2 1 0 0 — hp — str
  Unión

Gardner, John   (1917-)

Overture "Half Holiday" (1962)   4'
  2 1 3 1 — 2 2 1 0 — tmp+1 — str
  Novello

Gaslini, Giorgio   (1929-)

Canto Dalla Città Inquieta: From   11'
"Totale" (1965)
  2[1.pic] 1 1[bcl] 0 — 1 1 0 0 — gtr, tape — tmp+1
  — pf — str
  UE

Gaubert, Philippe   (1879-1941)

Madrigal   4'
  2 2 2 2 — 2 0 0 0 — hp — str
  Kalmus

Rhapsodie sur des thèmes   14'
populaires (1925)
  1 1 2 1 — 2 2 1 0 — tmp+1 — hp — str
  Orchestrated by L. Gaubert-Elgé.
  Fleisher; Lemoine

Gauldin, Robert   (1931-)

Diverse Dances (1957)   14'
  2[1.pic] 1 1 1 — 2 1 1 0 — tmp — hp — str
  Fleisher

Gebhard-Elsass, Hans   (1882-1947)

Ländliche Suite, op.23 (1935)   18'
  1 1 1 0 — 0 2 1 0 — tmp+1 — str
  Fleisher; Schott

Geiser, Walther   (1948-)

Concert Piece for Organ and   16'
Chamber Orchestra, op.30 (1944)
  solo org
  0 1 0 0 — 0 2 1 0 — tmp — str
  Bärenreiter

Fantasie I, op.31 (1948)
  tmp — pf — str
  Bärenreiter

Fantasie III für Streichorchester,   15'
op.39 (1949)
  str
  Bärenreiter

Geissler, Fritz   (1921-1984)

Chamber Concerto   16'
  solo fl, hpsd
  str[3.0.0.3.1]
  Breitkopf

Chamber Symphony (1954)   14'
  1 1 1 1 — 0 3 1 0 — tmp+1 — hp — str
  Breitkopf

Chamber Symphony (1970)   20'
  1 1 1 1 — 1 0 0 0 — 1perc — str
  Breitkopf

Five Miniatures   14'
  2 1 1 1 — 2 2 1 0 — tmp+1 — str
  Breitkopf

Italienische Lustspiel-Ouvertüre   8'
  2 2 2 2 — 2 2 1 0 — tmp+1 — hp — str
  Breitkopf

Regiser Festmusik   10'
  str
  Breitkopf

String Symphony; Symphony No.4   30'
  str
  Breitkopf

Symphony No.6; Concertante 25'
Symphony
    1 1 1 1 — 1 0 0 0 — str
Breitkopf

Gelbrun, Arthur   (1913-1985)

Lieder der Mädchen (Songs of the 25'
Girls) (1945)
    solo A
    2 2 2 0 — 2 0 0 0 — tmp+1 — hp — str
    perc: tam-tam
UE

Genzmer, Harald   (1909-2007)

Capriccio für Kammerorchester; 12'
(Nonett)
    0 1 1 1 — 1 0 0 0 — str[1.1.1.1.1]
Peters

Sinfonia da Camera 21'
    2 1 1 1 — 1 0 0 0 — tmp+1 — str
Peters

Gerhard, Roberto   (1896-1970)

Pandora: Orchestral suite from the 27'
ballet (1943)
    1[1/pic] 1[1/eh] 2[1.2/bcl] 1 — 2 1 1 0 — 3perc —
    hp — pf/cel — str
    perc: tmp, sd, tambn, 3 Chinese tom-tom, 3 Chinese cym, templeblk,
    woodblk, metalblk, 2 gongs, tri, xyl, glsp
Boosey & Hawkes

German, Sir Edward   (1862-1936)

Coronation March (1911) 6'
    2 2 2 2 — 2 2 3 0 — tmp+1 — str
Kalmus

The Conquerer: Incidental music, 8'
Romance and two Dances (1905)
    1[1/pic] 1 2 1 — 2 2 2 0 — tmp+1 — hp — pf —
    str
Kalmus

Gipsy Suite; Four characteristic 12'
dances (1892)
    2[1.2/pic] 2 2 2 — 4 2 3 0 — tmp+1 — hp — str
Kalmus

Tom Jones: Three Dances (1907) 11'
    2[1.2/pic] 1 2 1 — 2 2 3 0 — 1perc — pf — str
Kalmus

Gerster, Ottmar   (1897-1969)

Oberhessische Bauerntänze für 12'
Kleines Orchester (1937)
    1 1 2 1 — 2 2 1 0 — tmp+1 — str
Fleisher; Schott

Gianneo, Luis   (1897-1968)

Variaciones Sobre Tema de Tango 8'
    2 2 2 2 — 2 2 0 0 — tmp+1 — str
    perc: bd, tamburo, cym, tri, lija, cowbell, tam-tam, madera, legno,
    click, bongo
Peer

Giefer, Willy   (1930-)

Concerto per archi (1970) 12'
    str
Breitkopf

Pro - Kontra (1970) 16'
    1[1/pic] 1 1 1 — 1 0 0 0 — 1perc — str[1.0.1.1.1]
Breitkopf

Gielen, Michael   (1927-)

Musica (1954) 24'
    solo Bar
    0 0 0 0 — 0 0 1 0 — tmp — pf — str
UE

Gilbert, Anthony   (1934-)

Crow-Cry, op.27 (1976) 20'
    1[1/pic] 1 1[1/bcl] 1 — 1 1 1[ttbn/btbn] 0 — 1perc
    —elec pf — str[1.0.1.1.1]
    perc: marim, vib, glsp, chimes, 4 gongs
Schott

Sinfonia for Chamber Orchestra 10'
(1965)
    1[1/pic] 2 1[1/bcl] 1[1/cbn] — 2 1 0 0 — hp — str
Schott

Tree of Singing Names (1989)   15'
1[1/pic] 1[1/eh] 1[1/bcl] 1[1/cbn] — 2 1 0 0 —
1perc — str[6.6.4.4.2]
perc: sus cym, xyl, marim, vib, gong
Schott

Gill, Jeremy   (1975-)

Chamber Symphony (2005)   20'
1[1/pic] 1 1[1/Ebcl] 1 — 2 1 1 0 — str[3.0.3.3.2]
Fleisher

Gillis, Don   (1912-1978)

Four Scenes from Yesterday   16'
(1948)
1 1 1 1 — 0 0 0 0 — tmp+1 — hp — pf/cel — str
perc: glsp, chimes, vib, xyl, xym, sus cym, tri, templeblk, woodblk, sd
Boosey & Hawkes

Four Scenes from Yesterday: 5'
Courthouse Square (1948)
0 1 0 0 — 0 0 0 0 — tmp+1 — hp — pf/cel — str
perc: chimes, vib, xyl, sus cym, tri, woodblk
Boosey & Hawkes

Three Sketches (1942)   9'
str
Boosey & Hawkes

Ginastera, Alberto   (1916-1983)

Concerto per Corde, op.33 (1964)   23'
str
Boosey & Hawkes

Estancia: Four Dances from   13'
Estancia, op.8a (1941)
2[1/pic.pic] 2 2 2 — 4 2 0 0 — tmp+6 — pf — str
perc: tambn, cym, fd, tri, td, cast, tam-tam, sus cym, bd, xyl
Contents - 1. The Land Workers; 2. Wheat Dance; 3. The
Cattle Men; 4. Final Dance (Malambo)
mvt durations: 3' 4' 2' 4'
Boosey & Hawkes

Glosses sobre temes de Pau   18'
Casals, op.46; For String Orchestra
and String Quintet "in lontano"
(1976)
solo str 4t (in lontano)
str[8.6.4.4.2]
Boosey & Hawkes

Variaciones Concertantes, op.23   21'
(1953)
2[1.2/pic] 1 2 1 — 2 1 1 0 — tmp — hp — str
Boosey & Hawkes

Girnatis, Walter   (1894-1981)

Festmusik der Schiffergilde   13'
2 1 2 1 — 2 2 0 0 — tmp+2 — str
perc: tri, cym, tambn, bd, cast
Schott

Scherzo Fantastique; Rondo for   7'
Orchestra (1956)
2 2 2 2 — 2 2 1 0 — tmp+1 — str
Sikorski

Glass, Philip   (1937-)

Book of Longing (2007)   85'
solo 4 singers, actor
0 2[1.eh] 0 0 — 0 0 0 0 — 1perc — kybd —
str[1.0.0.1.1]
Dunvagen

Company (1983)   8'
str
Dunvagen

Concerto Grosso (1992)   19'
1 1 1 1 — 2 1 1 1 — str
Hn 2 can be replaced by a tpt. Tu can be replaced by a
btbn.
mvt durations: 6' 8' 5'
Dunvagen

Façades (1981)   7'
2sx[ssx.ssx] — str[1.1.1.1.1]
Two ssx can be replaced by two fl.
Dunvagen

Glassworks (1981)   40'
2 0 2[cl/ssx.bcl/tsx] 0 — 2 0 0 0 — 2sx[ssx.tsx] —
pf/synth — str[0.0.1.1.0]
Each movement can be performed separately.
Contents - 1. Opening; 2. Floe; 3. Islands; 4. Rubric; 5.
Façades; 6. Closing —> V. famous
Dunvagen

Interlude from "Orphée" (1992)   3'
1 0 1 1 — 1 1 1 0 — 1perc — str[6.4.4.3.2]
Dunvagen

Meetings along the Edge: From   8'
"Passages" (1990)
   1 0 0 0 — 0 0 0 0 — 2sx[ssx.ssx] — 1perc — str
Dunvagen

Mishima: Music from the Film   20'
(1985)
   gtr — 5perc — hp — str[1.1.2.2.1]
Dunvagen

Offering: From "Passages" (1990)   10'
   1 0 0 0 — 0 0 0 0 — 2sx[ssx.asx] — 1perc — hp
   — str
Dunvagen

Phaedra (1986)   13'
   gtr — tmp+1 — hp — str
Dunvagen

Runaway Horses: From "Mishima"   7'
(1985)
   hp — str[1.1.2.2.1]
Dunvagen

The Secret Agent: Three Pieces   11'
(1996)
   1 1[eh] 0 0 — 0 0 0 0 — 1perc — hp — cel — str
Contents - 1. The Secret Agent; 2. The First Meridian; 3.
The Secret Agent Ending
Dunvagen

Symphony No.3 (1995)   24'
   str[6.4.4.3.2]
   mvt durations: 4' 6' 10' 4'
Dunvagen

Glazunov, Alexander   (1865-1936)

Serenade for Small Orchestra No.2,   6'
op.11 (1888)
   2 1 2 2 — 2 0 0 0 — str
Belaieff; Fleisher

Gnessin, Mikhail   (1883-1957)

Fantaisie (1919)
   1 1 2 1 — 1 1 0 0 — tmp+1 — 2pf[pf.hpsd] — str
Schirmer

Jewish Orchestra at the   15'
Burgermaster's Ball (1926)
   1 1 2 1 — 1 1 0 0 — tmp+1 — 2pf[pf.hpsd] — str
Schirmer

Godfrey, Daniel Strong   (1949-)

Concentus (1985)   14'
   1[1/pic/afl] 1[1/eh] 1 1 — 1 1 1 0 — tmp/perc —
   str
Margun

Goeb, Roger   (1914-1997)

Prairie Songs   11'
   2 2 2 2 — 2 2 1 0 — tmp+1 — str
   perc: sd, bd, cym
Peer

Goehr, Alexander   (1932-)

Concert Piece, op.26 (1969)   12'
   solo pf
   1[1/pic] 2 0 2 — 2 0 0 0 — str
Schott

Concerto for Eleven, op.32 (1970)   17'
   1 0 2[1.2/bcl] 0 — 0 2 0 1 — 1perc —
   str[2.0.1.0.1]
   perc: tam-tam, 2 gongs, Chinese gong, sus cym, tom-tom, bd
Schott

Idées Fixes; Sonata for 13, op.63   17'
(1997)
   1[1/afl] 1 1 — 1 1 1 0 — 1perc — pf —
   str[1.1.1.1.0]
   perc: tmp, glsp, sd, tabor
Schott

...kein Gedanke, nur ruhiger Schlaf;   5'
In Memoriam Olivier Messiaen,
op.65 (1998)
   1 1 1 0 — 1 1 0 0 — 1perc — hp — pf —
   str[1.1.1.1.1]
   perc: marim
Schott

Little Symphony, op.15 (1963)   29'
   1[1/pic] 2 3[1.2.bcl] 0 — 2 0 0 1 — str
Schott

...a musical offering (J. S. B. 1985),   15'
op.46 (1985)
   1 0 2[1.bcl] 0 — 1 1 1 0 — 1perc — pf —
   str[3.0.2.0.1]
   perc: td, bd, wood dr, metal dr, tom-tom, 2 bongos, hi-hat, marac, claves
Schott

Sinfonia, op.42 (1979)   23'
    1[1/pic] 2 2 0 — 2 0 0 0 — str
Schott

Still Lands (1990)   15'
    2[1.2/afl] 1 2[1.2/bcl] 1 — 2 1 1 0 — tmp — str
Schott

Goldmark, Carl   (1830-1915)

Ballade (1913)   8'
    solo vn
    2 2 2 2 — 4 0 0 0 — hp — str
    Edited by Rudolf Nilius (1956).
UE

Goldstein, Mikhail   (1917-1989)

Ukranian Symphony in Old Style   25'
(1948)
    2 2 2 2 — 2 2 0 0 — tmp — str
Sikorski

Golijov, Osvaldo   (1960-)

Last Round (1996)   14'
    str
    Work can be performed in three different ways, depending
    on the size of the string ensemble: 9 string players
    (2.2.2.2.1), small string orchestra, large string orchestra.
    Boosey & Hawkes

ZZ's Dream (2008)   7'
    1 1 1 1 — 1 1 1 0 — 1perc — hp — cel — str
    perc: vib
    Boosey & Hawkes

Goossens, Eugene   (1893-1962)

Miniature Fantasy for String   8'
Orchestra, op.2 (1911)
    str
    Boosey & Hawkes

Pastorale, op.59 (1942)   8'
    str
    Boosey & Hawkes

Gordon, Michael   (1956-)

Acid Rain (1986)   8'
    1[1/pic/afl] 0 1[1/Ebcl/bcl] 0 — 0 0 0 0 — elec org
    — str[1.1.1.1.1]
    Red Poppy

Love Bead (1997)   10'
    1[1/pic] 1[1/eh] 1[bcl] 1[cbn] — 1 1 1 0 — ebtr,
    elec bgtr — sampler — str[1.0.1.1.0]
    All instruments amplified.
    Red Poppy

Who by Water (2004)   18'
    1[pic] 1 2 1 — 1 1 1 0 — elec gtr — 3perc — kybd
    — str[1.1.0.1.1]
    perc: cym, bd, marac, tambn
    Red Poppy

Górecki, Henryk Mikołaj   (1933-2010)

Each chamber piece deserves a listen

Concerto (1957)   10'
    1 0 1 0 — 0 1 0 0 — mand — 1perc —
    str[1.1.1.1.0]
    perc: xyl
    Chester Novello

Concerto for Harpsichord (or piano),   9'
op.40 (1980)
    solo hpsd
    str[6.6.4.4.2]
    If piano solo is used, strings should be (8.8.6.6.4).
    Boosey & Hawkes

Genesis II: Canti Strumentali,   8'
op.19/2 (1962)
    2[1.pic] 0 0 0 — 0 1 0 0 — mand, gtr — 2perc —
    2pf[4hand] — str[3.0.3.0.0]
    perc: 5 woodblk, 2 gongs, bd, very lg tam-tam, 4 bongo, 2 lg gongs,
    very lg bd, tam-tam
    Boosey & Hawkes

Kleines Requiem für eine Polka,   24'
op.66 (1993)
    1 1 1 1 — 1 1 1 0 — 1perc — pf — str[1.1.1.1.1]
    perc: chimes
    mvt durations: 10' 5' 3' 6'
    Boosey & Hawkes

Songs of Joy and Rhythm, op.7   14'
(1956)
    solo 2 pf
    2[1.pic] 0 1 1 — 0 1 1 0 — tmp+3 — cel —
    str[6.6.6.6.0]
    perc: sd, sd w/o snares, xyl
    Boosey & Hawkes

Three Dances, op.34 (1973) 12'
2[1.2/pic] 2 2 2 — 3 4 3 1 — tmp+2 — str
Boosey & Hawkes

Three Pieces in Old Style (1963) 10'
str
Chester Novello

Gough, Orlando (1953-)

Mungo Dances (1998) 16'
str[3.3.2.2.1]
Boosey & Hawkes

Gould, Morton (1913-1996)

1995 Pulitzer winner

Harvest (1945) 12'
1perc — pf — str
perc: vib
Schirmer

Serenade ("Orfeo") from "Audubon" 8'
(1970)
2 2 3[1.2.bcl] 2 — 0 0 0 0 — mand — hp — str
Schirmer

Grabner, Hermann (1886-1969)

Divertimento für Kleines Orchester, 22'
op.56 (1941)
1 1 2 1 — 2 2 1 0 — tmp — str
Fleisher; Kistner & Siegel

Grainger, Percy Aldridge (1882-1961)

Green Bushes; Passacaglia on an 10'
English folksong: British folkmusic
settings No.12 (1906)
2[1.pic] 1 1 2[1.cbn(opt)] — 2 1 0 0 — 2 — tmp+1
— 2pf[pf.harm] — str[3.0.2.2.1]
Kalmus

Hill Song (1921) 15'
2 4 0 2 — 1[opt] 1 0 1[euph] — 3[ssx.asx.tsx] —
1perc — 2pf[pf.harm] — str[2.0.2.2.1]
Study score available through www.musikmph.de
UE

My Robin is to the Greenwood 6'
Gone: Old English Popular Music
No.2 (1911)
1 1[eh] 0 0 — 0 0 0 0 — str[1.0.2.2.1]
Kalmus

Shepherd's Hey: British Folk Music 3'
Settings, No.3 (1908)
solo concertina
1 0 1 0 — 1 0 0 0 — str[3.0.2.2.1]
Kalmus

Youthful Rapture (1901) 5'
solo vc
1 0 0 0 — 1 1 0 0 — hp — harm — str
Kalmus

Granados, Enrique (1867-1916)

À la Cubana; Marche Militaire 8'
(1884)
1 1 2 1 — 2 2 1 0 — tmp+1 — str
Arranged by Otto Langey.
Kalmus

Danzas Espanolas: No.6: Jota 4'
(1890)
1 1 2 1 — 2 2 1 0 — tmp+1 — str
Arranged by Charles J. Roberts.
Kalmus

Goyescas: Intermezzo (1915) 5'
1 1 2 1 — 2 2 1 0 — tmp+1 — str
Arranged by Otto Langey.
Kalmus

Grandjany, Marcel (1891-1975)

Deux Chansons Populaires
solo hp
1 1 1 1 — 0 0 0 0 — pf — str[3.0.1.1.1]
Durand

Rhapsodie 8'
solo hp
1 1 1 0 — 1 0 0 0 — str
Presser

Grantham, Donald   (1947-)

Fantasy on Mr. Hyde's Song   7'
1 0 1[1/bcl] 0 — 0 0 0 0 — 1perc — pf/cel —
str[1.0.0.1.0]
perc: vib, glsp, trap set, tambn, templeblk, woodblk, 2 marac, guiro,
bell tree, tri, 3 sus cym, ratchet, cowbell, whistle
Peer

Slobberin' Goblins   7'
1[1/pic] 0 1[bcl] 0 — 1 0 0 0 — 1perc — pf/cel —
str[1.0.0.1.0]
perc: vib, marac, glsp, crot, bongos, tmp, bell tree, woodblk, sus
cym, tam-tam
Peer

Greenbaum, Matthew   (1950-)

Castelnau; For String Orchestra   15'
(2008)
str
ACA

Greenwood, Jonny   (1971-)

Doghouse (2010)   23'
solo vl, vla, vc
2 2 2 2 — 4 3 3 1 — 3perc — hp — str
Faber

Popcorn Superhet Receiver (2005)   18'
str(min)[18.0.6.6.4]
Faber

smear (2004)   10'
solo 2 ondes martenots
0 0 1 0 — 1 0 0 0 — 1perc — hp — str[1.1.1.1.1]
perc: vib, tam-tam
Faber

Gregson, Edward   (1945-)

Music for Chamber Orchestra   22'
(1968)
0 2 0 2 — 2 0 0 0 — str
Novello

Griffes, Charles Tomlinson   (1884-1920)

The Kairn of Koridwen; A Druid   52'
Legend (1917)
1 0 2 0 — 2 0 0 0 — hp — 2pf[pf.cel] — no str
Kallisti

Three Tone Pictures (1915)   5'
1 1 1 1 — 1 0 0 0 — pf — str(min)[1.1.1.1.1]
Schirmer

Grinberg, Alexander   (1961-)

Carillon (1988)   28'
3[1.2.pic] 1 2[1.Ebcl] 1 — 1 1 1 1 — ssx — 4perc
— str[4.3.2.2.1]
perc: tmp, 4 tri, 2 cowbells, 4 crot, 3 sus cym, 2 gongs, tam-tam,
chimes, vib, bell
Boosey & Hawkes

Grosse, Erwin   (1904-1982)

Kammersinfonie (Chamber   19'
Symphony), op.48 (1961)
2 0 3[1.2.bcl] 0 — 0 0 0 0 — str
Boosey & Hawkes

Grosskopf, Erhard   (1934-)

Sonata concertante 1 (1966)   16'
1 1 1 1 — 1 0 0 0 — pf — str
Boosey & Hawkes

Sonata concertante 2 (1967)   21'
solo vn
2[1.2/pic] 2[1.eh] 3[1.2.bcl] 1 — 2 1 1 0 — tmp+1
— hp — pf — str
Boosey & Hawkes

Gruber, HK   (1943-)

Manhattan Broadcast (1964)   11'
1 1 2 1 — 0 2 2 0 — elec gtr — 2perc — pf/cel —
str
perc: vib, 2 bongos, 4 tmp, hi-hat, cowbells, sus cym, ped bd, tom-
tom, sd
Boosey & Hawkes

Zeitfluren; Timescapes (2001)   23'
1[1/pic] 1[1/eh] 2[1/Ebcl.2/bcl] 1[1/cbn] — 1 1 1 1
— 2perc — hp — pf — str(min)[1.1.1.1.1]
perc: I=ped bd, 5 tom-tom, sd, hi-hat, sus cym, sus Chinese cym,
floor tom-tom, 2 sus cowbells, sus tambn, 2 bongos, lg Chinese tam-
tam, crot, glsp II=vib, marim, xylorimba
Boosey & Hawkes

Gruenberg, Louis   (1884-1964)

The Daniel Jazz, op.21 (1924)   18'
solo high voice
0 0 1 0 — 0 1 0 0 — 1perc — pf — str[1.1.1.1.0]
UE

Guarnieri, Camargo   (1907-1993)

Ponteios No.1 (1955)   2'
1 0 1 0 — 2 1 0 0 — str
Fleisher

Ponteios No.3 (1955)
2 0 2 1 — 2 0 0 0 — hp — str
Fleisher

Ponteios No.5 (1955)
str
Fleisher

Gubaidulina, Sofia   (1931-)

Concerto for Bassoon and Low   27'
Strings (1975)
solo bn
str[0.0.0.4.3]
Boosey & Hawkes

Concordanza (1971)   12'
1 1 1 1 — 1 0 0 0 — 1perc — str(min)[1.0.1.1.1]
perc: 5 bongos, sd, 5 sus cym, lg tam-tam, vib, marim
Sikorski

Detto II; Concerto for Cello and 13   15'
Instruments (1972)
solo vc
1 1 1 1 — 1 0 0 0 — 2perc — cel — str[1.1.1.1.1]
perc: I: 3 woodblks, 5 tom-tom, glsp, marim II: crot, 5 templeblks, 5 bongos, 3 sus cym, lg tam-tam
Boosey & Hawkes; Sikorski

Homage to T. S. Eliot (1987)   40'
solo S
0 0 1 1 — 1 0 0 0 — str[1.1.1.1.1]
Sikorski

Impromptu (1997)   18'
solo fl, vn
str
Boosey & Hawkes

Introitus; Concerto for Piano and   24'
Chamber Orchestra (1978)
solo pf
1 1 0 1 — 0 0 0 0 — str[6.4.4.3.1]
Boosey & Hawkes; Sikorski

Seven Words; For Cello, Bayan and   32'
Strings in 7 Movements (1982)
solo vc, bayan
str[5.4.3.2.1]
Boosey & Hawkes

Gudmundsen-Holmgreen,   (1932-)
Pelle

Caravanfanfan-farefare No.1   2'
(2001)
0 0 0 0 — 0 2[1.crt] 1 0 — 2sx[ssx.tsx] — gtr — 2perc — pf — str[0.0.0.0.1]
Hansen

Caravanfanfan-farefare No.3   2'
(2001)
0 0 0 0 — 0 1 1 0 — ssx — voice — 2perc — pf — str[0.0.0.3.0]
Hansen

Mester Jacob (Frère Jacques)   10'
(1964)
2[1.pic] 1 2[1.bcl] 2[1.cbn] — 2 2 2 0 — 2perc — pf — str[1.0.1.2.2]
Hansen

Nær og Fjern (Near and Distant)   16'
(1987)
1 1 1 1 — 1 0 0 0 — str[1.1.1.1.1]
Hansen

Variationer til Moster Rix (Variations   8'
for Aunt Rix) (1968)
1 1 1 1 — 1 0 0 0 — 1perc — pf — str
Hansen

Guenther, Felix   (1886-1951)

Deutsches Rokoko; Eine Suite für   20'
Kleines Orchester nach Alten
Meistern (1931)
1 1 2 1 — 2 0 0 0 — str
Contents - 1. Overture (Joseph Meck); 2. Siciliano (J . Ph. Kirnberger); 3. Andante grazioso (Fr. L. Benda); 4. Halb-steyrischer (Michael Haydn); 5. Aria (Emperor Joseph I); 6. Presto (Georg Böhm); 7. Finale (J. Ph. Kirnberger)
Fleisher; Ries & Erler

Guion, David (1892-1981)

Home on the Range (1930)   4'
solo voice (opt)
1 1 2 1 — 2 2 1 0 — tmp+1 — hp — pf — str
perc: vib (or bells)
Arranged by Adolf Schmid.
Schirmer

Gürsching, Albrecht (1934-)

Drei Plus Vier   3'
0 0 1 1 — 1 0 0 0 — str[1.0.1.1.1]
Peer

Piccola Sinfonia; Septett Nr.2   12'
0 0 1 1 — 1 0 0 0 — str[1.0.1.1.1]
Peer

Gutchë, Gene (1907-2000)

Rondo capriccioso, op.21   7'
2 2 2 0 — 2 0 0 0 — 1perc — str[0.0.1.0.1]
perc: cym, xyl
Fleisher

Guy, Barry (1947-)

Bitz! (1979)   15'
1[1/pic/afl] 1[1/eh] 1[1/Ebcl/bcl] 0 — 0 0 0 0 — pf
— str[1.0.1.1.0]
Novello

Play (1976)   22'
1 0 1 0 — 0 1 1 0 — 1perc — pf — str[1.0.1.1.1]
Novello

Gyring, Elizabeth (1909-1970)

Scherzo No.2 for Orchestra (1948)   9'
1 0 1 0 — 0 1 1 0 — str
Fleisher

H

Haas, Georg Friedrich (1953-)

He is fairly well-known

"..."; Double Concerto for Accordion and Viola (1994)   14'
solo accordion, va
0 2 0 0 — 0 0 2 0 — 1perc — hpsd —
str[1.1.1.2.1]
perc: marim, vib, crot, 2 cym, 2 tom-tom
UE

"...aus freier Lust...verbunden..." (1996)   11'
1[bfl] 0 1[bcl] 0 — 0 0 0 0 — 2perc —
str[0.0.1.1.1]
UE

"...Einklang freier Wesen..." (1996)   11'
1[bfl] 0 1[bcl] 0 — 0 1 1 1 — 2perc —
str[0.0.1.1.1]
UE

in vain; For 24 Instruments (2000)   70'
2[1/pic.2/pic/bfl] 1 2[1.2/bcl] 1 — 2 0 2 0 —
ssx/tsx — accordion — 2perc — hp — pf —
str[3.0.2.2.1]
To be performed with visual (light) effects.
UE

Monodie (1999)   15'
1[1/pic/afl] 1 2[1.bcl/Ebcl] 1 — 1 1 1 0 — 2perc —
hp — str[1.1.2.2.1]
UE

Quasi Una Tânpûrâ (1991)   28'
1[1/bfl] 0 1[1/bcl] 0 — 1 0 1 1 — 2perc — prepf —
str[3.0.2.2.1]
perc: vib, marim, 2 whips, 2 cast, 2 tom-tom, tmp, wood dr, td, ratchet, cel, 2 templeblks
UE

Wer, wenn ich schriee, hörte mich... (Who, if I screamed, would hear me...) (1999)   25'
solo perc
1[1/pic] 1[1/eh] 2[1/Ebcl.bcl/Ebcl] 1 — 1 2[1.2/flug]
2 1 — ssx/tsx — accordion — 1perc — str[3.0.2.2.1]
perc: crot, multiple sus cym, gongs, tam-tam, div. metal instruments
UE

Haas, Joseph   (1879-1960)

Lyrisches Intermezzo (1938)   7'
  1 1 1 0 — 0 1 1 0 — tmp — harm — str
Fleisher; Schott

Variationen-Suite; Über ein altes   40'
Rokoko-Thema, op.64 (1924)
  1 0 2 2 — 2 1 0 0 — tmp+1 — str
  perc: tri
Schott

Haas, Pavel   (1899-1944)

Study for Strings (1943)   10'
  str
Boosey & Hawkes

Hagen, Daron   (1961-)

Chimera; A Song Cycle for Speaker   11'
and Seven Players (1981)
  1[1/afl] 0 1 0 — 2 0 1 0 — narrator — 1perc —
  str[1.0.0.0.0]
Fleisher

Night Music; Five Scenes for   20'
Chamber Orchestra (1984)
  1[1/pic] 2 1 1 — 2 1 0 0 — tmp+1 — pf — str
  perc: roto toms
Fleisher

Hahn, Reynaldo   (1874-1947)

La Fête Chez Thérèse: Suite No.1   9'
(1910)
  1 1 2 1 — 2 2 1 0 — tmp+1 — str
  Arranged by Hubert Mouton.
  Contents - 1. La Contredanse des Grisettes; 2. Valse de
  Mimi Pinson; 3. Danse Violente
Kalmus

La Fête Chez Thérèse: Suite No.2   14'
(1910)
  1 1 2 1 — 2 2 1 0 — tmp+1 — str
  Arranged by Hubert Mouton.
  Contents - 1. Danse Galante; 2. Scene de l'Essayage; 3.
  Danse Triste; 4. Duo Mime; 5. Menuet Pompeux
Kalmus

Haieff, Alexei Vasilievich   (1914-1994)

Divertimento (1953)   12'
  2[1.2/pic] 1[1/eh] 1 0 — 0 2 2 0 — str
Boosey & Hawkes; Fleisher

Halffter, Cristóbal   (1930-)

Antiphonismoi (1967)   16'
  1 1 1 0 — 0 0 0 0 — pf — str[1.0.1.1.0]
UE

Dalíniana; Three Pieces on Three   16'
Paintings by Salvador Dalí (1994)
  2[1.2/pic/afl] 2 2 2 — 2 2 0 0 — 3perc — str
  Contents - 1. Relojes Blandos; 2. El Sueño; 3. Nacimiento
  de las Angustias Liquidas
UE

Double Concerto for Violin and   24'
Viola (1984)
  solo vn, va
  2 2 2 2 — 2 2 0 0 — 3perc — hpsd/cel —
  str[8.8.6.4.2]
UE

Halffter, Ernesto   (1905-1989)

Automne malade   8'
  solo voice
  1 1 1 0 — 1 0 0 0 — hp — str
Eschig

Cavatina (1934)   5'
  2 2 1 1 — 1 1 1 0 — sx — tmp+2 — hp — str
Eschig

El Cojo Enamorado: Ballet Suite   23'
(1955)
  2[1.2/pic] 1 2 1 — 2 2 1 0 — tmp+1 — str
Unión

Las Doncellas   12'
  1 1 1 1 — 2 1 0 0 — tmp — hp — pf — str
Eschig

Dos canciones (1927)   5'
  solo voice
  1 1 1 1 — 1 0 0 0 — hp — str
Eschig

Gerinaldo (1941)	6'

solo voice
1 2 1 0 — 0 0 0 0 — hp — str
No.2 from "Chansons portugaises."
Eschig

Minha mäe me deu um lenço	2'
(1940)	

solo 2 voices
2 2 2 2 — 0 2 0 0 — pf — str
No.4 from "Chansons portugaises."
Eschig

Sinfonietta (1927)	37'

solo vn, vc, db
1 1 1 1 — 2 1 1 0 — tmp+1 — str
mvt durations: 10' 11' 7' 9'
Eschig

Halffter, Rodolfo   (1900-1987)

Divertimento Para Nueve	11'
Instrumentos	

1 1 1 1 — 0 1 0 0 — str[1.1.1.1.0]
Peer

La Madrugada del Panadero: Suite	15'
del Ballet	

2 2 2 2 — 2 2 0 0 — tmp+1 — pf — str
perc: sd, tri, xyl
Peer

Obertura Festiva (Festive Overture)	6'

2 2 2 2 — 2 2 0 0 — tmp — str
Peer

Hallberg, Björn Wilho   (1938-)

Novelletten (1973)	13'

1[1/pic] 2[1.bcl] 1 — 1 1 1 0 — str
Nordiska

Hallén, Andreas   (1846-1925)

Om hösten (In Autumn) (1895)	12'

2 0 2 2 — 2 0 0 0 — tmp — str
Nordiska

Halvorsen, Johan   (1864-1935)

Sérénade, op.33 (1913)	

3[1.2.pic] 2 2 0 — 0 0 0 0 — hp — str
Fleisher; Norsk

Hamel, Peter Michael   (1947-)

Concerto for Violin in Two	40'
Movements (1986/1989)	

solo vn
3[pic.2.afl] 2[1.eh] 2[1.bcl] 2[1.cbn] — 1 1 1 1 —
3perc — hp — pf — str
Bärenreiter

Semiramis; Music in Three Parts (1983)	21'

0 2 5[1.2.3-5 basset hn] 1[cbn] — 2 0 0 0 —
1perc — hp — cel — str
Bärenreiter

Hamilton, Iain   (1922-2000)

The Alexandrian Sequence	24'

1 1 1 1 — 1 1 1 0 — str[1.1.1.1.1]
Presser

Arias (1962)	12'

1 1 1 1 — 1 1 1 0 — str
Schott

Concerto for Harp and Small	25'
Orchestra (1995)	

solo hp
1[1/pic] 1[1/eh] 1[1/bcl] 1 — 1 1 0 0 — 1perc —
str
Presser

Sinfonia Concertante	20'

solo vn, va
1 1 1 1 — 2 1 1 0 — hp — str
Presser

Sonata, op.34 (1957)	11'

2[1.pic] 1 1[bcl] 1 — 1 1 0 0 — cel — str
Schott

Symphony No.3	26'

2 2 2 2 — 2 0 0 0 — str
Presser

Voyage	18'

solo hn
1 1 1 0 — 0 2 1 0 — 1perc — pf — str[1.1.1.1.1]
Can be done with full strings.
Presser

Hansson, C.J. Gunnar

Suite No.1	8'

1 1 1 1 — 1 0 0 0 — tmp — str
Peer

Hanuš, Jan   (1915-2004)

Prazská Nokturna (Prague   25'
Nocturne), op.75 (1973)
   2[1.2/pic] 2[1.eh] 2 2 — 2 1 0 0 — tmp+1 —
str[6.6.4.4.2]
<small>perc: tri, gong, cym, sd</small>
Schott

Harbison, John Madison guy   (1938-)
1987 Pulitzer → The Flight into Egypt

Canonical American Songbook   15'
(2005)
   2[1.2/pic] 2[1.2/eh] 2[1.2/bcl] 2[1.2/cbn] — 2 2 0 0
— tmp+2 — hp — str
AMP

Confinement (1965)   15'
   1 1[1/eh] 1[1/bcl] 0 — 0 1 1 0 — asx — 1perc —
pf — str[1.0.1.1.1]
AMP

David's Fascinating Rhythm Method   2'
(1991)
   2 2 2 2 — 2 2 0 0 — tmp+4 — pf — str
AMP

Exequien for Calvin Simmons   5'
(1982)
   1[afl] 0 1[bcl] 0 — 0 0 0 0 — 1perc — pf —
str[0.0.2.1.0]
<small>perc: vib</small>
AMP

Incidental Music to Shakespeare's   12'
"The Merchant of Venice" (1971)
   str
AMP

The Most Often Used Chords (Gli   16'
Accordi Piu Usati) (1993)
   2 2 2 2 — 2 2 0 0 — tmp+1 — hp — pf/cel — str
AMP

Partita (2001)   18'
   2[1.2/pic] 2[1.2/eh] 2[1.2/bcl] 2[1.2/cbn] — 4 2 2 0
— tmp+3 — str
AMP

Remembering Gatsby; Foxtrot for   7'
Orchestra (1985) — DeMain did this in Madison
   2[1.2/pic] 2[1.2/eh] 2[1.2/ssx] 2 — 2 2 2 1 —
tmp+1 — pf — str
<small>Reduced orchestration by John Moody.</small>
AMP

Waltz-Passacaglia   1'
   2 2 2 3[1.2.cbn] — 4 2 3 0 — tmp — str
AMP

Harle, John   (1956-)

Cinéma (René Clair's "Entr'acte")   7'
(1995)
   0 1 1 0 — 0 0 0 0 — asx — 1perc — pf —
str[1.0.1.0.1]
Chester Novello

Harneit, Johannes   (1963-)

Ohne Leben Tod (Without Life   25'
Death), op.23 (2004)
   1[pic] 1 1 1[cbn] — 2 1 0 0 — 1perc — pf —
str[1.1.1.1.1]
Sikorski

Triptychon (13X3), op.20 (2003)   21'
   1 1 2[1.bcl] 1 — 2 1 0 0 — str[1.1.1.1.1]
Sikorski

Harris, Roy   (1898-1979)

Evening Piece   4'
   solo vn
   1 0 1 0 — 0 0 0 0 — str
Kalmus

Harrison, Lou   (1917-2003)

Alleluia   7'
   2 2 2 0 — 2 0 0 0 — hp — str
Presser

Seven Pastorales   7'
   2 1 0 1 — 0 0 0 0 — hp — str
Peer

Solstice   30'
   1 1 0 0 — 1 0 0 0 — 2pf[pf.cel] — str[0.0.0.2.1]
Peer

Suite No.2   7'
   str
Kalmus

Hartley, Walter Sinclair   (1927-)

Chamber Symphony (1954)   *14'*
1[1/pic] 1 1 1 — 2 1 1 0 — hp — str
Fleisher

Concertino for Chamber Ensemble   *15'*
(1952)
0 0 1 0 — 0 0 1 0 — 1perc — pf — str[4.0.0.4.0]
Fleisher

Concerto Breve for Bass Trombone   *8'*
solo btbn
2 2 2 2 — 2 2 0 1 — tmp — str
Kalmus

Psalm for Strings   *5'*
str
Kalmus

Sinfonia No.7   *8'*
2[1.2/pic] 1 2[1.2/bcl] 1 — 2 2 1 1 — tmp+1 — str
Kalmus

Three Patterns for Small Orchestra   *5'*
(1951)
2[1.2/pic] 2[1.2/eh] 2 2 — 2 2 1 0 — tmp+1 — hp
— str
Fleisher

Harty, Hamilton   (1879-1941)

Concerto for Violin in D minor   *27'*
solo vn
2 2 2 2 — 4 2 3 0 — tmp — str
Kalmus

Fantasy Scenes; From an Eastern   *12'*
Romance
2[1.2/pic] 1 1 1 — 2 1 1 0 — tmp+1 — hp — str
Kalmus

A John Field Suite (1939)   *18'*
1[1/pic] 1 1 1 — 1 1 0 0 — tmp+1 — hp — str
perc: glsp, chimes, tri, bd, sd, tambn
Orchestrations of piano pieces by John Field.
Boosey & Hawkes

Harvey, Jonathan   (1939-)

Bhakti (1982)   *50'*
1[1/pic] 1[1/eh] 2[1/Ebcl.bcl] 0 — 1 1[1/pic tpt] 1 0
— tape[or CD-ROM] — 1perc — hp — pf/glsp —
str[2.1.1.1.0]
perc: tam-tam, vib, 2 woodblks, 3 tom-tom, 2 sus cym, crot, marim,
gong, 2 templeblks, chimes, tri
Faber

Gong-Ring (1984)   *22'*
4perc — hp — 2pf[pf.cel] — str[8.0.3.3.1]
perc: 2 cup gong, 2 tri, xyl, marim, vib, chimes, finger cym, tam-tam,
2 gong, 2 sus cym, 2 woodblks, 2 templeblks, crot, tambn, Chinese
cym
Faber

Hidden Voice 1 (1995)   *7'*
1[pic] 1 1 1[1/cbn] — 2 0 0 0 — 1perc —
str[1.1.1.2.1]
perc: 4 templeblks, sm cym, crot, chimes
Faber

Hidden Voice 2 (1999)   *6'*
solo vn, va, vc
1[pic] 1 1 1 — 2 0 0 0 — CD — 1perc —
str[1.0.0.0.1]
perc: chimes, crot, sd, sus cym
Faber

Inner Light 1 (1973)   *30'*
1[1/pic] 0 1[1/bcl] 0 — 0 0 0 0 — tape — 1perc —
pf/org — str[1.0.1.1.0]
Novello

Jubilus (2003)   *15'*
solo va
1 0 1[cbcl] 0 — 0 1 0 0 — gtr — 1perc — hp —
str[1.0.0.1.0]
perc: 3 Taiwanese temple bowls, Javanese gong, 2 Korean sheung
cym, crot, 2 tam-tam, tri, 2 woodblks, 5 templeblks, cowbell, guiro,
ratchet vib
Faber

Moving Trees (2002)   *6'*
1[pic] 1 2 1 — 1 1 1 0 — gtr — 2perc — hp —
pf/cel — str[1.1.1.1.1]
perc: vib, mark tree, crot, 2 woodblks, Chinese cym, guiro, bamboo
cluster
Faber

Smiling Immortal (1977)   *17'*
1[1/pic] 1 1[1/Ebcl] 0 — 1 1 0 0 — CD — 1perc —
pf — str[1.1.1.1.0]
perc: 2 tam-tam, 2 sus cym, bongos, 3 tom-tom, sd, tmp, vib
Faber

Soleil Noir / Chitra (1995)　　　　　　　15'
　1[1/pic/afl/bfl] 0 0 0 — 0 0 1 1 —1perc — hp —
　synth — str[1.0.0.1.1]
　Electronics: 2 harmonizers and compressors, 7
　microphones, mixing desk (1 operator), amplification
　and speakers for stereo diffusion
　perc: bongos, tom-tom, oriental dr, tabla, bd, tambn, marac, guiro,
　tam-tam
　Tbn doubles on oriental dr. Tu doubles on woodblk. Vn
　doubles on crot. Vc doubles on cabaca. Synth: Yamaha
　SY77. Two operators needed for synth and electronics.
　Faber

Tendril (1987)　　　　　　　　　　　　14'
　1[1/pic] 1[1/eh] 1 1 — 1 0 0 0 — pf —
　str[1.1.1.1.1]
　Faber

Two Interludes for an Opera (2003)　　　20'
　1[1/pic] 1 2[1.2/bcl] 1[1/cbn] — 1 1 1 1 —
　electronics — 2perc — hp — kybd — str[2.2.2.2.1]
　perc: marim, crot, guiro, 2 bd, 2 gong, marac, rainstick, tam-tam, 2
　Tibetan bells, chimes, spring coil, vibraslap, glass chimes, bamboo
　cluster, mark tree, 2 sus cym, sd, 4 woodblks, 4 tom-tom, 3 bowls, 2
　high dr of skin or thin wood (for fingers)
　Electronics (2-3 players): 8 or 6 channel system/digital
　mixer/1 or 2 Mac computers with soundcards/Wacom
　Graphic Tablet/16 MIDI faders/Clip-on mics for all
　instruments and several close mics for percussion/CD Rom
　of patches and cue list in MAX/Msp
　Faber

Valley of Aosta (1988)　　　　　　　　14'
　1[1/pic] 1[1/eh] 0 0 — 0 1 0 0 — ssx — CD —
　1perc — 2hp — 2pf[pf.synth] — str[1.1.1.1.0]
　perc: 2 sus cym, marim, vib, 2 congas, tom-tom, gong, 2 woodblks,
　bongos, glsp, whip
　Two Synthesizers needed. Recommended: Yamaha DX7.
　Faber

Wheel of Emptiness (1997)　　　　　　16'
　1[1/pic/afl] 1 1[1/bcl] 1[1/cbn] — 1 1 1 0 — 2perc
　— 2pf[pf/sampler.kybd] — str[1.1.1.1.1]
　perc: marim, 2 sus cym, 3 cowbell, sm bell, guiro, slide whistle, 5
　templeblks, 2 woodblks, tam-tam, 5 button gong, crot, lion's roar
　Faber

Hasquenoph, Pierre　　　　(1922-1982)

Concertino for Strings　　　　　　　　8'
　str
　Presser

Concerto da Camera　　　　　　　　　23'
　solo pf
　str
　Presser

Symphony No.1, op.10　　　　　　　　21'
　2 2 2 2 — 2 2 2 0 — tmp — str
　Presser

Variations en Trois Mouvements　　　　12'
　2 2 2 2 — 2 3 2 0 — tmp+2 — str
　Presser

Variations Pour 14　　　　　　　　　23'
　1 1 1 1 — 1 0 0 0 — gtr — 1perc — hp — pf —
　str[1.1.1.1.1]
　Presser

Haubenstock-Ramati,　　　　(1919-1994)
Roman

Beaubourg Musique (1988)　　　　　　18'
　2 0 0 0 — 0 0 2 0 — 4perc — hp —
　3pf[pf.cel.hpsd] — str[2.2.2.2.0]
　UE

Concerto; Recitativo ed Aria for　　　　10'
Harpsichord and Orchestra (1954)
　solo hpsd
　2 0 2 0 — 0 2 0 0 — tmp+3 — hp — cel — str
　UE

Invocations (1990)　　　　　　　　　20'
　2 0 0 0 — 0 0 2 0 — 2perc — hp —
　3pf[pf.cel.hpsd] — str[2.2.2.2.0]
　UE

Papageno's Pocket-Size Concerto:　　　　3'
No.6 from "Divertimento for Mozart"
(1956)
　solo glsp
　2 2 2 2 — 2 2 0 0 — tmp — str
　For more information see: Mozart, Wolfgang Amadeus.
　UE

Polyphonien; For 2, 3 or 4 Chamber　　　25'
Orchestras (1993)
　2 0 0 0 — 0 0 2 0 — tape — 2perc — hp —
　3pf[pf.cel.hpsd] — str[4.4.4.4.0]
　Orchestra 1 plays live, others are pre-recorded on the tape.
　UE

Séquences (1958)　　　　　　　　　　13'
　solo vn
　3 0 0 0 — 0 0 0 0 — 4perc — hp — 2pf[pf.cel] —
　str[4.0.4.4.0]
　UE

Séquences 2 (1958)　　　　　　　　　13'
　2 0 0 0 — 0 0 0 0 — 5perc — hp — 2pf[pf.cel] —
　str[1.1.1.1.0]
　UE

Ständchen sur le nom de Heinrich   3'
Strobel: 3rd part of "Petite musique
de nuit" (1958)
    1 0 1 0 — 0 0 0 0 — 4perc — hp — 2pf[pf.cel] —
    str[4.4.2.2.0]
UE

Hauer, Josef Matthias   (1883-1959)

1. Tanzsuite, op.70 (1936)   14'
    1 1 1 1 — 0 0 0 0 — pf — str[1.1.1.1.0]
UE

2. Tanzsuite, op.71 (1936)   18'
    1 1 1 1 — 0 0 0 0 — pf — str[1.1.1.1.0]
UE

Emilie vor ihrem Brauttag (Emilie   15'
before her wedding day); Cantata,
op.58 (1928)
    solo A
    2 2 2 2 — 1 1 1 0 — tmp+2 — pf — str
UE

Romantische Phantasie, op.37   20'
(1925)
    2 2 2 2 — 2 2 0 0 — tmp — pf — str
UE

Zwölftonspiel XVII (Twelve-Tone   8'
game XVII)
    1 1 2 1 — 1 1 1 0 — hp — str
UE

Hayden, Sam   (1968-)

Collateral Damage (1999)   15'
    1[pic] 0 1[bcl] 1[cbn] — 0 1 1 1 — 2perc — pf —
    str[1.1.1.1.1]
    perc: xyl, 2 vib, crot, 3 tom-tom, sd, 3 bd, marim
Faber

Heath, Dave   (1956-)

Forest (1988)   20'
    1[1/pic/afl] 0 1[1/bcl] 0 — 0 0 0 0 — hp —
    str[1.1.1.1.0]
Chester Novello

Heiller, Anton   (1923-1979)

Kammersymphonie (Chamber   25'
Symphony) (1946)
    0 1 1 1 — 0 0 0 0 — str
    Strings without db.
UE

Heiß, Hermann   (1897-1966)

Duo-Konzert (1948)   21'
    solo vn, pf
    2 1 2[1.2/bcl] 2[1.2/cbn] — 0 2 1 0 — tmp — str
Breitkopf

Heitzeg, Steve   (1959-)

Aqua; Hommage à Jacques-Yves   6'
Cousteau (1999)
    2[1.2/pic] 2 2 2 — 4 3 3 1 — tmp+3 — hp — str
    perc: bd, button gong, 4 brake dr, chimes, claves, coral, 4 cowbells,
    crot, driftwood, fog bell, glsp, ocean dr, 2 plastic six-pack rings,
    rainstick, 2 sea shells, sea shell wind chime, 4 steel pipes, 2 river
    stones, tam-tam, templeblk
    Some of the more exotic percussion instruments are
    provided with the music rental.
Stone Circle Music

Flower of the Earth; Homage to   16'
Georgia O'Keeffe (1987)
    1 2 0 1 — 2 0 0 0 — str
Fleisher; Stone Circle Music

Helfer, Walter   (1896-1959)

A Fantasy on Children's Tunes   12'
    1[1/pic] 1 1 1 — 2 1 0 0 — tmp+1 — 2pf[pf.cel] —
    str
Fleisher

Prelude to a Midsummer Night's   13'
Dream
    1 1 1 2 — 1 1 0 0 — pf — str
Fleisher

A Water Idyll (1937)   8'
    1 1 1 1 — 1 0 0 0 — pf — str
Fleisher

Helm, Everett   (1913-1999)

Concerto for Strings   18'
    str
Bärenreiter

Italienische Suite   12'
    2[1.pic] 1 1 1 — 2 2 2 0 — str
Boosey & Hawkes

Serenade (1957)   14'
    0 1[eh] 1 1 — 0 0 0 0 — pf — str
Boosey & Hawkes

Hemberg, Eskil (1938-2004)

Migraine pour orchestre, op.19b   7'
(1973)
    1 1 1 1 — 1 0 0 0 — 1perc — str
Nordiska

Henze, Hans Werner (1926-)

Aria de la Folia Española (1977)   22'
    1[1/pic] 2[1.2/eh/ob d'am] 1[1/Ebcl/bcl] 2 — 2 0 0
    0 — mandolin — tmp+1 — 2pf[pf.cel] — str[5.4.4.4.1]
    perc: 3 sus cym, gong, 3 tom-tom, 3 bongos, 3 templeblks, marim,
    cast, crot
Schott

Arien des Orpheus (1981)   18'
    gtr — hp — hpsd — str[5.4.4.4.3]
Schott

Chamber Concerto 05 (2005)   17'
    1[1/pic/afl] 1[1/eh] 1[1/bcl] 1 — 1 1 1 0 — tmp —
    hp — pf — str[1.1.1.1.1]
    Version for 15 players of his "Symphony No.1."
Schott

Drei Dithyramben; In Memoriam   20'
Willy Strecker (1958)
    1 1 1 1 — 2 1 0 0 — tmp+2 — hp — pf —
    str[6.6.4.4.2]
    perc: 3 sus cym, 3 tam-tam, 3 tom-tom, bell tree, sd, sd w/o snares
Schott

Finale - Vivace assai: Nr.12 from   2'
"Divertimento for Mozart" (1956)
    2 2 2 2 — 2 2 0 0 — tmp — str
    For more information see: Mozart, Wolfgang Amadeus.
UE

Four Fantasies from
"Kammermusik" 1958 and Adagio
1963
    0 0 1 1 — 1 0 0 0 — str[1.1.1.1.1]
Luck's; Schott

L'heure bleu (2001)   10'
    2[1.afl] 2[eh.ob d'am] 2[1.bcl] 1 — 1 0 0 1[euph]
    — 1perc — hp — pf — str[1.1.1.1.1]
Chester Novello

Katharina Blum: Concerto suite   20'
(1975)
    1[1/pic/afl/amp bfl] 1[1/eh] 1[1/Ebcl/bcl] 1[1/cbn] —
    1 1 1 0 — tmp+2 — pf/cel — str
    perc: I: 3 sus cym, 1 amp tam-tam, 2 tam-tam, 3 bongos, log dr, loo-
    jon, vib II: 3 sus cym, 1 amp tam-tam, Trinidad steel dr, flexatone,
    watergong, lotos fl, boo-bam
Schott

Symphony No.1 (1947)   17'
    2[1/pic.afl/pic] 2[1.eh] 1[bcl] 0 — 2 2 0 0 — tmp —
    hp — 2pf[pf.cel] — str
    Revised by the composer in 1991.
Schott

Three Mozart Organ Sonatas for 14   14'
Players (1991)
    2[afl.bfl] 2[eh.ob d'am] 1[bcl] 1 — 0 0 0 0 — gtr,
    va d'amore — hp — str[0.0.2.2.1]
Schott

Herbert, Victor (1859-1924)

Al Fresco; Intermezzo (1904)   3'
    1 1 2 1 — 2 2[crt.crt] 1 0 — tmp+1 — pf — str
Fleisher

Herrera de la Fuente, Luis (1916-)

Fronteras; Ballet   15'
    2 2 2 2 — 2 2 0 0 — str
Peer

Herrmann, Peter (1941-)

Concerto for Trumpet and   16'
Orchestra
    solo tpt
    2 2 2 2 — 2 0 0 0 — tmp+1 — str
Breitkopf

Concerto for Violin and Orchestra   20'
    solo vn
    2 2 2 2 — 2 1 0 0 — tmp+1 — str
Breitkopf

Sinfonietta   22'
    str
Breitkopf

Sonata for Chamber Orchestra   20'
    1 1 0 0 — 0 1 0 0 — pf — str
Breitkopf

Sonatina for String Orchestra   8'
  str
Breitkopf

Three Pieces for Orchestra (1973)   20'
  2 2 2 2 — 4 2 3 0 — tmp+1 — str
Breitkopf

Hesketh, Kenneth   (1968-)

After Verdi!; Divertimento in Five   15'
Sections (2001)
  1[1/pic] 0 1 1 — 1 1 1 0 — 1perc — pf —
  str[3.3.3.2.1]
  perc: glsp, xyl, vib, tri, sus cym, sleigh bells, tambn, sd, bd, cast,
  whip
Schott

The Circling Canopy of Night   25'
(1999)
  1[1/pic/bfl] 1[1/eh/soprano rec] 2[1/Ebcl.2/bcl] 0 —
  1 0 0 0 — ssx — 3perc — hp — 2pf[pf.cel] —
  str[1.0.1.1.1]
  perc: vib, 2 sus cym, 2 conga, bongo, djembe, bd, 2 woodblks, 2 tri,
  tam-tam, marim, cym, marac, 2 tmp, glsp, crot, chimes
Faber

Danceries (1999)   12'
  2[1.2/pic] 2 2 2 — 4 3 3 1 — tmp+3 — hp — cel
  — str
  perc: glsp, tri, sleigh bells, sd, sus cym, tambn, cym, tam-tam, bd
  Contents - 1. Lull me beyond thee; 2. Catching of Quails; 3.
  My Lady's Rest; 4. Quodling's Delight
Faber

Detail from the Record (2001)   17'
  2[1.2/pic] 2[1.2/eh] 2[1.2/bcl] 1[1/cbn] — 1 1 1 0
  — 2perc — hp — pf/cel — str(min)[3.2.2.2.2]
  perc: glsp, xyl, vib, chimes, tri, sus cym, Chinese cym, cym, 2 ride
  cym, 3 gongs, tam-tam, metal chimes, sleigh bells, 3 tom-tom, td, bd,
  claves, marac, flexatone, woodblk, whip
Schott

Netsuke (2001)   15'
  1[1/pic/afl] 0 1[1/bcl] 1 — 0 0 0 0 — 1perc —
  pf/cel — str[1.0.1.1.0]
  perc: glsp, marim, vib, sus cym, tam-tam, bd, templeblk, woodblk,
  whip
  Revised version (2004).
Schott

Notte Oscura (2002)   6'
  2[1.2/pic] 1 2[1.2/bcl] 1[1/cbn] — 1 1 1 0 — 2perc
  — hp — pf/cel — str
  perc: glsp, vib, sus cym, tam-tam, 3 tmp
  Originally for piano, arranged by the composer in 2004.
Schott

Recit and Aria (1994)   11'
  solo S
  1 1[1/eh] 1[1/bcl/cbcl] 0 — 0 0 0 0 — 2perc — hp
  — str[1.0.1.1.0]
  perc: glsp, vib, chimes, tri, sus cym, tam-tam, td, bd, claves
Schott

Theatrum (1996)   19'
  1[1/pic] 1 2[1.2/bcl] 0 — 0 0 0 0 — 1[ssx/asx] —
  3perc — hp — 2pf[pf/hpsd/finger cym.pf/cel] —
  str[1.0.1.1.1]
  perc: glsp, crot, vib, marim, chimes, tri, cym, sus cym, sizzle cym,
  finger cym, bell tree, 3 gong, tam-tam, 3 log dr, bd
  Revised version (2002).
Schott

Three Movements from "Theatrum"   12'
(1996)
  1[1/pic] 1 2[1.2/bcl] 0 — 0 0 0 0 — 1[ssx/asx] —
  3perc — hp — 2pf[cel.pf/finger cym] — str[1.0.1.1.1]
  perc: lg bd, sus cym, cym, sizzle cym, finger cym, woodblk, ratchet,
  tri, tam-tam, 3 gongs, 3 log dr, marim, vib, glsp, crot, hand bells,
  chimes
  Requires 5 string db. Revised version (1998).
Schott

Torturous Instruments (1998)   12'
  1[1/pic/bfl] 1[1/eh] 1[bcl] 0 — 0 0 0 0 — 3perc —
  2pf[cel/synth/ 2 templeblks/ desk bell.pf] —
  str[1.0.0.1.1]
  perc: vib, xylorimba, chimes, 2 tri, sus cym, sizzle cym, cym,
  Chinese cym, tam-tam, Thai gong, 4 wood dr, bd, vibraslap, 3
  woodblks, police whistle
  Vn doubles on claves. Revised version (2009).
Schott

Hewitt, Harry   (1921-2003)

Overture: Taming of the Shrew   6'
  1 1 1 1 — 1 1 0 0 — tmp — str
Fleisher

Spoon River: Prelude and Elegy,   6'
op.26, No.3&4 (1959)
  str
  mvt durations: 4' 2'
Fleisher

Heyn, Volker   (1938-)

Phryh (1982)   9'
  pf — str[3.0.2.2.1]
Breitkopf

Hibbard, William (1939-)

Stabiles for 13 Instruments (1969)   8'
2[1.afl] 0 2[1/Ebcl.bcl] 0 — 0 1 1 0 — 1perc — hp
— pf — str[1.0.1.1.1]
AMP

Hidalgo, Manuel (1956-)

Einfache Musik (1989)   12'
str
Breitkopf

Gran Nada (1997)   17'
solo accordion
str
Breitkopf

Introduction and Fugue (2004)   13'
solo accordion
1[1/pic] 1 1[1/bcl] 1 — 1 1 1 0 — hp — str
Arrangement of the last movement of Beethoven's Sonata in
Bb major, op.106.
Breitkopf

Nahezu Stilles Auge des   15'
Wirbelsturms (1996)
1 1 1 1 — 1 0 0 0 — str[1.0.1.1.1]
Breitkopf

Nuut (1992)   16'
solo accordion
1[1/pic] 1 2[1.bcl] 1 — 1 1 1 0 — 2perc — hp —
pf — str[1.1.2.2.1]
Breitkopf

L'Obvio; For Conductor and 9   12'
Players (1982)
1 0 2 0 — 0 0 0 0 — 2perc — str[1.0.1.1.1]
Breitkopf

Variations on the Variations op.30   18'
by Webern (2001)
1 1 2[1.bcl] 0 — 1 1 1 1 — tmp — hp — cel — str
Breitkopf

Hier, Ethel Glenn (1889-1971)

Carolina Christmas; Suite for   12'
Chamber Orchestra
2 2 2 2 — 4 0 0 0 — str
Fleisher

Hill, Mabel Wood (1870-1954)

Reactions to "Prose Rhythms" of   10'
Fiona Macleod (1933)
1 1 1 1 — 1 0 0 0 — tmp — hp — str
Fleisher

Hiller, Lejaren (1924-1994)

Algorithms I; For 9 Instruments and   36'
Tape
1 0 1 1 — 0 1 0 0 — tape — 1perc — hp —
str[1.0.0.1.1]
In four versions, nine minutes each.
Presser

Algorithms II (With Ravi Kumra);   20'
For 9 Instruments and Tape
1 0 1 1 — 2 0 0 0 — tape — 1perc —
str[1.0.0.1.1]
In four versions, 5 minutes each.
Presser

Divertimento   36'
1 1 1 1 — 1 1 1 0 — gtr — 2perc — str[0.0.0.0.1]
Presser

Hindemith, Paul (1895-1963)

Concert Music for Strings and   16'
Brass, op.50 (1930)
0 0 0 0 — 4 4 3 1 — str
mvt durations: 8' 8'
Schott

Der Dämon: Konzertsuite aus der   25'
Tanzpantomime (1923)
1 0 1 0 — 1 1 0 0 — pf — str[1.1.1.1.1]
Schott

Hérodiade (1944)   22'
1 1 1 1 — 1 0 0 0 — 2 dancers[opt] — pf — str
Schott

In Sturm und Eis: Music to Arnold   87'
Fanck's film "Im Kampf mit dem
Berge" (1921)
1[1/pic] 1 1 0 — 0 1 1 0 — tmp+1 — 2pf[pf.harm]
— str[2.0.0.1.1]
perc: tri, tambn, sd, bd with cym
Schott

Kammermusik No.1 (with Finale   15'
1921), op.24, No.1 (1922)
   1[1/pic] 0 1 1 — 0 1 0 0 — accordion[or harm] —
   1perc — pf — str[1.1.1.1.1]
     perc: xyl, sd, sus cym, tambn, tri, siren, glsp, wood dr, metal shaker
   Kalmus; Luck's; Schott

Plöner Musiktag: Tafelmusik (1932)   10'
   1 0 0 0 — 0 1[or cl] 0 0 — str
   Fleisher; Schott

Der Schwanendreher; Concerto for   26'
Viola and Chamber Orchestra after
old Folksongs (1936)
   solo vla
   2[1.2/pic] 1 2 2 — 3 1 1 0 — tmp — hp —
   str[0.0.0.4.3]
   Schott

Sing- und Spielmusik für Liebhaber   5'
und Freunde: Ein Jäger aus
Kurpfalz, der reitet durch den
grünen Wald, op.45, No.3 (1928)
   1 1 1 1[opt] — 0 0 0 0 — str
   Fleisher; Schott

Sonata for 10 Instruments;   10'
(Fragment) (1917)
   1[1/pic] 0 2[1.bcl] 1 — 1 0 0 0 — str[1.1.1.1.1]
   Schott

Tuttifäntchen: Suite (1925)   20'
   1[1/pic] 1 1 1 — 1 1 0 0 — tmp+1 — str
     perc: tambn, sd, bd with cym, glsp
   Arranged by Franz Willms.
   Schott

Hindson, Matthew   (1968-)

Auto-Electric (2003)   5'
   2[1.pic] 2 2 2[1.cbn] — 4 3[1.2/flug(opt).3] 3 1 —
   tmp+2 — hp — str
     perc: vib, xyl, bongo, high timbale, 2 cowbells, tambn, sus cym, sm
     shaker, sleigh bells, tam-tam, glsp, crot, drum kit, bd, sd
   Faber

Balkan Connection (2003)   15'
   str
   Faber

Boom-Box (1999)   4'
   2 2 2 2 — 4 2 2 1 — 2perc — hp — str
     perc: vib, xyl, bongo, high timbale, 2 cowbells, tambn, sus cym, sm
     shaker, sleigh bells, tam-tam, glsp, crot, drum kit, bd
   Faber

Comin' Right Atcha (2006)   10'
   1[pic] 1 1 1 — 1 1 1 0 — 1perc — pf —
   str[1.1.1.1.1]
     perc: drum kit (bd, sd, 4 tom-tom, cym, hi-hat, splash, ride, Chinese
     cym, 2 cowbells)
   Faber

Comin' Right Atcha; For amplified   10'
Chamber Ensemble (2002)
   0 0 1 1 — 0 1 1 0 — 1perc — pf — str[1.0.0.0.1]
     perc: drum kit (bd, sd, 4 tom-tom, cym, hi-hat, splash, ride, Chinese
     cym, 2 cowbells)
   Faber

Dangerous Creatures; A Suite for   25'
Orchestra (2008)
   2[1.pic] 2[1.eh] 2 2[1.cbn] — 4 2 3 1 — tmp+2 —
   hp — str
     perc: tam-tam, ped bd, tom-tom, bd, sus cym, glsp, Chinese bell,
     drum kit, 2 sd, vibraslap, 2 marac, wind chimes, shell chimes,
     bamboo chimes, bowed cym, vib, cym, tri, whip, floor tom, flexatone,
     hi-hat
   Faber

Flash Madness (2006)   5'
   2[1.pic] 2[1.eh] 2 2 — 4 2 3 1 — tmp+2 — hp —
   str
     perc: cym, tambn, cowbell, whistle, mark tree or windchimes, sd, 2
     bongos, floor tom, bd
   Faber

Ictalurus Punctatus; For Amplified   7'
Cello and Orchestra (2008)
   solo amp vc
   2[1.pic] 2[1.eh] 2 2[1.cbn] — 4 2 2[1.btbn] 1 —
   tmp+1 — str
     perc: vib, 2 conga, bd, drum kit, high cowbell, 3 templeblks
   Faber

Lament (2006)   10'
   solo bn or vc
   2[1.pic] 2[1.2/eh] 2[1.bcl] 2[1.cbn] — 4 2 3 1 —
   tmp+5 — hp — pf/cel — str
     perc: bd, chimes, vib, glsp, cym
   Faber

LiteSPEED (1997)   6'
   2[1.2/pic] 2[1.eh] 2[1.2/bcl] 2[1.cbn] — 4 2 3 1 —
   tmp+1 — hp — str
     perc: kick dr, floor tom-tom, 4 tom-tom, 2 sd, 3 cym, ride cym,
     cowbell
   Faber

Lullaby (2003)   4'
   str
   Faber

RPM (1997)   4'
2[1/pic.2/pic] 2 2 2[1.cbn] — 2 2 0 0 — tmp+2 —
hp — str
perc: bd, 2 sd, tom-tom, 2 cym, ride cym, Chinese cym, glsp
Alternative orchestration uses 4 hn and 3 tbn. A version for
amateur orchestra is also available.
Faber

Song and Dance (2006)   10'
str
Faber

Speed (1997)   16'
2[1.2/pic] 2[1.eh] 2[1.2/bcl] 2[1.cbn] — 4 2 3 1 —
tmp+1 — hp — str
perc: drum kit (double kick dr, floor tom, 4 toms, 2 sd, crash, ride,
medium and splash cym, cowbell)
Faber

Technologic 1-2 (1998)   8'
1perc — str
Faber

Technologic 145 (1998)   14'
1[1/pic/claves] 1[1/guiro] 1[1/chicken shaker]
1[1/cbn] — 1[1/vibraslap] 1 1 0 — hp —
str[1.1.1.1.1]
Faber

Whitewater; For 12 Solo Strings   18'
(2000)
str[7.0.2.2.1]
Faber

Hochstetter, Armin Caspar   (1899-1978)

Concerto for Cello (1935)   22'
solo vc
1 1 1 1 — 0 0 0 0 — str
UE

Höller, York   (1944-)

Arcus (1978)   20'
1[1/pic] 1[1/eh] 2[1.bcl] 2[1.cbn] — 1 1 1 0 — tape
— tmp+1 — pf/elec org — str[1.1.1.1.1]
Breitkopf

Feuerwerk (2004)   9'
1 1 2[1.bcl] 1 — 1 1 1 0 — 2perc — pf —
str[1.1.1.1.1]
Boosey & Hawkes

Mythos (1979)   25'
1[1/pic] 0 1[1/bcl] 0 — 2 1 2 1 — tape — 2perc —
pf/cel — str[0.0.0.2.1]
Breitkopf

Résonance (1981)   20'
2[1/pic.2/afl] 2[1.2/eh] 2[1.2/bcl] 2[1.2/cbn] — 2 2 2
1 — tape — 2perc — hp — pf/cel — str[3.0.2.2.1]
Breitkopf

Holliger, Heinz   (1939-)

Ad Marginem (1983)   8'
2 0 2 0 — 0 0 0 0 — tape — str[1.1.2.2.1]
Schott

Choral à 8 (1983)   3'
0 0 2[1.bcl] 0 — 2 0 0 0 — str[1.1.2.2.0]
Schott

Engführung (1984)   8'
1[afl] 2[ob d'am.eh] 2 1 — 2 0 0 0 — str[1.1.2.2.1]
Schott

Der Ferne Klang (1984)   7'
2[1.pic] 2[ob d'am.eh] 2 1 — 1 0 0 0 — tape —
str[1.0.2.1.0]
Schott

Ostinato Funebre (1991)   8'
2[1.2/pic] 2 3[1.2/bcl.cbcl] 2 — 2 1 1 0 — tmp+3
— str[1.1.2.2.1]
Requires 5 string db.
Schott

Sommerkanon IV (1978)   2'
2[1(or hn).afl] 2[ob d'am.eh] 1 0 — 0 0 0 0 —
str[0.0.1.2.0]
Schott

Holloway, Robin   (1943-)

Concertino No.1, op.2 (1964)   20'
1[1/pic] 1 1 — 1 1 1 0 — str
Boosey & Hawkes

Concertino No.2, op.10 (1967)   25'
1 2[1.eh] 1 1 — 2 0 0 0 — str
Boosey & Hawkes

First Idyll, op.42 (1980)   11'
1 2[1.2/eh] 2[1.2/bcl] 2 — 2 0 0 0 — str[6.5.4.4.2]
Boosey & Hawkes

Fourth Idyll (2007)   23'
 2[1.2/pic] 2[1.2/eh] 2 2 — 2 2 0 0 — str
Boosey & Hawkes

Inquietus, op.66 (1986)   10'
 1 2[1.eh] 1 1 — 1 0 0 0 — hp — str[6.4.4.4.2]
Boosey & Hawkes

Ode, op.45 (1980)   14'
 0 2[1.2/eh] 0 0 — 2 0 0 0 — str
Boosey & Hawkes

Overture on a Nursery Rhyme,   6'
op.75a (1995)
 2[1.2/pic] 2 2 2 — 2 2 1 1 — tmp — str
Boosey & Hawkes

Second Idyll, op.54 (1983)   20'
 1[1/pic] 2[1.2/eh] 0 2 — 2 0 0 0 — str[6.5.4.3.2]
Boosey & Hawkes

Serenade in G, op.64a (1986)   12'
 str
Boosey & Hawkes

Third Idyll; Frost at Midnight, op.78 15'
(1993)
 2[1.2/pic] 2[1.2/eh] 0 2 — 0 2 0 0 — 1perc —
str[7.6.4.3.2]
perc: glsp
Boosey & Hawkes

Holmboe, Vagn   (1909-1996)

Chamber Concerto No.2 (1952)   17'
 solo fl, vn
 tmp+1 — cel — str
Edition Dania; Fleisher

Chamber Symphony No.1, op.53   19'
(1951)
 1 1 1 1 — 1 1 0 0 — tmp — str[6.4.3.2.2]
Hansen

Chamber Symphony No.2, op.100   30'
(1968)
 1 1 1 1 — 2 1 0 0 — tmp+1 — str[6.4.4.3.2]
Hansen

Chamber Symphony No.3, op.103a   25'
(1969)
 1 1 1 1 — 2 2 0 0 — tmp+1 — str
Hansen

Concerto for Orchestra, op.38   17'
(1945)
 2 2 2 2 — 2 2 0 0 — tmp — str
Hansen

Prelude to a Dolphin, op.166 (1986)   12'
 1 1 1 1 — 2 1 0 0 — 2perc — str[1.1.1.1.1]
Hansen

Prelude to a Living Stone, op.172   11'
(1989)
 1 1 1 1 — 2 1 0 0 — 2perc — str[1.1.1.1.1]
Hansen

Prelude to a Maple Tree, op.168   10'
(1986)
 1 1 1 1 — 2 1 0 0 — 3perc — str[1.1.1.1.1]
Hansen

Prelude to a Pine Tree, op.164   8'
(1986)
 1 1 1 1 — 2 1 0 0 — 1perc — pf — str[1.1.1.1.1]
Hansen

Prelude to a Willow Tree, op.170   6'
(1987)
 1 1 1 1 — 2 1 0 0 — tmp+2 — cel — str[1.1.1.1.1]
Hansen

Prelude to the Calm Sea, op.187   10'
(1991)
 1 1 1 1 — 2 1 0 0 — 2perc — cel — str[1.1.1.1.1]
Hansen

Prelude to the Pollution of Nature   9'
(1989)
 1 1 1 1 — 2 1 0 0 — 2perc — str[1.1.1.1.1]
Hansen

Prelude to the Seagulls and   7'
Cormorants, op.174 (1989)
 1 1 1 1 — 2 1 0 0 — 2perc — str
Hansen

Prelude to the Unsettled Weather,   10'
op.188 (1991)
 1 1 1 1 — 2 1 0 0 — 2perc — str[1.1.1.1.1]
Hansen

Prelude to the Victoria   12'
Embankment, op.184 (1990)
 1 1 1 1 — 2 1 0 0 — 3perc — str
Hansen

Sinfonia 1, op.73   12'
 str
Hansen

Sinfonia 2, op.73   *11'*
str
Hansen

Sinfonia 3, op.73   *15'*
str
Hansen

Sinfonia 4, op.73   *16'*
str
Hansen

Symphony No.1, op.4 (1935)   *16'*
1 1 1 1 — 1 1 1 0 — tmp+1 — str
Hansen

Vinter, op.194 (1994)   *13'*
2 2 2 2 — 4 2 0 0 — 2perc — str
Hansen

Holst, Gustav   (1874-1934)

Greeting   *2'*
2 1 2 1 — 0 0 0 0 — str
No score available from Kalmus.
Kalmus

Morris Dance Tunes; Set 1   *6'*
1 0 1 0 — 0 0 0 0 — str
Luck's

Morris Dance Tunes; Set 2   *6'*
1 0 1 0 — 0 0 0 0 — str
Luck's

St. Paul's Suite, op.29, No.2 (1913)   *12'*
str
Kalmus

Two Songs Without Words, op.22 /   *10'*
H88 (1906)
2 1 2 2 — 2 2 1 0 — tmp+1 — str
Contents - 1. Country Song; 2. Marching Song
mvt durations: 5' 5'
Kalmus

Hölszky, Adriana   (1953-)

Tragoedia; (Der unsichtbare Raum)   *60'*
(1996)
1[1/pic/afl/rec] 1 1[1/Ebcl/bcl/cbcl] 0 — 0 1 2 1 —
accordion, gtr, tape — 2perc — hp — 2pf[pf/cel.hpsd]
— str[1.0.1.1.1]
Breitkopf

Holt, Simon   (1958-)

Capriccio Spettrale (2008)   *12'*
1[1/afl] 0 1[1/bcl] 0 — 1 1[1/pic tpt] 0 0 —
str[2.0.2.1.1]
Chester Novello

Era Madrugada (1984)   *12'*
1[1/pic] 0 1[1/bcl] 0 — 1 0 0 0 — pf —
str[0.0.1.1.1]
Chester Novello

Kites (1983)   *15'*
1[1/pic] 1[1/eh] 1 1 — 1 0 0 0 — str[1.1.1.1.1]
Chester Novello

Lilith (1990)   *11'*
1[1/pic] 0 1[1/bcl] 0 — 1 0 0 0 — hp —
str[1.0.1.1.1]
Chester Novello

Homs, Joaquim   (1906-2003)

Nonet; Obra encàrrec Festival   *10'*
Internacional de Música de
Barcelona 1979 (1979)
1 0 1 0 — 0 1 1 0 — 1perc — pf — str[1.0.1.1.0]
Fleisher

Honegger, Arthur   (1892-1955)

Allegretto, H.221 (1938)   *2'*
1 2[1.2/eh] 1 1 — 2 2 0 0 — tmp — cel — str
Salabert

Blues, H.66a (1928)   *3'*
1 1 1 1 — 1 1 0 0 — str
Salabert

Concertino for Piano and Orchestra,   *12'*
H.55 (1924)
solo pf
2[1.2/pic] 2[1.2/eh] 2[1.2/bcl] 2 — 2 2 1 0 — str
Salabert

Concerto da Camera, H.196 (1948)   *17'*
solo fl, eh
str
Salabert

Concerto for Cello and Orchestra,   17'
H.72 (1929)
    solo vc
    2 2 2 2 — 2 2 0 1 — tmp+1 — str
Salabert

Deux Pièces pour "La Rédemption   5'
de François Villon," H.209 (1951)
    1 1 1 1 — 1 2 0 0 — 1perc — str
    Contents - 1. Neige; 2. Pluie et Vent
Salabert

Le Dit des Jeux du Monde: Suite   17'
d'orchestre en 4 mouvements
(1918)
    1[1/pic] 0 0 0 — 0 1 0 0 — 4perc — str[2.2.2.2.2]
Salabert

Le Dit des Jeux du Monde: 10   50'
Danses, 2 interludes et 1 épilogue
pour orchestre de chambre, pour le
poème de Paul Méral, H.19 (1918)
    1[1/pic] 0 0 0 — 0 1 0 0 — 4perc — str[2.2.2.2.2]
Salabert

Fantasio; Ballet pantomime de   10'
Georges Wague, H.46 (1922)
    1 1 1 1 — 1 1 1 0 — tmp+1 — str
Salabert

Interlude de "La Mort de Sainte   5'
Alméenne," H.20A (1920)
    1 1 2 2 — 2 1 0 0 — str
Salabert

Intrada (1947)   5'
    solo tpt
    0 2 0 0 — 2 0 0 0 — str
    Arranged by Marius Constant (1993).
Salabert

Largo, H.105 (1936)   3'
    str
Salabert

Mimaamaquim; Psaume 130, H.192   4'
(1947)
    solo low voice
    1 1 1 1 — 0 0 0 0 — hp[opt] — str
Salabert

Le Roi David is in the Daniel's

Les Misérables: Suite pour   20'
orchestre tirée de la musique du
film de Raymond Bernard, H.88A
(1934)
    1 1 2[1.2/bcl] 1 — 1 1 1 0 — asx — 1perc — hp
    — pf — str
    Strings without db.
Salabert

Napoleón: Danse des Enfants   2'
(1927)
    1 0 1 1 — 0 0 0 0 — str
    Strings without db.
Fleisher

Napoleón: La romance de Violine   3'
(1927)
    1 1 1 0 — 0 0 0 0 — str
Fleisher; Salabert

Pastorale d'été; Poème   8'
symphonique, H.31 (1920)
    1 1 1 1 — 1 0 0 0 — str
Kalmus; Luck's; Salabert

Prélude pour Aglavaine et   7'
Sélysette; D'après la pièce de
Maeterlinck, H.10 (1917)
    1 1 2 2 — 2 1 0 0 — str[5.5.3.3.1]
Salabert

Prière (1925)   3'
    solo S
    2 2 2 2 — 2 2 0 0 — 1perc — pf — str
Salabert

Regain: Suite d'orchestre tirée de la   16'
musique du film de Jean Giono et
Marcel Pagnol, H.117A (1937)
    1 1 1 1 — 0 2 2 0 — asx — 1perc — pf — str
Salabert

La Roue: Overture pour le film   4'
d'Abel Gance, H.44 (1922)
    2 0 2 2 — 0 0 0 0 — str
Salabert

Sérénade à Angélique, H.182   7'
(1945)
    1 1 1 1 — 2 1 1 0 — asx — 1perc — hp — str
Salabert

Six Poèmes d'Apollinaire, H.12:   18'
No.1: À la Santé (1916)
    solo voice
    2 0 0 0 — 0 0 0 0 — hp — str
Salabert

Six Poèmes d'Apollinaire, H.12:
No.3 Automne (1915)
    solo Mz
    1 0 0 0 — 1 0 1 0 — hp — str
Salabert

Six Poèmes d'Apollinaire, H.12:
No.4: Saltimbanques (1917)
    solo va, voice
    1[1/pic] 1 1 0 — 0 2 1 0 — hp — cel — str
    Strings without violins.
Salabert

Six Poèmes d'Apollinaire, H.12:   10'
No.5 L'Adieu (1917)
    solo voice
    1 0 0 0 — 2 0 0 0 — 1perc — cel — str[3.0.0.2.0]
Salabert

Six Poèmes d'Apollinaire, H.12:   8'
No.6: Les Cloches (1917)
    solo voice
    1 0 1 0 — 2 2 1 0 — 1perc — hp — cel — str
Salabert

Sous-marine; Ballet, H.58 (1925)   9'
    2 2[1.2/eh] 2[1.2/bcl] 2 — 4 0 0 0 — 1perc — hp
    — cel — str
    perc: cym
Salabert

Suite Archaïque, H.203 (1951)   14'
    2 2 2 2 — 0 2 2 0 — str
Salabert

Symphony No.2, H.153 (1941)   25'
    0 0 0 0 — 0 1[opt] 0 0 — str
    mvt durations: 11' 9' 5'
Salabert

Tête d'Or; Musique pour une pièce   20'
de Paul Claudel, H.199 (1950)
    1 1[1/eh] 1 1 — 0 3 3 0 — tmp+2 — str
Salabert

Toccata, H.207 (1951)   2'
    2 2 2 2 — 2 2 0 0 — str
Salabert

Vivace, H.220   4'
    1 1 2 2 — 2 0 0 0 — tmp — str
Salabert

Horne, David   (1970-)

Flicker (1997)   8'
    2 2 2[1.2/bcl] 2[1.2/cbn] — 2 2 0 0 — tmp — str
Boosey & Hawkes

Persistence (1995)   13'
    1[1/pic/afl] 1[1/eh] 1[1/bcl] 1[1/cbn] — 1 1 1 0 —
    2perc — str
    perc: vib, bd, tam-tam, sm, med and lg sus cym, guiro, claves, crot, 2
    bongos, marim, 4 templeblks, bass bow
Boosey & Hawkes

Horovitz, Joseph   (1926-)

Adagio Cantabile (1973)   6'
    1 1 1 0 — 0 0 0 0 — hp — str
Novello

Concertino Classico (1985)   10'
    0 0 0 0 — 0 2 0 0 — tmp — str
Novello

Horizon Overture (1972)   5'
    1[1/pic] 1 1 1 — 1 1 1 0 — tmp+1 — str
Novello

Sinfonietta for Light Orchestra   11'
(1971)
    2 1 2 1 — 2 2 3 0 — tmp+1 — str
    Arranged from his "Sinfonietta for Brass Band."
Novello

Valse (1973)   2'
    1 1 1 0 — 0 0 0 0 — 1perc — hp — str
Novello

Horváth, Josef Maria   (1931-)

Origines (1975)   15'
    1 0 1 1 — 0 1 1 0 — 2perc — pf — str[1.0.1.1.1]
UE

Hosokawa, Toshio   (1955-)

Garten Lieder (Garden Songs)   15'
(1995)
    1[1/pic/afl] 1[1/eh] 2[1.2/bcl] 1[1/cbn] — 2 1 0 0 —
    2perc — pf — str[2.2.2.2.1]
    perc: 2 tam-tam, gong, chimes, bd, 3 sus cym, 4 bongos, vib, crot
    Can be performed with an optional additional string group of
    [5.0.2.2.1]
Schott

Landscape VI; "Cloudscapes"   *16'*
(1994)
  1[1/pic/afl] 1[1/eh] 1[1/bcl] 1[1/cbn] — 1 1 0 0 —
  1perc — hp — str(min)[1.1.1.1.1]
  perc: tam-tam, bd, 3 sus cym, crot
Schott

Medea Fragments I (1996)   *8'*
  1[1/pic/afl] 1[1/eh] 2[1.2/bcl] 0 — 0 0 1 0 — 2perc
  — pf — str[1.1.1.1.1]
  perc: 2 bd, 2 tam-tam, 2 crot, 7 tom-tom, woodblk, 2 tri, 2 marac
Schott

Seascapes — Daybreak (1998)   *17'*
  2[1/pic.2/pic/afl/bfl] 1[1/eh] 2[1.2/bcl] 1[1/cbn] — 2
  1 1 0 — 2perc — hp — cel — str[1.1.1.1.1]
  perc: tam-tam, gong, 6 tri, 3 sus cym, 2 bd, crot, 8 bongos, 3 rins on
  tmp, vib, chimes, woodblk
Schott

Hovhaness, Alan   (1911-2000)

Saint Vartan Symphony   *36'*
  0 0 0 0 — 1 4 1 0 — asx — tmp+1 — pf — str
  perc: cym, sd, gong, tam-tam, vib
Peer

Zartik Parkim (Awake my Glory) (1949)   *15'*
  solo pf
  1 0 2 0 — 2 2 0 0 — tmp+1 — pf — str
  perc: cym, tam-tam
Peer

Howells, Herbert   (1892-1983)

Puck's Minuet, op.20, No.1   *4'*
  2 0 3[1.2.bcl] 1 — 0 0 0 0 — tmp+1 — pf — str
Kalmus

Hoyland, Vic   (1945-)

Andacht zum Kleinen (1980)   *17'*
  1 0 1 0 — 0 1 1 0 — 1perc — hp — str[1.0.1.1.0]
UE

Crazy Rosa - La Madre (1988)   *30'*
  solo Mz
  1 0 1 0 — 0 0 0 0 — 2perc — hp — pf —
  str[0.0.1.1.0]
UE

Fox (1983)   *17'*
  2 0 1 0 — 0 0 0 0 — 1perc — hp — pf —
  str[1.1.1.1.1]
UE

Hrabovsky, Leonid   (1935-)

Four Inventions for Chamber   *5'*
Orchestra (1965)
  1 1 1 1 — 1 1 1 1 — asx — elec gtr — 1perc —
  hp — pf/cel/hpsd — str
Schirmer

Hruby, Viktor   (1894-1978)

Drei Lieder nach Eichendorff   *12'*
(Three Songs after Eichendorff)
(1940)
  solo high voice
  2 2 2 2 — 3 0 0 0 — tmp+1 — hp — str
UE

Hubay, Jenö   (1858-1937)

Ende September, op.103/1 (1910)   *5'*
  solo medium voice
  2 2 2 2 — 4 0 0 0 — tmp — hp — str
UE

Huber, Nicolaus A.   (1939-)

Air mit Sphinxes (1987)   *17'*
  1 1 1 1 — 1 1 1 0 — 2perc — hp — str[1.1.1.1.1]
Breitkopf

Eröffnung und Zertrümmerung   *21'*
(1991)
  0 1 1 0 — 0 1 1 0 — accordion, tape, video or film
  productions — 2perc — pf — str[1.0.0.1.1]
Breitkopf

Hölderlin in Darkness: A Dedication   *19'*
(1992)
  1[1/pic] 1 1 1 — 1 1 1 0 — 2perc — hp — pf —
  str[1.0.1.1.1]
Breitkopf

Music on Canvas (2003)   *17'*
  1[1/pic] 1 1[1/bcl] 1 — 1 1 1 0 — CD, amplifier,
  jogger — 2perc — hp — pf/cast — str[1.1.1.1.1]
Breitkopf

Rose Selavy (2000)   *18'*
  1[1/pic] 1 1 1 — 1 1 1 0 — tape — hp —
  2pf[pf.cel] — str[1.1.1.1.1]
Breitkopf

Six Bagatelles (1981)   22'
  1[1/pic/bamboo panpipe] 1 1[1/bcl/cbcl] 1 — 0 0 0
  0 — elec bgtr[opt], tape — 1perc — hp —
  str[1.0.1.1.1]
  If no cbcl is available, the bn doubles on cbn.
  Breitkopf

Hübler, Klaus K.   (1956-)

Epiphyt (1988)   24'
  solo fl
  2 1 3 2 — 0 2 1 0 — 1perc — hp — str[3.0.2.3.1]
  Breitkopf

Kryptogramm (1989)   6'
  0 0 0 1 — 0 0 0 0 — 2perc — hp — 4pf[8hand] —
  str[0.0.0.1.2]
  Two pianos, each played 4-hands.
  Breitkopf

Hudec, Jiri   (1953-)

Drei Stilisierte Polkas im Volkston   10'
(1969)
  2 1 2 1 — 2 2 1 0 — tmp+1 — pf — str
  Sikorski

Huë, Georges Adolphe   (1858-1948)

Fantasie   6'
  solo fl
  1[pic] 2[1.eh] 2 2 — 2 0 0 0 — tmp+1 — hp[or pf]
  — str
  Kalmus

Gigue   4'
  solo fl
  0 2 2 2 — 1 0 0 0 — 1perc — hp — cel — str
  Kalmus

Nocturne   5'
  solo fl
  0 2[1.eh] 2 1 — 1 0 0 0 — hp — str
  Kalmus

Rêverie pour petit orchestre   3'
  1 1 1 1 — 0 0 0 0 — str
  Fleisher

Sérénade pour orchestre   4'
  1 1 1 1 — 0 0 0 0 — str
  Fleisher; Leduc

Huggler, John   (1928-1993)

Sinfonia for 13 Players, op.78 (1974)   12'
  1 1 1 1 — 0 1 1[btbn] 0 — 2perc — hp — pf —
  str[1.0.1.1.0]
  Margun

Hummel, Bertold   (1925-2002)

Drei Kleine Stücke, op.19b (1960)   9'
  str
  Boosey & Hawkes

Symphony for Strings, op.20 (1964)   22'
  str
  Boosey & Hawkes

Humperdink, Engelbert   (1854-1921)

Humoreske in E Dur   5'
  2 2 2 2 — 2 2 0 0 — tmp — str
  Fleisher

Hurd, Michael   (1928-2006)

Captain Coram's Kids (1988)   19'
  1 1 0 1 — 0 0 0 0 — str[1.1.1.1.0]
  Novello

Husa, Karel   (1921-)

Cayuga Lake; (Memories) (1992)   21'
  1 1 1 1 — 1 1 1 1 — 1perc — pf — str[1.1.1.1.0]
  AMP

Hutcheson, Jere   (1938-)

Concerto for Violin and Small   18'
Orchestra (1989)
  solo vn
  1 1 1 1 — 1 1 1 0 — tmp — cel — str[6.6.3.2.1]
  ACA

The Four Temperaments; Concerto   14'
for Trombone and Small Orchestra
(2009)
  solo tbn
  1 1 1 1 — 1 1 0 1 — 1perc — pf — str
  perc: marim, tom-toms, hi-hat
  ACA

Taj Mahal (2004)   *11'*
    2[1.2/pic] 2 2 2 — 2 2 0 0 — 1perc — str
    perc: glsp, 2 congas, templeblks
    ACA

Transitions for Orchestra (1973)   *10'*
    2 2 2 2 — 2 2 2 1 — 2perc — str
    perc: tmp, tom toms, bd, tam-tam, animal bells (or sleigh bells), crot
    (F#), 3 roto toms, tri, cym, hi-hat
    Seesaw

Wild Nights; Concertino for   *11'*
Bassoon and Mixed Ensemble
(2008)
    solo bn
    1 0 1 0 — 0 0 0 0 — 1perc — pf — str[1.0.0.1.0]
    perc: marim
    ACA

Hvidtfelt Nielsen, Svend   **(1958-)**

Flowerfall (1993)   *10'*
    1 0 1 0 — 0 1 0 0 — hp — pf — str[1.0.1.1.0]
    Hansen

Impromptu (1995)   *4'*
    1 0 1 0 — 1 0 0 0 — hp — str[1.1.1.1.1]
    Hansen

Movements (1999)   *17'*
    1 1 1 1 — 1 1 0 0 — tmp — hp — pf —
    str[1.1.1.1.1]
    Hansen

Singing the Dreams (1991)   *20'*
    2perc — pf — str[2.0.1.1.0]
    Hansen

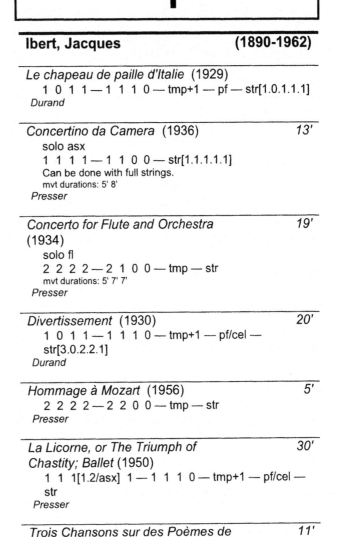

Ibert, Jacques   **(1890-1962)**

Le chapeau de paille d'Italie (1929)
    1 0 1 1 — 1 1 1 0 — tmp+1 — pf — str[1.0.1.1.1]
    Durand

Concertino da Camera (1936)   *13'*
    solo asx
    1 1 1 1 — 1 1 0 0 — str[1.1.1.1.1]
    Can be done with full strings.
    mvt durations: 5' 8'
    Presser

Concerto for Flute and Orchestra   *19'*
(1934)
    solo fl
    2 2 2 2 — 2 1 0 0 — tmp — str
    mvt durations: 5' 7' 7'
    Presser

Divertissement (1930)   *20'*
    1 0 1 1 — 1 1 1 0 — tmp+1 — pf/cel —
    str[3.0.2.2.1]
    Durand

Hommage à Mozart (1956)   *5'*
    2 2 2 2 — 2 2 0 0 — tmp — str
    Presser

La Licorne, or The Triumph of   *30'*
Chastity; Ballet (1950)
    1 1 1[1.2/asx] 1 — 1 1 1 0 — tmp+1 — pf/cel —
    str
    Presser

Trois Chansons sur des Poèmes de   *11'*
Charles Vildrac
    solo voice
    1 1 1 1 — 1 1 1 0 — tmp+1 — hp — str
    Presser

Tropismes pour les Amours   *25'*
Imaginaires
    2 2 2 2 — 2 2 2 0 — tmp+2 — pf/cel — str
    Presser

Ichiyanagi, Toshi   (1933-)

Symphony No.1; Time Current   20'
(1986)
   1 1 1 1 — 1 1 1 0 — 2perc — pf — str[1.1.1.1.1]
perc: vib, glsp, tam-tam, marim, sus cym
Schott

Ifukube, Akira   (1914-2006)

Triptyque aborigène; Trois tableaux   12'
pour orchestre de chambre (1939)
   1 1 1 1 — 2 1 0 0 — tmp+1 — str
Contents - 1. Payses; 2. Timbe; 3 Pakkai
Fleisher

Imbrie, Andrew   (1921-2007)

Chamber Symphony (1968)   18'
   1 1 1[Ebcl] 1 — 1 1 1 0 — hp — pf — str
Malcolm

Dandelion Wine (1967)   7'
   0 1 1 0 — 0 0 0 0 — pf — str[1.1.1.1.0]
Malcolm

From Time to Time (2000)   25'
   1 1 1 1 — 0 0 0 0 — 1perc — str[1.1.1.2.0]
AMP

Spring Fever (1996)   24'
   1 1 1 0 — 0 0 0 0 — 1perc — pf — str[1.1.1.1.1]
AMP

Ince, Kamran   (1960-)

Evil Eye Deflector (1996)   10'
   1[pic] 1 1[Ebcl] 1 — 1 1 1[btbn] 0 — 2sx[asx.bsx]
— elec bgtr — 1perc — 2pf[synth.elec pf] — str
perc: drum set
All strings amplified.
Schott

Turquoise (1996)   10'
   1 1 1 1 — 0 1 0 0 — asx — elec bgtr — 1perc —
pf/synth — str[1.0.1.1.0]
perc: glsp, sd, brake dr
Schott

Indy, Vincent d'   (1851-1931)

Andante   2'
   solo hn
   str
Arranged by Leloir.
Presser

Sérénade, op.16: Valse   5'
   1[1/pic] 1 1 1 — 0 1[1/crt] 0 0 — tmp — str
Fleisher; Hamelle

Suite dans le style ancien, op.24   12'
(1886)
   2 0 0 0 — 0 1 0 0 — str[1.1.1.1.0]
Kalmus; Fleisher; Hamelle

Inghelbrecht, D.E.   (1880-1965)

La Métamorphose d'Ève; Ballet   12'
(1928)
   1 1 2 1 — 2 1 1 0 — tmp+1 — hp[or pf] — str
Fleisher; Senart

Ireland, John   (1879-1962)

Concertino Pastorale (1939)   20'
   str
Boosey & Hawkes

Ishii, Maki   (1936-2003)

Präludium und Variationen (Prelude   7'
and Variations); For Nine Players
   1 0 1 1 — 1 0 0 0 — 1perc — pf — str[1.0.1.1.0]
Presser

Sieben Stücke (Seven Pieces)   12'
   1 0 1[bcl] 0 — 0 0 0 0 — 2perc — hp —
2pf[pf.cel] — str
Presser

Ives, Charles Edward   (1874-1954)

Adagio Sostenuto; At Sea   3'
   1 1[eh] 1[basset hn] 0 — 0 0 0 0 — hp[or pf] —
cel — str[3.0.0.1.0]
Vc is opt. Cel doubles on a high bell (opt).
Peer

Allegretto Sombreoso; Incantation
   1 1[eh] 1[basset hn] 0 — 0 1 0 0 — pf —
   str[3.0.0.0.0]
Peer

Central Park in the Dark, S.34   7'
(1906)
   2[1.pic] 1 1[1/Ebcl] 1 — 0 1 1 0 — 2perc — 2pf —
   str
   perc: sd, bd, cym
Boelke

Charlie Rutlage (1920)   3'
   solo voice (opt)
   1[pic] 1[eh] 1[Ebcl] 1 — 0 1 1 1 — 1perc — pf —
   str
   Arranged by Kenneth Singleton.
Luck's; AMP

Five Songs   11'
   solo voice
   2 2 2 2 — 1 1 0 0 — 1perc — hp — pf — str
   Arranged by John Adams.
Presser

Four Ragtime Dances   11'
   1[1/pic] 1 1 1 — 1 1 1 1 — 1[asx/bsx] — 1perc —
   pf — str
   perc: chimes, trap set
   Arranged by J. Sinclair.
Peer

The Gong on the Hook and Ladder;   3'
Firemen's Parade on Main Street,
S.38
   1 0 1 1 — 0 2 1 0 — tmp+2 — pf — str
   perc: sd, tri, gong[opt]
Peer

Gyp the Blood or Hearst!? Which is   3'
Worst?!
   1 0 1 1 — 0 1 0 0 — pf — str[3.3.3.2.1]
   Edited by Kenneth Singleton.
Peer

Hymn; Largo Cantabile, S.84, No.1   3'
   str
Peer

The Rainbow   2'
   1 1[eh] 1[basset hn] 0 — 0 0 0 0 — pf — str
   After the poem by Wordsworth.
Peer

Symphony No.3; The Camp   19'
Meeting, S.3 (1904)
   1 1 1 1 — 2 0 1 0 — 1perc[opt] — str
   perc: distant bells
   Edited by Kenneth Singleton.
   Contents - 1. Old Folks Gatherin'; 2. Children's Day; 3.
   Communion
   mvt durations: 7' 8' 4'
AMP

Tone Roads No.1, S.49 (1911)   3'
   1 0 1 1 — 0 0 0 0 — str
Peer; Fleisher

Tone Roads No.3, S.49 (1911)   3'
   1 0 1 0 — 0 1 1 0 — 1perc — pf — str
Peer; Fleisher

J

Jacob, Gordon (1895-1984)

Divertimento (1938)   *12'*
1[1/pic] 1 2 1 — 2 2 1 0 — tmp+1 — hp — str
perc: glsp, chimes, xyl, cym, tri, bd, sd, tambn
Boosey & Hawkes

Sinfonietta No.1 for Small Orchestra   *17'*
2 2 2 2 — 2 2 1 0 — tmp+1 — str
Kalmus

Suite in F for Small Orchestra   *14'*
1[1/pic] 1 2 1 — 2 2 1 0 — tmp+1 — hp — str
Kalmus

Jacobi, Frederick (1891-1952)

Concerto for Cello (1930)   *18'*
solo vc
2 2 2 2 — 2 2 0 0 — tmp+1 — str
UE

Jahn, Thomas (1940-)

Nonette "Zeitgeist"
0 0 1[1/asx] 0 — 0 1 1 0 — gtr/banjo — 1perc —
pf — str[1.0.1.1.0]
perc: tmp, jazz dr set, marim, 6 tam-tam, vib, 3 bongos, conga, 5
templeblks, bd
Peer

James, Dorothy (1901-1982)

Suite for Small Orchestra (1952)   *12'*
1 1 1 1 — 1 1 0 0 — str
Fleisher

Janáček, Leoš (1854-1928)

Adagio (1891)   *6'*
2 2 2 2 — 2 2 2 0 — tmp — str
UE

Jenufa-Rhapsodie (1894)   *25'*
2[1.2/pic] 2[1.2/eh] 2 2[1.2(opt)] — 4 2 3 1 —
tmp+1 — hp — str
Edited by Max Schönherr (1940).
UE

Mährische Volkstänze (Moravian   *9'*
Folk Dances) (1892)
2 2 2 2 — 3 2 2 0 — tmp+1 — hp — str
perc: glsp
Contents - 1. Kožich; 2. Kalamajka; 3. Trojky; 4. Silnice; 5.
Rožek
UE

Suite, op.3 (1891)   *16'*
2 2 2 2 — 3 2 0 0 — tmp+1 — hp — str
perc: tri
UE

Janssen, Werner (1899-1990)

Foster Suite (1937)
1[1/pic] 1 2 1 — 2 2 1 0 — tmp+1 — str
Fleisher; Birchard

Järnefelt, Armas (1869-1958)

Berceuse (1904)   *4'*
0 0 2 1 — 2 0 0 0 — str
Kalmus; Boosey & Hawkes

Präludium (1905)   *3'*
1 1 2 1 — 2 2 0 0 — tmp+1 — str
Kalmus; Fleisher; Breitkopf

Die Verlassene; Stimmungsbild   *5'*
nach einem finnischen Volkslied
str
Breitkopf

Jaroch, Jirí (1920-1986)

II. Nonet (1965)   *20'*
1 1 1 1 — 1 0 0 0 — str[1.0.1.1.1]
Schott

Jarre, Maurice (1924-2009)

Concertino: No.11 from   *3'*
"Divertimento for Mozart" (1956)
solo perc
str
For more information see: Mozart, Wolfgang Amadeus.
UE; Schott

Jekimowski, Viktor	**(1947-)**

Chamber Variations for 13 Players,   *8'*
op.15 (1974)
   1 1 1 1 — 1 1 1 0 — 1perc — hp — str[1.0.1.1.1]
Sikorski

Jelinek, Hanns	**(1901-1969)**

Parergon, op.15B (1957)   *18'*
   2 2 2 2 — 2 1 0 0 — 1perc — str
   Contents - 1. Walzer; 2. Sarabande; 3. Gavotte; 4. Musette;
   5. Siciliano; 6. Marsch
UE

Prelude, Passacaglia and Fugue,   *22'*
op.4 (1922)
   1 0 1 1 — 1 0 0 0 — str(min)[1.1.1.1.1]
UE

Jenkins, Karl	**(1944-)**

Palladio (1995)   *16'*
   str(min)[6.5.4.3.2]
Boosey & Hawkes

Passacaglia (1995)   *5'*
   str
Boosey & Hawkes

Jenner, Gustav	**(1865-1920)**

Serenade for Orchestra (1911/12)   *40'*
   2 2 2 2 — 2 2 0 0 — tmp — str
Bärenreiter

Jerger, Wilhelm	**(1902-1978)**

Symphony No.1; Classical   *20'*
Symphony
   2 2 2 2 — 2 2 2 0 — tmp — str
UE

Jirák, K. B.	**(1891-1972)**

Serenade for Small Orchestra,   *20'*
op.69 (1954)
   2 2 2 2 — 4 2 0 0 — tmp — str
Fleisher

Johnson, Hunter	**(1906-1998)**

Concerto for Small Orchestra   *20'*
   2 0 2 0 — 0 0 0 0 — pf — str
Fleisher

Jolivet, André	**(1905-1974)**

Symphonie pour cordes (1961)   *23'*
   str
Boosey & Hawkes

Jones, Charles	**(1910-1997)**

Suite for Small Orchestra
   1 1 1 1 — 2 1 0 0 — str
Fleisher

Jongen, Joseph	**(1873-1953)**

Sarabande Triste, op.58 (1925)
   solo vc
   1 1 1 1 — 1 0 0 0 — str
Bosworth

Jost, Christian	**(1963-)**

Mascarade: Tableau from the opera   *6'*
"Vipern" (2003)
   2[1.pic] 1[eh] 2[1.Ebcl] 1 — 2 1 1 0 —
   str[4.4.4.4.2]
Schott

Joubert, John	**(1927-)**

Octet, op.33 (1961)   *22'*
   0 0 1 1 — 1 0 0 0 — str[1.1.1.1.1]
Novello

Sinfonietta, op.38 (1962)   *19'*
   0 2 0 2 — 2 0 0 0 — str
Novello

Juon, Paul	**(1872-1940)**

Five Pieces for String Orchestra   *15'*
(1901)
   str
Kalmus

Kammersinfonie (Chamber   35'
Symphony), op.27 (1905)
    0 1 1 1 — 1 0 0 0 — pf — str
Fleisher

Serenade, op.40 (1909)   30'
    2 1 2 2 — 2 0 0 0 — tmp — str
Kalmus; Fleisher

K

Kagel, Mauricio   (1931-)

Finale mit Kammerensemble   22'
    1[1/pic] 1 2[1.bcl] 1 — 1 1 1 1 — 1perc — pf —
str[1.0.1.1.1]
Can be done with strings (12.0.8.6.4), in which case the title
of the work is "Finale mit Orchester"
Peters

Kahn, Erich Itor   (1905-1956)

Actus Tragicus (1955)   15'
    1 1 1 1 — 1 0 0 0 — str[1.1.1.1.1]
Fleisher

Petite Suite Bretonne (1936)   12'
    1 1 1 1 — 1 0 0 0 — hp[or pf] — str
Strings without db.
Fleisher; Pro Musica

Kahowez, Günther   (1940-)

Bardo-Puls; Musik nach dem   15'
tibetanischen Totenbuch (1974)
    1 0 1 0 — 1 1 0 0 — 2perc — pf — str[1.0.1.1.1]
UE

Kaipainen, Jouni   (1956-)

Accende Lumen Sensibus, op.52   22'
(1996)
    1 2 1 2 — 2 1 0 0 — tmp — str
Hansen

Kajanus, Robert   (1856-1933)

Sinfonietta in Bb major, op.16   25'
    2 2 2 2 — 3 0 0 0 — tmp+1 — str
Breitkopf

Kallstenius, Edvin   (1881-1967)

Berceuse (1939)   4'
    0 0 1 1 — 1 1 0 0 — 1perc — pf — str
Nordiska

Dalsland-Rhapsodie, op.22 (1936)   8'
     2 2 2 2 — 2 2 1 0 — 1perc — str
UE

Suite for 9 Instruments, op.23b   12'
(1949)
     1 1 1 — 1 0 0 0 — str[1.1.1.1.0]
Fleisher

Suite for 14 Instruments, op.23c   12'
(1949)
     1 1 2 1 — 2 1 0 0 — tmp — str[1.1.1.1.1]
Fleisher

Kalsons, Romualds   (1936-)

Symphony for Chamber Orchestra   17'
(1981)
     1perc — hpsd — str
     perc: flexatone
Sikorski

Kaminski, Heinrich   (1886-1946)

Brautlied: "Wo du hingehst..."   4'
(Bride's Song: "Where you are
going...") (1911)
     solo high voice
     2 1 2 1 — 2 0 0 0 — 1perc — hp — str
UE

Dorische Musik (Dorian Music)   29'
(1933)
     solo vn, va, vc
     2 2 3 3 — 2 2 0 0 — 1perc — str
UE

Kancheli, Giya   (1935-)

Abii ne Viderem (1992)   25'
     1[afl] 0 0 0 — 0 0 0 0 — bass gtr — pf — str
     Afl can be replaced by va.
Boosey & Hawkes

Besuch In Der Kindheit (Childhood   28'
Revisited) (1998)
     0 1 0 0 — 0 0 0 0 — bgtr — pf — str
Sikorski

Diplipito (1997)   27'
     solo vc, CT
     gtr, bgtr — 1perc — pf — str
     perc: diplipito [bongo], tam-tam, glsp
Sikorski

Kapote (2006)   32'
     solo accordion, perc, bgtr
     str
Schirmer

Largo and Allegro (1963)   15'
     tmp — pf — str
Sikorski; Boosey & Hawkes

A Life Without Christmas: The   23'
Morning Prayers; For Chamber
Orchestra and Tape (1990)
     1[afl] 0 0 0 — 0 0 0 0 — bass gtr, tape — amp pf
     — str[6.5.4.3.1]
Boosey & Hawkes

A Life Without Christmas: Midday   24'
Prayers; Concerto for Clarinet, Boy
Soprano and Chamber Ensemble
(1990)
     solo cl, boy soprano
     1[1/pic] 1 0 1[1/cbn] — 1 2 3 1 — bass gtr —
     2perc — amp pf/cel — str[1.0.1.1.1]
     perc: chimes, glsp, bd, tam-tam, cym, sus cym
Boosey & Hawkes

A Life Without Christmas: The   20'
Evening Prayers; For Chamber
Orchestra and 8 Alto Singers (1991)
     solo 8 alto singers
     1 1 0 0 — 1 2 2 1 — bass gtr — 3perc — pf — str
     perc: tambn, sd, bd, cym, sus cym, chimes, glsp
Boosey & Hawkes

A Life Without Christmas: The Night   23'
Prayers; For Soprano Saxophone,
Strings and Tape (1994)
     solo ssx
     tape — str
Boosey & Hawkes

Magnum Ignotum (1994)   22'
     1[1/afl] 2 2 2 — 2 0 0 0 — tape — str[0.0.0.0.1]
Sikorski

Sio (1998)   17'
     1perc — pf — str
     perc: sd, bd, glsp, marim
Boosey & Hawkes; Sikorski

Kander, Susan   (1957-)

She Never Lost A Passenger   2'
Overture (1996)
   2 0 2 0 — 0 1 1 0 — 1 — str
Boosey & Hawkes

Karayev, Kara   (1918-1982)

Symphony No.3 for Chamber   25'
Orchestra (1964)
   2 2 0 2 — 2 0 0 0 — 2pf[pf.hpsd] — str
Sikorski

Kasilag, Lucrecia   (1918-2008)

Legend of the Sarimanok   22'
   1 1 1 2 — 1 1 1 0 — tmp+1 — hp — cel — str
Peer

Kats-Chernin, Elena   (1957-)

Clocks; For Ensemble and Tape   21'
(1993)
   1[1/pic] 1 1 1[1/cbn] — 1 1 1 0 — asx — tape —
   2perc — hp — 2pf — str[3.0.2.2.1]
   perc: I=xyl, glsp, bd, 3 templeblks, cym, Chinese dr, crot, chimes,
   stones, Japanese woodblk II=xyl, glsp, 4 templeblks, cup chime, 3
   Chinese tom-tom, anvil, crot, chimes
Boosey & Hawkes

Torque (2002)   15'
   solo accordion
   pf — str
Boosey & Hawkes

Zoom and Zip (1997)   13'
   str
Boosey & Hawkes

Katz, Gil S.   (1968-)

Tribal (2010)   17'
   solo vc, db
   2perc — str
   perc: cym, splash cym, bd, 3 toms, bombo, high and low woodblk, 3
   congas, vibraslap, egg shaker, lg cowbell, lg shekere
Nona Music

Kauffmann, Leo Justinus   (1901-1944)

Concertino for Double Bass (1942)   10'
   solo db
   1 2 1 1 — 1 1 1 0 — tmp — str
UE

Kaun, Hugo   (1863-1932)

Elegie, op.70, No.5 (1907)   6'
   2 1 2 1 — 2 0 0 0 — str
Fleisher; Vieweg

Fröhliches Wandern, op.70, No.1   8'
(1906)
   2 0 2 1 — 2 0 0 0 — str
Fleisher; Vieweg

Idyll, op.70, No.2 (1907)   6'
   2 0 2 1 — 2 0 0 0 — str
Fleisher; Vieweg

Kelemen, Milko   (1924-)

Konstellationen (1959)   8'
   1 1 1 1 — 1 1 1 0 — str
Schott

Nonett (1989)   20'
   1 1 1 1 — 0 0 0 0 — str[1.1.1.1.1]
Sikorski

Kelly, Bryan   (1934-)

Concertante Dances (1980)   19'
   1 1 1 1 — 0 0 0 0 — str
Novello

Cookham Concertino (1969)   15'
   1 1 1 1 — 2 0 0 0 — tmp+1 — hp — str
Novello

Cookham Rondo (1969)   4'
   1 1 1 1 — 2 0 0 0 — tmp+1 — hp — str
Novello

Kelterborn, Rudolf   (1931-)

Four Movements for Classical   14'
Orchestra (1997)
   0 2[1.2/eh] 0 0 — 2 0 0 0 — str
Bärenreiter

Kammersinfonie II (1964) 13'
str
Boosey & Hawkes

Lamentationes (1961) 12'
str
Bärenreiter

Musica luminosa per orchestra 10'
(1983/84)
2 2 2 2 — 2 2 0 0 — tmp+1 — str
Bärenreiter

Passions (1998) 13'
str
Bärenreiter

Traummusik; 6 Stücke für kleines 13'
Orchester (1971)
1[1/pic/afl] 1[1/eh] 1[1/bcl] 0 — 1 0 1 0 — 1perc
— hp — str[6.6.4.4.2]
Requires 5-stringed basses.
Bärenreiter

Vier Nachtstücke für 13'
Kammerorchester (1963)
0 0 2[1.2/bcl] 0 — 2 0 0 0 — str
Bärenreiter

Kennan, Kent (1913-2003)

Dance Divertimento 7'
2[1.2/pic] 2 2 2 — 2 2 0 0 — tmp+1 — pf[opt] —
str
Contents - 1. Grand March; 2. Toe Dance; 3. Jig
mvt durations: 2' 2' 3'
Kalmus

Elegy 4'
solo ob
2 0 2 2 — 3 0 0 0 — tmp+1 — str
Kalmus

A Rome Dairy 7'
solo tpt (1.movement), vn (2.movement)
2[1.2/pic] 2 2 2 — 2 2 0 0 — tmp+1 — pf[opt] —
str
Contents - 1. Il Campo dei Fiori; 2. Notturno
mvt durations: 3' 4'
Kalmus

Kernis, Aaron Jay (1960-)

Invisible Mosaic II (1988) 16'
1[1/pic] 1 1[1/bcl] 1 — 1 1 1 1 — 2perc — hp —
pf/cel — str[1.1.1.1.1]
AMP

Ketèlbey, Albert W. (1875-1959)

My Lady Brocade (1933)
1perc — cel — str
perc: glsp
Bosworth

Keuning, Hans P. (1926-)

Remarkable Dances (1974)
1 1 1 0 — 0 0 0 0 — 1perc — pf — str
Fleisher; Harmonia

Killmayer, Wilhelm (1927-)

Führe mich, Alter, nur immer in 6'
deinen geschnörkelten Frühlings-
Garten! Noch duftet und taut frisch
und gewürzig sein Flor (1974)
1 0 1 0 — 0 0 1[atbn] 0 — 2perc — pf —
str[1.0.1.1.0]
perc: small bells attached to a string, sd, tri, chimes, vib, glsp
Schott

Sinfonia 2 (1969) 9'
1 1 0 1 — 0 0 0 0 — hpsd — str[6.0.2.1.1]
Schott

King, Alastair (1967-)

Dance Marathon ($1000 stake) 22'
solo narrator
0 0 1 1 — 0 1 1 0 — 1perc — str[1.0.0.0.1]
Chester Novello

Master Irpy (1999) 5'
2 2 2 2 — 4 0 0 0 — tmp — hp — str
Chester Novello

Kingman, Daniel (1924-)

A Revolutionary Garland 8'
2[1.2/pic] 2 2 2 — 2 2 0 0 — tmp+1 — str
Contents - 1. York Fusilliers; 2. Soldier's Joy; 3. St. Patrick's
Day in the Morning; 4. Gen'l Washington's March
Kalmus

Kirchner, Leon (1919-2009)

Music for Twelve (1985) 10'
1 1 1 1 — 1 1 1 0 — pf — str[1.0.1.1.1]
AMP

Kirchner, Volker David (1942-)

Bildnisse I (1982) 20'
2[1.2/pic] 3[1.2.eh] 2[1.2/bcl] 2[1.2/cbn] — 2 2 2 0
— str
Schott

Bildnisse II (1984) 12'
2[1.2/pic] 3[1.2.eh] 2[1.bcl] 2[1.cbn] — 2 2 2 0 —
hp — pf — str
Schott

Bildnisse III (1991) 15'
1 2[1.2/eh] 3[bcl.basset hn.basset hn] 1[cbn] —
2[natural in Eb] 0 0 0 — 1perc — str
perc: cym, tam-tam, bd
Schott

Kirk, Theron (1919-1999)

Adagietto 6'
1 2[1.eh] 1 1 — 2 0 0 0 — tmp — cel — str
Fleisher

Kisielewski, Stefan (1911-1991)

Concerto for Chamber Orchestra 14'
(1943)
1 2 1 1 — 0 0 0 0 — str
PWM

Rencontres dans un désert (1969) 12'
1 0 1 1 — 0 1 1 0 — 2perc — str[1.0.0.1.1]
PWM

Symphony for 15 Performers 15'
(1961)
2 1 1 1 — 1 1 1 0 — 2perc — str[1.1.1.1.1]
PWM

Kitzke, Jerome (1955-)

Present Music (1982) 15'
1 0 1 0 — 0 0 0 0 — 2perc — pf — str[1.0.0.1.0]
perc: trap set, xyl, vib
Peer

Klebe, Giselher (1925-2009)

Con moto, op.2 (1953) 9'
2 2 2 2 — 4 2 3 1 — str
Boosey & Hawkes

Divertissement joyeux, op.5 (1949) 11'
0 0 1 1 — 1 1 1 0 — 1perc — str
Boosey & Hawkes

Espressioni liriche: No.7 from 3'
"Divertimento for Mozart" (1956)
solo hn, tpt, tbn
2 2 2 2 — 2 2 0 0 — tmp — str
For more information see: Mozart, Wolfgang Amadeus.
UE; Schott

Moments musicaux, op.19 (1955) 4'
2[1.pic] 2[1.eh] 2[1.Ebcl] 2 — 4 2 3 1 — 2perc —
hp — str
Boosey & Hawkes

Scene und Arie, op.54 (1968) 12'
0 0 0 0 — 0 3 3 0 — 2pf — str[0.0.0.8.0]
Bärenreiter

Klenau, Paul von (1883-1946)

Altdeutsche Liedersuite (Old 17'
German Song Suite) (1934)
2 2 2 2 — 2 2 1 0 — hp — str
UE

Klengel, Julius (1859-1933)

Andante sostenuto, op.51 8'
solo vc
0 1 2 1 — 2 0 0 0 — str
Breitkopf

Concerto for Cello in A minor   22'
  solo vc
  2 2 2 2 — 2 2 0 0 — tmp — str
Breitkopf

Concerto for Cello in B minor   26'
  solo vc
  2 2 2 2 — 2 2 0 0 — tmp — str
Breitkopf

Concerto for Two Celli in E minor,   25'
op.45
  solo 2vc
  2 2 2 2 — 4 2 3 0 — tmp — str
Breitkopf

Concerto for Violin and Cello, op.61   22'
  solo vn, vc
  2[1.2/pic] 2 2 2 — 4 2 3 0 — tmp+1 — str
Breitkopf

Serenade in F major, op.24   26'
  str
Breitkopf

Knight, Edward   (1961-)

Cadillac Ranch (1998)   8'
  str
Subito

Concerto for Clarinet (1992)   15'
  solo cl
  1 1 1 1 — 1 0 0 0 — pf — str
Subito

Knipper, Lew   (1898-1974)

Wantsch; Turkmenische Suite,   20'
op.29 (1932)
  1 1 1 1 — 2 1 1 0 — 1 — tmp+1 — str
UE

Knussen, Oliver   (1952-)

Music for a Puppet Court; Puzzle   10'
pieces for 2 Chamber Orchestras,
op.11 (1983)
  2[1/pic/afl.2/pic] 2 2 2 — 2 0 0 0 — gtr — 2perc
  — hp — cel — str[4.4.4.4.2]
  perc: vib, chimes, 7 handbells, 2 tri, anvil, sus cym, marac, tam-tam,
  whip, ratchet, guiro, alarm clock
Faber

Notre Dame des Jouets; Organum   2'
from a Music Box, op.27, No.1 (1995)
  2 2[1.eh] 2 1 — 2 1 1 0 — 2perc — hp —
  2pf[pf.cel] — str[1.1.1.1.1]
  perc: vib, glsp, marac, vibraslap
Faber

Océan de Terre, op.10 (1976)   12'
  solo S
  1[1/afl] 0 1[1/bcl] 0 — 0 0 0 0 — 1perc —
  pf/cel/marac/templeblk — str[1.0.0.1.1]
  perc: vib, glsp, chimes, sus cym, gong, 2 tam-tam, xyl, woodblks,
  templeblk, claves, whip, marac, 2 tom-tom
Faber

Organum, op.27, No.2 (1994)   4'
  2[1.2/afl] 2[1.2h] 2 1 — 0 0 0 0 — 2perc — hp —
  2pf[pf.cel.harm] — str[1.1.1.1.1]
  perc: vib, glsp, chimes, tmp, bd, sus cym, tri, tam-tam
Faber

Processionals, op.2 (1978)   12'
  1 1 1 1 — 1 0 0 0 — str[1.1.1.1.0]
Faber

Requiem; Songs for Sue, op.33   12'
(2006)
  2[1.afl] 2 2[1.bcl] 0 — 2 0 0 0 — 1perc — hp —
  pf/cel — str[0.0.2.2.1]
  perc: marim, tam-tam
Faber

Symphony No.2 for High Soprano   17'
and Small Orchestra (1970)
  solo S
  2 2 2 2 — 2 0 0 0 — 1perc[opt] — str
  min[6.6.4.4.2]
  perc: 4 crot
Faber

Two Organa, op.27 (1995)   6'
  2[1.2/afl] 2[1.eh] 2 1 — 2 1 1 0 — 2perc — hp —
  3pf[pf.cel.harm] — str[1.1.1.1.1]
Faber

Koc, Marcelo   (1918-2006)

Tres Piezas Para Orquesta (1958)   15'
  1 1 1 1 — 2 1 0 0 — tmp — str
Fleisher

Koch, Erland von   (1910-2009)

Ballet Suite: Peter Tailless, the Cat   13'
(1948)
  1[1/pic] 1 1 1 — 1 1 1 0 — tmp+1 — str
Nordiska

Concertino pastorale, op.35 (1947)   15'
  solo fl
  str
Breitkopf

Concerto piccolo (1962)   13'
  solo ssx, asx
  str
Breitkopf

Dalecarlia Suite (1957)   10'
  1 0 1 0 — 0 0 0 0 — str
Breitkopf

Dance No.2 (1938)   3'
  2[1.2/pic] 2 2 2 — 2 2 0 0 — tmp+1 — str
Nordiska

Dance No.4 (1956)   5'
  1 0 1 0 — 0 0 0 0 — pf — str
Nordiska

Dance No.5 (1957)   4'
  1 0 1 0 — 0 0 0 0 — pf — str
Nordiska

Four Swedish Folk Melodies (1984)   12'
  1 1 1 1 — 1 0 0 0 — str
Fleisher

Kleine Lustspiel Ouvertüre (1952)   3'
  2 2 2 2 — 2 2 1 0 — tmp+1 — str
Breitkopf

Musica intima (1965)   16'
  str
Breitkopf

Oxberg Variations; On a Theme   18'
from Dalecarlien (1956)
  2[1.2/pic] 2 2 2 — 2 2 2 0 — 1perc — str
Breitkopf

Schwedische Tanz-Rhapsodie   16'
(1957)
  2[1.2/pic] 2[1.2/eh] 2 2 — 2 2 2 0 — tmp+1 — str
Breitkopf

Sechs Schwedische   10'
Bauernmelodien; Aus Dalekarlien
(1971)
  str
Breitkopf

Sicilienne (1942)   3'
  1 0 1 0 — 2 2 1 0 — 1perc — str
Nordiska

Skandinavische Tänze   56'
  2 2 2 2 — 2 2 1 0 — tmp+1 — str
  perc: sd, tri, cym
Peer

Three Miniatures for Orchestra   13'
(1951)
  2 2 2 2 — 2 2 1 0 — tmp+2 — str
Breitkopf

Kodály, Zoltán   (1882-1967)

Concerto for Orchestra (1940)   19'
  3[1.2.3/pic] 2 2 2 — 4 3 3 1 — tmp+1 — hp — str
  perc: tri
Boosey & Hawkes

Dances of Galanta (1933)   14'
  2[1.2/pic] 2 2 2 — 4 2 0 0 — tmp+2 — str
  perc: tri, glsp, sd
UE

Duet from "Háry János," No.8:   4'
Tiszán innen, Dunán túl (Far away
from the Danube) (1926)
  solo Mz, Bar
  1 0 2 0 — 2 0 0 0 — cimb — str
UE

Five Songs: From "Hungarian   16'
Folkmusic"
  solo high or medium voice
  1[1/pic] 1 1 1 — 1 0 0 0 — str
  Arranged by Paul Angerer (1957).
  Contents - 1. Kleines Vöglein; 2. Hochzeit der Grille; 3. Tief
  im Walde; 4. Dudelsack-Weise; 5. Winter kam durchs Land
  gezogen
  mvt durations: 4' 3' 3' 3' 3'
UE

Hungarian Rondo (1917)   8'
  0 0 2 2 — 0 0 0 0 — str
  Based on an old Hungarian soldiers' tune.
Boosey & Hawkes

Intermezzo: From "Háry János"   4'
(1927)
   3[1.2.3(opt)] 2 2 2 — 4 3[1.2.3(opt)] 0 0 —
   cimb[or pf] — tmp+3 — str
   <small>perc: bd, sd, tri, cym</small>
   Also available in a version for Salon-Orchestra arranged by
   Emil Bauer (1929):
   1110 - 0110 - 1perc - pf.harm - cimb - str(1.1.1.1.1)
   available from UE.
Luck's; UE

Kádár Kata; Transylvanian Folk   9'
Ballad (1943)
   solo A
   1[1/pic] 1 1 0 — 0 0 0 0 — pf/cel — str
UE

Marosszéker Tänze (1927)   12'
   2[1.2/pic] 2 2 2[1.cbn] — 4 2 0 0 — tmp+1 — str
UE

Minuetto Serio (1953)   7'
   2 2 2 2 — 4 2 0 0 — tmp — str
Kalmus; Boosey & Hawkes

Mónár Anna; Székler Ballade   9'
(1936)
   solo medium voice
   1 1 1 0 — 0 0 0 0 — pf — str
UE

Summer Evening (1906)   18'
   1 2[1.eh] 2 2 — 2 0 0 0 — str
UE

Symphony in C (1930s)   30'
   3[1.2.3/pic] 2 2 2 — 4 3 3 1 — tmp+1 — str
   <small>perc: cym, tri</small>
Boosey & Hawkes

Variations on a Hungarian   25'
Folksong; The Peacock (1939)
   3[1.2.3/pic] 2[1.2/eh] 2 2 — 4 3 3 0 — tmp+1 —
   hp — str
   <small>perc: glsp, cym, tri</small>
Boosey & Hawkes

Koechlin, Charles   (1867-1950)

Sur Les Flots Lointains (1933)   4'
   2 2[eh.ob d'am] 2[1.bcl] 2 — 2 2 0 0 — tmp — str
Schott

Kolb, Barbara   (1939-)

Voyants; For Piano and Chamber   20'
Orchestra (1991)
   solo pf
   2[1.2/pic] 1 1 1 — 1 1 1 0 — 1perc — str
   <small>perc: vib, cym, timbale, sd, chimes</small>
   Small string section or (1.1.1.1.1).
Boosey & Hawkes

The Web Spinner (2003)   10'
   2 2 2 2 — 2 0 0 0 — str
Boosey & Hawkes

Yet That Things Go Round (1987)   14'
   2[1.2/pic] 2 2[1.2/bcl] 2 — 2 2 1 0 — 2perc — pf
   — str
   <small>perc: vib, marim, sd, chimes, tmp</small>
Boosey & Hawkes

Komarova, Tatjana   (1968-)

Sonnenuntergänge auf B 612   10'
(Sunsets on B 612) (1998)
   1 1 1 1 — 0 0 0 0 — str(min)[1.1.1.1.1]
Schott

Komorous, Rudolf   (1931-)

Düstere Anmut (1968)   6'
   1 1 1 0 — 1 1 1 0 — nightingale[on tape] — 1perc
   — prepf — str[0.0.1.1.1]
   <small>perc: cowbell</small>
UE

Rossi (1975)   15'
   2[1.pic] 2[1.eh] 3[1.2.bcl] 0 — 0 1 0 0 — bass
   harmonica — 1perc — org — str[0.0.2.2.0]
   <small>org = small baroque organ.</small>
UE

York (1967)   5'
   1 1[or tpt] 0 1 — 0 0 0 0 — mand — 1perc —
   prepf — str[0.0.0.0.1]
   <small>perc: tri</small>
UE

Kopelent, Marek   (1932-)

Intimissimo (1971)   18'
   0 1[eh] 1 0 — 0 1 1 0 — asx — gtr, tape[opt] —
   1perc — prepf — str[1.1.2.1.1]
Breitkopf

Still-Leben (1968)   10'
1 1 1 0 — 1 1 1 0 — 1perc — pf — str
perc: marim
Breitkopf

Koppel, Anders   (1947-)

Concertino for Chamber Ensemble   15'
(1999)
1 1 1 1 — 1 0 0 0 — 1perc — str[1.1.1.1.1]
Hansen

Partita (1996)   30'
0 1 0 0 — 0 0 0 0 — asx — 1perc — pf —
str[1.0.0.1.1]
Norsk

Pogo (1997)   9'
0 1 0 0 — 0 0 0 0 — asx — 1perc — pf —
str[1.0.0.1.1]
Norsk

Seven Scenes from Everyday Cow   15'
Life (1998)
0 1 0 0 — 0 0 0 0 — ssx — 1perc — pf —
str[1.0.0.1.1]
Hansen

Korndorf, Nikolai   (1947-2001)

Confessiones; Chamber Symphony   21'
for 14 Instruments (1979)
2[1.rec] 1 1 0 — 1 1 1 0 — tape — tmp+1 — pf —
str[1.0.1.1.1]
Schirmer

Korngold, Erich Wolfgang   (1897-1957)

Dance in the Old Style (1919)   8'
2[1.2/pic] 2 2 2 — 2 2 0 0 — tmp+1 — str
perc: tri
Schott

Much Ado About Nothing: Suite,   16'
op.11 (1920)
1[1/pic] 1 1 1 — 2 1 1 0 — tmp+1 — hp —
2pf[pf.harm] — str[1.1.1.1.0]
perc: tri, chimes, tam-tam, tambn, sd, bd with cym, rute, ratchet, glsp
Also possible with strings (2.2.2.2.0).
Kalmus; Schott

Der Schneemann: Overture (1910)   5'
2[1.2/pic] 2 2 2 — 4 2 3 0 — tmp+2 — hp — str
perc: cym, glsp, tri, sd
Kalmus; Luck's

Straussiana (1920)   6'
3[1.2.pic] 1[opt] 2 1[opt] — 2[opt] 2 2 0 — tmp+2
— hp[opt] — pf — str
perc: cym, glsp, tri, sd
Kalmus

Kósa, György   (1897-1984)

Chamber Music (1928)   12'
1 1 2 1 — 1 1 0 0 — hp — str
UE

Suite; Three Ironic Portraits (1915)   10'
1 1 2 2 — 2 2 0 1 — 1perc — str
UE

Kozinski, Stefan   (1953-)

The Maloney Rag (1976)   4'
1[1/pic] 1 1 1 — 1 1 1 1 — 1perc — pf —
str[1.1.1.1.1]
perc: dr
Arranged by Gunther Schuller.
Margun

Krása, Hans   (1899-1944)

Brundibár: Suite from the Opera   14'
(1943)
1[1/pic] 0 2 1 — 0 1 0 0 — gtr — 1perc — pf —
str[4.0.0.1.1]
perc: sd, bd
Arr. By Petr Pokorny.
Boosey & Hawkes

Overture for Small Orchestra   7'
(1944)
0 0 2 0 — 0 2 0 0 — pf — str
Boosey & Hawkes

Symphony for Small Orchestra   17'
(1923)
solo A
3 0 4 2 — 2 2 0 0 — 1perc — hp — cel — str
UE

Krätzschmar, Wilfried (1944-)

Ballets imaginaires   12'
  1 1 0 1 — 2 0 0 0 — 1perc — str
Breitkopf

Krauze, Zygmunt (1938-)

Arabesque; For Piano and   13'
Chamber Ensemble (1983)
  solo pf (amp)
  1[1/soprano melodica] 1[1/soprano melodica] 1 1 —
  1[1/alto melodica] 1[1/alto melodica] 1 0 —
  str[2.2.4.2.1]
UE

Tableau Vivant (1982)   15'
  1 1 2 1 — 1 1 1 0 — pf — str[1.1.2.1.1]
UE

Krebs, Joachim (1952-)

Musik für Kleines Orchester (Music   25'
for Small Orchestra)
  1[1/pic/afl] 1[1/eh] 1[1/bcl] 1[1/cbn] — 1 1 1 0 —
  tmp+2 — pf/cel — str
  perc: marim, vib, bd, sd, 2 tam-tam, glsp, woodblk, hammer
Peer

Slow-Mobile   21'
  1[1/pic] 1[1/eh] 2[1.bcl] 2[1.cbn] — 2 0 0 0 —
  2perc — hp — str[1.0.1.1.1]
  perc: I: bells, vib, finger cym, 3 woodblk, long rod, 2 db bows, bd,
  tam-tam II: tmp, marim, finger cym, glsp, 3 woodblks, long rod, bd,
  tam-tam
Peer

Krek, Uroš (1922-2008)

Concertino (1967)   14'
  solo pic
  1 2[1.eh] 2[1.bcl] 1 — 3 1 0 1 — tmp+1 — hp —
  cel — str
Breitkopf

Concerto for Horn (1961)   15'
  solo hn
  str
Breitkopf

Simfonietta (1951)   28'
  2[1.2/pic] 2 2 2 — 4 2 3 0 — tmp+2 — str
Breitkopf

Sinfonia per archi (1973)   15'
  str
Breitkopf

Krenek, Ernst (1900-1991)

Campo Marzio, op.80 (1937)   5'
  1 1 1 1 — 2 2 1 0 — tmp+1 — 2pf[pf.cel] — str
UE

Capriccio for Cello and Chamber   10'
Orchestra, op.145 (1955)
  solo vc
  1 1 1 1 — 1 1 1 0 — tmp+2 — hp — cel — str
UE

Concerto for Harp and Chamber   20'
Orchestra, op.126 (1951)
  solo hp
  1 1 1 1 — 2 1 0 0 — str
UE

Concerto for Organ and Strings,   10'
op.230 (1979)
  solo org
  str
UE

Concerto for Piano No.1, op.18   30'
(1923)
  solo pf
  2 2 2 2 — 2 1 0 0 — str
UE

Concerto for Piano No.2, op.81   23'
(1937)
  solo pf
  2 2 2 2 — 4 2 2 1 — tmp+1 — str
UE

Concerto Grosso No.2, op.25   30'
(1924)
  solo vn, va, vc
  2 2 2 2 — 2 1 0 0 — str
UE

Double Concerto; For Violin, Piano   20'
and Chamber Orchestra, op.124
(1950)
  solo vn, pf
  1 1 1 1 — 2 1 1 0 — str
UE

Durch die Nacht (Through the   18'
Night), op.67a (1931)
  solo high voice
  2 0 2 1 — 0 1 0 0 — pf — str[1.1.1.1.0]
UE

Monolog der Stella (Stella's   10'
Monologue); Concert Aria, op.57a
(1928)
  solo S
  2 2 2 2 — 1 1 0 0 — str
UE

Die Nachtigall (The Nightingale),   8'
op.68 (1931)
  solo coloratura S
  2 0 0 0 — 0 0 0 0 — str
UE

Ouvertüre "Triumph der   2'
Empfindsamkeit" (Triumph of
Sensitivity), op.43a (1926)
  2 2 2 2 — 0 2 3 0 — tmp — str
UE

Small Symphony, op.58 (1928)   15'
  2 0 3 2 — 0 3 2 1 — 2 mand, 2 banjo, gtr —
  tmp+1 — hp — str[2.0.0.0.2]
UE

Suite from "Triumph der   17'
Empfindsamkeit" (Triumph of
Sensitivity), op.43a (1926)
  solo S
  2 2 2 2 — 0 2 3 0 — mand — tmp+1 — str
UE

Symphonische Musik für 9   27'
Soloinstrumente, op.11 (1922)
  1 1 1 1 — 0 0 0 0 — str[1.1.1.1.1]
Fleisher

Symphony No.3, op.16 (1922)   27'
  2 2 2 3 — 2 1 0 0 — tmp — str
UE

Von Vorn Herein, op.219 (1974)   9'
  1 1 2 0 — 1 0 1 0 — 2pf[pf.cel] — str
UE

Kreutz, Arthur   (1906-1991)

American Dances (1941)   18'
  2[1.2/pic] 2 2 2 — 0 0 0 0 — str
  Contents - 1. Jig Time; 2. Blues No.1; 3. Blues No.2;
  4.Boogie Woogie
Fleisher

Krol, Bernhard   (1920-)

Concerto Grosso, op.15 (1956)   14'
  0 2[1.eh] 0 1 — 0 2 0 0 — str
Boosey & Hawkes

Kubik, Gail   (1914-1984)

Folk Song Suite   10'
  1 1 2 1 — 2 2 1 0 — 1perc — pf — str
  perc: tmp, sd, sus cym, woodblk, cowbell, tri, tambn, xyl, glsp
Peer

Gerald McBoing Boing   9'
  solo narrator
  1 1 1 1 — 1 1 0 0 — 1perc — pf — str[0.0.1.1.0]
  perc: tmp, sd, bd, sus cym, woodblk, templeblk, tambn, cast, gourd,
  glsp, gong, vib, tam-tam, ratchet, cowbell
Peer

Music for Dancing   9'
  1[1/pic] 1 2 1 — 2 2 1 1 — tmp+1 — pf — str
  perc: sd, tambn, cym, cast, woodblk, templeblk, tri, xyl
Peer

Kubo, Mayako   (1947-)

Miniatur I (1981)   16'
  0 0 1 1 — 0 0 0 0 — 2perc — pf — str[1.0.0.0.1]
Breitkopf

Kühnl, Claus   (1957-)

Monodie; Music of the Silence,   8'
op.12 (1981)
  1 0 1 0 — 0 1 1 0 — 1perc — pf — str
  Strings without db.
Breitkopf

Vision; For 20 String Soloists (1983)   10'
  str[6.6.3.3.2]
Breitkopf

Kulenty, Hanna   (1961-)

Breathe (1987)   12'
  str[5.5.4.3.2]
PWM

Passacaglia (1992)   10'
  1 1 1 1 — 1 1 1 0 — 1perc — hp — pf — str
PWM

Trigon (1989)   *13'*
  1 1 1 1 — 1 1 1 0 — 3perc — hp — pf — str
PWM

Kunad, Rainer   (1936-1995)

Concerto per Archi, conatum 36   *18'*
  str
Breitkopf

Dialog, conatum 40   *16'*
  1 0 0 1 — 0 1 1 0 — 1perc — hp — str
Breitkopf

Kupferman, Meyer   (1926-2003)

Little Symphony (1952)   *22'*
  1[1/pic] 2 0 2 — 2 0 0 0 — str
Weintraub

Kupkovic, Ladislav   (1936-)

March for Violin and Orchestra   *6'*
(1978)
  solo vn
  2 2 2 2 — 2 1 1 0 — tmp+1 — str
UE

Kurtág, György   (1926-)

Four Capriccios, op.9 (1971)   *11'*
  solo S
  1[1/pic] 1 1 1 — 1 0 0 0 — cimb — 1perc — hp —
  pf/cel — str
  Contents - 1. La Dame à la Licorne; 2. Tour Saint Jacques;
  3. Nyelvlecke; 4. Ars Poetica
UE

Kurz, Siegfried   (1930-)

Chamber Concerto, op.31   *18'*
  solo fl, ob, cl, bn, hn
  str
Breitkopf

Concerto for Trumpet, op.23   *19'*
  solo tpt
  str
Breitkopf

Music for Brass, Kettledrums and   *10'*
Strings, op.36
  0 0 0 0 — 0 2 3 0 — tmp — str
Breitkopf

Sonatina for Orchestra, op.34   *12'*
  2 2 2 2 — 2 2 0 0 — tmp — str
Breitkopf

Kyburz, Hanspeter   (1960-)

Parts (1994)   *24'*
  1[1/pic/rec] 1 2[1/Ebcl/bcl.2/bcl/ssx] 0 — 2 2 2 0
  — gtr — 3perc — hp — pf — str[1.1.1.1.1]
Breitkopf

L

La Violette, Wesley (1894-1978)

Nocturne for Orchestra   9'
1[1/pic(opt)] 2 2 1 — 2 1 1 0 — tmp+1 — str
perc: bd, cym
Fleisher

Lachenmann, Helmut (1935-)

Notturno; Music for Julia (1968)   15'
solo vc
2[1.2/pic] 0 0 0 — 0 1 0 0 — tmp+3 — hp —
str[6.4.4.3.2]
Breitkopf

Laderman, Ezra (1924-)

Cadence (1978)   10'
2 0 0 0 — 0 0 0 0 — str[4.0.1.2.1]
Schirmer

Nonet of the Night (2004)   21'
1 0 1 0 — 0 0 0 0 — 1perc — pf — str[1.1.1.1.1]
Schirmer

Laks, Simon (1901-1983)

Sinfonietta for Strings (1936)   14'
str
Boosey & Hawkes

Symphony for Strings (1964)   23'
str
Boosey & Hawkes

Lam, Bun-Ching (1954-)

Saudades de Macau (1989)   20'
2[1.2/pic] 1 1 1 — 1 1 1 0 — 1perc — hp — str
Subito

Spring Yearning (1976)   5'
solo S
1 1 1 1 — 1 0 0 0 — 1perc — pf — str
Subito

Lambert, Constant (1905-1951)

Comus: Suite from the Ballet to   15'
Purcell's music
2 2 0 2 — 0 2 0 0 — tmp — hp — str
Boosey & Hawkes

Lampersberg, Gerhard (1928-2002)

Ahnung; Concerto for Violin and   15'
Orchestra (1980)
solo vn
1 1 1 1 — 1 1 1 1 — asx — 3perc — 2pf[pf.harm]
— str
UE

Music; For Oboe and 13   7'
Instruments (1956)
solo ob
0 0 1[bcl] 1 — 1 1 1 0 — 1perc — hp —
2pf[pf.cel] — str[1.0.1.1.1]
perc: sd
UE

Pfeffer und Salz (Pepper and Salt)   12'
(1981)
solo narrator
0 0 1 0 — 1 1 1 0 — 1 — 1perc — cel —
str[1.1.1.1.1]
UE

Symphony (1956)   11'
1 0 1 1 — 1 1 1 0 — gtr — hp — cel —
str[1.0.1.1.0]
UE

Verwirrung; Concerto for Cello (1984)   15'
solo vc
1 1 1 1 — 1 1 1 1 — asx — 1perc —
3pf[pf.cel.harm] — str
Strings without vc.
UE

Lang, David (1957-)

Child (2001)   42'
1[1/pic] 0 1[1/bcl] 0 — 0 0 0 0 — 1perc — pf —
str[1.0.1.1.0]
Red Poppy

increase (2002)   11'
1 1 1 1 — 1 1 1 0 — 2perc — 2pf[pf.synth] —
str[1.1.1.1.1]
All strings amplified.
Red Poppy

Open (2008)   3'
   2 2 2 2 — 4 0 0 0 — str[0.0.0.1.1]
Red Poppy

Spud (1986)   10'
   1 1 1[1/bcl] 0 — 1 0 0 0 — tmp — str[1.0.1.1.1]
Red Poppy

Larsson, Lars-Erik   (1908-1986)

Divertimento, op.15 (1935)   12'
   1 1 1 1 — 1 0 0 0 — str
UE

Gustaviansk Suite, op.28   12'
   1 0 0 0 — 0 0 0 0 — hpsd — str
Fleisher

Pastoral for liten orkester (1941)   4'
   1 0 1 0 — 0 0 0 0 — hp — pf[opt] — str
Fleisher; Gehrmans

Sinfonietta, op.10 (1932)   20'
   str
UE

Laufer, Kenneth   (1943-)

The Twelve-Note Rag (1977)   5'
   1 1 1 1 — 1 1 1 1 — gtr — 1perc — pf —
   str[1.1.1.1.1]
   perc: dr
   Arranged by Gunther Schuller.
GunMar

Lavista, Mario   (1943-)

Lacrymosa   13'
   0 2 1 2[1.cbn] — 0 0 4 0 — 1perc — str
   perc: 2 bd, tam-tam, chimes
Peer

Layton, Billy Jim   (1924-2004)

Divertimento, op.6 (1958)   11'
   0 0 1 1 — 0 0 1 0 — 1perc — hpsd —
   str[1.0.0.1.0]
Schirmer

Lazar, Filip   (1894-1936)

Concerto Grosso No.1, op.17   22'
(1930)
   0 2 0 2 — 2 1 0 0 — tmp — str
Fleisher; Durand

Concerto No.4; Concerto da   20'
Camera, op.24 (1935)
   1[1/pic] 1 1 1 — 1 1 1 0 — 1perc — pf —
   str[1.0.1.1.1]
Fleisher; Durand

Suite Valaque (1925)   10'
   2 2 2 2 — 2 2 0 0 — tmp — hp — cel — str
UE

Lazarof, Henri   (1932-)

Espaces (1966)   17'
   2 0 2[1.bcl] 0 — 0 0 0 0 — 2pf — str[0.0.2.2.0]
AMP

Le Grand, Robert   (1894-1964)

Dimanche d'été
   1 1 2 1 — 2 1 0 0 — tmp+1 — hp — str
   Contents - 1. En Forêt; 2. Au Fil de L'eau; 3. Guinguette
Salabert

Effets de Nuit   4'
   2 3 3 2 — 2 0 0 0 — str
   Contents - 1. Paysage Nocturne; 2. L'Heure du Berger
Salabert

Lecocq, Charles   (1832-1918)

Fricassée   4'
   2[1.pic] 2 2 2 — 2 2 1 0 — 1perc — str
   perc: tri
Boosey & Hawkes

Ledenjov, Roman   (1930-)

Notturni (1968)   7'
   1 1 1 1 — 1 0 0 0 — str
UE

Lees, Benjamin (1924-2010)

Concertante Breve (1959) 16'
0 1 0 0 — 2 0 0 0 — pf — str
Boosey & Hawkes

Concerto for Chamber Orchestra (1966) 18'
2[1.2/pic] 2[1.2/eh] 2[1.2/bcl] 2[1.2/cbn] — 2 2 0 0
— tmp+1 — str
perc: cym, tri, bd, sd
Boosey & Hawkes

Divertimento-Burlesca (1957) 22'
2[1.2/pic] 2[1.2/eh] 2 2 — 2 2 1 0 — 1perc — hp
— str
perc: glsp, xyl, cym, tri, bd, sd
Boosey & Hawkes

Interlude for String Orchestra (1957) 12'
str
Boosey & Hawkes

Intermezzo (1998) 6'
str
Boosey & Hawkes

LeFanu, Nicola (1947-)

Farne (1980) 20'
2 2 2 2 — 2 3 3 1 — 3perc — str
Novello

Preludio I (1967) 6'
1 1 1 1 — 1 0 0 0 — str
Novello

Preludio II (1976) 7'
1 1 1 1 — 2 0 0 0 — str
Novello

Lehmann, Hans Ulrich (1937-)

Chamber Music II (1979) 13'
2 2 2[1.bcl] 1 — 2 2 0 0 — 2perc — str[0.0.0.2.2]
Breitkopf

Composition for 19 (1965) 10'
1 2 2 1 — 1 1 1 0 — 2perc — hp — 2pf[pf.cel] —
str[1.1.1.1.1]
perc: chimes, gong, cym, tam-tam, 3 tom-tom, 2 sd, vib
Schott

Leigh, Walter (1905-1942)

Suite from Shakespeare's "A Midsummer Night's Dream" (1937) 15'
1 0 1 0 — 0 1 0 0 — tmp —hpsd [or pf] — str
Hansen

Lendvai, Erwin (1882-1949)

Archaische Tänze; Neun sinfonische Reigen für kleines Orchester, op.30 (1922)
1[1/pic] 1[1/eh] 1 1 — 1 1 1 0 — tmp+1 — hp —
str
Fleisher; Simrock

Kammersuite, op.32 (1923) 16'
1 1 1 1 — 1 0 0 0 — hp — str
Fleisher

Tafelmusik: From op.48 (1932)
0 2 0 0 — 2 0 0 0 — str
Fleisher; Kistner & Siegel

León, Tania (1943-)

Bele (1981) 15'
2 0 0 0 — 0 4 3 0 — 1perc — pf — str
Peer

The Beloved (1972) 10'
1 1 1 1 — 0 0 0 0 — pf — str[0.0.0.1.1]
Peer

The Golden Windows (1982) 30'
1[1/pic/afl] 1[1/eh] 0 0 — 0 1 0 0 — 1perc —
2pf[pf.hpsd] — str
perc: sd, bd, 3 tom-tom, tambn, sus cym, finger cym, tri, templeblk,
vib, bicycle horn
Peer

Hechizos (1995) 15'
1[1/pic] 1 2[1.bcl/ssx/tsx] 0 — 1 1 1 0 — gtr —
2perc — pf/cel/hpsd — str[1.0.1.1.1]
perc: I: cast, marac, 2 agogo, guiro, tambn, 2 bongo, 3 tom-tom,
zurdo, marim II: guiro, marac, claves, 2 conga, tom-tom, 4 rototom, 2
tmp, marim
Peer

Indigena (1991) 8'
1 1 1 1 — 1 1 0 0 — 1perc — pf — str[1.1.1.1.1]
perc: 2 rototoms, 2 tom-tom, 2 porcelain mugs, 1 shaker on stand,
sm bd, marim
Peer

sin normas ajenas (1994)   7'
1[1/pic] 1 1 0 — 0 0 0 0 — 2perc — pf —
str[1.1.1.1.0]
Peer

Tones (1970)   18'
2 2 1 0 — 1 0 1 1 — tmp+2 — pf — str
perc: I: templeblk, cym, bd, woodblk, gong, tri, vib, tom-tom II: tom-
tom, xyl, tri, bells
Peer

Leplin, Emanuel   (1917-1972)

Three Dances for Small Orchestra   14'
(1942)
2 2 2 2 — 2 2 0 0 — tmp — str
Strings without vc or db.
Fleisher

Leschetitzky, Theodor   (1896-1948)

Scherzo   10'
solo hn
2 2 2 2 — 2 2 0 0 — tmp+1 — str
UE

Levi, Paul Alan   (1941-)

Elegy and Recreations (1981)   16'
0 1 1 0 — 1 0 0 0 — pf — str[1.0.1.1.0]
Margun

Levinson, Gerald   (1951-)

Light Dances / Stones Sing (1978)   22'
1[1/pic] 1[1/eh] 2 1 — 1 2 1[btbn] 0 — 3perc —
pf/cel — str[1.1.1.1.1]
Margun

Levy, Marvin David   (1932-)

Trialogus I (1972)   18'
0 0 0 0 — 3 0 0 0 — hp — 2pf[pf.org] — str
Boosey & Hawkes

Trialogus II (1972)   15'
1 2 1 1 — 1 1 1 0 — hp — org — str
Boosey & Hawkes

Lewis, Harold Merrills

Two Preludes on Southern Folk   9'
Hymn Tunes
1 1 1 1 — 2 0 0 0 — tmp — str
Fleisher

Leyendecker, Ulrich   (1946-)

Jiddische Rumba (1977)   15'
0 0 1 0 — 0 0 1[btbn] 0 — tsx — elec gtr — 2perc
— pf/elec org — str[0.0.0.1.0]
Sikorski

Verwandlung; Four Pieces for   15'
Chamber Orchestra (1980)
3[1.2/pic.afl] 0 1[1/bcl] 0 — 2 1 1 1 — 1[asx/tsx]
— 2perc — hp — pf/cel — str[5.0.4.3.2]
Sikorski

Liebermann, Rolf   (1910-1999)

Lied der Yvette: From the Opera   2'
"Leonore 40/45" (1952)
solo S
2 2 3 0 — 0 0 0 0 — str
UE

Suite on Six Swiss Folksongs   10'
(1947)
2 2 2 2 — 2 0 0 0 — hp — str
Contents - 1. Es isch kei sölige Stamme; 2. Im Aargäu sind
zwei Liebi; 3. Schönster Abestärn; 4. Durs Oberland uf und
durs Oberland ab; 5. S'isch äben e Mönsch uf Ärde; 6. Üsen
Ätti.
UE

Lieberson, Peter   (1946-)

Accordance for 8 Instruments   12'
(1975)
1[afl] 1 1[bcl] 0 — 0 0 0 0 — 1perc — hp — pf —
str[0.0.1.0.1]
perc: vib (or glsp)
AMP

Free and Easy Wanderer (1998)   6'
1[pic] 1 2[1.2/bcl] 1 — 1 1 1 0 — 1perc — pf —
str[1.1.1.1.1]
AMP

Lalita; Chamber Variations (1984)   18'
   1[1/pic] 1 1[1/bcl] 0 — 1 0 0 0 — 1perc — pf —
   str[1.0.1.1.1]
AMP

Raising the Gaze (1988)   7'
   1[1/pic] 0 1[1/bcl] 0 — 0 0 0 0 — 1perc — pf —
   str[1.0.1.1.0]
AMP

Ligeti, György   (1923-2006)

Concerto for Piano (1988)   22'
   solo pf
   1[1/pic] 1 1[1/alto occarina] 1 — 1 1 1 0 — 2perc
   — str[1.1.1.1.1]
   perc: tri, 2 crot, 2 sus cym, 4 woodblks, 5 templeblks, tambour de
   basque, sd, 3 rototoms, 4 tom-tom, bd, guiro, cast, whip, siren
   whistle, alarm whistle, slide whistle, flexatone, Chromonica (Hohner),
   glsp, xyl
   Also possible with str(8.6.6.4.3).
Schott

Fragment (1961)   8'
   0 0 0 1[cbn] — 0 0 1[btbn] 1[cbtu] — 1perc — hp
   — 2pf[pf.hpsd] — str[0.0.0.0.3]
UE

Kammerkonzert (Chamber   21'
Concerto) (1970)
   1[1/pic] 1[1/eh/ob d'am] 2[1.2/bcl] 0 — 1 0 1 0 —
   2pf[pf/cel.hpsd/hamorg(or harm)] — str[1.1.1.1.1]
Schott

Melodien (1971)   13'
   1[1/pic] 1[1/ob d'am] 1 1 — 2 1 1 1 — 1perc[opt]
   — pf/cel — str(min)[1.1.1.1.1]
   perc: 3 tmp, crot, glsp, vib, xyl
Schott

Lincke, Paul   (1866-1946)

Hanako; Japanese Intermezzo   3'
(1939)
   1 1 1 0 — 0 1 1 0 — tmp+1 — harm — str
Fleisher; Schott

Träume vom Lido (1939)   4'
   1 1 1 0 — 0 1 1 0 — tmp+1 — harm — str
Fleisher; Schott

Lindberg, Magnus   (1958-)

Arena II (1996)   15'
   1[1/pic] 1 1 1[1/cbn] — 2 1 1 0 — 1perc — hp —
   pf/cel — str[1.1.1.1.1]
Chester Novello

Away (1994)   5'
   solo cl
   1perc — pf — str
Chester Novello

Corrente (1992)   14'
   1[1/afl] 1[1/eh] 1 1 — 2 1 1 0 — 1perc — hp — pf
   — str[1.1.1.1.1]
Chester Novello

Corrente; China Version (2000)   14'
   1[1/afl] 1[1/eh] 1 0 — 0 0 1 0 — 1perc — pf —
   str[1.1.1.1.1]
Chester Novello

Counter Phrases (2003)   6'
   1 1 1 1 — 1 1 1 0 — 2perc — 2pf — str[1.1.1.1.1]
   perc: vib, tri, mark tree, 3 Chinese cym, 4 sus cym, bongos, bd, tam-
   tam, marim, crot, glsp
Boosey & Hawkes

Coyote Blues (1993)   12'
   1 1 1 1 — 1 1 1 0 — 1perc — pf — str[1.1.1.1.1]
Chester Novello

Duo Concertante (1992)   13'
   solo cl, vc
   1 1[1/eh] 0 0 — 0 0 0 0 — gtr — 1perc — hp —
   str[0.0.1.0.1]
   perc: vib
Chester Novello

Engine (1996)   16'
   1[1/pic] 1 1 1[1/cbn] — 2 1 1 0 — 1perc — pf —
   str[1.1.1.1.1]
Chester Novello

Joy (1990)   30'
   2[1.2/pic] 1 3[1.2/Ebcl.bcl] 1[1/cbn] — 2 1 1 1 —
   2perc — 2pf[pf/cel.kybd] — str[1.1.2.2.1]
Hansen

Jubilees (2002)   15'
   1[1/pic] 1 1 1[1/cbn] — 2 1 1 0 — 2perc — hp —
   str[1.1.1.1.1]
   perc: vib, bd, mark tree, marim, glsp, 2 sus cym, tam-tam
Boosey & Hawkes

Marea (1990)   13'
   2[1.2/pic] 2[1.eh] 2[1.bcl] 2[1.cbn] — 2 1 1 1 —
tmp+1 — pf — str[6.6.5.4.3]
Hansen

Tendenza (1982)   12'
   1[pic] 1 3[1.Ebcl.bcl] 2[1.cbn] — 1 1 1 1 — asx —
2perc — hp — pf — str[1.1.1.1.1]
Chester Novello

Linke, Norbert   (1933-)

Divisioni   11'
   2[1.2/pic] 2 2 2 — 2 2 0 0 — str
Breitkopf

Konkretionen V (1969)   11'
   1[1/pic] 1 2[1.bcl] 1 — 1 1 1 0 — 2perc — str
Strings without db.
Breitkopf

Profit tout Clair (1967)   13'
   0 1 1 1 — 1 0 0 0 — str[1.1.1.1.1]
Can be done with full strings.
Breitkopf

Lloyd, Jonathan   (1948-)

Keir's Kick (1982)   5'
   str
Boosey & Hawkes

Symphony No.1 (1983)   28'
   2[1/afl.2/pic] 2[1.2/eh] 2[1.2/bcl] 2[1.2/cbn] — 2
2[1/pic tpt(opt). 2] 0 0 — tmp — str
Boosey & Hawkes

Symphony No.3 (1987)   31'
   1[1/pic/afl] 1[1/eh] 2[1.2/bcl] 1[1/cbn] — 2 0 0 0 —
str[3.3.2.2.1]
Boosey & Hawkes

Lobanov, Vasily   (1947-)

Sinfonietta for Chamber Orchestra,   20'
op.47 (1986)
   1 1 1 1 — 1 1 1 0 — tmp+1 — str[1.1.1.1.1]
perc: chimes
VAAP

Symphony No.1 for Chamber   25'
Orchestra (1977)
   4 0 0 0 — 0 1 0 0 — 3perc — hpsd —
str[8.7.6.5.4]
VAAP

Symphony No.2 for Chamber   28'
Orchestra; "Intermezzo," op.36
(1981)
   2 0 0 0 — 0 1 0 0 — tmp+1 — hp — 2pf[cel.hpsd]
— str
VAAP

Locklair, Dan   (1949-)

Dayspring; Fanfare/Concertino for   7'
Solo Guitar and Orchestra (1988)
   solo gtr
   2[1.2/pic] 2 2 2 — 2 2 2 0 — 2perc — str
Subito

In Memory H. H. L. (2005)   4'
   str
Subito

In the Autumn Days (1984)   14'
   1 2 1 2 — 2 1 0 0 — 1perc — pf — str
Subito

Loevendie, Theo   (1930-)

Back Bay Bicinium   14'
   1[pic] 0 1 0 — 0 0 0 0 — 1perc — pf —
str[1.0.1.1.0]
Peer

Laps   11'
   1[1/pic] 0 1[1/Ebcl] 1 — 0 1 1 0 — asx — 1perc
— pf — str[0.0.0.1.1]
perc: tri, woodblk, 2 templeblks, cym, sd, marim
Peer

Lopatnikoff, Nikolai   (1903-1976)

Symphonietta, op.27 (1942)   17'
   1[1/pic] 1 1 1 — 1 1 0 0 — tmp+1 — pf — str
Fleisher

Lord, David   (1944-)

Septet (1967)   12'
   1 0 1 0 — 0 0 0 0 — hp — str[1.1.1.1.0]
UE

Lorentzen, Bent   (1935-)

Paesaggio (1983)   12'
1 1 1 1 — 1 0 0 0 — str[1.0.1.0.0]
Hansen

Paradiesvogel (1983)   12'
1 0 1 0 — 0 0 0 0 — gtr — 1perc — pf —
str[1.0.0.1.0]
Hansen

Wunderblumen (1982)   14'
1 1 1 1 — 1 0 0 0 — 1perc — pf — str[1.1.1.1.1]
Hansen

Zauberspiegel (1998)   12'
1 0 1 0 — 1 0 0 0 — 1perc — hp — str[1.0.1.1.0]
Hansen

Losonczy, Andor   (1932-)

Phonophobie (1975)   18'
1 0 1 1 — 0 1 1 0 — pf — str[1.0.0.0.1]
UE

Lothar, Mark   (1902-1985)

Concertino, op.79 (1972)   30'
solo 2pf
1perc — str
Boosey & Hawkes

Ludewig, Wolfgang   (1926-)

Fantasia; On a Theme by W. A.   11'
Mozart (1977)
1 1 2[1.bcl] 0 — 0 1 1 0 — 1perc — pf — str
perc: marim
Breitkopf

Luening, Otto   (1900-1996)

Prelude to a Hymn Tune by William   10'
Billings (1943)
1 1 1 1 — 1 0 0 0 — pf — str
Fleisher

Lukáš, Zdenek   (1928-2007)

Concertino Dedicato, op.248   18'
solo vn
str
Boosey & Hawkes

Concerto for Piano No.3, op.258   25'
(1993)
solo pf
3[1.2.pic] 2 2 2 — 4 2 3 1 — 1perc — str
Boosey & Hawkes

Vox Cordis Mei, op.293 (1997)   16'
solo org
0 0 0 0 — 0 2 0 0 — str
Boosey & Hawkes

Lumsdaine, David   (1931-)

Salvation Creek with Eagle (1974)   18'
1 1 1 1 — 1 1 1 0 — pf — str[4.4.4.4.2]
Also possible with strings (8.8.8.8.4).
UE

Sunflower (1975)   20'
1 2 2 2 — 2 0 0 0 — str
UE

Lutosławski, Witold   (1913-1994)

Bucolics (1952)   7'
1 1 1 1 — 1 0 0 0 — str[1.0.1.1.1]
Arranged by Steven Stucky.
Chester Novello

Chain 1 [Launch 1] (1983)   9'
1[1/pic/afl] 1[1/eh] 1 1 — 1 1 1 0 — 1perc — hpsd
— str[1.1.1.1.1]
Chester Novello

Chain 2 [Launch 2]; Dialogue for   18'
Violin and Orchestra (1985)
solo vn
2[1/pic.2/pic] 2[1.2/eh] 2[1.2/bcl] 2 — 0 2 2 0 —
tmp+1 — pf/cel — str[6.6.4.4.2]
Chester Novello

Chantefleur et Chantefables (1990)   20'
solo S
1 1 2[1.Ebcl] 1 — 1 1 1 0 — tmp+1 — hp — pf/cel
— str[8.6.4.4.2]
Chester Novello

Dance Preludes; 2nd Version   7'
(1955)
    solo cl
    tmp+1 — hp — pf — str[8.8.6.6.4]
Chester Novello

Dance Preludes; 3rd Version (1959)   7'
    1 1 1 1 — 1 0 0 0 — str[1.1.1.1.0]
Chester Novello

Dance Preludes (1959)   7'
    1 1 1 1 — 1 0 0 0 — str[1.0.1.1.1]
    Version for 9 instruments.
PWM

Five Folk Melodies (1952)   9'
    str
Chester Novello

Grave; Metamorphosis (1981)   7'
    solo vc
    str[4.3.3.2.1]
Chester Novello

Interlude (1989)   6'
    1[pic] 1[1/eh] 2 1 — 0 1 1 0 — 1perc — hp —
    pf/cel — str[2.2.2.2.1]
Chester Novello

Jesien (Autumn) (1951)   7'
    solo Mz
    2 1 2 1 — 0 1 0 0 — str
    Contents - 1. W listopadzie [In October]; 2. Swierszcz [The
    Cricket]; 3. Mgla [Fog]; 4. Deszczyk jesienny [Light Autumn
    Rain]
Chester Novello

Jeux Vénitiens (Venetian Games)   13'
(1961)
    2[1.2/pic] 1 3[1.2.3/bcl] 1 — 1 1 1 0 — tmp+3 —
    hp — 2pf[pf4hand/cel] — str[4.0.3.3.2]
    perc: td, xyl, cym, tam-tam, vib, claves, 3 sd, 5 tom-tom, 3 sus cym
Moeck; PWM

Little Suite (1951)   11'
    2[1.pic] 2 2 2 — 4 3 3 1 — tmp+1 — str
Chester Novello

Little Suite (1951)   11'
    1 1 2 1 — 1 0 0 0 — tmp — str
    Version for Chamber Orchestra.
PWM

Musique funèbre (1958)   14'
    str[12.12.8.8.6]
    Can be done with larger string groups.
Chester Novello; PWM

Overture for Strings (1949)   5'
    str
Chester Novello

Paroles tissées (Woven words)   15'
(1965)
    solo T
    1perc — hp — pf — str[5.5.3.3.1]
Chester Novello

Partita (1988)   15'
    solo vn
    2[1/pic.2/pic] 0 2[1.2/bcl] 2[1.2/cbn] — 0 2 2 0 —
    tmp+1 — hp — 2pf[pf.cel] — str
Chester Novello; PWM

Prelude for Guildhall School of   2'
Music; Worldes Blis Ne Last No
Throwe (1989)
    2 2 2 2 — 2 2 2 1 — tmp+1 — hp — str
Chester Novello

Preludes and Fugue (1972)   34'
    str[7.0.3.2.1]
Chester Novello

Six Children's Songs (1947)   8'
    solo Mz
    1 1 2 1 — 0 0 0 0 — hp — str
Chester Novello

Slides; For 11 Soloists (1988)   4'
    1 1 1 1 — 1 0 0 0 — 1perc — pf/cel —
    str[1.0.1.1.1]
PWM; PWM

Spijze, spij (Sleep, sleep) (1954)   4'
    solo S
    1 0 1 1 — 2 0 0 0 — str
Chester Novello

Ten Polish Dances (1951)   12'
    1 1 2 1 — 1 1 0 0 — 2perc — str
PWM

Lutyens, Elisabeth   (1906-1983)

Six Tempi for 10 Instruments   12'
(1957)
    1 1 1 1 — 1 1 0 0 — pf — str[1.0.1.1.0]
EMI

M

Maasz, Gerhard   (1906-1984)

Musik (Nr.1)   14'
  1 0 1 0 — 0 0 0 0 — str
  Fleisher; Ries & Erler

Tripartita (1967)   15'
  3 0 0 0 — 0 0 0 0 — pf/hpsd — str
  Sikorski

Maayani, Ami   (1936-)

Songs of King Solomon (1962)   13'
  str[4.3.2.2.1]
  Boosey & Hawkes

MacKenzie, Sir Alexander C.   (1847-1935)

Benedictus, op.37, No.3   8'
  2 0 2 2 — 2 0 0 0 — str
  Kalmus

MacMillan, James   (1959-)

Cumnock Fair (1999)   12'
  solo pf
  str[8.6.4.4.2]
  Also possible with string quintet.
  Boosey & Hawkes

A Deep but Dazzling Darkness   22'
(2002)
  solo vn
  2[1/pic.afl] 1 2[1.cbcl] 0 — 1 2 1 1 — tape —
  2perc — hp — 2pf[pf.pf/cel] — str[1.1.1.1.1]
  perc: I=vib, 5 cowbells, 5 chimes, 2 bongos, bd, 4 gliss gongs
  II=tuned gongs, tambn, sd, ped bd, hi-hat, tam-tam, watergong
  2. pf is tuned a quarter-tone higher. Can also be performed
  with strings (8.6.4.4.2).
  Boosey & Hawkes

Í; A Meditation on Iona (1996)   17'
  1perc — str
  perc: chimes, steel pans, lg thundersheet
  Boosey & Hawkes

Kiss on Wood (1993)   9'
  solo vc
  str
  Boosey & Hawkes

Memoire imperiale; A Variation on   5'
General John Reid's March "Garb
of Gaul" (1993)
  2 2[1.eh] 2[1.cbl] 2[1.cbn] — 2 2 0 0 — tmp+1 —
  str
  perc: sd
  Boosey & Hawkes

The Sacrifice: Three Interludes   15'
(2006)
  2[1.2/pic] 2[1.2/eh] 2[1.2/bcl] 2[1.cbn] — 4 3 3 1
  — tmp+3 — hp — str
  perc: glsp, vib, tambn, bd, chimes, woodblk, sd, sus cym, crot, tuned
  gongs, guiro, vibraslap, tam-tam
  From his opera "The Sacrifice."
  Contents - 1. The Parting; 2. Passacaglia; 3. The Investiture
  mvt durations: 4' 5' 6'
  Boosey & Hawkes

Sinfonietta (1991)   19'
  1[afl/pic] 1[eh] 1[Ebcl/bcl] 1[cbn] — 1 1[pic tpt] 1 1
  — ssx — 2perc — hp — pf — str[6.6.4.4.2]
  perc: tri, vib, sd, woodblk, tam-tam, glsp, 2 cowbells, 2 congas, bd,
  sus cym, chimes, 2 tom-tom, anvil, lg tam-tam, lg sizzle cym
  Also possible with strings (1.1.1.1.1).
  Boosey & Hawkes

Symphony No.2 (1999)   24'
  2[1.2/pic] 2[1.2/eh] 2[1.2/bcl] 2[1.cbn] — 2 2 0 0
  — 2perc — hp — str
  perc: glsp, vib, chimes, bell tree, bongo, sd, bd, cym, tam-tam
  Boosey & Hawkes

Tryst (1989)   30'
  2[1.2/pic] 2[1.2/eh] 2[1.2/bcl] 2[1.2/cbn] — 2 2 0 0
  — tmp/perc — str
  perc: wind chimes, bell tree
  Boosey & Hawkes

MacRae, Stuart   (1976-)

The Broken Spectre (1996)   7'
  1 1 1 1 — 1 0 0 0 — str[1.1.1.1.1]
  Novello

The Broken Spectre (revisited)   7'
(1996)
  1 0 1 0 — 1 1 1 0 — 2perc — pf — str[1.0.0.1.0]
  Novello

Portrait (1999)   19'
  1[1/afl] 1[eh] 1[1/Ebcl] 1 — 2 1 1 0 —
  str[3.0.3.2.2]
  Novello

Portrait II (2000)   13'
  0 2 0 0 — 2 0 0 0 — 1perc — hp — str[4.0.3.2.1]
  perc: marim
  Novello

The Witch's Kiss (1997) 10'
1[1/afl] 1 1[1/bcl] 1 — 1 1 1 0 — 2perc — pf —
str[1.1.1.1.1]
Novello

Maganini, Quinto (1897-1974)

An Ornithological Suite, op.23 (1931) 15'
1[1/pic] 1 2[1.2(opt)] 1 — 2[1.2(opt)] 1 0 0 —
tmp+1 — hp[or pf] — str
Fleisher; Fischer (J.)

Magnard, Albéric (1865-1914)

Chant Funebre, op.9 (1895) 15'
2 2 2 2 — 4 1 3 0 — tmp — hp — str
Kalmus

Suite in Ancient Style, op.2 (1889) 20'
2 2 2 2 — 2 1 0 0 — tmp+1 — str
Kalmus

Symphony No.3 in B minor, op.11 30'
(1896)
2 2 2 2 — 4 2 3 0 — tmp — str
Kalmus

Malec, Ivo (1925-)

Tutti; Concert collectif (1962) 8'
2[1.2/pic] 1 2[1.bcl] 1[1/cbn] — 2 2 1 0 — tape —
3perc — hp — str
Breitkopf

Maler, Wilhelm (1902-1976)

Drei Festmusiken
1[opt] 1[opt] 1[opt] 0 — 0 0 0 0 — str
db is opt.
Fleisher; Tonger

Malipiero, Gian Francesco (1882-1973)

Endecatode; For 14 Instruments 15'
and Percussion (1966)
1 1 1 1 — 1 1 1 0 — 1perc — 2pf[pf.cel] —
str[1.1.1.1.1]
UE

Grottesco (1918) 9'
1[1/pic] 1 1 — 1 1 0 0 — 1perc — pf —
str[6.6.4.4.2]
Chester Novello

Oriente Immaginario; Tre stui per 15'
piccola Orchestra (1920)
1[1/pic] 1 0 1 — 0 0 0 0 — 1perc — hp —
2pf[pf.cel] — str[4.4.4.4.2]
Fleisher; Chester Novello

Ricercari (1925) 16'
1[1/pic] 1 1 1 — 1 0 0 0 — str[0.0.4.1.1]
Fleisher; UE

Ritrovari (1926) 15'
1 1 1 1 — 1 0 0 0 — str[0.0.4.1.1]
UE

Sette Canzonette Veneziane 10'
(1961)
solo medium voice
1 1 1 1 — 1 0 0 0 — pf — str
UE

Manén, Joan (1883-1971)

Caprice Nr. I, op.A-14 11'
solo vn
2 2 2 2 — 2 2 0 0 — 1perc — str
UE

Caprice Nr. II, op.A-15 9'
solo vn
2 2 2 2 — 2 2 0 0 — 1perc — str
UE

Chanson et Étude, op.A-8 8'
solo vn
str[5.5.3.2.2]
UE

Concerto da Camera Nr.2, op.A-24 32'
solo vn
hp — str
UE

Concerto Espagnol, op.A-7 28'
solo vn
1 1 1 1 — 4 2 0 0 — 1perc — hp — str
UE

Divertimento, op.A-32 (1937) 14'
2 2 2 2 — 2 0 0 0 — tmp+1 — str
perc: tambn
Fleisher; Eschig

Tartini-Variations; Introduction,   12'
Andante et Variazioni, op.A-2
solo vn
2 2 2 2 — 4 2 0 0 — tmp — str
UE

Manicke, Dietrich   (1923-)

Musica serena (1981)   18'
str
Boosey & Hawkes

Mansurian, Tigran   (1939-)

Da Ich Nicht Hoffe für 14   10'
Instrumentalisten; (In Memoriam
Igor Stravinsky) (1983)
1 1 1 1 — 1 1 1 0 — 2perc — pf/cel —
str[1.1.1.1.0]
Sikorski

Tovem for 15 Instruments (1979)   10'
1 1 1 1 — 1 1 1 0 — 1perc — 2pf[pf.hpsd] —
str[1.1.1.1.1]
Schirmer

Markevitch, Igor   (1912-1983)

Petite Suite d'après Schumann   16'
(1933)
1[1/pic] 2[1.2/eh] 2[1.2/bcl] 2[1.2/cbn] — 2 1 1 0
— 1perc — pf — str[3.0.2.2.1]
perc: tmp, sd w/o snares, tri, bd w/ cym
Boosey & Hawkes

Maros, Rudolf   (1917-1982)

Eufonia No.1   12'
4perc — 2hp — str
perc: I: xylorimba, tri, 2 sus cym, glsp, tmp, marac II: xylorimba, 3
crot, 3 bongo, sus cym, claves, guiro, chimes III: vib, 2 metal plates,
2 tom-tom, 3 templeblks, 2 gong IV: vib, metal plate, 2 dr, woodblk,
bd, tmp
Peer

Gemma; In Memoriam Zoltán   12'
Kodály
2[1.afl] 2[1.eh] 2[1.bcl] 0 — 4 2 0 0 — str
Peer

Musica da Camera per 11   10'
1[1/afl] 0 2 0 — 0 0 0 0 — 1perc — hp — hpsd —
str[1.1.1.1.1]
perc: vib, marim, sus cym, 2 gong, marac, metal blk
Peer

Sinfonietta No.1   6'
2[or rec] 0 0 0 — 0 2 0 0 — tmp+1 — str
perc: sm dr, tri
Peer

Marquez, Arturo   (1950-)

Danzón No.2 (1994)   11'
2[1.2/pic] 2 2 2 — 4 2 3 1 — tmp+3 — pf — str
perc: I: claves, sd, lg sus cym II: guiro, 3 tom-toms III: bd
Peer

Danzón No.3 (1994)   13'
solo gtr
0 1 3[1.Ebcl.bcl] 1 — 1 0 0 0 — 2perc — hp — pf
— str[1.1.0.1.1]
perc: I: tmp, claves, tam-tam II: guiro, sus cym
Also available in reduced orchestration: fl and gtr soli - 0020
- 2000 - 2perc - str.
Peer

Danzón No.4 (1996)   12'
2[1.2/pic] 2 2 2 — 4 2 3 1 — ssx — tmp+3 — pf
— str
Also available in reduced orchestration: 1111 - ssx - 1110 -
2perc - pf - str (1.1.1.1.1 - or small complements).
Peer

Espejos en la Arena (2000)   25'
solo vc
3[1.2.pic] 2 3[1.2.Ebcl] 2 — 2 0 0 0 — tmp+2 —
str
Peer

Paisajes Bajo el Signo de Cosmos   10'
(1993)
2 2 2 2 — 4 2 3 1 — tmp+4 — hp — str
perc: I: glsp, xyl, claves II: sd III: tambn, cym, sus cym, marac, guiro
IV: bd
Peer

Marsh, Roger   (1949-)

Dying for It (1988)   12'
1 1 1 1 — 0 0 0 0 — 1perc — str[1.1.1.1.1]
perc: marim
Novello

Marthinsen, Niels   (1963-)

A Bright Kind of High (1996)   7'
1 0 1 0 — 0 1 0 0 — hp — pf — str[1.0.1.1.0]
Hansen

Chimes at Midnight (1993)   18'
1 1 1 1 — 1 1 1 0 — 1perc — pf — str[1.1.1.1.1]
Hansen

Cupid and Death (1994)   20'
1 0 1[1/bcl] 0 — 0 0 0 0 — 1perc — pf —
str[1.0.1.1.0]
Hansen

A Miniature (1995)   8'
1 1 1 1 — 1 1 1 0 — 1perc — pf — str[1.1.1.1.1]
Hansen

Outland (1999)   10'
0 0 2[1/bcl.2/bcl] 0 — 3 2 0 0 — 2perc — pf —
str[4.0.0.2.0]
Hansen

Shadow Figures (1992)   21'
1 0 1 0 — 1 1 0 0 — pf — str[1.0.0.1.0]
Hansen

Martin, Frank   (1890-1974)

Concerto (1949)   22'
1 1 1 1 — 1 1 1 0 — tmp+2 — str
UE

Concerto for Cello (1966)   28'
solo vc
2 1 2 1 — 2 1 1 0 — asx — tmp+1 — hp —
2pf[pf.cel] — str
UE

Concerto for Harpsichord (1952)   20'
solo hpsd
2 1 1 1 — 2 1 0 0 — str
UE

Concerto for Violin (1951)   30'
solo vn
2[1.2/pic] 2 2 2 — 2 2 1 0 — tmp — hp — pf —
str
UE

Danse de la Peur (1936)   15'
solo 2 pf
0 0 2 0 — 0 2 3 1 — 2sx[asx.tsx] — tmp+1 — cel
— str
UE

Fox Trot (1927)   5'
1 1 1 1 — 1 1 1 0 — pf — str
UE

Overture to Racine's "Athalie"   9'
(1946)
2 2 2 2 — 4 2 1 0 — tmp+1 — hp — pf — str
UE

Passacaille (1944)   13'
str
UE

Die Weise von Liebe und Tod des   58'
Cornets Christoph Rilke (1943)
solo A
2[1.2/pic] 1[1/eh] 1 1 — 2 1 1 0 — asx — tmp+2
— hp — 2pf[pf.cel] — str
UE

Martino, Donald   (1931-2005)

Concerto for Alto Saxophone and   24'
Orchestra (1987)
solo asx
1 2 1 2 — 3 1 1 0 — 2perc — pf — str
Dantalian

Triple Concerto (1977)   26'
solo cl, bcl, cbcl
1 1 0 2 — 1 1 2 0 — 2perc — 2pf[pf.cel] —
str[1.1.1.1.1]
Dantalian

Martinů, Bohuslav   (1890-1959)

The Amazing Flight; Ballet   19'
mécanique, H.159 (1927)
0 0 2[1.2/tam-tam] 1[1/tam-tam] — 0 1 0 0 — pf
— str[1.1.2.1.0]
Schott

Comedy on the Bridge: Little Suite   6'
from the Opera (1935)
1[1/pic] 1 1 1 — 2 1 1 0 — tmp+1 — pf — str
perc: cym, bd, sd
Boosey & Hawkes

Concerto for 2 Violins and   17'
Orchestra, H.329 (1950)
solo 2 vn
2 2 2 2 — 4 2 3 1 — tmp+1 — str
Bärenreiter

Concerto for Harpsichord and Small   17'
Orchestra (1935)
    solo hpsd
    1 0 0 1 — 0 0 0 0 — pf — str[3.0.1.1.1]
UE

Concerto for Oboe and Small   17'
Orchestra, H.353 (1955)
    solo ob
    2 0 2 1 — 2 1 0 0 — pf — str
Eschig

Concerto for Violin and Orchestra   24'
No.1 in E (1932/33)
    solo vn
    2 2 2 2 — 4 2 3 0 — tmp+3 — str
Bärenreiter

Concerto Grosso, H.263 (1937)   16'
    1 3 3 0 — 2 0 0 0 — 2pf — str
UE

Divertimento; Serenata No.4 (1932)   7'
    solo vn, va, pf
    0 2 0 0 — 0 0 0 0 — str
Kalmus

Duo concertant, H.264 (1937)   25'
    solo 2vn
    2 2 2 2 — 2 2 1 0 — tmp/perc — pf — str
Bärenreiter

Échec au roi; Ballet en 1 acte.   27'
(1930)
    solo A
    2 2 2 2 — 2 2 3 0 — tmp+2 — pf — str
Eschig

Jazz Suite, H.172 (1928)   9'
    0 1 1 1 — 0 2 2 0 — pf — str[1.1.1.0.0]
Schott

Nonet, H.144 (1925)   5'
    1 1 1 1 — 1 0 0 0 — pf — str[1.0.1.1.0]
Schott

Nonet No.2, H.374 (1959)   17'
    1 1 1 1 — 1 0 0 0 — str[1.0.1.1.1]
Kalmus

Ouverture, H.345 (1953)   8'
    2 2 2 2 — 4 2 0 0 — tmp — str
Eschig

Rhapsody-Concerto; Concerto for   22'
Viola and Orchestra. H.337 (1952)
    solo va
    2 2 2 2 — 4 2 0 0 — tmp — str
Bärenreiter

Sérénade; Pour orchestre de   12'
chambre. H.199 (1931)
    1 2 1 2 — 2 2 1 0 — str[8.6.4.3.2]
    Two solo vn parts (to be covered by section players).
Fleisher

Serenata No.1 (1932)   10'
    0 1 1 0 — 1 0 0 0 — str[4.0.1.0.0]
Kalmus

Serenata No.3, H.218 (1932)   8'
    0 1 1 0 — 0 0 0 0 — str[4.0.0.1.0]
Kalmus

Sinfonietta la Jolla, H.328 (1950)   19'
    2[1.pic] 2 2 2 — 2 1 0 0 — tmp+1 — pf — str
    perc: tri, cym, sd
Boosey & Hawkes

Sonata da camera for Violoncello   28'
and Chamber Orchestra (1940)
    solo vc
    1 1 2 2 — 2 0 0 0 — str
Bärenreiter

Toccata e due canzoni, H.311   25'
(1946)
    1[pic] 2 1 1 — 0 1 0 0 — tmp+1 — pf — str
    perc: cym, tri, sd
Boosey & Hawkes

Tre Ricercari, H.267 (1938)   12'
    1[1/pic] 2 0 2 — 0 2 0 0 — 2pf — str[1.0.0.1.0]
Boosey & Hawkes

Martland, Steve   (1959-)

American Invention (1985)   22'
    2 0 2[bcl.bcl] 0 — 1 0 0 0 — bgtr — 1perc — 2pf
    — str[1.1.1.1.0]
    perc: ride cym, sus cym, break dr or anvil, 2 synth dr, ped bd
Schott

Remembering Lennon (1981)   12'
    1 0 1[1/wine glass in C# & A] 0 — 0 0 0 0 —
    1perc — pf/wine glass in G#/woodblk — str[1.0.1.1.0]
    perc: 3 bongos, 3 templeblks, marim, vib, glsp
    Vn doubles on wine glass in D#. Revised version (1985).
Schott

Marx, Joseph   (1882-1964)

Erinnerung: From "Lieder und   3'
Gesänge" (2.Folge Nr.2) (1911)
   solo medium voice
   2 2 2 2 — 2 0 0 0 — hp — cel — str
UE

Japanisches Regenlied: From   2'
"Lieder und Gesänge" (1.Folge
Nr.13) (1909)
   solo medium voice
   2 2 2 2 — 2 0 0 0 — hp — str
UE

Maienblüten: From "Lieder und   2'
Gesänge" (1.Folge Nr.16) (1909)
   solo high voice
   2 2[1.eh] 2 2 — 2 0 0 0 — tmp — hp — str
UE

Marienlied: From "Lieder und   3'
Gesänge" (1.Folge Nr.17) (1910)
   solo high voice
   0 0 0 0 — 2 0 0 0 — hp — str
UE

Selige Nacht: From "Lieder und   3'
Gesänge" (3.Folge Nr.9) (1914)
   solo medium voice
   1 0 0 0 — 4 0 0 0 — tmp+1 — hp — cel — str
   perc: tri
UE

Sommerlied: From "Lieder und   1'
Gesänge" (1.Folge Nr.22) (1909)
   solo high voice
   2 2[1.eh] 2 2 — 2 0 0 0 — tmp — hp — str
UE

Und gestern hat er mir Rosen   2'
gebracht: From "Lieder und
Gesänge" (1.Folge Nr.24) (1908)
   solo high voice
   2 2[1.eh] 3[1.2.bcl] 2 — 2 0 0 0 — hp — str
UE

Venetianisches Wiegenlied: From   3'
"Italienisches Liederbuch" (No.17)
(1912)
   solo medium voice
   2 1 2 3 — 2 0 0 0 — 1perc — hp — cel — str
   perc: tri, glsp
   Also available in a version for medium voice, harp and string
   orchestra.
UE

Zigeuner: From "Lieder und   3'
Gesänge" (3.Folge Nr.8) (1911)
   solo high voice
   2 2[1.eh] 3[1.2.3/bcl] 2 — 2 1 0 0 — hp — str
UE

Mason, Benedict   (1954-)

The Hinterstoisser Traverse (1986)   12'
   1 1 1 1 — 1 1 1 0 — 1perc — pf — str[1.0.1.1.0]
   perc: marim, vib, gong
   Chester Novello

Imposing a Regular Pattern in   15'
Chaos and Heterophony (1990)
   1 1 1 0 — 0 1 0 0 — 1perc — pf — str[1.1.1.1.1]
   Chester Novello

Matsudaira, Yoritsune   (1907-2001)

Pastorale (1935)   5'
   2 3 3 2 — 2 0 0 0 — hp — str
UE

Requiem (1992)   12'
   solo S
   1 1 1 1 — 0 0 0 0 — hp — pf — str[3.0.3.0.0]
   Durand

Matsushita, Shin-ichi   (1922-1990)

Composizione da Camera   10'
   1 0 1 0 — 0 1 1 0 — 1perc — pf — str[1.0.0.1.0]
   Presser

Correlaziono per 3 Gruppi   22'
   2[1.pic] 0 2[1.bcl] 0 — 0 0 0 0 — asx — 1perc —
   2pf[pf.claviolino] — str[1.0.1.1.1]
   Presser

Fresque Sonore   10'
   1 1 1 0 — 1 0 0 0 — hp — str[0.0.1.1.0]
   Presser

Haleines Astrals   15'
   1 1 1 1 — 1 1 1 0 — hp — pf — str[1.1.1.1.0]
   Presser

Matthews, Colin   (1946-)

Continuum (2000)   40'
solo Mz
2[1.afl] 1[eh] 3[1.bcl.bcl] 1[1/cbn] — 2 1 1 0 —
2perc — hp — pf — str[1.1.3.2.1]
perc: vib, glsp, crot, 2 tuned gongs, 2 tri, sus cym, 2 metal bars, 2 tam-tam
Faber

Contraflow (1992)   12'
1[1/afl/pic] 1[1/eh] 1[1/bcl] 1[1/cbn] — 1 1 1 0 —
1perc — pf — str[1.1.1.1.1]
perc: ped bd, hi-hat, 4 tom-tom, 3 tam-tam
Faber

Dowlandia (1997)   11'
1[1/afl/pic] 1[1/eh] 1[bcl/Ebcl] 1[1/cbn] — 1 1[flug]
1 0 — 1perc — hp — pf — str
perc: bd, td, tam-tam, sus cym, 4 Burmese gongs, glsp
Faber

Elegia: No.2 of "Two Tributes"   7'
(1998)
1[afl] 1[eh] 1[bcl] 1[cbn] — 1 1 1 0 — 1perc — hp
— pf — str[1.1.1.1.1]
perc: tam-tam
Faber

Flourish with Fireflies (2002)   4'
1[1/afl] 1 2[1.2/bcl] 1[1/cbn] — 1 1 1 0 — 1perc —
hp — pf — str[1.1.1.1.1]
perc: sus cym, sizzle cym, tam-tam, vib, glsp
Faber

Hidden Variables (1989)   13'
1 1 2[1.bcl] 1 — 1 1 0 0 — 1perc — hp —
pf/kybd[opt] — str[1.1.1.1.1]
perc: ped bd, hi-hat, woodblk, tam-tam, flexatone, vib, glsp, marim
Faber

L; bent (1993)   4'
1 1 1[bcl] 1 — 1 0 0 0 — pf — str[1.0.1.1.1]
Faber

Little Continuum: No.1 of "Two   4'
Tributes" (1999)
1[afl] 1[eh] 2[1.bcl] 1 — 1 1 1 0 — 1perc — hp —
pf — str[1.1.1.1.1]
perc: vib
Faber

Little Suite No.2, op.18b (1979)   8'
1[1/pic] 1[1/eh] 3[1.2.bcl] 1 — 1 1 0 0 — 1perc —
str[2.2.2.2.1]
perc: glsp, sus cym, vib, 2 gong, tam-tam
Also possible with strings (4.4.4.4.1).
Faber

Night Music, op.10 (1977)   19'
2 2[1.2/eh] 2[1.2/bcl] 2 — 2 1[opt] 0 0 — tmp/perc
— str[4.4.3.3.2]
Faber

Pursuit; Ballet (1987)   25'
1[pic/afl] 1 2[bcl.cbcl] 0 — 1 0 0 0 — asx[opt] —
1perc — str[2.2.2.2.2]
perc: gong, tam-tam, bell tree, crot
Faber

Suns Dance (1985)   17'
1[pic] 1 1[bcl] 1[cbn] — 1 0 0 0 — str[1.1.1.1.1]
Faber

...through the glass (1994)   16'
1[afl] 1[1/eh] 2[1.bcl/Ebcl(opt)] 1[1/cbn] — 2 1 0 0
— 1perc — hp — pf — str[1.1.1.1.1]
perc: bd, 4 tom-tom, vibraslap, sus cym, hi-hat, tam-tam, vib, marim
Faber

Tosca Revisited (1978)   14'
1 1 2[1.bcl] 1 — 2 1 0 0 — pf — str[2.2.2.2.1]
Novello

Two Part Invention (1988)   18'
2[1/pic.afl/pic] 1 4[1.2.bcl.bcl] 1 — 1 2 1 1 —
2perc — hp — pf — str[0.0.0.1.1]
perc: 2 anvil, spring coils, crot, 4 tam-tam, bell tree, 2 vib, 2 glsp, tri,
2 sizzle cym, chimes, hand bells
Strings to be amplified.
Faber

Two Tributes (1999)   11'
1[afl] 1[eh] 2[1.bcl] 1 — 1 1 1 0 — 1perc — hp —
pf — str[1.1.1.1.1]
perc: vib, 2 tam-tam
Faber

A Voice to Wake (2004)   12'
1[1/afl] 1 1[1/bcl] 0 — 1 0 0 0 — hp — pf —
str[1.0.1.1.0]
Faber

Matthews, David   (1943-)

Burnham Wick, op.73 (1997)   15'
1[1/pic] 1[1/eh] 1 1 — 1 0 0 0 — 1perc — hp —
str
perc: 6 crot, 3 tmp, 3 tuned gong, 2 conga, tambn, shaker, tam-tam
Faber

From Sea to Sky; Overture, op.59   4'
(1992)
0 2 0 0 — 2 0 0 0 — str[6.5.4.2.2]
Faber

Serenade, op.29 (1982)   16'
   1[1/pic/afl] 2[1.2/eh] 0 2 — 2 0 0 0 —
   str[6.4.4.3.2]
Boosey & Hawkes

Symphony No.4, op.51 (1990)   25'
   1[1/pic] 2[1.2/eh] 0 2 — 2 0 0 0 — str[6.5.4.3.2]
Faber

Matthus, Siegfried   (1934-)

Capriccio "Kraft-Variations"; On a   17'
Theme by Paganini (1999)
   solo vn
   2[1.pic] 2[1.eh] 2[1.bcl] 2[1.cbn] — 2 0 0 1 —
   3perc — synth — str
Breitkopf

Concerto for Oboe (1985)   15'
   solo ob
   0 3 0 3 — 0 0 0 0 — 2perc — hp — pf — str
Breitkopf

Concerto for Piano; Based on the   50'
Piano Quartet op.25 by J. Brahms
(1992)
   solo pf
   2[1.2/pic] 2 2[1.2/bcl] 2 — 2 2 3 1 — tmp+2 — hp
   — cel — str
Breitkopf

Concerto for Three Trumpets and   22'
String Orchestra; O namenlose
Freude (1990)
   solo 3tpt
   str
Breitkopf

Concerto for Trumpet and String   15'
Orchestra (2001)
   solo tpt
   str
Breitkopf

Concerto for Violin (1968)   17'
   solo vn
   2[1.2/pic] 2[1.2/eh] 2[1.2/bcl] 2 — 2 2 2 1 —
   tmp+1 — hp — str
Breitkopf

Divertimento for Orchestra; Triangle   24'
Concerto (1985)
   2 2 2 2 — 2 0 0 0 — tmp+2 — hp — str
Breitkopf

Drei Sommerbilder (1975)   10'
   1 1 0 1 — 0 0 0 0 — 1perc — pf — str
Breitkopf

Ich komm einen Weg (1989)   15'
   0 0 1 1 — 1 0 0 0 — str[1.1.1.1.1]
Breitkopf

Octet on an Octet (1976)   15'
   1 1 0 0 — 0 0 0 0 — 1perc — pf — str[1.1.1.1.0]
Breitkopf

Der See; Concerto for Harp (1989)   20'
   solo hp
   3 0 3 0 — 4 0 3 1 — tmp+1 — cel — str
Breitkopf

Small Concerto for Orchestra   9'
(1963)
   2 0 0 0 — 0 0 3 0 — 1perc — hp — pf — str
Breitkopf

Sonata by G. Gabrieli (1988)   10'
   2 2 0 2 — 2 2 2 0 — tmp — str
Breitkopf

Visionen (1978)   15'
   str
Breitkopf

Maw, Nicholas   (1935-2009)

Life Studies; Eight Studies for 15   40'
Solo Strings (1976)
   str[6.4.2.2.1]
Boosey & Hawkes

Serenade (1973)   36'
   1 2 0 2 — 2 0 0 0 — str[8.6.5.4.2]
Boosey & Hawkes

Sinfonia (1966)   30'
   1[1/pic] 2[1.2/eh] 2 2 — 2 0 0 0 — str[5.4.3.3.1]
Boosey & Hawkes

Sonata for Strings and Two Horns   17'
(1967)
   0 0 0 0 — 2 0 0 0 — str[5.4.3.3.2]
Boosey & Hawkes

Maxwell Davies, Peter   (1934-)

Canzona; (After Giovanni Gabrieli)   4'
(1969)
     1 1 1 1 — 1 0 0 0 — str
Chester Novello

Caroline Mathilde: Concert Suite   25'
from Act I of the ballet (1991)
     2[1/pic.2/afl] 2[1.2/eh] 2[1.2/bcl] 2[1.2/cbn] — 2 2 2
0 — tmp+2 — hp — str
Chester Novello

Caroline Mathilde: Concert Suite   25'
from Act II of the ballet (1991)
     2[1/pic.2/afl] 2[1.2/eh] 2[1.2/bcl] 2[1.2/cbn] — 2 2 2
0 — tmp+2 — hp — str
Chester Novello

Carolísima; Serenade for Chamber   17'
Orchestra (1994)
     1[1/pic] 1 2[1.bcl] 0 — 1 1 1 0 — 1perc —
str[1.1.1.1.1]
perc: crot, 2 sus cym, 2 sd, bd
Schott

Chat Moss (1994)   7'
     2 1 1 1 — 2 0 0 0 — tmp+2 — str
Chester Novello

Crossing Kings Reach (2001)   18'
     1[1/pic] 1 1 1[1/cbn] — 1 1 1 0 — asx — 1perc —
pf — str[1.1.1.1.1]
Chester Novello

De Assumtione Beatae Mariae   28'
Virginis (2001)
     1[1/pic] 1 1[1/bcl] 1[1/cbn] — 1 1 1 0 — 1perc —
pf/cel — str[1.1.1.1.1]
Chester Novello

Farewell to Stromness (1980)   4'
     str
Arranged by Rosemary Furniss (2005).
Boosey & Hawkes

Five Klee Pictures; For School,   10'
Amateur or Professional Orchestra
(1959)
     2 2 2 2 — 4 2 2 0 — 5perc — pf — str
perc: sd, bd, cym, cast, woodblk, 4 templeblks, tam-tam, tri,
nightingale, xyl
Revised in 1976.
Boosey & Hawkes

Jimmack the Postie (1986)   9'
     2[1/pic.2/afl] 2 2[1.2/bcl] 2 — 2 2 2 0 — tmp — str
Chester Novello

Ojai Festival Overture (1991)   6'
     2[1.2/pic] 2[1.2/eh] 2 2 — 2 2 0 0 — tmp — str
Boosey & Hawkes

An Orkney Wedding, with Sunrise;   13'
Version for Chamber Orchestra
(1985)
     2 2 2[1.2/bcl] 2 — 2 2 2 0 — highland bagpipes
— tmp+1 — str
perc: glsp, 4 woodblks, tambn, sd, ped bd, sus cym, cym
Boosey & Hawkes

Ricercar and Doubles on "To many   12'
a well" (1959)
     1 1 1 1 — 1 0 0 0 — hpsd — str[0.0.1.1.0]
Schott

Sinfonia (1962)   20'
     1 1 1 1 — 1 0 0 0 — str
Schott

Sinfonietta Accademica (1983)   26'
     2 2 2 2 — 2 2 0 0 — str
Chester Novello

Strathclyde Concerto No.10;   35'
Concerto for Orchestra (1996)
     2[1.2/pic/afl] 2[1.2/eh] 2[1.2/bcl] 2[1.2/cbn] — 2 2 0
0 — tmp — str
Boosey & Hawkes

Symphony No.4 (1989)   40'
     2[1.2/pic/afl] 2[1.2/eh] 2[1.2/bcl] 2[1.2/cbn] — 2 2 0
0 — tmp — str
Boosey & Hawkes

Threnody on a Plainsong for   4'
Michael Vyner (1989)
     0 2 0 2 — 2 2 0 0 — tmp — str
Chester Novello

Vanitas; Arrangement of a   3'
Fragment by Johan Ban for String
Orchestra (1991)
     str
To be performed with Strathclyde Concerto No.5.
Boosey & Hawkes

A Welcome to Orkney (1980)   3'
     1 1 1 1 — 1 0 0 0 — str[2.2.2.2.1]
Boosey & Hawkes

McAlister, Clark   (1946-)

A Christmas Pastorale   14'
  1 2 0 1 — 2 0 0 0 — narrator — str
Kalmus

McCabe, John   (1939-)

Concerto for Chamber Orchestra   13'
(1962)
  1 2 2 2 — 2 0 0 0 — 1perc[opt] — str
Novello

The Lion, the Witch and the   15'
Wardrobe: Suite (1971)
  1 1 2 1 — 1 2 1 0 — tmp+2 — pf — str
Novello

Rainforest I (1984)   20'
  1 0 1 0 — 0 0 0 0 — 1perc — pf — str[3.0.1.2.0]
  perc: glsp
Novello

Red Leaves (1991)   12'
  0 2 0 0 — 2 0 0 0 — str
Novello

Sam (1973)   5'
  2[1.2/pic] 0 2 0 — 0 1 0 0 — 1perc — str
Novello

Shepherd's Dream (2002)   2'
  0 2 0 1 — 0 2 0 0 — str
Novello

McGlaughlin, William   (1943-)

Aaron's Horizons (1998)   11'
  1 0 1 1 — 0 0 0 0 — pf — str
Subito

McGuire, John   (1942-)

Cadence Music (1982)   27'
  2 2 2 2 — 2 0 0 0 — 5perc — hp — 2pf[pf.cel] —
  str[2.0.2.2.1]
Breitkopf

McKay, George Frederick   (1899-1970)

Fantasy on a Western Folk Song;   11'
O! Bury me not on the lone prairie
  2 1[1/eh] 2 0 — 0 1 0 0 — str
Fleisher

Variants on a Texas Tune; Mustang   11'
grey
  2 1 2 1 — 2 0 0 0 — str
Fleisher

McKinley, William Thomas   (1938-)

Paintings No.6; (To hear the light   15'
dancing) (1981)
  1[1/afl] 0 1[1/bcl] 0 — 0 0 0 0 — 1perc — pf —
  str[1.0.1.1.0]
Margun

Meale, Richard   (1932-2009)

Variations (1970)   13'
  2 2 2 2 — 2 2 2 0 — tmp+1 — str
UE

Meester, Louis de   (1904-1987)

Sinfonietta Buffa (1949)   18'
  0 0 0 0 — 0 2 0 0 — tmp+2 — str
UE

Melby, John   (1941-)

Wind, Sand and Stars (1983)   16'
  1 1[1/eh] 1[1/bcl] 0 — 1 0 0 0 — tape —
  str[1.0.1.1.1]
Margun

Mendoza, Vicente   (1894-1964)

Impresiones de Estio I-IV
  0 0 1 1 — 0 1 0 0 — 1perc — pf — str
  perc: dr, sus cym, tri
Fleisher

Menotti, Gian Carlo (1911-2007)

Amahl and the Night Visitors: 7'
Introduction, March and Shepherd's
Dance (1951)
    1 2 1 1 — 1 1 0 0 — 1perc — hp — pf — str
Schirmer

Concerto for Violin (1952)   24'
    solo vn
    3[1.2.pic] 2 2 2 — 2 2 0 0 — tmp+1 — hp — str
Schirmer

The Consul: Lullaby (1950)   4'
    solo Mz
    1 1 1 1 — 2 1 1 0 — hp — pf — str
Schirmer

The Consul: Magda's Aria; (To this   5'
we've come) (1950)
    solo S
    1 1 1 1 — 2 2 1 0 — hp — pf — str
Schirmer

The Medium: Baba's Aria; (Afraid,   5'
am I afraid?) (1946)
    solo Mz
    1 1 1 1 — 1 1 0 0 — 2pf[4hand] — str
Schirmer

The Medium: The Black Swan   4'
(1946)
    solo S
    1 1 1 1 — 1 1 0 0 — 1perc — 2pf[4hand] — str
Schirmer

The Medium: Monica's Waltz   7'
(1946)
    solo S
    1 1 1 1 — 1 1 0 0 — 1perc — 2pf[4hand] — str
Schirmer

Pastorale (1933)   8'
    pf — str
Schirmer

The Telephone: Lucy's Aria; (Hello!   4'
Oh, Margaret it's you) (1947)
    solo S
    1 1 1 1 — 1 1 0 0 — 1perc — pf — str
Schirmer

Mercurio, Steven (1956-)

Sancta Maria (1998)   4'
    solo voice
    3[1.2.pic] 1 2 2 — 1 0 0 0 — 2hp — org[opt] — str
    Based on the "Intermezzo" from "Cavalleria Rusticana" by
    Mascagni.
Subito

Messiaen, Olivier (1908-1992)

Sept Haïkaï; Esquisses japonaises   25'
for Piano Solo, Xylophone and
Marimba
    solo pf, xyl, marim
    2[1.2/pic] 3[1.2.3/eh] 4[1.2.3/Ebcl.4/bcl] 2 — 0 1 1
    0 — 4perc — str[8.0.0.0.0]
Presser

Messner, Joseph (1893-1969)

Fünf Symphonische Gesänge,   30'
op.24 (1928)
    solo S
    1 2 2 1 — 2 1 0 0 — 1perc — hp — str
UE

Mieg, Peter (1906-1990)

Concerto Veneziano (1955)   17'
    str
Boosey & Hawkes

Milford, Robin (1903-1959)

Suite for Chamber Orchestra   12'
(1925)
    2[1.2(opt)] 1 2[1.2(opt)] 2[opt] — 1[or crt] 0 0 0 —
    str
Fleisher

Milhaud, Darius   (1892-1974)

Der 129. Psalm, op.53 (1919)   8'
   solo Bar
   2 1 2 1 — 0 1 0 0 — 1perc — hp — str[4.4.4.4.4]
UE

Actualités; Musik zu einer   7'
Filmwochenschau, op.104 (1928)
   0 0 2 0 — 0 2 1 0 — 1perc — str[1.1.2.2.1]
UE

Adages, op.120c (1932)   13'
   solo S, A, T, B
   1 0 1 1 — 1 0 0 0 — str[1.0.1.1.1]
Eschig; Salabert

Le Bal Martiniquais   16'
   2 2 2 2 — 2 2 2 0 — tmp+1 — hp — str
Presser

Le boeuf sur le toit, Ballet, op.58   15'
(1919)
   2[1.2/pic] 1 2 1 — 2 2 1 0 — 2perc — str
   perc: tambn, bd, guiro, tabor
   Also as version for solo vn and orchestra (same
   instrumentation), op.58b.
Eschig

Cantate de Psaumes, op.425   18'
(1967)
   solo Bar
   2 0 2 1 — 0 1 0 0 — 3perc — hp — str[2.2.2.2.1]
UE

La Carnaval de Londres: Suite sur   30'
les airs de "l' Opéra du Gueux,"
op.172 (1937)
   1[1/pic] 1 1 1 — 0 1 1 0 — asx — 1perc — hp —
   str
   perc: sd, td, cym, tri woodblk, tambn, bd
Salabert

Catalogue de fleurs, op.60 (1920)   6'
   solo voice
   1 0 1 1 — 0 0 0 0 — str[1.0.1.1.1]
   Contents - 1. La Violette; 2. Le Bégonia; 3. Les Fritillaire; 4.
   Les Jacinthes; 5. Les Crocus; 6. Le Brachycome; 7.
   L'Eremurus
Durand

Chamber Symphony No.1; Le   4'
Printemps, op.43 (1917)
   2[1.pic] 1 1 0 — 0 0 0 0 — hp — str[1.1.1.1.0]
Kalmus; Luck's; UE

Chamber Symphony No.2;   5'
Pastorale, op.49 (1918)
   1 1[eh] 0 1 — 0 0 0 0 — str[1.0.1.1.1]
Kalmus; Luck's; UE

Chamber Symphony No.3;   4'
Sérénade, op.71 (1921)
   1 0 1 1 — 0 0 0 0 — str[1.0.1.1.1]
Kalmus; Luck's; UE

Chamber Symphony No.4; Dixtuor   6'
à Cordes, op.74 (1921)
   str[2.2.2.2.2]
Kalmus; Luck's; UE

Chamber Symphony No.5; Dixtuor   6'
d'Instruments à Vent, op.75 (1922)
   2[1.2/pic] 2[1.eh] 2[1.bcl] 2 — 2 0 0 0 — no str
Kalmus; Luck's; UE

Cinq Chansons de Charles Vildrac,   12'
op.167 (1937)
   solo T
   1 1 2 1 — 0 2 1 0 — 1 — 1perc — hp — str
   Contents - 1. Les Quatre Petits Lions; 2. La Pomme et
   l'Escargot; 3. Le Malpropre; 4. Poupette et Patata; 5. Le
   Jardinier Impatient
Salabert

Cinq Études pour Piano et   10'
Orchestre, op.63 (1920)
   solo pf
   1 1 1 1 — 1 1 1 0 — tmp+1 — str
UE

Concert de chambre, op.389 (1961)   15'
   1 1 1 1 — 1 0 0 0 — pf — str[1.1.1.1.1]
Eschig

Concertino de Printemps, op.135   9'
(1934)
   solo vn
   1 1 1 1 — 1 1 0 0 — tmp+1 — str[1.1.1.1.1]
   Possible with full strings.
Salabert

Concerto for Clarinet and Orchestra   12'
   solo cl
   2 2 2 2 — 2 2 2 1 — tmp+1 — hp — str
Presser

Concerto for Harpsichord and   17'
Orchestra, op.407 (1964)
   solo hpsd
   1 1 1 1 — 0 1 0 0 — tmp+3 — hp — str
Salabert

Concerto for Two Pianos and   18'
Orchestra
   solo 2pf
   2 2 2 2 — 2 2 2 1 — tmp — str
Presser

Concerto for Viola, op.108 (1929)   15'
   solo va
   2 2 3[1.2.bcl] 2 — 2 2 1 1 — tmp+1 — hp — pf —
   str
UE

Concerto for Viola, op.108 (1929)   15'
   solo va
   2[1.pic] 1 2[1.bcl] 1 — 1 1 1 0 — 1perc —
   str[1.1.1.1.1]
   Version for va and ensemble.
UE

Couronne de Gloire; Cantata for   17'
Baritone and Small Orchestra
   solo Bar
   1 0 0 0 — 0 1 0 0 — str
Presser

La creation du monde; Ballet,   15'
op.81a (1923)
   2 1 2 1 — 1 2 1 0 — asx — tmp+1 — pf —
   str[1.1.0.1.1]
   perc: tambn, cowbell, woodblk, cym, sd, td, tabor, ped bd w/cym, 2
   high tmp
Eschig

Fantasie Pastorale, op.188 (1938)   10'
   solo pf
   1 1 1 1 — 1 1 1 1 — 1perc — hp — str
Salabert

L'Homme et son Désir, op.48   20'
(1918)
   2 2 2 1 — 1 2 0 0 — 2perc — hp — str[1.1.1.1.1]
UE

Jeux de Printemps, op.243 (1944)   20'
   1[1/pic] 0 1 1 — 0 1 0 0 — str[1.1.1.1.1]
Salabert

Machines Agricoles; 6 Pastoral   12'
Songs, op.56 (1919)
   solo medium voice
   1 0 1 1 — 0 0 0 0 — str[1.0.1.1.1]
UE

Music for Boston   13'
   solo vn
   1 0 1 1 — 0 0 0 0 — str
Presser

Musique pour Ars Nova, op.432   12'
(1969)
   1 0 2 1 — 1 1 1 0 — 2perc — hp — pf —
   str[1.0.0.1.0]
Eschig

Musique pour Graz, op.429 (1969)   15'
   1 1 1 1 — 0 1 0 0 — str[1.0.1.1.1]
UE

Musique pour Lisbonne, op.420   21'
(1966)
   0 2 0 0 — 2 0 0 0 — str
Eschig

Musique pour San Francisco,   11'
op.436 (1971)
   2 2 2 2 — 2 2 2 0 — 1perc — str
Eschig

Opus Americanum No.2 (Moïse)   18'
   2 2 2 2 — 2 2 2 0 — tmp+1 — hp — str
Presser

Un petit peu d'exercice (1934)   30'
   solo voice
   2 2 2 1 — 0 1 0 0 — tmp+1 — hp — str[1.1.1.1.0]
   Orchestrated by Roger Calmel.
Durand

Protée, op.17 (1919)   30'
   1 2 0 0 — 4 2 2 0 — 2perc — str[1.1.1.1.0]
Durand

La Rose des Vents; Ballet, op.367   22'
(1957)
   2 1 2 1 — 2 2 2 1 — 1perc — hp — pf — str
Salabert

Sérénade, op.62 (1921)   14'
   2 2 2 2 — 2 2 0 0 — 1perc — str
UE

Les Songes; Ballet, op.124 (1933)   30'
   1 1 1 1 — 1 1 1 0 — tmp+1 — pf — str
Salabert

Stanford Serenade, op.430 (1969)   12'
   solo ob
   1 0 1 1 — 0 1 0 0 — tmp — hp — str[1.1.1.1.1]
Eschig

Suite; For Ondes Martenot (or   10'
Piano) and String Orchestra
   solo Ondes Martenot (or pf)
   str
   Arranged by R. Calmel.
Presser

Trois Rag-Caprices (1922)   8'
  1 1 1 1 — 2 1 1 0 — 1perc — str
Fleisher; UE

Trois Valses (1945)   4'
  2[1.2/pic] 1 2 1 — 2 2 1 0 — tmp+1 — hp — str
Enoch & Cie

Vendanges; Ballet, op.317 (1952)   50'
  2 2 2 2 — 2 3 3 1 — tmp+1 — hp — str
Eschig

Milner, Anthony   (1925-2002)

Chamber Symphony (1968)   15'
  1 2 1 2 — 2 0 0 0 — str
Novello

Concerto for String Orchestra (1982)   15'
  str
Novello

Mirzoyan, Edvard   (1921-)

Symphony for Strings and Timpani (1962)   31'
  tmp — str
Boosey & Hawkes

Mitsukuri, Shukichi   (1895-1971)

Sinfonietta in D Major (1934)   15'
  2[1.2/pic] 2[1.eh] 2 2 — 2 2 1 0 — tmp+1 — pf — str
  perc: tri, cym
UE

Mochizuki, Misato   (1969-)

4 D (2003)   12'
  1[1/afl] 0 1[Ebcl/bcl] 0 — 0 0 1 0 — 2perc — pf — str[0.0.1.1.1]
Breitkopf

La Chambre Claire (1998)   13'
  1[1/pic/lotos fl] 1 2[1/Ebcl.2/bcl] 1 — 1 1 1 0 — 2perc — str[1.1.1.1.1]
Breitkopf

Chimera (2000)   11'
  0 0 1[bcl] 0 — 0 1 1 0 — ssx/tsx — 3perc — pf — str[1.0.1.1.0]
Breitkopf

Wise Water (2002)   16'
  1[1/afl] 0 1[1/bcl] 0 — 0 0 1 0 — 2perc — pf — str[0.0.1.1.1]
Breitkopf

Moeran, E. J.   (1894-1950)

Whythorne's Shadow (1932)   7'
  1 1 1 0 — 1 0 0 0 — str
Novello

Moeschinger, Albert   (1897-1985)

Fantasie, op.64 (1944)   14'
  str
Boosey & Hawkes

Quatre pièces brèves (1953)   8'
  str
Boosey & Hawkes

Symphony No.2, op.73 (1948)   25'
  1 1 1 1 — 2 0 0 0 — tmp+1 — str
  perc: cym, tri, bd, sd
Boosey & Hawkes

Le Voyage (1958)   12'
  str
Boosey & Hawkes

Molina Pinillos, José

Cromos Nacionales; Rapsodia guatemalteca Nr.2 (1939)
  1 1 1 0 — 0 1 1 0 — str
Fleisher

Mommer, Hans Günter   (1925-)

Concerto for Strings (1958)   23'
  str
Boosey & Hawkes

Moncayo, José Pablo   (1912-1958)

Cumbres   10'
2[1.2/pic] 2[1.2/eh] 2 2 — 4 2 3 1 — tmp+1 — hp
— str
perc: field dr, bd, cym
Peer

Homenaje a Cervantes   8'
0 2 0 0 — 0 0 0 0 — str
Peer

Huapango   8'
3[1.2.pic] 2 3[1.2.Ebcl] 2 — 4 3 3 1 — tmp+3 —
hp — str
perc: guiro, marac, sd, Indian dr, bd, claves, xyl
Also available in reduced orchestration: 1121 - 2210 - 1perc
- pf(or hp) - str.
Peer

Montsalvatge, Xavier   (1912-2002)

Cinco Invocaciones al Crucificado   23'
(1969)
1 2 2 1 — 2 1 0 0 — 1perc — hp — 2pf[pf.cel] —
str[0.0.0.0.1]
Unión

Serenade a Lydia de Cadaques   10'
(1972)
2[1.pic] 2 2 1 — 2 2 1 0 — tmp+1 — hp — str
Unión

Moore, Douglas   (1893-1969)

Farm Journal; Suite for Chamber   16'
Orchestra (1950)
2[1.2/pic] 2 2 2 — 2 1 0 0 — tmp+1 — str
Fleisher; Fischer (C.)

Village Music (1942)   11'
2[1.pic] 1[opt] 2 1[opt] — 2[opt] 2 1 0 — tmp+1 —
str
Kalmus; Fleisher

Moravec, Paul   (1957-)

Adelphony (1997)   8'
2 2 2 2 — 2 2 1 0 — tmp — str
Subito

Ancient Lights (1990)   15'
2[1.2/pic] 2 2 2 — 2 2 1 0 — tmp+1 — str
Subito

Aubade (1990)   15'
str
Subito

Northern Lights Electric (1994)   15'
1 0 1 0 — 0 0 0 0 — pf — str[1.1.1.1.1]
Revised version for full orchestra is also available.
Subito

Sempre Diritto!; (Straight Ahead)   14'
(1991)
0 2 0 0 — 2 0 0 0 — str
Subito

Streamline (1988)   15'
2[1.2/pic] 2 2 2 — 2 2 1 0 — tmp+1 — str
Subito

Morawetz, Oskar   (1917-2007)

Carnival Overture (1946)   7'
3 2 2 2 — 4 3 2 1 — tmp+1 — hp — str
Boosey & Hawkes

Overture to a Fairy Tale (1956)   12'
2[1.2/pic] 2 2 2 — 4 2 0 0 — tmp — str
Boosey & Hawkes

Moross, Jerome   (1913-1983)

Paeans (1933)   5'
2[1.pic] 1 1 1 — 2 2 1 0 — tmp+1 — pf — str
Fleisher

Morris, Harold   (1890-1964)

Suite for Small Orchestra   16'
1 1 1 1 — 1 1 1 0 — tmp+1 — pf — str
Fleisher

Variations on the American Negro   14'
Spiritual "I was way down a-yonder"
1 1 1 1 — 1 0 0 0 — pf — str
Fleisher

Morthenson, Jan Wilhelm   (1940-)

Antiphonia I (1963)   12'
2[1.2/pic] 2[eh.ob d'am] 2[1/bcl.2/bcl] 2 — 2 0 0 2
— asx — elec gtr, elec bgtr[or hp] — 4perc —
3pf[pf.org.cel] — str[0.0.0.4.0]
Nordiska

Antiphonia II (1965)   5'
  3[1.2/pic.3/pic] 0 2[1.2/bcl] 0 — 0 0 0 0 —
  str[3.0.2.1.1]
Nordiska

Labor (1974)   12'
  1 1 1 1 — 1 0 1 0 — pf — str[1.1.1.1.0]
UE

Mossolow, Alexander   (1900-1973)

Concerto for Piano, op.14 (1927)   23'
  solo pf
  1[1/pic] 1 1 1 — 2 1 1 0 — 1perc — str
  perc: tri, cym, tam-tam, military dr, bd
UE

Moyzes, Alexander   (1906-1984)

Slowakische Volkslieder, op.15   12'
(1933)
  2 1 2 1 — 2 2 1 0 — tmp+1 — pf — str
UE

Mozart, Wolfgang Amadeus   (1756-1791)

Divertimento for Mozart; 12 Aspects   40'
of the Aria "Ein Mädchen oder
Weibchen wünscht Papageno sich"
(1956)
  Commissioned by the South West German Radio to mark
  the 200th birthday of Mozart. See individual composers for
  detailed information.
  Contents - I Introduktion: Wandlungen (von Einem); II
  Variazioni (Berio); III Allegro-Lento-Allegro (Erbse); IV
  Fantasie (Fricker); V Brillantes Concertino (Bentzon); VI
  Papageno's Pocket-Size Concerto (Haubenstock-Ramati);
  VII Espressioni liriche (Klebe); VIII Allegro Giocoso
  (Wimberger)
UE; Schott

Muhly, Nico   (1981-)

By All Means (2004)   9'
  1 1 1 0 — 1 1 1 0 — pf — str[1.0.1.1.0]
Chester Novello

Muldowney, Dominic   (1952-)

Concerto for Saxophone (1984)   20'
  solo asx
  1[1/pic/afl] 1[1/eh] 1[1/bcl] 1[1/cbn] — 1 1 1 0 —
  1perc — pf — str
UE

Double Helix (1977)   6'
  2[1/pic.pic] 0 1[1/bcl] 0 — 0 1 0 0 — hp — pf —
  str[1.0.0.1.1]
Novello

The Duration of Exile (1983)   20'
  solo Mz
  1 1 1 0 — 0 0 1 0 — hp — str[1.0.1.0.0]
  Contents - 1. Everything Changes (Prelude); 2. The
  Wireless; 3. The Smoke; 4. On Sterility; 5. Things Change;
  6. From "Finland 1940"; 7. Firs; 8. The Mask of Evil; 9.
  Everything Changes (Postlude)
UE

The Earl of Essex Galliard (1976)   40'
  0 0 1 1 — 0 1[1/crt] 1 0 — 1perc — str[1.0.0.0.1]
Novello

Entr'acte (1976)   12'
  1 0 1 0 — 0 1 0 0 — tape — 1perc — pf —
  str[1.0.1.1.0]
  perc: vib
Novello

Lonely Hearts; Song Cycle for   30'
Mezzo Soprano, 14 Players, Two
Conductors and Click-Track Tape
(1988)
  solo Mz
  1[1/pic] 0 1 0 — 0 1 1 0 — asx — gtr/banjo, tape
  — 2perc — hp — pf — str[1.1.1.0.1]
  perc: vib, glsp, 2 tambn, 3 boobam, 2 choke cym, 2 templeblks, 2
  woodblks, 2 drum kit (sus cym, hi-hat, sd, ped bd), marac, claves, 3
  Chinese dr
  Requires pre-recorded 4-track tape, 4 pairs of headphones
  for the 2 conductors and 2 percussionists.
Faber

Maxim's (1986)   10'
  solo Bar
  2 2 2 2 — 2 2 2 0 — 1perc — hp — str[1.1.1.1.1]
  perc: vib
UE

Sinfonietta (1986)   18'
  1 1 1 1 — 1 1 1 0 — 1perc — pf — str[1.1.1.1.1]
UE

Solo / Ensemble (1974)　　　　　　　15'
　1[1/pic] 0 1 0 — 0 0 0 0 — 3perc — pf —
　str[0.0.1.1.0]
Novello

Three-Part Motet (1976)　　　　　　10'
　1 0 2 0 — 1 1 1 0 — 2perc — str[0.0.1.1.1]
Novello

Variations on "Mein junges Leben　　7'
hat ein End" (1976)
　1[1/pic] 0 1[1/bcl] 0 — 0 1 0 0 — hp — pf —
　str[1.0.1.1.0]
Novello

Mulè, Giuseppe　　　　　　　(1885-1951)

Largo (1931)
　hp — 2pf[pf.harm] — str
Fleisher

Müller, Sigfrid Walther　　　(1905-1946)

Concerto in B-flat Major; For Flute　22'
and Chamber Orchestra, op.62
(1940)
　solo fl
　0 2 0 0 — 2 0 0 0 — str
Schott

Concerto in F Major; For Bassoon　18'
and Orchestra, op.56 (1938)
　solo bn
　2 2 2 2 — 4 3 3 0 — tmp+1 — str
　perc: tri, bd w/ cym
Schott

Müller-Hornbach, Gerhard　　(1951-)

Passacaglia II (1981)　　　　　　　15'
　1 1 1[bcl] 1 — 1 1 2 0 — str[1.1.1.1.1]
Breitkopf

Müller-Siemens, Detlev　　　　(1957-)

Pavane (1985)　　　　　　　　　　11'
　1 1 1 1 — 0 0 0 0 — pf — str[1.1.1.1.0]
Schott

Phoenix 1 (1993)　　　　　　　　　14'
　1 1 1[1/bcl] 1 — 1 1 1 0 — pf — str[1.1.1.1.1]
Schott

Phoenix 2 (1994)　　　　　　　　　16'
　1 1 1 1 — 1 1 1 0 — pf — str[1.1.1.1.1]
Schott

Phoenix 3 (1995)　　　　　　　　　14'
　1 1 1[1/bcl] 1 — 1 1 1 0 — pf — str[1.1.1.1.1]
Schott

Refuge (1998)　　　　　　　　　　11'
　1 1 1 1 — 1 0 0 0 — pf — str[1.1.1.1.1]
Schott

Variationen über einen Ländler von　13'
Schubert (Variations on a Landler
by Schubert) (1978)
　1[1/pic] 1 1 1 — 1 0 0 0 — str[1.1.1.2.0]
Schott

Zwei Stücke (Two Pieces) (1977)　　9'
　2 2 2 2 — 2 0 0 0 — str[3.0.1.1.1]
Schott

Müller-Wieland, Jan　　　　　　(1966-)

Allegria (1991)　　　　　　　　　　2'
　0 1 1[bcl] 0 — 1 1 0 0 — hp — str[1.0.0.0.1]
Sikorski

Amtsantritt von Leonce und Lena;　20'
Zweite imaginäre Theaterszene
nach dem Schluss von Georg
Büchner (1998)
　tsx — 1perc — str[1.0.1.2.1]
　perc: marim
Sikorski

Narrativo e Sonnambulo (1989)　　15'
　1[1/afl] 0 1 0 — 0 0 0 0 — 1perc — pf —
　str[1.0.1.1.1]
Sikorski

Der Revolutionsplatz (1989)　　　11'
　1 2 1 1 — 1 1 1 0 — 2perc — pf — str[1.0.1.1.1]
Sikorski

Two Pieces for Chamber Orchestra　9'
(1986)
　1[1/pic] 1 1 1 — 1 1 1 0 — 1perc — hp — cel —
　str
Sikorski

Müller-Zürich, Paul   **(1898-1993)**

Marienleben, op.8   25'
  1 1 1 0 — 1 0 0 0 — str
Schott

Mundry, Isabel   **(1963-)**

Panorama ciego (2001)   12'
  solo pf
  2[1.2/pic] 2 2[1.2/bcl] 2 — 2 2 0 0 — 2tmp —
  str[4.0.2.2.2]
Breitkopf

Schwankende Zeit (2008)   16'
  1[1/pic] 1 1[1/cbcl] 1 — 1 1 1 1 — 2perc — hp —
  pf — str[1.1.2.1.1]
Breitkopf

Le Silence; Tystnaden (1993)   13'
  1[1/pic] 1[1/eh] 1 0 — 1 1 1 0 — 2perc —
  str[1.1.1.1.0]
Breitkopf

Le Voyage (1996)   22'
  2[1/pic/afl.2/pic/rec] 1 1[1/Ebcl/bcl] 0 — 1 1 1 0 —
  2perc — str[1.1.2.2.2]
Breitkopf

Muñoz Molleda, José   **(1905-1988)**

Circo; Suite (1964)   10'
  2[1.2/pic] 2[1.eh] 2 2 — 2 2 2 1 — tmp+2 — hp —
  pf — str
Unión

Miniaturas medievales (1974)
  2 2[1.2/eh] 1 2 — 2 2 0 0 — hp — str
Unión

Musgrave, Thea   **(1928-)**

Chamber Concerto No.1 (1962)   11'
  0 1 1 1 — 1 1 1 0 — str[1.0.1.1.0]
Chester Novello

Chamber Concerto No.2 (1966)   14'
  1[1/pic/afl] 0 1[1/bcl] 0 — 0 0 0 0 — pf —
  str[1.0.0.1.0]
  Vn doubles on va.
Chester Novello

Lamenting with Ariadne (1999)   16'
  1 0 1[1/bcl] 0 — 0 1 0 0 — 1perc — hp —
  str[1.0.1.1.0]
Novello

Night Music (1969)   18'
  1[1/pic] 2 0 1 — 2 0 0 0 — str
Chester Novello

The Seasons (1988)   22'
  2[1.2/pic] 2[1.2/eh] 2[1.2/bcl] 2[1.2/cbn] — 2 2 0 0
  — tmp+1 — pf — str
Novello

Space Play (1974)   19'
  1 1 1 1 — 1 0 0 0 — str[1.0.1.1.1]
Novello

Musto, John   **(1954-)**

Divertimento   20'
  1 0 1 0 — 0 0 0 0 — 1perc — pf — str[0.0.1.1.0]
  perc: bd, sus cym, sd, templeblk, marim, hi-hat
Peer

Myaskovsky, Nikolai   **(1881-1950)**
Yakovlevich

Concertino Lyrico, op.32 (1929)   18'
  1 0 1 1 — 1 0 0 0 — hp — str
Boosey & Hawkes

Military March No.1   4'
  1 1 2 1 — 2 2 1 0 — 1perc — str
Kalmus

Sinfonietta, op.32 (1929)   25'
  str
Boosey & Hawkes

Mykietyn, Paweł   **(1971-)**

Eine Kleine Herbstmusik (A Little   12'
Autumn Music) (1995)
  1 1 1 0 — 1 0 0 0 — 1perc — pf — str[1.0.1.1.1]
PWM

N

Nabokoff, Nicholas   (1903-1978)

Le Fiance, op.9 (1934)   6'
   2 2 2 2 — 2 2 1 0 — tmp+1 — cel — str
Boosey & Hawkes

Naginski, Charles   (1909-1940)

Suite for Small Orchestra
   2[1.2/pic] 2[1.2/eh] 2 2 — 2 1 1 0 — tmp+1 — hp
   — str
Fleisher

Nancarrow, Conlon   (1912-1997)

Study No.1 (1995)   3'
   1[pic] 1 1 1 — 1 1 1 0 — ssx/bcl — tmp+1 —
   3pf[pf.hpsd.synth] — str
   perc: xyl, marim (or vib)
   Orchestrated by Yvar Mikhashoff. A gtr can be used instead
   of the synth.
Schott

Study No.2 (1995)   4'
   1 1[1/eh] 2[1.bcl] 1 — 1 1 1 0 — ssx — 1perc —
   cel/hpsd — str[1.1.1.1.1]
   perc: xyl, marim, vib
   Orchestrated by Yvar Mikhashoff.
Schott

Study No.3c (1995)   3'
   1[1/pic] 1 4[Ebcl.2/ssx.bcl.cbcl] 1[1/cbn] — 0 1 0 0
   — tsx — 1perc — 2pf[pf.hpsd] — str[0.0.0.0.1]
   perc: marim
   Orchestrated by Yvar Mikhashoff.
Schott

Study No.5 (1995)   3'
   1[pic] 1[(or cl)] 1[bcl(or tsx)] 1[(or bcl)] — 0 3 0 0
   — 1perc — 2pf — str[1.1.1.1.1]
   perc: xyl, marim
   Orchestrated by Yvar Mikhashoff.
Schott

Study No.6 (1995)   4'
   1[1/pic] 1[1/eh] 1[1/bcl] 0 — 1 0 0 0 — 1perc —
   3pf[2pf.cel] — str[1.1.1.0.2]
   perc: glsp, marim
   Orchestrated by Yvar Mikhashoff.
Schott

Study No.7 (1995)   10'
   1[pic] 1 2[1/Ebcl.2/bcl/asx/tsx] 1 — 1 1 1 0 —
   1perc — 2pf[pf.hpsd] — str[1.1.1.1.1]
   perc: xyl, marim
   Orchestrated by Yvar Mikhashoff.
Schott

Study No.9 (1995)   4'
   1[pic] 1 2[Ebcl.bcl] 1 — 1 1 1 0 — 1perc —
   2pf[pf/cel.hpsd] — str[1.0.1.1.1]
   perc: xyl, marim
   Orchestrated by Yvar Mikhashoff.
Schott

Study No.12 (1995)   8'
   1[pic] 1[1/eh] 2[1/Ebcl.bcl/asx] 1 — 1 1 0 0 — gtr,
   accordion — 1perc — 2pf[pf/cel.hpsd] —
   str[1.1.1.1.1]
   perc: xyl, vib, marim
   Orchestrated by Yvar Mikhashoff.
Schott

Study No.16 (1995)   3'
   0 1 0 1 — 1 0 0 0 — 1perc — 2pf[cel.hpsd] —
   str[0.0.0.1.0]
   perc: vib, marim
   Orchestrated by Yvar Mikhashoff.
Schott

Three Movements (1993)   12'
   1 1 1 0 — 1 1 1 0 — 1perc — pf — str[1.1.1.1.1]
   perc: xyl, marim, tabla
   Arranged by Thomas Adès.
Schott

Naylor, Bernard   (1907-1986)

Variations (1960)   10'
   1 1 1 1 — 2 2 0 0 — tmp+1 — str
UE

Neikrug, Marc   (1946-)

Chetro Ketl (1986)   15'
   1 2[1.2/eh] 2 2 — 2 2 0 0 — tmp/perc —
   str[6.6.4.4.2]
Chester Novello

Concertino (1977)   17'
   1 1 1 0 — 0 0 0 0 — pf — str[1.0.1.1.0]
Chester Novello

Concerto for 2 Violins, Viola,   16'
Violoncello and Orchestra
   solo str 4t
   1 2 2 2 — 2 2 0 0 — 3perc — str
Presser

Concerto for Clarinet (2004)   25'
  solo cl
  2 2 2 2 — 4 2 0 1 — 4perc — hp — pf/cel — str
Presser

Concerto for Piano (1995)   18'
  solo pf
  2 2 2 2 — 2 2 0 1 — 2perc — str
Presser

Concerto for Violin and Orchestra   21'
No.2 (1998)
  solo vn
  2 2 2 2 — 4 2 0 1 — tmp+2 — hp — pf — str
Presser

Mobile (1981)   17'
  2 1 3[1.2.3/bcl] 0 — 0 0 0 0 — 2perc — pf —
  str[1.1.1.1.1]
Chester Novello

Suite from Los Alamos (1998)
  2 2[1.2/eh] 2 2 — 2 2 0 0 — 1perc — str
Chester Novello

Nelson, Larry   (1944-)

Catena (1986)   18'
  1[1/pic] 1 1[1/bcl] 0 — 1 1 1[1/btbn] 0 — 2perc —
  str
Presser

In Silence, In Memory (1994)   18'
  solo pf
  1 1 1 1 — 1 1 1 0 — 1perc — pf — str
Presser

Loose Leaves (1989)   19'
  1 1 2[1.bcl] 0 — 0 0 0 0 — 1perc — str[1.0.1.1.1]
Presser

Neubert, Günter   (1936-)

Concertante Suite (1971)   17'
  solo vn
  1 1 1 1 — 1 1 1 0 — 1perc — str
Breitkopf

Music for Orchestra on a Theme by   11'
Robert Schumann (1969)
  2 1 1 2 — 2 1 1 0 — 3perc — str
Breitkopf

Music for Strings in Three Parts   11'
(1967)
  str
Breitkopf

Nieder, Fabio   (1957-)

"das ewig liecht"; Canon cancrizans   9'
per augmentationem in contrario
motu (from J. S. Bach's "Kunst der
Fuge") (2001)
  solo S, A, T, B
  2[1.pic] 0 2[1.bcl] 0 — 0 1[pic tpt in F] 1 0 —
  3perc — hp — 2pf[pf.sampler] — str[0.0.2.0.1]
UE

Nielsen, Carl   (1865-1931)

At the Bier of a Young Artist, F.58   5'
(1910)
  str
Kalmus

Bohemian Danish Folksong, F.130   8'
(1928)
  str
Kalmus

Festival Prelude (1900)   2'
  2[1.pic] 2 2 2 — 2 2 2 0 — tmp+1 — str
Hansen

Romanze, op.2, No.1 (1889)   9'
  solo vn
  0 0 2 2 — 2 0 0 0 — str
Kalmus; Hansen

Suite for Strings; (Little Suite) op.1 /   15'
F.6 (1888)
  str
Kalmus; Luck's; Hansen

Nilsson, Bo   (1937-)

Bombi Bitt (1966)   60'
  2 0 1 0 — 0 0 0 0 — pf — str
Nordiska

Hemsoborna (1964)   60'
  1 0 0 0 — 0 0 0 0 — pf — str
Nordiska

Taqsim-Caprice-Maqam (1973)   15'
  2 0 2 2 — 2 2 0 1 — elec bgtr, tape — 4perc — pf
  — str
  Nordiska

Nono, Luigi   (1924-1990)

Canti Per 13 (1955)   12'
  1[1/pic] 1 2[1.bcl] 1 — 1 1 1 0 — ssx —
  str[1.0.1.1.1]
  Schott

Incontri (1955)   7'
  2[1.2/pic] 2 2 2 — 2 1 1 0 — 2tmp — str[2.2.2.2.2]
  Schott

Nordentoft, Anders   (1957-)

The City of Threads (1994)   10'
  1 1 1 1 — 1 0 0 0 — str[1.1.1.1.1]
  Hansen

Entgegen (1985)   12'
  1 1 1 1 — 1 1 1 0 — 1perc — pf — str[1.1.1.1.1]
  Hansen

Hymne (1996)   16'
  1 0 1 0 — 1 1 0 0 — pf — str[1.0.1.1.0]
  Hansen

Zenerva Sesio (1992)   10'
  1 0 1 0 — 0 0 0 0 — 1perc — pf — str[1.1.1.1.0]
  Hansen

Nordheim, Arne   (1931-2010)

Tractatus (1986)   15'
  1 1[eh] 1[bcl] 1[cbn] — 0 0 0 0 — 2perc — hp —
  2pf[pf.cel] — str[1.1.1.1.1]
  Hansen

Nørgård, Per   (1932-)

Adagio Di Preludio (1951)   4'
  str
  Hansen

Amled; Prince of Jutland (1993)   35'
  1 1 1 1 — 1 1 0 0 — 1perc — str[1.1.1.1.1]
  Hansen

Amled: Suite (1993)   20'
  1 1 1 1 — 1 1 0 0 — 1perc — str
  Hansen

Aspects of Leaving (1997)   15'
  2 1 3 2 — 2 2 1 1 — 1perc — str
  Hansen

Bach to the Future (1996)   20'
  solo 2perc
  2 2 2 2 — 2 2 2 0 — hp — str
  Strings without vn.
  Hansen

Bright Dances, op.24 (1959)   10'
  1 1 1 1 — 2 1 0 0 — tmp — str
  Hansen

Concerto for Viola No.1;   23'
Remembering Child (1986)
  solo va
  1 2 1 2 — 2 1 0 0 — 1perc — pf — str
  Hansen

Concerto for Violin No.2;   23'
Borderlines (2002)
  solo vn
  1perc — str
  Hansen

Constellations, op.22 (1958)   22'
  str
  Hansen

Dream Play (1975)   10'
  2 1 2 1 — 2 2 0 0 — 1perc — 2pf[pf.cel] — str
  Hansen

For a Change (1982)   25'
  solo perc
  2 2 2 2 — 4 3 3 0 — str
  Hansen

Four Observations - From an   5'
Infinite Rapport; Hommage a Béla
Bartók (1995)
  str
  Hansen

Fugitive Summer (1992)   10'
  str
  Hansen

Lysning (2006)   6'
  str
  Hansen

Metamorphose, op.4 (1953)   *11'*
   str
   Hansen

Night-Symphonies; Day Breaks   *20'*
(1992)
   1 1 1 1 — 1 1 1 0 — 1perc — pf — str[1.1.1.1.1]
   Hansen

Nocturnes; Fragment VII (1961)   *8'*
   solo S
   1 1 1 1 — 0 1 1 0 — 2perc — hp — pf —
   str[2.2.2.2.1]
   Hansen

Out Of This World — Parting   *7'*
(1994)
   str
   Hansen

Pastorale: From Babette's Feast   *6'*
(1988)
   str
   Hansen

Pictures from Lake Arre   *16'*
   solo sx
   pf — str
   Hansen

Prelude and Fugue (With a Crab   *14'*
Canon) (1982)
   1 0 1 0 — 0 0 0 0 — gtr, mand — 1perc —
   str[1.0.0.0.1]
   Hansen

Recall (1968)   *12'*
   solo accordion
   2 2 2 2 — 2 2 1 0 — tmp+1 — cel — str
   Hansen

Rhapsody (1952)   *11'*
   solo pf
   2 2 2 2 — 2 2 2 0 — tmp+1 — str
   Hansen

Scintillation (1993)   *16'*
   1 0 1 0 — 1 0 0 0 — pf — str[1.0.1.1.0]
   Hansen

Shaking Hands (2000)   *4'*
   solo perc
   2[1/pic.2/afl] 2[1.eh] 2[1.bcl] 2 — 2 2 1 0 — str
   Hansen

Snip Snap (2006)   *2'*
   1 1 1 1 — 1 0 0 0 — pf — str[1.0.1.1.0]
   Alternative orchestration: 1111 - 1000 - str (1.1.1.1.0).
   Hansen

Surf (1983)   *10'*
   2 0 2 0 — 2 2 0 0 — accordion — 1perc — pf —
   str[2.0.0.2.0]
   Hansen

Tango Chikane; (reduced version)   *12'*
   1 2 2 2 — 2 1 1 0 — elec gtr — tmp+1 — elec org
   — str
   Also available in an arrangement by Karl Aage Rasmussen:
   1111 - 1000 - tmp+1 - elec org - str (1.1.1.1.1).
   Hansen

Towards Freedom? (1977)   *5'*
   2 2 2 2 — 4 2 2 0 — tmp+2 — str
   Hansen

Tributes; Album for Strings (1994-   *17'*
1995)
   str
   Contents - 1. Four Observations - From an Infinite Rapport
   (Hommage a Bartók); 2. Out of this World (Hommage a
   Lutoslawski); 3. Voyage into the Broken Screen (Hommage
   a Sibelius)
   mvt durations: 5' 7' 5'
   Hansen

Voyage into the Broken Screen;   *5'*
Hommage a Sibelius (1995)
   str
   Hansen

Voyage into the Golden Screen   *18'*
(1968)
   2 1 1 1 — 2 2 1 0 — 2perc — hp — str
   Hansen

Without Jealousy (1984)   *5'*
   1 0 1 1 — 0 1 0 0 — bandoneon (or accordion) —
   hp — pf — str[1.0.1.1.0]
   Hansen

Nørholm, Ib   (1931-)

The Garden With The Paths That   *14'*
Part, op.86 (1982)
   1 0 1 0 — 0 0 0 0 — gtr — 1perc — pf —
   str[1.0.0.1.0]
   Hansen

Novák, Vítêzslav   (1870-1949)

Serenade, op.36 (1905)   *26'*
   2 2 2 2 — 4 0 0 0 — hp — str
   UE

Nussio, Otmar   (1902-1990)

Boccaccio-Suite; Novelle dal   *12'*
Decamerone
> 2 2 2 2 — 2 2 1 0 — tmp+1 — str
> Contents - 1. Burlesca di Frate Cipolla; 2. Lamento
> d'Isabella; 3. Marinaresca di Paganin da Mare
> *UE*

Divertimento (1951)   *18'*
> 0 0 1 1 — 1 0 0 0 — str
> *Boosey & Hawkes*

Suite from the Tessin   *20'*
> 1 1 2 1 — 2 2 1 0 — tmp+1 — hp — 2pf[pf.cel] —
> str
> Contents - 1. Overture; 2. Serenata; 3. Girotondo; 4.
> Notturno Valmaggino; 5. Danza Ticinese
> mvt durations: 4' 3' 2' 6' 5'
> *UE*

Nyman, Michael   (1944-)

Concert Suite from Prospero's   *25'*
Books (1994)
> 2[1.2/pic] 2 2[1.2/bcl] 2 — 2 2 1 0 — pf — str
> *Chester Novello*

Drowning by Numbers for Chamber   *20'*
Orchestra (1998)
> solo vn, va
> 2[1.2/pic] 2[1.eh] 2[1.2/bcl] 2 — 2 2 1[btbn] 0 — pf
> — str[8.6.4.4.2]
> Solos can be played by the leaders of the orchestral
> sections.
> *Chester Novello*

Strong on Oaks; Strong on the   *17'*
Causes of Oaks (1997)
> 2[1.pic] 2 2 2 — 2 2 0 0 — tmp — str
> *Chester Novello*

O

Obst, Michael   (1955-)

Kristallwelt (1983)   *18'*
> 1 1 2[1.bcl] 1 — 1 2 1 0 — tape — 2perc —
> 2pf[pf.cel/elec org/synth] — str[3.0.2.2.1]
> *Breitkopf*

Nachtstücke (1990)   *35'*
> 1 0 1 0 — 0 0 1[1/atbn] 0 — electronics — 2perc
> — synth — str[0.0.0.0.1]
> *Breitkopf*

Nosferatu: Music to the Silent Film   *93'*
by Friedrich Wilhelm Murnau (2002)
> 1[1/afl] 0 2[1.bcl] 1[1/cbn] — 0 2 2 0 — 1perc —
> pf — str[1.0.1.1.1]
> *Breitkopf*

Shadow (...of a doubt) (1997)   *20'*
> solo perc
> 1 1 2[1.bcl] 1 — 1 1 1 0 — 2perc — str[1.0.1.1.1]
> *Breitkopf*

Ohse, Reinhard   (1930-)

Serenade   *18'*
> str
> *Breitkopf*

Oldham, Arthur   (1926-2003)

Divertimento (1951)   *14'*
> str
> *Boosey & Hawkes*

Variations on a Carol Tune (1949)   *10'*
> 1 1 1 1 — 1 0 0 0 — 1perc — hp — str
> perc: cym, bd, sd
> *Boosey & Hawkes*

Oliver, Stephen   (1950-1992)

Nicholas Nickelby; (incidental   *55'*
music) (1980)
> 1[1/pic] 0 1[1/bcl/asx] 1 — 1 2[1/crt.2/crt] 1[1/tu] 0
> — banjo[or gtr] — 1perc — pf — str[1.1.0.0.1]
> Vn2 doubles on va. Pf part to be played by conductor.
> *Novello*

Olivier, François   (1907-1947)

Suite Pour Petit Orchestre   *16'*
1 1 1 1 — 2 1 0 0 — str
UE

Orbón, Julián   (1925-1991)

Partita No.2   *9'*
1perc — 2pf[cel.harm] — str[1.1.1.1.0]
perc: vib
Peer

Osborne, Nigel   (1948-)

Alba (1984)   *17'*
solo Mz
1 1 1 0 — 1 1 1 0 — tape — 1perc — hp — str[1.1.1.1.1]
UE

The Art of the Fugue (1993)   *20'*
solo vc
2 2 2 2 — 2 2 0 0 — 1perc — str
UE

The Cage (1981)   *14'*
solo T
1[afl] 1 1 1 — 1 1 0 0 — str[1.1.0.1.0]
UE

Concerto for Flute (1980)   *16'*
solo fl
0 2 0 0 — 2 0 0 0 — str[6.4.3.2.1]
UE

Eulogy (1990)   *8'*
1 1 1 1 — 1 1 1 0 — 1perc — str[1.1.1.1.1]
UE

Fantasia (1983)   *12'*
1 1 1 1 — 1 0 0 0 — pf — str[1.0.1.1.1]
UE

In Camera (1979)   *19'*
1 1 1 1 — 1 1 1 0 — gtr — str[1.1.1.1.1]
UE

Pornography (1985)   *13'*
solo Mz
1 0 1 0 — 1 0 0 0 — gtr — 1perc — str[1.0.1.1.0]
UE

Prelude and Fugue (1975)   *17'*
1 0 1 0 — 0 1 1 0 — 1perc — pf — str[1.0.1.1.1]
UE

Stone Garden (1988)   *15'*
1 1 1 1 — 1 1 1 0 — 1perc — hp — str[1.1.1.1.1]
UE

Wildlife (1984)   *20'*
1 0 1 0 — 1 1 0 0 — ebtr, electronics — 1perc — hp — str[1.0.1.1.0]
UE

Zansa (1985)   *20'*
1 1 1 1 — 1 1 1 0 — zansa — 1perc — pf — str[1.1.1.1.1]
UE

Ostendorf, Jens-Peter   (1944-2006)

Septett "Geschichte Vom..." (1990)   *26'*
0 0 1 1 — 0 1 1 0 — 1perc — str[1.0.0.0.1]
Sikorski

P

Paccagnini, Angelo   (1930-1999)

Actuelles 1968 (1968)   *19'*
  solo S
  2 1 1 0 — 1 1 0 0 — tape — str
UE

Dialoghi (1963)   *14'*
  2 2 2 0 — 2 2 0 0 — tmp+1 — str
UE

Musica da Camera (1960)   *11'*
  2[1.pic] 0 1[bcl] 0 — 1 0 0 0 — 1perc — hp —
  str[1.0.0.1.1]
    perc: vib
UE

Pade, Steen   (1956-)

Sinfonietta (1998)   *20'*
  1 1 1 1 — 1 1 1 0 — 1perc — pf — str[1.1.1.1.1]
  Hansen

Palau Boix, Manuel   (1893-1967)

Homenaje a Debussy (1929)   *6'*
  2 2 2 2 — 2 2 0 0 — tmp — str
  Unión

Palmer, Robert   (1915-)

Memorial Music
  1 1 1 1 — 2 1 1 0 — str
  Peer

Panufnik, Andrzej   (1914-1991)

Divertimento for Strings (1947)   *15'*
  str
  Arranged from his string trios by Janiewicz.
  Boosey & Hawkes

Jagiellonian Triptych (1966)   *7'*
  str
  Boosey & Hawkes

Landscape (1962)   *7'*
  str
  Boosey & Hawkes

Lullaby (1947)   *7'*
  2hp[1.2(opt)] — str[6.6.6.6.5]
  Boosey & Hawkes

Metasinfonia; Symphony No.7   *25'*
(1978)
  solo org
  tmp — str
  Boosey & Hawkes

Old Polish Suite (1950)   *12'*
  str
  Boosey & Hawkes

Sinfonia Mistica; Symphony No.6   *22'*
(1977)
  2 2 2 2 — 2 0 0 0 — str[6.6.3.3.2]
  Boosey & Hawkes

Panufnik, Roxanna   (1968-)

The Frog and the Nightingale   *16'*
(2003)
  solo S, Mz, Bar
  2 2 2 2 — 2 0 0 0 — tmp+1 — hp — str
UE

Powers & Dominions; Concertino   *14'*
for Harp (2001)
  solo hp
  2 0 2 2 — 1 1 0 0 — 1perc — hp — str[6.6.6.4.2]
    perc: vib
UE

Papandopulo, Boris   (1906-1991)

Concerto da Camera, op.11 (1928)   *20'*
  solo coloratura S
  2[1.2/pic] 2[1.2/eh] 2[1.2/bcl] 1 — 0 0 0 0 — pf —
  str[1.0.0.0.0]
UE

Concerto for Doublebass (1968)   *20'*
  solo db
  str
  Breitkopf

Concerto for Harpsichord   *20'*
  solo hpsd (or pf)
  str
  Breitkopf

Pape, Andy   (1955-)

Clarino Concerto (1990)   25'
  solo pic tpt
  1 1 1 1 — 1 1 1 0 — 2perc — hp — str
Hansen

Min Fynske Barndom: Suite (2004)   15'
  1 1 1 1 — 1 0 0 0 — str[1.1.1.1.1]
Hansen

Pärt, Arvo   (1935-)

An den Wassern zu Babel saßen   7'
wir und weinten; Psalm 137 (1976)
  solo tbn
  0 0 2 0 — 1 0 0 0 — str
  Year of composition: 1976. This version: 1995.
UE

An den Wassern zu Babel saßen   7'
wir und weinten; Psalm 137 (1976)
  solo S, A, T, B
  1[1/pic] 1 1 1 — 1 0 0 0 — str[1.0.1.1.1]
  Original version 1976.
UE

Cantus in Memory of Benjamin   6'
Britten (1977)
  1perc — str
  perc: chime (A natural)
UE

Collage on B-A-C-H (1964)   9'
  0 2 0 0 — 0 0 0 0 — 2pf[pf.hpsd] — str
  Pf and hpsd can be executed by one player.
  Contents - 1. Toccata; 2. Sarabande; 3. Ricercare
  mvt durations: 3' 4' 2'
Sikorski

Concerto Piccolo after B-A-C-H   10'
(1994)
  solo tpt
  2pf[pf.hpsd] — str
Sikorski

Darf ich... (1995)   3'
  solo vn
  1perc[opt] — str
  perc: chime (C#)
UE

Festina Lente (1988)   8'
  hp[opt] — str
UE

Fratres; For Cello, Strings and   10'
Percussion (1977)
  solo vc
  1perc — str
UE

Fratres; For Chamber Ensemble   10'
(1977)
  1 1 1 1 — 1 0 0 0 — 1perc — str[1.1.1.1.1]
  perc: clav, bd (or tom-tom)
UE

Fratres; For Strings and Percussion   10'
(1977)
  1perc — str
  perc: claves, bd
  Original composition 1977. This version: 1991.
UE

Fratres; For Trombone, Strings and   10'
percussion (1977)
  solo tbn
  1perc — str
  Original composition 1977. This version arranged by
  Christian Lindberg (1993).
UE

Fratres; For Violin, Strings and   10'
Percussion (1977)
  solo vn
  1perc — str
  Original composition 1977. This version: 1992.
UE

Lamentate; Homage to Anish   37'
Kapoor and his sculpture "Marsyas"
(2002)
  solo pf
  3[1.pic.3/afl] 2[1.2/eh] 2 2 — 4 2 2 0 — tmp+3 —
  str
UE

Mein Weg; For 14 Strings and   7'
Percussion (1999)
  1perc — str[3.3.2.4.2]
  perc: chime in E, bd
UE

Orient & Occident (2000)   7'
  str
UE

Pari Intervallo (1995)   6'
  0 0 1 0 — 0 0 1 0 — str
UE

Pro Et Contra; Concerto for Cello   9'
(1966)
    solo vc
    1 1 1 1 — 1 1 1 0 — asx — tmp+3 — hp — pf —
    str
Sikorski

Psalom (1995)   6'
    str
UE

Silouans Song; "My soul yearns   6'
after the Lord..." (1991)
    str
UE

Summa (1991)   6'
    str
UE

Symphony No.1; "Polyphonic," op.9   17'
(1963)
    1[1/pic] 1 1 1 — 2 1 1 0 — tmp+3 — str
    perc: tri, cym, hi-hat, tamburo, bd, xyl
    Contents - 1. Canon; 2. Preludio e Fuga
    mvt durations: 10' 7'
Sikorski

Symphony No.4; "Los Angeles"   34'
(2008)
    tmp+3 — hp — str
UE

Tabula Rasa; Double Concerto   27'
(1977)
    solo 2 vn
    pf[prepf] — str
    Also available for solo vn and va (same instrumentation).
    (UE)
    Contents - 1. Ludus; 2. Silentium
    mvt durations: 10' 17'
UE

These Words... (2008)   15'
    2perc — str
    perc: crot, marim, tri, sus cym, bd
UE

Trisagion (1994)   12'
    str
UE

Wenn Bach Bienen gezüchtet   7'
hätte... (1976/2001)
    1[1/pic] 1 1 1 — 1 0 0 0 — 1perc — pf —
    str[4.4.4.4.2]
    Also possible with strings (8.8.8.8.4).
UE

Pasatieri, Thomas   (1945-)

Concerto for Piano (1994)   30'
    solo pf
    2 2 2 2 — 2 2 2 0 — 2perc — hp — str
Subito

Serenade for Violin and Orchestra   9'
(1994)
    solo vn
    1 1 1 1 — 2 1 0 0 — str
Subito

Pasquet, Yves-Marie   (1947-)

Atemkristal   45'
    solo S
    1 2 2 1 — 2 2 1 0 — tape — hp — pf —
    str[0.0.0.0.1]
Presser

Suaire de Sons
    solo Mz
    2 1 0 0 — 1 1 1 1 — bsx — 3perc — str
Presser

Patterson, Paul   (1947-)

At the Still Point of the Turning   14'
World, op.41 (1980)
    1 1 1 0 — 1 0 0 0 — str[1.0.1.1.1]
UE

Europhony, op.55 (1985)   15'
    0 2 0 0 — 2 0 0 0 — str
UE

Pauels, Heinz   (1908-1985)

Capriccio; For Piano, five Solo   14'
Instruments and Percussion, op.92b
(1960)
    1 0 1 0 — 0 1 0 0 — 1perc — hp — pf —
    str[0.0.1.0.0]
    perc: tri, cym, tom-tom, military dr, sd, cast, glsp, xyl, vib
Schott

Paumgartner, Bernhard   (1887-1971)

Divertimento; Five Old-English   *12'*
Dances
   1 1 1 1 — 1 1 0 0 — 1perc — hpsd —
   str[0.0.1.1.0]
UE

Suite in G minor (1930)   *15'*
   2 2 2 2 — 2 2 0 0 — tmp+1 — hp — 2pf[pf.cel] —
   str
UE

Pavlenko, Sergei   (1952-)

Symphony No.3 for Chamber   *15'*
Orchestra; (For the Centenary of
Igor Stravinsky) (1982)
   1 1 1 1 — 1 1 1 0 — tmp+1 — hp — cel —
   str[1.1.1.1.1]
   perc: cym, tam-tam
Schirmer

Payne, Anthony   (1936-)

Hidden Music (1992)   *10'*
   1 1 1 1 — 1 0 0 0 — str[5.4.2.2.1]
Chester Novello

Orchestral Variations; "The Seeds   *20'*
Long Hidden" (1994)
   2 2 2 2 — 2 2 0 0 — tmp — str
Chester Novello

A Sea Change (1988)   *12'*
   1 0 1 0 — 0 0 0 0 — hp — str[1.1.1.1.0]
Chester Novello

Songs and Seascapes (1984)   *18'*
   str[8.6.4.4.2]
   Also possible with (3.3.2.2.1).
Chester Novello

Spring's Shining Wake (1982)   *15'*
   1 1 2 1 — 2 0 0 0 — 1perc — str[3.3.3.3.2]
Chester Novello

The Stones and Lonely Places Sing   *18'*
(1979)
   1[1/pic] 0 1[1/bcl] 0 — 1 0 0 0 — pf —
   str[1.0.1.1.0]
Chester Novello

Symphonies of Wind and Rain   *15'*
(1992)
   1 1 2 1 — 1 0 0 0 — 1perc — str[1.1.1.1.1]
Chester Novello

Paz, Juan Carlos   (1901-1972)

Obertura Para Doce Instrumentos   *6'*
(Overture for 12 Instruments)
   1 1 1 1 — 2 1 1 0 — str[1.0.1.1.1]
Peer

Pepping, Ernst   (1901-1981)

Invention für Kleines Orchester: *4'*
From "Musiken für Orchester"
(1930)
   2 2 2 2 — 2 2 0 0 — str
Fleisher; Schott

Pergament, Moses   (1893-1977)

Vision; Ballet (1923)   *10'*
   2 2 2 2 — 2 1 1 0 — tmp — org[opt] — str
Nordiska

Pernes, Thomas   (1956-)

Gesänge (1983)   *15'*
   0 1 2 1 — 1 0 0 0 — str[1.1.1.1.0]
UE

Petyrek, Felix   (1892-1951)

Arabian Suite (1925)   *8'*
   2 1 2 2 — 2 0 1 0 — 1perc — hp — str[0.0.0.0.1]
UE

Pfitzner, Hans   (1869-1949)

Das Christ-Elflein, op.20 (1906)   *12'*
   2 2 2 2 — 2 0 0 0 — tmp+1 — hp — str
   perc: tri, tam-tam, tambn
Boosey & Hawkes

Pfundt, Reinhard   (1951-)

Bartók-Reflexionen (1983)   10'
2 2 2 2 — 2 2 2 0 — tmp+1 — hp — str
Breitkopf

Musique Pour Sanssouci   17'
2 2 2 2 — 2 2 2 0 — tmp+1 — hp — str
Breitkopf

Phibbs, Joseph   (1974-)

Cayuga (1999)   15'
1[1/pic] 1 1[1/Ebcl/bcl] 1 — 1 1 1 0 — 1perc — hp
— pf — str[1.1.1.1.1]
perc: sus cym, hi-hat, sd, bd, 4 tom-tom, marac, police whistle,
marim, vib, xyl, glsp
Faber

Piazzolla, Astor   (1921-1992)

Aconcagua; (Concierto para   22'
Bandoneón) (1979)
solo bandoneon
tmp+1 — hp — pf — str
perc: bd, tri, guiro
mvt durations: 7' 7' 8'
Tonos

Las Cuatro Estaciones Porteñas   26'
(1964-1970)
2 2 2 2 — 4 3 3 1 — tmp+1 — str
Orchestrated by Carlos Franzetti.
Contents - 1. Primavera Porteña; 2. Verano Porteño; 3.
Otoño Porteño; 4. Invierno Porteño
mvt durations: 6' 7' 6' 7'
Tonos

Danza Criolla (1950)   2'
1[1/pic] 1 1 — 2 2 1 0 — tmp+1 — hp — pf —
str
Tonos; Peer

Milonga del Ángel (1987)   6'
2 2[1.2/eh] 2 1 — 4 0 0 0 — 1perc — hp — pf —
str
Orchestrated by José Bragato.
Tonos

Oblivion (1982)   5'
solo ob
str
Tonos

Tangazo; Variations on Buenos   15'
Aires (1969)
2 2 2 2 — 2 0 0 0 — 1perc — pf — str
perc: guiro, tri, chimes, xyl, 3 tom-tom, cym
Tonos

Picker, Tobias   (1954-)

The Blue Hula (1981)   10'
1 0 1 0 — 0 0 0 0 — 3perc — pf — str[1.0.0.1.0]
perc: vib, glsp, marim
Schott

Pierné, Gabriel   (1863-1937)

Album Pour Mes Petites Amis   2'
(Album for My Little Friends):
Farandole, op.14, No.2
1[pic] 1 1 1 — 1 1[opt] 0 0 — 1perc — str
Kalmus

Album Pour Mes Petites Amis   3'
(Album for My Little Friends): La
Veillee de l'Ange Gardien, op.14,
No.3
str
Kalmus

Album Pour Mes Petites Amis   2'
(Album for My Little Friends): Petite
Gavotte, op.14, No.4
1 1 1 0 — 1 0 0 0 — str
Kalmus

Album Pour Mes Petites Amis   3'
(Album for My Little Friends):
Chanson d'Autrefois, op.14, No.5
str
Kalmus

Album Pour Mes Petites Amis   4'
(Album for My Little Friends):
Marche des Petits Soldats de
Plomb (March of the Little Lead
Soldiers), op.14, No.6
1 0 1 0 — 0 1 0 0 — 1perc — hp — str
Kalmus

Ballet de Cour, No.1: Rigaudon   3'
(1901)
1 1 1 2[1.2(opt)] — 1 1[opt] 0 0 — tmp[opt] — str
Kalmus

Ballet de Cour, No.2: Passepied   4'
(1901)
   str
Kalmus

Ballet de Cour, No.3: La Canarie   2'
(1901)
   1 1 1 1 — 0 0 0 0 — str
Kalmus

*Ballet de Cour, No.4: Pavane et
Saltarello* (1901)   7'
   1 1 1 1 — 1 0 0 0 — 1perc — str
Kalmus

*Ballet de Cour, No.5: Menuet de
Roy* (1901)   4'
   str
Kalmus

Ballet de Cour, No.6: Passamezzo
(1901)   2'
   2 2 2 2 — 2 2 3 0 — tmp+1 — str
   Optional instruments: fl2, ob2, cl2, bn2, hn2, all tpt, all tbn,
   tmp, perc.
Kalmus

*Canzonetta for Clarinet and
Orchestra*   4'
   solo cl
   2 1 1 1 — 1 0 0 0 — str
Kalmus

Concert Piece in G-flat, op.39
(1903)   13'
   solo hp
   2 2 2 2 — 4 2 3 0 — tmp+1 — str
Kalmus

*Giration; Divertissement
choréographique* (1935)   9'
   1 0 1 1 — 0 1 1 0 — pf — str
Fleisher

Serenade, op.7 (1883)   3'
   str
Kalmus

Pilati, Mario   (1903-1938)

*Alla Culla; Ninna-nanna per piccola
Orchestra* (1940)   5'
   1 1 1 1 — 1 0 0 0 — hp — cel — str
Fleisher; Ricordi

Pillney, Karl Hermann   (1896-1980)

*Eskapaden eines Gassenhauers;
Für Hörer mit Sinn für musikalische
Eulenspiegeleien* (1968)   30'
   1 1 1 1 — 1 1 0 0 — 1perc — pf — str
   perc: chimes
Breitkopf

Pintscher, Matthias   (1971-)

*La Metamorfosi di Narciso;
Allegoria sonora per un violoncello
principale e gruppo strumentale*
(1992)   36'
   solo vc
   1[1/pic] 0 1[1/bcl] 1 — 1 1 2 0 — 2perc — pf/hpsd
   — str[1.0.1.1.1]
Bärenreiter

Pisk, Paul Amadeus   (1893-1990)

Partita, op.10 (1924)   29'
   2 2 2 2 — 2 2 1 0 — 1perc — hp — str
UE

Piston, Walter   (1894-1976)

Divertimento (1946)   11'
   1 1 1 1 — 0 0 0 0 — str[1.1.1.1.1]
AMP

Sinfonietta (1941)   17'
   2 2 2 2 — 2 0 0 0 — str
Boosey & Hawkes

Pittaluga, Gustavo   (1906-1975)

*Petite Suite: D'après la musique
écrite pour "Un torero hermosisimo"*
(1934)
   1[1/pic] 0 1 1 — 0 1 1 0 — hp — str
   Strings without va.
Fleisher; Leduc

Platz, Robert H. P.   (1951-)

CHLEBNICOV (1979)   30'
   1 1 1 0 — 1 1 1 0 — tape — str[0.0.0.2.1]
Breitkopf

From Fear of Thunder, Dreams...   13'
(1987)
    1[afl/bfl] 0 1[1/bcl] 0 — 1 0 0 0 — 2perc — pf —
str[1.0.0.1.0]
Breitkopf

PIECE NOIRE (1989)   20'
    2[afl.bfl] 1 1[1/cbcl] 0 — 1 1 1 0 — tape — pf —
str[1.0.1.1.1]
Breitkopf

Pokorný, Petr   (1932-)

Hommage a "Brundibár"; Overture   8'
for Small Orchestra (1999)
    1 0 1 0 — 1 0 0 0 — 1perc — pf — str[1.0.0.1.1]
A contemplative piece in the "Terezin" instrumentation,
suitable as a sensitive introduction to Hans Krása's opera
"Brundibár."
Boosey & Hawkes

Polovinkin, Leonid   (1894-1949)

Tänze der Rätsel (1930)   15'
    1[1/pic] 1 1 2 — 2 1 0 0 — tmp+1 — str
Fleisher; UE

Pompey, Angel Martin   (1902-2001)

Serenata madrilena (1949)   10'
    2[1.2/pic] 2[1.2/eh] 2 2 — 2 2 0 0 — tmp — str
Boosey & Hawkes

Ponce, Manuel   (1882-1948)

Gavota   5'
    2 1 1 1 — 2 0 0 0 — tmp — str
Fleisher; Peer

Instantáneas Mexicanas, No.3:   4'
Cielito lindo (1938)
    1 1 2 1 — 0 0 0 0 — str
Fleisher

Instantáneas Mexicanas, No.4: Si   1'
algún ser
    1 1 2 1 — 0 0 0 0 — str
Fleisher

Instantáneas Mexicanas, No.6:   2'
Mañanitas de los niños
    1 1 2 0 — 0 0 0 0 — gtr — str
Strings without va or db.
Fleisher

Instantáneas Mexicanas, No.7:
Jugando
    1 1 1 0 — 0 0 0 0 — gtr — str
Fleisher

Suite en Estilo Antiguo   10'
    1 1 1 1 — 4 0 0 0 — str
Peer

Poot, Marcel   (1901-1988)

Ballade (1952)   13'
    solo vn
    2 2 2 2 — 2 0 0 0 — tmp — str
Eschig

Fantasia (1942)   10'
    1 1 1 1 — 2 1 1 0 — str
UE

Fête à Thélème (1957)   6'
    1 1 2 1 — 2 2 1 0 — tmp+1 — str
Eschig

Musique Legère (1943)   9'
    2[1.2(opt)] 1 2[1.2(opt)] 1 — 2 2 1 0 — tmp+1 —
str
UE

Musique pour cordes (1963)   9'
    str
Eschig

Musiquette (1930)   5'
    solo pf
    1 1 2 1 — 2 2 1 0 — str
Eschig

Ouverture Joyeuse (1934)   5'
    2 2 2 2 — 2 2 2 0 — 1perc — str
UE

Rondo (1928)   10'
    solo pf
    1 1 2 1 — 2 1 1 0 — 1perc — str
Eschig

Porrino, Ennio   (1910-1959)

Notturno e Danza (1936)   13'
  1 1 2 1 — 2 1 1 0 — hp — str
UE

Tre Canzoni Italiane (1939)   9'
  2[1.2/pic] 1 2 1 — 2 1 1 0 — str
UE; Fleisher

Poulenc, Francis   (1899-1963)

Airs chantés (1928)   8'
  solo S
  1 1[1/eh] 1 2 — 1 1 0 0 — tmp — hp — str
  Orchestrated by Elsa Barraine.
Salabert

La Bal masqué; Cantate profane   17'
sur un texte de Max Jacob (1932)
  solo Bar (or Mz)
  0 1 1 1 — 0 1[crt] 0 0 — 1perc — pf —
  str[1.0.0.1.0]
Salabert

Bucolique (1954)   2'
  2[1.2/pic] 2[1.2/eh] 2 2 — 2 0 0 0 — tmp — str
Salabert

Chansons villageoises (1942)   10'
  solo voice
  2 2 2 2 — 2 1 0 0 — tmp+2 — hp — str
Eschig

Deux Marches et un Intermède   6'
(1938)
  1 1 1 1 — 0 1 0 0 — str
Fleisher; Salabert

L'embarquement pour Cythère   3'
  2 2 2 2 — 2 1 1 0 — tmp+3 — hp — str
  No.3 of "Musique pour faire plaisir." Orchestrated by Jean
  Françaix.
Eschig

Esquisse d'une Fanfare: Ouverture   2'
pour le Ve acte de "Romeo et
Juliette"
  1[1/pic] 1 1 1 — 1 1 1[btbn] 0 — str
  Strings without db.
Fleisher

Flute Sonata (1957)   14'
  solo fl
  1 2 2 2 — 2 0 0 0 — tmp — str
Chester Novello

L'histoire de Babar, le petit éléphant   22'
(1940)
  2[1/pic.2/pic] 2[1.2/eh] 2[1.2/bcl] 2[1.2/cbn] — 2
  2[1/crt.2] 1 1 — narrator — tmp — hp — str
Chester Novello

Hoops, Ballet (1963)   20'
  1 1 1 1 — 2 1 1 0 — tmp/perc — pf[opt] — str
  Orchestrated by Leighton Lucas. Possible with 1111-0100-
  tmp/perc-pf-str.
Chester Novello

Matelote provençale (1952)   2'
  2[1.2/pic] 2 2 2 — 2 2 0 0 — tmp+1 — str
Salabert

Mouvements perpétuels for nine   5'
instruments (1918)
  1 1 1 1 — 1 0 0 0 — str[1.0.1.1.1]
Chester Novello

Mouvements perpétuels; Nos. 1 & 2   5'
(1918)
  1 1 2 1 — 2 2 1 0 — 1perc — hp — cel — str
  Orchestrated by Manuel E. Gomez.
Chester Novello

Overture (1965)   5'
  2 2 2 2 — 2 2 1 0 — tmp/perc — hp — str
  Orchestrated by Jean Françaix. Not to be confused with
  "Overture" (1939) arr. by Milhaud.
Chester Novello

Overture (1939)   5'
  2 1 2 1 — 2 2 1 0 — 1perc — str
  Orchestrated by Darius Milhaud.
Chester Novello

Pièce brève; On the Name of Albert   2'
Roussel
  2 2 2 2 — 2 1 0 0 — tmp — hp — str
Presser

Sinfonietta (1947)   24'
  2 2 2 2 — 2 2 0 0 — tmp — hp — str
Chester Novello

Valse (1932)   2'
  1 1 1 1 — 1 1 1 0 — tmp+1 — str
  Excerpt from "L'album des six."
Eschig

Pousseur, Henri   (1929-2009)

Symphonies à Quinze Solistes   13'
(1954)
  1 1 1 1 — 2 1 1 0 — 2hp — pf — str[1.1.1.1.0]
UE

Powell, Mel   (1923-1998)

Modules; An Intermezzo for   15'
Chamber Orchestra (1985)
    1 1 1 1 — 2 1 1[btbn] 0 — 2perc — hp — pf/cel
    — str[1.0.1.1.1]
Schirmer

Stanzas (1965)   7'
    2 1 2 1 — 2 2 1 0 — 1perc — str
Schirmer

Price, Florence   (1887-1953)

Suite of Dances
    2 0 2 1 — 2 2 0 0 — tmp+1 — str
Fleisher

Primosch, James   (1956-)

Five Miniatures (1982)   7'
    1 1 1[1/bcl] 0 — 1 1 1 0 — str[1.0.1.1.0]
Margun

Septet (1985)   15'
    1[1/pic] 1[1/eh] 1[1/bcl] 0 — 0 0 0 0 — pf —
    str[1.0.1.1.0]
Margun

Prokofiev, Sergei   (1891-1953)

Andante, op.50a (1930)   9'
    str
    Arranged from String Quartet No.1.
Boosey & Hawkes

Autumn; A Symphonic Sketch for   7'
Small Orchestra, op.8 (1910)
    2 2 3[1.2.bcl] 2 — 4 1 0 0 — hp — str
Boosey & Hawkes

Cinderella; Ballet in Three Acts,   100'
op.87 (1944)
    1[1/pic] 1[1/eh] 2[1.2/bcl] 1 — 2 2 1 0 — tmp+1 —
    hp — pf/cel — str
    Reduced orchestration by Daryl Griffith.
Boosey & Hawkes

Cinq Melodies (sans paroles), op.35   13'
(1920)
    solo vc
    2[1.2/pic] 2 2 2 — 3 0 0 0 — hp — str
    Arranged by Rodion Shchedrin (Nos.1,3,4,5) and Prokofiev
    (No.2). Shchedrin arrangement from 2007.
Boosey & Hawkes

Classical Symphony in D;   15'
Symphony No.1, op.25 (1917)
    2 2 2 2 — 2 2 0 0 — tmp — str
Boosey & Hawkes

Concerto for Cello in E minor, op.58   35'
(1938)
    solo vc
    2 2 2 2 — 2 2 0 1 — tmp+1 — str
    perc: cym, cast, bd, sd, tambn
    See also the composer's *Sinfonia Concertante, op.125.*
Boosey & Hawkes

Concertino for Cello in G minor,   21'
op.132 (1952)
    solo vc
    2[1.2/pic] 2[1.2/eh] 2[1.2/bcl] 2 — 2 1 0 0 —
    tmp+1 — pf[opt] — str
    perc: tri, tambn, sd, bd, glsp
    Reduced orchestration by Vladimir Blok.
Boosey & Hawkes

Divertimento, op.43 (1929)   15'
    2 2 2 2 — 4 2 3 1 — tmp+1 — str
    perc: cym, bd, sd, tambn
Boosey & Hawkes

Eugene Onegin; For Narrator,   57'
Actors and Orchestra, op.71 (1936)
    2 2 2[1/asx.2/tsx] 1 — 2 3[1.2.btpt] 2 1 —
    narrator, actors — tmp+1 — hp — 2pf — str
Boosey & Hawkes

Festive Poem "Thirty Years,"   15'
op.113 (1947)
    2 2 2 2 — 4 2 3 1 — tmp+1 — pf — str
    perc: tri, sd, cym, bd
Boosey & Hawkes

Hamlet, op.77 (1938)   24'
    solo S, Bar
    1 1 1 1 — 2 1 1 0 — accordion — 1perc — pf[opt]
    — str
    perc: tri, tambn, sd, bd, cym
Boosey & Hawkes

Lieutenant Kije: Troika, op.60   2'
(1934)
 2[1.pic] 1 2 1 — 2 2 3 0 — tsx — 1perc — hp[or
pf] — str
 perc: sleigh bells, tri, bd, tambn
 Arranged by David Lloyd-Jones.
Boosey & Hawkes

March in B-flat Major, op.99 (1944)   3'
 1 1 1 1 — 0 0 0 0 — 1perc — pf — str[1.1.1.1.1]
 Edited by Helmut Schmidinger.
UE

Overture; American, op.42 (1926)   8'
 1 1 2 2 — 0 2 1 0 — tmp+1 — 2hp — 2pf — str
 perc: cym, bd, sd
Boosey & Hawkes

Overture on Hebrew Themes,   9'
op.34a (1919)
 2 2 2 2 — 2 2 0 0 — 1perc — pf — str
 perc: bd
 Klezmer tunes arranged by the composer.
Boosey & Hawkes

Peter and the Wolf, op.67 (1936)   25'
 1 1 1 1 — 3 1 1 0 — narrator — tmp+1 — str
 perc: bd, sd, cast, cym, sus cym, tri, tambn
 For alternate text see Schickele, Peter: "Sneaky Pete and
 the Wolf."
Boosey & Hawkes; UE

Peter and the Wolf, op.67 (1936)   25'
 1 1 1 1 — 0 0 0 0 — narrator — 1perc — pf —
str[1.1.1.1.1]
 Arranged for ensemble by Helmut Schmidinger.
UE; Boosey & Hawkes

Sinfonia Concertante, op.125   35'
(1952)
 solo vc
 2[1.2/pic] 2 2 2 — 4 3[1.2.3(opt)] 3 1 — tmp+1 —
 cel — str
 perc: cym, tri, bd, sd, tambn
 A reworking of his "Concerto for Cello," op.58.
Boosey & Hawkes

Sinfonietta, op.48 (1909)   21'
 2 2 2 2 — 4 2 0 0 — str
 Revised version of his "Sinfonietta," op.5.
Boosey & Hawkes

A Summer Day, op.65a (1941)   15'
 2 2 2 2 — 2 2 0 0 — tmp+1 — str
 perc: cym, tri, cast, bd, sd
 Orchestrations of some of his piano pieces "Music for
 Children."
Boosey & Hawkes

The Ugly Duckling, op.18 (1914)   12'
 solo Mz
 2[1.2/pic] 2 3[1.2.bcl] 2 — 2 2 2 0 — 1perc — hp
 — str
 perc: glsp, cym, sd, bd
Boosey & Hawkes

Visions fugitives, op.22 (1917)   20'
 str
 Arranged by Rudolf Barshai.
Boosey & Hawkes

Proto, Frank   (1941-)

Concerto for Double Bass and   28'
Orchestra No.3; Four Scenes after
Picasso
 solo db
 2[1.2/pic] 2 2[1.2/bcl] 1 — 0 0 0 0 — 2perc — hp
 — pf — str
Liben

Fantasy for Double Bass and   14'
Orchestra
 solo db
 2[1.2/pic] 0 0 0 — 0 0 0 0 — 4perc — hp — pf —
 str
Liben

Nine Variations on Paganini; For   20'
Double Bass and Orchestra
 solo db
 2[1.2/pic] 2[1.2/eh] 2[1.2/bcl] 1 — 0 0 0 0 —
 tmp+1 — hp — pf — str
Liben

Provazník, Anatol   (1887-1950)

Ländliche Suite, op.53 (1935)   16'
 2 1 2 1 — 2 2 1 0 — tmp+1 — hp — str[1.1.1.1.1]
UE

Q

R

Qu, Xiao-song   (1952-)

Ji No.1   12'
  1 0 1 0 — 0 0 0 0 — 1perc — pf — str[1.0.1.0.1]
  perc: xyl, vib, chimes, bd
  Peer

String Symphony   21'
  tmp+1 — hp — pf — str
  perc: side dr, bd, tri, cym, xyl
  Peer

Quilter, Roger   (1877-1953)

As you like it: Suite, op.21 (1920)   9'
  1 1 2 1 — 2 2 1 0 — tmp+1 — hp — str
  perc: cym, tri, sd, tambn
  Kalmus; Boosey & Hawkes

A Children's Overture, op.17   11'
  1[1/pic] 1 2 1 — 2 2 1 0 — tmp+1 — hp — str
  Kalmus

Three English Dances, op.11   8'
(1910)
  2[1.2/pic] 2 2 2 — 2 2 3 1[euph] — 3sx[opt] —
  tmp+1 — str
  Kalmus

Where the Rainbow Ends: Suite   11'
  1 1 2 1 — 2 2 1 0 — tmp+1 — hp — str
  Contents - 1. Rainbow Land; 2. Rosamund; 3. Will o' the
  Wisp
  Kalmus

Quinet, Marcel   (1915-1986)

Sinfonietta (1953)   15'
  1 1 1 1 — 1 0 0 0 — tmp — str
  UE

Raasted, N.O.   (1888-1966)

Sinfonia da Chiesa, op.76 (1947)   30'
  0 0 0 0 — 0 2 2 0 — tmp — org — str
  Fleisher; Edition Dania

Rachmaninoff, Sergei   (1873-1943)

Caprice bohémien, op.12 (1894)   20'
  3[1.2.pic] 2 2 2 — 4 2 3 1 — tmp+1 — hp — str
  perc: cym, tri, bd, sd, tambn
  Boosey & Hawkes

Vocalise, op.34 (1912)   6'
  2 3[1.2.eh] 2 2 — 2 0 0 0 — str
  Arranged by the composer.
  Boosey & Hawkes

Vocalise, op.34 (1912)   6'
  str
  Arranged by Dubensky.
  Boosey & Hawkes

Rangström, Ture   (1884-1947)

Partita (1933)   12'
  solo vn
  2 2 2 2 — 2 2 0 0 — 1perc — str
  UE

Raphael, Günter   (1903-1960)

Chamber Concerto in D minor,   25'
op.24
  solo vc
  2 2 3[1.2.bcl] 2 — 0 0 0 0 — str
  Breitkopf

Concertino, op.71   16'
  solo asx
  1 1 0 1 — 1 1 1 0 — 2perc — str
  Breitkopf

Concertino, op.82   18'
  solo fl
  0 1 1 1 — 1 1 0 0 — str
  Breitkopf

Concertino in D 9'
solo va
1 1 1 1 — 1 1 1 0 — 1perc — str
Breitkopf

Concerto for Violin in C major, 25'
op.21
solo vn
2[1.2/pic] 2 0 2 — 3 2 0 0 — tmp+1 — str
Breitkopf

Concerto for Violin No.2, op.87 27'
solo vn
2[1.2/pic] 2 2 2[1.2/cbn] — 3 2 0 0 — tmp+1 —
cel — str
Breitkopf

Variationen über eine Schottische 20'
Volksweise, op.23
2 1 1[bcl] 2 — 2 0 0 0 — hp — str
Breitkopf

Rapoport, Eda   (1900-1969)

Israfel; Tone Picture after Edgar 10'
Allan Poe
1 0 0 0 — 0 0 0 0 — hp — str
Fleisher

Rasch, Kurt   (1902-1986)

Balletsuite 19'
solo cel
1 2 1 1 — 2 2 1 0 — tmp+1 — str
UE

Rasmussen, Karl Aage   (1947-)

A Ballad of Game and Dream 19'
(1974)
1 0 1 0 — 0 0 0 0 — elec gtr — 1perc — pf/hpsd
— str[1.0.0.1.0]
Hansen

Berio Mask (1977) 12'
1 0 1 0 — 0 0 0 0 — elec gtr — 1perc — pf —
str[1.0.0.1.0]
Hansen

Italian Concerto (1981) 12'
1 0 1 0 — 0 0 0 0 — gtr — 1perc — pf —
str[1.0.0.1.0]
Hansen

Movements on a Moving Line 17'
(1987)
1 1 1 1 — 1 1 1 0 — 2perc — pf — str[1.1.1.1.1]
Also available in a version for 1010-0000-1perc-pf-gtr-
str(1.0.0.1.0).
Hansen

Symphonie Classique (1969) 14'
1 2 1 1 — 2 1 1 0 — elec gtr — 1perc —
2pf[org.hpsd] — str
Hansen

Rathaus, Karol   (1895-1954)

Music for Strings; Adagio for 10'
Strings, op.49 (1941)
str
Boosey & Hawkes

Suite, op.27 (1929) 15'
solo vn
1 1 2 2 — 2 2 1 0 — banjo — 1perc — str
UE

Ratner, Leonard   (1916-)

Suite for Strings 16'
str
Boosey & Hawkes

Rautavaara, Einojuhani   (1928-)

Adagio Celeste (2000) 6'
str
Fennica Gehrman

Autumn Gardens (1999) 28'
2 2 2 2 — 2 0 0 0 — tmp+1 — str
Fennica Gehrman

Bird Gardens; Hommage a Zoltán 15'
Kodály (1982)
str
Fennica Gehrman

Canto IV (1992) 17'
str
Fennica Gehrman

Cantos (1960)   23'
str
Contents - 1. Canto I; 2. Canto II; 3. Canto III "A Portrait of
the Artist at a Certain Moment"
mvt durations: 6' 8' 9'
Fennica Gehrman

Cantus Arcticus; Concerto for Birds   18'
and Orchestra (1972)
2 2 2 2 — 2 2 1 0 — tape — tmp[opt]+1perc —
hp — cel — str
perc: cym, tam-tam
Contents - 1. The Bog; 2. Melancholy; 3. Swans Migrating
mvt durations: 7' 4' 7'
Warner; Fennica Gehrman

Concerto for Cello, op.41 (1968)   17'
solo vc
2 1 1 1 — 4 2 2 0 — tmp — hp — str
Breitkopf

Concerto for Flute; Dances with the   21'
Winds, op.69
solo fl
0 0 0 3[1.2.cbn] — 3 3 0 0 — tmp+3 — hp — str
Breitkopf

Concerto for Piano, op.45   20'
solo pf
2 0 2 0 — 4 2 2 0 — tmp+1 — str
Breitkopf

Divertimento (1953)   12'
str
Fennica Gehrman

Epitaph for Béla Bartók (1956)   6'
str
Fennica Gehrman

Garden of Spaces (1971)   12'
3 0 0 0 — 3 1 0 0 — tmp+1 — pf — str
Previous title: "Regular Sets of Elements in a Semiregular
Situation."
Fennica Gehrman

Hommage a Ferenc Liszt (1989)   6'
str
Fennica Gehrman

Incantations (2008)   25'
solo perc
2 2 2 2 — 2 3 2 0 — tmp — str
Solo perc requires: marim, 4 rototoms, 3 tam-tam, 2
bongos, 2 conga, vib, crot, chimes, 3 gongs, ped bd,
thunderstick
Boosey & Hawkes

Lintukoto (Isle of Bliss) (1995)   10'
2 2 2 2 — 2 1 1 0 — tmp+2 — hp — str
Fennica Gehrman

Pelimannit (The Fiddlers) (1952)   9'
str
Orchestrated by the composer in 1972.
Fennica Gehrman

Praevariata (1957)   7'
2 2 2 2 — 4 4 3 1 — tmp+2 — str
Fennica Gehrman

Suite for Strings (1952)   12'
str
Fennica Gehrman

Suomalainen Myytti (A Finnish   7'
Myth) (1977)
str
Fennica Gehrman

Symphony No.1 (1956)   22'
2 2 2 2 — 4 3 2 1 — tmp+2 — str
Revised in 2003.
Fennica Gehrman

Symphony No.2 (1957)   21'
2 2 2 2 — 2 1 1 0 — tmp+2 — str
Revised in 1984.
Fennica Gehrman

Symphony No.7; Angel of Light (1994)   35'
2 2 2 2 — 4 3 3 1 — tmp+2 — hp — str
perc: sus cym, sd, glsp, xyl, marim, vib, 4 tom-tom, 3 tam-tam
Warner; Fennica Gehrman

Three Meditations: Suite from   10'
"Children's Mass," op.71 (1973)
str
Fennica Gehrman

Ravel, Maurice   (1875-1937)

D'Anne jouant de l'espinette (1898)   3'
solo voice
2 2 2 2 — 2 1 0 0 — hp — str
Excerpt No.2 from "Deux Épigrammes de Clément Marot."
Orchestrated by Maurice Delage.
Eschig

Chanson hébraïque (1910)   5'
solo medium voice
2 2 2 2 — 2 0 0 0 — tmp — hp — str
From "Quatre Chants Populaires." Orchestrated by Maurice
Delage.
Durand

Cinq Mélodies populaires grecques   7'
(Five Greek Folk Melodies) (1906)
    2[1/pic.2/pic] 2[1.2/eh] 2 2 — 2 1 0 0 — tmp+4 —
hp — cel — str
Orchestrated by the composer and Manuel Rosenthal.
Kalmus; Durand

Deux Mélodies hébraïques (1919)   6'
    solo Mz
    2 2 2 2 — 2 2 0 0 — 1perc — hp — str
Contents - 1. Kaddisch; 2. L'Énigme Éternelle
Kalmus; Durand

Don Quichotte à Dulcinée (1933)   8'
    solo Bar
    2 2[1.2/eh] 2 2 — 2 1 0 0 — 1perc — hp — str
Contents - 1. Chanson Romanesque; 2. Chanson Épique; 3.
Chanson à Boire
Durand

Fanfare   2'
    2 2 2 2 — 2 1 0 0 — 1perc — str
Presser

Histoires naturelles (1906)   16'
    solo medium voice
    2 1 2 1 — 2 1 0 0 — 3perc — hp — cel — str
Contents - 1. Le Paon; 2. Le Grillon; 3. Le Cygne; 4. Le
Martin-Pêcheur; 5. La Pintade
Durand

Introduction et Allegro (1905)   12'
    solo hp
    1 0 1 0 — 0 0 0 0 — str[1.1.1.1.0]
Kalmus; Luck's

Ma Mère l'Oye (Mother Goose):   28'
Ballet en un acte, cinq tableaux et
un apothéose (1912)
    2[1.2/pic] 2[1.2/eh] 2 2[1.2/cbn] — 2 0 0 0 —
tmp+4 — hp — cel — str
perc: bd, cym, tri, sd, tam-tam, xyl, glsp
Kalmus; Durand; Luck's

Ma Mère l'Oye (Mother Goose):   16'
Cinq pièces enfantines (Suite)
(1912)
    2[1.2/pic] 2[1.2/eh] 2 2[1.2/cbn] — 2 0 0 0 —
tmp+3 — hp — cel — str
perc: bd, cym, tri, tam-tam, xyl, glsp
Contents - 1. Pavane de la Belle au bois dormant (Pavane
of the Sleeping Beauty); 2. Petit Poucet (Tom Thumb); 3.
Laideronnette, Impératrice des Pagodes ("Little Ugly,"
Empress of the Toy Mandarins); 4. Les entretiens de la
Belle et de la Bête (The Conversations of Beauty and the
Beast); 5. Le jardin féerique (The Fairy Garden)
mvt durations: 2' 3' 3' 4' 4'
Kalmus; Durand; Luck's

Ma Mère l'Oye (Mother Goose):   6'
Prelude et Danse du Rouet (1912)
    2[1.2/pic] 2[1.2/eh] 2 2 — 2 0 0 0 — tmp+3 — hp
— cel — str
perc: sus cym, cym, tri, tam-tam, sd, glsp, xyl
Kalmus; Durand; Luck's

Pavane pour une infante défunte   6'
(1910)
    2 1 2 2 — 2 0 0 0 — hp — str
A reduced version (by David Walter) is also available from
Eschig: 1111-1000-hp-str.
Eschig; Kalmus; Luck's

Ronsard à son âme (1935)   2'
    solo Bar
    2 2 2 2 — 0 0 0 0 — 2perc — str
Durand

Le Tombeau de Couperin (1917)   16'
    2[1.2/pic] 2[1.2/eh] 2 2 — 2 1 0 0 — hp — str
Contents - 1. Prélude; 2. Forlane; 3. Menuet; 4. Rigaudon
mvt durations: 3' 5' 4' 3'
Durand; Kalmus; Luck's

Trois poèmes de Stéphane   11'
Mallarmé (1913)
    solo medium voice
    2[1.pic] 0 2[1.bcl] 0 — 0 0 0 0 — pf —
str[1.1.1.1.0]
Durand

Read, Gardner   (1913-2005)

Partita for Small Orchestra, op.70   11'
(1946)
    1 1 1 1 — 1 1 1 0 — tmp — str
Fleisher

Petite Pastorale, op.40a   2'
    1 1 2 2 — 2 0 0 0 — str
Fleisher

Rechberger, Herman   (1947-)

Consort Music 1 (1976)   20'
    solo rec
    0 0 0 0 — 0 0 1 0 — tape — 1perc — hpsd — str
Hansen

Consort Music 2 (1977)   20'
    solo 2 rec
    0 0 0 0 — 0 2 2 0 — 4perc — str
Hansen

Redel, Martin Christoph   (1947-)

Dispersion, op.16 (1972)   11'
   1[1/pic] 1 1 0 — 0 0 0 0 — 1perc —
   hpsd/typewriter — str[1.0.1.1.0]
Boosey & Hawkes

Kammersinfonie II (Chamber   14'
Symphony II), op.17 (1972)
   1 1 1 0 — 0 0 0 0 — str
Boosey & Hawkes

Traumtanz, op.30 (1981)   15'
   1perc — str
Boosey & Hawkes

Reger, Max   (1873-1916)

Eine Balletsuite, op.130 (1913)   20'
   2 2 2 2 — 4 2 0 0 — tmp+1 — str
Kalmus

Christmas, op.145, No.3 (1916)   6'
   str
   From his "7 Organ Pieces," op.145, orchestrated by the
   composer.
Kalmus

Five Orchestra Songs (1901)   13'
   solo medium voice
   1 1 2 1 — 1 0 0 0 — 1perc — str
   Contents - 1. Mein Traum (op.31/5); 2. Fiedler (op.35/4); 3.
   Glückes genug (op.37/3); 4. Wiegenlied (op.43/5); 5. Fromm
   (op.62/11)
   mvt durations: 5' 2' 2' 2' 2'
UE

Suite, op.44 (1900)   8'
   2 2 2 2 — 3 2 0 0 — tmp+1 — str
   perc: sd
   Arranged from his "10 Small Pieces," op.44 by Wilhelm
   Rohm (1941).
   Contents - 1. Burletta (No.2); 2. Scherzo (No.6); 3. Fughette
   (No.8); 4. Gigue (No.9)
UE

Suite in A minor, op.103a   25'
   1 1 1 1 — 1 0 0 0 — str
   Arranged by Baranski.
Boosey & Hawkes

Symphonic Rhapsody, op.147   22'
   solo vn
   2 2 2 2 — 4 2 0 0 — tmp — str
   Edited by Florizel von Reuter (1931).
UE

Two Romances (1900)   11'
   solo vn
   2 2 2 2 — 2 0 0 0 — tmp — str
   mvt durations: 5' 6'
UE

Reich, Steve   (1936-)

City Life (1995)   24'
   2 2 2 0 — 0 0 0 0 — 3perc — 4pf[2pf.2sampler]
   — str[1.1.1.1.1]
   perc: 2 vib, cym, sd, gong, 2 bd
   All instruments amplified except for bd, sd, cym.
Boosey & Hawkes

Duet (1993)   5'
   solo 2vn
   str
Boosey & Hawkes

Eight Lines (1983)   17'
   2[1/pic.2/pic] 0 2[1/bcl.2/bcl] 0 — 0 0 0 0 — 2pf —
   str[2.2.2.2.0]
   Reorchestration of his "Octet." For performances in concert
   halls with a capacity of more than 200 seats, the flutes (but
   not the pic) and the clarinets (and bcl) must be amplified.
Boosey & Hawkes

Reimann, Aribert   (1936-)

Invenzioni (1979)   17'
   1[1/pic/afl] 1[1/eh] 1[1/bcl] 1 — 1 1 1 0 —
   str[1.1.1.1.1]
Schott

Metamorphosen über ein Menuett   11'
von Franz Schubert (1997)
   1[1/pic] 1 1 1 — 1 0 0 0 — str[1.1.1.1.1]
Schott

Reizenstein, Franz   (1911-1968)

Capriccio (1957)   5'
   1[1/pic] 1 2 1 — 2 2 0 0 — 1perc — str
Fleisher

Serenade in F, op.29a (1951)   27'
   2[1.2/pic] 2 2 2 — 2 0 0 0 — tmp — str
Boosey & Hawkes

Respighi, Ottorino   (1879-1936)

Antiche Danze ed Arie: Suite 1   16'
(1917)
2 3[1.2.eh] 0 2 — 2 1 0 0 — hp — hpsd — str
Contents - 1. Balletto Detto "Il Conte Orlando" (Simone
Molinaro); 2. Gagliarda (Vincenzo Galilei); 3. Villanella
(Anon.); 4. Passo Mezzo e Mascherada (Anon.)
mvt durations: 3' 4' 5' 4'
Kalmus; Luck's

Revueltas, Silvestre   (1899-1940)

Alcancias (1932)   10'
1[1/pic] 1 2[1.2/Ebcl] 0 — 1 2 1 0 — tmp+1 — str
Peer

Batik (1926)   4'
1 0 2 0 — 0 0 0 0 — str[1.1.1.1.0]
Peer

Colorines (1932)   8'
1[1/pic] 1 2[1.2/Ebcl] 2[1.2(opt)] — 1 1 1 0 —
1perc — str[1.1.0.0.1]
perc: xyl, tom-tom, cym, bd, marac
Peer

Homenaje a Federico Garccía   10'
Lorca (1936)
1[pic] 0 1[Ebcl] 0 — 0 2 1 1 — 1perc — pf —
str[1.1.0.0.1]
perc: 2 tam-tam, xyl
Contents - 1. Baile (Dance); 2. Duelo (Sorrow); 3. Son
(Sound)
mvt durations: 3' 4' 3'
Peer

Hora de Junio (1938)   13'
0 1 3[1.2.bcl] 2 — 2 2 1 1 — narrator — tmp+1 —
pf — str
perc: tam-tam
Peer

Janitzio (1933)   7'
3[1.2.pic] 2 2[1.Ebcl] 2 — 4 2 2 1 — 3perc — str
perc: cym, sd, bd, tam-tam
Peer

Musica Para Charlar (1938)   30'
1[1/pic] 1 1 1 — 2 2 2 1 — tmp+1 — pf — str
perc: sd, bd, sus cym, tri, xyl
Peer

Le Noche de los Mayas: Suite (1939)   12'
2[1.2/pic] 1 2 1 — 4 1 1 1 — tmp+1 — str
perc: tam-tam, bd, cym, Indian dr, marac, guiro, xyl
A two movement suite arranged by Paul Hindemith (1939)
and different from the well-known Limantour arrangement.
Peer

Ocho Por Radio, Eight Musicians   6'
Broadcasting (1933)
0 0 1 1 — 0 1 0 0 — 1perc — str[1.1.0.1.1]
perc: cym, marac, Indian dr
Peer

Paisajes (Landscapes) (1938)   20'
1 0 1 1 — 1 2 1 1 — tmp+1 — pf — str
perc: sd, xyl, sus cym, bd, tri
Peer

Planos (Planes) (1934)   9'
0 0 2[1.bcl] 1 — 0 1 0 0 — pf — str
Strings without va.
Peer

Ranas (1931)   3'
solo S
2 1 0 1 — 1 1 0 0 — 1perc — str[1.1.0.1.0]
Originally for voice and pf. This version arranged in 1932.
perc: guiro
Peer

El Renacuajo Paseador   8'
1[pic] 0 2[1.Ebcl] 0 — 0 2 1 0 — tmp+1 — str
perc: bd, sus cym, sd, guiro, marac
Strings without va or vc.
Peer

Sensemayá; (for Chamber   7'
Ensemble) (1937)
1[pic] 0 3[Ebcl.2.bcl] 1 — 0 2 1 0 — 4perc — pf
— str[1.1.0.0.1]
Schirmer

El Tecolote (The Owl) (1931)   3'
solo S
1 2 0 1 — 1 0 0 0 — pf — str[1.0.0.1.0]
Originally for voice and pf. This version arranged in 1932.
Peer

Toccata sin Fuga (Toccata without   6'
a Fugue) (1933)
1[pic] 0 3[1.2.3/Ebcl] 0 — 1 1 0 0 — tmp —
str[1.0.0.0.0]
Peer; Fleisher

Troka; Music for a Puppet Show (1933)   9'
1[pic] 1 2[1.Ebcl] 1 — 1 2 1 1 — tmp+1 — str
perc: xyl, dr, sus cym, bd, gong
Peer

Reznicek, Emil Nikolaus von   (1860-1945)

Symphony in the Old Style   35'
2 2 2 2 — 4 2 0 0 — tmp — str
UE

Vier Bet- und Bussgesänge (1915)   *12'*
  solo A (or B)
  1 2 2 2 — 2 0 0 0 — hp — str
UE

Riedel, Georg (1934-)

Nursery Rhymes (1986)   *18'*
  0 0 0 0 — 1 2 1 1 — 2sx[asx.tsx] — gtr — 1perc
  — pf — str[0.0.0.0.1]
Nordiska

Riege, Ernst (1885-1976)

Rondo Giocoso (1934)   *12'*
  2 2 2 2 — 2 2 0 0 — tmp+3 — str
Sikorski

Serenade (1963)   *28'*
  2 2 2 2 — 2 2 0 0 — tmp+2 — hp — str
Sikorski

Riegger, Wallingford (1885-1961)

Dichotomy, op.12 (1932)   *12'*
  1[1/pic] 1 1 1 — 1 2 0 0 — tmp+1 — pf — str
Fleisher

Scherzo   *7'*
  1 1 1 1 — 1 1 0 0 — 1perc — str
  perc: tmp, xyl, sd, bd, woodblk, cym, glsp
Peer

Rieti, Vittorio (1898-1994)

Due Pastorali (1925)   *14'*
  1 1 1 2 — 2 1 0 0 — str
Fleisher; UE

Sinfonietta per Piccola Orchestra   *15'*
(1934)
  1[1/pic] 1 1 2 — 2 2 2 0 — tmp+1 — str
Fleisher; Ricordi

Rihm, Wolfgang (1952-)

abgewandt 1 (1989)   *7'*
  1[1/pic] 1[eh] 1[bcl] 1[cbn] — 1 0 0 0 — pf/tam-
  tam — str[1.1.1.1.1]
UE

abgewandt 2; Musik in Memoriam   *16'*
Luigi Nono (3. Versuch) (1990)
  0 0 1[1/bcl] 1[cbn] — 1 1 1[cbtbn] 0 — 2perc — pf
  — str[1.1.1.1.1]
UE

Abschiedsstücke (1993)   *20'*
  solo female voice
  1[1/pic] 1 1[1/bcl] 1[cbn] — 1 1 1 0 — accordion
  — 2perc — hp — pf — str[0.0.1.1.1]
UE

Aria / Ariadne; "Szenarie" (2001)   *30'*
  solo S
  0 1 0 0 — 2 0 0 0 — hp — str[3.3.2.2.1]
UE

Bild; (eine Chiffre) (1984)   *9'*
  0 0 0 0 — 1 1 1 0 — 2perc — pf — str[0.0.1.1.1]
UE

Cantus Firmus; Musik in Memoriam   *4'*
Luigi Nono (1. Versuch) (1990)
  0 0 1 1 — 1 1 1 0 — 2perc — pf — str[1.1.1.2.1]
UE

Chiffre-Cycle (1982-1988)   *75'*
  This work consists of the following compositions: Chiffre I, II,
  III, IV, Bild, Chiffre V, VI, VII, VIII. See individual listings for
  details. Movements may be performed separately.
UE

Chiffre I (1982)   *8'*
  solo pf
  0 0 1[1/bcl] 1 — 0 1 1 0 — str[0.0.0.2.1]
UE

Chiffre II; Silence to be Beaten   *14'*
(1983)
  1[1/pic] 1[1/eh] 1[1/Ebcl/bcl] 1[1/cbn] — 1 1[1/pic
  tpt] 1 0 — 2perc — pf — str[1.1.1.1.1]
  Version with only one percussionist is available too.
UE

Chiffre III (1983)   *10'*
  0 1 1 1 — 1 1[btpt] 1 0 — 2perc — pf —
  str[0.0.0.2.1]
UE

Chiffre IV (1984)   *9'*
  0 0 1[bcl] 0 — 0 0 0 0 — pf — str[0.0.0.1.0]
UE

Chiffre V (1984)   *8'*
  1 1 1 1 — 1 2[1.btpt] 1 0 — 2perc — pf —
  str[1.1.1.2.1]
UE

Chiffre VI (1985)   6'
    0 0 1[bcl] 1[cbn] — 1 0 0 0 — str[1.1.1.1.1]
UE

Chiffre VII (1985)   15'
    1 1 1 1 — 1 2[1.btpt] 1 0 — 2perc — pf —
    str[1.1.1.2.1]
UE

Chiffre VIII (1988)   4'
    0 0 1[bcl] 1[cbn] — 1 0 1 0 — pf — str[0.0.0.2.1]
UE

Concerto for Piano (1969)   6'
    solo pf
    1 1 0 1 — 0 1 1 0 — str[1.0.1.1.0]
UE

Cuts and Dissolves;   17'
Orchesterskizzen (1976)
    2[1/pic.2/pic/afl] 2[1.2/eh] 2[1.2/bcl] 2[1.cbn] — 2 2
    2 1 — 3perc — hp — pf — str[3.0.2.2.2]
    <small>perc: chimes, vib, xyl</small>
UE

Dunkles Spiel (1990)   15'
    0 0 1 1 — 2 0 2 0 — 4perc — hp — pf —
    str[0.0.2.4.2]
UE

Form / 2 Formen; For 20   9'
Instrumentalists in 4 Groups of 5
Players (1994)
    2[1/pic.2/pic] 0 2[bcl.bcl] 0 — 2 3[1.2.pic tpt] 3
    2[1.cbtu] — 5perc — str[0.0.0.0.1]
    <small>perc: I: chimes, 3 sus cym, cym, sd II: chimes, tam-tam, cym, 3
    bongos III: chimes, 2 sus cym, cym IV: vib, gong, cym, 3 tom-tom V:
    chimes, 3 sus cym, cym, bd</small>
UE

Frage (Question) (2000)   40'
    solo female voice
    0 1[eh] 1[1/bcl] 0 — 0 0 0 0 — 1perc — hp — pf
    — str[0.0.1.1.1]
UE

Fusées (1984)   4'
    1[pic] 2[eh.eh] 3[1.2.bcl] 2[1.cbn] — 2 0 0 0 —
    2perc — pf — str[0.0.1.1.1]
UE

Gedrängte Form (1998)   6'
    1 1 1[eh] 1[bcl] 0 — 0 1 1 0 — gtr — 2perc — hp —
    pf — str[1.0.1.1.1]
UE

Gesungene Zeit (1992)   25'
    2[1.2/pic] 2 2[1.bcl] 2[1.cbn] — 1 2 1 0 — 2perc
    — hp — str[1.1.4.4.2]
    <small>perc: I: 5 crot, 2 bongos, tam-tam, db bow II: 3 crot, 2 chimes, sd, 2
    tom-tom, db bow</small>
UE

In Frage (2000)   17'
    0 1[eh] 1[bcl] 0 — 0 0 0 0 — 1perc — hp — pf —
    str[0.0.1.1.1]
UE

Jagden und Formen (2001)   55'
    2 1[eh] 2[1/bcl.2/bcl/cbcl] 1[1/cbn] — 2 2 2
    1[1/cbtu] — gtr — 3perc — hp — pf — str[1.1.1.1.1]
UE

Kein Firmament (1988)   35'
    0 0 1[bcl] 1[cbn] — 1 1 1 0 — 2perc — pf —
    str[1.1.1.2.1]
UE

Kolchis (1991)   5'
    1perc — hp — pf — str[0.0.0.1.1]
    Can also be performed as part of "Pol - Kolchis - Nucleus."
UE

Music-Hall Suite (1979)   6'
    0 0 1 0 — 0 1 0 0 — 1[asx/tsx] — 1perc — pf —
    str[1.0.0.0.1]
    Contents - 1. Vorspiel; 2. Pussy's Lied; 3. Intermezzo; 4.
    Charleston
UE

Nach-Schrift; Eine Chiffre (2004)   10'
    1 1 1[1/bcl] 1 — 1 2[1.btpt] 1 0 — 2perc — pf —
    str[1.1.1.2.1]
UE

Nucleus (1996)   7'
    0 0 2[1.bcl] 0 — 1 2 1 0 — 2perc — hp — pf —
    str[0.0.1.1.1]
    <small>perc: I: tam-tam, 2 bongos, sus cym, 3 gongs, 6 chimes II: marim</small>
    Can also be performed as part of "Pol - Kolchis - Nucleus."
UE

O Notte (1975)   7'
    solo Bar
    1 0 2[1.bcl] 1[cbn] — 0 0 0 0 — hp —
    str[0.0.2.2.1]
UE

Pol (1996)   6'
    0 0 2[1.bcl] 0 — 1 2 1 0 — 2perc — hp — pf —
    str[0.0.1.1.1]
    Can also be performed as part of "Pol - Kolchis - Nucleus."
UE

Pol - Kolchis - Nucleus (1996)   *18'*
0 0 2[1.bcl] 0 — 1 2 1 0 — 2perc — hp — pf —
str[0.0.1.1.1]
See Pol, Kolchis and Nucleus for details. All three
compositions can also be performed separately.
mvt durations: 6' 5' 7'
UE

Ricercare; Musik in Memoriam Luigi   *9'*
Nono (2.Versuch) (1990)
0 0 1[bcl] 1[cbn] — 1 1 1[cbtbn] 0 — 2perc — pf
— str[1.1.1.2.1]
perc: 2 crot, 2 chimes, 2 gongs
UE

Segmente, op.12   *10'*
str[8.0.4.4.2]
Breitkopf

Sicut Cervus Desiderat ad Fontes   *9'*
Aquarum, op.7 (1970)
solo S
0 0 1[bcl] 1 — 0 0 1 0 — 1perc — 2pf[pf.org] —
str[0.0.0.1.1]
perc: sd, lg sus cym, woodblk, tri, Chinese gong, tam-tam, chimes,
vib
UE

Sotto Voce 2, Capriccio (2007)   *17'*
solo pf
2 2 1 1 — 2 0 0 0 — tmp — str
UE

Sphäre um Sphäre (2003)   *30'*
1 1 1 0 — 0 0 0 0 — 1perc — hp — 2pf —
str[1.0.1.1.1]
UE

Eine Stimme 1-3 (2005)   *15'*
solo Mz
1[1/pic] 0 1[1/Ebcl] 0 — 0 0 0 0 — 6perc — pf —
str[0.0.1.1.1]
UE

Die Stücke des Sängers (2001)   *17'*
solo hp
2[afl.afl] 1[eh] 3[1.bcl.cbcl] 1[cbn] — 2 0 2 1[cbtu]
— 3perc — pf — str[0.0.2.2.1]
perc: I: 7 gongs, 2 sus cym, 2 sd, 3 tom-tom II: 2 sus cym, 3 tam-
tam, 3 bongos III: marim, bd
UE

Umsungen (1984)   *30'*
solo Bar
0 0 1 1 — 1 0 0 0 — str[1.1.1.1.1]
UE

Verborgene Formen (1997)   *15'*
2 1[eh] 2[1.bcl] 1 — 2 2 2 1 — 3perc — hp — pf
— str[0.0.1.1.1]
UE

Riisager, Knudåge   (1897-1974)

Valse Lente (1935)
1 0 2 0 — 0 2 1 0 — pf — str
Hansen

Variations on a Theme by   *20'*
Mezangeau, op.12 (1926)
2 2 2 2 — 4 2 0 0 — tmp+1 — str
Hansen

Rochberg, George   (1918-2005)

Chamber Symphony for 9   *18'*
Instruments (1953)
0 1 1 1 — 1 1 1 0 — str[1.0.1.1.0]
Fleisher

Cheltenham Concerto (1960)   *15'*
1 1 1 1 — 1 1 1 0 — str
Fleisher; Zerboni

Rodrigo, Joaquín   (1901-1999)

Cántico de la Esposa (1934)   *4'*
solo S
1 2[1.eh] 0 1 — 1 0 0 0 — 3perc — str
perc: sd, cym, tambn
Schott

Concierto Como Un Divertimento   *21'*
(1981)
solo vc
2[1.2/pic] 2 2 0 — 1 2 0 0 — 1perc — cel —
str[5.4.3.2.1]
Schott

Concierto heroico (1942)   *30'*
solo pf
2[1/pic.2/pic] 2 2 2 — 4 2 3 0 — tmp+1 — str
AMP

Concierto In Modo Galante (1949)   *20'*
solo vc
2[1.2/pic] 2 2 2 — 2 2 0 0 — str
Schott

Concierto Pastoral (1977) 25'
solo fl
0 1[1/eh] 1 0 — 1 1 0 0 — str
Schott

Concierto Serenata (1952) 24'
solo hp
2[1.2/pic] 2 2 — 2 2 0 0 — str
Unión

Cuatre Cançons En llengua Catalana (1946) 12'
solo S
2[1.pic] 1 1 1 — 2 2 0 0 — tmp+1 — 2hp — str
perc: tri, cym
Schott

Cuatro Madrigales Amatorios 9'
solo S
2[1.2/pic] 2 1 0 — 1 1 0 0 — 1perc — str
Contents - 1. Con Que la Lavare; 2. Vos me Matastes; 3. De Donde Venis Amore; 4. De los Alamos Vengo Madre
mvt durations: 3' 3' 1' 2'
Also available in a version for medium voice.
Chester Novello

Cyrano de Bergerac; Music for Edmond Rostand's Play of the Same Name (1955) 5'
1[1/pic] 0 0 0 — 0 1 0 0 — 1perc — str
perc: td
Schott

Dos Danzas Españolas; Suite for Castanets and Orchestra (1969) 9'
2[1.2/pic] 2 2 2 — 2 2 0 0 — 1perc — str
perc: improvisation on cast
Schott

Duérmete, Niño (1952) 4'
solo S, Bar
1 1[eh] 0 0 — 0 0 0 0 — str
Schott

La Espera (1952) 4'
solo S
1 1[eh] 0 0 — 0 0 0 0 — hp — str
Schott

Homenaje a la Tempranica (1939) 5'
2[1.pic] 1 1 1 — 2 2 0 0 — tmp+2[opt] — hp[opt] — str
perc: tri, cym, sd, cast, glso
Schott

Musica para un Jardín (1957) 12'
2[1.pic] 2[1.eh] 1 0 — 1 1 0 0 — 2perc — hp — cel — str
perc: cym, xyl, glsp
Schott

Palillos y Panderetas; Música para una tonadilla imaginaria (1982) 13'
2[1.2/pic] 2 2 2 — 2 2 0 0 — tmp+3 — str
perc: tri, cym, tambn, sd, cast, whip
Schott

Pavana Real; Ballet in Three Acts (1955) 30'
solo S
2[1.pic] 2[1.2/eh] 2 2 — 4 2 2 1 — gtr[or hp] — tmp+2 — str
perc: tri, sd, cym, cast, glsp, xyl
Soprano sings only in one number (No.7).
Schott

Retablo de Navidad (1952) 8'
solo S
2[1.2/pic] 1[1/eh] 1 1 — 2 1 0 0 — 1perc — hp — str
perc: xyl, tri
Schott

Rosaliana (1965) 12'
solo S
1 1 1 0 — 1 0 0 0 — 1perc — str
perc: sd
Schott

Serranilla (1928) 3'
solo S
1 1 1 1 — 2 1 0 0 — str
Schott

Soleriana; Suite for Chamber Orchestra (1953) 41'
2[1.pic] 1 1 1 — 1 1 0 0 — str
Fleisher; Unión

Tres Viejos Aires de Danza (1929) 10'
1 1 1 1 — 2 0 0 0 — str
Schott

Tríptic de Mossén Cinto (1935) 12'
solo S
2[1.2/pic] 2[1.eh] 1 1 — 2 2 0 0 — 1perc — hp — cel — str
perc: sd
Schott

Rodríguez, Robert Xavier (1946-)

Adagio for Small Orchestra (1967)   5'
1 1 1 2 — 2 0 0 0 — str
Alhambra

Estampie; Ballet for Small   18'
Orchestra (1981)
2[1.2/pic] 2[1.2/eh] 2[1.2/asx] 2 — 2 2 2 0 —
4perc — hp — pf — str
Alhambra

Five Études (1983)   15'
0 0 1 1 — 0 1 1 0 — 1perc — pf — str[1.0.0.1.0]
Schirmer

A Midsummer Night's Dream;   45'
Incidental Music (2001)
0 0 1[1/bcl] 0 — 1 1 0 0 — accordion — 1perc —
hp — pf — str[1.1.1.1.1]
Alhambra

Roentgen, Julius (1855-1932)

Old Netherlands Dances, op.46   9'
2 2 0 2 — 4 2 0 0 — tmp+1 — hp — str
Kalmus

Rogers, Bernard (1893-1968)

Elegy: From Symphony No.3   5'
0 3[1.2.eh] 0 0 — 0 0 0 0 — str
Presser

Elegy: To the Memory of Franklin D.   8'
Roosevelt
1 0 0 0 — 2 0 0 0 — tmp — str
Presser

Five Fairy Tales (Once Upon a   12'
Time) (1936)
2[1/pic.2/pic] 2 2 2 — 2 2 1 0 — tmp+1 — hp —
pf — str
Kalmus

A Letter from Pete   26'
1 0 1 0 — 1 1 1 0 — tmp — pf — str
perc: bd, cym, tri, gong, td, sd
Peer

The Musicians of Bremen   22'
2 1 1 1 — 1 1 0 0 — narrator — tmp+1 — str
Presser

The Plains   14'
1 1 2 1 — 2 1 0 0 — tmp — str
Presser

Roldán, Amadeo (1900-1939)

La Muerte Alegre
1 1 1 1 — 0 1 1 0 — 1perc — hp — pf — str
Peer

Ropartz, Joseph Guy Marie (1864-1955)

Cinq pièces brèves   14'
1 1 1 1 — 2 0 0 0 — tmp — str
Fleisher; Heugel

Pastorale et Danses   13'
solo ob
2 0 2 2 — 2 1 0 0 — tmp — hp — str
Kalmus

Sons de Cloches   11'
1 1 1 1 — 1 0 0 0 — tmp+1 — hp — str
perc: tri
Kalmus; Fleisher

Rorem, Ned (1923-)

Design (1953)   18'
2[1.2/pic] 2 2 2 — 4 2 2 0 — tmp+1 — hp —
2pf[pf.cel] — str
perc: gong, xyl, cym, tri, bd, sd
Boosey & Hawkes

Ideas; For Easy Orchestra (1961)   13'
1 1 1 1 — 2 1 1 0 — tmp+1 — hp — pf — str
perc: gong, cym, tri, sd, tambn
Boosey & Hawkes

Pilgrims (1958)   6'
str
Boosey & Hawkes

A Quaker Reader: Suite (1976)   20'
2[1.2/pic] 2[1.2/eh] 2 2 — 2 1 1 0 — str
Boosey & Hawkes

String Symphony (1985)   23'
str
Contents - 1. Waltz; 2. Berceuse; 3. Scherzo; 4. Nocturne;
5. Rondo
mvt durations: 5' 2' 2' 8' 6'
Boosey & Hawkes

Symphony No.2 (1956)　　　　　　　　22'
2[1.2/pic] 2[1.2/eh] 2 2 — 2 1 0 0 — tmp+1 — hp
— pf — str
perc: gong, xyl, cym, tri, sd, tambn
mvt durations: 15' 4' 3'
Boosey & Hawkes

Triptych; Three Pieces for Chamber　　　10'
Orchestra (1992)
2 2 2 2 — 2 2 0 0 — tmp — str
Boosey & Hawkes

Waiting (1996)　　　　　　　　　　　2'
2 2 2 2 — 2 2 2 0 — 3perc — pf — str
perc: tri, gong, vib
Boosey & Hawkes

Roselius, Ludwig　　　　　　(1902-1977)

Friesische Musik, op.30 (1957)　　　　21'
1 2[1.eh] 2 1 — 1 0 0 0 — str
Boosey & Hawkes

Lilofee Suite, op.16 (1937)　　　　　17'
2 2[1.eh] 2 2 — 2 1 1 0 — tmp+1 — hp — str
Also available as chamber version (op.16a): eh-cl-tmp-
1perc-hp-str (1.1.1.1.1).
Boosey & Hawkes

Rosenberg, Hilding　　　　　(1892-1985)
Constantin

Bianca-Nera; Overture (1946)　　　　10'
str
Kalmus

Concerto for Viola (1942)　　　　　21'
solo va
2 2 2 2 — 3 2 0 0 — tmp — hp — str
Kalmus

Concerto No.1 for String Orchestra　　23'
(1946)
str
Kalmus

Dance Suite from the Grand Opera　　11'
"The Marionettes" (1938)
2 2 2 2 — 2 2 0 0 — tmp+1 — str
Nordiska

Ouvertura Piccola (1934)　　　　　4'
2 1 0 2 — 2 2 1 0 — 2 — tmp+1 — pf — str
Kalmus

Sinfonia da Chiesa No.1 (1923)　　　20'
1 1 1 1 — 2 0 0 0 — tmp+1 — org — str
Nordiska

Sinfonia da Chiesa No.2 (1924)　　　22'
2 2 2 2 — 4 2 0 0 — tmp — str
Kalmus

Suite for Violin and Orchestra　　　17'
solo vn
2 1 2 1 — 0 0 0 0 — str
Kalmus

Suite on Popular Swedish Folk　　　15'
Melodies (1927)
str
Kalmus

Rosenman, Leonard　　　　　(1924-2008)

Chamber Music No.1 (1960)
1[1/pic] 0 2[1.bcl] 1 — 1 2 1 0 — 3perc — hp —
pf/cel — str[1.0.0.1.1]
perc: xyl, vib, sd, 3 tom-tom, bd, tam-tam, tri, tambn, sus cym, rattle,
cast, 3 bongos
Peer

Chamber Music No.2　　　　　　22'
1[afl] 1[eh] 2[1.bcl] 0 — 0 0 0 0 — asx — tape, S
— hp — pf — str[1.0.1.1.1]
Peer

Rosing-Schow, Niels　　　　　(1954-)

Canon and Corale (1984)　　　　　6'
2 0 2 0 — 1 2 1 0 — accordion — 1perc — pf —
str[2.0.0.2.0]
Also as version for Sinfonietta: 1111 - 1110 - 2perc - hp - pf
- str (1.1.1.1.1) (1991).
Hansen

Equinoxe (2003)　　　　　　　　13'
1[1/pic/afl] 1 1[1/bcl] 0 — 1 0 0 0 — 1perc — hp
— str[1.0.1.1.0]
Hansen

Meeting (1985)　　　　　　　　　15'
0 1 1 1 — 1 0 0 0 — str[0.0.1.1.1]
Hansen

Roslavets, Nikolai Andreyevich   (1881-1944)

Chamber Symphony (1926)   *14'*
1[1/pic] 1[1/eh] 1[1/Ebcl/bcl] 1 — 2 1 1 0 — 2perc
— hp — pf/cel — str[1.1.1.1.1]
perc: tmp, tri, sd, cym, gong, water gong, tam-tam, chimes, glsp, xyl
Boosey & Hawkes

Chamber Symphony; For 18 Solo   *12'*
Instruments (1935)
2[1.pic] 2[1.eh] 3[1.2.bcl] 2[1.cbn] — 2 1 0 0 — pf
— str[1.1.1.1.1]
Schott

Rota, Nino   (1911-1979)

Canzona (1935)   *10'*
1 1 1 1 — 1 1 0 0 — str
Schott

Cristallo di Rocca (1950)   *22'*
1 0 0 0 — 0 0 0 0 — 2pf[pf.org(opt)] —
str[1.0.1.1.1]
Schott

Roters, Ernst   (1892-1961)

Tanzsuite, op.23   *16'*
2 2 2 2 — 2 2 1 0 — 1perc — hp[opt] — str
Alternative instrumentation: 1121 - 0000 - 1perc - pf - str
UE

Röttger, Heinz   (1909-1977)

Concerto for Piano (1951)   *25'*
solo pf
0 1 1 1 — 0 1 0 0 — pf — str
Breitkopf

Sinfonietta per archi (1968)   *16'*
str
Breitkopf

Sinfonische Meditationen   *18'*
2 2 2 2 — 0 3 3 1 — tmp+1 — pf — str
Breitkopf

Roumain, Daniel Bernard (DBR)   (1971-)

Call Them All; Fantasy Projections   *18'*
for Film, Laptop and Chamber
Orchestra (2006)
1 1 1 1 — 1 1 1 1 — laptop, digital video — 1perc
— pf — str
perc: vib
Subito

Harvest (2004)   *7'*
solo Bar
2 2 2 2 — 2 2 0 0 — tmp+1 — str
perc: sd
Subito

Voodoo Violin Concerto No.1   *24'*
(2002)
solo vn
1 0 1 0 — 0 1 1 0 — 1perc — pf — str[1.0.0.1.1]
perc: drum kit
Version for chamber ensemble.
Subito

Voodoo Violin Concerto No.1   *24'*
(2002)
solo vn
2 2 2 2 — 2 2 2 1 — tmp+1 — hp — pf — str
Subito

Rouse, Christopher   (1949-)

Concerto per Corde (1990)   *27'*
str
Boosey & Hawkes

Iscariot (1989)   *13'*
1[1/pic] 2[1.eh] 1 2 — 3 1 0 0 — 2perc — cel —
str
perc: 4 tom-tom, field dr, bongo, Chinese cym, bd, tam-tam,
slapstick, sd, td, 2 chimes, sus cym, cym, hammer
Boosey & Hawkes

Roussel, Albert   (1869-1937)

À un Jeune Gentilhomme (1908)   *2'*
solo S
2 2 0 2 — 2 0 0 0 — str
Salabert

Aria; For Orchestra, or Divers Soli   *2'*
and Orchestra
possible solo: voice, va, vc, fl, ob, cl
2 0 2 2 — 2 1 0 0 — 1perc — hp — cel — str
perc: tri
Presser

Le bachelier de Salamanque,   2'
op.20, No.1 (1919)
     solo voice
     2 2 2 2 — 2 2 0 0 — 1perc — hp — str
     Durand

Concert; pour petit orchestre, op.34   15'
(1927)
     2 2 2 2 — 2 1 0 0 — tmp — str
     Durand

Concertino, op.57 (1936)   12'
     solo vc
     2 2 2 2 — 2 2 0 0 — tmp — str
     Durand

Concerto for Piano, op.36 (1927)   16'
     solo pf
     2 2 2 2 — 2 2 0 0 — tmp+2 — str
     Durand

Le festin de l'araignée; Ballet-   38'
pantomime en un acte, op.17
(1912)
     2 2 2 2 — 2 2 0 0 — tmp+2 — hp — cel — str
     Durand

Le Marchand de Sable qui Passe   19'
(The Sandman Passing By), op.13
(1908)
     1 0 1 0 — 1 0 0 0 — hp — str
     Contents - 1. Prelude; 2. Scene; 3. Interlude and Scene IV;
     4. Scene Finale
     Kalmus; Eschig

Roux, Maurice le   (1923-1992)

Allegro Moderato: No.9 from   3'
"Divertimento for Mozart" (1956)
     2 2 2 2 — 2 2 0 0 — tmp+1 — str
     perc: glsp
     For more information see: Mozart, Wolfgang Amadeus.
     UE; Schott

Rovsing Olsen, Poul   (1922-1982)

Schicksalslieder von Hölderlin,
op.28 (1953)
     solo high voice
     1 0 1 0 — 0 0 0 0 — str
     Fleisher

Rózsa, Miklós   (1907-1995)

Concerto, op.17 (1943)   26'
     str
     Breitkopf

Hungarian Serenade, op.25   21'
     1 1 1 1 — 1 1 0 0 — tmp+1 — str
     Breitkopf

Kaleidoscope; Six Short Pieces for   10'
Small Orchestra, op.19a
     1[1/pic] 1 1 1 — 1 1 1 0 — tmp+1 — hp — str
     Fleisher

Nordungarische Bauernlieder und   9'
Tänze; Kleine Suite, op.5 (1929)
     solo vn
     1 1 1 1 — 1 1 0 0 — tmp+1 — hp — str
     Breitkopf

Notturno ungherese, op.28   9'
     2 2 2 2 — 4 2 3 0 — tmp+1 — hp — cel — str
     Breitkopf

Rhapsody, op.3 (1929)   20'
     solo vc
     2 2 2 2 — 2 2 0 0 — tmp+1 — hp — str
     Breitkopf

Tema con variazioni, op.29a   11'
     solo vn, vc
     0 2 0 0 — 2 0 0 0 — tmp — str
     Breitkopf

Variations on a Hungarian Peasant   12'
Song, op.4 (1929)
     solo vn
     1 1 1 1 — 1 1 1 0 — tmp+1 — hp — str
     Breitkopf

Ruders, Poul   (1949-)

Abysm (2000)   23'
     1[1/pic/afl] 1 1[1/bcl] 0 — 1 1 1 0 — 1perc — pf —
     str[1.0.1.1.1]
     Hansen

Corpus Cum Figuris (1985)   20'
     1 1 2 2 — 1 1 1 0 — 2perc — hp — pf —
     str[1.1.2.2.1]
     Hansen

Diferencias (1980)   8'
  1 0 1 0 — 0 0 0 0 — gtr — 1perc — pf —
  str[1.0.0.1.0]
  perc: vib
Hansen

Four Dances in One Movement   18'
(1983)
  1 1 1 1 — 1 1 1 0 — 2perc — pf — str[1.1.1.1.1]
Hansen

Greeting Concertino (1982)   10'
  0 0 0 0 — 1 1[crt] 1 0 — 1perc — pf —
  str[1.0.0.1.1]
Hansen

Nightshade (1987)   9'
  1 1 1[cbcl] 1[cbn] — 1 0 1 0 — 1perc — pf —
  str[1.0.0.0.1]
Hansen

Trapeze (1992)   8'
  0 2 0 0 — 2 0 0 0 — str[5.4.3.2.1]
Hansen

Rueda, Jesús   (1961-)

Elephant Skin (2002)   12'
  2[1.2/pic] 2 2[1.bcl] 2 — 2 2 0 0 — 1perc — str
Tritó

Runswick, Daryl   (1946-)

I Am A Donut; Dialectic II. Concerto   20'
Grosso for Flute, Trumpet, Bass
Clarinet and 11 Players (1993)
  solo fl, tpt, bcl
  1[pic] 1 0 1[cbn] — 1 1[flug] 1 0 — 2perc —
  str[1.0.1.0.1]
Faber

Songs of Love and Farewell (1987)   20'
  1[1/pic] 1[1/eh] 1[Ebcl] 2[1.2/cbn] — 0 1[1/flug]
  3[1.2.btbn] 0 — 2perc — 2pf[pf.sampler] —
  str[1.0.0.0.0]
Faber

Rushton, Edward   (1973-)

Lost City Life (1998)   15'
  1[1/pic] 0 2[1.2/bcl] 1 — 2 1 1 0 — 1perc — pf —
  str[2.0.0.2.0]
  perc: party siren, sus cym, splash cym, glsp, 2 chimes, tmp, bd, tri,
  cowbell, templeblk, 2 bongo, tom-tom, crot, vib, talking dr, woodblk
Faber

Russo, William   (1928-2003)

The Golden Bird, op.77 (1984)   44'
  solo S, Bar, narrator
  1 2 1 1 — 2 1 1[btbn] 0 — 2perc — pf — str
GunMar

Ruzicka, Peter   (1948-)

Der die Gesänge Zerschlug (1985)   22'
  solo Bar
  1 0 1 0 — 0 1 0 0 — 2perc — hp — pf — str
Sikorski

Ryden, William   (1939-)

Concertino (1999)   8'
  solo cl
  0 2[1.eh] 0 1 — 2 0 0 0 — 1perc — str
Kalmus

S

Saariaho, Kaija   (1952-)

Aer: Part 7 of "Maa" (1991)   17'
 1 0 0 0 — 0 0 0 0 — electronics — 1perc — hp —
 pf/hpsd — str[1.0.1.1.0]
Hansen

Aile Du Songe (2001)   18'
 solo fl
 tmp+3 — hp — cel — str
Chester Novello

Château de l'âme (1996)   22'
 solo S, A
 2[1.2/pic] 2 2 2 — 4 2 2 1 — tmp+3 — hp — pf —
 str
Chester Novello

Forty Heartbeats (1998)   3'
 1[1/pic] 1 1 1 — 1 2 1 1 — tmp+2 — hp — pf —
 str
Chester Novello

Graal Théâtre; (Chamber Version)   29'
(1997)
 solo vn
 1[1/pic] 1 2[1.bcl] 1 — 2 1 1[btbn] 0 — 2perc —
 hp — pf — str[1.1.1.1.1]
 mvt durations: 18' 11'
Chester Novello

Io (1987)   18'
 3[1/pic.2/pic/afl.bfl] 0 0 0 — 2 0 1 1 — electronics,
 tape — 2perc — hp — pf/cel — str[1.1.1.1.1]
Hansen

Leino Songs (2007)   13'
 solo S
 2 2 2 2 — 4 2 2 0 — tmp+2 — hp — cel — str
Chester Novello

Lichtbogen (1986)   17'
 1[1/pic/afl] 0 0 0 — 0 0 0 0 — electronics — 1perc
 — hp — pf — str[1.1.1.1.1]
Hansen

Message Pour Gérard (2000)   4'
 solo Mz
 1[afl/pic] 0 0 0 — 0 0 0 0 — 1perc — hp —
 str[1.0.1.1.1]
Chester Novello

Nymphéa Reflection (2001)   27'
 str(min)[6.6.4.4.2]
Chester Novello

Quatre Instants (2002)   23'
 solo S
 2 2 2 2 — 2 0 0 0 — tmp+1 — hp — cel —
 str[8.7.6.4.3]
Chester Novello

Solar (1993)   18'
 1[1/pic] 1 1 0 — 0 1 0 0 — electronics — 2perc —
 hp — 2pf[pf/kybd.kybd] — str[1.0.1.0.1]
Chester Novello

The Tempest Songbook (2004)   21'
 solo S, Bar
 1 0 1 0 — 0 0 0 0 — gtr, mand — hp —
 str[1.0.1.1.1]
Chester Novello

Verblendungen (1984)   14'
 2[1.afl/pic] 1 1 1[1/cbn] — 4 1 1 1 — asx — tape
 — 2perc — hp — pf — str[4.4.5.3.2]
Hansen

Sackman, Nicholas   (1950-)

Corranach (1985)   20'
 1[1/pic/afl] 0 1[1/Ebcl] 0 — 1 0 0 0 — 1perc — pf
 — str[1.0.0.1.0]
 perc: 2 sm sd, lg sus cym, bd, sus Chinese cym, lg tam-tam, vib,
 lion's roar, sus Bamboo wind chimes
Schott

Saint-Saëns, Camille   (1835-1921)

Africa, op.89 (1891)   10'
 solo pf
 2 2 2 2 — 2 2 3 0 — tmp+1 — str
 perc: cym, tri
Durand; Kalmus; Luck's

Allegro appassionato, op.43 (1875)   3'
 solo vc
 2 2 2 2 — 2 0 0 0 — str
Durand; Kalmus; Luck's

Allegro appassionato, op.70 (1884)   7'
 solo pf
 2 2 2 2 — 2 2 0 0 — str
Durand; Kalmus; Leduc

L'assassinat de Duc de Guise;   18'
Tableux d'histoire, op.128 (1908)
    1 1 1 1 — 1 0 0 0 — pf — str
Durand

Le carnaval des animaux; Grande   20'
fantasie zoologique (1886)
    solo 2 pf
    1[1/pic] 0 1 0 — 0 0 0 0 — glass harmonica[or
    glsp or cel] — 1perc — str[1.1.1.1.1]
    perc: xyl
Durand; Kalmus; Luck's

Concerto for Cello No.2, op.119   17'
(1902)
    solo vc
    2 2 2 2 — 4 2 0 0 — tmp — str
Kalmus

Les fées (1892)   4'
    solo voice
    2 2 2 2 — 2 0 0 0 — tmp — hp — str
Durand

Havanaise, op.83 (1887)   10'
    solo vn
    2 2 2 2 — 2 2 0 0 — tmp — str
Kalmus

La Libellule (1894)   5'
    solo voice
    2 2 2 2 — 2 0 0 0 — str
Durand

Morceau de concert, op.62 (1880)   8'
    solo vn
    2 2 2 2 — 2 0 0 0 — tmp — str
Durand; Kalmus

Morceau de concert, op.94 (1887)   10'
    solo hn
    2 2 2 2 — 0 0 3 0 — tmp — str
Durand; Kalmus; Luck's

Morceau de concert, op.154   16'
    solo hp
    2 2 2 2 — 2 2 0 0 — tmp — str
Durand; Kalmus; Luck's

Ô beaux rêves évanouis: "Air de   3'
Béatrix" (1879)
    solo S
    2 2 2 2 — 4 0 0 0 — str
Durand

Odelette, op.162 (1920)   7'
    solo fl
    0 2 0 2 — 0 0 0 0 — str
Durand; Kalmus; Luck's

Où nous avons aimé   2'
    solo T
    0 1 2 1 — 0 0 0 0 — str
Dunvagen

Papillons   4'
    solo S
    2 0 0 0 — 0 0 0 0 — str
Durand

Rigaudon, op.93, No.2 (1892)   3'
    2 2 2 2 — 2 0 2 0 — tmp — str
Durand; Kalmus

Suite in D major   22'
    2 3[1.2.3/eh] 2 2 — 2 2 0 0 — tmp — str
    Edited by Pietro Spada.
Presser

Symphony in A   23'
    2 2 2 2 — 2 2 0 0 — tmp — str
Presser

Symphony in F; Urbs Roma   40'
    3 2 2 2 — 4 2 0 0 — tmp — str
Presser

Une nuit à Lisbonne, op.63 (1880)   4'
    1 1 1 1 — 2 0 0 0 — hp — str
Kalmus; Fleisher

Sallinen, Aulis   (1935-)

Concerto for Chamber Orchestra   22'
(1960)
    1[1/pic] 1 2 1 — 1 0 0 0 — str
Novello

Sunrise Serenade (1989)   6'
    0 0 0 0 — 0 2 0 0 — pf — str
Novello

Salmhofer, Franz   (1900-1975)

Overture (1922)   12'
    2 2 2 2 — 2 2 1 0 — tmp — hp — pf — str
UE

Wonne der Wehmut   2'
  solo medium voice
  2 2 2 2 — 4 0 0 0 — hp — str
UE

Salviucci, Giovanni   (1907-1937)

Sinfonia da Camera (1936)   15'
  1 1 1 1 — 1 1 0 0 — str
Fleisher; Ricordi

Samazeuilh, Gustave   (1877-1967)

Divertissement et Musette (1912)   15'
  1 1 1 1 — 1 0 0 0 — str[1.1.1.1.0]
Fleisher; Durand

Sandström, Sven-David   (1942-)

In the Meantime (1970)   10'
  1 1 2 1 — 1 1 1 0 — tmp+1 — hp — 2pf — str
Nordiska

Santander, Manuel   (1908-)

Ritmos de Cadiz (1963)   6'
  1 1 1 1 — 2 2 1 0 — tmp+1 — hp — str
Unión

Santórsola, Guido   (1904-1994)

Prelúdio No.3 (1936)   3'
  1 1 2 1 — 2 0 0 0 — hp — str
Fleisher

Satie, Erik   (1866-1925)

La belle excentrique; Fantasie sérieuse pour Orchestra de music-hall (1920)   8'
  1 1 1 1 — 1 1 1 0 — 2perc — pf — str
Eschig

Carnet de croquis et d'esquisses (1914)   5'
  2 2 2 2 — 0 0 0 0 — 1perc — str[2.2.1.1.0]
  Orchestrated by Robert Caby.
Salabert

Cinéma: Entr'acte symphonique du ballet "Relâche" (1924)   15'
  1 1 1 1 — 2 2 1 0 — tmp+1 — str
Salabert

La Diva de l'Empire (1904)   3'
  2[1.2/pic] 0 1 1 — 1 1[crt] 1 0 — 1perc — str
Salabert

Illusion [Tendrement] (1902)   3'
  1 1 2 1 — 2 2[crt] 3 0 — str
Salabert

Jack in the Box, op.post (1899)   6'
  2 2 2 2 — 2 2 0 0 — tmp+1 — str
  Edited by Darius Milhaud (1928).
UE

Je te veux (1902)   5'
  2[1.2/pic] 1 2 1 — 2 2[crt] 3 0 — 1perc — str
Salabert

Mercure; Poses plastiques, op.post (1924)   19'
  1[1/pic/afl] 1[1/eh] 1[1/bcl] 1[1/cbn] — 1 1 1 0 —
  1perc — pf — str[1.1.1.1.1]
  Arranged by Sir Harrison Birtwistle (1980).
UE

Mercure; Poses plastiques, op.post (1924)   20'
  2[1.pic] 1 2 1 — 2 2 1 1 — 2perc — str
UE

Mort de Socrate (1918)   10'
  solo voice
  1 2 1 1 — 1 1 0 0 — tmp — hp — str
  Excerpt No.3 from "Socrate."
Eschig

Les Pantins Dansent (1913)   3'
  1 1 1 1 — 1 1 0 0 — str
Salabert

Le Piège de Méduse: Sept toutes petites danses (1913)   25'
  0 0 1 0 — 0 1 1 0 — 2perc — str[1.0.0.1.1]
  perc: tri, tambn
Salabert

Poudre d'or (1902)   2'
  2[1.2/pic] 1 2 1 — 2 2[crt] 3 0 — 1perc — str
Salabert

Relâche; Ballet (1924)   25'
  1 1 1 1 — 2 2 1 0 — tmp+1 — str
  Can be performed with "Cinéma" as interlude.
Salabert

Socrate; Drame symphonique en 3   25'
parties (1918)
   solo 4 voices
   1 2 1 1 — 1 1 0 0 — tmp — hp — str
Eschig

Sports et Divertissements (1914)   15'
   1[1/pic] 1 1 1 — 1 0 0 0 — pf — str[1.0.1.1.1]
   Arranged by Dominic Muldowney (1981).
UE

Trois Mélodies de 1916 (1916)   5'
   2 2[1.2/eh] 2 2 — 1 1 1 1 — 2perc — str
   Orchestrated by Robert Caby.
   Contents - 1. La Statue de Bronze; 2. Daphénéo; 3. Le
   Chapelier
   mvt durations: 2' 2' 1'
Salabert

Trois petites pièces montées   3'
(1919)
   1 1 1 1 — 1 2 1 0 — 1perc — str
Eschig

Saturen, David   (1939-)

Expression; Lyric Piece for Small   5'
Orchestra
   1 1 2 0 — 2 2 2 0 — str
Fleisher

Sawer, David   (1961-)

Cat's-eye (1986)   25'
   0 0 2[1/bcl.2/bcl] 0 — 0 1 1 0 — hp — pf —
   str[0.0.1.1.0]
UE

Take Off (1987)   18'
   1[1/pic/afl] 0 2[1.2/bcl] 0 — 0 0 0 0 — pf —
   str[1.0.1.1.0]
UE

Tiroirs (1996)   12'
   1[1/pic/afl] 1 2[1/Ebcl/bcl.2/bcl] 1 — 2 1 1 0 —
   2perc — hp — pf/cel — str[1.1.2.2.1]
   Requires 5-string db.
UE

Saxton, Robert   (1953-)

Birthday Music for Sir William Glock   3'
(1988)
   1 0 1[1/bcl] 0 — 1 0 0 0 — 1perc — pf —
   str[1.0.1.1.0]
Chester Novello

Canzona; In Memoriam Igor   13'
Stravinsky (1978)
   1 1 1 0 — 1 0 0 0 — hp — str[1.0.1.1.0]
Chester Novello

Chamber Symphony; The Circles of   19'
Light (1986)
   1[1/pic/afl] 1[1/eh] 1[1/Ebcl/bcl] 1[1/cbn] — 1 1 1 0
   — 1perc — pf — str[1.1.1.1.1]
Chester Novello

Elijah's Violin (1988)   21'
   1[1/pic] 2[1.2/eh] 0 2 — 2 0 0 0 — str[4.3.2.2.1]
Chester Novello

Processions and Dances (1981)   12'
   1[1/pic/afl] 1[1/eh] 1 0 — 0 0 0 0 — 1perc — hp
   — str[1.0.1.1.0]
Chester Novello

The Ring of Eternity (1983)   14'
   2[1.2/pic] 2[1.2/eh] 2[1.2/Ebcl] 2 — 2 2 0 0 —
   1perc — pf/cel — str[6.6.4.4.2]
Chester Novello

Traumstadt (1980)   13'
   2 2 2 2 — 2 2 1 0 — pf — str[1.1.1.1.1]
Chester Novello

Variation on "Sumer is Icumen In"   6'
(1987)
   2 2 2 2 — 2 2 0 0 — tmp — hp — str
Chester Novello

Saygun, A. Adnan   (1907-1991)

Bir Orman Masali; A Forest Tale   27'
   1 1 1 1 — 1 1 1 0 — 1 — tmp+1 — cel — str
Peer

Symphony No.1   25'
   1 2 2 2 — 2 0 0 0 — str
Peer

Schaathun, Asbjørn   (1961-)

"S" (1992)   4'
  1 1 1 0 — 1 1 0 0 — electronics — 1perc — pf —
  str[1.0.1.1.1]
  Hansen

Schaeuble, Hans   (1906-1988)

Music for two violins and string   22'
orchestra, op.18 (1959)
  solo 2vn
  str
  Boosey & Hawkes

Schafer, Robert Murray   (1933-)

Arcana (1972)   18'
  solo voice
  2 2 2 2 — 2 2 2 0 — 2perc — hp — pf — str
  Also available in a version for chamber ensemble: 1010 -
  0110 - 1perc - hp - pf - str (1.0.0.1.1) - solo voice.
  UE

Cortège (1977)   15'
  2 2 2 2 — 2 2 0 0 — 1perc — str
  UE

Hymn to the Night (1976)   16'
  solo S
  1 0 1 0 — 0 1 1 0 — 2perc — hp — pf/elec org —
  str[1.0.0.1.1]
  Also available in a version for chamber orchestra: 1111 -
  1110 - 2perc - hp - pf - str - solo S
  UE

Scharwenka, Franz Xaver   (1850-1924)

À la Hongroise, op.43, No.6   4'
  1 1 2 1 — 2 2 1 0 — 1perc — str
  Kalmus

A Polish Dance Theme   4'
  1 1 2 1 — 2 2 1 0 — tmp+1 — str
  Orchestrated by Otto Langey.
  Kalmus

Schauss, Ernst   (1882-1953)

Serenade   11'
  str
  Boosey & Hawkes

Schelling, Ernest   (1876-1939)

Tarantella   3'
  1 1 0 1 — 0 0 0 0 — str
  Fleisher

Schenker, Friedrich   (1942-)

Concerto for Bassoon (1970)   22'
  solo bn
  str
  Breitkopf

Concerto for Oboe (1969)   30'
  solo ob
  str
  Breitkopf

Concerto for Viola (1975)   28'
  solo va
  1 1 1 1 — 1 1 1 0 — 1perc — hp — hpsd — str
  Breitkopf

Gute Behandlung der Pferde   32'
(1986)
  0 2[1.eh] 0 0 — 0 0 1 0 — 1perc — pf —
  str[1.0.1.1.1]
  Breitkopf

Hades di Orfeo; Dramma per   25'
musica (1977)
  0 2[1.eh] 0 0 — 0 0 1 0 — 1perc — str[0.0.1.1.1]
  Breitkopf

Jessenin-Majakowski-Recital   50'
(1981)
  0 2[1.eh] 0 0 — 0 0 1 0 — accordion, tape —
  1perc — pf — str[0.0.0.1.1]
  Breitkopf

Little Symphony (1966)   14'
  str
  Breitkopf

Solo for a Percussionist with Small   20'
Orchestra (1997)
  solo perc
  1 1 2[1/Ebcl.bcl] 1[cbn] — 1 1 1 0 — hp — pf —
  str
  Breitkopf

Triple Concerto; Overture,   23'
Variations and Finale on Rocco's
Aria from Beethoven's "Fidelio"
(1969)
    solo ob, bn, pf
    1perc — str
Breitkopf

Scherchen, Tona   (1938-)

Bien (1973)   20'
    0 0 1 0 — 1 1 1 0 — 2perc — pf — str[1.1.1.1.1]
UE

L'Invitation au voyage (1977)   23'
    1[1/pic] 1 3[1.2.bcl] 1 — 1 2 2 0 — amp speaking
    voice[also playing jew's harp] — 2perc — hp — pf —
    str[1.0.1.1.1]
    perc: 2 ant crot, 2 crot, 2 cym, deep gong, claves, xyl, 2 congas,
    glsp, Chinese cym, very deep tam-tam, snail-shell chimes, whip, 3
    Chinese templeblks, deep guiro, lg dr, lg crystal glass
Boosey & Hawkes

Khouang (1968)   11'
    1 1 2 1 — 1 1 1 0 — 2pf[cel.hpsd] — str
UE

Tjao-Houen (1973)   14'
    1 1 0 0 — 0 0 1 0 — 3perc — pf — str[0.0.1.1.0]
UE

Schickele, Peter   (1935-)

Broadway Boogie   5'
    1 0 1 0 — 0 0 0 0 — hp — pf — str
Presser

Concerto for Cello and Orchestra;   22'
In Memoriam F.D.R. (2000)
    solo vc
    2[1.2/pic] 2 2[1.2/bcl] 2 — 2 3 0 0 — tmp+3 — pf
    — str
Presser

Concerto for Chamber Orchestra   27'
(1998)
    2 2 2 2 — 2 2 0 0 — 2perc — str
Presser

Concerto for Flute and Orchestra   18'
    solo fl
    2 2 2 2 — 2 2 1 0 — tmp+1 — str
Presser

Elegy for String Orchestra   8'
    str
Presser

If Love Is Real (1991)   3'
    solo 2 voices
    1 1 1 1 — 1 1 1 0 — 1perc — pf — str
    Text by Peter Schickele.
Presser

Legend   22'
    2 2 2 2 — 3 2 2 1 — 2perc — str
    Instrumental version of his "The Chenoo Who Stayed To
    Dinner."
Presser

The Maiden on the Moor   8'
    solo CT or Contralto
    0 1 0 0 — 2 0 0 0 — 1perc — str
    perc: finger cym
Presser

Requiem (1968)   5'
    str
Presser

Sneaky Pete and the Wolf (1991)   26'
    Alternate text written by Schickele for performance with
    Prokofiev's "Peter and the Wolf."
Presser

Songs from Shakespeare   6'
    2 2 2 2 — 2 2 1 0 — tmp+1 — str
Presser

Symphony No.2; The Sweet   22'
Season
    2[1.2/pic] 2 2[1.2/bcl] 2 — 2 2 0 0 — tmp/perc —
    hp — pf — str[6.6.4.4.2]
Presser

Three Girls, Three Women   22'
    2 2 2 2 — 3 2 1 1 — 1perc — hp — cel — str
Presser

Three Strange Cases   6'
    solo narrator
    1 1 1 1 — 0 0 0 0 — 2perc — str
Presser

Thurber's Dogs   20'
    2[1.2/pic] 2 2 2 — 2 2 0 0 — tmp+1 — hp — str
Presser

What Did You Do Today at Jeffey's   5'
House? (1994)
    2 2 2 2 — 2 2 1 0 — tmp+2 — pf — str
Presser

Schifrin, Lalo   (1932-)

Variants on a Madrigal by Gesualdo   *18'*
(1969)
    1[afl] 1 1 1 — 1 1[1/crt] 1 1 — pf/hpsd/cel —
    str[1.1.1.1.0]
AMP

Schiske, Karl   (1916-1969)

Chamber Concerto, op.28 (1949)   *23'*
    1 1 1 1 — 2 1 0 0 — tmp+1 — str
UE

Concerto for Violin, op.33 (1952)   *25'*
    solo vn
    1 1 1 1 — 2 1 1 0 — tmp+2 — str
UE

Synthese; For 4X4 Instruments,
op.47 (1958)
    1 1 1 1 — 2 1 1 0 — 3perc — pf —
    str(min)[1.0.1.1.1]
    Variable duration.
UE

Schlee, Thomas Daniel   (1957-)

Concertino, op.36   *15'*
    solo 2 pictp
    0 1 0 0 — 0 0 0 0 — str
Bärenreiter

Sonata da Camera, op.42   *13'*
    0 1 0 0 — 2 0 0 0 — str
Bärenreiter

Schleiermacher, Steffen   (1960-)

Keil (1998)   *21'*
    solo asx/tsx/barsx
    2 2 2 2 — 2 2 2 1 — 3perc — hp — str[6.5.4.3.2]
Breitkopf

Trotz Reaktion I (1994)   *7'*
    0 1[1/eh] 1[1/bcl] 0 — 0 1 0 0 — 1perc — hp —
    str[0.0.1.1.0]
Breitkopf

Trotz Reaktion II (1996)   *6'*
    0 1 1 0 — 0 1 0 0 — 1perc — hp — str[0.0.1.1.0]
Breitkopf

Trotz Reaktion III (1997)   *8'*
    0 1[eh] 1[bcl] 0 — 0 1 0 0 — 1perc — hp —
    str[0.0.1.1.0]
Breitkopf

Trotz Reaktion IV (1997)   *6'*
    0 1[1/eh] 1[1/bcl] 0 — 0 1 0 0 — 1perc — hp —
    str[0.0.1.1.0]
Breitkopf

Zeit Verschiebung (1997)   *17'*
    1[pic] 1 1 1 — 0 0 0 0 — 2perc — pf —
    str[1.1.1.1.0]
Breitkopf

Schlemm, Gustav Adolf   (1902-1987)

Polka-Fughetta   *9'*
    2 2 2 2 — 3 2 3 0 — 1perc — hp — cel — str
UE

Serenade   *16'*
    2 2 2 2 — 2 2 0 0 — tmp+1 — hp — str
UE

Schmidt, Christfried   (1932-)

Chamber Music IV (1972)
    0 2[1.eh] 0 0 — 0 0 1 0 — 1perc — str[0.0.1.1.1]
Breitkopf

Schmidt, Franz   (1874-1939)

Concerto for Piano in E-flat Major   *46'*
(1934)
    2 2 2 2 — 4 2 0 0 — tmp — str
UE

Schmitt, Florent   (1870-1958)

Cançunik; Suite No.1, op.79 (1929)   *5'*
    1 1 1 1 — 2 2 2 0 — tmp+1 — 2hp — str
Durand

Chanson à Bercer, op.19, No.1   *3'*
(1898)
    solo vn (or vc)
    1 1 1 1 — 0 0 0 0 — str
Kalmus

Enfants, op.94 (1941)   *13'*
    2 1 1 1 — 1 1 0 0 — tmp+2 — str
Durand

Hymne à Tanit (1925)   *4'*
    1 1 1 1 — 1 0 0 0 — 1perc — str
From his music to the silent film *Salammbô*.
Durand

Kerob-shal, op.67 (1924)   *7'*
    solo medium voice
    2 0 2 0 — 0 0 0 0 — pf — str
Durand

Pupazzi, op.36 (1907)   *15'*
    2 2 2 2 — 2 0 0 0 — tmp+1 — hp — str
    Contents - 1. Scaramouche; 2. Damis; 3. Elegé; 4. Atys; 5.
    Clymène
Salabert

Quatre poèmes de Ronsard, op.100   *15'*
(1941)
    solo voice
    2 2 2 2 — 2 0 0 0 — tmp — str
Durand

Reflets d'Allemagne: Heidelberg,   *5'*
op.28 (1905)
    1 1 1 1 — 1 0 0 0 — tmp — str
    Reduced orchestration by P. O. Ferroud.
Salabert

Reflets d'Allemagne: Suite for   *11'*
Orchestra, op.28 (1905)
    3[1.2.pic] 2 2 2 — 4 2 3 1 — tmp+1 — hp — str
    perc: bd, tri, cym
    Contents - 1. Nuremberg; 2. Dresden; 3. Werder; 4. Munich
    mvt durations: 3' 2' 2' 4'
Durand; Kalmus

Soirs, op.5 (1896)   *24'*
    1 1 1 1 — 0 0 0 0 — tmp+2 — str
Durand

Suite, op.129 (1954)   *20'*
    solo fl
    1 2 2 2 — 2 0 0 0 — str
Durand

Schmitt, Meinrad   (1935-)

Concerto for Harp and Strings   *15'*
(1983)
    solo hp
    str
Boosey & Hawkes

Schneid, Tobias P.M.   (1963-)

Umbrellas & Sewing Machines   *20'*
    1 1 1 0 — 0 0 0 0 — 1perc — pf — str[1.0.0.1.0]
Peer

Schnittke, Alfred   (1934-1998)

3 X 7 (1989)   *3'*
    0 0 1 0 — 1 0 1 0 — hpsd — str[1.0.0.1.1]
Sikorski

Concerto for Piano 4 hands and   *15'*
Chamber Orchestra (1988)
    solo pf 4 hands
    1 1 1 1 — 1 1 1 1 — tmp+3 — str
UE

Concerto for Violin No.2 (1966)   *20'*
    solo vn
    1 1 1 1 — 1 1 1 0 — 2perc — pf — str
Sikorski

Concerto for Violin No.3 (1978)   *28'*
    solo vn
    2 2 3 2 — 2 1 1 0 — str[1.0.1.1.1]
Sikorski

Concerto Grosso No.1 (1977)   *31'*
    solo 2vn
    2pf[hpsd.prep-pf] — str
Boosey & Hawkes

Concerto Grosso No.3 (1985)   *24'*
    solo 2vn
    1perc — 2pf[hpsd/cel.pf] — str[4.4.3.2.1]
    perc: glsp
Sikorski

Four Aphorisms (1988)   *10'*
    1 1 2 1 — 2 1 1 0 — 3perc — 3pf[hpsd.cel.pf] —
    str
    perc: drums, chimes, glsp, vib
Boosey & Hawkes

Gogol Suite: Suite from the   *35'*
incidental music to "The Dead
Souls Register" (1980)
    2[1/pic.2(opt)] 1[1/eh] 2[1/Ebcl.2/bcl] 1[1/cbn] — 2
    1 1[btbn(opt)] 1 — elec gtr, bgtr — tmp+4 —
    4pf[prepf.org.hpsd.cel] — str
    perc: glsp, bells, sd, bd, cym, sus cym, tam-tam, templeblk,
    flexatone, rattle, whistle, xyl
Boosey & Hawkes; Schirmer

Hymn IV (1979) 5'
  0 0 0 1 — 0 0 0 0 — tmp+1 — hp — hpsd —
  str[0.0.0.1.1]
  perc: chimes
Schirmer; Sikorski

Labyrinths: Ballet Suite (1971) 38'
  1perc — 2pf[hpsd.cel] — str[3.3.3.3.1]
  perc: glsp, marim, 2 tom-tom, vib
Boosey & Hawkes

Little Tragedies: Suite from the 15'
Music to the Film (1994)
  1 1 1 1 — 1 1 1 0 — 2perc — hp — 2pf[pf.cel] —
  str[1.1.1.1.1]
  Arranged by Yuri Kasparov.
Sikorski

Monologue (1989) 18'
  solo va
  str[6.5.5.4.1]
Boosey & Hawkes

Moz-Art à la Haydn; Play on Music 12'
for 2 Violins, 2 Small String
Orchestras, double bass and
conductor (1977)
  soli 2vn, db
  str[6.0.2.2.0]
Boosey & Hawkes

Music for Piano and Chamber 25'
Orchestra (1964)
  solo pf
  1 1 1 0 — 1 1 0 0 — 1perc — str[1.1.1.1.1]
Sikorski

Pantomime; Suite for Chamber 15'
Orchestra, op.102 (1975)
  1 0 1 0 — 0 0 0 0 — 2perc — org — str[3.0.1.1.1]
  Instrumentation of W. A. Mozart's fragment K.416d.
Sikorski

Polyphonic Tango (1979) 5'
  1 1 1 1 — 1 1 1 0 — 2perc — pf — str[1.1.1.1.1]
Sikorski

Quasi una Sonata (1987) 20'
  solo vn
  2 2 2 2 — 2 0 0 0 — pf/hpsd — str
UE

Sonata for Violin and Chamber 23'
Orchestra (1968)
  solo vn
  hpsd — str[4.4.3.3.1]
Sikorski

Suite in Old Style (1972) 23'
  0 2 0 0 — 2 0 0 0 — hpsd — str
Sikorski

Trio-Sonata (1987) 25'
  str
  Chamber version of his String Trio.
Boosey & Hawkes

Schoeck, Othmar (1886-1957)

Besuch in Urach, op.62/40 (1950) 17'
  solo high voice
  2 2 2 2 — 2 1 0 0 — tmp+1 — pf — str
UE

Five Songs, op.60 (1946) 10'
  solo high voice
  1 1 1 0 — 1 0 0 0 — pf — str
  Also available in a version for medium voice.
UE

Nachhall, op.70 (1956) 39'
  solo medium voice
  1[1/pic] 2[1.2/eh] 2 2 — 2 1 0 0 — 1perc — pf —
  str
  perc: tmp, tam-tam, cym, xyl
UE

Serenade, op.1 (1907) 10'
  1 1 1 1 — 1 0 0 0 — str
Fleisher; Hug

Serenade (Interlude) (1917) 6'
  0 2[1.eh] 0 0 — 0 0 0 0 — str
Breitkopf; Fleisher

Schollum, Robert (1913-1987)

Concerto Grosso, Werk 34 (1948) 25'
  solo cl
  1 1 0 1 — 1 2 0 0 — asx — 1perc — pf — str
UE

Romanze, Werk 25 (1942) 7'
  solo vn
  2 1 1 2 — 3 1 0 0 — tmp+1 — str
UE

Serenade, Werk 39a (1952) 17'
  2 2 2 2 — 2 1 1 0 — 1perc — str
UE

Sonate (1952) 11'
  2 2 2 3 — 3 2 2 1 — 3perc — str
UE

Tanzsuite, Werk 21　　　　　　　　　　15'
　　2 1 1 1 — 3 3 1 0 — 1perc — hp — str
UE

Schönberg, Arnold　　　　　　(1874-1951)

Concerto for Cello; (After G. M.　　　　18'
Monn) (1933)
　　solo vc
　　2[1.2/pic] 2 2 2 — 2 2 1[btbn] 0 — tmp+2 — hp —
　　cel — str
Schirmer

Concerto for String Quartet; (After　　　27'
G. F. Händel's Concerto Grosso,
op.6, No.7) (1933)
　　solo str 4t
　　2 2 2 2 — 2 2 1 0 — 1perc — hp — pf — str
Schirmer

Four Pieces　　　　　　　　　　　　　8'
　　1 1 1 1 — 1 1 1 0 — 1perc — hp — cel —
　　str[1.1.1.1.1]
　　From his "Six Small Piano Pieces." Arranged by Hans
　　Abrahamsen.
Hansen

Kammersymphonie Nr.1 (Chamber　　　22'
Symphony No.1), op.9 (1906)
　　1 2[1.eh] 3[1.bcl.Ebcl] 2[1.cbn] — 2 0 0 0 —
　　str[1.1.1.1.1]
Kalmus

Kammersymphonie Nr.2 (Chamber　　　24'
Symphony No.2), op.38 (1940)
　　2[1.2/pic] 2[1.2/eh] 2 2 — 2 2 0 0 — str
　　First movement composed in 1906 and reorchestrated in
　　1935. Second movement composed and orchestrated in
　　1940.
Schirmer

Lied der Waldtaube: From "Gurre-　　　13'
Lieder" (1922)
　　solo S
　　1[1/pic] 2[1.eh] 3[1.2/Ebcl.bcl] 2[1.cbn] — 2 0 0 0
　　— 2pf[pf.harm] — str[1.1.1.1.1]
UE

Nature, op.8/1 (1904)　　　　　　　　4'
　　solo high or medium voice
　　1 1 1 1[opt] — 1[opt] 0 0 0 — 2pf[pf.harm] —
　　str[1.1.1.1.1]
　　From "Sechs Orchesterlieder," op.8. Arranged by Hanns
　　Eisler (1921).
UE

Nie Ward Ich, Herrin, Müd', op.8/4　　　4'
(1904)
　　solo high or medium voice
　　1 1 1 1[opt] — 1[opt] 0 0 0 — 2pf[pf.harm] —
　　str[1.1.1.1.1]
　　From "Sechs Orchesterlieder," op.8. Reconstructed from
　　sketches by Schönberg and arranged for chamber
　　ensemble by Klaus Simon (2007).
UE

Notturno in A-flat Major (1896)　　　　3'
　　hp — str
UE

Ode to Napoleon (1942)　　　　　　　16'
　　solo reciter
　　pf — str
Schirmer

Pierrot lunaire, op.21; Three Times　　　34'
Seven Poems from Albert Giraud's
"Pierrot lunaire" (1912)
　　solo Sprechstimme
　　1[1/pic] 0 1[1/bcl] 0 — 0 0 0 0 — pf —
　　str[1.0.1.1.0]
　　Contents - Part 1: Mondestrunken; Columbine; Der Dandy;
　　Eine blasse Wäscherin; Valse de Chopin; Madonna; Der
　　kranke Mond - Part 2: Nacht; Gebet an Pierrot; Raub; Rote
　　Messe; Galgenlied; Enthauptung; Die Kreuze - Part 3:
　　Heimweh; Gemeinheit; Parodie; Der Mondfleck; Serenade
　　Heimfahrt (Barcarole); O alter Durft
　　mvt durations: 12' 11' 11'
Belmont; Luck's; UE

Sechs Orchesterlieder, op.8 (1905)　　　23'
　　solo voice
　　1 1 1 1[opt] — 1[opt] 0 0 0 — 2kybd[pf.harm] —
　　str[1.1.1.1.1]
　　Arranged for chamber ensemble and voice by Erwin Stein,
　　Hanns Eisler and Klaus Simon. See also "Verein für
　　Musikalische Privataufführungen" (Appendix p.399). Each
　　song can be performed separately. See individual listings
　　for details.
　　Contents - 1. Natur (Eisler); 2. Das Wappenschild (Stein); 3.
　　Sehnsucht (Simon); 4. Nie ward ich, Herrin, müd' (Simon);
　　5. Voll jener Süße (Stein); 6. Wenn Vöglein klagen (Simon)
UE

Sehnsucht, op.8/3 (1904)　　　　　　2'
　　solo high or medium voice
　　2 2 2 2 — 4 0 0 0 — str
　　From "Sechs Orchesterlieder," op.8.
UE

Six Little Piano Pieces, op.19　　　　　8'
(1911)
　　1[1/pic] 1[1/eh] 2[1.2/bcl] 0 — 1 1 1 0 — 2perc —
　　hp — pf — str[1.0.1.1.1]
　　Orchestrated by Bernhard Wulff (1983).
UE

String Quartet No.2 in F-sharp   29'
minor, op.10 (1908)
    solo S
    str
    Version for Soprano and String Orchestra arranged by the
    composer (1929).
    UE

Suite (1934)   30'
    str
    Schirmer

Verklärte Nacht, op.4; Version for   30'
String Orchestra (1899/1916)
    str
    String orchestra version arranged by the composer.
    UE; Belmont; Luck's

Verklärte Nacht, op.4; Revised   30'
version 1943 (1899/1943)
    str
    String orchestra version arranged and revised by the
    composer.
    UE; Belmont; Luck's

Voll jener Süße, op.8/5 (1904)   5'
    solo high or medium voice
    1 1 1 1[opt] — 1[opt] 0 0 0 — 2pf[pf.harm] —
    str[1.1.1.1.1]
    From "Sechs Orchesterlieder," op.8. Arranged by Erwin
    Stein (1921).
    UE

Das Wappenschild, op.8/2 (1904)   4'
    solo high or medium voice
    1 1 1 1[opt] — 1[opt] 0 0 0 — 2pf[pf.harm] —
    str[1.1.1.1.1]
    From "Sechs Orchesterlieder," op.8. Arranged by Erwin
    Stein (1921).
    UE

Wenn Vöglein klagen, op.8/6 (1904)   5'
    solo high or medium voice
    1 1 1 1[opt] — 1[opt] 0 0 0 — 2pf[pf.harm] —
    str[1.1.1.1.1]
    From "Sechs Orchesterlieder" op.8. Reconstructed from
    sketches by Schönberg and arranged for chamber
    ensemble by Klaus Simon (2007).
    UE

Schönherr, Max   (1903-1984)

Concertino   12'
    solo pf
    2 2 2 2 — 0 0 0 0 — tmp — str
    UE

Festa Musicale   15'
    solo pf
    2 2 0 2 — 2 2 0 0 — 2perc — str
    UE

Tänze aus Salzburg   7'
    1 1 2 1 — 2 0 0 0 — tmp+1 — str
    UE

Das trunkene Mücklein   9'
    2 2 0 0 — 0 0 0 0 — 2perc — hp — str
    UE

Schreker, Franz   (1878-1934)

Fünf Gesänge (Five Songs) (1909)   20'
    solo Mz (or A, or Bar)
    2[1.2/pic] 2[1.eh] 2[1.basset hn/bcl] 2[1.cbn] — 2 1
    1 0 — tmp+2 — 2hp — cel — str
    perc: glsp, bd, tam-tam, cym
    Originally for piano and voice, arranged for orchestra and
    voice in 1922.
    Contents - 1. Ich frag' nach dir jedwede Morgensonne; 2.
    Dies aber kann mein Sehnen nimmer fassen; 3. Die
    Dunkelheit sinkt schwer wie Blei; 4. Sie sind so schön, die
    milden, sonnenreichen; 5. Einst gibt ein Tag mir alles Glück
    zu eigen
    UE

Fünf Gesänge (Five Songs);   20'
Chamber Ensemble Version (1909)
    solo low voice
    1 1[1/eh] 1[1/bcl] 1 — 1 1 1 0 — tmp+1 — hp —
    2pf[pf.cel] — str[2.2.2.3.1]
    Arranged for chamber ensemble and voice by Gösta
    Neuwirth (1976).
    Contents - 1. Ich frag' nach dir jedwede Morgensonne; 2.
    Dies aber kann mein Sehnen nimmer fassen; 3. Die
    Dunkelheit sinkt schwer wie Blei; 4. Sie sind so schön, die
    milden, sonnenreichen; 5. Einst gibt ein Tag mir alles Glück
    zu eigen
    UE

Kammersymphonie (Chamber   25'
Symphony) (1916)
    1 1 1 1 — 1 1 1 0 — tmp+1 — hp —
    3pf[pf.cel.harm] — str[2.2.2.3.2]
    perc: glsp, xyl, tri, cym, tambn
    mvt durations: 6' 4' 7' 2' 6'
    Kalmus; Luck's; UE

Scherzo (1900)   7'
    str
    Boosey & Hawkes

Symphony in A minor, op.1 (1899)   30'
    2 2 2 2 — 4 2 3 1 — tmp+2 — str
    perc: cym, tri
    Boosey & Hawkes

Valse Lente; Weißer Tanz (1908)   5'
  2 1 1 1 — 0 0 0 0 — 2perc — hp —
  str(min)[6.4.2.2.2]
  perc: glsp, tri
UE

Vom Ewigen Leben (1923)   20'
  solo S
  1[1/pic] 1[1/eh] 1[1/bcl] 1 — 1 1 1 0 —
  1[ssx/asx/tsx/bcl] — tmp+4 — hp — 2pf[pf/harm.cel]
  — str[1.1.1.1.1]
  Arranged for chamber ensemble and voice by Gösta
  Neuwirth (1976).
UE

Schroeder, Hermann   (1904-1984)

Concertino, op.42   12'
  solo pf
  2[1.2/pic] 2[1.2/eh] 2[1.2/bcl] 2 — 2 2 1 0 —
  tmp+1 — str[0.0.0.0.2]
Breitkopf

Concerto for Clarinet, op.47   17'
  solo cl
  2 2 2 2 — 2 2 0 0 — tmp+1 — str
Breitkopf

Concerto for Piano, op.35   18'
  solo pf
  2 2 2 2 — 4 3 3 0 — tmp+1 — str
Breitkopf

Concerto for Viola, op.45 (1973)   18'
  solo va
  2 0 2 2 — 0 0 0 0 — 1perc — str
Breitkopf

Double Concerto, op.41   21'
  solo 2vn
  2 2[1.2/eh] 0 2 — 2 2 0 0 — tmp+1 — str
Breitkopf

Schubert, Heino   (1928-)

Concerto (1975)   20'
  1 1 1 1 — 0 0 0 0 — str
Breitkopf

Schubert, Manfred   (1937-)

Nachtstück und Passacaglia (1967)   17'
  0 0 1 1 — 1 0 0 0 — str[1.1.1.1.1]
Breitkopf

Septet in Two Movements (1967)   11'
  0 0 1 1 — 1 0 0 0 — str[1.0.1.1.1]
Breitkopf

Schulhoff, Erwin   (1894-1942)

Hot-Sonate (1930)   15'
  solo asx
  1 1 1 1 — 1 1 0 0 — str(min)[1.1.1.1.1]
  Orchestrated by Harry White (2002).
Schott

Suite (1921)   18'
  1[1/pic] 2[1.eh] 2[1/Ebcl.bcl] 1 — 2 1 0 0 — 4perc
  — hp — str
  perc: tri, cym, tambn, military dr, td, bd with cym, cast, ratchet, siren,
  car horn, xyl, glsp, rute
Schott

Suite for Chamber Orchestra   18'
(1921)
  0 0 1 1 — 0 1 1 0 — 1perc — str[1.0.0.0.1]
  perc: vib, glsp, siren, tri, cast, cym, 2 templeblks, tambn, sd, ratchet,
  td, ped bd, hi-hat
  Arranged for chamber ensemble from his "Suite" by
  Andreas N. Tarkmann (2004).
Schott

Schuller, Gunther   (1925-)

Automation; (Music for a Real or   7'
Imagined Film Score) (1962)
  1 0 1[1/bcl] 1 — 1 0 0 0 — 2perc — hp — pf —
  str[1.0.0.0.1]
Margun

Chamber Symphony (1989)   14'
  2[1.pic] 2[1.2/eh] 2[1.2/bcl] 2[1.2/cbn] — 1 1 1 1
  — hp — str
  Contents - 1. Calmo; 2. Arioso; 3. Vivo
  mvt durations: 5' 3' 6'
AMP

Chimeric Images (1988)   15'
  1 0 1 1 — 1 1 0 0 — hp — pf/cel — str[1.0.1.1.1]
Margun

Contours (1958)   21'
  1 1 2 1 — 1 1 1 0 — 1perc — hp — str
  perc: 6 cym, 2 td, tambn, 2 tom-tom, tri, 2 gongs, glsp, xyl
Schott

Journey to the Stars (1962)   15'
  solo narrator (opt)
  1[1/pic] 0 2[1.2/bcl] 1 — 2 2 2 2 — tmp+2 — hp
  — pf/cel — str
  Strings without va.
AMP

Little Fantasy (1957)   4'
  1 1 1 1 — 2 1 1 0 — tmp+1 — str
Margun

Schultz, Wolfgang-Andreas   (1948-)

Was mir die Aeolsharfe erzählt...   15'
(2004)
  str[6.4.4.3.1]
Boosey & Hawkes

Schuman, William   (1910-1992)

Amaryllis; Variants on an Old   10'
English Round
  str
Presser

Night Journey   20'
  1 1 1 1 — 1 0 0 0 — pf — str[2.2.2.2.1]
Presser

A Song of Orpheus; Fantasy for   20'
Cello
  solo vc
  2 2 3 2 — 1 0 0 0 — hp — str
  Version for chamber orchestra.
Presser

The Witch of Endor; Ballet   30'
  1 1 1 1 — 1 1 1 1 — tmp+1 — pf — str
Presser

Schurmann, Gerard   (1924-)

Sonata for String Orchestra (2004)   25'
  str
Novello

Variants (1970)   18'
  1[1/pic] 2[1.2/eh] 0 2 — 2 0 0 0 — str
Novello

Schwaen, Kurt   (1909-2007)

Zwingerserenade   9'
  1 1 1 1 — 0 0 0 0 — str
Breitkopf

Schwantner, Joseph   (1943-)

Angelfire; Fantasy for Amplified   18'
Violin and Orchestra (2002)
  solo vn (amp)
  2 2[1.eh] 2[1.2/bcl] 2 — 4 2 2 0 — tmp+3 — hp —
  amp pf — str
Schott

Chasing Light (2008)   22'
  2[1.2/pic] 2 2 2 — 2 2 1 0 — tmp+1 — amp pf —
  str
  perc: vib, xyl, crot, lg tam-tam, tri, bd, 3 tom-tom
Schott

Concerto for Piano (1988)   30'
  solo pf
  2[1.2/pic] 2[1.2/eh] 2[1.2/bcl] 2 — 2 2 2 1 — 2perc
  — cel — str
  perc: bongo, tom-tom, bd, timbales, sus cym, water gong, lg tam-
  tam, crot, vib, glsp, marim, xyl, chimes, bell tree, tri
Schott

Distant Runes and Incantations   15'
(1983)
  solo pf (amp)
  2[1.2/pic] 2[1.2/eh] 2[1.2/bcl] 2 — 2 2 0 0 — 2perc
  — cel — str
  perc: tmp, bongo, tom-tom, bd, timbales, sus cym, water gong, crot,
  vib, glsp, marim, chimes, bell tree, tri
Schott

Dreamcaller (1984)   21'
  solo S, vn
  1[1/afl] 2[1.2/eh] 1[1/bcl] 2 — 2 1 0 0 — 1perc —
  pf/cel — str
  perc: tam-tam, bd, 2 tom-tom, 2 timbales, lg sus cym, 4 tri, bell tree,
  vib, glsp, crot, chimes, marim
Schott

...from Afar (1987)   16'
  solo gtr
  2[1.2/pic] 2[1.eh] 2[1.2/bcl] 2 — 2 1 1 0 — tmp+3
  — hp — pf/cel — str
  perc: vib, tam-tam, tri, 2 sus cym, woodblk, 2 gong, marim, glsp, bd,
  timbales, bell tree, 5 templeblks, crot, xyl, bd, 3 tom-tom, chimes
Schott

New Morning for the World;   23'
"Daybreak of Freedom" (2004)
    narrator
    2[1.2/pic] 2[1.2/eh] 2[1.2/bcl] 2 — 2 2 0 0 — 1perc
    — pf — str
    perc: vib, chimes, crot, xyl, glsp, lg tam-tam, button gong, bd, 3 tom-
    tom, timbales, lg sus cym, tri
    With texts by Dr. Martin Luther King Jr.
    Schott

Sparrows (1978)   17'
    solo S
    1[1/pic] 0 1 0 — 0 0 0 0 — 1perc — hp — pf —
    str[1.0.1.1.0]
    Schott

Schwartz, Francis   (1940-)

Flaming June (1998)   12'
    1 1 1 0 — 1 0 0 1 — 1perc — str[4.0.2.2.1]
    perc: templeblks, tam-tam, tri
    SchwartzWorks

Grimaces "Commande d'Etat"   16'
(1984)
    solo S
    1 1 1 0 — 1 0 0 0 — asx — gtr — 2perc —
    str[1.0.0.1.1]
    perc: drum kit, vib
    Two conductors needed: one for the ensemble, one for the
    audience participation.
    SchwartzWorks

Songs of Loneliness (1991)   15'
    solo Mz
    0 2 0 0 — 0 0 0 0 — pf — str[6.0.0.0.0]
    SchwartzWorks

Un Sourire Festif (A Festive Smile)   12'
(1981)
    str
    SchwartzWorks

Schwarz-Schilling, Reinhard   (1904-1985)

Introduction and Fugue (1948)   11'
    str
    Bärenreiter

Partita (1934/35)   33'
    1 1 1 1 — 2 2 0 0 — tmp+1 — hp — str
    Bärenreiter

Schwehr, Cornelius   (1953-)

Aber die Schönheit des Gitters   20'
(1992)
    1 0 1 0 — 0 0 0 0 — film projection[opt] — 1perc
    — pf — str[1.0.1.1.0]
    Breitkopf

Schweitzer, Benjamin   (1973-)

flekkicht; For Baroque Orchestra   14'
(2004)
    2[1.2/pic] 2[1.2/ob da cacc] 0 1 — 2 0 0 0 —
    lute[opt] — hpsd — str[4.4.2.2.1]
    Schott

unplugged. unperfumed (2001)   12'
    0 0 1[bcl] 1 — 0 1 1 0 — A (voice) — 2perc — pf
    — str[0.0.1.0.1]
    perc: vib, marim, 2 sus cym, Chinese cym, thunder sheet, cowbell, 2
    bongo, 2 tom-tom, sd, 2 congitas, 2 congas, bd, 5 templblks, marim,
    sandpaper, paper, schlitztrommel, angklung
    Schott

Schwertsik, Kurt   (1935-)

Compagnie Masquerade; Ein   22'
Divertissement für kleines
Orchester, einer Idee & teilweise
erhaltenen Violinstimme Mozarts
folgend. op.93 (2005)
    2[1.2/pic] 2 2[basset hn.basset hn] 2 — 2 1 1 0 —
    str
    Boosey & Hawkes

Möbelmusik-Klassisch, op.68   12'
(1994)
    str
    Boosey & Hawkes

Mond-Lichtung; Eine Nacht-partie   10'
für Streichorchester, op.75 (1997)
    str
    Boosey & Hawkes

Mozart, auf und davon, op.94   9'
(2005)
    2[1.2/pic] 2 2 — 2 1 1 0 — tmp — str
    Boosey & Hawkes

Now you hear me, now you don't   15'
(2008)
    solo marim
    str
    Boosey & Hawkes

Schrumpf-Symphonie, op.80 (1999)   5'
  2[1.2/pic] 2 2 2 — 2 2 0 0 — tmp — str
Boosey & Hawkes

Scott, Cyril   (1879-1970)

Suite Phantastique   15'
  1 1 1 1 — 1 0 0 0 — 1perc — hp — str
UE

Summer Gardens   8'
  1 1 1 1 — 1 0 0 0 — 1perc — hp — str
  perc: tri, tambn
Schott

Search, Frederick   (1889-1959)

Sinfonietta   20'
  1 1 1 1 — 1 1 1 0 — tmp+1 — str
Fleisher

Searle, Humphrey   (1915-1982)

Night Music (1947)   9'
  1[1/pic] 1 1[1/bcl] 1[1/cbn] — 1 1 1 0 — tmp — str
Fleisher

Three Songs of Jocelyn Brooke,   18'
op.25b (1954)
  2[1.pic] 1 2[1.bcl] 1[1/cbn] — 1 1 0 0 — hp[or pf]
  — str[1.0.1.1.1]
Faber

Variations and Finale, op.34 (1958)   18'
  1[pic] 1 1 1 — 1 0 0 0 — str[1.1.1.1.1]
Schott

Sekles, Bernhard   (1872-1934)

Serenade for 11 Solo Instruments,   15'
op.14 (1913)
  1 1 1 1 — 1 0 0 0 — hp — str[1.1.1.1.1]
Kalmus

Sessions, Roger   (1896-1985)

Concertino   17'
  1[1/pic/afl] 1[1/eh] 1[1/Ebcl/bcl] 1[cbn] — 2 1 1 0
  — tmp+1 — str
Presser

Romualdo's Song from "The Black   4'
Maskers"
  solo S
  1 1 2 1 — 1 2 1 0 — 1perc — pf — str
Presser

Sgrizzi, Luciano   (1910-1994)

Englische Suite nach Werken der   14'
Virginalisten (1952)
  2 1 2 1 — 2 2[opt] 0 0 — hpsd — str
UE

Suite Belge; D'après des œuvres   15'
de clavecinistes belges du 18ème
siècle (1953)
  2 1 2 1 — 0 0 0 0 — str
UE

Sharp, Elliott   (1951-)

Akadak (2004)   30'
  1[pic] 0 1[bcl] 0 — 0 0 0 0 — accordion, gtr, tape
  — pf — str[1.0.0.1.0]
zOaR

Calling (2002)   27'
  2[pic.afl] 1 2[bcl.bcl] 1 — 1 2 2 1 — tmp+1 — pf
  — str
  perc: bongos, crot, China crash, dome cym, sizzle cym, med tom, 2
  bd
zOaR

Dark Matters (2008)   15'
  1 0 1[bcl] 0 — 0 0 1 0 — cimbalom, gtr, accordion
  — 2pf[pf.synth] — str[1.0.1.1.0]
zOaR

Evolute (2007)   15'
  2[pic.afl] 2[1.eh] 1[bcl] 0 — 0 0 0 0 — 1perc — pf
  — str[0.0.1.0.1]
  perc: marim
zOaR

No Time Like The Stranger (2004)   10'
  solo S
  1 0 1[bcl] 1 — 1 0 0 0 — 1perc — pf —
  str[1.0.1.1.0]
  perc: unpitched metallophones, hi-hat, med and low tom-tom, 2 bd
zOaR

On Corlear's Hook (2007)   20'
  2[pic.afl] 2[1.eh] 2[bcl.bcl] 2 — 1 2 2[1.btbn] 0 —
  tmp+1 — hp — pf — str
  perc: glsp, crot, hi-hat, dome cym, sizzle cym, med tom, 2 bd
zOaR

Points & Fields (2009)   12'
    1 1 2[1.bcl] 1 — 1 1 1 0 — 2perc — pf — str
perc: marim, crot, glsp, hi-hat, bd
zOaR

Polymerae (2008)   50'
    1[afl] 0 2[1.bcl] 0 — 0 1 1 0 — tmp+3 — pf —
str[1.0.1.0.0]
perc: marim, vib, crot, glsp, 8 dome cym, 8 tam-tam (different sizes),
8 floor toms (different sizes)
zOaR

Proof Of Erdös (2005)   21'
    str[7.0.2.2.1]
zOaR

Racing Hearts (2001)   15'
    2 2 2 2 — 2 2 2 1 — tmp+1 — pf — str
perc: bongos, crot, China crash, dome cym, sizzle cym, med tom, 2
bd
zOaR

Re/Iterations (1986)   12'
    str[8.8.4.4.2]
zOaR

Ripples & Heats (2004)   15'
    0 0 1[Ebcl] 0 — 0 1 1 0 — asx — 2perc — pf —
str[1.0.0.1.1]
perc: vib, jazz drum set
zOaR

Spring & Neap (1996)   30'
    2 shamisen, koto — 1perc — hp — pf —
str[1.0.1.1.1]
perc: low drums (bd, floor toms, taiko)
zOaR

Shchedrin, Rodion   (1932-)

The Frescoes of Dionysus for Nine   12'
Instruments (1981)
    1 1[eh] 1 1 — 1 0 0 0 — 1perc — cel —
str[0.0.1.1.0]
VAAP

The Geometry of Sound (1987)   15'
    1 1 1 1 — 1 1 1 0 — 1perc — hp —
3pf[hpsd.cel.synth] — str[1.1.1.1.1]
VAAP

Music for the Town of Köthen   18'
(1984)
    0 2 0 2 — 0 0 0 0 — hpsd — str[6.4.4.3.1]
Also possible with strings (4.4.3.3.1).
Sikorski

Shepherd's Pipes of Vologda   8'
(1995)
    0 2[1.eh] 0 0 — 1 0 0 0 — str
Schott

Shchetinsky, Alexander   (1960-)

Glossolalie (1989)   14'
    2 1 2 1 — 1 1 1 0 — tsx — elec gtr — 2perc — hp
— pf — str
perc: 5 tom-tom, chimes, bell, vib
Boosey & Hawkes

Sheinkman, Mordechai   (1926-)

Serenade (1957)   14'
    str
Boosey & Hawkes

Sheng, Bright   (1955-)

H'un (Lacerations): In Memoriam   22'
1966-76 (1988)
    2[1/pic.2/pic/afl] 2 2[1/bcl.2/bcl] 2[1.2/cbn] — 3 2 2
0 — 2perc — hp — pf — str
Schirmer

Postcards (1997)   15'
    1[1/pic] 2[1.2/eh] 1[1/Ebcl/bcl] 2 — 2 1 0 0 —
2perc — pf/cel — str
Schirmer

Shostakovich, Dmitri   (1906-1975)

Chamber Symphony, op.73a (1946)   33'
    1 2[1.2/eh] 1 1 — 0 0 0 0 — tmp — hp — str
Arranged from String Quartet No.3 by Rudolf Barshai.
Boosey & Hawkes

Chamber Symphony, op.83a (1949)   19'
    1 2[1.eh] 1[1/bcl] 1 — 2 1 0 0 — 1perc — str
perc: whip, sd, 4 tom-tom, tam-tam, xyl, marim, cel
Arranged from String Quartet No.4 by Rudolf Barshai.
Boosey & Hawkes

Chamber Symphony, op.110a   19'
(1960)
    str
Arranged from String Quartet No.8 by Rudolf Barshai.
Boosey & Hawkes

Five Fragments, op.42 (1935)　　　　　　9'
2[1.pic] 2[1.eh] 3[1.bcl.Ebcl] 2[1.cbn] — 2 1 1 1 —
1perc — hp — str
perc: sd
Boosey & Hawkes

Hamlet; Incidental Music to　　　　　　45'
Shakespeare's Tragedy, op.32
(1932)
solo Mz, Bar
2[1.pic] 1 1 1 — 2 2 1 1 — female and male actor
— tmp+1 — str
perc: tri, tambn, cym, sd, bd, gong
Boosey & Hawkes

Hamlet: Suite from the Theatre　　　　　23'
Music, op.32a (1932)
1 1 1 1 — 2 2 1 1 — tmp+1 — str
Contents - 1. Introduction and Night Watch; 2. Funeral
March; 3. Flourish and Dance Music; 4. Hunting; 5. Actors'
Pantomime; 6. Procession; 7. Musical Pantomime; 8.
Banquet; 9. Ophelia's Song; 10. Lullaby; 11. Requiem; 12.
Tournament; 13. Fortinbras' March
Boosey & Hawkes

The Human Comedy: Suite, op.37　　　　23'
(1934)
1 1 1 1 — 2 2 1 1 — Bb baritone saxhorn —
tmp+1 — pf — str
perc: tri, sd, cym, tambn
Incidental music to a play by Pavel Sukhotin, adapted from
"La Comedie Humaine" by Balzac.
Boosey & Hawkes

New Babylon, op.18 (1929)　　　　　　85'
1 1 1 1 — 2 2 1 0 — 3perc — pf — str
perc: tri, tambn, sd, cym, bd, gong, xyl, flexatone
Music for the movie *New Babylon.*
Boosey & Hawkes

The Nose: Suite, op.15a (1928)　　　　　25'
solo T, Bar
1[1/pic] 1[1/eh] 1[1/Ebcl/bcl] 1[1/cbn] — 1 1[1/crt]
1[1/btbn] 0 — 2 balalaikas — 1perc — 2hp — pf —
str
perc: tri, cast, flexatone, tom-tom, tambn, sd, bd, cym, tam-tam, glsp,
xyl
To be performed with small string section.
Contents - 1. Overture; 2. Kovalyov's Aria from Scene 5; 3.
Percussion Interlude to Scene 3; 4. Interlude to Scene 6; 5.
Ivan's aria from Scene 6; 6. Kovalyov's Monologue from
Scene 6; 7. Galop from Scene 3
Boosey & Hawkes

Symphony for Strings, op.118a　　　　　26'
(1964)
str
Arranged from String Quartet No.10 by Rudolf Barshai.
mvt durations: 5' 4' 6' 11'
Boosey & Hawkes

Two Pieces, Prelude and Scherzo,　　　　11'
op.11 (1925)
str
Also available as string octet or string orchestra without
basses. Full string orchestra version by Lazar Gozman.
Boosey & Hawkes

Shulman, Alan　　　　　　(1915-2002)

Vodka Float (1947)　　　　　　3'
0 0 1 0 — 0 0 0 0 — gtr — hp — str
Shawnee

Sibelius, Jean　　　　　　(1865-1957)

Belsazars Gaestabud (Belshazzar's　　　14'
Feast); Incidental Music, op.51
(1906)
2[1.2/pic] 1 2 0 — 2 0 0 0 — 3perc — str
perc: bd, cym, tri, tambn
Kalmus; Luck's

Canzonetta, op.62a (1911)　　　　　　3'
str
Breitkopf; Kalmus

Dance Intermezzo, op.45, No.2　　　　　4'
(1904)
2 1 2 1 — 4 2 0 0 — tmp+1 — hp — str
Kalmus; Luck's; Breitkopf

Impromptu; On the Impromptus　　　　　6'
op.5/5 and 5/6
str
Breitkopf

Laetare Anima Mea, op.77a (1914)　　　4'
solo vn
2 0 1 0 — 2 0 0 0 — tmp — hp — str
Kalmus

Pelleas & Melisande, op.46 (1905)　　　28'
1[1/pic] 1[1/eh] 2 2 — 2 0 0 0 — tmp — str
Kalmus; Luck's

Rakastava, op.14 (1911)　　　　　　15'
tmp+1 — str
perc: tri
Kalmus; Breitkopf

Romance in C major, op.42 (1903)　　　5'
str
Breitkopf; Kalmus

Scaramouche; Tragic Pantomime,   56'
op.71 (1913)
     2[1.2/pic] 0 0 2 — 4 0 0 0 — tmp — str[2.2.1.1.1]
     Also calls for banda: 0220 - 0100 - 1perc - pf - str(0.0.1.1.0).
     Kalmus

Scenes Historique I, op.25 (1911)   15'
     2[1.2/pic] 2 2 2 — 4 3 3 0 — tmp+3 — str
     Contents - 1. All'Overtura; 2. Scena; 3. Festivo (Bolero)
     mvt durations: 5' 5' 5'
     Breitkopf; Kalmus

Scenes Historiques, op.66 (1912)   20'
     3[1.2.pic] 2 2 2 — 4 0 0 0 — tmp+1 — hp — str
     Contents - 1. Die Jagd; 2. Minnelied; 3. An der Zugbrücke
     mvt durations: 8' 5' 7'
     Breitkopf; Kalmus

Serenata No.1 in D major, op.69a   9'
(1913)
     solo vn
     2 2 2 2 — 4 0 0 0 — tmp — str
     Breitkopf; Kalmus

Serenata No.2 in G minor, op.69b   8'
(1913)
     solo vn
     2 2 2 2 — 4 0 0 0 — tmp+1 — str
     Breitkopf; Kalmus

Suite Mignonne, op.98a (1921)   8'
     2 0 0 0 — 0 0 0 0 — str
     Kalmus

Svanevit Suite (Swanwhite Suite)   30'
op.54 (1909)
     2 2 2 2 — 4 0 0 0 — tmp+1 — hp — str
     Contents - 1. The Peacock; 2. The Harp; 3. The Maiden with
     the Roses; 4. Listen, the Robin Sings; 5. The Prince Alone;
     6. Swanwhite and the Prince; 7. Song of Praise
     Kalmus

Swan of Tuonela: From   9'
Lemminkäinen Suite, op.22 (1893)
     solo eh
     0 1 1[bcl] 2 — 4 0 3 0 — tmp+1 — hp — str
     perc: bd
     Breitkopf; Luck's

Valse Chevaleresque, op.96c   4'
(1920)
     2 2 2 2 — 4 2 3 0 — tmp+1 — str
     Kalmus

Valse Romantique, op.62b (1911)   5'
     2 0 2 0 — 2 0 0 0 — tmp — str
     Composed for a 1911 production of "Kuolema" (op.44).
     Breitkopf; Kalmus; Luck's

Valse Triste: From "Kuolema,"   5'
op.44, No.1 (1904)
     1 0 1 0 — 2 0 0 0 — tmp — str
     Breitkopf; Kalmus; Luck's

Siegl, Otto   (1896-1978)

Lyrische Tanzmusik, op.82 (1934)   17'
     2 2 2 2 — 2 1 1 0 — tmp — pf[opt] — str
     Can also be performed with strings and piano alone or with
     strings, piano and several winds.
     UE

Sierra, Roberto   (1953-)

Alegría (1996)   6'
     3[1.2.pic] 2 2 2 — 4 3 3 1 — tmp+3 — str
     Subito

Concertino (1995)   15'
     1 1 1[1/Ebcl] 1 — 1 1 1 0 — CD — 1perc — pf —
     str[1.1.1.1.1]
     Subito

Concierto Barroco; (Guitar   10'
Concerto) (1996)
     solo gtr
     2 2 2 2 — 2 2 0 0 — 1perc — str
     Subito

Concierto Caribe (1993)   20'
     solo fl
     1 1 1 1 — 2 1 0 0 — 2perc — pf/cel — str
     Subito

Cuatro Versos; (Cello Concerto)   20'
(1999)
     solo vc
     2 2 2 2 — 2 1 1 0 — 2perc — pf — str
     Subito

Cuentos (1997)   12'
     1[1/pic] 1 1[1/Ebcl] 1 — 1 1 1 0 — asx — 2perc
     — pf — str[1.1.1.1.1]
     perc: glsp, xyl, vib, marim, ratchet, whip, marac, 2 cencerros,
     Chinese gong, bongos, 2 congas, vibraslap, 5 templeblks, guiro, 5
     sus cym, bd, cabata, 5 brake dr
     Subito

Danzas Concertantes; (Guitar   20'
Concerto) (2007)
  solo gtr
  2 2 2 2 — 2 2 1 0 — tmp+1 — str
Subito

Descarga; (Orchestral Version) (1988)   13'
  1 1 1 1 — 2 1 1 0 — 3perc — hp — pf — str
Subito

Doce Bagatelas (2000)   20'
  str
Subito

Folias; (Guitar Concerto) (2002)   12'
  solo gtr
  2 2 2 2 — 2 2 0 0 — 1perc — str
Subito

The Güell Concerto (2006)   13'
  1 1 1 1 — 1 1 1 0 — 1perc — pf — str
Subito

Imágenes; (Double Concerto)   23'
(1993)
  solo vn, gtr
  2 2[1.eh] 2[1.bcl] 2 — 2 1 0 0 — 2perc — str
Subito

Of Discoveries (1992)   22'
  solo 2 gtr
  2 2 2 2 — 2 2 2 0 — 2perc — str
Subito

Serenata (2005)   15'
  2[1.2/pic] 2 2 2 — 2 2 0 0 — tmp+1 — pf — str
Subito

Sinfonía No.1 (2002)   16'
  2[1.2/pic] 2 2 2 — 2 2 0 0 — tmp+2 — pf — str
  perc: bongos, sus cym, ped bd, marim, xyl, sd, cencerros, vib, hi-hat,
  cym
  mvt durations: 5' 4' 3' 4'
Subito

Sonatina: From "Let's Make a   3'
Symphony" (1997)
  2 2 2 2 — 4 2 2 1 — tmp+2 — str
Subito

Silverman, Stanley   (1938-)

Planh; For Chamber Ensemble   11'
(1965)
  1[1/afl] 0 1[1/bcl] 0 — 0 0 0 0 — mand, gtr —
  2perc — str[1.0.1.1.0]
EMI

Silvestrov, Valentin   (1937-)

Symphony No.2 (1965)   24'
  1 0 0 0 — 0 0 0 0 — 2perc — pf — str[8.0.3.2.1]
Schirmer

Sinding, Christian   (1856-1941)

Abendstimmung, op.120   6'
  solo vn
  2 2 2 2 — 4 0 0 0 — tmp — hp — str
Breitkopf

Romance in D major, op.100   10'
  solo vn
  2 2 2 2 — 4 2 0 0 — tmp — hp — str
Breitkopf; Luck's

Sinigaglia, Leone   (1868-1944)

Concerto for Violin in A major,   40'
op.20
  solo vn
  2 2 2 2 — 4 2 0 0 — tmp — str
Breitkopf

Rhapsodia piemontese, op.26   4'
  solo vn
  2 2 2 2 — 4 2 0 0 — tmp — str
Breitkopf

Sjöblom, Heimer   (1910-2001)

Liten Svit I Spelmanston (1973)   13'
  1 1 1 1 — 1 0 0 0 — str
Fleisher

Slonimsky, Nicolas   (1894-1995)

Little March for the Big Bowl;   2'
Marche grotesque (1943)
  1[pic] 0 0 0 — 2 2 1 0 — 1perc — pf — str
Fleisher

Slonimsky, Sergei   (1932-)

Concerto Buffo   12'
   1[1/pic] 0 0 0 — 0 1 0 0 — 1perc — pf —
   str[8.0.3.2.1]
   perc: cym, gong, 3 tom-tom, conga, bongos, claves, templeblk,
   woodblk, recco-recco, tartaruga, cabaza, vib, marim, upright piano
   with action removed
   Boosey & Hawkes

Smalley, Roger   (1943-)

Missa Parodia II (1967)   16'
   solo pf
   1[1/pic] 1 1 0 — 1 1 1 0 — str[1.0.1.0.0]
   Faber

Smirnov, Dmitri   (1948-)

Between Scylla and Charybdis,   20'
op.104 (1998)
   str[6.6.4.4.2]
   Boosey & Hawkes

Elegie In Memoriam Edison   6'
Denissow for 16 Players, op.97b
(1997)
   1 1 1 1 — 1 1 1 0 — 2perc — hp — cel —
   str[1.1.1.1.1]
   Sikorski

Jacob's Ladder, op.58 (1990)   13'
   1 1 1 1 — 1 1 1 0 — 2perc — hp — cel —
   str[1.1.1.1.1]
   Schirmer

The River of Life, op.66 (1992)   14'
   1 1 1 1 — 1 1 1 0 — 2perc — str[1.1.1.1.1]
   After the drawing of William Blake.
   Boosey & Hawkes

Two Ricercares (1983)   8'
   str[7.0.3.2.1]
   Boosey & Hawkes

Smit, Andre-Jean   (1926-)

Suite Pittoresque   8'
   1 1 2 1 — 2 0 0 0 — tmp — str
   Schott

Smolka, Martin   (1959-)

Octet (2001)   20'
   0 0 1 1 — 1 0 0 0 — str[1.1.1.1.1]
   Breitkopf

Oh, My Admired C minor (2002)   10'
   1[afl] 0 1[Ebcl] 0 — 0 0 0 0 — 1perc — pf —
   str[1.0.1.1.0]
   Breitkopf

Rain, A Window, Roofs, Chimneys,   20'
Pigeons And So (1991)
   1[pic/rec] 1[eh] 1[bcl/Ebcl] 1 — 1 1 1 1 —
   accordion, elec gtr — 2perc — 2pf — str[1.0.1.1.1]
   Breitkopf

Solitudo (2003)   14'
   1[1/pic] 1 1 1 — 1 1 0 1 — gtr — 2perc — hp —
   pf — str[0.0.0.1.0]
   Breitkopf

Sobanski, Hans Joachim   (1906-1959)

Romantic Concerto   28'
   solo va
   2 2 2 2 — 2 2 0 0 — tmp+1 — str
   UE

Sørensen, Bent   (1958-)

Clairobscur (1987)   10'
   1 1 1 1 — 1 0 0 0 — str[1.1.1.1.1]
   Hansen

Funeral Procession (1989)   9'
   solo vn, va
   1 0 1 0 — 0 0 0 0 — 1perc — pf — str[1.0.0.1.0]
   Hansen

Minnelieder — Zweites Minnewater   12'
(1994)
   1 1 1 1 — 1 1 1 0 — 1perc — pf — str[1.1.1.1.1]
   Hansen

Minnewater; Thousands of Canons   12'
(1988)
   2 1 1 0 — 2 1 1 0 — 2perc — str[1.1.1.1.1]
   Hansen

Shadowland   20'
   1 1 1 1 — 1 0 0 0 — str[1.1.1.1.1]
   mvt durations: 6' 7' 4' 3
   Hansen

Sirenengesang (1994)   14'
1[1/pic] 1 1[1/Ebcl] 0 — 1 1 1 0 — 1perc — pf —
str[1.1.1.1.0]
Hansen

The Weeping White Room (2002)   8'
1[1/pic/bfl] 0 1[1/bcl] 0 — 0 0 0 0 — 1perc — pf —
str[1.1.1.1.1]
Hansen

Sotelo, Mauricio   (1961-)

Chalan (2003)   18'
solo perc
2[1/pic/afl.2/pic/bfl] 1 2[1.2/bcl] 1 — 1 1 2 1[cbtu]
— 2perc — pf — str[1.1.1.2.1]
UE

De Imaginum, Signorum, et   14'
Idearum Compositione I (1996)
1 0 1 0 — 0 0 0 0 — 2sx[asx.tsx] — 2perc — pf
— str[0.0.0.1.1]
UE

Wall of Light Black (2006)   16'
1 1 1[1/bcl] 1 — 1 1 1 1 — 2perc — pf —
str[1.1.1.1.1]
UE

Wall of Light Red (2004)   17'
solo sx
1[1/pic/bfl] 1 1[1/bcl] 1[1/cbn] — 0 1 1 0 — 3perc
— pf — str[1.1.1.1.1]
UE

Spinner, Leopold   (1906-1980)

Ricercata, op.21 (1965)   16'
2[1.afl] 2[1.eh] 2[1.bcl] 0 — 1 1 1 1 — hp — cel —
str[3.3.3.3.0]
Boosey & Hawkes

Spitzmüller, Alexander   (1894-1962)

40. Mai; Suite, op.25 (1941)   21'
2 1 1 1 — 2 2 0 0 — 2perc — cel — str
UE

Spratlan, Lewis   (1940-)

Diary Music I (1972)   14'
1 1 1 1 — 0 1 0 0 — 1perc — str[1.0.1.1.1]
Margun

Staempfli, Edward   (1908-2002)

Präludium und Variationen (1945)   12'
1 1 1 1 — 2 1 1 0 — tmp+1 — str
Boosey & Hawkes

Stahmer, Klaus Hinrich   (1941-)

Dans Une Lumière Eclatante   15'
(1989)
1[pic] 0 1 0 — 0 0 0 0 — electronics — 1perc —
pf — str[1.0.1.1.1]
Breitkopf

Standford, Patric   (1939-)

Nocturne (1968)   8'
2 1 3 0 — 1 0 0 0 — tmp — pf — str[1.2.2.3.2]
Novello

Notte (1968)   13'
1 2 0 1 — 2 0 0 0 — str[6.0.2.2.1]
Novello

Suite for Small Orchestra (1966)   16'
2 1 2 1 — 2 0 0 0 — str
Novello

Stanford, Charles Villiers   (1852-1924)

Songs of the Sea, op.91 (1904)   17'
2[1.pic] 1 2 1 — 2 2 2 0 — tmp+1 — str
perc: cym, bd, sd
Suite arranged for chamber orchestra by Thomas F. Dunhill.
Boosey & Hawkes

Suite of Ancient Dances, op.58   15'
(1895)
2 2 2 2 — 2 2 0 0 — tmp+1 — str
perc: tri, sd
Boosey & Hawkes

Staud, Johannes Maria   (1974-)

Berenice: Suite 1 (2003)   20'
1[1/pic/afl/bfl] 0 1 0 — 1 2[1/pic tpt.2/flug]
2[1.cbtbn/cbtu] 0 — ssx/asx/tsx/bsx — tape — 2perc
— 2pf[pf.harm] — str[1.1.2.2.1]
perc: I: glsp, vib, gong, 2 cym, 2 Chinese cym, shell cym, ride cym, 2
tri, tambn, thundersheet, 3 darabukkas, 2 woodboxes, tam-tam II:
crot, marim, gong, cym, 2 Chinese cym, ride cym, sizzle cym, 4 dr, 2
wooddr, woodchimes, sandblk, thundersheet, 2 tam-tam, bd
UE

Berenice: Suite 2 (2003)   10'
    1[1/pic/bfl] 0 1[1/cbcl] 0 — 1[1/wag tu] 2[1/pic
    tpt.2/flug] 1 1[cbtu] — ssx/tsx/bsx — 2perc —
    2pf[pf.harm] — str[1.1.2.2.1]
UE

Berenice: Lied vom Verschwinden   12'
(2003)
    solo S
    0 0 1 0 — 0 1 1 0 — tape — 2perc — pf —
    str[0.0.1.2.1]
    perc: I: crot, vib, shell chimes, cym, Chinese cym, ride cym, tam-tam,
    7 templeblks, db bow, thin metal stick II: crot, marim, 2 Chinese cym,
    cym, tam-tam, wood chimes, 5 wood dr, db bow, thin metal stick
UE

Configurations / Reflet (2002)   10'
    0 1[1/eh] 1[1/bcl/hi-hat] 1 — 1[1/ped bd] 0 0 0 —
    str[1.1.1.1.0]
    Strings double on percussion: 2.vn/ped bd and va/hi-hat.
UE

Die Ebene (1997)   12'
    solo narrator
    0 0 0 0 — 1 0 2 0 — 2perc — pf — str[0.0.0.2.1]
UE

A Map is not the Territory (2001)   18'
    1[1/pic/afl] 1[1/eh] 2[1/Ebcl.2/bcl] 1[1/cbn] — 2 1 1
    0 — accordion — 3perc — pf — str[1.1.2.2.1]
    The first movement (ca. 8') may be performed separately
    under the title "A Map."
UE

Steffen, Wolfgang   (1923-1993)

Kammerkonzert, op.48 (1978)   13'
    1 1 1[1/bcl] 1 — 1 0 0 0 — 1perc — pf — str
Boosey & Hawkes

Stenhammar, Wilhelm   (1871-1927)

Lodolezzi Sjunger: Suite, op.39   18'
(1941)
    1 0 0 0 — 0 0 0 0 — gtr, mand — 1perc — str
    perc: tambn
Fleisher

Stern, Robert   (1934-)

Ricordanza (1955)   8'
    2[1.2/pic] 1 2 1 — 2 1 0 0 — str
Fleisher

Stevens, Bernard   (1916-1983)

Eclogue (1946)   8'
    1 1 1 1 — 2 0 0 0 — tmp — str
Lengnick

Introduction, Variations & Fugue on   13'
a Theme of Giles Farnaby (1972)
    2 2 2 2 — 2 2 0 0 — tmp — str
Lengnick

Stiller, Andrew   (1946-)

A Periodic Table of the Elements   8'
(1988)
    1[1/afl] 1[1/eh] 1[1/bcl] 1 — 1 2 1 0 — 1perc — str
Fleisher; Kallisti

Stock, David   (1939-)

Capriccio (1963)   7'
    1 1 1 1 — 1 1 0 0 — str
ACA; Fleisher

Stockhausen, Karlheinz   (1928-2007)

Drei Lieder (Three Songs;, Nr.1/10   19'
(1950)
    solo A
    1 0 2 1 — 0 1 1 0 — 2perc — 2pf[pf.hpsd] — str
    Contents - 1. Der Rebell; 2. Frei; 3. Der Saitenmann
    mvt durations: 4' 9' 6'
UE

Formel; Nr.1/6 (1951)   13'
    0 3 3 3 — 3 0 0 0 — 1perc — hp — 2pf[pf.cel] —
    str[6.0.0.3.3]
    perc: vib, glsp
UE

Kontra-Punkte Nr.1 (1953)   14'
    1 0 2[1.bcl] 1 — 0 1 1 0 — hp — pf —
    str[1.0.0.1.0]
UE

Stöhr, Richard   (1874-1967)

Kammersymphonie, op.32 (1921)   36'
    0 1 1 1 — 1 0 0 0 — hp — str[1.1.1.1.0]
Fleisher; Kahnt

Stranz, Ulrich   (1946-)

Anstieg — Ausblick für Orchester   12'
(2002)
  2 2[1.eh] 2 2 — 2 2 2 0 — tmp+1 — hp — str
Bärenreiter

Contrasubjekte; Passacaglia über   9'
B-A-C-H für Streicher (1980)
  str[4.4.3.2.1]
Bärenreiter

Déjà vu (1973)   20'
  solo ob d'am
  0 0 1 0 — 0 1 0 0 — tmp+2 — hp — str[4.4.3.2.1]
Bärenreiter

Sieben Feld-, Wald- und   15'
Wiesenstücke (1983)
  str[4.3.2.2.1]
Bärenreiter

Strauss, Richard   (1864-1949)

Ariadne auf Naxos: Overture and   9'
Dance Scene, op.60 (1916)
  2 2 2 2 — 2 0 0 0 — str
Boosey & Hawkes

Das Bächlein, op.88/1 (1933)   2'
  solo high voice
  2 2 3[1.2.bcl] 2 — 2 0 0 0 — hp — str
  Original key (G major). Also available for medium voice (F
  major).
UE

Le Bourgeois Gentilhomme (Der   35'
Bürger als Edelmann): Suite, op.60
(1918)
  2[1/pic.2/pic] 2[1.2/eh] 2 2[1.2/cbn] — 2 1 1 0 —
  tmp+4 — hp — pf — str[6.0.4.4.2]
  perc: tambn, tri, sd, cym, bd, glsp
Kalmus; Luck's

Burleske, AV 85 (1886)   19'
  solo pf
  3[1.2.pic] 2 2 — 4 2 0 0 — tmp — str
Kalmus; Luck's

Freundliche Vision, op.48, No.1   4'
(1900)
  solo voice
  2 0 0 2 — 4 2 1 0 — str
Kalmus

Meinem Kinde, op.37/3 (1897)   2'
  solo medium voice
  2 0 0 2 — 0 0 0 0 — hp — str[1.1.1.1.1]
  Original key (G-flat Major). Also available for low voice (F
  major).
UE

Metamorphosen; For 23 Solo   25'
Strings (1945)
  str[10.0.5.5.3]
Boosey & Hawkes

Morgen (1894)   3'
  solo S
  1 0 2 0 — 1 1 1 0 — 2perc — pf — str[1.0.0.1.0]
  Orchestrated by Costin Miereanu (1991).
Salabert

Morgen, op.27/4 (1894)   3'
  solo high, medium or low voice, vn
  0 0 0 0 — 3 0 0 0 — hp — str
  Available for medium voice (F major), high voice (G major)
  or low voice (E major).
Kalmus; Luck's; UE

Muttertändelei, op.43, No.2 (1899)   3'
  solo voice
  2 3[1.2.eh] 2 2 — 2 0 0 0 — str
  Strings without db. Available in F and G.
Kalmus

Romanze in Es Dur, op.61 (1879)   10'
  solo cl
  0 2 0 2 — 2 0 0 0 — str
Schott

Das Rosenband, op.31/1 (1897)   2'
  solo high or low voice
  3[1.2.pic] 2 3[1.2.bcl] 2 — 2 0 0 0 — str
  Available for high voice (A major) or low voice (UE only, F-
  sharp major).
Kalmus; Luck's; UE

Tanzsuite nach Couperin (1923)   28'
  2 2[1.2/eh] 2 2 — 2 1 1 0 — 1perc — hp —
  2pf[cel.hpsd] — str[4.3.2.2.2]
  perc: chimes, tambn
Boosey & Hawkes

Traum durch die Dämmerung,   3'
op.29/1 (1895)
  solo high or medium voice
  2 0 3[1.2.bcl] 2 — 4 0 1 0 — hp — str
  Orchestrated by Robert Heger (1929).
Luck's; UE

Waldseligkeit, op.49, No.1 (1901)   3'
  solo voice
  2 0 3[1.2.bcl] 2 — 2 0 0 0 — hp — harm — str
Kalmus

Stravinsky, Igor   (1882-1971)

Bluebird Pas de Deux (1941)   6'
  1 1 2 1 — 1 2 2 0 — tmp — pf — str[5.0.3.2.1]
  Arrangement of music from Tchaikovsky's "Sleeping
  Beauty." Even though the music is not by Stravinsky it is
  published under his name.
Chester Novello

Circus Polka; Composed for a   4'
Young Elephant (1942)
  2[1.pic] 2 2 2 — 4 2 3 1 — tmp+3 — str
  perc: sd, cym, bd
Schott

Concertino for 12 Instruments   6'
(1952)
  1 2[1.eh] 1 2 — 0 2 2 0 — str[1.0.0.1.0]
Hansen

Concerto in D (1946)   12'
  str[8.8.6.6.4]
Boosey & Hawkes

Concerto in E-flat "Dumbarton   15'
Oaks" (1938)
  1 0 1 1 — 2 0 0 0 — str[3.0.3.2.2]
Schott

Danses Concertantes (1942)   20'
  1 1 1 1 — 2 1 1 0 — tmp — str[6.0.4.3.2]
Schott; Schott

Eight Instrumental Miniatures   6'
(1962)
  2 2 2 2 — 1 0 0 0 — str[1.1.2.2.0]
Chester Novello

L'Histoire du Soldat (The Soldier's   25'
Tale): Suite (1920)
  0 0 1 1 — 0 1[crt] 1 0 — 1perc — str[1.0.0.0.1]
  perc: bd, sus cym, tambn, tri, field dr, 2 sd
Chester Novello

Praeludium (1937)
  0 0 0 0 — 0 3 1 0 — 4sx[asx.asx.tsx.bsx] — gtr
  — tmp+1 — cel — str
  perc: sd
  Arranged for Jazz ensemble.
Fleisher

Pulcinella: Suite (1920)   22'
  solo str 5t
  2[1.2/pic] 2 0 2 — 2 1 1 0 — str[4.4.4.3.3]
  Revised in 1949.
  Contents - 1. Sinfonia; 2. Serenata; 3. Scherzino —
  Allegretto — Andantino; 4. Tarantella; 5. Toccata; 6.
  Gavotta (con due variazioni); 7. Vivo; 8. Minuetto — Finale
Boosey & Hawkes

Ragtime (1918)   4'
  1 0 1 0 — 1 1[crt] 1 0 — cimb — 1perc —
  str[1.1.1.0.1]
Chester Novello; Kalmus; Luck's

Scenes de Ballet (1944)   18'
  2[1.2/pic] 2 2 1 — 2 3 3 1 — tmp — pf — str
Boosey & Hawkes; AMP

Suite No.1 for Small Orchestra   6'
(1925)
  2[1.2/pic] 1 2 2 — 1 1 1 1 — 1perc — str
  perc: bd
  mvt durations: 2' 2' 1' 1'
Chester Novello; Kalmus

Suite No.2 for Small Orchestra   7'
(1921)
  2[1.2/pic] 1 2 2 — 1 2 1 1 — 3perc — pf — str
  perc: sd, cym, bd
  mvt durations: 1' 2' 2' 2'
Chester Novello; Kalmus

Tango (1953)   3'
  1 2 1 1 — 2 0 0 0 — hpsd — str
  Arranged by Avner Dorman.
Schirmer

Strohbach, Siegfried   (1929-)

Serenade in D major   13'
  str
Breitkopf

Stroman, Scott   (1958-)

Clown Dances (1984)   8'
  0 0 1 1 — 0 1 1 0 — 2perc — str[1.0.0.0.1]
Chester Novello

Studer, Hans   (1911-1984)

Chamber Concerto (1947)   19'
  solo pf
  0 0 2 1 — 0 0 0 0 — tmp+1 — str
Bärenreiter

Stürmer, Bruno   (1892-1958)

Suite für Neun Solo-Instrumente,   20'
op.9 (1923)
   1 1 1 1 — 0 0 0 0 — str[1.1.1.1.1]
   Fleisher; Schott

Tanzsuite (Dance Suite), op.24   10'
   1 1 1 1 — 1 1 0 0 — tmp+1 — pf — str[4.4.2.2.2]
   perc: tri, cym, tam-tam
   Schott

Šulek, Stjepan   (1914-1986)

Concerto Classique (1952)   12'
   2 2 2 2 — 4 2 0 0 — str
   UE

Surinach, Carlos   (1915-1997)

Acrobats of God; Ballet for   23'
Chamber Orchestra (1960)
   1[1/pic] 1[1/eh] 1 1 — 1 1 1 1[opt] — tmp+1 — hp
   — str
   Fleisher

Apasionada; Ballet for Chamber   35'
Orchestra (1960)
   1[1/pic] 1[1/eh] 1 1 — 1 1 1 1[opt] — tmp+1 — pf
   — str[0.0.0.0.1]
   AMP; Fleisher

Danza Andaluza   4'
   1 1 1 1 — 1 1 0 0 — tmp+1 — str
   Peer

Embattled Garden; Ballet for   21'
Chamber Orchestra (1957)
   1[1/pic] 1[1/eh] 1 1 — 1 1 1 0 — tmp+1 — hp —
   str
   AMP; Fleisher

Suter, Robert   (1919-2008)

Epitaffio (1968)   12'
   0 0 0 0 — 3 3 0 0 — tmp+2 — str
   Bärenreiter

Sutermeister, Heinrich   (1910-1995)

Sérénade pour Montreux (1970)   13'
   0 2 0 0 — 2 0 0 0 — str
   Schott

Swafford, Jan   (1946-)

Chamber Sinfonietta   14'
   1 1 1 1 — 1 1 1 0 — 1perc — hp — pf — str
   Peer

Late August   8'
   1[1/pic] 2 2[1.2/Ebcl] 2 — 2 2 0 0 — 1perc — str
   perc: tmp, bd, sd, 6 tom-tom, marim, glsp, sus cym
   Peer

Swanson, Howard   (1907-1978)

Short Symphony (1948)   11'
   2[1.2/pic] 2 2 2 — 2 2 1 0 — tmp — str
   Weintraub

Swayne, Giles   (1946-)

Into the Light (1986)   20'
   0 0 1[1/Ebcl/bcl] 1 — 0 1 1 0 — 1perc —
   str[1.0.0.0.1]
   Novello

PP, op.46 (1987)   1'
   1 1 1 1 — 1 1 1 0 — 1perc — cel — str[1.1.1.1.1]
   Novello

Symphony for Small Orchestra   25'
(1984)
   1 2 0 2[1.2/cbn] — 2 0 0 0 — str
   Novello

Szabelski, Bolesław   (1896-1979)

Preludes (1963)   7'
   2 1 1 0 — 2 2 1 0 — 1perc — pf — str[4.0.3.2.0]
   PWM

Szalonek, Witold   (1927-2001)

Connections (1972)   14'
   1 1 1 0 — 1 0 0 0 — pf — str[1.1.1.1.0]
   Also possible with strings (1.0.1.1.1).
   PWM

Szeryng, Henryk   (1918-1988)

Preludio Classico   4'
   solo vn
   2 2 0 0 — 2 0 0 0 — tmp — str
   First version.
   Presser

Preludio Classico   4'
   solo vn
   2 2 1 1 — 4 0 0 0 — tmp — str
   Second version.
   Presser

Szymanowski, Karol   (1882-1937)

Lieder des verliebten Muezzin,   11'
op.42 (1934)
   solo high voice
   2[1.2/pic] 2[1.2/eh] 2 1 — 2 2 0 0 — tmp+2 — pf
   — str
   UE

Three Berceuses, op.48 (1922)   6'
   solo voice
   1perc — hp — str[8.0.8.8.0]
   perc: tam-tam
   Arranged by Jan Krenz (1967).
   UE

Szymanski, Pawel   (1954-)

Intermezzo (1977)   8'
   2 0 0 0 — 0 0 0 0 — 1perc — str[4.0.3.2.1]
   Chester Novello

Quasi una Sinfonietta (1990)   20'
   1[1/pic] 1 1 1 — 1 1 1 0 — 1perc — pf —
   str[1.1.1.1.1]
   Chester Novello

Sixty-Odd Pages (1987)   15'
   1[1/pic] 1 1 1 — 1 1 1 0 — 2perc — str[12.0.6.4.4]
   Chester Novello

Through the Looking Glass I (1987)   13'
   · 1 1 1 0 — 1 0 0 0 — gtr, 3 mand — 5perc — hp
   — 3pf[pf.cel.hpsd] — str[1.1.1.1.1]
   Chester Novello

T

Takács, Jenö   (1902-2005)

Eisenstädter Divertimento; Suite,   11'
op.75 (1962)
   2 2 2 2 — 4 2 1 0 — tmp+2 — hp — str
   Contents - 1. Arie; 2. Präludium; 3. Reigen; 4. Soldatentanz;
   5. Winzertanz
   UE

Ländliches Barock; Suite, op.48   18'
(1941)
   2 2 2 2 — 2 2 1[opt] 0 — tmp+1 — hp[or pf] — str
   Contents - 1. Intrada; 2. Aria; 3. Steirischer Tanz; 4.
   Hirtenszene; 5. Springtanz; 6. Preghiera; 7. Dudelsack
   UE

Overtura Semiseria, op.69 (1959)   8'
   2 2 2 2 — 4 2 2 0 — tmp+2 — hp — str
   UE

Tarantella, op.39 (1937)   13'
   solo pf
   2[1.2/pic] 2 2 2 — 2 2 1 1 — tmp+1 — str
   UE

Ungarische Burgmusik; Antiqua   17'
hungarica, op.47 (1941)
   2 2 2 2 — 4 3 3 0 — tmp+1 — hp — 2pf[pf.cel] —
   str
   Contents - 1. Cantus Finalis; 2. Cantus Initialis; 3.
   Nordungarischer Tanz; 4. Südungarischer Tanz
   UE

Volkstänze aus dem Burgenland,   8'
op.57 (1952)
   2 1 2 1 — 2 1 1 0 — tmp+1 — str
   Contents - 1. Aufmarsch; 2. Pascher; 3. Polstertanz -
   Kroatischer Tanz; 4. Volkslied
   UE

Von fremden Ländern und   19'
Menschen, op.37 (1937)
   2 2 2 2 — 2 1 1 0 — tmp+1 — hp — cel — str
   Contents - 1. Aus Großbritannien; 2. Dudelsack, Ungarn; 3.
   Kirschblütenlied, Japan; 4. Lied der spanischen Kolonisten,
   Philippinen; 5. Negro Spiritual, USA; 6. Saltarello, Italien; 7.
   Straßenmusikanten, Spanien; 8. Tanz der Medizinmannes,
   Südsee
   mvt durations: 3' 2' 2' 3' 2' 2' 3' 2'
   UE

Takemitsu, Tōru   (1930-1996)

Archipelago S. (1993)   *14'*
1[1/afl] 1[1/ob d'am] 2 1 — 2 1 2 0 — 2perc — hp
— cel — str[2.0.2.2.1]
perc: vib, crot, 2 cym on pedal tmp, glsp, chimes, sus cym
Schott

Eucalypts I (1970)   *11'*
1 1 0 0 — 0 0 0 0 — hp — str[8.6.4.4.2]
Salabert

Rain Coming (1982)   *10'*
1[1/afl] 1 1 1 — 1 1 1 0 — 1perc — pf/cel —
str[1.1.1.1.1]
perc: vib, 3 tam-tam, crot
Schott

Tree Line (1988)   *13'*
1[1/afl] 1 2[1.2/bcl] 1[1.cbn] — 2 1 1 0 — 2perc —
hp — pf/cel — str[1.1.1.1.1]
perc: vib, crot, chimes, glsp, 2 cym on pedal tmp
Schott

Water Ways (1978)   *12'*
0 0 1 0 — 0 0 0 0 — 2perc — hp — str[1.0.0.1.0]
perc: 2vib
Salabert

Talbot, Joby   (1971-)

Animisation (1995)   *13'*
1[1/pic] 1 1[1/Ebcl] 1 — 1 1 1 0 — str[0.0.0.0.1]
Chester Novello

Arbor Low (1994)   *2'*
1 1 1 1 — 1 0 0 0 — str[1.1.1.1.0]
Chester Novello

Compound Fracture (1995)   *5'*
2[1.pic] 0 0 0 — 0 0 0 0 — 2sx[ssx.asx] — 1perc
— kybd — str[0.0.0.1.1]
Chester Novello

Minus 1500 (2001)   *7'*
0 0 0 1 — 0 0 0 0 — 1perc — str[1.1.1.1.1]
Chester Novello

Tan, Dun   (1957-)

Circle with Four Trios, Conductor   *14'*
and Audience (1992)
solo pf, perc, db, mand, gtr, hp
1[pic] 1 1[bcl] 0 — 0 0 0 0 — str[1.0.1.1.0]
Schirmer

Tanaka, Karen   (1961-)

Echo Canyon (1995)   *9'*
1[1/afl] 1[1/eh] 1 1[1/cbn] — 1 1 1 0 — 2perc —
str[1.1.1.1.1]
Requires 5-string db.
Chester Novello

Water and Stone (1999)   *9'*
0 0 1 0 — 0 0 0 0 — 2perc — hp — str[1.0.1.1.1]
Chester Novello

Wave Mechanics (1994)   *9'*
2[1/pic.2/pic] 1[1/eh] 2[1.2/bcl] 1[1/cbn] — 2 2 0 0
— 2perc — str[3.0.2.2.1]
perc: 2 vib
Requires 5-string db.
Chester Novello

Tansman, Alexandre   (1897-1986)

Des Kaisers neue Kleider; Musik zu   *16'*
einem Andersen-Ballett (1959)
2 2 2 2 — 2 2 1 0 — tmp+1 — pf/cel — str
UE

Musique de Cour; D'après les   *24'*
themes de Robert de la Visée
(1960)
solo gtr
1 1 1 0 — 1 0 0 0 — tmp+1 — str[6.4.4.4.2]
perc: tri
UE

Sinfonia Piccola (1952)   *17'*
2 2 2 2 — 2 1 1 0 — tmp+1 — pf — str
UE

Sinfonietta (1924)   *16'*
1 1 1 1 — 1 1 2 0 — 1perc — pf — str
UE

Suite Baroque (1958)   *11'*
2 2 2 2 — 2 0 0 0 — tmp+1 — 2pf[pf.cel(opt)] —
str
perc: tri
Contents - 1. Entrée; 2. Sarabande; 3. Divertissement; 4.
Aria; 5. Rigaudon
UE

Tavener, John   (1944-)

Grandma's Footsteps (1968)   *15'*
0 1 0 1 — 1 0 0 0 — 5 musical boxes —
str[2.2.2.2.0]
Chester Novello

Remembering Lennox through   *3'*
Michael (2004)
   str
   Chester Novello

Variations on "Three Blind Mice"   *5'*
(1972)
   2[1/pic.2/pic] 0 0 0 — 0 2 2 0 — tmp — hp — 2pf
   — str
   Chester Novello

Taylor, Deems   (1885-1966)

The Portrait of a Lady, op.14 (1932)   *12'*
   1 1 1 1 — 1 0 0 0 — pf — str[1.1.1.1.1]
   Fischer (J.); Fleisher

Tcherepnin, Alexander   (1899-1977)

La Femme et son Ombre, Ballet   *15'*
Suite (1948)
   2 1 2 1 — 2 1 1 0 — 1perc — hp — str
   AMP

Suite populaire russe   *6'*
   1 1 1 1 — 2 1 1 0 — tmp+4 — str
   Breitkopf

Three Pieces for Chamber   *30'*
Orchestra, op.37 (1927)
   solo vc
   1 0 1 2 — 0 2[crt.crt] 0 0 — tmp+1 — str
   Solo vc in 2. movement only.
   Fleisher; UE

Terzakis, Dimitri   (1938-)

Hommage à Dionysos (1980)   *13'*
   2 2 2 2 — 2 2 2 1 — 2perc — hp — str
   Breitkopf

Hommage à Morse (1970)   *6'*
   1 1 1 0 — 0 0 1 0 — str[1.1.1.1.0]
   Breitkopf

Ichochronos II (1972)   *9'*
   2[1.lotos fl] 0 1 0 — 1 0 0 1 — tmp+1 —
   str[1.1.1.1.1]
   Breitkopf

Tropi (1978)   *15'*
   2 2 2 2 — 2 2 2 0 — 2perc — hp — str
   Breitkopf

Thärichen, Werner   (1921-2008)

Divertimento, op.57   *11'*
   str
   Boosey & Hawkes

Theodorakis, Mikis   (1925-)

Oedipus Tyrannos; Ode for String   *10'*
Orchestra (1964)
   str
   Boosey & Hawkes

Thiele, Siegfried   (1934-)

Concerto for Orchestra (1997)   *18'*
   2 2 2 2 — 2 1 1 0 — tmp+1 — str
   Breitkopf

Drei Orchestermotetten nach   *10'*
Machaut (1972)
   1 2 2 1 — 2 1 2 0 — str
   Breitkopf

Intrada, Cantus, Toccata (1968)   *12'*
   2 2 2 2 — 2 2 1 0 — tmp+1 — str
   Breitkopf

Sonatina (1974)   *17'*
   2 2 2 2 — 2 1 0 0 — tmp — str
   Breitkopf

Trauermusik (1966)   *7'*
   str
   Breitkopf

Übungen im Verwandeln (1978)   *23'*
   str
   Breitkopf

Wolkenbilder; Four Movements   *14'*
(1977)
   1 2 0 0 — 2 0 0 0 — str
   Breitkopf

Thomas, Augusta Read   (1964-)

Capricious Angels (2009)   *8'*
   1 1 1 0 — 1 0 0 0 — str[3.0.1.0.0]
   Schirmer

Murmurs in the Mist of Memory   12'
(2001)
   str[3.3.2.2.1]
Schirmer

Passion Prayers (1999)   9'
   solo vc
   1 0 1 0 — 0 0 0 0 — 1perc — hp — pf —
   str[1.0.0.0.0]
Schirmer

Thomas, Kurt   (1904-1973)

Concerto for Piano, op.30   30'
   solo pf
   2 2 2 2 — 2 2 0 0 — tmp — str
Breitkopf

Serenade, op.10   20'
   1 1 1 1 — 1 1 1 0 — tmp+1 — str
Breitkopf

Thomson, Virgil   (1896-1989)

Autumn; Concertino for Harp,   10'
Percussion and Strings (1964)
   1perc — hp — str
Schirmer

Suite from "The River"   25'
   1 2 2 1 — 2 2 2 0 — banjo — tmp+1 — str
   perc: sd, bd, cym, tri, gong, ratchet, iron bars, bells
Peer

Thoughts for Strings (1982)   4'
   str
Boosey & Hawkes

Tishchenko, Boris   (1939-)

Symphony No.3; For Soprano and   31'
Baritone (or Tape) and Chamber
Orchestra
   solo S, Bar (or tape)
   2[1.pic] 2[1.eh] 2[1.bcl] 1 — 1 1 1 0 — tmp+2 —
   pf — str[1.0.1.1.1]
   perc: bd, tom-tom, tam-tam, cym, tambn, sd, xyl, woodblk, flexatone
Boosey & Hawkes

Toch, Ernst   (1887-1964)

Circus Overture (1953)   6'
   2[2.1/pic] 2 2 2 — 3 3 3 1 — 1perc — pf[opt] —
   str
Kalmus

Epilogue (1959)   3'
   3[1.2.pic] 2 2 2 — 2 2 0 0 — tmp+1 — str
Kalmus

Fünf Stücke (Five Pieces), op.33   20'
(1924)
   2 0 2[1.bcl] 0 — 0 0 0 0 — tmp+2 — str[1.0.1.0.1]
   perc: tri, gong, cym, bd
Schott

Intermezzo (1959)   5'
   2 2 2 2 — 2 2 0 0 — 1perc — hp[or pf] — str
Kalmus

Tomlinson, Ernest   (1924-)

A Georgian Miniature   12'
   2 1 2 1 — 0 0 0 0 — str
Boosey & Hawkes

Little Serenade   3'
   2 1 2 1 — 0 0 0 0 — accordion — 1perc — hp —
   pf — str
Boosey & Hawkes

Toovey, Andrew   (1962-)

Mozart (1991)   6'
   str
Boosey & Hawkes

Torke, Michael   (1961-)

Adjustable Wrench (1987)   11'
   0 1 2 1 — 1 2 1 0 — 1perc — 2pf[pf.synth] —
   str[1.0.1.1.1]
   perc: marim
Boosey & Hawkes

Ash (1988)   17'
   1 2 1 2 — 3 1 0 0 — tmp — synth — str
Boosey & Hawkes

Tower, Joan   (1938-)

Chamber Dance (2006)   *16'*
2[1.2/pic] 2 2 2 — 2 2 0 0 — tmp+1 — str
AMP

Duets (1994)   *19'*
2 2 2 2 — 2 2 0 0 — tmp+1 — str
AMP

In Memory (2002)   *12'*
str
AMP

Island Rhythms (1985)   *8'*
2[1.2/pic] 2 2 2 — 2 2 1[btbn] 1 — tmp+2 — str
AMP

The Last Dance (2000)   *14'*
2[1.2/pic] 2 2 2 — 2 2 1[btbn] 0 — tmp+2 — str
AMP

Made in America (2004)   *14'*
2[1.2/pic] 2 2 2 — 2 2 1 0 — tmp+1 — str
AMP

Paganini Trills (1996)   *2'*
2 2 2 2 — 2 2 2 0 — 2perc — str
AMP

Stepping Stones; Ballet (1993)   *25'*
2[1.2/pic] 2 2 2 — 4 2 2 0 — 2perc — hp — pf/cel
— str
AMP

Trantow, Herbert   (1903-1993)

Kleine Tafelmusik (1958)   *10'*
1 1 0 0 — 0 0 0 0 — hpsd — str
Boosey & Hawkes

Trapp, Max   (1887-1971)

Divertimento für Kammerorchester,   20'
op.27 (1931)
1 1 1 1 — 1 1 1 1 — tmp — str
Eulenburg; Fleisher

Treibmann, Karl Ottomar   (1936-)

Capriccio 71   *10'*
2 2 2 2 — 2 2 2 1 — 1perc — hp — pf — str
Peters

First Symphonic Essay   *20'*
1 1 1 1 — 2 1 1 0 — 1perc — hp — pf — str
Peters

Second Symphonic Essay; For Ten   15'
Instruments*
1 1 1 1 — 1 0 0 0 — str[1.1.1.1.1]
Peters

Symphony for 15 Strings (1979)   *15'*
str[9.0.3.2.1]
Breitkopf

Symphony No.2 (1981)   *37'*
2 2 2 2 — 1 1 1 0 — 1perc — hp — str
Breitkopf

Trexler, Georg   (1903-1979)

Concerto for Cello (1952)   *18'*
solo vc
2 3 2 3 — 2 2 0 0 — tmp — str
Breitkopf

Concerto for Orchestra (1962)   *21'*
2 2 2 2 — 2 2 0 0 — tmp+1 — str
Breitkopf

Introduzione e Scherzo   *12'*
2 2 2 2 — 2 2 3 0 — tmp+1 — hp — str
Breitkopf

Music   *14'*
solo ob
2 0 0 2 — 2 0 0 0 — tmp — str
Breitkopf

Music for Orchestra   *25'*
2 2 2 3 — 2 2 0 0 — tmp — str
Breitkopf

Small Suite (1954)   *15'*
1 1 1 1 — 2 0 0 0 — tmp — str
Breitkopf

Trojahn, Manfred   (1949-)

Mit durchscheinender Melancholie   *8'*
(1995)
2 2 2 2 — 4 2 2 0 — tmp — str
Bärenreiter

Notturni trasognati (1977) 14'
solo fl/afl
0 1[eh] 1[bcl] 1 — 2 1 1 0 — 1perc — hp — cel — str
Bärenreiter

Trojan, Václav (1907-1983)

Sinfonietta Armoniosa (1970) 17'
1[1/pic] 0 1 0 — 0 1 1 0 — tmp+2 — str
Schott

Tubin, Eduard (1905-1982)

Symphony No.7 (1958) 24'
2 2 2 2 — 2 2 0 0 — str
Nordiska

Valse Triste (1939) 4'
1 1 2 1 — 2 1 0 0 — tmp — hp — str
Nordiska

Tull, Fisher (1934-1994)

Capriccio (1980) 9'
2 1 1 1 — 2 1 1 0 — tmp+1 — pf — str
Boosey & Hawkes

Turina, Joaquin (1882-1949)

Cinq Danzas Gitanas, op.55 (1931) 16'
2 2 2 2 — 2 2 0 0 — tmp+1 — pf — str
Contents - 1. Zambra; 2. Danza de la Seduccion; 3. Danza Ritual; 4. Generalife; 5. Sacro-Monte
Salabert

Oración del Torero, op.34 (1926) 8'
str
Salabert

Turnage, Mark-Anthony (1960-)

Dark Crossing (2000) 20'
2[1/pic.2/afl] 1[1/eh] 2[1/bcl.bcl/cbcl] 1[1/cbn] — 2 1[1/flug] 1[1/btbn/euph] 0 — 1[ssx/asx] — 2perc — hp — pf/cel — str[3.0.2.2.2]
perc: crot, vib, marim, 2 gong, tambn, tmp, bd, claves, woodblk
Schott

On All Fours (1985) 13'
1[1/bfl] 1[1/eh/bass ob] 1[1/bcl] 1 — 0 1[1/flug/steel bar/desk bell] 1[1/log dr/desk bell] 0 — asx/ssx/break dr/desk bell — 1perc — str[3.0.3.2.1]
perc: vib, marim, bells, mark tree, sus cym, hi-hat, 2 bongos, sd, log dr, ped bd, glass chimes, spring coil
VI doubles on woodblk.
Schott

Turok, Paul (1929-)

Antoniana; Suite for Small Orchestra after Vivaldi, op.47 (1977) 20'
1 1 1 1 — 2 1 1 0 — tmp — hp[or pf] — str
Schirmer

Tuthill, Burnet (1888-1982)

Intrada (1934)
1 1 1 1 — 1 1 0 0 — pf — str
Fleisher

U

V

Uhl, Alfred   (1909-1992)

Kleines Konzert (1963)   21'
  solo vn
  2 2 2 2 — 2 2 2 1 — str
  UE

Vergnügliche Musik aus einer   16'
deutschen Kleinstadt (1944)
  1 2 2 1 — 2 2 2 0 — 1perc — hp — str
  UE

Wiener Walzer (1942)   6'
  2 2 2 2 — 4[3.&4. opt] 2 2 0 — tmp+2 — str
  UE

Ullmann, Jakob   (1958-)

Composition for 10 Instruments I-V   11'
(1982)
  1 0 1 0 — 1 0 0 0 — str[4.0.1.1.1]
  Breitkopf

Vactor, David van   (1906-1994)

Divertimento   20'
  1[1/pic] 1 1 1 — 1 1 1 0 — 1perc — pf — str
  Fleisher

Vate, Nancy van de   (1930-)

Variations for Chamber Orchestra   10'
(1959)
  1 1 1 1 — 0 0 0 0 — str
  Fleisher

Vaughan Williams, Ralph   (1872-1958)

English Folk Song Suite (1923)   10'
  2[1.2/pic] 1 2 1 — 2 2 2 0 — tmp+1 — str
  perc: sd, bd, tri, cym
  Orchestration by Gordon Jacob.
  Boosey & Hawkes

English Folk Song Suite (1923)   10'
  str
  Boosey & Hawkes

Vercoe, Elizabeth   (1941-)

Changes; A Little Music for Mozart   10'
(1991)
  2 2 2 2 — 2 2 0 0 — 2perc — hp — str
  Fleisher

Villa-Lobos, Heitor   (1887-1959)

Canções típicas brasileiras (1935)   15'
  solo voice
  2 1 2 2 — 3 0 0 0 — tmp+1 — hp — pf — str
  Eschig

Concerto for Guitar and Small   20'
Orchestra (1951)
  solo gtr
  1 1 1 1 — 1 0 1 0 — str
  Eschig

Francette et Pia (1958)22'
1 1 1 1 — 2 1 1 0 — tmp+2 — hp — cel — str
Eschig

Ouverture de l'homme tel... (1952)4'
1 1 1 1 — 1 1 1 0 — tmp+1 — 2pf[pf.cel] — str
From "Suít Sugestiva."
Eschig

Sinfonietta No.120'
2 2 2 2 — 2 2 2 0 — tmp — str
Peer

Sinfonietta No.220'
1[1/pic] 1[1/eh] 1[1/bcl] 1 — 3 2 2 1 — asx —
tmp+1 — str
perc: xyl, tam-tam, cym
Peer

Suíte Sugestiva; Cinémas (1929)18'
solo S, Bar
1 1 1 1 — 0 1 1 0 — tmp+2 — 2pf[pf.cel] —
str[1.1.1.1.1]
Eschig

Vincent, John(1902-1977)

The House that Jack Built: From the17'
Ballet "Three Jacks" (1942)
2 2 2 2 — 2 1 1 0 — tmp+2 — str
EMI

Suite from the Ballet "Three Jacks"15'
(1942)
2 2 2 2 — 2 1 1 0 — tmp+1 — str
perc: xyl, glsp
EMI

Vinci, Albert(1937-)

Dance Suite15'
1 1 1 1 — 1 2 1 0 — 1perc — str
Kalmus

Vines, Nicholas(1976-)

Firestick (1999)15'
0 0 3[1.bcl.Ebcl] 0 — 2 0 0 0 — 1perc —
str[2.2.2.2.1]
perc: sus cym, tam-tam, whip, templeblk, bongos, conga, crot, vib
Faber

Vinter, Gilbert(1909-1969)

Christmas Sinfonietta (1956)10'
2 1 2 1 — 2 2 3 0 — 1perc — hp — cel — str
UE

Dance of the Marionettes (1956)12'
2 1 2 1 — 0 0 0 0 — str
Boosey & Hawkes

The Poet Speaks; Suite from16'
Pieces by Robert Schumann (1959)
0 0 1 0 — 0 0 0 0 — hp — str
Boosey & Hawkes

Vir, Param(1952-)

Before Krishna (1987)8'
str[8.6.4.4.2]
Novello

Contrapulse (1985)10'
1[1/pic] 1[1/eh/ratchet] 1[1/Ebcl/bcl] 0 — 0 0 0 0
— 1perc — pf/cel/anvil/whistle — str[1.0.0.1.0]
Novello

The Field of Opportunity (1994)10'
2[1.2/pic] 2[1.2/eh] 2 2[1.2/cbn] — 2 2 2 0 —
2perc — hp — pf/cel — str[5.4.3.3.2]
Novello

Hayagriva (2005)13'
1[1/pic/afl] 1[1/eh] 1[1/bcl] 1 — 1 1 1 0 — 1perc
— hp — pf/cel — str[1.1.1.1.1]
Novello

The Theatre of Magical Beings29'
(2003)
1[1/pic/afl] 1[1/eh] 1[1/cbcl] 1 — 2 2 1[ttbn/btbn] 0
— 2perc — hp — kybd — str[3.3.3.2.1]
Novello

Vivier, Claude(1948-1983)

Deva et Asura (1972)15'
2 2 2 2 — 2 3 2 0 — str[1.1.1.1.1]
Boosey & Hawkes

Zipangu (1980)16'
str[7.0.3.2.1]
Boosey & Hawkes

Vlad, Roman (1919-)

Immer Wieder... (1965) 10'
solo S
0 1[eh] 1 1 — 0 0 0 0 — 1perc — hp — pf —
str[0.0.1.1.0]
perc: marim, xyl
UE

In Memoriam di Valentino Bucchi 16'
1 1 1 1 — 1 0 1 0 — tmp — pf — str
Presser

Ode Super "Chrysea Phorminx" 10'
(1964)
solo gtr
2 2 2 2 — 2 2 2 0 — str
UE

Volans, Kevin (1949-)

Concerto for Cello (1997) 22'
solo vc
2[1.2/pic] 2[1.2/eh] 2[1.2/Ebcl] 2[1.2/cbn] — 4 2 2
0 — hp — str
Chester Novello

Joining Up The Dots (2006) 13'
2pf — str[1.1.1.1.1]
Chester Novello

Volkonsky, André (1933-)

Les Plaintes de Chtchaza (1962) 17'
solo voice
0 1[eh] 0 0 — 0 0 0 0 — 3perc — hpsd —
str[1.0.1.0.0]
perc: tambn, marim, vib
UE

Voss, Friedrich (1930-)

Concerto da camera (1953) 12'
str
Breitkopf

Epitaph (1960) 8'
str
Breitkopf

Fantasia (1956) 12'
str
Breitkopf

Résonances; 12 Poems (1957) 17'
1 1 1 1 — 2 1 1 0 — hp — str
Breitkopf

Tragic Overture; In Memoriam D. 8'
Hammarskjoeld (1961)
str
Breitkopf

Vostřák, Zbyněk (1920-1985)

Tao, op.41 (1967) 10'
1 1 1 1 — 0 0 0 0 — 1perc — str[1.0.1.1.1]
UE

Vries, Klaas de (1944-)

Bewegingen, (Movements) 8'
1 1 1 1 — 1 0 0 0 — 2perc — hp — 2pf[pf.cel] —
str[1.1.1.1.1]
Presser

...Ibant Obscuri Sola sub Nocte per
Umbras...
1 2 3 1 — 1 1 1 0 — 2perc — hp — pf —
str[1.1.1.1.1]
Presser

Refrains 14'
solo 2pf
1 1 2 2 — 2 1 2 1 — 2perc — str
Presser

Vuataz, Roger (1898-1988)

Petit Concert, op.39 (1939) 14'
1[1/pic] 1 1 1 — 2 1 1 0 — tmp+1 — hp — cel —
str
perc: sd, bd, chimes, cym, tri
Boosey & Hawkes

W

Wagenaar, Bernard   (1894-1971)

Sinfonietta (1930)   12'
1 1 1 1 — 1 1 1 1 — tmp — hp[or pf] — str
Fleisher

Song of Mourning; A Reflection   6'
Upon the Slain Dutch Patriots
(1944)
1 1 1 0 — 2 2 0 0 — 1perc — hp — str
perc: bd, sd
Fleisher

Wagner, Joseph   (1900-1974)

Four Miniatures   12'
2 2 2 2 — 2 2 0 0 — tmp — str
Peer

Pastoral costarricense; Un recuerdo   10'
sentimental
1 1 1 1 — 2 0 0 0 — tmp+1 —cel[or pf] — str
Fleisher

Walker, Robert   (1946-)

Chamber Symphony No.1 (1981)   23'
1[1/afl] 1 1 1 — 0 1 0 0 — 1perc — pf — str
Novello

Wallin, Rolf   (1957-)

Appearances (2002)   25'
2[1.2/pic] 2[1.2/eh] 2[1.cbcl] 2[1.cbn] — 2 2 1 1 —
2perc — pf — str[3.0.2.2.1]
Chester Novello

Boyl (1995)   17'
1 1 1 1 — 2 1 1 0 — 2perc — kybd —
str[1.1.1.1.1]
Chester Novello

Solve et Coagula (1992)   13'
1[1/pic/afl] 0 1[1/bcl] 0 — 0 0 0 0 — 1perc — pf —
str[1.1.1.1.0]
Chester Novello

Walton, William   (1902-1983)

Siesta (1929)   7'
1[1/pic] 1 2 1 — 2 0 0 0 — str
Fleisher; Oxford

Warlock, Peter   (1894-1930)

An Old Song (1923)   3'
1 1 1 0 — 1 0 0 0 — str
Chester Novello; Fleisher

Watkins, Huw   (1976-)

Rondo (2005)   17'
1[1/pic] 1[1/eh] 1[1/bcl] 1[1/cbn] — 1 1 1 0 —
1perc — hp — pf — str[1.1.1.1.1]
perc: glsp, tri, sus cym, cym, metal block, sd, bd, 2 templeblks, whip
Schott

Sonata for Cello and Eight   15'
Instruments (1998)
solo vc
1 0 1 1 — 0 0 0 0 — pf — str[1.1.1.0.1]
Faber

Watkins, Michael Blake   (1948-)

Concertante (1973)   30'
1[1/pic] 1[1/eh] 1 0 — 1 1 0 0 — 2perc — pf —
str[1.0.1.1.0]
Novello

Sinfonietta (1982)   16'
1[1/pic] 1 1 1 — 1 1 1 0 — str[1.1.1.1.1]
Novello

Youth's Dream and Time's Truths   16'
(1973)
solo T
0 0 0 0 — 0 1 0 0 — hp — str
Novello

Webern, Anton   (1883-1945)

Fünf Sätze, op.5 (1909)   12'
str
UE

Fünf Stücke, op.10 (1913)   6'
1[1/pic] 1 2[Ebcl.2/bcl] 0 — 1 1 1 0 — mand, gtr
— 4perc — hp — 2pf[cel.harm] — str[1.0.1.1.1]
perc: glsp, xyl, chimes, herdenglocken, tri, cym, sd, bd
UE

Konzert; Anton Schönberg zum 60.   8'
Geburtstag, op.24 (1934)
1 1 1 0 — 1 1 0 0 — pf — str[1.0.1.0.0]
Fleisher; UE

Orchesterstücke, op.6 (1909)   13'
1 1 1 0 — 0 0 0 0 — 3perc — 2kybd[pf.harm] —
str[1.1.1.1.1]
Chamber Version of op.6 arranged by the composer (1920).
See also "Verein für Musikalische Privataufführungen"
(Appendix p.399).
mvt durations: 1' 2' 1' 4' 3' 2'
UE

Passacaglia, op.1 (1908)   11'
1[1/pic] 1 1 1 — 1 0 1 0 — 2perc — synth —
str[1.0.1.1.1]
Arranged by Henri Pousseur (1987).
UE

Symphony, op.21 (1928)   10'
0 0 2[1.bcl] 0 — 2 0 0 0 — hp — str
Strings without db.
mvt durations: 7' 3'
UE

Variations, op.30 (1941)   8'
1 1 2[1.bcl] 0 — 1 1 1 1 — tmp — hp — cel — str
UE

Vier Lieder, op.13 (1918)   7'
solo voice
1[1/pic] 0 2[1.bcl] 0 — 1 1 1 0 — 1perc — hp —
cel — str[1.0.1.1.1]
perc: glsp
Contents - 1. Wiese im Park; 2. Der Einsame; 3. In der
Fremde; 4. Ein Winterabend
UE

Zwei Lieder, op.8 (1910)   4'
solo medium voice
0 0 1[1/bcl] 0 — 1 1 0 0 — hp — cel —
str[1.0.1.1.0]
Contents - 1. Du, der ichs nicht sage; 2. Du machst mich
allein
UE

Weigl, Karl   (1881-1949)

Comedy Overture, op.32 (1933)   10'
2 2 2 2 — 4 2 0 0 — 1perc — str
UE; Fleisher

Music for the Young (1939)   7'
2 2 2 2 — 2 1 0 0 — tmp+1 — str
perc: cym, tri, sd
Boosey & Hawkes

Pictures and Tales; Suite for Small   13'
Orchestra, op.2
2[1.2/pic] 2 2 2 — 2 2 0 0 — tmp+1 — hp — str
perc: tri
Fleisher

Weill, Kurt   (1900-1950)

Aufstieg und Fall der Stadt   7'
Mahagonny (Rise and Fall of the
City of Mahagonny): Alabama Song
(1927)
solo voice
1 1 2 0 — 0 2 1 0 — 3[2asx.tsx] — banjo — 1perc
— 2pf[pf.harm] — str[1.0.0.1.1]
Arranged by Richard Etlinger.
UE

Aufstieg und Fall der Stadt   17'
Mahagonny (Rise and Fall of the
City of Mahagonny): Suite (1929)
2[1/pic.2/pic] 1 1 2 — 2 2 2 1[1/tbn3] —
2sx[asx.tsx/ssx] — bgtr, banjo — tmp+2 — pf — str
Arranged by Wilhelm Brückner-Rüggeberg (1959).
mvt durations: 3' 3' 3' 2' 3' 3'
UE

Berlin im Licht-Song (1928)   5'
solo voice
1 1 2 0 — 0 2 2 0 — 3[2asx.tsx] — banjo — 1perc
— 2pf[pf.harm] — str
Edited by Otto Liebermann.
UE

Die Dreigroschenoper: Ballade von   3'
der sexuellen Hörigkeit (1928)
solo A
0 0 2[1.bcl] 0 — 0 0 0 0 — accordion — 1perc —
str[1.0.1.1.1]
perc: vib
UE

Happy End: Surabaya Johnny   5'
(1929)
solo Mz
1 0 1 0 — 0 1 0 0 — gtr — 1perc — str[1.0.1.1.1]
Arranged by Luciano Berio (1972).
UE

Marie Galante: Le Grand Lustucru   3'
(1934)
> solo Mz
> 2[1.pic] 1 3 1 — 0 1 0 0 — 1perc — str[1.0.1.1.1]
> Arranged by Luciano Berio (1972).
> UE

Der neue Orpheus; Cantata for   18'
Soprano, Violin and Orchestra,
op.16 (1925)
> solo S, vn
> 2[1/pic.2/pic] 2 2 2 — 0 2 2 0 — tmp+2 — hp —
> str[0.0.8.6.2]
> UE

Quodlibet: Suite aus "Zaubernacht."   23'
Eine Unterhaltungsmusik, op.9
(1922)
> 2 2 2 2 — 2 2 2 0 — tmp+3 — str
> UE

Der Silbersee: Suite aus dem   23'
Wintermärchen (1933)
> 2[1.2/pic] 2[1.2/eh] 2 2 — 2 2 2 0 — 1perc —
> hp[opt] — pf — str
> Arranged by Karel Salomon (1952).
> UE

Weinberger, Jaromir   (1896-1967)

Overture to a Knightly Play (1931)   10'
> 1 1 1 1 — 2 2 1 0 — 1perc — 2pf[pf.harm] — str
> perc: chimes[opt], tri, tam-tam, sd, cym
> Boosey & Hawkes

Weiner, Leo   (1885-1960)

Concertino, op.15 (1923)   19'
> solo pf
> 2 2 2 2 — 2 2 0 0 — tmp — str
> UE

Divertimento No.1; On old   9'
Hungarian folk dances, op.20
(1934)
> 1[pic] 0 0 0 — 1 1 0 0 — str
> Kalmus

Divertimento No.2 in A minor;   13'
Hungarian Folk Melodies, op.24
(1938)
> str
> Kalmus

Fasching; Carnival Humoresque,   7'
op.5 (1907)
> 2[1.2/pic] 1 2 1 — 2 2 1 0 — tmp+1 — str
> perc: tri
> Fleisher; Kalmus

Serenade for Small Orchestra in F   9'
minor, op.3 (1906)
> 2 2 2 2 — 2 2 0 0 — tmp+1 — str
> perc: tri
> Kalmus

Soldatenspiel, op.16 (1924)   4'
> 2 2 2 2 — 4 2 3 0 — 1perc — str
> UE

Weingartner, Felix   (1863-1942)

Concerto for Violin in G major,   25'
op.52
> solo vn
> 2 2 2 2 — 4 2 0 0 — tmp — str
> Breitkopf

Concerto in A minor, op.60 (1916)   15'
> solo vc
> 2 2 2 2 — 3 2 0 0 — tmp — str
> UE

Gottvertrauen, op.55/1 (1914)   3'
> solo voice
> 0 1 2 2 — 2 0 0 0 — str
> UE

Overture to Shakespeare's "The   15'
Tempest," op.65 (1919)
> 2 2 2 2 — 4 2 3 1 — tmp+2 — hp — str
> UE

Sinfonietta, op.83 (1935)   25'
> solo vn, va, vc
> 2 2 2 2 — 2 2 0 0 — tmp — hp — str
> UE

Symphony No.4 in F Major, op.61   20'
(1917)
> 2 2 2 3 — 4 2 3 0 — tmp — hp — str
> UE

Weir, Judith (1954-)

Isti Mirant Stella (1981)   12'
2[1.2/pic] 2 2 2 — 2 2 0 0 — str
Novello

Musicians Wrestle Everywhere   13'
(1994)
1 1 1[bcl] 0 — 1 0 1 0 — 1perc — pf —
str[0.0.0.1.1]
Chester Novello

Sederunt Principes (1987)   10'
1 1 2 1 — 1 1 1 0 — 1perc — hp — pf —
str(min)[3.0.2.1.1]
Chester Novello

Still, Glowing (2008)   4'
2 0 2 0 — 0 0 0 0 — 1perc — str
Chester Novello

Tiger under the Table (2002)   15'
1[1/pic] 1 1 1 — 1 1 1 0 — 1perc — pf —
str[1.1.1.1.1]
Chester Novello

Winter Song (2006)   17'
2[1.pic] 2[1.2/eh] 2 2[1.2/cbn] — 2 2 0 0 — str
Chester Novello

Weiss, Manfred (1935-)

Abendmusik (1989)   15'
2 2 2 2 — 3 2 2 0 — tmp+1 — str
Breitkopf

Concerto for Cello   23'
solo vc
2 2 2 2 — 3 2 3 1 — tmp+1 — str
Breitkopf

Concerto for Organ (1977)   17'
solo org
1perc — str
Breitkopf

Five Pieces   10'
str
Breitkopf

Music for Strings   11'
str
Breitkopf

Wellejus, Henning (1919-2002)

Postvognen Ruller (The Mailcoach   3'
is Rolling), op.16 (1959)
2 2 2 2 — 2 2 1 0 — tmp+1 — str
Hansen

Vor Barndoms Venner (Our   13'
Childhood Friends), op.15 (1950)
2 2 2 2 — 2 2 1 0 — tmp+1 — str
Hansen

Wellesz, Egon (1885-1974)

Amor Timido, op.50 (1933)   14'
solo coloratura S
1 2 2 1 — 2 0 0 0 — str
UE

Concerto for Piano, op.49 (1934)   20'
solo pf
2 2 2 2 — 4 2 1 0 — str
UE

Pastorale (1935)   3'
1 1 0 0 — 0 1 1 0 — asx — 1perc — str[1.1.0.1.1]
perc: tri
UE

Westergaard, Peter (1931-)

Fünf Sätze (1958)   6'
1 0 2[1.bcl] 1 — 2 1 1 0 — 1perc — hp — pf —
str
Boosey & Hawkes

L'Homme Armé, op.22a   20'
2[1.pic] 2 2 2 — 2 2 0 0 — 1perc — hp — str
Hansen

Westerman, Gerhart von (1894-1963)

Kleine Suite, op.3 (1940)   12'
1 1 2 1 — 2 2 1 0 — tmp+1 — hp — str
Boosey & Hawkes

Serenade, op.7 (1937)   20'
1[1/pic] 1 1 1 — 2 0 1 0 — tmp+1 — hp — str
Boosey & Hawkes

Widmann, Jörg   (1973-)

ad absurdum; Concerto for Trumpet (2002)   *17'*
  solo tpt
  2[1.2/pic] 0 2[bcl.cbcl] 2[1.cbn] — 0 0 0 0 —
  1perc — hand organ — str[6.5.4.3.1]
  perc: xylorimba, tri, Chinese cym, Peking opera gong, 2 high tambn,
  6 ped tmp, 5 woodblks
  Requires 5-string db.
  Schott

Freie Stücke (2002)   *25'*
  2[1.2/pic] 1[1/eh] 2[1/bcl.2/cbcl] 1[1/cbn] — 1 1 1
  0 — 2perc — str(min)[1.1.1.1.1]
  perc: crot, lotos fl, watergong, tam-tam, xylorimba, bd, cym, glsp, 5
  woodblks, 2 Peking opera gongs, police whistle, tom-tom, 2 tambn,
  steel dr, rototoms, buckelgongs, Chinese cym, ped tmp with cym, 5
  cym, whip,flexatone, guiro, chimes
  Both cl also double on ped bd. Bn and tpt double on lotos fl.
  Requires 5-string db.
  Schott

Ikarische Klage (1999)   *14'*
  str[4.0.3.2.1]
  Also possible with str[8.0.6.4.3]. Requires 5-string db.
  Schott

...umdüstert... (2000)   *18'*
  0 0 1[bcl] 0 — 0 0 0 0 — 1perc — pf —
  str[1.0.1.1.1]
  perc: bd, crot
  Schott

Wiechowicz, Stanisław   (1893-1963)

Nocturne (1960)
  1 1 1 0 — 0 0 0 0 — str
  PWM

Wiegold, Peter   (1949-)

The Flowers Appear on the Earth   *20'*
(1978)
  1 0 1 0 — 0 0 0 0 — gtr — 1perc — hp —
  str[0.0.1.1.0]
  UE

Wielecki, Tadeusz   (1954-)

Melody with Accompaniment   *9'*
(1981)
  0 0 1 0 — 0 0 1 0 — 1perc — pf — str[5.0.3.3.0]
  PWM

Wiener, Karl   (1891-1942)

Kammerstück für 12   *10'*
Soloinstrumente, op.7 (1932)
  0 1 2[1.bcl] 1 — 2 0 0 0 — tmp — hp — str
  Fleisher

Wilby, Philip   (1949-)

An Imagined Fable (1993)   *11'*
  1[1/pic] 1[1/eh] 1[1/bcl] 1 — 2 1 1 0 — 2perc — pf
  — str[1.1.1.1.1]
  Also possible with full strings.
  Chester Novello

The Wings of Morning (1988)   *12'*
  0 2 0 0 — 2 0 0 0 — str
  Chester Novello

Wildberger, Jacques   (1922-2006)

Liebestoto: No.10 from   *4'*
"Divertimento for Mozart" (1956)
  solo S
  2 2 2 2 — 2 2 0 0 — tmp — str
  For more information see: Mozart, Wolfgang Amadeus.
  Schott; UE

Wilkinson, Marc   (1929-)

Aliquant (1959)   *16'*
  solo vn
  2 2 0 1 — 2 0 0 0 — 2perc — str
  UE

Willi, Herbert   (1956-)

Für 16; Kleines Kammerkonzert   *12'*
(For 16; Small Chamber Concerto)
(1990)
  1[1/pic] 1 2[1.bcl] 1 — 1 1 1 0 — tmp+2 — pf —
  str
  perc: 8 cym, 2 bongos, 2 conga, 2 tom-tom, wood tom-tom, sd, metal
  block, woodblk, xyl, marim
  Schott

Williams, Graham   (1940-)

Cerberus (1977)   *9'*
  1 1 1 1 — 1 0 0 0 — hp — str[0.0.0.0.1]
  Chester Novello

Wilson, Ian   (1964-)

An Angel Serves a Small Breakfast;   19'
Concerto No.2 (1999)
    solo vn
    0 0 0 0 — 4 2 3[1.2.btbn] 0 — 2perc — hp — str
UE

...and flowers fall... (1990)   11'
    0 0 1 1 — 1 0 0 0 — pf — str[1.0.1.1.0]
UE

Inquieto; Concerto for Marimba   18'
(2001)
    solo marim
    2[1.2/pic] 2 2[1.2/bcl] 2 — 2 2 0 0 — 1perc — str
UE

Mutazione; Concerto for Piano   18'
(2003)
    solo pf
    2 2 2 2 — 2 2 0 0 — 1perc — str
UE

Near the Western Necropolis   25'
(1998)
    solo Mz
    1 1 1 1 — 1 1 0 0 — 1perc — str
UE

Running, Thinking, Finding (1989)   19'
    2 2 2 2 — 4 2 2 0 — tmp+4 — pf — str
UE

Shining Forth; Concerto for Cello   25'
(1998)
    solo vc
    2[1.afl] 0 2[1.bcl] 0 — 2 2 0 0 — str
UE

What we can see of the sky has   5'
fallen (1999)
    2 1 2 2 — 2 1 0 0 — tmp — str
UE

Who's Afraid of Red, Yellow and   19'
Blue?; Concerto for Alto Saxophone
(1998)
    solo asx
    2[1.2/pic/afl] 2[1.2/eh] 2[1/Ebcl.2/bcl] 2 — 4 2
    3[1.2.btbn] 1 — 2tmp+1 — str
UE

Wilson, Richard   (1941-)

Contentions   13'
    1[afl] 1[eh] 1[bcl] 1[cbn] — 0 0 0 0 — 2perc — hp
    — pf/elec pf — str[0.0.1.0.1]
Peer

Fantasy and Variations   8'
    1 0 1 1 — 0 1 1 0 — 2perc — str[1.0.1.1.1]
    perc: tambn, 2 templeblks, bongos, 2 tom-toms, sd, bd, lg cym, 2 sus
    cym, gong, tri, crot, chimes, glsp, xyl, vib, 2 tmp
Peer

Wimberger, Gerhard   (1923-)

Allegro Giocoso: No.8 from   4'
"Divertimento for Mozart" (1956)
    2[1.2/pic] 2 2 2 — 2 2 0 0 — tmp — str
    For more information see: Mozart, Wolfgang Amadeus.
Schott; UE

Concertino per orchestra (1981)   11'
    2 2 2 2[1.cbn] — 3 2 1 0 — tmp+1 — cel — str
Bärenreiter

Concerto for Piano No.2 (1980/81)   27'
    solo pf
    2[1.2/pic] 2 2 3[1.2.cbn] — 3 2 2 0 — gtr —
    tmp+2 — hp — str
Bärenreiter

Multiplay; Kanonische Reflexionen   13'
für 23 Spieler (Kammerorchester)
(1973)
    1 1 1 1 — 1 1 1 0 — 2perc — cel — str[3.3.3.3.1]
    perc: marim, vib
Bärenreiter

Partita Giocosa (1961)   18'
    1 1 2 1 — 1 1 1 0 — tmp+2 — str
    perc: tri, 2 sd, woodblk, glsp, xyl
Schott

Winkler, Gerhard   (1906-1977)

Wolken über Samland (1941)   5'
    1 1 1 0 — 0 2[1.2/crt] 1 0 — tmp+1 —
    2pf[pf.harm] — str
    Strings without va.
Fleisher; Schott

Winters, Geoffrey   (1928-)

Concertino, op.18 (1959)   13'
   0 0 0 0 — 2 0 0 0 — pf — str
Fleisher

Wirth, Carl Anton   (1912-1986)

Serenade (1962)
   1[1/pic] 1 1 1 — 0 0 0 0 — str
Fleisher

Wittinger, Robert   (1945-)

Compensazioni, op.9 (1967)   8'
   1 1[1/eh/perc] 1 0 — 1 1 1 0 — str[1.0.1.0.0]
Schirmer

Sinfonia, op.18 (1964)   15'
   str
Schirmer

Wolf-Ferrari, Ermanno   (1876-1948)

Chamber Symphony, op.8 (1901)   36'
   1 1 1 1 — 1 0 0 0 — pf — str[1.1.1.1.1]
Boosey & Hawkes

Serenade for Strings in E-flat
(1896)
   str
Kalmus

Sinfonia da Camera in B-flat, op.8   20'
(1901)
   1 1 1 1 — 1 0 0 0 — pf — str
Kalmus

Wolpe, Michael   (1960-)

Caprisma 2   20'
   2 1 1 0 — 0 0 0 0 — gtr — tmp+1 — str[1.0.1.1.1]
Presser

Wolpe, Stefan   (1902-1972)

Chamber Piece No.1   9'
   1 2[1.eh] 1 1 — 1 1 1 0 — pf — str[1.1.1.1.1]
Peer

Chamber Piece No.2   4'
   1 1 1 1 — 1 1 1 0 — 1perc — pf — str[1.0.1.1.1]
   perc: tmp, vib, glsp, dr, bd
Peer

Piece for Two Instrumental Units   12'
   1 1 0 0 — 0 0 0 0 — 1perc — pf — str[1.0.0.1.1]
   perc: gong, rubber sticks, vib, glsp, xyl, tam-tam
Peer

Wolschina, Reinhard   (1952-)

Concerto for Piano (1988)   20'
   solo pf
   2 1 2 1 — 2 1 1 1 — tmp — str
Breitkopf

Klangspiele I (1987)   17'
   solo fl
   0 0 2 1 — 0 1 1 0 — 3perc — str[4.0.3.2.1]
Breitkopf

Klangspiele II (1989)   16'
   solo va
   3 1 3 1 — 0 0 0 0 — str[0.0.0.4.2]
Breitkopf

Klangspiele III (1990)   11'
   solo marim, vib
   str
Breitkopf

Three Dialogues (1975)   15'
   solo hn
   str[8.0.3.3.1]
Breitkopf

Three Novels (1980)   17'
   solo vn, va, vc
   2 1 3 1 — 2 0 0 0 — 1perc — hp — str
Breitkopf

Vier Aphorismen (1981)   11'
   str
Breitkopf

Wandlungen (1985)   17'
   str
Breitkopf

Wood, Hugh   (1932-)

Chamber Concerto, op.15 (1971)   28'
   2[1/pic.2/pic/afl] 1 2[1.2/bcl] 1 — 1 1 1 1 — 3perc
   — hp — pf/cel — str[1.1.1.1.1]
Chester Novello

Comus Quadrilles (1988)   3'
    1 1 0 0 — 1 1 0 0 — 1perc — pf — str[1.0.1.1.0]
    Chester Novello

Woolrich, John   (1954-)

After the Clock (2005)   12'
    1 1 1 1 — 1 1 1 0 — 1perc — pf — str[1.1.1.1.1]
    perc: marim, bd, sleigh bells
    Also possible with small string section.
    Faber

Black Riddle; Five Songs for   9'
Soprano and Large Chamber
Ensemble (1984)
    solo S
    1 0 1 1 — 2 0 0 0 — 2perc — hp — str[3.0.3.2.2]
    perc: 4 spring coils, 2 tam-tam, bd
    Faber

Caprichos (1997)   7'
    1[pic/afl] 0 1[Ebcl/bcl] 0 — 1 1 1 0 — ssx — 1perc
    — pf — str[1.0.1.1.1]
    perc: marim, bd, tam-tam, 2 Peking opera gong
    Faber

Cutting a Caper (2001)   15'
    solo group: ob, cl/bcl, tpt, vn, vc
    2 2 2 2 — 0 2 1[btbn] 0 — 1perc — str
    perc: bd, 2 gongas, log dr, wood dr, tam-tam
    Faber

Darlington Doubles (1988)   5'
    1[afl] 0 0 0 — 1 1 0 0 — ssx — 2perc — pf —
    str[1.0.1.1.0]
    perc: boobams, bd
    Faber

From the Shadow (1994)   7'
    1[1/pic/afl] 0 1[1/Ebcl/bcl] 0 — 1 1 0 0 — ssx —
    1perc — pf — str[1.0.1.1.1]
    perc: 12 or more tin cans, 4 car wheels, 2 break dr, anvil, hi-hat, 8
    scaffold bars, 3 scaffold feet
    Faber

Lending Wings (1989)   14'
    1 1 1 1[1/cbn] — 1 1 1 0 — 2perc — hp — pf —
    str[1.1.1.1.1]
    perc: 2 tam-tam, 12 templeblks, 12 cowbells, 2 hi-hat, 2 log dr, 2 ped
    bd
    Faber

Music from the House of Crossed   8'
Desires (1996)
    1[pic/hand bell] 1 2[1/Ebcl/ssx.bcl] 1[cbn] —
    1[1/whistle] 1[1/whistle] 1 1 — 2perc — pf/whistle
    — str[0.0.0.1.1]
    perc: bd, crot, 10 tin cans, 2 templeblks, whistle, gongs, tam-tam,
    sus cym, ped bd, guiro, log dr, claves, whip, hand bell
    Faber

Stealing a March (2000)   7'
    1[1/pic] 1 1[Ebcl] 1 — 2 1 1 0 — 2perc — hp — pf
    — str[1.1.1.1.1]
    perc: taiko, sus cym, hi-hat, Chinese cym, sleigh bells, tam-tam, tin
    cans
    Faber

Suite from Bitter Fruit (2002)   20'
    1[1/pic/afl] 1 1[1/bcl] 1[1/cbn] — 1 1 2 1 — ssx —
    2perc — str[1.0.1.1.1]
    perc: 2 tam-tam, 2 bd, sd, 2 whip, anvil, flexatone, car wheel, 2
    Peking opera gongs, 2 hi-hat, 2 sus cym, 2 sm cym, 5 tuned gongs,
    10 tin cans, dustbin, woodblk, cuica, military dr, rattle, thunder sheet,
    2 spring coils
    Faber

Wunsch, Hermann   (1884-1954)

Fest auf Monbijou; Suite in fünf   14'
Sätzen, op.50
    2 2 2 2 — 2 2 0 0 — tmp — str
    Schott

Wyner, Yehudi   (1929-)

Amadeus' Billiard (1991)   8'
    0 0 0 2 — 2 0 0 0 — str[1.0.1.0.1]
    AMP

Passage (1983)   9'
    1 0 1 0 — 0 1 0 0 — pf — str[1.0.1.1.0]
    AMP

Serenade for Seven Instruments   18'
(1958)
    1 0 0 0 — 1 1 1 0 — pf — str[0.0.1.1.0]
    AMP

X

Xenakis, Iannis   (1922-2001)

À l'île de Gorée (1986)   *14'*
  solo amp hpsd
  0[1/pic] 1 1 1 — 1 1 1 0 — str[1.1.1.1.1]
  Salabert

Akanthos; Phonèmes de Iannis   *11'*
Xenakis (1977)
  solo S
  1[1/pic/afl] 0 1[1/bcl] 0 — 0 0 0 0 — pf —
  str[1.1.1.1.1]
  Salabert

Alax; Pour 30 musiciens divises en   *22'*
3 ensembles (1985)
  3 0 3 0 — 6 0 3 0 — 3perc — 3hp — str[3.0.0.6.0]
  Salabert

Anaktoria (1969)   *11'*
  0 0 1 1[1/cbn(opt)] — 1 0 0 0 — str[1.1.1.1.1]
  Salabert

Atrées (1960)   *15'*
  1 0 1[1.bcl] 0 — 1 1 1 0 — 3perc — str[1.0.0.1.0]
  Salabert

Échange (1989)   *14'*
  solo bcl
  1 1 1 1 — 1 1 1 1 — str[1.1.1.1.1]
  Salabert

Epicycle (1989)   *12'*
  solo vc
  1 1 1 1 — 1 1 1 1 — str[1.1.1.0.1]
  Salabert

Jalons (1986)   *15'*
  1[1/pic] 1 2[1/bcl.2/cbcl] 1[1/cbn] — 1 1 1 1 — hp
  — str[1.1.1.1.1]
  Salabert

Kaï (1995)   *8'*
  1 0 1 1 — 0 1 1 0 — str[1.0.1.1.1]
  Salabert

O-Mega (1997)   *4'*
  solo perc
  1 1 1 1 — 1 1 1 1 — str[1.1.1.1.1]
  Salabert

Palimpsest (1979)   *11'*
  0 1[1/eh] 1[1/bcl] 1 — 1 0 0 0 — 1perc — pf —
  str[1.1.1.1.1]
  Salabert

Phlegra (1975)   *14'*
  1[1/pic] 1 1[1/bcl] 1 — 1 1 1 0 — str[1.0.1.1.1]
  Salabert

Thalleïn (1984)   *17'*
  1[1/pic] 1 1 1 — 1 1[1/pic tpt] 1 0 — 1perc — pf
  — str[1.1.1.1.1]
  Salabert

Waarg (1988)   *16'*
  1[1/pic] 1 1 1 — 1 1 1 1 — str[1.1.1.1.1]
  Salabert

Y

Yanov-Yanovsky, Dmitri (1963-)

Chamber Music for Twelve 17'
Musicians (1993)
1 1 2 0 — 0 1 1 0 — 1perc — pf — str[1.0.1.1.1]
Schirmer

Message (2001) 9'
str
Boosey & Hawkes

Night Music; Voice in the Leaves 16'
(2000)
solo vc
1 0 1 0 — 0 0 0 0 — tape — 2perc — hp — pf —
str[1.0.1.0.1]
Schirmer

Ye, Xiaogang (1955-)

Nine Horses, op.19 (1993) 9'
1 1 1 0 — 0 0 0 0 — 2perc — pf — str[1.0.1.1.1]
perc: vib, marim, tri, sus cym, Chinese sus cym, 2 Chinese cym, 2
gongs, Chinese gong, tom-tom
Schott

Strophe (1985) 12'
1 1 1 0 — 1 1 1 0 — tmp+2 — hp — pf —
str[1.1.1.1.1]
Schott

Yu, Julian (1957-)

Ballade Concertante; For Zheng 19'
and String Orchestra (1999)
solo zheng
str
UE

Concerto; For Marimba and Small 21'
Orchestra, op.38 (1996)
solo marim
1[1/pic] 1 1 0 — 1 1 0 0 — 1perc — str
UE

First Australian Suite, op.22 (1990) 13'
1 1 1 1 — 1 1 1 0 — 1perc — hp — str
UE

Great Ornamented Fuga Canonica, 10'
op.17 (1988)
2 2 2 2 — 4 2 3 0 — 3perc — hp — pf — str
UE

Lyrical Concerto, op.39 (1997)
solo fl
1[pic] 0 2 0 — 1 1 0 0 — 2perc — hp — pf — str
UE

Not a Stream but an Ocean (2000) 13'
2[1.2/pic] 2[1.2/eh] 2[1.2/bcl] 2[1.cbn] — 4 2 3 1
— tmp+2 — hp — cel — str
UE

Philopentatonia, op.32 (1994) 12'
2[1/pic.pic] 1 1 0 — 1 1 1 0 — 1perc — hp —
pf/cel — str[1.1.1.1.1]
UE

Yuasa, Joji (1929-)

Projection (2008) 7'
2 1 2 1 — 1 1 1 1 — 2perc — hp — pf —
str[1.1.1.1.1]
Schott

Projection for Seven Players 17'
(1955)
1[1/pic] 1 1[1/bcl] 0 — 1 1 0 0 — pf —
str[0.0.0.1.0]
Schott

Yun, Isang (1917-1995)

Colloides sonores (1961) 16'
str
Boosey & Hawkes

Impression (1986) 13'
2[1.2/pic/afl] 2 2[1.bcl] 1 — 1 1 1 0 — 2perc — hp
— str[1.1.1.1.1]
Boosey & Hawkes

Kammerkonzert II (Chamber 13'
Concerto II) (1990)
0 1[1/eh] 0 0 — 0 0 1 0 — 1perc — pf —
str[0.0.1.1.1]
perc: 5 tom-tom, 3 cym, xyl, glsp, 3 gongs, 3 templeblks, 5 woodblks
Boosey & Hawkes

Kammersinfonie I (Chamber 24'
Symphony I) (1987)
0 2 0 0 — 2 0 0 0 — str
Boosey & Hawkes

Kammersinfonie II (Chamber   *33'*
Symphony II) (1989)
   1[1/pic] 1 2[1.bcl] 1 — 1 1 0 0 — 2perc — hp —
   pf — str
     perc: 5 tom-tom, glsp, 5 sus cym, 2 marac, rattle, claves, 5
     woodblks, 5 gongs, claves
   Boosey & Hawkes

Konzertante Figuren (1972)   *20'*
   2[1/pic.2/afl] 2 1 1 — 2 1 1 0 — str
   Boosey & Hawkes

Z

Zbinden, Julien-François   (1917-)

Ballad, op.33 (1961)   *7'*
   solo bn
   2 2 2 2 — 2 2 1 0 — tmp+2 — str
   Breitkopf

Concerto breve, op.36 (1962)   *15'*
   solo vc
   2 2 2 2 — 2 2 0 0 — tmp — hp — str
   Breitkopf

Concerto for Violin, op.37 (1965)   *25'*
   solo vn
   2 2 2 2 — 2 2 2 0 — tmp+1 — pf — str
   Breitkopf

Fantasia, op.22 (1954)   *7'*
   solo fl
   0 1 1 1 — 2 0 0 0 — pf — str
   Breitkopf

Orchalau Concerto, op.38   *7'*
   2[1.2/pic] 2 2 2 — 2 2 0 0 — tmp — pf — str
   Breitkopf

Rhapsody, op.25   *9'*
   solo vn
   2 2 2 2 — 2 2 0 0 — tmp+1 — hp — str
   Breitkopf

Symphony No.1, op.18   *20'*
   2[1.pic] 2[1.eh] 2[1.bcl] 1 — 2 1 0 0 — tmp — str
   Breitkopf

Zechlin, Ruth   (1926-2007)

Concertino   *16'*
   solo ob
   1 0 0 0 — 0 1 1 0 — tmp+1 — pf — str
   Breitkopf

Gedanken über ein Klavierstück   *10'*
von Prokofjew (1967)
   solo pf
   1 1 1 1 — 0 1 0 0 — 1perc — str[1.0.1.1.1]
   Breitkopf

Zemlinsky, Alexander — (1871-1942)

Das Mädchen mit den verbundenen   3'
Augen: From "Sechs Gesänge,"
op.13/2 (1914)
 solo medium voice
 1 0 1 0 — 0 0 0 0 — 2pf[pf.harm] — str[1.1.1.1.1]
 Arranged by Erwin Stein (1921). See also "Verein für
 Musikalische Privataufführungen" (Appendix p.399).
 UE

Sechs Gesänge, op.13 (1913)   16'
 solo medium voice
 1[1/pic/afl] 1[1/eh] 1[1/bcl] 1 — 1 1 1 1 —
 asx/tsx/ssx — accordion — 3perc — hp — cel —
 str[4.4.2.2.1]
 Arranged for chamber orchestra by Gösta Neuwirth (1994).
 UE

Sinfonietta, op.23 (1934)   22'
 2[1.2/pic] 2[1.2/eh] 2[1.2/Ebcl] 2 — 4 3 3 0 —
 tmp+1 — hp — str
 UE

String Quartet No.4, op.25 (1936)   25'
 str
 Arranged for string orchestra by Simeon Pironkoff (1992).
 UE

Symphony No.2 in Bb major (1897)   40'
 2 2 2 2 — 4 2 3 1 — tmp — str
 UE

Und kehrt er einst Heim: From   3'
"Sechs Gesänge," op.13/5 (1914)
 solo medium voice
 1 0 1 0 — 0 0 0 0 — 2pf[pf.harm] — str[1.1.1.1.1]
 Arranged by Erwin Stein. See also "Verein für Musikalische
 Privataufführungen" (Appendix p.399).
 UE

Zender, Hans — (1936-)

4 Enso (LO-SHU VII) (1997)   14'
 0 2 0 0 — 2 2 2 0 — accordion — 4perc — pf —
 str[1.1.2.2.0]
 Breitkopf

Bardo (2000)   26'
 solo vc (opt with curved bow)
 2[1.2/pic] 2 2 0 — 2 2 2 1 — tmp+3 — 2pf —
 str[6.5.4.4.2]
 Breitkopf

Concerto for Flute; Loshu 5 (1987)   27'
 solo fl
 2 2 2 0 — 2 2 2 1 — hp — pf — str
 UE

Kalligraphie II (1998)   8'
 0 0 0 0 — 0 3 2 0 — 4perc — hp — pf —
 str[6.6.2.4.3]
 Breitkopf

Zilcher, Hermann — (1881-1948)

Concert Piece in One Movement,   20'
op.21
 solo vc
 2 2 2 2 — 2 2 0 0 — tmp — str
 Breitkopf

Concert Piece on a Theme by W. A.   15'
Mozart (K.251), op.81
 solo fl
 1 2 2 2 — 2 2 0 0 — tmp+1 — str
 Breitkopf

Concerto for Violin in B minor,   20'
op.11
 solo vn
 2 2 2 2 — 2 2 0 0 — tmp+1 — str
 Breitkopf

Klage, op.22   15'
 solo vn
 2 2 2 2 — 2 2 0 0 — tmp — hp — str
 Breitkopf

Lustspielsuite; Der Widerspenstigen   19'
Zähmung, op.54b
 1[1/pic] 1 1 1 — 2 1 0 0 — str
 Breitkopf

Variations on a Theme by W. A.   20'
Mozart, op.95
 solo vc
 2[1.2/pic] 2 2 2 — 2 2 0 0 — tmp+1 — str
 Breitkopf

Zimmermann, Bernd Alois — (1918-1970)

Metamorphose; Music for the Film   25'
of the same Title by Michael
Wolgensinger (1954)
 1 1 1 1 — 1 1 0 0 — asx — gtr — tmp+3 — hp —
 pf/hpsd/elec org — str[2.2.2.2.1]
 perc: tri, cym, hi-hat, tam-tam, bongo, 2 tom-tom, 2 wood dr, bd, sd,
 templeblk, glsp, xyl, vib
 Schott

Un "Petit Rien" (1964)   6'
3[1/pic.2/pic.3/pic/afl] 0 0 0 — 0 0 0 0 — gtr —
3perc — 2pf[cel.hpsd] — str[3.0.2.1.1]
perc: sd, 2 wood dr, 3 templeblks, guiro, hi-hat, vib, xyl
Schott

Zimmermann, Udo   (1943-)

Music for Strings (1968)   14'
str
Breitkopf

Nouveaux Divertissements (1987)   20'
solo hn
2 2 2 0 — 2 2 2 0 — tmp+1 — 2pf — str
Breitkopf

Songerie Pour Orchestre de   20'
Chambre (1982)
4 0 0 0 — 0 3 0 0 — tmp+1 — 2hp — str
Breitkopf

Tänzerinnen; Choreographies   12'
based on E. Degas (1973)
3 2 2 0 — 0 2 0 0 — 1perc — hp — str[0.0.5.4.0]
Breitkopf

Zipp, Friedrich   (1914-1997)

Sonne der Gerechtigkeit;
Choralkonzert für Blechbläser und
Streicher
0 0 0 0 — 0 2 2 0 — str
Bärenreiter

Zwilich, Ellen Taaffe   (1939-)

Concerto for Bass Trombone   18'
solo btbn
tmp+1 — str
perc: cym
Presser

Concerto for Bassoon and   17'
Orchestra (1992)
solo bn
2[1.2/pic] 2[1.2/eh] 2[1.2/bcl] 0 — 2 1 1 0 — 1perc
— str
Presser

Concerto for Clarinet (2002)   26'
solo cl
1 1 0 1 — 2 1[1/crt] 0 0 — 1perc — str
Presser

Concerto for Flute and Orchestra   18'
solo fl
0 2[1.2/eh] 2 2 — 0 2[1.2/crt] 3 0 — tmp+1 — hp
— str
Presser

Concerto for Horn and String   14'
Orchestra
solo hn
str
Presser

Concerto for Piano, Violin and   24'
Cello; Triple Concerto
solo pf, vn, vc
1 2 2 2 — 2 2 0 0 — tmp — str
Presser

Concerto for Violin and Orchestra   26'
(1997)
solo vn
2[1.2/pic] 2[1.2/eh] 2[1.2/bcl] 2[1.2/cbn] — 2 2 0 0
— tmp — hp — str
Presser

Concerto for Violin and Violoncello;   18'
Double Concerto
solo vn, vc
2 2[1.2/eh] 2 2 — 2 2 0 0 — tmp — str
Presser

Images   18'
solo 2pf
2 2 2 2 — 2 1 1 1 — 1perc — str
Presser

Millennium Fantasy   20'
solo pf
2[1.2/pic] 2[1.2/eh] 2[1.2/bcl] 2[1.2/cbn] — 2 2 0 0
— 1perc — str
Presser

Partita   18'
solo vn
str
Presser

Peanuts® Gallery (1996)   13'
solo pf
1 2 2 2 — 2 0 0 0 — 1perc — str
Presser

Prologue and Variations   *13'*
   str
 Presser

Romance   *7'*
   solo vn
  1 1 0 1 — 0 0 0 0 — str
 Presser

APPENDIX

HOW TO USE THIS APPENDIX

Exact and Maximum Instrumentation

Duration

This appendix lists all of the almost four thousand compositions in this catalog according to certain criteria in an effort to help you find repertoire that best meets your requirements. Once you have found a piece in the appendix, refer back to the composer listings for complete information on the composition.

If a category has more than 25 pieces listed it will be subdivided by duration: Smaller categories usually subdivide pieces that are 10 minutes or less (10' or less) and pieces that are longer than this (over 10'). Larger categories will break the selection down further (5' or less, etc.).

Exact and Maximum Instrumentation

While sometimes it is helpful to be able to search for pieces in a specific instrumentation, my experience is that mostly we search for compositions that can be performed with a certain size orchestra. It usually does not matter if a composition does not use every single player. But it is crucial that the composition at hand is not *larger* than the orchestra that is available to us.

Therefore, there are two different ways to search the categories "Ensemble" and "Chamber Orchestra." If you are looking for a piece with a very specific instrumentation you can search for the **Exact Instrumentation**. Compositions listed in this category use exactly the given instrumentation.

Example:
The category **1111 - 1000 - str** will only list pieces in exactly this instrumentation.

If you are searching for pieces that are not larger than the group that is available to you, you can of course search all the "exact" categories smaller or equal to your orchestra's size. In addition you can search by **Maximum Instrumentation**. Compositions listed in these categories use either the exact given instrumentation or call for *smaller* forces.

Example:
The category **1010 - 0110 - str** can return a piece in this very instrumentation but it can also list pieces that require, i.e., **1000 - 0110 - str** or **0010 - 0010 - str**.

Maximum Instrumentations are listed with the exact woodwind, brass, or string count in brackets at the end of each entry.

All listings will indicate if a given category represents the Exact or the Maximum Instrumentation. The categories "Ensemble" and "Chamber Orchestra" are organized roughly from small to large groups.

SOLO VOICES

SOPRANO

10' or Less

Albin, Roger
- Chantefables pour les enfants sages; Pour Soprano et 20 musiciens

Aperghis, Georges
- Il Gigante Golia; Texte d'un petit motet sarde pour Soprano et orchestre de 16 musiciens

Banfield, Raffaello de
- Liebeslied (Love Song)
- Serale
- Der Tod der Geliebten (The Death of the Beloved)

Bartók, Béla
- Two Village Scenes (Slovak Folksongs)

Ben-Haim, Paul
- Lift Up Your Heads; Motet

Berio, Luciano
- Air: From "Opera"
- E vó: Sicilian Lullaby from "Opera"

Birtwistle, Sir Harrison
- An die Musik
- Four Poems by Jaan Kaplinski
- Songs by Myself
- Words Overheard

Blech, Leo
- Six Children's Songs

Debussy, Claude
- Coquetterie Posthume
- Musique
- Trois Poèmes de Stéphane Mallarmé

Finnissy, Michael
- From the Revelations of St. John the Divine

Honegger, Arthur
- Prière

Kaminski, Heinrich
- Brautlied: "Wo du hingehst…" (Bride's Song: Where you are going…)

Krenek, Ernst
- Monolog der Stella (Stella's Monologue); Concert Aria, op.57a
- Die Nachtigall (The Nightingale), op.68

Lam, Bun-Ching
- Spring Yearning

Liebermann, Rolf
- Lied der Yvette: From the opera "Leonore 40/45"

Lutosławski, Witold
- Spijze, spij (Sleep, sleep)

Marx, Joseph
- Maienblüten: From "Lieder und Gesänge" (1.Folge Nr.16)
- Marienlied: From "Lieder und Gesänge" (1.Folge Nr.17)
- Sommerlied: From "Lieder und Gesänge" (1.Folge Nr.22)
- Und gestern hat er mir Rosen gebracht: From "Lieder und Gesänge" (1.Folge Nr.24)
- Zigeuner: From "Lieder und Gesänge" (3.Folge Nr.8)

Menotti, Gian Carlo
- The Consul: Magda's Aria (To this we've come)
- The Medium: The Black Swan
- The Medium: Monica's Waltz
- The Telephone: Lucy's Aria (Hello! Oh, Margaret it's you)

Nørgård, Per
- Nocturnes; Fragment VII

Poulenc, Francis
- Airs chantés

Revueltas, Silvestre
- Ranas
- El Tecolote (The Owl)

Rihm, Wolfgang
- Sicut Cervus Desiderat ad Fontes Aquarum, op.7

Rodrigo, Joaquín
- Cántico de la Esposa
- Cuatro Madrigales Amatorios
- La Espera
- Retablo de Navidad
- Serranilla

Roussel, Albert
- À un Jeune Gentilhomme

Saint-Saëns, Camille
- Ô beaux rêves évanouis: "Air de Béatrix"
- Papillons

Schoeck, Othmar
- Five Songs, op.60

Schönberg, Arnold
- Nature, op.8/1
- Nie Ward Ich, Herrin, Müd', op.8/4
- Sehnsucht, op.8/3
- Voll jener Süße, op.8/5
- Wenn Vöglein klagen, op.8/6

Sessions, Roger
- Romualdo's Song from "The Black Maskers"

Strauss, Richard
- Das Bächlein, op.88/1
- Morgen
- Das Rosenband, op.31, No.1
- Traum durch die Dämmerung, op.29/1

Vlad, Roman
- Immer Wieder…

Wildberger, Jacques
- Liebestoto: No.10 from "Divertimento for Mozart"

Woolrich, John
- Black Riddle; Five Songs for Soprano and Large Chamber Ensemble

Over 10'

Aa, Michel van der
- Here trilogy; for soprano, chamber orchestra and soundtrack
Albert, Stephen
- Flower of the Mountain: From "Distant Hills"
- Flower of the Mountain: From "Distant Hills." Version for full orchestra
Bacri, Nicolas
- Notturni; Concerto da camera quasi una sinfonia piccola, op.14
Barber, Samuel
- Knoxville: Summer of 1915, op.24
Bavicchi, John
- Farewell & Hail, op.28
- There is sweet music here, op.93
Blacher, Boris
- Parergon zum "Eugen Onegin"
Bolcom, William
- Medusa; A Monodrama for dramatic soprano and string orchestra
Boone, Charles
- Fields / Singing
Boucourechliev, André
- Lit de Neige
Britten, Benjamin
- Quatre Chansons Françaises
Brizzi, Aldo
- Le Erbe Nella Thule
Carter, Elliott
- A Mirror on Which to Dwell; For Soprano and Ensemble
Danielpour, Richard
- Sonnets to Orpheus; Book 1
Del Tredici, David
- Haddock's Eyes
Engelmann, Hans Ulrich
- Nocturnos
Falla, Manuel de
- Seven Popular Spanish Songs
Feldman, Morton
- Voice and Instruments 1
Furrer, Beat
- Illuminations
Gruenberg, Louis
- The Daniel Jazz, op.21
Gubaidulina, Sofia
- Homage to T. S. Eliot
Hesketh, Kenneth
- Recit and Aria

Hruby, Viktor
- Drei Lieder nach Eichendorff (Three Songs after Eichendorff)
Knussen, Oliver
- Océan de Terre, op.10
Kodály, Zoltán
- Five Songs: From "Hungarian Folkmusic"
Krenek, Ernst
- Durch die Nacht (Through the Night), op.67a
- Suite from "Triumph der Empfindsamkeit" (Triumph of Sensitivity), op.43a
Kurtág, György
- Four Capriccios, op.9
Lutosławski, Witold
- Chantefleur et Chantefables
Matsudaira, Yoritsune
- Requiem
Messner, Joseph
- Fünf Symphonische Gesänge, op.24
Paccagnini, Angelo
- Actuelles 1968
Papandopulo, Boris
- Concerto da Camera, op.11
Pasquet, Yves-Marie
- Atemkristal
Rihm, Wolfgang
- Aria / Ariadne; "Szenarie"
Rodrigo, Joaquín
- Cuatre Cançons En llengua Catalana
- Pavana Real; Ballet in three acts
- Rosaliana
- Tríptic de Mossén Cinto
Saariaho, Kaija
- Leino Songs
- Quatre Instants
Schafer, Robert Murray
- Hymn to the Night
Schoeck, Othmar
- Besuch in Urach, op.62/40
Schönberg, Arnold
- Lied der Waldtaube: From "Gurre-Lieder"
- String Quartet No.2 in F-sharp minor; For Soprano and String Orchestra, op.10
Schreker, Franz
- Vom Ewigen Leben
Schwantner, Joseph
- Sparrows
Schwartz, Francis
- Grimaces "Commande d'Etat"
Staud, Johannes Maria
- Berenice: Lied vom Verschwinden

Szymanowski, Karol
- Lieder des verliebten Muezzin, op.42
Wellesz, Egon
- Amor Timido, op.50
Xenakis, Iannis
- Akanthos; Phonèmes de Iannis Xenakis

ALTO or MEZZO-SOPRANO

10' or Less

Ast, Max
- Es ist alles wie ein wunderbarer Garten
Berg, Alban
- Five Orchestra Songs, op.4
Carter, Elliott
- Three Poems of Robert Frost
Castelnuovo-Tedesco, Mario
- Three Sephardic Songs
Falla, Manuel de
- El Amor Brujo: Chanson du Feu Follet
- El Amor Brujo: Récit du Pécheur et Pantomime
Hubay, Jenö
- Ende September, op.103/1
Kodály, Zoltán
- Kádár Kata; Transylvanian Folk Ballad
- Mónár Anna; Székler Ballade
Lutosławski, Witold
- Jesien (Autumn)
- Six Children's Songs
Malipiero, Gian Francesco
- Sette Canzonette Veneziane
Marx, Joseph
- Erinnerung: From "Lieder und Gesänge" (2.Folge Nr.2)
- Japanisches Regenlied: From "Lieder und Gesänge" (1.Folge Nr.13)
- Selige Nacht: From "Lieder und Gesänge" (3.Folge Nr.9)
- Venetianisches Wiegenlied: From "Italienisches Liederbuch" (No.17)
Menotti, Gian Carlo
- The Consul: Lullaby
- The Medium: Baba's Aria (Afraid, am I afraid?)
Ravel, Maurice
- Chanson hébraïque
- Deux Mélodies hébraïques
Rodrigo, Joaquín
- Cuatro Madrigales Amatorios
Saariaho, Kaija
- Message Pour Gérard

Salmhofer, Franz
- Wonne der Wehmut
Schmitt, Florent
- Kerob-shal, op.67
Schönberg, Arnold
- Nature, op.8/1
- Nie Ward Ich, Herrin, Müd', op.8/4
- Sehnsucht, op.8/3
- Voll jener Süße, op.8/5
- Wenn Vöglein klagen, op.8/6
Strauss, Richard
- Meinem Kinde, op.37/3
- Traum durch die Dämmerung, op.29/1
Webern, Anton
- Zwei Lieder, op.8
Weill, Kurt
- Die Dreigroschenoper: Ballade von der sexuellen Hörigkeit
- Marie Galante: Le Grand Lustucru
- Surabaya Johnny: From "Happy End"
Zemlinsky, Alexander
- Das Mädchen mit den verbundenen Augen: From "Sechs Gesänge," op.13/2
- Und kehrt er einst Heim: From "Sechs Gesänge," op.13/5

Over 10'

Aperghis, Georges
- Dark Side
Bartók, Béla
- Five Songs, op.15
Berio, Luciano
- Calmo
- Folk Songs
Britten, Benjamin
- Phaedra; Cantata for Mezzo-Soprano and Small Orchestra, op.93
Copland, Aaron
- Eight Poems of Emily Dickinson
- Old American Songs; First Set
- Old American Songs; Second Set
Einem, Gottfried von
- Kammergesänge, op.32
Falla, Manuel de
- El Amor Brujo (First Version)
- El Amor Brujo (Second Version)
- El Corregidor y la Molinera
- Seven Popular Spanish Songs
Gelbrun, Arthur
- Lieder der Mädchen (Songs of the Girls)

Hauer, Josef Matthias
- Emilie vor ihrem Brauttag (Emilie before her wedding day); Cantata, op.58
Hoyland, Vic
- Crazy Rosa - La Madre
Kodály, Zoltán
- Five Songs: From "Hungarian Folkmusic"
Krása, Hans
- Symphony for Small Orchestra
Martin, Frank
- Die Weise von Liebe und Tod des Cornets Christoph Rilke
Martinů, Bohuslav
- Échec au roi; Ballet en 1 acte
Matthews, Colin
- Continuum
Milhaud, Darius
- Machines Agricoles, 6 pastoral songs, op.56
Muldowney, Dominic
- The Duration of Exile
- Lonely Hearts;Song Cycle for Mezzo Soprano, 14 Players, Two Conductors and Click-Track Tape
Osborne, Nigel
- Alba
- Pornography
Prokofiev, Sergei
- The Ugly Duckling, op.18
Ravel, Maurice
- Histoires naturelles
Reger, Max
- Five Orchestra Songs
Rihm, Wolfgang
- Eine Stimme 1-3
Schoeck, Othmar
- Nachhall, op.70
Schwartz, Francis
- Songs of Loneliness
Stockhausen, Karlheinz
- Drei Lieder (Three Songs), Nr.1/10
Wilson, Ian
- Near the Western Necropolis
Zemlinsky, Alexander
- Sechs Gesänge, op.13

TENOR

10' or Less

Birtwistle, Sir Harrison
- Prologue
Blech, Leo
- Six Children's Songs
Braunfels, Walter
- Abschied vom Walde

Burt, Francis
- The Skull; Cantata for Tenor and Orchestra
Foss, Lukas
- Measure for Measure
Kaminski, Heinrich
- Brautlied: "Wo du hingehst..." (Bride's Song: Where you are going...)
Marx, Joseph
- Maienblüten: From "Lieder und Gesänge" (1.Folge Nr.16)
- Marienlied: From "Lieder und Gesänge" (1.Folge Nr.17)
- Sommerlied: From "Lieder und Gesänge" (1.Folge Nr.22)
- Und gestern hat er mir Rosen gebracht: From "Lieder und Gesänge" (1.Folge Nr.24)
- Zigeuner: From "Lieder und Gesänge" (3.Folge Nr.8)
Saint-Saëns, Camille
- Où nous avons aimé
Schoeck, Othmar
- Five Songs, op.60
Schönberg, Arnold
- Nature, op.8/1
- Nie Ward Ich, Herrin, Müd', op.8/4
- Sehnsucht, op.8/3
- Voll jener Süße, op.8/5
- Wenn Vöglein klagen, op.8/6
Strauss, Richard
- Das Bächlein, op.88/1
- Das Rosenband, op.31, No.1
- Traum durch die Dämmerung, op.29/1

Over 10'

Albert, Stephen
- Into Eclipse; Chamber with voice version.
Bolcom, William
- Open House
Corigliano, John
- Poem in October
Denisov, Edison
- Fünf Geschichten vom Herrn Keuner (Five Stories of Mr. Keuner)
Falla, Manuel de
- Seven Popular Spanish Songs
Füssl, Karl Heinz
- Dialogue in Praise of the Owl and the Cuckoo
Gruenberg, Louis
- The Daniel Jazz, op.21
Hruby, Viktor
- Drei Lieder nach Eichendorff (Three Songs after Eichendorff)

Kodály, Zoltán
- Five Songs: From "Hungarian Folkmusic"
Krenek, Ernst
- Durch die Nacht (Through the Night), op.67a
Lutosławski, Witold
- Paroles tissées (Woven words)
Milhaud, Darius
- Cinq Chansons de Charles Vildrac, op.167
Osborne, Nigel
- The Cage
Schoeck, Othmar
- Besuch in Urach, op.62/40
Szymanowski, Karol
- Lieder des verliebten Muezzin, op.42
Watkins, Michael Blake
- Youth's Dream and Time's Truths

BARITONE or BASS

10' or Less

Asia, Daniel
- V'shamru; For Baritone (Cantor) and Chamber Orchestra
Honegger, Arthur
- Mimaamaquim; Psaume 130, H.192
Milhaud, Darius
- Der 129. Psalm, op.53
Muldowney, Dominic
- Maxim's
Ravel, Maurice
- Ronsard à son âme
- Don Quichotte à Dulcinée
Rihm, Wolfgang
- O Notte
Roumain, Daniel Bernard
- Harvest
Schönberg, Arnold
- Nature, op.8/1
- Nie Ward Ich, Herrin, Müd', op.8/4
- Sehnsucht, op.8/3
- Voll jener Süße, op.8/5
- Wenn Vöglein klagen, op.8/6
Strauss, Richard
- Traum durch die Dämmerung, op.29/1

Over 10'

Ben-Haim, Paul
- Melodies from the East
Cerha, Friedrich
- Lichtenberg-Splitter
Danielpour, Richard
- Sonnets to Orpheus, Book 2

Falla, Manuel de
- Seven Popular Spanish Songs
Gielen, Michael
- Musica
Kodály, Zoltán
- Five Songs: From "Hungarian Folkmusic"
Milhaud, Darius
- Cantate de Psaumes, op.425
- Couronne de Gloire; Cantata for Baritone and Small Orchestra
Rihm, Wolfgang
- Umsungen
Ruzicka, Peter
- Der die Gesänge Zerschlug
Schreker, Franz
- Fünf Gesänge (Five Songs); Chamber Ensemble version

VOICE (UNSPECIFIED)

10' or Less

Aubert, Louis
- La Mauvaise Prière
- Le Nez de Martin
- Sérénade
- Sérénade mélancolique
- Silence
- Le sommeil de colombes
- Visage penché
Beydts, Louis
- Chansons pour les oiseaux
Büsser, Henri
- Dors là-bas petit Baya; Berceuse d'Afrique
- Soupir, op.109, No.3
Elgar, Edward
- Grania and Diarmid: There are seven that pull the thread, op.42
Fauré, Gabriel
- L'Horizon chimérique, op.118
Halffter, Ernesto
- Automne malade
- Dos canciones
- Gerinaldo
Honegger, Arthur
- Six Poèmes d'Apollinaire, H.12: No.5 L'Adieu
- Six Poèmes d'Apollinaire, H.12: No.6: Les Cloches
Mercurio, Steven
- Sancta Maria
Milhaud, Darius
- Catalogue de fleurs, op.60
Poulenc, Francis
- Chansons villageoises
Ravel, Maurice
- D'Anne jouant de l'espinette

Roussel, Albert
- Le bachelier de Salamanque, op.20, No.1
Saint-Saëns, Camille
- Les fées
- La Libellule
Satie, Erik
- Mort de Socrate
Strauss, Richard
- Freundliche Vision, op.48, No.1
- Muttertändelei, op.43, No.2
- Waldseligkeit, op.49, No.1
Szymanowski, Karol
- Three Berceuses, op.48
Webern, Anton
- Vier Lieder, op.13
Weill, Kurt
- Aufstieg und Fall der Stadt Mahagonny: Alabama Song
- Berlin im Licht-Song
Weingartner, Felix
- Gottvertrauen, op.55/1

Over 10'

Corigliano, John
- The Cloisters
Finnissy, Michael
- Folk-Song Set
Franceschini, Romulus
- White Spirituals
Honegger, Arthur
- Six Poèmes d'Apollinaire, H.12: No.1: À la Santé
Ibert, Jacques
- Trois Chansons sur des Poèmes de Charles Vildrac
Ives, Charles Edward
- Five Songs
Milhaud, Darius
- Un petit peu d'exercice
Ravel, Maurice
- Trois poèmes de Stéphane Mallarmé
Schafer, Robert Murray
- Arcana
Schmitt, Florent
- Quatre poèmes de Ronsard, op.100
Schönberg, Arnold
- Sechs Orchesterlieder, op.8
Villa-Lobos, Heitor
- Canções típicas brasileiras
Volkonsky, André
- Les Plaintes de Chtchaza

MULTIPLE SOLO VOICES

Albert, Stephen
- Distant Hills; Chamber Version (S, T)
- TreeStone (S, T)

Aperghis, Georges
- B.W.V. (S, Mz, Counter T, T, 2 Bar)

Ballif, Claude
- Alma redemptoris mater, op.7, No.1 (2 S, A, CT, T, B)
- Quatre antiennes à la Sainte Vierge, op.7 (2 S, A, CT, T, Bar)

Bartók, Béla
- Three Village Scenes (four or eight female voices)

Bedford, David
- That White and Radiant Legend (S, narrator)

Boone, Charles
- Linea Meridiana (S, A, CT)

Burgan, Patrick
- Oiseau d'éternité; Five Poems for Soprano, Mezzo-Soprano and Baritone (S, Mz, Bar)

Denisov, Edison
- Die Sonne der Inkas; Cantata (S, 3 narrators)

Farkas, Ferenc
- Kalender (S, T)

Halffter, Ernesto
- Minha mäe me deu um lenço (2 voices)

Kancheli, Giya
- A Life Without Christmas: The Evening Prayers; For Chamber Orchestra and 8 Alto Singers (8 alto singers)

Milhaud, Darius
- Adages, op.120c (S, A, T, B)

Nieder, Fabio
- "das ewig liecht"; Canon cancrizans per augmentationem in contrario motu (from J. S. Bach's "Kunst der Fuge") (S, A, T, B)

Panufnik, Roxanna
- The Frog and the Nightingale (S, Mz, Bar)

Pärt, Arvo
- An den Wassern zu Babel saßen wir und weinten; Psalm 137 (S, A, T, B)

Prokofiev, Sergei
- Hamlet, op.77 (S, Bar)

Rodrigo, Joaquín
- Duérmete, Niño (S, Bar)

Russo, William
- The Golden Bird, op.77 (S, Bar, narrator)

Saariaho, Kaija
- Château de l'âme (S, A)
- The Tempest Songbook (S, Bar)

Satie, Erik
- Socrate; Drame symphonique en 3 parties (4 voices)

Schickele, Peter
- If Love Is Real (2 voices)

Tishchenko, Boris
- Symphony No.3; For soprano and baritone (or tape) and chamber orchestra (S, Bar)

Villa-Lobos, Heitor
- Suíte Sugestiva, Cinémas (S, Bar)

NARRATOR (OR SPEAKER)

Abels, Michael
- Frederick's Fables

Adolphe, Bruce
- Marita and Her Heart's Desire; A Chamber Music Fairy Tale for Family Audiences

Amy, Gilbert
- Écrits Sur Toiles; Pour Ensemble de Chambre & Voix récitée

Antheil, George
- Music to a World's Fair Film

Bacon, Ernst
- Fables for Narrator and Orchestra; Or the Secretary Bird and Associates: Studies in the Ecology of Academic Democracy

Baltakas, Vykintas
- about to drink dense clouds

Bedford, David
- That White and Radiant Legend

Braun, Yehezkel
- Apartment To Let

Britten, Benjamin
- Young Person's Guide to the Orchestra, op.34

Corigliano, John
- Creations: Two Scenes from Genesis

Danielpour, Richard
- Washington Speaks

Denisov, Edison
- Die Sonne der Inkas; Cantata

Einem, Gottfried von
- Prinz Chocolat; Musical fairytale in 5 episodes, op.66

Furrer, Beat
- Narcissus-Fragment; For 2 narrators and 26 players

Hagen, Daron
- Chimera; A song cycle for speaker and seven players

King, Alastair
- Dance Marathon ($1000 stake)

Kubik, Gail
- Gerald McBoing Boing

Lampersberg, Gerhard
- Pfeffer und Salz (Pepper and Salt)

McAlister, Clark
- A Christmas Pastorale

Poulenc, Francis
- L'histoire de Babar, le petit éléphant

Prokofiev, Sergei
- Eugene Onegin; For narrator, actors and orchestra, op.71
- Peter and the Wolf, op.67

Revueltas, Silvestre
- Hora de Junio

Rogers, Bernard
- The Musicians of Bremen

Russo, William
- The Golden Bird, op.77

Schickele, Peter
- Three Strange Cases

Schönberg, Arnold
- Ode to Napoleon

Schuller, Gunther
- Journey to the Stars

Schwantner, Joseph
- New Morning for the World; "Daybreak of Freedom"

Staud, Johannes Maria
- Die Ebene

SOLO INSTRUMENTS

VIOLIN

10' or Less

Aubert, Louis
- Caprice
Bernstein, Leonard
- Mass: Meditation No.1
Fauré, Gabriel
- Romance, op.28
Finzi, Gerald
- Introit
Foerster, Josef Bohuslav
- Ballata, op.92
Goldmark, Carl
- Ballade
Harris, Roy
- Evening Piece
Kupkovic, Ladislav
- March for Violin and Orchestra
Manén, Joan
- Caprice Nr. II, op.A-15
- Chanson et Étude, op.A-8
Milhaud, Darius
- Concertino de Printemps, op.135
Nielsen, Carl
- Romanze, op.2, No.1
Pärt, Arvo
- Darf ich…
- Fratres; For violin, strings and percussion
Pasatieri, Thomas
- Serenade for Violin and Orchestra

Rózsa, Miklós
- Nordungarische Bauernlieder und Tänze; Kleine Suite, op.5
Saint-Saëns, Camille
- Havanaise, op.83
- Morceau de concert, op.62
Schmitt, Florent
- Chanson à Bercer, op.19, No.1
Schollum, Robert
- Romanze, Werk 25
Sibelius, Jean
- Laetare Anima Mea, op.77a
- Serenata No.1 in D major, op.69a
- Serenata No.2 in G minor, op.69b
Sinding, Christian
- Abendstimmung, op.120
- Romance in D major, op.100
Sinigaglia, Leone
- Rhapsodia piemontese, op.26
Szeryng, Henryk
- Preludio Classico
Zbinden, Julien-François
- Rhapsody, op.25
Zwilich, Ellen Taaffe
- Romance

11' - 20'

Aa, Michel van der
- Imprint; for baroque orchestra
Antoniou, Theodore
- Concerto for Violin and Orchestra, op.28

Auerbach, Lera
- Concerto for Violin No.2, op.77
Bartók, Béla
- Rhapsody No.1
- Rhapsody No.2
Berio, Luciano
- Corale (su Sequenza VIII)
Blacher, Boris
- Concerto for Violin
Bolcom, William
- Concerto for Violin and Orchestra
- Concerto Serenade for Violin and String Orchestra
Burkhard, Willy
- Concerto for Violin, op.69
David, Johann Nepomuk
- Concerto for Violin No.2, Wk50
Dillon, James
- Vernal Showers
Erdmann, Dietrich
- Concerto
Haubenstock-Ramati, Roman
- Séquences
Herrmann, Peter
- Concerto for Violin and Orchestra
Hutcheson, Jere
- Concerto for Violin and Small Orchestra
Lampersberg, Gerhard
- Ahnung
Lukáš, Zdenek
- Concertino Dedicato, op.248

Lutosławski, Witold
- Chain 2 [Launch 2]; Dialogue for Violin and Orchestra
- Partita
Manén, Joan
- Caprice Nr. I, op.A-14
- Tartini-Variations; Introduction, Andante et Variazioni, op.A-2
Matthus, Siegfried
- Capriccio "Kraft-Variations"; On a Theme by Paganini
- Concerto for Violin
Milhaud, Darius
- Music for Boston
Neubert, Günter
- Concertante Suite
Poot, Marcel
- Ballade
Rangström, Ture
- Partita
Rathaus, Karol
- Suite, op.27
Reger, Max
- Two Romances
Rosenberg, Hilding Constantin
- Suite for Violin and Orchestra
Rózsa, Miklós
- Variations on a Hungarian Peasant Song, op.4
Schnittke, Alfred
- Concerto for Violin No.2
- Quasi una Sonata
Schwantner, Joseph
- Angelfire; Fantasy for Amplified Violin and Orchestra
Wilkinson, Marc
- Aliquant
Wilson, Ian
- An Angel Serves a Small Breakfast; 2. Concerto
Zilcher, Hermann
- Concerto for Violin in B minor, op.11
- Klage, op.22
Zwilich, Ellen Taaffe
- Partita

Over 20'

Atterberg, Kurt
- Concerto for Violin in E minor, op.7
Auerbach, Lera
- Concerto for Violin No.1, op.56
Barber, Samuel
- Concerto for Violin, op.14
Ballif, Claude
- Deuxième concert symphonique "Haut les Rêves!"; En homage à Gaston Bachelard, op.49, No.2

Baur, Jürg
- Concerto for Violin No.2; In form of a ballad
Ben-Haim, Paul
- Concerto for Violin and Orchestra
Bernstein, Leonard
- Serenade; After Plato's "Symposium"
Beyer, Frank Michael
- Musik der Frühe; Concerto for violin and orchestra
Boelter, Karl
- Concerto for Violin and Orchestra
Britten, Benjamin
- Concerto for Violin No.1, op.15
Bruns, Victor
- Concerto for Violin, op.36
- Concerto for Violin, op.53
Busch, Adolf
- Concerto for Violin
Corigliano, John
- The Red Violin: Suite for Violin and Orchestra
David, Johann Nepomuk
- Concerto for Violin No.1, Wk45
- Concerto for Violin No.3, Wk56
Fauré, Gabriel
- Concerto for Violin in D minor
Gál, Hans
- Concerto for Violin, op.39
Grosskopf, Erhard
- Sonata concertante 2
Hamel, Peter Michael
- Concerto for Violin in Two Movements
Harty, Hamilton
- Concerto for Violin in D minor
MacMillan, James
- A Deep but Dazzling Darkness
Manén, Joan
- Concerto da Camera Nr.2, op.A-24
- Concerto Espagnol, op.A-7
Martin, Frank
- Concerto for Violin
Martinů, Bohuslav
- Concerto for Violin and Orchestra No.1 in E
Menotti, Gian Carlo
- Concerto for Violin
Neikrug, Marc
- Concerto for Violin and Orchestra No.2
Nørgård, Per
- Concerto for Violin No.2; Borderlines
Raphael, Günter
- Concerto for Violin in C major, op.21
- Concerto for Violin No.2, op.87

Reger, Max
- Symphonic Rhapsody, op.147
Roumain, Daniel Bernard
- Voodoo Violin Concerto No.1
Saariaho, Kaija
- Graal Théâtre
Schiske, Karl
- Concerto for Violin, op.33
Schnittke, Alfred
- Sonata for Violin and Chamber Orchestra
- Concerto for Violin No.3
Sinigaglia, Leone
- Concerto for Violin in A major, op.20
Uhl, Alfred
- Kleines Konzert
Weingartner, Felix
- Concerto for Violin in G major, op.52
Zbinden, Julien-François
- Concerto for Violin, op.37
Zwilich, Ellen Taaffe
- Concerto for Violin and Orchestra

VIOLA

Bartel, Hans-Christian
- Concerto for Small Orchestra and Solo Viola
Baur, Jürg
- Concerto for Viola
Beyer, Frank Michael
- Concerto for Viola and Orchestra
Bialas, Günter
- Trauermusik
Blacher, Boris
- Concerto for Viola
Boivin, Philippe
- Concerto for Alto and Orchestra
Britten, Benjamin
- Lachrymae, op.48a
Bruns, Victor
- Concerto for Viola, op.69
Burkhard, Willy
- Concerto for Viola and Orchestra, op.93
Denisov, Edison
- Es ist genug; Variations on a Theme by J. S. Bach
Harvey, Jonathan
- Jubilus
Hindemith, Paul
- Der Schwanendreher; Concerto for Viola and Chamber Orchestra after old Folksongs
Honegger, Arthur
- Six Poèmes d'Apollinaire, H.12: No.4: Saltimbanques

Martinů, Bohuslav
- Rhapsody-Concerto; Concerto for
  Viola and Orchestra
Milhaud, Darius
- Concerto for Viola, op.108
Nørgård, Per
- Concerto for Viola No.1,
  Remembering Child
Raphael, Günter
- Concertino in D
Rosenberg, Hilding Constantin
- Concerto for Viola
Schenker, Friedrich
- Concerto for Viola
Schnittke, Alfred
- Monologue
Schroeder, Hermann
- Concerto for Viola, op.45
Sobanski, Hans Joachim
- Romantic Concerto
Wolschina, Reinhard
- Klangspiele II

CELLO

10' or Less

Bantock, Granville
- Hamabdil; Hebrew melody for
  Violoncello with Accompaniment of
  Strings, Kettledrum and Harp
Daugherty, Michael
- Jackie's Song
Grainger, Percy Aldridge
- Youthful Rapture
Hindson, Matthew
- Ictalurus Punctatus; For amplified
  cello and orchestra
Klengel, Julius
- Andante sostenuto, op.51
Krenek, Ernst
- Capriccio for Cello and Chamber
  Orchestra, op.145
Lutosławski, Witold
- Grave; Metamorphosis
MacMillan, James
- Kiss on Wood
Pärt, Arvo
- Fratres; For cello, strings and
  percussion
- Pro Et Contra; Concerto for Cello
Saint-Saëns, Camille
- Allegro appassionato, op.43
Thomas, Augusta Read
- Passion Prayers

11' - 20'

Antoniou, Theodore
- Jeux for Violoncello and String
  Orchestra, op.22
Baker, David
- Concerto for Cello
Berio, Luciano
- Ritorno Degli Snovidenia (The
  return of the dreams)
Beyer, Frank Michael
- Canto di giorno; For cello and
  orchestra
Bialas, Günter
- Concerto for Violoncello and
  Orchestra
- Concerto for Violoncello and
  Orchestra No.2
Cassadó, Gaspar
- Concerto for Cello
Cerha, Friedrich
- Phantasiestück in C.'s Manier
Crumb, David
- Variations
Engelmann, Hans Ulrich
- Concerto for Cello
Firsova, Elena
- Chamber Concerto No.2, op.26,
  Concerto for Cello No.2
- Concerto for Cello, op.10
Gubaidulina, Sofia
- Detto II; Concerto for cello and 13
  instruments
Honegger, Arthur
- Concerto for Cello and Orchestra
Jacobi, Frederick
- Concerto for Cello
Lachenmann, Helmut
- Notturno; Music for Julia
Lampersberg, Gerhard
- Verwirrung; Concerto for Cello
Prokofiev, Sergei
- Cinq Melodies (sans paroles), op.35
Rautavaara, Einojuhani
- Concerto for Cello, op.41
Rodrigo, Joaquín
- Concierto In Modo Galante
Roussel, Albert
- Concertino, op.57
Rózsa, Miklós
- Rhapsody, op.3
Saint-Saëns, Camille
- Concerto for Cello No.2, op.119
Schönberg, Arnold
- Concerto for Cello (After G. M.
  Monn)
Schuman, William
- A Song of Orpheus; Fantasy for
  Cello

Sierra, Roberto
- Cuatro Versos (Cello Concerto)
Trexler, Georg
- Concerto for Cello
Watkins, Huw
- Sonata for Cello and Eight
  Instruments
Weingartner, Felix
- Concerto in A minor, op.60
Xenakis, Iannis
- Epicycle
Yanov-Yanovsky, Dmitri
- Night Music: Voice in the Leaves
Zbinden, Julien-François
- Concerto breve, op.36
Zilcher, Hermann
- Variations on a Theme by W. A.
  Mozart, op.95

Over 20'

Atterberg, Kurt
- Concerto for Cello in C minor, op.21
Biggs, John
- Concerto for Cello and Chamber
  Orchestra
Blacher, Boris
- Concerto for Cello
Britten, Benjamin
- Symphony for Cello and Orchestra,
  op.68
Bruns, Victor
- Concerto for Cello, op.29
Dohnanyi, Ernest von
- Concert Piece in D, op.12
Erdmann, Dietrich
- Concerto
Gál, Hans
- Concerto for Cello, op.67
Hochstetter, Armin Caspar
- Concerto for Cello
Klengel, Julius
- Concerto for Cello in A minor
- Concerto for Cello in B minor
Marquez, Arturo
- Espejos en la Arena
Martin, Frank
- Concerto for Cello
Martinů, Bohuslav
- Sonata da camera for Violoncello
  and Chamber Orchestra
Osborne, Nigel
- The Art of the Fugue
Pintscher, Matthias
- La Metamorfosi di Narciso;
  Allegoria sonora per un violoncello
  principale e gruppo strumentale

Prokofiev, Sergei
- Concertino for Cello in G minor, op.132
- Concerto for Cello in E minor, op.58
- Sinfonia Concertante, op.125

Raphael, Günter
- Chamber Concerto in D minor, op.24

Rodrigo, Joaquín
- Concierto Como Un Divertimento

Schickele, Peter
- Concerto for Cello and Orchestra; In Memoriam F.D.R.

Tcherepnin, Alexander
- Three Pieces for Chamber Orchestra, op.37

Volans, Kevin
- Concerto for Cello

Weiss, Manfred
- Concerto for Cello

Wilson, Ian
- Shining Forth; Concerto for Cello

Zilcher, Hermann
- Concert Piece in One Movement, op.21

DOUBLE BASS

Bruns, Victor
- Concerto for Doublebass, op.73

Conyngham, Barry
- Concerto for Double Bass, Shadows of Noh

Kauffmann, Leo Justinus
- Concertino for Double Bass

Papandopulo, Boris
- Concerto for Doublebass

Proto, Frank
- Concerto for Double Bass and Orchestra No.3; Four scenes after Picasso
- Fantasy for Double Bass and Orchestra
- Nine Variations on Paganini; For Double Bass and orchestra

MULTIPLE STRINGS

10' or Less

Bolcom, William
- Commedia for (Almost) 18th Century Orchestra (2vn, vc)

Denisov, Edison
- Happy End (2vn, vc, db)

Harvey, Jonathan
- Hidden Voice 2 (vn, va, vc)

Reich, Steve
- Duet (2vn)

Schnittke, Alfred
- Moz-Art à la Haydn; Play on music for 2 violins, 2 small string orchestras, double bass and conductor (2vn, db)

Sørensen, Bent
- Funeral Procession (vn, va)

11' - 20'

Abels, Michael
- Delights & Dances (str 4t)

Atterberg, Kurt
- Suite pastorale in modo antico (2vn, va)

Beyer, Frank Michael
- Deutsche Tänze (German Dances) (vc, db)

Cooper, Paul
- Double Concerto (vn, va)

David, Johann Nepomuk
- Concerto for Violin and Cello, Wk68 (vn, vc)

Hamilton, Iain
- Sinfonia Concertante (vn, va)

Katz, Gil
- Tribal (vc, db)

Martinů, Bohuslav
- Concerto for 2 Violins and Orchestra (2 vn)

Neikrug, Marc
- Concerto for 2 Violins, Viola, Violoncello and Orchestra (str 4t)

Nyman, Michael
- Drowning by Numbers for Chamber Orchestra (vn, va)

Wolschina, Reinhard
- Three Novels (vn, va, vc)

Zwilich, Ellen Taaffe
- Concerto for Violin and Violoncello; Double Concerto (vn, vc)

Over 20'

Auerbach, Lera
- Fragile Solitudes; Shadowbox for String Quartet and Orchestra (str 4t)

Britten, Benjamin
- Concerto for Violin and Viola; Double Concerto (vn, va)

Halffter, Cristóbal
- Double Concerto for Violin and Viola (vn, va)

Halffter, Ernesto
- Sinfonietta (vn, vc, db)

Kaminski, Heinrich
- Dorische Musik (Dorian Music) (vn, va, vc)

Klengel, Julius
- Concerto for Violin and Cello, op.61 (vn, vc)

Krenek, Ernst
- Concerto Grosso No.2, op.25 (vn, va, vc)

Martinů, Bohuslav
- Duo concertant (2vn)

Pärt, Arvo
- Tabula Rasa; Double Concerto (2 vn)

Rózsa, Miklós
- Tema con variazioni, op.29a (vn, vc)

Schaeuble, Hans
- Music for two violins and string orchestra, op.18 (2vn)

Schnittke, Alfred
- Concerto Grosso No.1 (2vn)
- Concerto Grosso No.3 (2vn)

Schönberg, Arnold
- Concerto for String Quartet (After G. F. Händel's Concerto Grosso, op.6, No.7) (str4)

Schroeder, Hermann
- Double Concerto, op.41 (2vn)

Stravinsky, Igor
- Pulcinella: Suite (str 5t)

Weingartner, Felix
- Sinfonietta, op.83 (vn, va, vc)

PIANO
(or HARPSICHORD or ORGAN)

10' or Less

Adès, Thomas
- Concerto Conciso, op.18

Bentzon, Niels Viggo
- Brillantes Concertino: No.5 from "Divertimento for Mozart"

Busoni, Ferruccio
- Romanza e Scherzoso in F minor; Concertino Part II, op.54 (Busoni Verz. 290)
- Rondo concertante (Busoni Verz. B87)

Dean, Brett
- Etüdenfest

Górecki, Henryk Mikołaj
- Concerto for Harpsichord (or piano), op.40

Haubenstock-Ramati, Roman
- Concerto; Recitativo ed Aria for Harpsichord and Orchestra

Krenek, Ernst
- Concerto for Organ and Strings, op.230

Milhaud, Darius
- Cinq Études pour Piano et
  Orchestre, op.63
- Fantasie Pastorale, op.188
Poot, Marcel
- Musiquette
- Rondo
Rihm, Wolfgang
- Chiffre I
- Concerto for Piano
Saint-Saëns, Camille
- Africa, op.89
- Allegro appassionato, op.70
Zechlin, Ruth
- Gedanken über ein Klavierstück
  von Prokofjew

11' - 20'

Albright, William Hugh
- Gothic Suite; For organ, strings and
  percussion
Antoniou, Theodore
- Concertino for Piano, Strings and
  Percussion
Arnold, Malcolm
- Concerto for Organ and Orchestra
Bates, Mason
- Sounds for His Animation; Concerto
  for Synthesizer and Chamber
  Orchestra
Berio, Luciano
- "points on the curve to find..."
Blacher, Boris
- Concerto for Piano No.1, op.28
- Concerto for Piano No.2; In variable
  Metres
- Variations on a Theme of Muzio
  Clementi
Bolcom, William
- Orphée Sérénade
Brunner, Adolf
- Partita for Piano and Orchestra
Cage, John
- Fourteen
Carter, Elliott
- Dialogues; For piano and large
  ensemble
Erb, Donald
- Chamber Concerto
Erickson, Robert
- Concerto for Piano and 7
  Instruments
Farkas, Ferenc
- Concertino for Harpsichord and
  String Orchestra
Fauré, Gabriel
- Ballade, op.19
- Fantasie, op.111

Firsova, Elena
- Chamber Concerto No.3; For piano
  and orchestra, op.33
- Chamber Concerto No.6; The
  Temple of Mnemosyne, op.80
Furrer, Beat
- Nuun
Geiser, Walther
- Concert Piece for Organ and
  Chamber Orchestra, op.30
Goehr, Alexander
- Concert Piece, op.26
Honegger, Arthur
- Concertino for Piano and Orchestra,
  H.55
Hovhaness, Alan
- Zartik Parkim (Awake my Glory)
Kolb, Barbara
- Voyants; For piano and chamber
  orchestra
Krauze, Zygmunt
- Arabesque; For piano and chamber
  ensemble
Lukáš, Zdenek
- Vox Cordis Mei, op.293
MacMillan, James
- Cumnock Fair
Martin, Frank
- Danse de la Peur
- Concerto for Harpsichord
Martinů, Bohuslav
- Concerto for Harpsichord and Small
  Orchestra
Milhaud, Darius
- Concerto for Harpsichord and
  Orchestra, op.407
- Concerto for Two Pianos and
  Orchestra
Mundry, Isabel
- Panorama ciego
Neikrug, Marc
- Concerto for Piano
Nelson, Larry
- In Silence, In Memory
Nørgård, Per
- Rhapsody
Papandopulo, Boris
- Concerto for Harpsichord
Rasch, Kurt
- Balletsuite
Rautavaara, Einojuhani
- Concerto for Piano, op.45
Rihm, Wolfgang
- Sotto Voce 2; Capriccio
Roussel, Alber
- Concerto for Piano, op.36
Saint-Saëns, Camille
- Le carnaval des animaux; Grande
  fantasie zoologique

Schnittke, Alfred
- Concerto for Piano 4 hands and
  Chamber Orchestra
Schönherr, Max
- Concertino
- Festa Musicale
Schroeder, Hermann
- Concertino, op.42
- Concerto for Piano, op.35
Schwantner, Joseph
- Distant Runes and Incantations
Smalley, Roger
- Missa Parodia II
Strauss, Richard
- Burleske, AV 85
Studer, Hans
- Chamber Concerto
Takács, Jenö
- Tarantella, op.39
Vries, Klaas de
- Refrains
Weiner, Leo
- Concertino, op.15
Weiss, Manfred
- Concerto for Organ
Wellesz, Egon
- Concerto for Piano, op.49
Wilson, Ian
- Mutazione; Concerto for Piano
Wolschina, Reinhard
- Concerto for Piano
Xenakis, Iannis
- À l'île de Gorée
Zwilich, Ellen Taaffe
- Images
- Millennium Fantasy
- Peanuts® Gallery

Over 20'

Acker, Dieter
- Texturae II
Adler, Samuel
- Concerto No.2 for Piano and
  Orchestra
Aguila, Miguel del
- Concerto for Piano
Bialas, Günter
- Concerto lirico for Piano and
  Orchestra
Boucourechliev, André
- Concerto for Piano and Orchestra
Brandmüller, Theo
- Concerto for Organ
- Si j'etais Domenico...;
  Phantasmagorie für Streicher mit
  konzertierendem Cembalo

Britten, Benjamin
- Concerto for Piano No.1; Original
  version, op.13
Busoni, Ferruccio
- Concert Piece in D major;
  Concertino Part I, op.31a
- Indian Fantasia, op.44 (Busoni
  Verz. 264)
Cage, John
- Concerto for Prepared Piano and
  Chamber Orchestra
Casella, Alfredo
- Concerto Romano, op.43
Castelnuovo-Tedesco, Mario
- Concerto for Piano in G Major,
  op.46
Danielpour, Richard
- Metamorphosis; Piano Concerto
  No.1
David, Johann Nepomuk
- Concerto for Organ, Wk61
Eben, Petr
- Concerto for Organ No.2
Einem, Gottfried von
- Concerto for Organ, op.62
Engelmann, Hans Ulrich
- Trias
Erbse, Heimo
- Concerto for Piano, op.22
Erdmann, Dietrich
- Concerto for Piano
Falla, Manuel de
- Noches en los Jardines de España
  (Nights in the Gardens of Spain)
Ferguson, Howard
- Concerto for Piano and String
  Orchestra, op.12
Füssl, Karl Heinz
- Refrains, op.13
Gál, Hans
- Concerto for Piano, op.57
Gubaidulina, Sofia
- Introitus; Concerto for piano and
  chamber orchestra
Hasquenoph, Pierre
- Concerto da Camera
Krenek, Ernst
- Concerto for Piano No.1, op.18
- Concerto for Piano No.2, op.81
Ligeti, György
- Concerto for Piano
Lothar, Mark
- Concertino, op.79
Lukáš, Zdenek
- Concerto for Piano No.3, op.258
Matthus, Siegfried
- Concerto for Piano; Based on the
  Piano Quartet op.25 by J. Brahms

Mossolow, Alexander
- Concerto for Piano, op.14
Panufnik, Andrzej
- Metasinfonia; Symphony No.7
Pärt, Arvo
- Lamentate; Homage to Anish
  Kapoor and his sculpture "Marsyas"
Pasatieri, Thomas
- Concerto for Piano
Rodrigo, Joaquín
- Concierto heroico
Röttger, Heinz
- Concerto for Piano
Schwantner, Joseph
- Concerto for Piano
Thomas, Kurt
- Concerto for Piano, op.30
Wimberger, Gerhard
- Concerto for Piano No.2

HARP

Bialas, Günter
- Music in Two Movements for Harp
  and String Orchestra
Coolidge, Peggy Stuart
- Rhapsody for Harp
Farkas, Ferenc
- Concertino for Harp and Orchestra
Firsova, Elena
- Postlude; For harp and orchestra,
  op.18
Grandjany, Marcel
- Rhapsodie
- Deux Chansons Populaires
Hamilton, Iain
- Concerto for Harp and Small
  Orchestra
Krenek, Ernst
- Concerto for Harp and Chamber
  Orchestra, op.126
Matthus, Siegfried
- Der See; Concerto for Harp
Panufnik, Roxanna
- Powers & Dominions; Concertino
  for Harp
Pierné, Gabriel
- Concert Piece in G-flat, op.39
Ravel, Maurice
- Introduction et Allegro
Rihm, Wolfgang
- Die Stücke des Sängers
Rodrigo, Joaquín
- Concierto Serenata
Saint-Saëns, Camille
- Morceau de concert, op.154
Schmitt, Meinrad
- Concerto for Harp and Strings

GUITAR

Adler, Samuel
- Concerto for Guitar and Orchestra
Arnold, Malcolm
- Concerto for Guitar and Chamber
  Orchestra
Bennett, Richard Rodney
- Concerto for Guitar and Chamber
  Ensemble
Berio, Luciano
- Chemins V (su Sequenza XI)
Brouwer, Léo
- Concerto for Guitar No.1
- Concerto for Guitar No.4; Concierto
  de Toronto
- Retrats catalans
Castelnuovo-Tedesco, Mario
- Concerto for 2 Guitars and
  Orchestra, op.201
Corigliano, John
- Troubadours (Variations for Guitar
  and Chamber Orchestra)
Erdmann, Dietrich
- Concerto for Mandolin
Foss, Lukas
- Orpheus
Locklair, Dan
- Dayspring; Fanfare/Concertino for
  solo guitar and orchestra
Marquez, Arturo
- Danzón No.3
Schwantner, Joseph
- ...from Afar
Sierra, Roberto
- Concierto Barroco (Guitar
  Concerto)
- Danzas Concertantes (Guitar
  Concerto)
- Folias (Guitar Concerto)
- Of Discoveries
Tansman, Alexandre
- Musique de Cour; D'après les
  themes de Robert de la Visée
Villa-Lobos, Heitor
- Concerto for Guitar and Small
  Orchestra
Vlad, Roman
- Ode Super "Chrysea Phorminx"

PERCUSSION

Ali-Zadeh, Franghiz
- Silk Road; Concerto for Percussion
  and Chamber Orchestra
Aperghis, Georges
- Parenthèses; Pour Percussion Solo
  et 16 Instrumentistes

Brandmüller, Theo
- Ach, trauriger Mond; Klage um
  Federico Garcia Lorca
Colgrass, Michael
- Rhapsodic Fantasy
Corigliano, John
- Conjurer; Concerto for
  Percussionist and String Orchestra
Edwards, Ross
- Yarrageh; Nocturne
Foss, Lukas
- Concerto for Percussion and
  Chamber Orchestra
Haas, Georg Friedrich
- Wer, wenn ich schriee, hörte
  mich... (Who, if I screamed, would
  hear me...)
Haubenstock-Ramati, Roman
- Papageno's Pocket-Size Concerto:
  No.6 from "Divertimento for Mozart"
Jarre, Maurice
- Concertino: No.11 from
  "Divertimento for Mozart"
Nørgård, Per
- Bach to the Future
- For a Change
- Shaking Hands
Obst, Michael
- Shadow (...of a doubt)
Rautavaara, Einojuhani
- Incantations
Schenker, Friedrich
- Solo for a Percussionist with Small
  Orchestra
Schwertsik, Kurt
- Now you hear me, now you don't
Sotelo, Mauricio
- Chalan
Wilson, Ian
- Inquieto; Concerto for Marimba
Wolschina, Reinhard
- Klangspiele III
Xenakis, Iannis
- O-Mega
Yu, Julian
- Concerto; For Marimba and Small
  Orchestra, op.38

FLUTE

10' or Less

Antoniou, Theodore
- Katharsis; After the poem by Toula
  S. Tolia with illustrations by Kostas
  Andreou
Boulez, Pierre
- Mémoriale: (...explosante-
  fixe...Originel)

- Originel: From "...explosante-fixe..."
Burkhard, Willy
- Canzona, op.76
Corigliano, John
- Voyage; For flute and string
  orchestra
Daugherty, Michael
- Mxyzptlk: From "Metropolis
  Symphony"
Delius, Frederick
- Air and Dance
Huë, Georges Adolphe
- Fantasie
- Gigue
- Nocturne
Saint-Saëns, Camille
- Odelette, op.162
Yu, Julian
- Lyrical Concerto, op.39
Zbinden, Julien-François
- Fantasia, op.22

Over 10'

Bacri, Nicolas
- Concerto for Flute and Orchestra,
  op.63
Bartók, Béla
- Suite Paysanne Hongroise
Baur, Jürg
- Concerto da camera; Auf der Suche
  nach der verlorenen Zeit
Berio, Luciano
- Tempi Concertati
Bernstein, Leonard
- Halil; Nocturne for solo flute and
  small orchestra
Beyer, Frank Michael
- Meridian; Concerto for flute and
  string ensemble
Bjelinski, Bruno
- Concerto for Flute and Strings
Boone, Charles
- Trace
Boulez, Pierre
- Transitoire V: From "...explosante-
  fixe..."
- Transitoire VII
Braun, Yehezkel
- Et Laetitia Cordis
Bruns, Victor
- Concerto for Flute, op.51
Carter, Elliott
- Concerto for Flute
Chen, Qigang
- Un Pétale de Lumière
David, Johann Nepomuk
- Concerto for Flute

Dubois, Pierre-Max
- Concerto for Flute and Chamber
  Orchestra
Firsova, Elena
- Chamber Concerto No.1; For flute
  and strings, op.19
Hübler, Klaus K.
- Epiphyt
Ibert, Jacques
- Concerto for Flute and Orchestra
Koch, Erland von
- Concertino pastorale, op.35
Krek, Uroš
- Concertino
Müller, Sigfrid Walther
- Concerto in B-flat Major; For Flute
  and Chamber Orchestra, op.62
Osborne, Nigel
- Concerto for Flute
Poulenc, Francis
- Flute Sonata
Raphael, Günter
- Concertino, op.82
Rautavaara, Einojuhani
- Concerto for Flute; Dances with the
  winds, op.69
Rechberger, Herman
- Consort Music 1
- Consort Music 2
Rodrigo, Joaquín
- Concierto Pastoral
Saariaho, Kaija
- Aile Du Songe
Schickele, Peter
- Concerto for Flute and Orchestra
Schmitt, Florent
- Suite, op.129
Sierra, Roberto
- Concierto Caribe
Trojahn, Manfred
- Notturni trasognati
Wolschina, Reinhard
- Klangspiele I
Zender, Hans
- Concerto for Flute; Loshu 5
Zilcher, Hermann
- Concerto Piece on a Theme by W.
  A. Mozart (K.251), op.81
Zwilich, Ellen Taaffe
- Concerto for Flute and Orchestra

OBOE

Amy, Gilbert
- Jeux et formes; For Oboe and
  Chamber Ensemble
Auric, Georges
- Imaginées VI

Barlow, Wayne
- The Winter's Passed
Becker, Günther
- Concerto
Berio, Luciano
- Chemins IV (su Sequenza VII)
Beyer, Frank Michael
- Canzona di Ombra; For solo oboe and strings
- Concerto for Oboe and String Orchestra
Bolcom, William
- Spring Concertino
Britten, Benjamin
- Temporal Variations
Bruns, Victor
- Concerto, op.61
Burt, Francis
- Blind Visions
Carter, Elliott
- Concerto for Oboe; For oboe, concertino group and orchestra
- Pastoral
Chen, Qigang
- Extase
- Extase II
Cowell, Henry
- Hymn and Fuguing Tune No.10
Dittrich, Paul-Heinz
- Concerto for Oboe
Eder, Helmut
- Concerto for Oboe and Orchestra, op.35
Kennan, Kent
- Elegy
Lampersberg, Gerhard
- Music; For oboe and 13 instruments
Martinů, Bohuslav
- Concerto for Oboe and Small Orchestra, H.353
Matthus, Siegfried
- Concerto for Oboe
Milhaud, Darius
- Stanford Serenade, op.430
Ropartz, Joseph Guy Marie
- Pastorale et Danses
Schenker, Friedrich
- Concerto for Oboe
Sibelius, Jean
- Swan of Tuonela: From Lemminkäinen Suite, op.22
Stranz, Ulrich
- Déjà vu
Trexler, Georg
- Music
Zechlin, Ruth
- Concertino

CLARINET

Adler, Samuel
- Beyond the Pale; A Portrait of a Klezmer for Clarinet and String Orchestra
Aguila, Miguel del
- Concerto for Clarinet
Amrhein, Karen Amanda
- Event Horizon; For Clarinet and Orchestra
Aperghis, Georges
- Babil
Arnold, Malcolm
Concerto for Clarinet and Orchestra, op.115
Avshalomov, Jacob
- Evocations for Clarinet and Chamber Orchestra
Bacon, Ernst
- Remembering Ansel Adams
Bacri, Nicolas
- Capriccio notturno; In memoriam Carl Nielsen, op.20
Bavicchi, John
- Concerto for Clarinet and String Orchestra, op.11
Becker, Günther
- Correspondences I
Bernstein, Leonard
- Clarinet Sonata
- Prelude, Fugue and Riffs; For solo clarinet and orchestra
Boulez, Pierre
- Domaines
Braun, Yehezkel
- Concerto for Clarinet and Chamber Orchestra
Bruns, Victor
- Concerto for Clarinet, op.76
Carter, Elliott
- Concerto for Clarinet
Copland, Aaron
- Concerto for Clarinet
Cotton, Jeffery
- Concerto for Clarinet, Strings and Harp
Knight, Edward
- Concerto for Clarinet
Lindberg, Magnus
- Away
Lutosławski, Witold
- Dance Preludes; 2nd Version
Milhaud, Darius
- Concerto for Clarinet and Orchestra
Neikrug, Marc
- Concerto for Clarinet

Pierné, Gabriel
- Canzonetta for Clarinet and Orchestra
Ryden, William
- Concertino
Schollum, Robert
- Concerto Grosso, Werk 34
Schroeder, Hermann
- Concerto for Clarinet, op.47
Strauss, Richard
- Romanze in Es Dur, op.61
Xenakis, Iannis
- Échange
Zwilich, Ellen Taaffe
- Concerto for Clarinet

BASSOON

Aguila, Miguel del
- Hexen
Alonso-Crespo, Eduardo
- Concerto for Bassoon
Bondon, Jacques
- Trois images concertantes
Bruns, Victor
- Concerto for Bassoon, op.41
Daugherty, Michael
- Dead Elvis
Gubaidulina, Sofia
- Concerto for Bassoon and Low Strings
Hutcheson, Jere
- Wild Nights; Concertino for Bassoon and Mixed Ensemble
Schenker, Friedrich
- Concerto for Bassoon
Zbinden, Julien-François
- Ballad, op.33
Zwilich, Ellen Taaffe
- Concerto for Bassoon and Orchestra

SAXOPHONE

Benson, Warren
- Aeolian Song
Boutry, Roger
- Sérénade
Cowell, Henry
- Air and Scherzo
Ibert, Jacques
- Concertino da Camera
Kancheli, Giya
- A Life Without Christmas: The Night Prayers; For Soprano Saxophone, Strings and Tape
Martino, Donald
- Concerto for Alto Saxophone and Orchestra

Muldowney, Dominic
- Concerto for Saxophone
Nørgård, Per
- Pictures from Lake Arre
Raphael, Günter
- Concertino, op.71
Schulhoff, Erwin
- Hot-Sonate
Sotelo, Mauricio
- Wall of Light Red
Wilson, Ian
- Who's Afraid of Red, Yellow and
  Blue?; Concerto for Alto Saxophone

HORN

Adler, Samuel
- Concerto for Horn and Orchestra
Atterberg, Kurt
- Concerto for Horn in A minor, op.28
Boelter, Karl
- Images from Goldsmith
Bresgen, Cesar
- Concerto for Horn
Bruns, Victor
- Concerto for Horn, op.63
Dennison, Sam
- Adagio for Solo Horn and Chamber
  Symphony
Dubois, Pierre-Max
- Concerto for Horn and Chamber
  Orchestra
Dukas, Paul
- Villanelle
Firsova, Elena
- Chamber Concerto No.4; For horn
  and 13 performers, op.37
Hamilton, Iain
- Voyage
Indy, Vincent d'
- Andante
Krek, Uroš
- Concerto for Horn
Leschetitzky, Theodor
- Scherzo
Saint-Saëns, Camille
- Morceau de concert, op.94
Wolschina, Reinhard
- Three Dialogues
Zimmermann, Udo
- Nouveaux Divertissements
Zwilich, Ellen Taaffe
- Concerto for Horn and String
  Orchestra

TRUMPET

Addison, John
- Concerto for Trumpet and Strings
Asia, Daniel
- Three Movements for Trumpet and
  Orchestra
Bacri, Nicolas
- Concerto; Épisodes pour trompette
  et orchestre, op.39
Bainbridge, Simon
- For Miles
Birtwistle, Sir Harrison
- Endless Parade
Blacher, Boris
- Concerto for High Trumpet and
  String Orchestra
Boßler, Kurt
- Metamorphosen
Bruns, Victor
- Concerto for Trumpet, op.50
Herrmann, Peter
- Concerto for Trumpet and
  Orchestra
Honegger, Arthur
- Intrada
Kennan, Kent
- A Rome Dairy
Kurz, Siegfried
- Concerto for Trumpet, op.23
Matthus, Siegfried
- Concerto for Three Trumpets and
  String Orchestra; O namenlose
  Freude
- Concerto for Trumpet and String
  Orchestra
Pape, Andy
- Clarino Concerto
Pärt, Arvo
- Concerto Piccolo after B-A-C-H
Schlee, Thomas Daniel
- Concertino, op.36
Widmann, Jörg
- ad absurdum; Concerto for Trumpet

TROMBONE

Bondon, Jacques
- Chant et Danse
Bresgen, Cesar
- Concerto for Trombone
Bruun, Peter
- Twelve to Remember, Twelve to
  Come
Hartley, Walter Sinclair
- Concerto Breve for Bass Trombone
Hutcheson, Jere
- The Four Temperaments; Concerto
  for Trombone and Small Orchestra

Pärt, Arvo
- An den Wassern zu Babel saßen
  wir und weinten; Psalm 137
- Fratres; For trombone, strings and
  percussio
Zwilich, Ellen Taaffe
- Concerto for Bass Trombone

TUBA

Becker, Günther
- Un poco giocoso; Concertante
  Scenes

MULTIPLE DIVERSE SOLOISTS

10' or Less

Auerbach, Lera
- Serenade for a Melancholic Sea,
  op.68 (soli: vn, vc, pf)
Copland, Aaron
- Quiet City (soli: tpt, eh [or ob])
Crawford, Ruth
- Three Songs (soli: contralto, ob,
  perc, pf)
Klebe, Giselher
- Espressioni liriche: No.7 from
  "Divertimento for Mozart" (soli: hn,
  tpt, tbn)
Martinů, Bohuslav
- Divertimento; Serenata No.4 (soli:
  vn, va, pf)
Piazzolla, Astor
- Oblivion (soli: ob, bandoneon)
Roussel, Albert
- Aria; For Orchestra, or Divers Soli
  and Orchestra (soli: possible soli:
  voice, va, vc, fl, ob, cl)

11' - 20'

Adler, Samuel
- Time In Tempest Everywhere; For
  Soprano, Oboe and Chamber
  Orchestra
Amy, Gilbert
- Echos 13; For Horn, Trombone,
  Harp, Piano and 9 instruments
- Shin'anim Sha'ananim (soli: Mz, cl,
  vc)
Antoniou, Theodore
- Events I (soli: vn, pf)
Aperghis, Georges
- Le Reste du temps (soli: vc, cimb)
Barber, Samuel
- Capricorn Concerto (soli: fl, ob, tpt)
Baur, Jürg
- Concertino (soli: fl, ob, cl)

Berio, Luciano
- Concertino (soli: vn, cl, hp, cel)
Blacher, Boris
- Dialog (soli: fl, vn, pf)
Bruns, Victor
- Concerto for Flute and English
  Horn, op.74
Burkhard, Willy
- Concertino, op.94 (soli: 2 fl, hpsd)
Carter, Elliott
- Syringa (soli: Mz, db, gtr)
Castelnuovo-Tedesco, Mario
- Figures (soli: hpsd, vn, va, vc)
Cerha, Friedrich
- Concertino; For violin, accordion
  and chamber orchestra
Ekimovsky, Viktor
- Brandenburg Concerto for Flute,
  Oboe, Violin, Strings and
  Harpsichord
Felder, David
- Coleccion Nocturna (soli: cl/bcl, pf)
Geissler, Fritz
- Chamber Concerto (soli: fl, hpsd)
Górecki, Henryk Mikołaj
- Songs of Joy and Rhythm, op.7
  (soli: 2pf)
Gubaidulina, Sofia
- Impromptu (soli: fl, vn)
Holmboe, Vagn
- Chamber Concerto No.2 (soli: fl, vn)
Krenek, Ernst
- Double Concerto; For Violin, Piano
  and Chamber Orchestra, op.124
  (soli: vn, pf)
Kurz, Siegfried
- Chamber Concerto, op.31 (soli: fl,
  ob, cl, bn, hn)
Lindberg, Magnus
- Duo Concertante (soli: cl, vc)
Runswick, Daryl
- I Am A Donut; Dialectic II. Concerto
  Grosso for Flute, Trumpet, Bass
  Clarinet and 11 Players
Tan, Dun
- Circle with Four Trios, Conductor
  and Audience (soli: pf, perc, db,
  mand, gtr, hp)
Weill, Kurt
- Der neue Orpheus; Cantata for
  Soprano, Violin and Orchestra,
  op.16

Woolrich, John
- Cutting a Caper (soli: Solo group:
  ob, cl/bcl, tpt, vn, vc)

Over 20'

Asia, Daniel
- Songs from the Page of Swords
  (soli: Bar, ob)
Auerbach, Lera
- Dialogues on Stabat Mater (soli: vn,
  va, vib)
- Suite Concertante, op.60 (soli: vn,
  pf)
Baur, Jürg
- Sentimento del tempo (soli: ob, cl,
  bn)
Bolcom, William
- Concertante for Violin, Flute and
  Oboe
Bräutigam, Helmut
- Concerto for Flute, Oboe and
  Bassoon
Bresgen, Cesar
- Elenka (soli: balalaika, hp)
Del Tredici, David
- Syzygy (soli: S, hn)
Denisov, Edison
- Concerto for Flute and Harp
Eckhardt-Gramatté, Sophie Carmen
- Triple Concerto (soli: cl, bn, tpt)
Frazelle, Kenneth
- The Four Winds (After Mozart) (soli:
  fl, ob, bn, hn)
Gubaidulina, Sofia
- Seven Words; For cello, bayan and
  strings in 7 movements
Heiß, Hermann
- Duo-Konzert (soli: vn, pf)
Kancheli, Giya
- Diplipito (soli: vc, counter T)
Martino, Donald
- Triple Concerto (soli: cl, bcl, cbcl)
Messiaen, Olivier
- Sept Haïkaï; Esquisses japonaises
  for Piano Solo, Xylophone and
  Marimba

Schenker, Friedrich
- Triple Concerto; Overture,
  Variations and Finale on Rocco's
  Aria from Beethoven's "Fidelio" (soli:
  ob, bn, pf)
Schleiermacher, Steffen
- Keil (soli: asx/tsx/barsx)
Schwantner, Joseph
- Dreamcaller (soli: S, vn)
Sierra, Roberto
- Imágenes (Double Concerto) (soli:
  vn, gtr)
Zwilich, Ellen Taaffe
- Concerto for Piano, Violin and
  Cello; Triple Concerto

OTHER

Ali-Zadeh, Franghiz
- Mirage for Ud and Chamber
  Ensemble
Cowell, Henry
- Concerto No.1 for Koto and
  Orchestra
Grainger, Percy Aldridge
- Shepherd's Hey; British Folk Music
  Settings, No.3 (solo: concertina)
Greenwood, Jonny
- smear (soli: 2 ondes martenots)
Haas, Georg Friedrich
- "...", Double Concerto for Accordion
  and Viola
Hidalgo, Manuel
- Gran Nada (solo: accordion)
- Introduction and Fugue (solo:
  accordion)
- Nuut (solo: accordion)
Kancheli, Giya
- Kápote (soli: accordion, perc, bgtr)
Kats-Chernin, Elena
- Torque (solo: accordion)
Milhaud, Darius
- Suite; For Ondes Martenot (or
  Piano) and String Orchestra
Nørgård, Per
- Recall (solo: accordion)
Piazzolla, Astor
- Aconcagua (Concierto para
  Bandoneón)
Yu, Julian
- Ballade Concertante; For Zheng
  and String Orchestra

STRING ORCHESTRA

Only String Orchestra repertoire is listed (no solo repertoire).

STRING ORCHESTRA

5' or Less

Antheil, George
- Lithuanian Night

Berners, Lord
- Adagio, Variations and Hornpipe: From "The Triumph of Neptune"

Binkerd, Gordon
- Two Meditations for Strings

Bridge, Frank
- Rosemary

Carter, Elliott
- Sound Fields

Chávez, Carlos
- Sarabande: From "The Daughter of Colchis"

Cowell, Henry
- Hymn and Fuguing Tune No.2
- Movement

Danielpour, Richard
- Nocturne

Finzi, Gerald
- Prelude, op.25

Hartley, Walter Sinclair
- Psalm for Strings

Hindson, Matthew
- Lullaby

Honegger, Arthur
- Largo, H.105

Ives, Charles Edward
- Hymn; Largo Cantabile

Järnefelt, Armas
- Die Verlassene; Stimmungsbild nach einem finnischen Volkslied

Jenkins, Karl
- Passacaglia

Lloyd, Jonathan
- Keir's Kick

Locklair, Dan
- In Memory H. H. L.

Lutosławski, Witold
- Overture for Strings

Maxwell Davies, Peter
- Farewell to Stromness

- Vanitas; Arrangement of a fragment by Johan Ban for string orchestra

Nielsen, Carl
- At the Bier of a Young Artist, F.58

Nørgård, Per
- Adagio Di Preludio
- Four Observations; From an Infinite Rapport, Hommage a Béla Bartók
- Voyage into the Broken Screen; Hommage a Sibelius

Pierné, Gabriel
- Album Pour Mes Petites Amis (Album for My Little Friends): La Veillee de l'Ange Gardien, op.14, No.3
- Album Pour Mes Petites Amis (Album for My Little Friends): Chanson d'Autrefois, op.14, No.5
- Ballet de Cour, No.2: Passepied
- Ballet de Cour, No.5: Menuet de Roy
- Serenade, op.7

Rachmaninoff, Sergei
- Vocalise, op.34

Schickele, Peter
- Requiem

Sibelius, Jean
- Canzonetta, op.62a
- Romance in C major, op.42

Tavener, John
- Remembering Lennox through Michael

Thomson, Virgil
- Thoughts for Strings

6' - 10'

Adler, Samuel
- Concertino for Strings

Alonso-Crespo, Eduardo
- Sinfonietta for Strings

Bacewicz, Grażyna
- Symphoniette

Barber, Samuel
- Adagio for Strings
- Serenade, op.1

Bartók, Béla
- Rumanian Folk Dances

Baumann, Herbert
- Nordic Impressions; Suite for String Orchestra

Bayoras, Feliksas
- Präludium und Toccata für Streichorchester

Blacher, Boris
- Divertimento

Blackford, Richard
- Music for Carlow

Blomdahl, Karl-Birger
- Preludio and Allegro

Boyle, Rory
- Moel Bryn Divisions

Brandmüller, Theo
- Carillon joyeux

Bridge, Frank
- Two Old English Songs

Britten, Benjamin
- Prelude and Fugue, op.29

Chávez, Carlos
- Sonante

Corigliano, John
- Voyage (for String Orchestra)

Cowell, Henry
- Hymn and Fuguing Tune No.5
- Hymn, Chorale and Fuguing Tune No.8

Danielpour, Richard
- Adagietto for String Orchestra
- Swan Song

Daugherty, Michael
- Strut

Denisov, Edison
- Aquarell

Fine, Irving
- Serious Song; A Lament for String Orchestra

Finzi, Gerald
- Romance, op.11

Foulds, John
- Music-Pictures (Group IV), op.55

Geissler, Fritz
- Regiser Festmusik

Gillis, Don
- Three Sketches
Glass, Philip
- Company
Goossens, Eugene
- Miniature Fantasy for String
  Orchestra, op.2
- Pastorale, op.59
Górecki, Henryk Mikołaj
- Three Pieces in Old Style
Haas, Pavel
- Study for Strings
Harrison, Lou
- Suite No.2
Hasquenoph, Pierre
- Concertino for Strings
Herrmann, Peter
- Sonatina for String Orchestra
Hewitt, Harry
- Spoon River: Prelude and Elegy,
  op.26, No.3&4
Hindson, Matthew
- Song and Dance
Hummel, Bertold
- Drei Kleine Stücke, op.19b
Knight, Edward
- Cadillac Ranch
Koch, Erland von
- Sechs Schwedische
  Bauernmelodien; Aus Dalekarlien
Kühnl, Claus
- Vision; For 20 String Soloists
Lees, Benjamin
- Intermezzo
Lutosławski, Witold
- Five Folk Melodies
Milhaud, Darius
- Chamber Symphony No.4; Dixtuor
  à Cordes, op.74
Moeschinger, Albert
- Quatre pièces brèves
Nielsen, Carl
- Bohemian Danish Folksong, F.130
Nørgård, Per
- Fugitive Summer
- Lysning
- Out Of This World – Parting
- Pastorale: From Babette's Feast
Panufnik, Andrzej
- Jagiellonian Triptych
- Landscape
Pärt, Arvo
- Psalom
- Orient & Occident
- Silouans Song; "My soul yearns
  after the Lord…"
- Summa
Poot, Marcel
- Musique pour cordes

Prokofiev, Sergei
- Andante, op.50a
Rathaus, Karol
- Music for Strings; Adagio for
  Strings, op.49
Rautavaara, Einojuhani
- Adagio Celeste
- Epitaph for Béla Bartók
- Hommage a Ferenc Liszt
- Pelimannit (The Fiddlers)
- Suomalainen Myytti (A Finnish
  Myth)
- Three Meditations: Suite from
  "Children's Mass," op.71
Reger, Max
- Christmas, op.145, No.3
Rihm, Wolfgang
- Segmente, op.12
Rorem, Ned
- Pilgrims
Rosenberg, Hilding Constantin
- Bianca-Nera; Overture
Schickele, Peter
- Elegy for String Orchestra
Schreker, Franz
- Scherzo
Schuman, William
- Amaryllis; Variants on an Old
  English Round
Schwertsik, Kurt
- Mond-Lichtung; Eine Nacht-partie
  für Streichorchester, op.75
Sibelius, Jean
- Impromptu; On the Impromptus
  op.5/5 and 5/6
Smirnov, Dmitri
- Two Ricercares
Stranz, Ulrich
- Contrasubjekte; Passacaglia über
  B-A-C-H für Streicher
Theodorakis, Mikis
- Oedipus Tyrannos; Ode for String
  Orchestra
Thiele, Siegfried
- Trauermusik
Toovey, Andrew
- Mozart
Turina, Joaquin
- Oración del Torero, op.34
Vaughan Williams, Ralph
- English Folk Song Suite
Vir, Param
- Before Krishna
Voss, Friedrich
- Epitaph
- Tragic Overture; In memoriam D.
  Hammarskjoeld
Weiss, Manfred
- Five Pieces

Yanov-Yanovsky, Dmitri
- Message

11' - 15'

Antheil, George
- Serenade
Antoniou, Theodore
- Kinesis ABCD for two String
  Groups, op.31
Armstrong, Craig
- Slow Movement
Arnell, Richard
- Classical Variations in C
Arnold, Malcolm
- Variations on a Ukranian Folk Song,
  op.9a
Bacewicz, Grażyna
- Simfonietta
Bäck, Sven-Erik
- Sumerkei
Bates, Mason
- Icarian Rhapsody
Baur, Jürg
- Abbreviaturen
- Fresken
Bavicchi, John
- Canto I, op.96
Benjamin, Arthur
- Ballade
Bennett, Richard Rodney
- Metamorphoses
- Reflections on a 16th-Century Tune
- Reflections on a Theme of William
  Walton; For 11 solo strings
Bentzon, Jørgen
- Sinfonietta, op.41
Bentzon, Niels Viggo
- Copenhagen Concerto No.3,
  op.169
Berkeley, Lennox
- Antiphon
- Serenade for Strings
- Suite for Strings
Beyer, Frank Michael
- Passionato con Arietta
- Streicherfantasien; On a motif by
  Johann Sebastian Bach
- Versi
Blake, David
- Nocturne
Bliss, Arthur
- Two Contrasts for String Orchestra
Britten, Benjamin
- Variations on "Sellenger's Round";
  Aldeburgh Variations
Burkhard, Willy
- Toccata, op.55

Copland, Aaron
- Two Pieces
D'Alessandro, Raffaele
- Concerto Grosso, op.57
David, Johann Nepomuk
- Concerto No.2, Wk40/2
Dean, Brett
- Short Stories; Five Interludes for
  String Orchestra
Dessau, Paul
- Musik für 15 Streichinstrumente
Diamond, David
- Rounds for String Orchestra
Einem, Gottfried von
- Concertino Carintico, op.86
Elgar, Edward
- Serenade in E minor, op.20
Erdmann, Dietrich
- Serenità notturna
Fennelly, Brian
- Sigol for Strings
Geiser, Walther
- Fantasie III für Streichorchester,
  op.39
Giefer, Willy
- Concerto per archi
Golijov, Osvaldo
- Last Round
Greenbaum, Matthew
- Castelnau; For String Orchestra
Harbison, John
- Incidental Music to Shakespeare's
  "The Merchant of Venice"
Hidalgo, Manuel
- Einfache Musik
Hindson, Matthew
- Balkan Connection
Holloway, Robin
- Serenade in G, op.64a
Holmboe, Vagn
- Sinfonia 1, op.73
- Sinfonia 2, op.73
- Sinfonia 3, op.73
Holst, Gustav
- St. Paul's Suite, op.29, No.2
Juon, Paul
- Five Pieces for String Orchestra
Kats-Chernin, Elena
- Zoom and Zip
Kelterborn, Rudolf
- Kammersinfonie II
- Lamentationes
- Passions
Krek, Uroš
- Sinfonia per archi
Kulenty, Hanna
- Breathe
Laks, Simon
- Sinfonietta for Strings

Lees, Benjamin
- Interlude for String Orchestra
Lutosławski, Witold
- Musique funèbre
Maayani, Ami
- Songs of King Solomon
Martin, Frank
- Passacaille
Matthus, Siegfried
- Visionen
Milner, Anthony
- Concerto for String Orchestra
Moeschinger, Albert
- Fantasie, op.64
- Le Voyage
Moravec, Paul
- Aubade
Neubert, Günter
- Music for Strings in Three Parts
Nielsen, Carl
- Suite for Strings (Little Suite), op.1 /
  F.6
Nørgård, Per
- Metamorphose, op.4
Oldham, Arthur
- Divertimento
Panufnik, Andrzej
- Divertimento for Strings
- Old Polish Suite
Pärt, Arvo
- Trisagion
Rautavaara, Einojuhani
- Bird Gardens; Hommage a Zoltán
  Kodály
- Divertimento
- Suite for Strings
Rosenberg, Hilding Constantin
- Suite on Popular Swedish Folk
  Melodies
Schauss, Ernst
- Serenade
Schenker, Friedrich
- Little Symphony
Schultz, Wolfgang-Andreas
- Was mir die Aeolsharfe erzählt…
Schwartz, Francis
- Un Sourire Festif
Schwarz-Schilling, Reinhard
- Introduction and Fugue
Schwertsik, Kurt
- Möbelmusik-Klassisch, op.68
Sharp, Elliot
- Re/Iterations
Sheinkman, Mordechai
- Serenade
Shostakovich, Dmitri
- Two Pieces; Prelude and Scherzo,
  op.11

Stranz, Ulrich
- Sieben Feld-, Wald- und
  Wiesenstücke
Stravinsky, Igor
- Concerto in D
Strohbach, Siegfried
- Serenade in D major
Thärichen, Werner
- Divertimento, op.57
Thomas, Augusta Read
- Murmurs in the Mist of Memory
Tower, Joan
- In Memory
Treibmann, Karl Ottomar
- Symphony for 15 Strings
Voss, Friedrich
- Concerto da camera
- Fantasia
Webern, Anton
- Fünf Sätze, op.5
Weiner, Leo
- Divertimento No.2 in A minor;
  Hungarian Folk Melodies, op.24
Weiss, Manfred
- Music for Strings
Widmann, Jörg
- Ikarische Klage
Wittinger, Róbert
- Sinfonia, op.18
Wolschina, Reinhard
- Vier Aphorismen
Zimmermann, Udo
- Music for Strings
Zwilich, Ellen Taaffe
- Prologue and Variations

16' - 20'

Arutiunian, Alexander
- Sinfonietta
Bäck, Sven-Erik
- Four Motets for Strings
- Sinfonia per archi
Baird, Tadeusz
- String Quartet (Arranged for String
  Orchestra)
Bennett, Richard Rodney
- Music for Strings
Bentzon, Niels Viggo
- Concerto per archi, op.114
- Copenhagen Concerto, op.167
- Copenhagen Concerto No.2,
  op.168
- Divertimento, op.19
- Lille Suite, op.60
Beyer, Frank Michael
- Liturgia
Blacher, Boris
- Concerto for String Orchestra

Braun, Peter Michael
- Problems and Solutions
Britten, Benjamin
- Simple Symphony, op.4
Cooper, Paul
- Symphony No.3; "Lamentations"
Cowell, Henry
- Ensemble; Revised Version of
  String Quintet and Thundersticks
David, Johann Nepomuk
- Concerto No.3
- Sinfonia per archi, Wk54
Gál, Hans
- Musik, op.73
Ginastera, Alberto
- Glosses sobre temes de Pau
  Casals, op.46; For string orchestra
  and string quintet "in lontano"
Gough, Orlando
- Mungo Dances
Greenwood, Jonny
- Popcorn Superhet Receiver
Helm, Everett
- Concerto for Strings
Hindson, Matthew
- Whitewater; For 12 solo strings
Holmboe, Vagn
- Sinfonia 4, op.73
Ireland, John
- Concertino Pastorale
Jenkins, Karl
- Palladio
Koch, Erland von
- Musica intima
Kunad, Rainer
- Concerto per Archi; conatum 36
Larsson, Lars-Erik
- Sinfonietta, op.10
Manicke, Dietrich
- Musica serena
Mieg, Peter
- Concerto Veneziano
Nørgård, Per
- Tributes; Album for Strings
Ohse, Reinhard
- Serenade
Payne, Anthony
- Songs and Seascapes
Prokofiev, Sergei
- Visions fugitives, op.22
Ratner, Leonard
- Suite for Strings
Rautavaara, Einojuhani
- Canto IV
Röttger, Heinz
- Sinfonietta per archi
Shostakovich, Dmitri
- Chamber Symphony, op.110a

Sierra, Roberto
- Doce Bagatelas
Smirnov, Dmitri
- Between Scylla and Charybdis
Vivier, Claude
- Zipangu
Wolschina, Reinhard
- Wandlungen
Yun, Isang
- Colloides sonores

21' - 25'

Adams, John
- Shaker Loops
Arnold, Malcolm
- Symphony for Strings
Beyer, Frank Michael
- Griechenland; For three groups of
  strings
Blacher, Boris
- Pentagramm
Bliss, Arthur
- Music for Strings
Borges, Joaquin
- Suite Sofia
Britten, Benjamin
- Variations on a Theme of Frank
  Bridge, op.10
Cage, John
- Twenty Three
Chávez, Carlos
- Sinfonía No.5
David, Johann Nepomuk
- Concerto No.1, Wk40/1
Erdmann, Dietrich
- Divertimento
Füssl, Karl Heinz
- Szenen, op.6
Ginastera, Alberto
- Concerto per Corde, op.33
Herrmann, Peter
- Sinfonietta
Hummel, Bertold
- Symphony for Strings, op.20
Jolivet, André
- Symphonie pour cordes
Laks, Simon
- Symphony for Strings
Mommer, Hans Günter
- Concerto for Strings
Myaskovsky, Nikolai Yakovlevich
- Sinfonietta, op.32
Nørgård, Per
- Constellations, op.22
Rautavaara, Einojuhani
- Cantos
Rorem, Ned
- String Symphony

Rosenberg, Hilding Constantin
- Concerto No.1 for String Orchestra
Schnittke, Alfred
- Trio-Sonata
Schurmann, Gerard
- Sonata for String Orchestra
Sharp, Elliot
- Proof Of Erdös
Strauss, Richard
- Metamorphosen; For 23 solo strings
Thiele, Siegfried
- Übungen im Verwandeln
Zemlinsky, Alexander
- String Quartet No.4, op.25

Over 25'

Adler, Samuel
- Elegy for String Orchestra
Alwyn, William
- Sinfonietta for String Orchestra
Atterberg, Kurt
- Suite No.7, op.29
Bacewicz, Grażyna
- Symphony for String Orchestra
Bäck, Sven-Erik
- String Symphony
Bartók, Béla
- Divertimento
Brott, Alexander
- Three Astral Visions
Corigliano, John
- Symphony No.2 for String
  Orchestra
Cotton, Jeffery
- Symphony for Strings
Geissler, Fritz
- String Symphony; Symphony No.4
Glass, Philip
- Symphony No.3
Klengel, Julius
- Serenade in F major, op.24
Lutosławski, Witold
- Preludes and Fugue
Maw, Nicholas
- Life Studies; Eight studies for 15
  solo strings
Rouse, Christopher
- Concerto per Corde
Rózsa, Miklós
- Concerto, op.17
Saariaho, Kaija
- Nymphéa Reflection
Schönberg, Arnold
- Suite
- Verklärte Nacht, op.4
Shostakovich, Dmitri
- Symphony for Strings, op.118a

**STRING ORCHESTRA
with PERCUSSION and/or
HARP and/or PIANO**

10' or Less

Argento, Dominick
- Valse Triste
Bedford, David
- Piece for Mo
Bernstein, Leonard
- Mass: Two Meditations
Elgar, Edward
- Sospiri, op.70
Glass, Philip
- Runaway Horses: From "Mishima"
Heyn, Volker
- Phryh
Hindson, Matthew
- Technologic 1-2
Menotti, Gian Carlo
- Pastorale
Orbón, Julián
- Partita No.2
Panufnik, Andrzej
- Lullaby
Pärt, Arvo
- Cantus in Memory of Benjamin
  Britten
- Festina Lente
- Fratres; For strings and percussion
- Mein Weg; For 14 strings and
  percussion

Rihm, Wolfgang
- Kolchis
Schönberg, Arnold
- Notturno in A-flat Major
Thomson, Virgil
- Autumn; Concertino for Harp,
  Percussion and Strings

Over 10'

Adamo, Mark
- Alcott Music: Suite from "Little
  Women"
Apostel, Hans Erich
- Adagio, op.11
Bäck, Sven-Erik
- A Game Around A Game
Bantock, Granville
- Celtic Symphony
Bartók, Béla
- Music for Strings, Percussion and
  Celesta
Becker, Günther
- Correspondences II
Blacher, Boris
- Partita
Danielpour, Richard
- Apparitions
Erbse, Heimo
- Capriccio, op.4
Frank, Gabriela Lena
- Manchay Tiempo (Time of Fear)
Glass, Philip
- Mishima: Music from the Film
- Phaedra

Gould, Morton
- Harvest
Harvey, Jonathan
- Gong-Ring
Henze, Hans Werner
- Arien des Orpheus
Hvidtfelt Nielsen, Svend
- Singing the Dreams
Kalsons, Romualds
- Symphony for Chamber Orchestra
Kancheli, Giya
- Largo and Allegro
- Sio
MacMillan, James
- Í; A Meditation on Iona
Maros, Rudolf
- Eufonia No.1
Mirzoyan, Edvard
- Symphony for Strings and Timpani
Pärt, Arvo
- These Words…
Qu, Xiao-song
- String Symphony
Redel, Martin Christoph
- Traumtanz
Schnittke, Alfred
- Labyrinths: Ballet Suite
Sharp, Elliot
- Spring & Neap
Sibelius, Jean
- Rakastava, op.14
Volans, Kevin
- Joining Up The Dots

ENSEMBLE

All listings may include Harp, Piano, Percussion or Auxiliary Instruments.
Only Ensemble repertoire is listed (no solo repertoire).

ENSEMBLES WITH STRINGS IN 1

STRINGS SMALLER THAN [1.1.1.1.1] with
Exact String Count, **Any** Woodwinds, **Any** Brass

STRINGS EXACTLY [1.1.1.1.1] with
Exact Woodwinds and Brass

STRINGS EXACTLY [1.1.1.1.1] with
Maximum Woodwinds and Brass

ENSEMBLES WITH STRINGS IN 2

STRINGS MAXIMUM with
Any Woodwinds, **Any** Brass

EXACT & MAXIMUM INSTRUMENTATION
(for the Categories "Ensemble" and "Chamber Orchestra")

Exact (E):   Will return pieces in exactly the given instrumentation

Maximum (M):   Will return pieces in exactly the given instrumentation OR SMALLER
                        Example No.1: "1010 - 0110 - str" can also return a piece that uses 1010 - 0100 - str
                        Example No.2: "str with a maximum of [1.1.2.2.2]" can also return a piece that uses [1.0.2.1.2]
                        Maximum Searches will list the woodwind and brass count in brackets, i.e., (1111 - 1111)

STRINGS IN 1

SMALLER THAN [1.1.1.1.1] ANY WOODWINDS, ANY BRASS

Strings [0.0.0.0.1]

10' or Less

Babbitt, Milton
- All Set

Bentzon, Niels Viggo
- Two Monkton-Blues, op.127

Dillon, James
- ...Once Upon A Time

Françaix, Jean
- Onze Variations sur un Thème de Haydn

Gudmundsen-Holmgreen, Pelle
- Caravanfanfan-farefare No.1

Komorous, Rudolf
- York

Nancarrow, Conlon
- Study No.3c

Petyrek, Felix
- Arabian Suite

Rihm, Wolfgang
- Form / 2 Formen; For 20 instrumentalists in 4 groups of 5 players

Williams, Graham
- Cerberus

Over 10'

André, Mark
- Fatal

Aperghis, Georges
- Pièce pour douze, op.99

Benson, Warren
- Shadow Wood; Six Poems of Tennessee Williams

Bentzon, Niels Viggo
- Chamber Concerto for 11 Instruments, op.52

Braun, Yehezkel
- Emek Hayarden (The Yordan Valley): Ballet Suite

Bryars, Gavin
- Four Elements

Hiller, Lejaren
- Divertimento

Kancheli, Giya
- Magnum Ignotum

Montsalvatge, Xavier
- Cinco Invocaciones al Crucificado

Obst, Michael
- Nachtstücke

Riedel, Georg
- Nursery Rhymes

Surinach, Carlos
- Apasionada; Ballet for chamber orchestra

Talbot, Joby
- Animisation

Strings [0.0.0.1.1]

10' or Less

Bermel, Derek
- Hot Zone

Lang, David
- Open

León, Tania
- The Beloved

Rihm, Wolfgang
- Kolchis

Schnittke, Alfred
- Hymn IV

Talbot, Joby
- Compound Fracture

Woolrich, John
- Music from the House of Crossed Desires

Over 10'

Eisler, Hanns
- Suite for Orchestra No.2: From the music to the film *Niemandsland*, op.24
- Suite for Orchestra No.3: From the music to the film *Kuhle Wampe*, op.26
- Suite for Orchestra No.5: From the music to the film *Dans les Rules*, op.34
- Suite for Orchestra No.6: From the music to the film *Le Grand Jeu*, op.40

Loevendie, Theo
- Laps

Matthews, Colin
- Two Part Invention

Schenker, Friedrich
- Jessenin-Majakowski-Recital

Sotelo, Mauricio
- De Imaginum, Signorum, et Idearum Compositione I

Weir, Judith
- Musicians Wrestle Everywhere

Strings [0.0.1.1.0]

10' or Less

Bolcom, William
- Session I
Matsushita, Shin-ichi
- Fresque Sonore
Schleiermacher, Steffen
- Trotz Reaktion I
- Trotz Reaktion II
- Trotz Reaktion III
- Trotz Reaktion IV

Over 10'

Ballif, Claude
- Le Taille-Lyre, op.64, No.1
Berio, Luciano
- Chemins II (su Sequenza VI)
Casken, John
- Amarantos
Delás, José Luis de
- Denkbild - Kurze Schatten
Glass, Philip
- Glassworks
Maxwell Davies, Peter
- Ricercar and Doubles on "To many
  a well"
Muldowney, Dominic
- Solo / Ensemble
Musto, John
- Divertimento
Paumgartner, Bernhard
- Divertimento; 5 old-english dances
Sawer, David
- Cat's-eye
Scherchen, Tona
- Tjao-Houen
Shchedrin, Rodion
- The Frescoes of Dionysus for Nine
  Instruments
Wiegold, Peter
- The Flowers Appear on the Earth
Wyner, Yehudi
- Serenade for Seven Instruments

Strings [0.0.1.1.1]

10' or Less

Chávez, Carlos
- Energia; for Nine Instruments
Komorous, Rudolf
- Düstere Anmut
Muldowney, Dominic
- Three-Part Motet

Rihm, Wolfgang
- Bild (eine Chiffre)
- Fusées
- Nucleus
- Pol

Over 10'

Aperghis, Georges
- In extremis; Pour 8 Instrumentistes
Franke, Bernd
- Konform - Kontraform
Haas, Georg Friedrich
- "...aus freier Lust...verbunden..."
- "...Einklang freier Wesen..."
Holt, Simon
- Era Madrugada
Mochizuki, Misato
- 4 D
- Wise Water
Rihm, Wolfgang
- In Frage
- Pol - Kolchis - Nucleus
- Verborgene Formen
Rosing-Schow, Niels
- Meeting
Schenker, Friedrich
- Hades di Orfeo; Dramma per
  musica
Yun, Isang
- Kammerkonzert II (Chamber
  Concerto II)

Strings [1.0.0.0.1]

10' or Less

Hindson, Matthew
- Comin' Right Atcha; For amplified
  chamber ensemble
Müller-Wieland, Jan
- Allegria
Rihm, Wolfgang
- Music-Hall Suite
Ruders, Poul
- Nightshade
Schuller, Gunther
- Automation (Music for a real or
  imagined film score)
Stroman, Scott
- Clown Dances

Over 10'

Einfeldt, Dieter
- Apokalypse
King, Alastair
- Dance Marathon ($1000 stake)

Kubo, Mayako
- Miniatur I
Losonczy, Andor
- Phonophobie
Muldowney, Dominic
- The Earl of Essex Galliard
Nørgård, Per
- Prelude and Fugue (With a Crab
  Canon)
Ostendorf, Jens-Peter
- Septett "Geschichte Vom..."
Schulhoff, Erwin
- Suite for Chamber Orchestra
Stravinsky, Igor
- L'Histoire du Soldat (The Soldier's
  Tale): Suite
Swayne, Giles
- Into the Light

Strings [1.0.0.1.0]

10' or Less

Buck, Ole
- Aquarelles
Felder, David
- Passageways IIA
Grantham, Donald
- Fantasy on Mr. Hyde's Song
- Slobberin' Goblins
MacRae, Stuart
- The Broken Spectre (revisited)
Matsushita, Shin-ichi
- Composizione da Camera
Picker, Tobias
- The Blue Hula
Ruders, Poul
- Diferencias
Stravinsky, Igor
- Concertino for 12 Instruments
Vir, Param
- Contrapulse

Over 10'

Ballif, Claude
- Imaginaire No.1, op.41, No.1
Bennett, Richard Rodney
- Commedia III
Braun, Peter Michael
- Terms
Cage, John
- Sixteen Dances
Davis, Anthony
- Undine
- Wayang IV

Einem, Gottfried von
- Steinbeis-Serenade; Variations,
  op.61
Feldman, Morton
- For Frank O'Hara
Kitzke, Jerome
- Present Music
Layton, Billy Jim
- Divertimento, op.6
Lorentzen, Bent
- Paradiesvogel
Marthinsen, Niels
- Shadow Figures
Martinů, Bohuslav
- Tre Ricercari, H.267
Milhaud, Darius
- Musique pour Ars Nova, op.432
Musgrave, Thea
- Chamber Concerto No.2
Nørholm, Ib
- The Garden With The Paths That
  Part, op.86
Platz, Robert H. P.
- From Fear of Thunder, Dreams...
Rasmussen, Karl Aage
- A Ballad of Game and Dream
- Berio Mask
- Italian Concerto
Rodríguez, Robert Xavier
- Five Études
Sackman, Nicholas
- Corranach
Schneid, Tobias P.M.
- Umbrellas & Sewing Machines
Sharp, Elliot
- Akadak
Stockhausen, Karlheinz
- Kontra-Punkte Nr.1
Takemitsu, Tōru
- Water Ways
Xenakis, Iannis
- Atrées

Strings [1.0.0.1.1]

10' or Less

Chen, Yi
- Sparkle, Octet
Davis, Anthony
- Wayang II
Delás, José Luis de
- Cinco Sellos
Dessau, Paul
- Alice the Firefighter
- Alice's Monkey Business
Koppel, Anders
- Pogo

Muldowney, Dominic
- Double Helix
Pokorný, Petr
- Hommage a "Brundibár"; Overture
  for small orchestra
Ruders, Poul
- Greeting Concertino
Schnittke, Alfred
- 3 X 7

Over 10'

Bermel, Derek
- Three Rivers
Glass, Philip
- Book of Longing
Harvey, Jonathan
- Soleil Noir / Chitra
Hesketh, Kenneth
- Torturous Instruments
Hiller, Lejaren
- Algorithms I; For 9 Instruments and
  Tape
- Algorithms II (With Ravi Kumra) for
  9 Instruments and Tape
Huber, Nicolaus A.
- Eröffnung und Zertrümmerung
Kisielewski, Stefan
- Rencontres dans un désert
Koppel, Anders
- Partita
- Seven Scenes from Everyday Cow
  Life
Paccagnini, Angelo
- Musica da Camera
Rosenman, Leonard
- Chamber Music No.1
Satie, Erik
- Le Piège de Méduse; Sept toutes
  petites danses
Sharp, Elliot
- Ripples & Heats
Wolpe, Stefan
- Piece for Two Instrumental Units

Strings [1.0.1.1.0]

10' or Less

Becker, Günther
- Game for Nine
Bennett, Richard Rodney
- Calendar; For Chamber Ensemble
Blake, David
- Scherzo and Two Dances
Bonnet, Antoine
- La terre habitable II; Aubrac

Bruun, Peter
- Bag Den Kan Fredens Ranker Gro
  (Behind it grow the branches of
  peace)
Buck, Ole
- Landscapes IV
Burt, Francis
- Echoes
Dallapiccola, Luigi
- Piccola Musica Notturna
Dillon, James
- Zone (...de azul)
Döhl, Friedhelm
- Medeas Lied
Fundal, Karsten
- Zoom; Figure and Ground Study III
Gordon, Michael
- Love Bead
Homs, Joaquim
- Nonet; Obra encàrrec Festival
  Internacional de Música de
  Barcelona 1979
Hvidtfelt Nielsen, Svend
- Flowerfall
Ince, Kamran
- Turquoise
Ishii, Maki
- Präludium und Variationen (Prelude
  and Variations); For Nine Players
Killmayer, Wilhelm
- Führe mich, Alter, nur immer in
  deinen geschnörkelten Frühlings-
  Garten! Noch duftet und taut frisch
  und gewürzig sein Flor
Lieberson, Peter
- Raising the Gaze
Marthinsen, Niels
- A Bright Kind of High
Martinů, Bohuslav
- Nonet, H.144
Muhly, Nico
- By All Means
Muldowney, Dominic
- Variations on "Mein junges Leben
  hat ein End"
Nørgård, Per
- Snip Snap
- Without Jealousy
Primosch, James
- Five Miniatures
Saxton, Robert
- Birthday Music for Sir William Glock
Sharp, Elliot
- No Time Like The Stranger
Smolka, Martin
- Oh, My Admired C minor
Wood, Hugh
- Comus Quadrilles

Woolrich, John
- Darlington Doubles
Wyner, Yehudi
- Passage

11' - 15'

Banks, Don
- Sonata da Camera; In memoriam
  Matyas Seiber
Dazzi, Gualtiero
- Sable; In memoriam Edmond Jabès
Delás, José Luis de
- Imago
Engelmann, Hans Ulrich
- Ciacona
Erdmann, Dietrich
- Epitaph
Guy, Barry
- Bitz!
Hesketh, Kenneth
- Netsuke
Huggler, John
- Sinfonia for 13 Players, op.78
Lampersberg, Gerhard
- Symphony
Loevendie, Theo
- Back Bay Bicinium
Lorentzen, Bent
- Zauberspiegel
Lutyens, Elisabeth
- Six Tempi for 10 Instruments
Martland, Steve
- Remembering Lennon
Mason, Benedict
- The Hinterstoisser Traverse
Matthews, Colin
- A Voice to Wake
McKinley, William Thomas
- Paintings No.6 (To hear the light
  dancing)
Mochizuki, Misato
- Chimera
Muldowney, Dominic
- Entr'acte
Musgrave, Thea
- Chamber Concerto No.1
Primosch, James
- Septet
Redel, Martin Christoph
- Dispersion, op.16
Rosing-Schow, Niels
- Equinoxe
Saxton, Robert
- Canzona; In memoriam Igor
  Stravinsky
- Processions and Dances
Sharp, Elliot
- Dark Matters

Silverman, Stanley
- Planh; For chamber ensemble
Wilson, Ian
- ...and flowers fall...

Over 15'

Berkeley, Lennox
- Diversions for Eight Instruments,
  op.63
Birkenkötter, Jörg
- Schwebende Form
Blake, David
- Seasonal Variants
Boulez, Pierre
- Dérive 2 (Work in progress)
Brandmüller, Theo
- Missa Morgenstern
Brødsgaard, Anders
- Ghostorchestra
Brown, Earle
- Centering
Buck, Ole
- Landscapes I
- Landscapes II
- Landscapes III
Burgon, Geoffrey
- Goldberg's Dream (Running
  Figures)
Cordero, Roque
- Dodecaconcerto
Denisov, Edison
- Chamber Symphony
Einfeldt, Dieter
- Sinfonia da Camera
Feldman, Morton
- Samuel Beckett, Words & Music
Fuchs, Kenneth
- Face of the Night (After a Painting
  by Robert Motherwell)
Furrer, Beat
- Gaspra
Halffter, Cristóbal
- Antiphonismoi
Harvey, Jonathan
- Inner Light 1
Hoyland, Vic
- Andacht zum Kleinen
Lang, David
- Child
Levi, Paul Alan
- Elegy and Recreations
Marthinsen, Niels
- Cupid and Death
Musgrave, Thea
- Lamenting with Ariadne
Neikrug, Marc
- Concertino

Nordentoft, Anders
- Hymne
Nørgård, Per
- Scintillation
Osborne, Nigel
- Wildlife
Payne, Anthony
- The Stones and Lonely Places Sing
Rochberg, George
- Chamber Symphony for 9
  Instruments
Saariaho, Kaija
- Aer: Part 7 of "Maa"
Sawer, David
- Take Off
Schwehr, Cornelius
- Aber die Schönheit des Gitters
Watkins, Michael Blake
- Concertante
Wilson, Ian
- A City Called Heaven

Strings [1.0.1.1.1]

10' or Less

Anderson, Julian
- Tiramisu
Babbitt, Milton
- Composition for 12 Instruments
Czernowin, Chaya
- Afatsim
Gürsching, Albrecht
- Drei Plus Vier
Hibbard, William
- Stabiles for 13 Instruments
Jekimowski, Viktor
- Chamber Variations for 13 Players,
  op.15
Kirchner, Leon
- Music for Twelve
Lang, David
- Spud
Lutosławski, Witold
- Bucolics
- Dance Preludes
- Slides; For 11 Soloists
Matthews, Colin
- L, bent
Milhaud, Darius
- Chamber Symphony No.2;
  Pastorale, op.49
- Chamber Symphony No.3;
  Sérénade, op.71
Nancarrow, Conlon
- Study No.9
Paz, Juan Carlos
- Obertura Para Doce Instrumentos
  (Overture for 12 Instruments)

Poulenc, Francis
- Mouvements perpétuels for nine instruments

Rihm, Wolfgang
- Gedrängte Form

Schaathun, Asbjørn
- "S"

Schönberg, Arnold
- Six Little Piano Pieces, op.19

Tanaka, Karen
- Water and Stone

Vostřák, Zbyněk
- Tao, op.41

Webern, Anton
- Fünf Stücke, op.10

Wilson, Richard
- Fantasy and Variations

Wolpe, Stefan
- Chamber Piece No.2

Woolrich, John
- Caprichos
- From the Shadow

Xenakis, Iannis
- Kaï

Ye, Xiaogang
- Nine Horses, op.19

11' - 15'

Anderson, Allen
- Charrette

Banks, Don
- Equation I and II

Bawden, Rupert
- The Donkey Dances

Bentzon, Niels Viggo
- Sonata for 12 Instruments, op.257

Bonnet, Antoine
- La terre habitable IV; La presqu'île

Cassuto, Alvaro
- Song of Loneliness

Dobbins, Lori
- Music for Chamber Orchestra

Erdmann, Dietrich
- Musica Multicolore
- Nuancen

Fontyn, Jacqueline
- Nonetto

Gubaidulina, Sofia
- Concordanza

Gürsching, Albrecht
- Piccola Sinfonia; Septett Nr.2

Harbison, John
- Confinement

Hesketh, Kenneth
- Three Movements from "Theatrum"

Hidalgo, Manuel
- L'Obvio

- Nahezu Stilles Auge des Wirbelsturms

Holt, Simon
- Lilith

Horváth, Josef Maria
- Origines

Kahowez, Günther
- Bardo-Puls; Musik nach dem tibetanischen Totenbuch

León, Tania
- Hechizos

Milhaud, Darius
- Musique pour Graz, op.429

Müller-Wieland, Jan
- Narrativo e Sonnambulo
- Der Revolutionsplatz

Mykietyn, Paweł
- Eine Kleine Herbstmusik (A Little Autumn Music)

Nono, Luigi
- Canti Per 13

Osborne, Nigel
- Fantasia

Patterson, Paul
- At the Still Point of the Turning World, op.41

Powell, Mel
- Modules; An Intermezzo for Chamber Orchestra

Satie, Erik
- Sports et Divertissements

Schubert, Manfred
- Septet in Two Movements

Schuller, Gunther
- Chimeric Images

Spratlan, Lewis
- Diary Music I

Stahmer, Klaus Hinrich
- Dans Une Lumière Eclatante

Torke, Michael
- Adjustable Wrench

Webern, Anton
- Passacaglia, op.1

Xenakis, Iannis
- Phlegra

Over 15'

Amy, Gilbert
- La Variation Ajoutée; Pour 17 Instruments & Bande Électroacoustique

Aperghis, Georges
- Von Zeit zu Zeit; Pour 16 Instrumentistes

Bawden, Rupert
- The Angel and the Ship of Souls

Bennett, Richard Rodney
- Dream Dancing

Beyer, Frank Michael
- Musikalisches Opfer; Ricercare a 3, Fuga canonica & 9 Kanons

Birkenkötter, Jörg
- Klaenge Schatten

Bolcom, William
- Octet

Braun, Peter Michael
- Quanta

Butting, Max
- Sinfonietta mit Banjo; 1. Rundfunkmusik, op.37

Conyngham, Barry
- Dwellings

Dalby, Martin
- Chamber Symphony (O Bella e Vaga Aurora)

Dittrich, Paul-Heinz
- Concert Avec Plusieurs Instruments No.1

Einfeldt, Dieter
- Mobiles

Ferrari, Luc
- Entrée; For 15 instruments

Frankel, Benjamin
- Catalogue of Incidents

Furrer, Beat
- Studie 2; A un moment de terre perdue

Giefer, Willy
- Pro - Kontra

Gilbert, Anthony
- Crow-Cry

Guy, Barry
- Play

Hesketh, Kenneth
- The Circling Canopy of Night
- Theatrum

Hölszky, Adriana
- Tragoedia (Der unsichtbare Raum)

Huber, Nicolaus A.
- Hölderlin in Darkness: A Dedication
- Six Bagatelles

Jaroch, Jiří
- II. Nonet

Kagel, Mauricio
- Finale mit Kammerensemble

Korndorf, Nikolai
- Confessiones; Chamber Symphony for 14 Instruments

Krebs, Joachim
- Slow-Mobile

Lieberson, Peter
- Lalita; Chamber Variations

Martinů, Bohuslav
- Nonet No.2

Matsushita, Shin-ichi
- Correlaziono per 3 Gruppi
Melby, John
- Wind, Sand and Stars
Musgrave, Thea
- Space Play
Nelson, Larry
- Loose Leaves
Obst, Michael
- Nosferatu
Osborne, Nigel
- Prelude and Fugue
Platz, Robert H. P.
- PIECE NOIRE
Rihm, Wolfgang
- Sphäre um Sphäre
Rosenman, Leonard
- Chamber Music No.2
Rota, Nino
- Cristallo di Rocca
Ruders, Poul
- Abysm
Schenker, Friedrich
- Gute Behandlung der Pferde
Scherchen, Tona
- L'Invitation au voyage
Searle, Humphrey
- Three Songs of Jocelyn Brooke,
  op.25b
Smolka, Martin
- Rain, A Window, Roofs, Chimneys,
  Pigeons And So
Widmann, Jörg
- ...umdüstert...
Wolpe, Michael
- Caprisma 2
Woolrich, John
- Suite from Bitter Fruit
Yanov-Yanovsky, Dmitri
- Chamber Music for Twelve
  Musicians

Strings [1.1.1.1.0]

10' or Less

Bedford, David
- Trona For 12
Brown, Earle
- Novara
Buck, Ole
- Chamber Music I
- Chamber Music II
Debussy, Claude
- Deux Arabesques
Fundal, Karsten
- Hoquetus
Górecki, Henryk Mikołaj
- Concerto

Imbrie, Andrew
- Dandelion Wine
Lutosławski, Witold
- Dance Preludes; 3rd Version
Mansurian, Tigran
- Da Ich Nicht Hoffe für 14
  Instrumentalisten (In memoriam Igor
  Stravinsky)
Milhaud, Darius
- Chamber Symphony No.1; Le
  Printemps, op.43
Nordentoft, Anders
- Zenerva Sesio
Orbón, Julián
- Partita No.2
Revueltas, Silvestre
- Batik
Staud, Johannes Maria
- Configurations / Reflet
Stravinsky, Igor
- Ragtime
Talbot, Joby
- Arbor Low
Terzakis, Dimitri
- Hommage à Morse

11' - 15'

Ali-Zadeh, Franghiz
- Dilogie II for Nine Players
Ballif, Claude
- La musique d'Erich Zahn
Becker, Günther
- Correspondences II
Birtwistle, Sir Harrison
- Tragoedia
Boccadoro, Carlo
- Ae Fond Kiss; For 7 instruments
Denisov, Edison
- Femme et Oiseaux
Döhl, Friedhelm
- Octet (Varianti)
Engelmann, Hans Ulrich
- Sinfonia da Camera
Firsova, Elena
- Music for Twelve
Fuchs, Kenneth
- Out of the Dark (After Three
  Paintings by Helen Frankenthaler)
Halffter, Rodolfo
- Divertimento Para Nueve
  Instrumentos
Harvey, Jonathan
- Valley of Aosta
Haubenstock-Ramati, Roman
- Séquences 2
Hauer, Josef Matthias
- 1. Tanzsuite, op.70

Indy, Vincent d'
- Suite dans le style ancien, op.24
Kallstenius, Edvin
- Suite for 9 Instruments, op.23b
Knussen, Oliver
- Processionals, op.2
León, Tania
- sin normas ajenas
Lord, David
- Septet
Matsushita, Shin-ichi
- Haleines Astrals
Matthus, Siegfried
- Octet on an Octet
Morthenson, Jan Wilhelm
- Labor
Mundry, Isabel
- Le Silence; Tystnaden
Müller-Siemens, Detlev
- Pavane
Payne, Anthony
- A Sea Change
Pernes, Thomas
- Gesänge
Pousseur, Henri
- Symphonies à Quinze Solistes
Samazeuilh, Gustave
- Divertissement et Musette
Szalonek, Witold
- Connections
Sørensen, Bent
- Sirenengesang
Wallin, Rolf
- Solve et Coagula

Over 15'

Bawden, Rupert
- Ultima Scena
- Wanderjahr
Bergman, Erik
- Silence and Eruptions, op.91
Cage, John
- Ten
- Thirteen
Chávez, Carlos
- Suite for Double Quartet
Goehr, Alexander
- Idées Fixes; Sonata for 13, op.63
Harvey, Jonathan
- Smiling Immortal
Hauer, Josef Matthias
- 2. Tanzsuite, op.71
Heath, Dave
- Forest
Hurd, Michael
- Captain Coram's Kids
Husa, Karel
- Cayuga Lake (Memories)

Imbrie, Andrew
- Spring Fever
Korngold, Erich Wolfgang
- Suite from the Music to
  Shakespeare's "Much Ado About
  Nothing," op.11
Martland, Steve
- American Invention
Milhaud, Darius
- Protée, op.17
Schifrin, Lalo
- Variants on a Madrigal by Gesualdo
Schleiermacher, Steffen
- Zeit Verschiebung
Stöhr, Richard
- Kammersymphonie, op.32

Other Combinations of Strings Smaller Than [1.1.1.1.1]

10' or Less

Arnold, Malcolm
- Trevelyan Suite, op.96 [0.0.0.1.0]
Bruun, Peter
- Himmel og Jord (Heaven and Earth)
  [0.0.1.0.1]
Chávez, Carlos
- Cantos de México [2.0.0.0.0]
Chou, Wen-Chung
- Yu ko [1.0.0.0.0]
Cordero, Roque
- Permutaciones 7 [1.0.1.0.1]
Frounberg, Ivar
- En Vue de Roesnaes [0.0.1.0.0]
Gutchë, Gene
- Rondo capriccioso, op.21 [0.0.1.0.1]
Harle, John
- Cinéma (René Clair's "Entr'acte")
  [1.0.1.0.1]
Martinů, Bohuslav
- Jazz Suite, H.172 [1.1.1.0.0]
Nancarrow, Conlon
- Study No.16 [0.0.0.1.0]
Revueltas, Silvestre
- Colorines [1.1.0.0.1]
- Homenaje a Federico Garccía
  Lorca [1.1.0.0.1]
- Ocho Por Radio; Eight Musicians
  Broadcasting [1.1.0.1.1]
- Sensemayá (for chamber
  ensemble) [1.1.0.0.1]
Rihm, Wolfgang
- Chiffre IV [0.0.0.1.0]
Webern, Anton
- Konzert; Anton Schönberg zum 60.
  Geburtstag, op.24 [1.0.1.0.0]

Wellesz, Egon
- Pastorale [1.1.0.1.1]
Wittinger, Róbert
- Compensazioni, op.9 [1.0.1.0.0]
Wyner, Yehudi
- Amadeus' Billiard [1.0.1.0.1]

Over 10'

Ardevol, José
- Concerto Grosso No.2 [1.1.0.1.0]
Bryars, Gavin
- Aus den Letzten Tagen [1.1.0.1.0]
Burkhard, Willy
- Serenade, op.77 [1.0.1.0.1]
Cerha, Friedrich
- Quellen [1.1.0.0.0]
Dickinson, Peter
- Juilliard Dances [0.0.0.1.0]
Gordon, Michael
- Who by Water [1.1.0.1.1]
Hagen, Daron
- Chimera; A song cycle for speaker
  and seven players [1.0.0.0.0]
Leyendecker, Ulrich
- Jiddische Rumba [0.0.0.1.0]
Lieberson, Peter
- Accordance for 8 Instruments
  [0.0.1.0.1]
Lorentzen, Bent
- Paesaggio [1.0.1.0.0]
Milhaud, Darius
- La creation du monde; Ballet,
  op.81a [1.1.0.1.1]
Oliver, Stephen
- Nicholas Nickelby (incidental music)
  [1.1.0.0.1]
Pauels, Heinz
- Capriccio; For piano, five solo
  instruments and percussion, op.92b
  [0.0.1.0.0]
Qu, Xiao-song
- Ji No.1 [1.0.1.0.1]
Runswick, Daryl
- Songs of Love and Farewell
  [1.0.0.0.0]
Saariaho, Kaija
- Solar [1.0.1.0.1]
Schweitzer, Benjamin
- unplugged. unperfumed [0.0.1.0.1]
Sharp, Elliot
- Evolute [0.0.1.0.1]
- Polymerae [1.0.1.0.0]
Smolka, Martin
- Solitudo [0.0.0.1.0]
Toch, Ernst
- Fünf Stücke (Five Pieces), op.33
  [1.0.1.0.1]

Wilson, Richard
- Contentions [0.0.1.0.1]
Yuasa, Joji
- Projection for Seven Players
  [0.0.0.1.0]

STRINGS [1.1.1.1.1]

1111 - 0000 - str[1.1.1.1.1]
Exact Winds, Exact Strings

Boone, Charles
- San Zeno / Verona
Kelemen, Milko
- Nonett
Komarova, Tatjana
- Sonnenuntergänge auf B 612
  (Sunsets on B 612)
Krenek, Ernst
- Symphonische Musik für 9
  Soloinstrumente, op.11
Marsh, Roger
- Dying for It
Nordheim, Arne
- Tractatus
Piston, Walter
- Divertimento
Prokofiev, Sergei
- March in B-flat Major, op.99
- Peter and the Wolf, op.67 (arr.
  Schmidinger)
Stürmer, Bruno
- Suite für Neun Solo-Instrumente,
  op.9

1111 - 1000 - str[1.1.1.1.1]
Exact Winds, Exact Strings

10' or Less

Boccadoro, Carlo
- Adagio
Brødsgaard, Anders
- Magam
Davico, Vincenzo
- Poemetti Pastorali
Griffes, Charles Tomlinson
- Three Tone Pictures
MacRae, Stuart
- The Broken Spectre
Nordentoft, Anders
- The City of Threads
Pärt, Arvo
- Fratres; For chamber ensemble
Rihm, Wolfgang
- abgewandt 1

Schönberg, Arnold
- Das Wappenschild, op.8/2
Sørensen, Bent
- Clairobscur
Vries, Klaas de
- Bewegingen (Movements)

Over 10'

Apostel, Hans Erich
- Kammersymphonie (Chamber
  Symphony), op.41
Bennett, Richard Rodney
- A Book of Hours
Bon, André
- Travelling
Boyle, Rory
- Night Pictures
Britten, Benjamin
- Sinfonietta, op.1
Davis, Anthony
- Litany of Sins
Frankel, Benjamin
- Bagatelles "Cinque Pezzi Notturni"
Gudmundsen-Holmgreen, Pelle
- Nær og Fjern (Near and Distant)
Harvey, Jonathan
- Tendril
Hasquenoph, Pierre
- Variations Pour 14
Holt, Simon
- Kites
Kahn, Erich Itor
- Actus Tragicus
Koppel, Anders
- Concertino for Chamber Ensemble
Lorentzen, Bent
- Wunderblumen
Matthews, Colin
- Suns Dance
Milhaud, Darius
- Concert de chambre, op.389
Müller-Siemens, Detlev
- Refuge
Pape, Andy
- Min Fynske Barndom: Suite
Reimann, Aribert
- Metamorphosen über ein Menuett
  von Franz Schubert
Searle, Humphrey
- Variations and Finale, op.34
Sekles, Bernhard
- Serenade for 11 Solo Instruments,
  op.14
Sørensen, Bent
- Shadowland
Taylor, Deems
- The Portrait of a Lady, op.14

Treibmann, Karl Ottomar
- Second Symphonic Essay; For ten
  instruments
Wolf-Ferrari, Ermanno
- Chamber Symphony, op.8

**1111 - 1110 - str[1.1.1.1.1]
Exact Winds, Exact Strings**

10' or Less

Benjamin, George
- Fanfare for Aquarius
Bose, Hans-Jürgen von
- Concertino Per Il H. W. H.
Cowell, Henry
- Polyphonica; For 12 Instruments or
  Chamber Orchestra
Denisov, Edison
- Epitaph
Françaix, Jean
- Sérénade
Hindson, Matthew
- Comin' Right Atcha
Lindberg, Magnus
- Counter Phrases
Lutosławski, Witold
- Chain 1 [Launch 1]
MacRae, Stuart
- The Witch's Kiss
Mansurian, Tigran
- Tovem for 15 Instruments
Marthinsen, Niels
- A Miniature
Matthews, Colin
- Elegia: No.2 of "Two Tributes"
Osborne, Nigel
- Eulogy
Schnittke, Alfred
- Polyphonic Tango
Schönberg, Arnold
- Four Pieces
Smirnov, Dmitri
- Elegie In Memoriam Edison
  Denissow for 16 Players, op.97b
Swayne, Giles
- PP, op.46
Takemitsu, Tōru
- Rain Coming
Tanaka, Karen
- Echo Canyon

Over 10'

Abrahamsen, Hans
- Märchenbilder
Adès, Thomas
- Living Toys, op.9

Anderson, Julian
- Alhambra Fantasy
- Khorovod
Anderson, T.J.
- Chamber Symphony
Bates, Mason
- Omnivorous Furniture
Benjamin, George
- At First Light
Bermel, Derek
- Natural Selection
Beyer, Frank Michael
- Architettura per musica
Birtwistle, Sir Harrison
- Carmen Arcadiae Perpetuum
- Secret Theatre
- Silbury Air
Buck, Ole
- Flower Ornament Music
Casken, John
- Vaganza
Chapple, Brian
- Venus Fly Trap
Denhoff, Michael
- Einsamkeit; In memoriam W.
  Buchebner
Denisov, Edison
- Chamber Symphony No.2
Ferrari, Luc
- Flashes; For 14 instruments
Górecki, Henryk Mikołaj
- Kleines Requiem für eine Polka,
  op.66
Hamilton, Iain
- The Alexandrian Sequence
Harvey, Jonathan
- Wheel of Emptiness
Henze, Hans Werner
- Chamber Concerto 05
Hindson, Matthew
- Technologic 145
Huber, Nicolaus A.
- Air mit Sphinxes
- Music on Canvas
- Rose Selavy
Ichiyanagi, Toshi
- Symphony No.1; Time Current
Lang, David
- increase
Lindberg, Magnus
- Coyote Blue
Lobanov, Vasily
- Sinfonietta for Chamber Orchestra,
  op.47
Malipiero, Gian Francesco
- Endecatode; For 14 instruments
  and percussion
Marthinsen, Niels
- Chimes at Midnight

Matthews, Colin
- Contraflow
Maxwell Davies, Peter
- Crossing Kings Reach
- De Assumtione Beatae Mariae
  Virginis
Muldowney, Dominic
- Sinfonietta
Müller-Siemens, Detlev
- Phoenix 1
- Phoenix 2
- Phoenix 3
Nordentoft, Anders
- Entgegen
Nørgård, Per
- Night-Symphonies; Day Breaks
Osborne, Nigel
- In Camera
- Stone Garden
- Zansa
Pade, Steen
- Sinfonietta
Pavlenko, Sergei
- Symphony No.3 for Chamber
  Orchestra (For the Centenary of
  Igor Stravinsky)
Phibbs, Joseph
- Cayuga
Rasmussen, Karl Aage
- Movements on a Moving Line
Reimann, Aribert
- Invenzioni
Rihm, Wolfgang
- Chiffre II; Silence to be beaten
Ruders, Poul
- Four Dances in One Movement
Satie, Erik
- Mercure; Poses plastiques, op.post
Saxton, Robert
- Chamber Symphony; The Circles of
  Light
Schnittke, Alfred
- Little Tragedies: Suite from the
  music to the film
Shchedrin, Rodion
- The Geometry of Sound
Sierra, Roberto
- Concertino
- Cuentos
Smirnov, Dmitri
- Jacob's Ladder, op.58
- The River of Life, op.66
Sørensen, Bent
- Minnelieder - Zweites Minnewater
Szymanski, Pawel
- Quasi una Sinfonietta
Vir, Param
- Hayagriva

Watkins, Huw
- Rondo
Watkins, Michael Blake
- Sinfonietta
Weir, Judith
- Tiger under the Table
Woolrich, John
- After the Clock
- Lending Wings
Xenakis, Iannis
- Thalleïn

0011 - 1110 - str[1.1.1.1.1]
Maximum Winds, Exact Strings

Dalby, Martin
- De Patre Ex Filio (0011-1000)
Denhoff, Michael
- O Orpheus singt (0011-1000)
Eberhard, Dennis
- Endgame (0011-1000)
Henze, Hans Werner
- Four Fantasies from "Kammermusik
  1958 and Adagio 1963" (0011-1000)
Joubert, John
- Octet, op.33 (0011-1000)
Matthus, Siegfried
- Ich komm einen Weg (0011-1000)
Rihm, Wolfgang
- abgewandt 2; Musik in memoriam
  Luigi Nono (3. Versuch) (0011-
  1110)
- Chiffre VI (0011-1000)
Rodríguez, Robert Xavier
- A Midsummer Night's Dream;
  Incidental Music (0010-1100)
Scherchen, Tona
- Bien (0010-1110)
Schubert, Manfred
- Nachtstück und Passacaglia (0011-
  1000)
Smolka, Martin
- Octet (0011-1000)
Talbot, Joby
- Minus 1500 (0001-0000)
Xenakis, Iannis
- Anaktoria (0011-1000)

1111 - 1111 - str[1.1.1.1.1]
Maximum Winds, Exact Strings

10' or Less

Bermel, Derek
- Continental Divide (1111-1111)
Del Tredici, David
- Acrostic Song (1010-0100)

Goehr, Alexander
- ...kein Gedanke, nur ruhiger Schlaf;
  In memoriam Olivier Messiaen,
  op.65 (1110-1100)
Gordon, Michael
- Acid Rain (1010-0000)
Hvidtfelt Nielsen, Svend
- Impromptu (1010-1000)
Kozinski, Stefan
- The Maloney Rag (1111-1111)
Laufer, Kenneth
- The Twelve-Note Rag (1111-1111)
León, Tania
- Indigena (1111-1100)
Sørensen, Bent
- The Weeping White Room (1010-
  0000)

Over 10'

Aa, Michel van der
- Above; for ensemble and
  soundtrack (1111-0100)
Adolphe, Bruce
- Marita and Her Heart's Desire; A
  Chamber Music Fairy Tale for
  Family Audiences (1111-0010)
Aguila, Miguel del
- A Conga Line in Hell, op.43 (1111-
  1111)
Bacewicz, Grażyna
- Contradizione (1111-1100)
Ballif, Claude
- Suite Dracoula (1100-1010)
Bentzon, Niels Viggo
- Sinfonia da Camera, op.139 (1111-
  1111)
Buck, Ole
- A Tree (1111-1100)
Dalby, Martin
- Man Walking; Serenade for Octet
  (0101-1000)
Debussy, Claude
- Petite suite (1111-1100)
Erbse, Heimo
- For String and Wind Players (0111-
  1000)
Genzmer, Harald
- Capriccio für Kammerorchester
  (Nonett) (0111-1000)
Hayden, Sam
- Collateral Damage (1011-0111)
Hindemith, Paul
- Der Dämon: Konzertsuite aus der
  Tanzpantomime (1010-1100)
- Kammermusik No.1 (with Finale
  1921), op.24, No.1 (1011-0100)
Hosokawa, Toshio
- Landscape VI (1111-1100)

Hvidtfelt Nielsen, Svend
- Movements (1111-1100)
Jelinek, Hanns
- Prelude, Passacaglia and Fugue, op.4 (1011-1000)
Kernis, Aaron Jay
- Invisible Mosaic II (1111-1111)
Laderman, Ezra
- Nonet of the Night (1010-0000)
Lindberg, Magnus
- Corrente; China Version (1110-0010)
Mason, Benedict
- Imposing a Regular Pattern in Chaos and Heterophony (1110-0100)
Milhaud, Darius
- Jeux de Printemps, op.243 (1011-0100)
Moravec, Paul
- Northern Lights Electric (1010-0000)
Nancarrow, Conlon
- Three Movements (1110-1110)
Nørgård, Per
- Amled; Prince of Jutland (1111-1100)
Saariaho, Kaija
- Lichtbogen (1000-0000)
Schnittke, Alfred
- Music for Piano and Chamber Orchestra (1110-1100)
Sotelo, Mauricio
- Wall of Light Black (1111-1111)
Szymanski, Pawel
- Through the Looking Glass I (1110-1000)
Webern, Anton
- Sechs Stücke, op.6 (1110-0000)
Xenakis, Iannis
- Palimpsest (0111-1000)
- Waarg (1111-1111)
Ye, Xiaogang
- Strophe (1110-1110)

1111 - 2111 - str[1.1.1.1.1]
Maximum Winds, Exact Strings

Harneit, Johannes
- Ohne Leben Tod (Without Life Death), op.23 (1111-2000)
Holmboe, Vagn
- Prelude to a Dolphin, op.166 (1111-2100)
- Prelude to a Living Stone, op.172 (1111-2100)
- Prelude to a Maple Tree, op.168 (1111-2100)
- Prelude to a Pine Tree (1111-2100)

- Prelude to a Willow Tree (1111-2100)
- Prelude to the Calm Sea, op.187 (1111-2100)
- Prelude to the Pollution of Nature (1111-2100)
Ligeti, György
- Melodien (1111-2111)
Lindberg, Magnus
- Arena II (1111-2110)
- Corrente (1111-2110)
- Engine (1111-2110)
- Jubilees (1111-2110)
Roslavets, Nikolai Andreyevich
- Chamber Symphony (1111-2110)
Wallin, Rolf
- Boyl (1111-2110)
Wilby, Philip
- An Imagined Fable (1111-2110)
Woolrich, John
- Stealing a March (1111-2110)

1121 - 2221 - str[1.1.1.1.1]
Maximum Winds, Exact Strings

10' or Less

Brown, Earle
- Available Forms I (1120-1110)
Daugherty, Michael
- Snap! (1120-1110)
Harvey, Jonathan
- Moving Trees (1121-1110)
Hindemith, Paul
- Sonata for 10 Instruments (1021-1000)
Höller, York
- Feuerwerk (1121-2100)
Hosokawa, Toshio
- Medea Fragments I (1120-0010)
Lieberson, Peter
- Free and Easy Wanderer (1121-1110)
Maros, Rudolf
- Musica da Camera per 11 (1020-0000)
Matthews, Colin
- Flourish with Fireflies (1121-1110)
- Little Continuum: No.1 of "Two Tributes" (1121-1110)
Nancarrow, Conlon
- Study No.2 (1121-1110)
- Study No.7 (1121-1110)
- Study No.12 (1121-1100)

Over 10'

Aa, Michel van der
- Attach (0121-0100)
Adès, Thomas
- Chamber Symphony, op.2 (1120-1110)
Beltrami, Marco
- Iskios; City of Shadows (1121-1110)
Birkenkötter, Jörg
- Four Pieces for Ensemble (1121-1110)
- Halt! (1121-1110)
Bose, Hans-Jürgen von
- Prozess (1121-1110)
Brown, Earle
- Sign Sounds (1021-0110)
Carter, Elliott
- Penthode (1121-1211)
Cerha, Friedrich
- Jahrlang ins Ungewisse Hinab (1021-2220)
Dillon, James
- Überschreiten (1121-1111)
Gruber, HK
- Zeitfluren; Timescapes (1121-1111)
Harneit, Johannes
- Triptychon (13X3), op.20 (1121-2100)
Kallstenius, Edvin
- Suite for 14 Instruments, op.23c (1121-2100)
Kyburz, Hanspeter
- Parts (1120-2220)
Levinson, Gerald
- Light Dances / Stones Sing (1121-1210)
Ligeti, György
- Kammerkonzert (Chamber Concerto) (1120-1010)
Matthews, Colin
- Hidden Variables (1121-1100)
- ...through the glass (1121-2100)
- Two Tributes (1121-1110)
Maxwell Davies, Peter
- Carolisima, Serenade for Chamber Orchestra (1120-1110)
Mochizuki, Misato
- La Chambre Claire (1121-1110)
Müller-Hornbach, Gerhard
- Passacaglia II (1111-1120)
Payne, Anthony
- Symphonies of Wind and Rain (1121-1000)
Takemitsu, Tōru
- Tree Line (1121-2110)
Xenakis, Iannis
- Jalons (1121-1111)

2121 - 2221 - str[1.1.1.1.1]
Maximum Winds, Exact Strings

Anderson, Julian
- Book of Hours (2121-1110)
Antoniou, Theodore
- Cheironomiës - Gesten (2010-0010)
Barreau, Gisèle
- Piano-piano (2121-1110)
Benjamin, Arthur
- Olicantus (2010-2000)
Bousch, François
- Spirales Insolites (2020-1000)
Cerha, Friedrich
- Scherzino (2121-1110)
Henze, Hans Werner
- L'heure bleu (2121-1001)
Hosokawa, Toshio
- Seascapes - Daybreak (2121-2110)
Hoyland, Vic
- Fox (2010-0000)
Kisielewski, Stefan
- Symphony for 15 Performers (2111-1110)
Provazník, Anatol
- Ländliche Suite, op.53 (2121-2210)
Rihm, Wolfgang
- Jagden und Formen (2121-2221)
Sørensen, Bent
- Minnewater; Thousands of Canons (2110-2110)
Terzakis, Dimitri
- Ichochronos II (2010-1001)
Widmann, Jörg
- Freie Stücke (2121-1110)
Wood, Hugh
- Chamber Concerto, op.15 (2121-1111)
Yu, Julian
- Philopentatonia, op.32 (2110-1110)
Yuasa, Joji
- Projection (2121-1111)

2222 - 2221 - str[1.1.1.1.1]
Maximum Winds, Exact Strings

Bedford, David
- Symphony for 12 Musicians (1201-1000)
Feldman, Morton
- For Samuel Beckett; For 23 players (2222-2221)
Höller, York
- Arcus (1122-1110)
Knussen, Oliver
- Notre Dame des Jouets; Organum from a Music Box, op.27, No.1 (2221-2110)
- Organum, op.27, No.2 (2221-0000)
- Two Organa, op.27 (2221-2110)
Lehmann, Hans Ulrich
- Composition for 19 (1221-1110)
Milhaud, Darius
- L'Homme et son Désir, op.48 (2221-1200)
Reich, Steve
- City Life (2220-0000)
Saxton, Robert
- Traumstadt (2222-2210)
Wolpe, Stefan
- Chamber Piece No.1 (1211-1110)
Yun, Isang
- Impression (2221-1110)

Winds Larger Than
2222 - 2221 - str[1.1.1.1.1]
Exact Strings

Cage, John
- Cheap Imitation (3221-1111)
Lindberg, Magnus
- Tendenza (1132-1111)
Nancarrow, Conlon
- Study No.5 (1111-0300)
Neikrug, Marc
- Mobile (2130-0000)
Roslavets, Nikolai Andreyevich
- Chamber Symphony; For 18 solo instruments (2232-2100)
Saariaho, Kaija
- Io (3000-2011)
Schönberg, Arnold
- Kammersymphonie Nr.1 (Chamber Symphony No.1), op.9 (1232-2000)
Vivier, Claude
- Deva et Asura (2222-2320)
Vries, Klaas de
- ...Ibant Obscuri Sola sub Nocte per Umbras... (1231-1110)

STRINGS IN 2

Maximum Strings [1.1.2.2.2]
Any Woodwinds, Any Brass
String Count Given in Brackets

10' or Less

Aperghis, Georges
- Heysel; Pour 18 Instrumentistes [1.1.1.2.1]

Argento, Dominick
- Valse Triste [1.1.2.2.1]

Bolcom, William
- Session IV [0.0.2.1.0]

Bonnet, Antoine
- La terre habitable III; Les hautes terres du Sertalejo [1.1.2.2.1]
- La terre habitable V; Liberté grande [1.1.2.2.1]

Feldman, Morton
- Madame Press Died Last Week at Ninety [0.0.0.2.2]

Glass, Philip
- Runaway Horses: From "Mishima" [1.1.2.2.1]

Grainger, Percy Aldridge
- My Robin is to the Greenwood Gone; Old English Popular Music No.2 [1.0.2.2.1]

Gudmundsen-Holmgreen, Pelle
- Mester Jacob (Frère Jacques) [1.0.1.2.2]

Harbison, John
- Exequien for Calvin Simmons [0.0.2.1.0]

Harvey, Jonathan
- Hidden Voice 1 [1.1.1.2.1]

Holliger, Heinz
- Ad Marginem [1.1.2.2.1]
- Choral à 8 [1.1.2.2.0]
- Der Ferne Klang [1.0.2.1.0]
- Engführung [1.1.2.2.1]
- Ostinato Funebre [1.1.2.2.1]
- Sommerkanon IV [0.0.1.2.0]

Hübler, Klaus K.
- Kryptogramm [0.0.0.1.2]

Milhaud, Darius
- Actualités; Musik zu einer Filmwochenschau, op.104 [1.1.2.2.1]

Nancarrow, Conlon
- Study No.6 [1.1.1.0.2]

Rihm, Wolfgang
- Cantus Firmus; Musik in memoriam Luigi Nono (1. Versuch) [1.1.1.2.1]
- Chiffre III [0.0.0.2.1]
- Chiffre V [1.1.1.2.1]
- Chiffre VIII [0.0.0.2.1]
- Nach-Schrift; Eine Chiffre [1.1.1.2.1]
- Ricercare; Musik in memoriam Luigi Nono (2.Versuch) [1.1.1.2.1]

Stravinsky, Igor
- Eight Instrumental Miniatures [1.1.2.2.0]

Over 10'

Amy, Gilbert
- 7 Sites; For 14 players [1.1.2.2.0]

André, Mark
- ...Das O...: From ...22,1... [0.0.0.2.2]

Baggiani, Guido
- Double [0.0.0.0.2]

Baird, Tadeusz
- Four Novelettes [1.1.2.2.1]

Ballif, Claude
- Imaginaire No.3, op.41, No.3 [0.0.2.1.1]

Bartholomée, Pierre
- Fancy as a Ground [1.1.2.1.1]

Bonnet, Antoine
- La terre habitable I; Les eaux étroites [1.1.2.2.1]

Boone, Charles
- Second Landscape [1.1.1.1.2]

Bose, Hans-Jürgen von
- Scene [1.1.2.2.2]

Brown, James Francis
- Sinfonietta [1.0.2.2.1]

Dalby, Martin
- Aleph [0.0.0.0.2]
- Cancionero Para Una Mariposa [0.0.0.2.0]

Delás, José Luis de
- Concetti; Musica para Gesualdo di Venosa [1.1.2.1.2]

Furrer, Beat
- In der Stille des Hauses wohnt ein Ton (In the silence of the house there lives a sound) [1.0.1.2.1]

Glass, Philip
- Mishima (Music from the Film) [1.1.2.2.1]

Haas, Georg Friedrich
- Monodie [1.1.2.2.1]

Harrison, Lou
- Solstice [0.0.0.2.1]

Henze, Hans Werner
- Three Mozart Organ Sonatas for 14 Players [0.0.2.2.1]

Höller, York
- Mythos [0.0.0.2.1]

Imbrie, Andrew
- From Time to Time [1.1.1.2.0]

Knussen, Oliver
- Requiem; Songs for Sue, op.33 [0.0.2.2.1]

Komorous, Rudolf
- Rossi [0.0.2.2.0]

Kopelent, Marek
- Intimissimo [1.1.2.1.1]

Krauze, Zygmunt
- Tableau Vivant [1.1.2.1.1]

Lazarof, Henri
- Espaces [0.0.2.2.0]

Lehmann, Hans Ulrich
- Chamber Music II [0.0.0.2.2]

Lindberg, Magnus
- Joy [1.1.2.2.1]

Martinů, Bohuslav
- The Amazing Flight; Ballet mécanique, H.159 [1.1.2.1.0]

Müller-Siemens, Detlev
- Variationen über einen Ländler von Schubert [1.1.1.2.0]

Müller-Wieland, Jan
- Amtsantritt von Leonce und Lena; Zweite imaginäre Theaterszene nach dem Schluss von Georg Büchner [1.0.1.2.1]

Mundry, Isabel
- Schwankende Zeit [1.1.2.1.1]
- Le Voyage [1.1.2.2.2]

Platz, Robert H. P.
- CHLEBNICOV [0.0.0.2.1]

Rihm, Wolfgang
- Chiffre VII [1.1.1.2.1]
- Kein Firmament [1.1.1.2.1]

Ruders, Poul
- Corpus Cum Figuris [1.1.2.2.1]

Sawer, David
- Tiroirs [1.1.2.2.1]

Staud, Johannes Maria
- Berenice: Suite 1 [1.1.2.2.1]
- Berenice: Suite 2 [1.1.2.2.1]
- A Map is not the Territory [1.1.2.2.1]

Zender, Hans
- 4 Enso (LO-SHU VII) [1.1.2.2.0]

Maximum Strings [2.2.2.2.2]
Any Woodwinds, Any Brass
String Count Given in Brackets

10' or Less

Auric, Georges
- La fontaine de jouvence [2.0.2.2.1]
Bedford, David
- Piece for Mo [3.0.0.1.1]
Berio, Luciano
- Re-Call [2.0.2.2.1]
Carter, Elliott
- Réflexions [2.1.2.2.1]
Crawford, Ruth
- Music for Small Orchestra
  [2.2.0.2.0]
Françaix, Jean
- 85 Measures et un Da Capo
  [3.0.1.1.0]
Grainger, Percy Aldridge
- Green Bushes; Passacaglia on an
  English folksong: British folkmusic
  settings No.12 [3.0.2.2.1]
Heyn, Volker
- Phryh [3.0.2.2.1]
Ives, Charles Edward
- Adagio Sostenuto; At Sea
  [3.0.0.1.0]
- Allegretto Sombreoso; Incantation
  [3.0.0.0.0]
Laderman, Ezra
- Cadence [4.0.1.2.1]
Lutosławski, Witold
- Interlude [2.2.2.2.1]
Marthinsen, Niels
- Outland [4.0.0.2.0]
Martinů, Bohuslav
- Serenata No.1 [4.0.1.0.0]
- Serenata No.3 [4.0.0.1.0]
Matthews, Colin
- Little Suite No.2, op.18b [2.2.2.2.1]
Maxwell Davies, Peter
- A Welcome to Orkney [2.2.2.2.1]
Milhaud, Darius
- Chamber Symphony No.4; Dixtuor
  à Cordes, op.74 [2.2.2.2.2]
Morthenson, Jan Wilhelm
- Antiphonia II [3.0.2.1.1]
Müller-Siemens, Detlev
- Zwei Stücke (Two Pieces)
  [3.0.1.1.1]
Nono, Luigi
- Incontri [2.2.2.2.2]
Nørgård, Per
- Surf [2.0.0.2.0]
Rosing-Schow, Niels
- Canon and Corale [2.0.0.2.0]

Satie, Erik
- Carnet de croquis et d'esquisses
  [2.2.1.1.0]
Tanaka, Karen
- Wave Mechanics [3.0.2.2.1]
Thomas, Augusta Read
- Capricious Angels [3.0.1.0.0]
Weir, Judith
- Sederunt Principes [3.0.2.1.1]
Zimmermann, Bernd Alois
- Un "Petit Rien" [3.0.2.1.1]

Over 10'

Atterberg, Kurt
- Barocco-Suite No.5, op.23
  [3.0.0.1.1]
Baggiani, Guido
- Memoria [2.1.1.1.1]
Bainbridge, Simon
- Landscape and Memory [4.0.2.2.1]
Benjamin, George
- Three Inventions for Chamber
  Orchestra [2.1.2.2.2]
Bennett, Richard Rodney
- Metamorphoses [2.2.2.2.0]
Blomdahl, Karl-Birger
- Game for Eight [2.0.2.2.2]
Bolcom, William
- Summer Divertimento [3.0.2.2.2]
Bose, Hans-Jürgen von
- Travesties in a Sad Landscape
  [2.0.1.1.1]
Chen, Qigang
- Luminères de Guang-Ling
  [3.0.1.1.1]
Copland, Aaron
- Appalachian Spring: Suite (original
  version) [2.2.2.2.1]
Cowell, Henry
- Sinfonietta [2.2.1.1.1]
Duddell, Joe
- Alberti Addict [2.0.2.1.1]
Eötvös, Peter
- Chinese Opera [2.0.2.2.1]
Goehr, Alexander
- Concerto for Eleven, op.32
  [2.0.1.0.1]
- ...a musical offering (J. S. B. 1985)
  [3.0.2.0.1]
Grainger, Percy Aldridge
- Hill Song [2.0.2.2.1]
Haas, Georg Friedrich
- Quasi Una Tânpûrâ [3.0.2.2.1]
Harvey, Jonathan
- Two Interludes for an Opera
  [2.2.2.2.1]

- Bhakti [2.1.1.1.0]
Haubenstock-Ramati, Roman
- Beaubourg Musique [2.2.2.2.0]
- Invocations [2.2.2.2.0]
Hindemith, Paul
- In Sturm und Eis: Music to Arnold
  Fanck's film *Im Kampf mit dem
  Berge* [2.0.0.1.1]
Höller, York
- Résonance [3.0.2.2.1]
Holt, Simon
- Capriccio Spettrale [2.0.2.1.1]
Honegger, Arthur
- Le Dit des Jeux du Monde: Suite
  d'orchestre en 4 mouvements
  [2.2.2.2.2]
- Le Dit des Jeux du Monde: 10
  Danses, 2 interludes et 1 épilogue
  pour orchestre de chambre, pour le
  poème de Paul Méral, H.19
  [2.2.2.2.2]
Hosokawa, Toshio
- Garten Lieder (Garden Songs)
  [2.2.2.2.1]
Hvidtfelt Nielsen, Svend
- Singing the Dreams [2.0.1.1.0]
Ibert, Jacques
- Divertissement [3.0.2.2.1]
Kats-Chernin, Elena
- Clocks; For ensemble and tape
  [3.0.2.2.1]
Krása, Hans
- Brundibár: Suite from the opera
  [4.0.0.1.1]
Krenek, Ernst
- Small Symphony, op.58 [2.0.0.0.2]
Markevitch, Igor
- Petite Suite d'après Schumann
  [3.0.2.2.1]
Matthews, Colin
- Tosca Revisited [2.2.2.2.1]
- Pursuit; Ballet [2.2.2.2.2]
McCabe, John
- Rainforest I [3.0.1.2.0]
McGuire, John
- Cadence Music [2.0.2.2.1]
Obst, Michael
- Kristallwelt [3.0.2.2.1]
Reich, Steve
- Eight Lines [2.2.2.2.0]
Rihm, Wolfgang
- Cuts and Dissolves;
  Orchesterskizzen [3.0.2.2.2]
Rushton, Edward
- Lost City Life [2.0.0.2.0]
Schnittke, Alfred
- Pantomime; Suite for Chamber
  Orchestra [3.0.1.1.1]

Schuman, William
 - Night Journey [2.2.2.2.1]
Sibelius, Jean
 - Scaramouche; Tragic Pantomime,
   op.71 [2.2.1.1.1]
Takemitsu, Tōru
 - Archipelago S. [2.0.2.2.1]

Tavener, John
 - Grandma's Footsteps [2.2.2.2.0]
Turnage, Mark-Anthony
 - Dark Crossing [3.0.2.2.2]
Ullmann, Jakob
 - Composition for 10 Instruments I-V
   [4.0.1.1.1]
Vines, Nicholas
 - Firestick [2.2.2.2.1]

Wallin, Rolf
 - Appearances [3.0.2.2.1]
Zimmermann, Bernd Alois
 - Metamorphose; Music for the film of
   the same title by Michael
   Wolgensinger [2.2.2.2.1]

CHAMBER ORCHESTRA

All listings may include Harp, Piano, Percussion or Auxiliary Instruments.
Only Chamber Orchestra repertoire is listed (no solo repertoire).

	Woodwinds	Brass	Strings	Maximum (M) or Exact (E)	Page
No Woodwinds	0000	4431	str	M	265
Full Orchestra	0032	4321	str	M	265
	0222	2210	str	M	266
	2000	2220	str	M	266
	0200	2000	str	E	267
	1111	1000	str	E	267
	1111	1100	str	E	268
	1111	1110	str	E	268
	1111	1111	str	E	269
	1111	2000	str	E	269
	1111	2100	str	E	269
	1101	2200	str	M	270
	1111	2110	str	E	270
	1111	2210	str	M	270
	1011	2211	str	M	271
	1111	2221	str	M	272
	1121	1110	str	E	272
	1121	2210	str	E	272
	1121	2231	str	M	273
	2121	2110	str	M	274
	2121	4231	str	M	274
	1212	3221	str	M	275
	1222	2321	str	M	275
	2112	2221	str	M	276
	2222	2000	str	E	276
	2222	2000	str	M	277
	2222	2100	str	E	278
	2222	2110	str	E	278
	2222	2200	str	E	278
	2222	2210	str	E	280
	2222	2220	str	E	281
	2022	2211	str	M	281
	2222	2221	str	E	282
	2222	2331	str	M	282
	2222	3331	str	M	283
	2222	4200	str	E	283
	2222	4200	str	M	283
	2222	4230	str	E	284
	2222	4231	str	E	284
	2222	4331	str	M	284
	3222	4331	str	M	285
	Other Combinations with Woodwinds in 3		str	M	286
	Larger than all previous		str	M	287
No Brass	1010	0000	str	E	287
	1110	0000	str	E	287
	1111	0000	str	E	287
	3332	0000	str	M	288

265

EXACT & MAXIMUM INSTRUMENTATION
(for the Categories "Ensemble" and "Chamber Orchestra")

Exact (E): Will return pieces in exactly the given instrumentation

Maximum (M): Will return pieces in exactly the given instrumentation OR SMALLER
Example No.1: "1010 - 0110 - str" can also return a piece that uses 1010 - 0100 - str
Example No.2: "str with a maximum of [1.1.2.2.2]" can also return a piece that uses [1.0.2.1.2]
Maximum Searches will list the woodwind and brass count in brackets, i.e., (1111 - 1111)

NO WOODWINDS

0000 - 4431 - str
Maximum

10' or Less

Arnold, Malcolm
- Symphonic Study "Machines," op.30 (0000-4331)
Babbitt, Milton
- All Set (0000-0110)
Bentzon, Jørgen
- Sinfonia Buffo, op.35 (0000-0100)
Brant, Henry
- Prelude and Fugue (0000-2221)
Daugherty, Michael
- Ghost Ranch; Above Clouds (0000-4000)
Erdmann, Dietrich
- Concert Piece (0000-2000)
Gudmundsen-Holmgreen, Pelle
- Caravanfanfan-farefare No.1 (0000-0210)
- Caravanfanfan-farefare No.3 (0000-0110)
Horovitz, Joseph
- Concertino Classico (0000-0200)
Kurz, Siegfried
- Music for Brass, Kettledrums and Strings, op.36 (0000-0230)
Sallinen, Aulis
- Sunrise Serenade (0000-0200)
Zender, Hans
- Kalligraphie II (0000-0320)

Over 10'

Ardevol, José
- Musica para Pequena Orquesta. Himno (Music for small orchestra. Hymn) (0000-2000)
Bjelinski, Bruno
- Serenade (0000-0100)
Burt, Francis
- Blind Visions (0000-0220)
Engelmann, Hans Ulrich
- Partita (0000-0300)
Essl, Karl-Heinz
- Et Consumimur Igni (0000-2220)
Hindemith, Paul
- Concert Music for Strings and Brass, op.50 (0000-4431)
Honegger, Arthur
- Symphony No.2, H.153 (0000-0100)
Hovhaness, Alan
- Saint Vartan Symphony (0000-1410)
Klebe, Giselher
- Scene und Arie, op.54 (0000-0330)
Levy, Marvin David
- Trialogus I (0000-3000)
Maw, Nicholas
- Sonata for Strings and Two Horns (0000-2000)
Meester, Louis de
- Sinfonietta Buffa (0000-0200)
Raasted, N.O.
- Sinfonia da Chiesa, op.76 (0000-0220)
Suter, Robert
- Epitaffio (0000-3300)
Winters, Geoffrey
- Concertino, op.18 (0000-2000)

FULL ORCHESTRA

0032 - 4321 - str
Maximum

Adès, Thomas
- The Origin of the Harp, op.13 (0030-0000)
Berio, Luciano
- Variazione sull'aria di Papageno: No.2 from "Divertimento for Mozart" (0020-0000)
Ferguson, Howard
- Serenade (0011-1000)
Fortner, Wolfgang
- Suite for Orchestra; After music by Jan Pieters Sweelinck (0002-0200)
Hartley, Walter Sinclair
- Concertino for Chamber Ensemble (0010-0010)
Järnefelt, Armas
- Berceuse (0021-2000)
Kallstenius, Edvin
- Berceuse (0011-1100)
Kelterborn, Rudolf
- Vier Nachtstücke für Kammerorchester (0020-2000)
Klebe, Giselher
- Divertissement joyeux, op.5 (0011-1110)
Kodály, Zoltán
- Hungarian Rondo (0022-0000)
Krása, Hans
- Overture for Small Orchestra (0020-0200)
Ligeti, György
- Fragment (0001-0011)
Marthinsen, Niels
- Outland (0020-3200)
Mendoza, Vicente
- Impresiones de Estio I-IV (0011-0100)

Nussio, Otmar
- Divertimento (0011-1000)
Pärt, Arvo
- Pari Intervallo (0010-0010)
Revueltas, Silvestre
- Planos (Planes) (0021-0100)
Rihm, Wolfgang
- Dunkles Spiel (0011-2020)
Shulman, Alan
- Vodka Float (0010-0000)
Vinter, Gilbert
- The Poet Speaks; Suite from pieces by Robert Schumann (0010-0000)
Webern, Anton
- Symphony, op.21 (0020-2000)
Wielecki, Tadeusz
- Melody with Accompaniment (0010-0010)

0222 - 2210 -str
Maximum

10' or Less

Alfvén, Hugo
- Elegi; För liten orkester, ur orkestersviten Gustav II Adolf (0121-0000)
Bauer, Marion
- Concertino (0110-0000)
Diehl, Paula
- Insiders (0101-0110)
Dubois, Pierre-Max
- Trois Sérénades (0111-0000)
Fuleihan, Anis
- Divertimento (0211-1100)
Gillis, Don
- Four Scenes from Yesterday: Courthouse Square (0100-0000)
Maxwell Davies, Peter
- Threnody on a Plainsong for Michael Vyner (0202-2200)
McCabe, John
- Shepherd's Dream (0201-0200)
Moncayo, José Pablo
- Homenaje a Cervantes (0200-0000)
Pärt, Arvo
- Collage on B-A-C-H (0200-0000)
Schoeck, Othmar
- Serenade (Interlude) (0200-0000)
Shchedrin, Rodion
- Shepherd's Pipes of Vologda (0200-1000)
Wiener, Karl
- Kammerstück für 12 Soloinstrumente, op.7 (0121-2000)

Over 10'

Amram, David
- Shakespearean Concerto (0100-2000)
Bavicchi, John
- Concertante, op.44 (0101-0000)
Gregson, Edward
- Music for Chamber Orchestra (0202-2000)
Heiller, Anton
- Kammersymphonie (Chamber Symphony) (0111-0000)
Helm, Everett
- Serenade (0111-0000)
Joubert, John
- Sinfonietta, op.38 (0202-2000)
Juon, Paul
- Kammersinfonie (Chamber Symphony), op.27 (0111-1000)
Kancheli, Giya
- Besuch In Der Kindheit (Childhood Revisited) (0100-0000)
Krol, Bernhard
- Concerto Grosso, op.15 (0201-0200)
Lazar, Filip
- Concerto Grosso No.1, op.17 (0202-2100)
Lees, Benjamin
- Concertante Breve (0100-2000)
Schlee, Thomas Daniel
- Sonata da Camera, op.42 (0100-2000)
Shchedrin, Rodion
- Music for the City of Köthen (0202-0000)

2000 - 2220 -str
Maximum

10' or Less

Banks, Don
- Elizabethan Miniatures (1000-0000)
Cheslock, Louis
- Theme and Variations (1000-1000)
Glass, Philip
- Meetings along the Edge: From "Passages" (1000-0000)
- Offering: From "Passages" (1000-0000)
Górecki, Henryk Mikołaj
- Genesis II: Canti Strumentali, op.19/2 (2000-0100)
Hindemith, Paul
- Plöner Musiktag: Tafelmusik (1000-0100)

Laderman, Ezra
- Cadence (2000-0000)
Maros, Rudolf
- Sinfonietta No.1 (2000-0200)
Rapoport, Eda
- Israfel; Tone Picture after Edgar Allan Poe (1000-0000)
Rodrigo, Joaquín
- Cyrano de Bergerac; Music for Edmond Rostand's play of the same name (1000-0100)
Rogers, Bernard
- Elegy; To the Memory of Franklin D. Roosevelt (1000-2000)
Sibelius, Jean
- Suite Mignonne, op.98a (2000-0000)
Slonimsky, Nicolas
- Little March for the Big Bowl; Marche grotesque (1000-2210)
Szymanski, Pawel
- Intermezzo (2000-0000)
Tavener, John
- Variations on "Three Blind Mice" (2000-0220)
Weiner, Leo
- Divertimento No.1; On old Hungarian folk dances, op.20 (1000-1100)

Over 10'

Arnold, Malcolm
- Sinfonietta No.2, op.65 (2000-2000)
David, Johann Nepomuk
- Sinfonia preclassica super nomen H-A-S-E, Wk44 (2000-2000)
Haubenstock-Ramati, Roman
- Polyphonien; For 2, 3 or 4 chamber orchestras (2000-0020)
Kancheli, Giya
- Abii ne Viderem (1000-0000)
- A Life Without Christmas: The Morning Prayers; For Chamber Orchestra and Tape (1000-0000)
Larsson, Lars-Erik
- Gustaviansk Suite, op.28 (1000-0000)
Lobanov, Vasily
- Symphony No.2 for Chamber Orchestra; "Intermezzo," op.36 (2000-0100)
Nilsson, Bo
- Hemsoborna (1000-0000)
Silvestrov, Valentin
- Symphony No.2 (1000-0000)
Slonimsky, Sergei
- Concerto Buffo (1000-0100)

Stenhammar, Wilhelm
- Lodolezzi Sjunger: Suite, op.39
  (1000-0000)

0200 - 2000 - str
Exact

Arnold, Malcolm
- Sinfonietta No.1, op.48
Blake, David
- Sonata alla Marchia
Davison, John
- Symphony No.6
Holloway, Robin
- Ode, op.45
Kelterborn, Rudolf
- Four Movements for Classical
  Orchestra
Lendvai, Erwin
- Tafelmusik: From op.48
MacRae, Stuart
- Portrait II
Matthews, David
- From Sea to Sky; Overture, op.59
McCabe, John
- Red Leaves
Milhaud, Darius
- Musique pour Lisbonne, op.420
Moravec, Paul
- Sempre Diritto! (Straight Ahead)
Patterson, Paul
- Europhony, op.55
Ruders, Poul
- Trapeze
Schnittke, Alfred
- Suite in Old Style
Sutermeister, Heinrich
- Sérénade pour Montreux
Wilby, Philip
- The Wings of Morning
Yun, Isang
- Kammersinfonie I (Chamber
  Symphony I)

1111 - 1000 - str
Exact

10' or Less

Arbeau, Pierre
- Paysage d'Auvergne; Danse
  paysanne pour orchestre
- Poème slave
Bavicchi, John
- Fantasy, op.36
Beyer, Johanna
- Fragment for Chamber Orchestra
Britten, Benjamin
- Irish Reel

De Brant, Cyr
- A Song of Yesteryear: Sarabande
Earls, Paul
- And On The Seventh Day
Finzi, Gerald
- Love's Labour's Lost: Three
  Soliloquies, op.28
Gudmundsen-Holmgreen, Pelle
- Variationer til Moster Rix (Variations
  for Aunt Rix)
Hansson, C.J. Gunnar
- Suite No.1
Helfer, Walter
- A Water Idyll
Hemberg, Eskil
- Migraine pour orchestre, op.19b
Hill, Mabel Wood
- Reactions to "Prose Rhythms" of
  Fiona Macleod
Honegger, Arthur
- Pastorale d'été; Poème
  symphonique, H.31
Ledenjov, Roman
- Notturni
LeFanu, Nicola
- Preludio I
Luening, Otto
- Prelude to a Hymn Tune by William
  Billings
Maxwell Davies, Peter
- Canzona (After Giovanni Gabrieli)
Oldham, Arthur
- Variations on a Carol Tune
Pärt, Arvo
- Wenn Bach Bienen gezüchtet
  hätte…
Payne, Anthony
- Hidden Music
Pierné, Gabriel
- Ballet de Cour, No.4: Pavane et
  Saltarello
Pilati, Mario
- Alla Culla; Ninna-nanna per piccola
  orchestra
Schmitt, Florent
- Hymne à Tanit
- Reflets d'Allemagne: Heidelberg,
  op.28
Schoeck, Othmar
- Serenade, op.1
Scott, Cyril
- Summer Gardens
Williams, Graham
- Cerberus

Over 10'

Alizade, Akshin
- Symphony No.4
Ali-Zadeh, Franghiz
- Sturm und Drang for Chamber
  Orchestra
Bennett, Richard Rodney
- Nocturnes
Bentzon, Niels Viggo
- Pupitre 14, op.339
Bloch, Ernest
- Four Episodes
Braun, Yehezkel
- Apartment To Let
- Serenade for Chamber Orchestra
- Serenade II
Burgon, Geoffrey
- Suite from Martin Chuzzlewit
David, Johann Nepomuk
- Kume, kum, Geselle min;
  Divertimento nach alten
  Volksliedern, Wk24
Geissler, Fritz
- Chamber Symphony (1970)
- Symphony No.6; Concertante
  Symphony
Grosskopf, Erhard
- Sonata concertante 1
Hindemith, Paul
- Hérodiade
Kahn, Erich Itor
- Petite Suite Bretonne
Koch, Erland von
- Four Swedish Folk Melodies
Larsson, Lars-Erik
- Divertimento, op.15
Lendvai, Erwin
- Kammersuite, op.32
Malipiero, Gian Francesco
- Grottesco
- Ricercari
- Ritrovari
Matthews, David
- Burnham Wick, op.73
Maxwell Davies, Peter
- Sinfonia
Morris, Harold
- Variations on the American Negro
  Spiritual "I was way down a-yonder"
Quinet, Marcel
- Sinfonietta
Reger, Max
- Suite in A minor, op.103a
Ropartz, Joseph Guy Marie
- Sons de Cloches
Saint-Saëns, Camille
- L'assassinat de Duc de Guise;
  Tableux d'histoire, op.128

Scott, Cyril
- Suite Phantastique
Sjöblom, Heimer
- Liten Svit I Spelmanston
Steffen, Wolfgang
- Kammerkonzert, op.48
Wolf-Ferrari, Ermanno
- Sinfonia da Camera in B-flat, op.8

1111 - 1100 - str
Exact

10' or Less

Beydts, Louis
- À travers Paris; Images
  symphoniques
Copland, Aaron
- Symphony No.1: Prelude
Daniels, Mabel W.
- Deep Forest; Prelude for Little
  Symphony Orchestra, op.34, No.1
Hewitt, Harry
- Overture: Taming of the Shrew
Honegger, Arthur
- Blues, H.66a
Pierné, Gabriel
- Album Pour Mes Petites Amis
  (Album for My Little Friends):
  Farandole, op.14, No.2
Riegger, Wallingford
- Scherzo
Rota, Nino
- Canzona
Satie, Erik
- Les Pantins Dansent
Stock, David
- Capriccio
Stürmer, Bruno
- Tanzsuite (Dance Suite), op.24
Surinach, Carlos
- Danza Andaluza
Tuthill, Burnet
- Intrada

Over 10'

Becker, John J.
- When the Willow Nods: Second
  Suite in one Movement from Stage
  Work No.5-b
Cohn, James
- Symphony No.4 in A, op.29
Harty, Hamilton
- A John Field Suite
Hindemith, Paul
- Tuttifäntchen: Suite
Holmboe, Vagn
- Chamber Symphony No.1, op.53

James, Dorothy
- Suite for Small Orchestra
Lopatnikoff, Nikolai
- Symphonietta, op.27
Nørgård, Per
- Amled: Suite
Pillney, Karl Hermann
- Eskapaden eines Gassenhauers;
  Für Hörer mit Sinn für musikalische
  Eulenspiegeleien
Rózsa, Miklós
- Hungarian Serenade, op.25
Salviucci, Giovanni
- Sinfonia da Camera

1111 - 1110 - str
Exact

10' or Less

Beydts, Louis
- Hue!; Croquis parisien pour petit
  orchestre
Brant, Henry
- Lyric Piece
Buck, Ole
- Preludes I - V
Capanna, Robert
- Concerto for Chamber Orchestra
Clarke, Henry
- Saraband for the Golden Goose
Cohn, James
- Homage
Farago, Marcel
- Divertimento for Chamber
  Orchestra, op.18
Franco, Johan
- Sinfonia
Golijov, Osvaldo
- ZZ's Dream
Honegger, Arthur
- Fantasio; Ballet pantomime de
  Georges Wague, H.46
Horovitz, Joseph
- Horizon Overture
Ince, Kamran
- Evil Eye Deflector
Kelemen, Milko
- Konstellationen
Kulenty, Hanna
- Passacaglia
Lendvai, Erwin
- Archaische Tänze; Neun
  sinfonische Reigen für kleines
  Orchester, op.30
Martin, Frank
- Fox Trot
Müller-Wieland, Jan
- Two Pieces for Chamber Orchestra

Nancarrow, Conlon
- Study No.1
Poulenc, Francis
- Esquisse d'une Fanfare: Ouverture
  pour le Ve acte de "Romeo et
  Juliette"
- Valse
Rózsa, Miklós
- Kaleidoscope; Six short pieces for
  small orchestra, op.19a
Satie, Erik
- La belle excentrique; Fantasie
  sérieuse pour orchestra de music-
  hall
Searle, Humphrey
- Night Music
Villa-Lobos, Heitor
- Ouverture de l'homme tel...

Over 10'

Abendroth, Walter
- Divertimento für Kammerorchester,
  op.24
Asia, Daniel
- Rivalries
Boucourechliev, André
- Le Chevelure de Bérénice
Cohn, James
- Variations on The Wayfaring
  Stranger
- Symphony No.3 in G, op.27
- Symphony No.5
Cooper, Paul
- Love Songs and Dances;
  Concertante for 21 Players
Cordero, Roque
- Ocho Miniaturas
Donato, Anthony
- Serenade for Small Orchestra
Eisler, Hanns
- Five Pieces for Orchestra: From the
  music to the film *The 400 Million*
- Three Pieces for Orchestra: From
  the music to the film *The 400 Million*
Engelmann, Hans Ulrich
- Shadows; Scenes for Orchestra
- Strukturen; Den Taten der neuen
  Bildhauer
Essl, Karl-Heinz
- O Tiempo Tus Piramides
Fundal, Karsten
- Oscillation
Gál, Hans
- Zauberspiegel-Suite;
  Weihnachtsmusik. Musik zu einem
  Märchenspiel, op.38

Godfrey, Daniel Strong
- Concentus
Hamilton, Iain
- Arias
Henze, Hans Werner
- Katharina Blum: Concerto suite
Holloway, Robin
- Concertino No.1, op.2
Holmboe, Vagn
- Symphony No.1, op.4
Horne, David
- Persistence
Ibert, Jacques
- La Licorne, or The Triumph of
  Chastity; Ballet
Imbrie, Andrew
- Chamber Symphony
Koch, Erland von
- Ballet Suite: Peter Tailless, the Cat
Krebs, Joachim
- Musik für Kleines Orchester (Music
  for Small Orchestra)
Kulenty, Hanna
- Trigon
Lazar, Filip
- Concerto No.4; Concerto di
  Camera, op.24
Lumsdaine, David
- Salvation Creek with Eagle
Martin, Frank
- Concerto
Matthews, Colin
- Dowlandia
Milhaud, Darius
- Les Songes; Ballet, op.124
Morris, Harold
- Suite for Small Orchestra
Read, Gardner
- Partita for Small Orchestra, op.70
Rochberg, George
- Cheltenham Concerto
Saygun, A. Adnan
- Bir Orman Masali; A Forest Tale
Schreker, Franz
- Kammersymphonie (Chamber
  Symphony)
Search, Frederick
- Sinfonietta
Sierra, Roberto
- The Güell Concerto
Surinach, Carlos
- Embattled Garden; Ballet for
  chamber orchestra
Swafford, Jan
- Chamber Sinfonietta
Szymanski, Pawel
- Sixty-Odd Pages
Thomas, Kurt
- Serenade, op.10

Vactor, David van
- Divertimento
Wimberger, Gerhard
- Multiplay; Kanonische Reflexionen
  für 23 Spieler (Kammerorchester)
Yu, Julian
- First Australian Suite, op.22

1111 - 1111 - str
Exact

Engelmann, Hans Ulrich
- Capricciosi
Hrabovsky, Leonid
- Four Inventions for Chamber
  Orchestra
Ives, Charles Edward
- Four Ragtime Dances
MacMillan, James
- Sinfonietta
Roumain, Daniel Bernard
- Call Them All
Schuman, William
- The Witch of Endor; Ballet
Surinach, Carlos
- Acrobats of God; Ballet for chamber
  orchestra
Trapp, Max
- Divertimento für Kammerorchester,
  op.27
Wagenaar, Bernard
- Sinfonietta

1111 - 2000 - str
Exact

Absil, Jean
- Petite Suite, op.20
Arbeau, Pierre
- Polichinelle
Arnell, Richard
- Sonata for Chamber Orchestra,
  op.18
Barlow, Fred
- Lune de miel
Britten, Benjamin
- Sinfonietta, op.1
David, Johann Nepomuk
- Symphony No.8, Wk59
Ficher, Jacobo
- Dos Poemas; De El Jardino de R.
  Tagore, op.10, No.16
Kelly, Bryan
- Cookham Concertino
- Cookham Rondo
LeFanu, Nicola
- Preludio II

Lewis, Harold Merrills
- Two Preludes on Southern Folk
  Hymn Tunes
Moeschinger, Albert
- Symphony No.2, op.73
Rodrigo, Joaquín
- Tres Viejos Aires de Danza
Ropartz, Joseph Guy Marie
- Cinq pieces brèves
Rosenberg, Hilding Constantin
- Sinfonia da Chiesa No.1
Saint-Saëns, Camille
- Une nuit à Lisbonne, op.63
Stevens, Bernard
- Eclogue
Trexler, Georg
- Small Suite
Wagner, Joseph
- Pastoral costarricense; Un recuerdo
  sentimental

1111 - 2100 - str
Exact

Blake, David
- Chamber Symphony
Boelter, Karl
- Dharma
Brandmüller, Theo
- Venezianische Schatten
Busch, Adolf
- Divertimento, op.30
Diamond, David
- Concerto for Small Orchestra
Gilbert, Anthony
- Tree of Singing Names
Halffter, Ernesto
- Las Doncellas
Helfer, Walter
- A Fantasy on Children's Tunes
Henze, Hans Werner
- Drei Dithyramben; In memoriam
  Willy Strecker
Holmboe, Vagn
- Chamber Symphony No.2, op.100
- Prelude to the Seagulls and
  Cormorants, op.174
- Prelude to the Unsettled Weather,
  op.188
- Prelude to the Victoria
  Embankment, op.184
Ifukube, Akira
- Triptyque aborigène; Trois tableaux
  pour orchestre de chambre
Jones, Charles
- Suite for Small Orchestra
Koc, Marcelo
- Tres Piezas Para Orquesta

Nørgård, Per
- Bright Dances, op.24
Olivier, François
- Suite Pour Petit Orchestre
Schiske, Karl
- Chamber Concerto, op.28
Zilcher, Hermann
- Lustspielsuite; Der Widerspenstigen
  Zähmung, op.54b

1101 - 2200 - str
Maximum

Alwyn, William
- Concerto Grosso No.1 in Bb (1100-2100)
Ardevol, José
- Concerto Grosso No.1 (1101-0200)
Bedford, Herbert
- The Lonely Dancer of Gedār;
  Oriental Dance for Small Orchestra,
  op.36 (1101-1000)
Beydts, Louis
- Le Voyage de Tchong-Li (1101-0000)
Blomdahl, Karl-Birger
- Adagio from "Vaknatten": Incidental
  music from the play (1100-2000)
Burgon, Geoffrey
- Brideshead Variations (1101-1100)
- The Chronicles of Narnia Suite
  (1101-1100)
Degen, Helmut
- Kleine Weihnachtsmusik (1100-0000)
Diamond, David
- Elegies (1100-0000)
Eaton, John
- Adagio and Allegro (1100-0000)
Franze, Juan Pedro
- Lamento quechua, op.6 (1101-2000)
Glass, Philip
- The Secret Agent: Three Pieces
  (1100-0000)
Herrmann, Peter
- Sonata for Chamber Orchestra
  (1100-0100)
Honegger, Arthur
- Concerto da Camera, H.196 (1100-0000)
Killmayer, Wilhelm
- Sinfonia 2 (1101-0000)
Krätzschmar, Wilfried
- Ballets imaginaires (1101-2000)
León, Tania
- The Golden Windows (1100-0100)

Malipiero, Gian Francesco
- Oriente Immaginario; Tre stui per
  piccola orchestra (1101-0000)
Matthus, Siegfried
- Drei Sommerbilder (1101-0000)
Schelling, Ernest
- Tarantella (1101-0000)
Takemitsu, Tōru
- Eucalypts I (1100-0000)
Trantow, Herbert
- Kleine Tafelmusik (1100-0000)

1111 - 2110 - str
Exact

10' or Less

Honegger, Arthur
- Sérénade à Angélique, H.182
Martinů, Bohuslav
- Comedy on the Bridge: Little Suite
  from the opera
Milhaud, Darius
- Trois Rag-Caprices
Palmer, Robert
- Memorial Music
Poot, Marcel
- Fantasia
Schuller, Gunther
- Little Fantasy
Tcherepnin, Alexander
- Suite populaire russe

Over 10'

Bäck, Sven-Erik
- Fantasia on "Dies Sind Die Heiligen
  Zehn Gebot"
Barraud, Henry
- Concerto da Camera
Baur, Jürg
- Triton-Sinfonietta; Drei Grotesken
Brauel, Henning
- Les Fenêtres Simultanées
Danielpour, Richard
- First Light; Concerto for Chamber
  Orchestra in One Movement
Etler, Alvin
- Music for Chamber Orchestra
Gill, Jeremy
- Chamber Symphony
Hartley, Walter Sinclair
- Chamber Symphony
Knipper, Lew
- Wantsch; Turkmenische Suite,
  op.29
Korngold, Erich Wolfgang
- Much Ado About Nothing: Suite,
  op.11

MacRae, Stuart
- Portrait
Pärt, Arvo
- Symphony No.1; "Polyphonic," op.9
Poulenc, Francis
- Hoops, Ballet
Rorem, Ned
- Ideas; For easy orchestra
Sessions, Roger
- Concertino
Sierra, Roberto
- Descarga
Staempfli, Edward
- Präludium und Variationen
Stravinsky, Igor
- Danses Concertantes
Treibmann, Karl Ottomar
- First Symphonic Essay
Turok, Paul
- Antoniana; Suite for Small
  Orchestra after Vivaldi, op.47
Villa-Lobos, Heitor
- Francette et Pia
Voss, Friedrich
- Résonances, 12 Poems
Vuataz, Roger
- Petit Concert, op.39

1111 - 2210 - str
Maximum

10' or Less

Bruun, Peter
- Tre Små Stykker (1110-0210)
Cowell, Henry
- Teheran Movement (1111-0100)
Dessau, Paul
- Alice Helps the Romance (1110-0110)
- Alice in the Wooly West (1110-0110)
Finzi, Gerald
- A Severn Rhapsody, op.3 (1110-1000)
Haas, Joseph
- Lyrisches Intermezzo (1110-0110)
Honegger, Arthur
- Deux Pièces pour "La Rédemption
  de François Villon," H.209 (1111-1200)
Indy, Vincent d'
- Sérénade, op.16: Valse (1111-0100)
Kopelent, Marek
- Still-Leben (1110-1110)

Lincke, Paul
- Hanako; Japanese Intermezzo (1110-0110)
- Träume vom Lido (1110-0110)
Moeran, E. J.
- Whythorne's Shadow (1110-1000)
Naylor, Bernard
- Variations (1111-2200)
Pierné, Gabriel
- Album Pour Mes Petites Amis (Album for My Little Friends): Petite Gavotte, op.14, No.4 (1110-1000)
Poulenc, Francis
- Deux Marches et un Intermède (1111-0100)
Satie, Erik
- Trois petites pièces montées (1111-1210)
Stiller, Andrew
- A Periodic Table of the Elements (1111-1210)
Wagenaar, Bernard
- Song of Mourning; A reflection upon the slain Dutch patriots (1110-2200)
Warlock, Peter
- An Old Song (1110-1000)
Winkler, Gerhard
- Wolken über Samland (1110-0210)

Over 10'

Antheil, George
- Music to a World's Fair Film (1111-1210)
Brust, Herbert
- Ostpreußische Fischertänze, op.34 (1110-0110)
Copland, Aaron
- Music for Movies (1111-1210)
- Music for the Theatre (1111-0210)
- Three Latin American Sketches (1111-0100)
Delás, José Luis de
- Conjuntos (1110-1000)
Donovan, Richard
- Symphony for Chamber Orchestra (1111-0100)
Ettinger, Max
- An den Wassern Babylons; Songs of Babylonian Jews for Small Orchestra (1110-0210)
Felder, David
- Journal (1110-1110)
Gebhard-Elsass, Hans
- Ländliche Suite, op.23 (1110-0210)
Holmboe, Vagn
- Chamber Symphony No.3 (1111-2200)

Ives, Charles Edward
- Symphony No.3; The Camp Meeting, S.3 (1111-2010)
Kelterborn, Rudolf
- Traummusik; 6 Stücke für kleines Orchester (1110-1010)
Milhaud, Darius
- La Carnaval de Londres: Suite sur les airs de "l' Opéra du Gueux," op.172 (1111-0110)
Müller-Zürich, Paul
- Marienleben, op.8 (1110-1000)
Nelson, Larry
- Catena (1110-1110)
Riegger, Wallingford
- Dichotomy, op.12 (1111-1200)
Schwarz-Schilling, Reinhard
- Partita (1111-2200)
Vinci, Albert
- Dance Suite (1111-1210)
Vlad, Roman
- In Memoriam di Valentino Bucchi (1111-1010)
Walker, Robert
- Chamber Symphony No.1 (1111-0100)
Westerman, Gerhart von
- Serenade, op.7 (1111-2010)

1011 - 2211 - str
Maximum

10' or Less

Adams, John
- Christian Zeal and Activity (1011-0000)
Asia, Daniel
- B for J (1010-0010)
Beck, Jeremy
- Sparks and Flame (Ash) (1011-2000)
Glass, Philip
- Interlude from "Orphée" (1011-1110)
Guarnieri, Camargo
- Ponteios No.1 (1010-2100)
Gyring, Elizabeth
- Scherzo No.2 for Orchestra (1010-0110)
Honegger, Arthur
- Napoleón: Danse des Enfants (1011-0000)
Ives, Charles Edward
- The Gong on the Hook and Ladder; Firemen's Parade on Main Street, S.38 (1011-0210)
- Gyp the Blood or Hearst!? Which is Worst?! (1011-0100)

- Tone Roads No.1, S.49 (1011-0000)
- Tone Roads No.3, S.49 (1010-0110)
Koch, Erland von
- Sicilienne (1010-2210)
Kühnl, Claus
- Monodie; Music of the silence, op.12 (1010-0110)
Pierné, Gabriel
- Album Pour Mes Petites Amis: Marche des Petits Soldats de Plomb, op.14, No.6 (1010-0100)
- Giration, Divertissement chorégraphique (1011-0110)
Sibelius, Jean
- Valse Triste: From "Kuolema," op.44, No.1 (1010-2000)

Over 10'

Bäck, Sven-Erik
- Chamber Symphony (1011-1110)
- Movimento I (1010-0110)
Barraud, Henry
- Images pour un Poète Maudit; Pour 25 musiciens (1011-0100)
Bavicchi, John
- Fireworks, op.48 (1010-1000)
Bergman, Erik
- Tutti e soli, op.113 (1011-0000)
Bergsma, William
- Symphony for Chamber Orchestra (1010-2100)
Blomdahl, Karl-Birger
- Concerto grosso (1011-1000)
Burgon, Geoffrey
- Suite from Bleak House (1011-1100)
Burkhard, Willy
- Toccata for Chamber Orchestra, op.86 (1011-0100)
Frackenpohl, Arthur
- Divertimento in F (1010-1110)
Hesketh, Kenneth
- After Verdi!; Divertimento in five sections (1011-1110)
Kunad, Rainer
- Dialog; conatum 40 (1001-0110)
Leigh, Walter
- Suite from Shakespeare's "A Midsummer Night's Dream" (1010-0100)
McGlaughlin, William
- Aaron's Horizons (1011-0000)
Myaskovsky, Nikolai Yakovlevich
- Concertino Lyrico, op.32 (1011-1000)

Revueltas, Silvestre
- Paisajes (1011-1211)
Rogers, Bernard
- A Letter from Pete (1010-1110)
Roussel, Albert
- Le Marchand de Sable qui Passe
  (The Sandman Passing By), op.13
  (1010-1000)
Stravinsky, Igor
- Concerto in E-flat "Dumbarton
  Oaks" (1011-2000)
Trojan, Václav
- Sinfonietta Armoniosa (1010-0110)

1111 - 2221 - str
Maximum

Aguila, Miguel del
- Toccata; Chamber Orchestra
  version, op.28 (1111-2111)
Berlin, David
- Structures for Chamber Orchestra
  (1111-1120)
Birtwistle, Sir Harrison
- Three Movements with Fanfares
  (1111-2220)
Converse, Frederick Shepherd
- Three Old Fashioned Dances for
  Chamber Orchestra, op.102 (1111-
  2210)
Cowell, Henry
- American Melting Pot Set (1111-
  2111)
Dessau, Paul
- Sonatine; For small orchestra and
  obbligato piano (1111-2220)
Glass, Philip
- Concerto Grosso (1111-2111)
Honegger, Arthur
- Regain: Suite d'orchestre tirée de la
  musique du film de Jean Giono et
  Marcel Pagnol, H.117A (1111-0220)
Krenek, Ernst
- Campo Marzio, op.80 (1111-2210)
Piazzolla, Astor
- Danza Criolla (1111-2210)
Revueltas, Silvestre
- Musica Para Charlar (1111-2221)
Saariaho, Kaija
- Forty Heartbeats (1111-1211)
Santander, Manuel
- Ritmos de Cadiz (1111-2210)
Satie, Erik
- Cinéma: Entr'acte symphonique du
  ballet "Relâche" (1111-2210)
- Relâche; Ballet (1111-2210)
Schmitt, Florent
- Cançunik, Suite No.1, op.79 (1111-
  2220)

Schwartz, Francis
- Flaming June (1110-1001)
Shostakovich, Dmitri
- Hamlet: Suite from the Theatre
  Music, op.32a (1111-2211)
- New Babylon, op.18 (1111-2210)
Tansman, Alexandre
- Sinfonietta (1111-1120)
Turnage, Mark-Anthony
- On All Fours (1111-1011)
Vir, Param
- The Theatre of Magical Beings
  (1111-2210)
Weinberger, Jaromir
- Overture to a Knightly Play (1111-
  2210)

1121 - 1110 - str
Exact

Hallberg, Björn Wilho
- Novelletten
Hauer, Josef Matthias
- Zwölftonspiel XVII (Twelve-tone
  game XVII)
Honegger, Arthur
- Les Misérables: Suite pour
  orchestre tirée de la musique du film
  de Raymond Bernard, H.88A
Linke, Norbert
- Konkretionen V
Sandström, Sven-David
- In the Meantime
Scherchen, Tona
- Khouang
Schuller, Gunther
- Contours
Sharp, Elliot
- Points & Fields
Weir, Judith
- Sederunt Principes
Willi, Herbert
- Für 16; Kleines Kammerkonzert
  (For 16; Small Chamber Concerto)
Wimberger, Gerhard
- Partita Giocosa

1121 - 2210 - str
Exact

10' or Less

Bales, Richard
- Primavera
Bartók, Béla
- Bartók Suite
Berners, Lord
- For a Statesman: No.1 of "Three
  Small Funeral Marches"

Blumer, Theodor
- Lyrisches Intermezzo
Bridge, Frank
- Norse Legend
- Two Entr'actes
- Two Intermezzi: From the incidental
  music to the play "Threads"
- Vignettes de danse
Crawford, Ruth
- Rissolty-Rossolty
Elgar, Edward
- May Song
Filippi, Amedeo De
- Raftsman's Dance
Granados, Enrique
- À la Cubana; Marche militaire
- Danzas Espanolas, No.6: Jota
- Goyescas: Intermezzo
Hahn, Reynaldo
- La Fête Chez Thérèse: Suite No.1
Herbert, Victor
- Al Fresco; Intermezzo
Janssen, Werner
- Foster Suite
Kubik, Gail
- Folk Song Suite
Myaskovsky, Nikolai Yakovlevich
- Military March No.1
Poot, Marcel
- Fête à Thélème
Poulenc, Francis
- Mouvements perpétuels; Nos. 1 & 2
Quilter, Roger
- As you like it: Suite, op.21
Scharwenka, Franz Xaver
- À la Hongroise, op.43, No.6
- A Polish Dance Theme

Over 10'

Antheil, George
- Dreams
Gaubert, Philippe
- Rhapsodie sur des thèmes
  populaires
Gerster, Ottmar
- Oberhessische Bauerntänze für
  Kleines Orchester
Grabner, Hermann
- Divertimento für Kleines Orchester,
  op.56
Hahn, Reynaldo
- La Fête Chez Thérèse: Suite No.2
Jacob, Gordon
- Divertimento
- Suite in F for Small Orchestra
Nussio, Otmar
- Suite from the Tessin

Prokofiev, Sergei
- Cinderella; Ballet in three acts, op.87
Quilter, Roger
- A Children's Overture, op.17
- Where the Rainbow Ends: Suite
Westerman, Gerhart von
- Kleine Suite, op.3

**1121 - 2231 - str
Maximum**

10' or Less

Almand, Claude
- Chorale for Chamber Orchestra (1120-2000)
Argento, Dominick
- The Boor: Overture to the opera (1121-2110)
Benjamin, Arthur
- From San Domingo (1121-2100)
- Two Jamaican Pieces (1121-2100)
Bittner, Julius
- Der Musikant; Serenade (1121-2000)
Bridge, Frank
- There Is A Willow Grows Aslant A Brook (1121-1000)
Copland, Aaron
- Billy the Kid: Prairie Night & Celebration Dance (1121-1220)
- Billy the Kid: Waltz (Billy and his Sweetheart) (1121-1210)
Cowell, Henry
- Saturday Night at the Firehouse (1121-2200)
Delius, Frederick
- Five Little Pieces (1121-2100)
Elgar, Edward
- Chanson de Matin, op.15, No.2 (1121-2000)
- Chanson de Nuit, op.15, No.1 (1121-2000)
- Minuet, op.21 (1121-2000)
Felder, David
- Three Lines from Twenty Poems (1121-1121)
German, Sir Edward
- The Conquerer: Incidental music, Romance and two Dances (1121-2220)
Järnefelt, Armas
- Präludium (1121-2200)
Krenek, Ernst
- Von Vorn Herein, op.219 (1120-1100)
Kubik, Gail
- Music for Dancing (1121-2211)

Ponce, Manuel
- Instantáneas Mexicanas, No.3: Cielito lindo (1121-0000)
- Instantáneas Mexicanas, No.4: Si algún ser (1121-0000)
- Instantáneas Mexicanas, No.6: Mañanitas de los niños (1120-0000)
Reizenstein, Franz
- Capriccio (1121-2200)
Revueltas, Silvestre
- Troka (1121-1211)
- Alcancias (1120-1210)
Santórsola, Guido
- Prelúdio No.3 (1121-2000)
Satie, Erik
- Illusion [Tendrement] (1121-2230)
Saturen, David
- Expression; Lyric piece for small orchestra (1120-2220)
Schnittke, Alfred
- Four Aphorisms (1121-2110)
Schönherr, Max
- Tänze aus Salzburg (1121-2000)
Smit, Andre-Jean
- Suite Pittoresque (1121-2000)
Stravinsky, Igor
- Bluebird Pas de Deux (1121-1220)
Tubin, Eduard
- Valse Triste (1121-2100)
Walton, William
- Siesta (1121-2000)
Webern, Anton
- Variations, op.30 (1120-1111)

Over 10'

Antoniou, Theodore
- Op Ouvertüre für Orchester und drei Lautsprechergruppen (Tonband) (1120-2221)
Bedford, David
- With 100 Kazoos; For chamber ensemble and 100 kazoos (1120-1110)
Berkeley, Lennox
- Partita, op.66 (1121-2110)
Britten, Benjamin
- Johnson Over Jordan: Suite (1121-0210)
Brødsgaard, Anders
- Procession II (1120-1110)
Brust, Herbert
- Kurische Nehrung, op.36 (1120-1110)
Campo, Frank
- Partita for Two Chamber Orchestras, op.45 (1121-1000)
Cohn, James
- Sinfonietta in F (1121-2000)

Coolidge, Peggy Stuart
- Pioneer Dances (1121-1210)
Dubois, Pierre-Max
- Sérieux s'abstenir (1121-1111)
Forst, Rudolf
- Divertimento for Chamber Orchestra (1121-1100)
Gerhard, Roberto
- Pandora: Orchestral suite from the ballet (1121-2110)
Gnessin, Mikhail
- Jewish Orchestra at the Burgermaster's Ball (1121-1100)
Griffes, Charles Tomlinson
- The Kaim of Koridwen; A Druid Legend (1020-2000)
Gruber, HK
- Manhattan Broadcast (1121-0220)
Guenther, Felix
- Deutsches Rokoko; Eine Suite für Kleines Orchester nach alten Meistern (1121-2000)
Hidalgo, Manuel
- Variations on the Variations op.30 by Webern (1120-1111)
Inghelbrecht, D.E.
- La Métamorphose d'Ève; Ballet (1121-2110)
Kósa, György
- Chamber Music (1121-1100)
Lloyd, Jonathan
- Symphony No.3 (1121-2000)
Ludewig, Wolfgang
- Fantasia; On a Theme by W. A. Mozart (1120-0110)
Lutosławski, Witold
- Little Suite (1121-1000)
- Ten Polish Dances (1121-1100)
Maganini, Quinto
- An Ornithological Suite, op.23 (1121-2100)
McCabe, John
- The Lion, the Witch and the Wardrobe: Suite (1121-1210)
Payne, Anthony
- Spring's Shining Wake (1121-2000)
Porrino, Ennio
- Notturno e Danza (1121-2110)
Rogers, Bernard
- The Plains (1121-2100)
Sallinen, Aulis
- Concerto for Chamber Orchestra (1121-1000)
Yun, Isang
- Kammersinfonie II (Chamber Symphony II) (1121-1100)

2121 - 2110 - str
Maximum

Bainbridge, Simon
- Landscape and Memory (2121-1110)

Bennett, Richard Rodney
- Suite Française for Small Orchestra (2121-2110)

Brown, Earle
- Module 3 (2121-1210)

Casella, Alfredo
- Divertimento Per Fulvia: Suite from "La camera dei diseegni," op.64 (2121-2100)

Copland, Aaron
- Down a Country Lane (2121-2110)

Cowell, Henry
- Symphony No.7 (2121-2110)

Dubois, Pierre-Max
- Queue Leu Leu; File de Danses (2121-2110)

Finzi, Gerald
- Love's Labour's Lost: Suite, op.28b (2121-2100)

Ginastera, Alberto
- Variationes Concertantes, op.23 (2121-2110)

Goehr, Alexander
- Still Lands (2121-2110)

Hesketh, Kenneth
- Notte Oscura (2121-1110)

Jost, Christian
- Mascarade: Tableau from the opera "Vipern" (2121-2110)

McKay, George Frederick
- Fantasy on a Western Folk Song; O! Bury me not on the lone prairie (2120-0100)

Porrino, Ennio
- Tre Canzoni Italiane (2121-2110)

Shchetinsky, Alexander
- Glossolalie (2121-1110)

Stern, Robert
- Ricordanza (2121-2100)

Takács, Jenö
- Volkstänze aus dem Burgenland, op.57 (2121-2110)

Tcherepnin, Alexander
- La Femme et son Ombre; Ballet Suite (2121-2110)

2121 - 4231 - str
Maximum

10' or Less

Barlow, Fred
- Cinq Enfantines (2121-2200)

Benjamin, Arthur
- Caribbean Dance; A New Jamaican Rumba (2121-2210)

Falla, Manuel de
- El Amor Brujo: Ritual Fire Dance (2121-2200)

Farkas, Ferenc
- Two Hungarian Dances (2121-2210)

Hartley, Walter Sinclair
- Sinfonia No.7 (2121-2211)

Hudec, Jiri
- Drei Stilisierte Polkas im Volkston (2121-2210)

Malec, Ivo
- Tutti, Concert collectif (2121-2210)

Milhaud, Darius
- Trois Valses (2121-2210)

Nørgård, Per
- Dream Play (2121-2200)

Poot, Marcel
- Musique Legère (2121-2210)

Poulenc, Francis
- Overture (2121-2210)

Powell, Mel
- Stanzas (2121-2210)

Prokofiev, Sergei
- Lieutenant Kije: Troika, op.60 (2121-2230)

Satie, Erik
- Poudre d'or (2121-2230)
- Je te veux (2121-2230)

Vaughan Williams, Ralph
- English Folk Song Suite (2121-2220)

Vinter, Gilbert
- Christmas Sinfonietta (2121-2230)

Weiner, Leo
- Fasching; Carnival Humoresque, op.5 (2121-2210)

Over 10'

Absil, Jean
- Introduction et Valses (2121-3210)

Bolcom, William
- Symphony No.1 (2111-4210)

Bruns, Victor
- Sinfonietta, op.23 (2121-3200)

Bush, Alan
- Partita Concertante, op.63 (2121-2210)

Copland, Aaron
- Dance Panels; Ballet in Seven Sections (2121-2210)

Creston, Paul
- Out of the Cradle Endlessly Rocking; After the poem by Walt Whitman (2121-1111)

Eisler, Hanns
- Suite No.1: From the movie *Opus III*, op.23 (2121-0211)

Ferguson, Howard
- Four Diversions on Ulster Airs, op.7 (2212-4230)

German, Sir Edward
- Tom Jones: Three Dances (2121-2230)

Girnatis, Walter
- Festmusik der Schiffergilde (2121-2200)

Haas, Georg Friedrich
- in vain (2121-2020)

Halffter, Ernesto
- El Cojo Enamorado: Ballet Suite (2121-2210)

Horovitz, Joseph
- Sinfonietta for Light Orchestra (2121-2230)

Milhaud, Darius
- Le boeuf sur le toit; Ballet, op.58 (2121-2210)
- La Rose des Vents; Ballet, op.367 (2121-2221)

Moore, Douglas
- Village Music (2121-2210)

Moyzes, Alexander
- Slowakische Volkslieder, op.15 (2121-2210)

Revueltas, Silvestre
- Le Noche de los Mayas (2121-4111)

Saariaho, Kaija
- Verblendungen (2111-4111)

Satie, Erik
- Mercure; Poses plastiques, op.post (2121-2211)

Sgrizzi, Luciano
- Englische Suite nach Werken der Virginalisten (2121-2200)

Sharp, Elliot
- Calling (2121-1221)

Stanford, Charles Villiers
- Songs of the Sea, op.91 (2121-2220)

1212 - 3221 - str
Maximum

Abendroth, Walter
- Sinfonietta, op.32 (1212-1220)

Bond, Victoria
- Journal (1212-2200)

Chávez, Carlos
- Discovery (1211-2100)
- Sinfonía de Antígona (Symphony No.1) (1210-0100)

Delius, Frederick
- Hassan: Intermezzo and Serenade (1211-2100)

Diamond, David
- Heroic Piece (1211-2111)

Gilbert, Anthony
- Sinfonia for Chamber Orchestra (1211-2100)

Hagen, Daron
- Night Music; Five Scenes for Chamber Orchestra (1211-2100)

Holloway, Robin
- Inquietus, op.66 (1211-1000)

Honegger, Arthur
- Allegretto, H.221 (1211-2200)

Kaipainen, Jouni
- Accende Lumen Sensibus, op.52 (1212-2100)

Kisielewski, Stefan
- Concerto for Chamber Orchestra (1211-0000)

Levy, Marvin David
- Trialogus II (1211-1110)

Locklair, Dan
- In the Autumn Days (1212-2100)

Martinů, Bohuslav
- Sérénade; Pour orchestre de chambre (1212-2210)
- Toccata e due canzoni, H.311 (1211-0100)

Menotti, Gian Carlo
- Introduction, March and Shepherd's Dance: From "Amahl and the Night Visitors" (1211-1100)

Prokofiev, Sergei
- Peter and the Wolf, op.67 (1111-3110)

Rasmussen, Karl Aage
- Symphonie Classique (1211-2110)

Rouse, Christopher
- Iscariot (1212-3100)

Sheng, Bright
- Postcards (1212-2100)

Shostakovich, Dmitri
- Chamber Symphony, op.73a (1211-0000)
- Chamber Symphony, op.83a (1211-2100)

Torke, Michael
- Ash (1212-3100)

Villa-Lobos, Heitor
- Sinfonietta No.2 (1111-3221)

1222 - 2321 - str
Maximum

10' or Less

Aperghis, Georges
- Ascoltare stanca; Pour 18 Instrumentistes (1200-2000)

Ben-Haim, Paul
- Chorale Prelude by J. S. Bach (1201-1110)

Bentzon, Niels Viggo
- Overture for Chamber Orchestra, op.14 (1200-1000)

Blacher, Boris
- Hommage à Mozart; Metamorphoses on a group of Mozart themes for orchestra (1202-2200)

Cohn, James
- The Little Circus, op.51 (1021-2221)

Engelmann, Hans Ulrich
- Ezra Pound Music (1201-0010)

Honegger, Arthur
- Interlude de "La Mort de Sainte Alméene," H.20A (1122-2100)
- Prélude pour Aglavaine et Sélysette; D'après la pièce de Maeterlinck, H.10 (1122-2100)

Kósa, György
- Suite; Three ironic portraits (1122-2201)

La Violette, Wesley
- Nocturne for Orchestra (1221-2110)

Pierné, Gabriel
- Ballet de Cour, No.1: Rigaudon (1112-1100)

Prokofiev, Sergei
- Overture; American, op.42 (1122-0210)

Revueltas, Silvestre
- El Renacuajo Paseador (1020-0210)

Rodríguez, Robert Xavier
- Adagio for Small Orchestra (1112-2000)

Swafford, Jan
- Late August (1222-2200)

Thiele, Siegfried
- Drei Orchestermotetten nach Machaut (1221-2120)

Westergaard, Peter
- Fünf Sätze (1021-2110)

Over 10'

Abendroth, Walter
- Konzertante Phantasie für Orchester, op.23 (1202-0320)

Angerer, Paul
- Sinfonia (1102-1200)

Apostel, Hans Erich
- Variations on Three Folksongs, op.23 (1122-2100)

Argento, Dominick
- Royal Invitation (Homage to the Queen of Tonga) (1202-2000)

Arnold, Malcolm
- Concerto for 28 Players, op.105 (1201-2000)

Berkeley, Lennox
- Windsor Variations, op.75 (1202-2000)

Bialas, Günter
- Der Weg nach Eisenstadt; Haydn Phantasies for Small Orchestra (1202-2000)

Britten, Benjamin
- Plymouth Town (1122-2110)

Chapple, Brian
- Little Symphony (1202-2000)

Conyngham, Barry
- Glimpses of Bennelong (1200-2000)

David, Johann Nepomuk
- Variations on a Theme by J. S. Bach, Wk29a (1201-2000)

Firsova, Elena
- Autumn Music, op.39 (1202-2000)

Geissler, Fritz
- Chamber Symphony (1954) (1111-0310)

Grinberg, Alexander
- Carillon (1221-1111)

Haas, Joseph
- Variationen-Suite; Über ein altes Rokoko-Thema, op.64 (1022-2100)

Heitzeg, Steve
- Flower of the Earth; Homage to Georgia O'Keeffe (1201-2000)

Helfer, Walter
- Prelude to a Midsummer Night's Dream (1112-1100)

Holloway, Robin
- Second Idyll, op.54 (1202-2000)

Kasilag, Lucrecia
- Legend of the Sarimanok (1112-1110)

Kupferman, Meyer
- Little Symphony (1202-2000)

Matthews, David
- Serenade, op.29 (1202-2000)
- Symphony No.4, op.51 (1202-2000)

Maw, Nicholas
- Serenade (1202-2000)
McAlister, Clark
- A Christmas Pastorale (1201-2000)
Musgrave, Thea
- Night Music (1201-2000)
Neikrug, Marc
- Chetro Ketl (1222-2200)
Nørgård, Per
- Tango Chikane (reduced version) (1222-2110)
Polovinkin, Leonid
- Tänze der Rätsel (1112-2100)
Rieti, Vittorio
- Due Pastorali (1112-2100)
- Sinfonietta per Piccola Orchestra (1112-2220)
Saxton, Robert
- Elijah's Violin (1202-2000)
Schulhoff, Erwin
- Suite (1221-2100)
Schurmann, Gerard
- Variants (1202-2000)
Standford, Patric
- Notte (1201-2000)
Swayne, Giles
- Symphony for Small Orchestra (1202-2000)
Thiele, Siegfried
- Wolkenbilder; Four Movements (1200-2000)
Thomson, Virgil
- Suite from "The River" (1221-2220)
Uhl, Alfred
- Vergnügliche Musik aus einer deutschen Kleinstadt (1221-2220)

2112 - 2221 - str
Maximum

10' or Less

Finke, Fidelio
- Festliche Musik (2112-1220)
Harrison, Lou
- Seven Pastorales (2101-0000)
Ives, Charles Edward
- Central Park in the Dark (2111-0110)
Moross, Jerome
- Paeans (2111-2210)
Rodrigo, Joaquín
- Homenaje a la Tempranica (2111-2200)
Rosenberg, Hilding Constantin
- Ouvertura Piccola (2102-2210)
Schreker, Franz
- Valse Lente; Weißer Tanz (2111-0000)

Szabelski, Bolesław
- Preludes (2110-2210)
Tull, Fisher
- Capriccio (2111-2110)

Over 10'

Abrahamsen, Hans
- Foam (2111-1110)
Antheil, George
- Serenade II (2111-2110)
Benjamin, Arthur
- Light Music Suite (2111-2210)
Borkovec, Pavel
- Sinfonietta da Camera (2111-2100)
Braun, Yehezkel
- Illuminations to the Book of Ruth (2101-2110)
David, Johann Nepomuk
- Magische Quadrate; Symphonische Phantasie, Wk52 (2111-2110)
Degen, Helmut
- Chamber Symphony (Symphony No.2) (2101-2100)
Diamond, David
- Music for Chamber Orchestra (2111-2110)
Dubois, Pierre-Max
- Analogie; Suite for Orchestra (2111-2111)
Gaslini, Giorgio
- Canto Dalla Città Inquieta: From "Totale" (2110-1100)
Gauldin, Robert
- Diverse Dances (2111-2110)
Geissler, Fritz
- Five Miniatures (2111-2210)
Haieff, Alexei Vasilievich
- Divertimento (2110-0220)
Hamilton, Iain
- Sonata, op.34 (2111-1100)
Harty, Hamilton
- Fantasy Scenes; From an Eastern Romance (2111-2110)
Helm, Everett
- Italienische Suite (2111-2220)
Lam, Bun-Ching
- Saudades de Macau (2111-1110)
Neubert, Günter
- Music for Orchestra on a Theme by Robert Schumann (2112-2110)
Nørgård, Per
- Voyage into the Golden Screen (2111-2210)
Rodrigo, Joaquín
- Soleriana; Suite for chamber orchestra (2111-1100)

Rogers, Bernard
- The Musicians of Bremen (2111-1100)
Schmitt, Florent
- Enfants, op.94 (2111-1100)
Spitzmüller, Alexander
- 40. Mai; Suite, op.25 (2111-2200)
Weill, Kurt
- Aufstieg und Fall der Stadt Mahagonny (Rise and Fall of the City of Mahagonny): Suite (2112-2221)

2222 - 2000 -str
Exact

10' or Less

Aubert, Louis
- La Lettre
Bentzon, Niels Viggo
- Prelude and Rondo, op.56
Delius, Frederick
- Petite Suite No.2
Dohnanyi, Ernest von
- The Veil of Pierette: Waltz, op.18, No.2
Duparc, Henri
- Aux étoiles
Elgar, Edward
- Serenade Lyrique
Elias, Alfonso de
- El Jardín Encantado; Tríptico Sinfoníco
Faust, George
- Adagio for Small Orchestra
Fenney, William
- Romance in Early Spring
Gaubert, Philippe
- Madrigal
Knussen, Oliver
- Music for a Puppet Court; Puzzle pieces for 2 Chamber Orchestras, op.11
Kolb, Barbara
- The Web Spinner
Liebermann, Rolf
- Suite on Six Swiss Folksongs
Milhaud, Darius
- Chamber Symphony No.5; Dixtuor d'Instruments à Vent, op.75
Poulenc, Francis
- Bucolique
Ravel, Maurice
- Ma Mère l'Oye (Mother Goose): Prelude et Danse du Rouet
Strauss, Richard
- Ariadne auf Naxos: Overture and Dance Scene, op.60

Over 10'

Amy, Gilbert
- D'Après "Ecrits Sur Toiles"; Pour Orchestre de Chambre

Bacri, Nicolas
- Symphony No.4; Symphonie Classique Sturm und Drang, op.49

Bentzon, Niels Viggo
- Symphony No.6, op.66
- Symphony No.11, op.158

Berkeley, Lennox
- Nocturne, op.25
- Sinfonietta, op.34

Bon, André
- Ode; Pour orchestre "Mozart"

Coleman, Linda Robbins
- For A Beautiful Land

Cowie, Edward
- Leonardo

Gál, Hans
- Idyllikon; Four movements for small orchestra, op.79

Hamilton, Iain
- Symphony No.3

Manén, Joan
- Divertimento, op.A-32

Matthus, Siegfried
- Divertimento for Orchestra; Triangle Concerto

Panufnik, Andrzej
- Sinfonia Mistica; Symphony No.6

Pfitzner, Hans
- Das Christ-Elflein, op.20

Piazzolla, Astor
- Tangazo; Variations on Buenos Aires

Piston, Walter
- Sinfonietta

Rautavaara, Einojuhani
- Autumn Gardens

Ravel, Maurice
- Ma Mère l'Oye (Mother Goose): Ballet en un acte, cinq tableaux et un apothéose
- Ma Mère l'Oye (Mother Goose): Cinq pièces enfantines (Suite)

Reizenstein, Franz
- Serenade in F, op.29a

Schmitt, Florent
- Pupazzi, op.36

Tansman, Alexandre
- Suite Baroque

2222 - 2000 - str
Maximum

10' or Less

Baird, Tadeusz
- Overture in Old Style (2202-2000)

Barnett, Carol
- Sumervar (2212-2000)

Bartók, Béla
- Suite, op.14 (2212-2000)

Bond, Victoria
- Concertino (1212-2000)

Bossi, Marco Enrico
- Siciliana e Giga (stile antico) per Orchestra, op.73 (2111-1000)

Busoni, Ferruccio
- Berceuse elegiaque (2122-2000)

Delius, Frederick
- A Song Before Sunrise (2122-2000)

Diamond, David
- Hommage à Satie; À mémoire for chamber orchestra (2111-2000)

Dohnanyi, Ernest von
- The Veil of Pierette: Menuett, op.18, No.5 (1122-2000)

Elgar, Edward
- Salut d'Amour, op.12 (1222-2000)

Etler, Alvin
- Elegy for Small Orchestra (1122-2000)

Glazunov, Alexander
- Serenade for Small Orchestra No.2, op.11 (2122-2000)

Harrison, Lou
- Alleluia (2220-2000)

Honegger, Arthur
- Vivace, H.220 (1122-2000)

Kaun, Hugo
- Elegie, op.70, No.5 (2121-2000)

Kirk, Theron
- Adagietto (1211-2000)

Maxwell Davies, Peter
- Chat Moss (2111-2000)

Ponce, Manuel
- Gavota (2111-2000)

Ravel, Maurice
- Pavane pour une infante défunte (2122-2000)

Read, Gardner
- Petite Pastorale, op.40a (1122-2000)

Stravinsky, Igor
- Tango (1211-2000)

Over 10'

Arnold, Malcolm
- Sinfonietta No.3 (2202-2000)

Bolcom, William
- Symphony No.3 (1212-2000)

Bon, André
- Ode II; Pour orchestre de chambre (2201-2000)

Cage, John
- Quartets I-VIII; For an Orchestra of 24 Instruments (1212-2000)

Delius, Frederick
- Two Pieces for Small Orchestra (1122-2000)

Dillon, James
- Windows and Canopies (2201-2000)

Druckman, Jacob
- Nor Spell, Nor Charm (1222-2000)

Genzmer, Harald
- Sinfonia da Camera (2111-1000)

Goehr, Alexander
- Sinfonia, op.42 (1220-2000)

Henze, Hans Werner
- Aria de la Folia Española (1212-2000)

Holloway, Robin
- Concertino No.2, op.10 (1211-2000)
- First Idyll, op.42 (1222-2000)

Juon, Paul
- Serenade, op.40 (2122-2000)

Karayev, Kara
- Symphony No.3 for Chamber Orchestra (2202-2000)

Kodály, Zoltán
- Summer Evening (1222-2000)

Lumsdaine, David
- Sunflower (1222-2000)

Maw, Nicholas
- Sinfonia (1222-2000)

McCabe, John
- Concerto for Chamber Orchestra (1222-2000)

McKay, George Frederick
- Variants on a Texas Tune; Mustang grey (2121-2000)

Milford, Robin
- Suite for Chamber Orchestra (2122-1000)

Milner, Anthony
- Chamber Symphony (1212-2000)

Raphael, Günter
- Variationen über eine Schottische Volksweise, op.23 (2112-2000)

Roselius, Ludwig
- Friesische Musik, op.30 (1221-1000)

Saygun, A. Adnan
- Symphony No.1 (1222-2000)
Schweitzer, Benjamin
- flekkicht; For baroque orchestra
(2201-2000)
Sibelius, Jean
- Belsazars Gaestabud (Belshazzar's
Feast); Incidental Music, op.51
(2120-2000)
- Pelleas & Melisande, op.46 (1122-
2000)
Standford, Patric
- Suite for Small Orchestra (2121-
2000)

2222 - 2100 - str
Exact

Brouk, Joanna
- Lalinia electra; Part 1
Castro, José Maria
- Concerto Grosso
Cruft, Adrian
- Partita, op.7
Debussy, Claude
- Lindaraja
Delius, Frederick
- Fennimore and Gerda: Intermezzo
Hanuš, Jan
- Prazská Nokturna (Prague
Nocturne), op.75
Jelinek, Hanns
- Parergon, op.15B
Magnard, Albéric
- Suite in Ancient Style, op.2
Martinů, Bohuslav
- Sinfonietta la Jolla, H.328
Matthews, Colin
- Night Music, op.10
Moore, Douglas
- Farm Journal; Suite for Chamber
Orchestra
Poulenc, Francis
- Pièce brève; On the name of Albert
Roussel
Ravel, Maurice
- Cinq Mélodies populaires grecques
(Five Greek Folk Melodies)
- Fanfare
- Le Tombeau de Couperin
Rorem, Ned
- Symphony No.2
Roussel, Albert
- Concert pour petit orchestre, op.34
Thiele, Siegfried
- Sonatina
Weigl, Karl
- Music for the Young

2222 - 2110 - str
Exact

Bentzon, Niels Viggo
- Mini-Symphony, op.231
Corigliano, John
- Creations: Two Scenes from
Genesis
- Elegy
Erdmann, Eduard
- Ständchen, op.16
Naginski, Charles
- Suite for Small Orchestra
Pergament, Moses
- Vision; Ballet
Poulenc, Francis
- L'embarquement pour Cythère
Rautavaara, Einojuhani
- Lintukoto (Isle of Bliss)
- Symphony No.2
Rorem, Ned
- A Quaker Reader; Suite
Roselius, Ludwig
- Lilofee Suite, op.16
Schollum, Robert
- Serenade, Werk 39a
Schwertsik, Kurt
- Compagnie Masquerade; Ein
Divertissement für kleines
Orchester, einer Idee & teilweise
erhaltenen Violinstimme Mozarts
folgend
- Mozart, auf und davon, op.94
Siegl, Otto
- Lyrische Tanzmusik, op.82
Strauss, Richard
- Le Bourgeois Gentilhomme (Der
Bürger als Edelmann): Suite, op.60
- Tanzsuite nach Couperin
Takács, Jenö
- Von fremden Ländern und
Menschen, op.37
Tansman, Alexandre
- Sinfonia Piccola
Thiele, Siegfried
- Concerto for Orchestra
Vincent, John
- The House that Jack Built: From the
ballet "Three Jacks"
- Suite from the Ballet "Three Jacks"

2222 - 2200 - str
Exact

10' or Less

Absil, Jean
- Sérénade
Adamo, Mark
- Overture to Lysistrata
Adler, Samuel
- Show An Affirming Flame; A Poem
for Orchestra ("September 1, 1939"
by W. H. Auden)
Albeniz, Isaac
- Iberia: Evocación
- Iberia: Lavapiés
- Iberia: Triana
Atterberg, Kurt
- Eine Värmlandsrhapsodie, op.36
Auric, Georges
- Ecossaise
Bacri, Nicolas
- Folia; Chaconne symphonique pour
orchestre, op.30
Bavicchi, John
- Music for Small Orchestra, op.81
Bennett, Richard Rodney
- Sinfonietta
Bjelinski, Bruno
- Pinocchio; Ballet in 4 acts
Black, Stanley
- A Costume Comedy Overture
- Percussion Fantasy
Boccadoro, Carlo
- Mouvement for Orchestra
Buck, Ole
- Overture
Cowell, Henry
- Carol
Daugherty, Michael
- Tell My Fortune
Einem, Gottfried von
- Introduktion - Wandlungen: No.1
from "Divertimento for Mozart,"
op.21
Fricker, Peter Racine
- Fantasie: No.4 from "Divertimento
for Mozart"
Fujiie, Keiko
- Beber, op.31
Gianneo, Luis
- Variaciones Sobre Tema de Tango
Halffter, Rodolfo
- Obertura Festiva (Festive Overture)
Harbison, John
- David's Fascinating Rhythm Method
Henze, Hans Werner
- Finale - Vivace assai: Nr.12 from
"Divertimento for Mozart"

Hindson, Matthew
- RPM
Honegger, Arthur
- Toccata, H.207
Horne, David
- Flicker
Humperdinck, Engelbert
- Humoreske in E Dur
Ibert, Jacques
- Hommage à Mozart
Kelterborn, Rudolf
- Musica luminosa per orchestra
Kennan, Kent
- Dance Divertimento
Kingman, Daniel
- A Revolutionary Garland
Koch, Erland von
- Dance No.2
Korngold, Erich Wolfgang
- Dance in the Old Style
Lazar, Filip
- Suite Valaque
MacMillan, James
- Memoire imperiale; A variation on
  General John Reid's March "Garb of
  Gaul"
Maxwell Davies, Peter
- Ojai Festival Overture
Neikrug, Marc
- Suite from Los Alamos
Palau Boix, Manuel
- Homenaje a Debussy
Pepping, Ernst
- Invention für Kleines Orchester:
  From "Musiken für Orchester"
Pompey, Angel Martin
- Serenata madrilena
Poulenc, Francis
- Matelote Provençale
Prokofiev, Sergei
- Overture on Hebrew Themes,
  op.34a
Rodrigo, Joaquín
- Dos Danzas Españolas; Suite for
  castanets and orchestra
Rorem, Ned
- Triptych; Three Pieces for Chamber
  Orchestra
Roux, Maurice le
- Allegro Moderato: No.9 from
  "Divertimento for Mozart"
Satie, Erik
- Jack in the Box, op.post
Saxton, Robert
- Variation on "Sumer is Icumen In"
Schwertsik, Kurt
- Schrumpf-Symphonie, op.80
Toch, Ernst
- Intermezzo

Vercoe, Elizabeth
- Changes; A little music for Mozart
Weiner, Leo
- Serenade for Small Orchestra in F
  minor, op.3
Wimberger, Gerhard
- Allegro Giocoso: No.8 from
  "Divertimento for Mozart"
Zbinden, Julien-François
- Orchalau Concerto, op.38

11' - 15'

Alnar, Hasan Ferit
- Zwei Türkische Orchesterstücke;
  Improvisation und zwei Tänze
Arnold, Malcolm
- Serenade for Small Orchestra
Bedford, David
- This One For You
Bennett, Richard Rodney
- Country Dances; Book 1
Binkerd, Gordon
- Movement for Orchestra
Britten, Benjamin
- Suite on English Folk Tunes, op.90
Cowell, Henry
- Ongaku
Dalby, Martin
- Nozze di Primavera
Daugherty, Michael
- Sunset Strip
Dean, Brett
- Testament; Music for orchestra,
  after "Testament: Music for twelve
  violas"
Falla, Manuel de
- El Sombrero des Tres Picos: Suite
  No.1
Fauré, Gabriel
- Masques et Bergamasques, op.112
Frank, Gabriela Lena
- Elegía Andina
Frazelle, Kenneth
- Laconic Variations
Halffter, Rodolfo
- La Madrugada del Panadero: Suite
  del Ballet
Harbison, John
- Canonical American Songbook
Herrera de la Fuente, Luis
- Fronteras; Ballet
Hutcheson, Jere
- Taj Mahal
Kurz, Siegfried
- Sonatina for Orchestra, op.34
Leplin, Emanuel
- Three Dances for Small Orchestra

Linke, Norbert
- Divisioni
Milhaud, Darius
- Sérénade, op.62
Paumgartner, Bernhard
- Suite in G minor
Prokofiev, Sergei
- Classical Symphony in D,
  Symphony No.1, op.25
- A Summer Day, op.65a
Riege, Ernst
- Rondo Giocoso
Rodrigo, Joaquín
- Palillos y Panderetas; Música para
  una tonadilla imaginaria
Rosenberg, Hilding Constantin
- Dance Suite from the Grand Opera
  "The Marionettes"
Rueda, Jesús
- Elephant Skin
Saxton, Robert
- The Ring of Eternity
Schafer, Robert Murray
- Cortège
Sierra, Roberto
- Serenata
Stanford, Charles Villiers
- Suite of Ancient Dances, op.58
Stevens, Bernard
- Introduction, Variations & Fugue on
  a Theme of Giles Farnaby
Wagner, Joseph
- Four Miniatures
Weigl, Karl
- Pictures and Tales; Suite for small
  orchestra, op.2
Weir, Judith
- Isti Mirant Stella
Wunsch, Hermann
- Fest auf Monbijou; Suite in fünf
  Sätzen, op.50

Over 15'

Adolphe, Bruce
- Three Pieces; For Kids in the
  Audience and Chamber Orchestra
Aitken, Robert
- Spiral
Bacri, Nicolas
- Symphony No.5; Concerto pour
  orchestre, op.55
Bedford, David
- The Valley Sleeper, the Children,
  the Snakes and the Giant
Bräutigam, Helmut
- Tänzerische Suite
Cowell, Henry
- Symphony No.10

Ficher, Jacobo
- Seis Fabulas (Six Falbes)
Frazelle, Kenneth
- Concerto for Chamber Orchestra
Goldstein, Mikhail
- Ukranian Symphony in Old Style
Halffter, Cristóbal
- Dalíniana; Three pieces on three
  paintings by Salvador Dalí
Harbison, John
- The Most Often Used Chords (Gli
  Accordi Piu Usati)
Hauer, Josef Matthias
- Romantische Phantasie, op.37
Holloway, Robin
- Fourth Idyll
Holmboe, Vagn
- Concerto for Orchestra, op.38
Jenner, Gustav
- Serenade for Orchestra
Lees, Benjamin
- Concerto for Chamber Orchestra
Lloyd, Jonathan
- Symphony No.1
MacMillan, James
- Symphony No.2
- Tryst
Maxwell Davies, Peter
- Sinfonietta Accademica
- Strathclyde Concerto No.10;
  Concerto for Orchestra
- Symphony No.4
Musgrave, Thea
- The Seasons
Nyman, Michael
- Strong on Oaks; Strong on the
  Causes of Oaks
Payne, Anthony
- Orchestral Variations; "The Seeds
  Long Hidden"
Poulenc, Francis
- Sinfonietta
Riege, Ernst
- Serenade
Roussel, Albert
- Le festin de l'araignée; Ballet-
  pantomime en un acte, op.17
Saint-Saëns, Camille
- Symphony in A
Schickele, Peter
- Concerto for Chamber Orchestra
- Symphony No.2; The Sweet
  Season
- Thurber's Dogs
Schlemm, Gustav Adolf
- Serenade
Schönberg, Arnold
- Kammersymphonie Nr.2 (Chamber
  Symphony No.2), op.38

Sierra, Roberto
- Sinfonia No.1
Tower, Joan
- Chamber Dance
- Duets
Trexler, Georg
- Concerto for Orchestra
Tubin, Eduard
- Symphony No.7
Turina, Joaquin
- Cinq Danzas Gitanas, op.55
Weir, Judith
- Winter Song
Westergaard, Peter
- L'Homme Armé, op.22a

2222 - 2210 - str
Exact

10' or Less

Alonso-Crespo, Eduardo
- Yubarta: Overture
Blumer, Theodor
- Vagabund; Scherzo for Orchestra
Copland, Aaron
- John Henry
Csonka, Paul
- Prisma Sinfonico (Symphonic
  Prism)
Eitler, Esteban
- Divertimento 1950
Fenby, Eric
- Rossini on Ilkla Moor; Overture
Geissler, Fritz
- Italienische Lustspiel-Ouvertüre
Girnatis, Walter
- Scherzo Fantastique
Hartley, Walter Sinclair
- Three Patterns for Small Orchestra
Kallstenius, Edvin
- Dalsland-Rhapsodie, op.22
Koch, Erland von
- Kleine Lustspiel Ouvertüre
Lecocq, Charles
- Fricassée
Moravec, Paul
- Adelphony
Nabokoff, Nicholas
- Le Fiance, op.9
Poulenc, Francis
- Overture
Schickele, Peter
- Songs from Shakespeare
- What Did You Do Today at Jeffey's
  House?
Wellejus, Henning
- Postvognen Ruller (The Mailcoach
  is Rolling), op.16

Over 10'

Aguila, Miguel del
- Salon Buenos Aires
Apostel, Hans Erich
- Five Austrian Miniatures
Auric, Georges
- La Peintre et son Modèle; Ballet in
  one act
Bentzon, Niels Viggo
- Sinfonia, op.402
Berkeley, Lennox
- Divertimento in Bb, op.18
Bondon, Jacques
- Symphonie latine
Burkhard, Willy
- Kleine konzertante Suite
  (Kaleidoskop) für Orchester, op.79
Carter, Elliott
- Symphony No.1
Consoli, Marc-Antonio
- Odefonia
Fletcher, Horace Grant
- Two Orchestral Pieces for Small
  Orchestra
Gál, Hans
- Ballet Suite "Scaramussio," op.36
Goeb, Roger
- Prairie Songs
Jacob, Gordon
- Sinfonietta No.1 for Small Orchestra
Klenau, Paul von
- Altdeutsche Liedersuite (Old
  German Song Suite)
Koch, Erland von
- Skandinavische Tänze
- Three Miniatures for Orchestra
Kolb, Barbara
- Yet That Things Go Round
Lees, Benjamin
- Divertimento-Burlesca
Mitsukuri, Shukichi
- Sinfonietta in D Major
Moravec, Paul
- Ancient Lights
- Streamline
Nussio, Otmar
- Boccaccio-Suite; Novelle dal
  Decamerone
Nyman, Michael
- Concert Suite from Prospero's
  Books
Pisk, Paul Amadeus
- Partita, op.10
Rautavaara, Einojuhani
- Cantus Arcticus; Concerto for Birds
  and Orchestra

Rogers, Bernard
- Five Fairy Tales (Once Upon a Time)
Roters, Ernst
- Tanzsuite, op.23
Salmhofer, Franz
- Overture
Schwantner, Joseph
- Chasing Light
Swanson, Howard
- Short Symphony
Takács, Jenö
- Ländliches Barock; Suite, op.48
Tansman, Alexandre
- Des Kaisers neue Kleider; Musik zu einem Andersen-Ballett
Thiele, Siegfried
- Intrada, Cantus, Toccata
Tower, Joan
- The Last Dance
- Made in America
Wellejus, Henning
- Vor Barndoms Venner (Our Childhood Friends), op.15

2222 - 2220 -str
Exact

10' or Less

Blacher, Boris
- Kleine Marschmusik
- Orchester-Capriccio über ein Volkslied
Döhl, Friedhelm
- Ikaros; Ballet nach einem Gedicht von E. Lindgren
Janáček, Leoš
- Adagio
Maxwell Davies, Peter
- Jimmack the Postie
Nielsen, Carl
- Festival Prelude
Pfundt, Reinhard
- Bartók-Reflexionen
Poot, Marcel
- Ouverture Joyeuse
Rorem, Ned
- Waiting
Tower, Joan
- Paganini Trills
Vir, Param
- The Field of Opportunity

Over 10'

Barber, Samuel
- Medea: Ballet Suite, op.23
Blacher, Boris
- Feste im Süden: Suite
Cage, John
- The Seasons; Ballet in One Act
Copland, Aaron
- Appalachian Spring: Suite (full orchestra version)
Cowell, Henry
- Symphony No.9
Danielpour, Richard
- Souvenirs
David, Johann Nepomuk
- Partita No.2, Wk27
Einem, Gottfried von
- Münchner Symphonie, op.70
Feldman, Morton
- The Turfan Fragments
Hasquenoph, Pierre
- Symphony No.1, op.10
Ibert, Jacques
- Tropismes pour les Amours Imaginaires
Jerger, Wilhelm
- Symphony No.1; Classical Symphony
Koch, Erland von
- Oxberg Variations; On a Theme from Dalekarlien
- Schwedische Tanz-Rhapsodie
Maxwell Davies, Peter
- Caroline Mathilde: Concert Suite from Act I of the ballet
- Caroline Mathilde: Concert Suite from Act II of the ballet
- An Orkney Wedding, with Sunrise; Version for Chamber Orchestra
Meale, Richard
- Variations
Milhaud, Darius
- Le Bal Martiniquais
- Musique pour San Francisco, op.436
- Opus Americanum No.2 (Moïse)
Pfundt, Reinhard
- Musique Pour Sanssouci
Rodríguez, Robert Xavier
- Estampie; Ballet for Small Orchestra
Stranz, Ulrich
- Anstieg - Ausblick für Orchester
Terzakis, Dimitri
- Tropi
Villa-Lobos, Heitor
- Sinfonietta No.1

Weill, Kurt
- Quodlibet: Suite aus "Zaubernacht." Eine Unterhaltungsmusik, op.9
- Der Silbersee: Suite aus dem Wintermärchen

2022 -2211 - str
Maximum

Bartók, Béla
- Rumanian Folk Dances (2022-2000)
Bonnet, Antoine
- D'une Source Oubliée I (2020-1010)
- Trajectoires (2020-2110)
Chou, Wen-Chung
- Two Miniatures from T'ang (2010-1000)
Denisov, Edison
- Hommage à Pierre (2020-1000)
Freyhan, Michael
- Toy Symphony (2020-0200)
Ganne, Louis
- Deux Airs de Ballet: Pasquinade (2020-0000)
Guarnieri, Camargo
- Ponteios No.3 (2021-2000)
Hallén, Andreas
- In Autumn (Om hösten) (2022-2000)
Honegger, Arthur
- La Roue: Overture pour le film d'Abel Gance, H.44 (2022-0000)
Johnson, Hunter
- Concerto for Small Orchestra (2020-0000)
Kander, Susan
- She Never Lost A Passenger Overture (2020-0110)
Kaun, Hugo
- Fröhliches Wandern, op.70, No.1 (2021-2000)
- Idyll, op.70, No.2 (2021-2000)
MacKenzie, Sir Alexander C.
- Benedictus, op.37, No.3 (2022-2000)
McCabe, John
- Sam (2020-0100)
Nilsson, Bo
- Bombi Bitt (2010-0000)
- Taqsim-Caprice-Maqam (2022-2201)
Price, Florence
- Suite of Dances (2021-2200)
Satie, Erik
- La Diva de l'Empire (2011-1110)

Sibelius, Jean
- Valse Romantique, op.62b (2020-2000)
Weir, Judith
- Still, Glowing (2020-0000)

2222 - 2221 - str
Exact

Bartók, Béla
- Hungarian Folksongs
Bermel, Derek
- Tag Rag
- Turning Variations
Bernstein, Leonard
- 1600 Pennsylvania Avenue: Suite for Orchestra
Britten, Benjamin
- Death in Venice: Suite, op.88a
Brown, Earle
- Modules 1 & 2
Cowell, Henry
- Symphony No.16; Icelandic
Davis, Anthony
- Notes from the Underground
Einem, Gottfried von
- Symphony No.4, op.80
Harbison, John
- Remembering Gatsby; Foxtrot for Orchestra
Hutcheson, Jere
- Transitions for Orchestra
Lutosławski, Witold
- Prelude for Guildhall School of Music: Worldes Blis Ne Last No Throwe
Muñoz Molleda, José
- Circo; Suite
Sharp, Elliot
- Racing Hearts
Terzakis, Dimitri
- Hommage à Dionysos
Treibmann, Karl Ottomar
- Capriccio 71

2222 - 2331 - str
Maximum

10' or Less

Abrahamsen, Hans
- Stratifications (2221-2210)
Adler, Samuel
- City By The Lake; A Portrait of Rochester, NY (2222-2231)
Chou, Wen-Chung
- Landscapes (2200-2020)
Engelmann, Hans Ulrich
- Kaleidoskop (1111-0330)

German, Sir Edward
- Coronation March (2222-2230)
Halffter, Ernesto
- Cavatina (2211-1110)
Holloway, Robin
- Overture on a Nursery Rhyme, op.75a (2222-2211)
Holst, Gustav
- Two Songs Without Words, op.22 / H88 (2122-2210)
Krenek, Ernst
- Ouvertüre "Triumph der Empfindsamkeit" (Triumph of Sensitivity), op.43a (2222-0230)
Matthus, Siegfried
- Small Concerto for Orchestra (2000-0030)
- Sonata by G. Gabrieli (2202-2220)
Montsalvatge, Xavier
- Serenade a Lydia de Cadaques (2221-2210)
Pierné, Gabriel
- Ballet de Cour, No.6: Passamezzo (2222-2230)
Quilter, Roger
- Three English Dances, op.11 (2222-2231)
Saint-Saëns, Camille
- Rigaudon, op.93, No.2 (2222-2020)
Satie, Erik
- Trois Mélodies de 1916 (2222-1111)
Stravinsky, Igor
- Suite No.1; For Small Orchestra (2122-1111)
- Suite No.2; For Small Orchestra (2122-1211)
Tower, Joan
- Island Rhythms (2222-2211)
Wilson, Ian
- What we can see of the sky has fallen (2122-2100)

Over 10'

Bantock, Granville
- Russian Scenes (2222-2230)
Baur, Jürg
- Frammenti; Erinnerungen an Schubert (2222-2230)
- Sentieri musicali; Auf Mozarts Spuren. Sinfonietta (2222-2230)
Bennett, Richard Rodney
- Serenade for Small Orchestra (2221-2210)
Berio, Luciano
- Chemins IIb (2122-2321)
Biersack, Anton
- Bagatellen (2222-0100)

Blacher, Boris
- Collage (2222-1111)
- Demeter: Suite (2222-1110)
Britten, Benjamin
- Matinées musicales, op.24; Second Suite of Five Movements from Rossini (2222-2230)
Buck, Ole
- Pastorals (2221-1200)
Busoni, Ferruccio
- Concertante Suite from W. A. Mozart's Opera "Idomeneo" (Busoni Verz. B85) (2222-2230)
Casella, Alfredo
- Serenata, op.46b (2122-2110)
Cerha, Friedrich
- Sinfonie (2222-2111)
Copland, Aaron
- Prairie Journal (2221-2321)
Cowell, Henry
- Old American Country Set (2222-2211)
David, Johann Nepomuk
- Symphonic Variations on a Theme by H. Schütz, Wk29b (2222-0220)
Döhl, Friedhelm
- Passion (2122-2320)
Falla, Manuel de
- Fuego Fatuo (2122-2230)
Finke, Fidelio
- Eight Bagatelles (2222-2230)
Fitelberg, Jerzy
- Suite No.3 (2122-0220)
Foulds, John
- Keltic Suite, op.29 (2222-2231)
Hasquenoph, Pierre
- Variations en Trois Mouvements (2222-2320)
Hesketh, Kenneth
- Detail from the Record (2221-1110)
Honegger, Arthur
- Suite Archaïque, H.203 (2222-0220)
- Tête d'Or; Musique pour une pièce de Paul Claudel, H.199 (1111-0330)
LeFanu, Nicola
- Farne (2222-2331)
León, Tania
- Tones (2210-1011)
Lindberg, Magnus
- Marea (2222-2111)
Milhaud, Darius
- Vendanges; Ballet, op.317 (2222-2331)
Morthenson, Jan Wilhelm
- Antiphonia I (2222-2002)

Poulenc, Francis
- L'histoire de Babar, le petit éléphant (2222-2211)

Prokofiev, Sergei
- Eugene Onegin; For narrator, actors and orchestra, op.71 (2221-2321)

Rihm, Wolfgang
- Gesungene Zeit (2222-1210)

Röttger, Heinz
- Sinfonische Meditationen (2222-0331)

Schnittke, Alfred
- Gogol Suite (2121-2111)

Schuller, Gunther
- Chamber Symphony (2222-1111)

Sharp, Elliot
- On Corlear's Hook (2222-1220)

Spinner, Leopold
- Ricercata, op.21 (2220-1111)

Stravinsky, Igor
- Scenes de Ballet (2221-2331)

Treibmann, Karl Ottomar
- Symphony No.2 (2222-1110)

Trexler, Georg
- Introduzione e Scherzo (2222-2230)

Yun, Isang
- Konzertante Figuren (2211-2110)

Zbinden, Julien-François
- Symphony No.1, op.18 (2221-2100)

2222 - 3331 - str
Maximum

10' or Less

Antheil, George
- Suite for Orchestra (2220-3001)

Argento, Dominick
- The Dream of Valentino: Dances from Valentino (2222-3211)

Bleyle, Karl
- Bacchanten-Overture, op.52 (2222-3201)

Janáček, Leoš
- Mährische Volkstänze (Moravian Folk Dances) (2222-3230)

Reger, Max
- Suite, op.44 (2222-3200)

Schlemm, Gustav Adolf
- Polka-Fughetta (2222-3230)

Toch, Ernst
- Circus Overture (2222-3331)

Over 10'

Aguila, Miguel del
- Conga for Orchestra, op.44 (2222-3221)

Angerer, Paul
- Musica Fera (2222-3321)

Atterberg, Kurt
- De Fåvitska Jungfrurna; The wise and the foolish virgins. Rhapsody on old Swedish folksongs (2222-3000)

Bartel, Hans-Christian
- Concerto (2222-3321)

Bartók, Béla
- Suite No.2, op.4 (2222-3200)

Baur, Jürg
- Carmen Variations; Theme, Variations and Finale on a Theme from Bizet's "Carmen" (2222-3230)

Bleyle, Karl
- Schneewittchensuite, op.50 (2222-3201)

Busch, Adolf
- Variations on a Theme by W. A. Mozart (2222-3200)

Gál, Hans
- Symphony No.2, op.53 (2222-3230)

Janáček, Leoš
- Suite, op.3 (2222-3200)

Kajanus, Robert
- Sinfonietta in Bb major, op.16 (2222-3000)

Schickele, Peter
- Legend (2222-3221)
- Three Girls, Three Women (2222-3211)

Schollum, Robert
- Tanzsuite, Werk 21 (2111-3310)

Sheng, Bright
- H'un (Lacerations): In Memoriam 1966-76 (2222-3220)

Weiss, Manfred
- Abendmusik (2222-3220)

Wimberger, Gerhard
- Concertino per orchestra (2222-3210)

2222 - 4200 - str
Exact

Abendroth, Walter
- Concerto for Orchestra, op.14

Barclay, Robert Lenard
- Symphony in One Movement

Blacher, Boris
- Two Inventions

Bräutigam, Helmut
- Music for Orchestra, Wk.8

David, Johann Nepomuk
- Symphony No.1 in A minor, Wk18
- Symphony No.3, Wk28
- Symphony No.7, Wk49

Duparc, Henri
- Danse Lente

Ginastera, Alberto
- Estancia: Four Dances from Estancia, op.8a

Holmboe, Vagn
- Vinter, op.194

Jirák, K. B.
- Serenade for Small Orchestra, op.69

Kodály, Zoltán
- Dances of Galanta
- Marosszéker Tänze
- Minuetto Serio

Martinů, Bohuslav
- Ouverture, H.345

Morawetz, Oskar
- Overture to a Fairy Tale

Prokofiev, Sergei
- Sinfonietta, op.48

Reger, Max
- Eine Balletsuite, op.130

Reznicek, Emil Nikolaus von
- Symphony in the Old Style

Riisager, Knudåge
- Variations on a Theme by Mezangeau, op.12

Rosenberg, Hilding Constantin
- Sinfonia da Chiesa No.2

Schmidt, Franz
- Concerto for Piano in E-flat Major

Sibelius, Jean
- Dance Intermezzo, op.45, No.2

Šulek, Stjepan
- Concerto Classique

Weigl, Karl
- Comedy Overture, op.32

2222 - 4200 - str
Maximum

10' or Less

Absil, Jean
- Deux Danses Rituelles (2122-3000)
- Triptique (2122-3000)

Bräutigam, Helmut
- Festliche Musik (2200-0200)

Bruns, Victor
- Minna von Barnhelm: Overture, op.39 (2122-2200)

Dohnanyi, Ernest von
- The Veil of Pierette: Pierrot's complaint of love, op.18, No.1 (1222-4000)

Elgar, Edward
- Dream Children, op.43 (2222-4000)
Honegger, Arthur
- Sous-marine; Ballet, H.58 (2222-4000)
King, Alastair
- Master Irpy (2222-4000)
Koechlin, Charles
- Sur Les Flots Lointains (2122-2200)
Piazzolla, Astor
- Milonga del Ángel (2221-4000)
Ponce, Manuel
- Suite en Estilo Antiguo (1111-4000)
Roentgen, Julius
- Old Netherlands Dances, op.46 (2202-4200)

Over 10'

Abels, Michael
- More Seasons (2202-2200)
Besch, Otto
- Divertimento (2122-2200)
Braunfels, Walter
- Divertimento, op.42 (2222-1200)
Eppert, Carl
- A Little Symphony; Symphony No.2 (2122-2200)
Fauré, Gabriel
- Symphony in F major (2222-4000)
Henze, Hans Werner
- Symphony No.1 (2210-2200)
Hier, Ethel Glenn
- Carolina Christmas; Suite for Chamber Orchestra (2222-4000)
Holloway, Robin
- Third Idyll; Frost at Midnight, op.78 (2202-0200)
Lambert, Constant
- Comus: Suite from the Ballet to Purcell's music (2202-0200)
Maros, Rudolf
- Gemma; In Memoriam Zoltán Kodály (2220-4200)
Novák, Vítězslav
- Serenade, op.36 (2222-4000)
Paccagnini, Angelo
- Dialoghi (2220-2200)
Rodrigo, Joaquín
- Musica para un Jardín (2210-1100)
Sibelius, Jean
- Svanevit Suite, op.54 (2222-4000)

2222 - 4230 - str
Exact

Bartók, Béla
- Concerto for Piano No.1
Benjamin, Arthur
- Overture to an Italian Comedy
Bresgen, Cesar
- Intrada
Britten, Benjamin
- Soirées musicales, op.9; Suite of Five Movements from Rossini
Bruns, Victor
- Das Edelfräulein als Bäuerin: Orchestersuite, op.69
Busoni, Ferruccio
- Tanzwalzer, op.53 (Busoni Verz. 288)
David, Johann Nepomuk
- Chaconne, Wk71
Dohnanyi, Ernest von
- The Veil of Pierette: Wedding March, op.18, No.4
Ferguson, Howard
- Overture for an Occasion, op.16
German, Sir Edward
- Gipsy Suite; Four characteristic dances
Herrmann, Peter
- Three Pieces for Orchestra
Korngold, Erich Wolfgang
- Der Schneemann: Overture
Krek, Uroš
- Simfonietta
Magnard, Albéric
- Symphony No.3 in B minor, op.11
Rózsa, Miklós
- Notturno ungherese, op.28
Sibelius, Jean
- Valse Chevaleresque, op.96c
Weiner, Leo
- Soldatenspiel, op.16
Yu, Julian
- Great Ornamented Fuga Canonica, op.17

2222 - 4231 - str
Exact

10' or Less

Benjamin, Arthur
- Waltz and Hyde Park Gallop: From the film *An Ideal Husband*
Blacher, Boris
- Musica giocosa
Britten, Benjamin
- Gloriana: The Courtly Dances

Hindson, Matthew
- Flash Madness
- Lament
- LiteSPEED
Klebe, Giselher
- Moments musicaux, op.19
- Con moto, op.2
Marquez, Arturo
- Paisajes Bajo el Signo de Cosmos
Moncayo, José Pablo
- Cumbres
Stravinsky, Igor
- Circus Polka; Composed for a Young Elephant

Over 10'

Blacher, Boris
- Concertante Musik
Carter, Elliott
- Variations for Orchestra
Copland, Aaron
- Orchestral Variations
Hindson, Matthew
- Dangerous Creatures
- Speed
Janáček, Leoš
- Jenufa-Rhapsodie
Marquez, Arturo
- Danzón No.2
- Danzón No.4
Prokofiev, Sergei
- Divertimento, op.43
- Festive Poem "Thirty Years," op.113
Schreker, Franz
- Symphony in A minor, op.1
Weingartner, Felix
- Overture to Shakespeare's "The Tempest," op.65
Yu, Julian
- Not a Stream but an Ocean
Zemlinsky, Alexander
- Symphony No.2 in Bb major

2222 - 4331 - str
Maximum

10' or Less

Antheil, George
- Archipelago "Rhumba" (2222-4321)
Barber, Samuel
- Essay No.1, op.12 (2222-4331)
Bernstein, Leonard
- Fancy Free: Three Dance Variations (2222-4331)
Blacher, Boris
- Alla Marcia (2222-4331)

Cowell, Henry
- Hymn and Fuguing Tune No.3 (2222-4221)

Daugherty, Michael
- Oh Lois!: From "Metropolis Symphony" (2222-4330)
- Pachelbel's Key; For Youth Orchestra (2222-4221)

Engelmann, Hans Ulrich
- Impromptu (1111-4331)

Heitzeg, Steve
- Aqua; Hommage à Jacques-Yves Cousteau (2222-4331)

Hindson, Matthew
- Auto-Electric (2222-4221)
- Boom-Box (2222-4221)

Martin, Frank
- Overture to Racine's "Athalie" (2222-4210)

Maxwell Davies, Peter
- Five Klee Pictures; For school, amateur or professional orchestra (2222-4220)

Nørgård, Per
- Towards Freedom? (2222-4220)

Sierra, Roberto
- Sonatina (From "Let's Make a Symphony") (2222-4221)

Takács, Jenö
- Overtura Semiseria, op.69 (2222-4220)

Trojahn, Manfred
- Mit durchscheinender Melancholie (2222-4220)

Uhl, Alfred
- Wiener Walzer (2222-4220)

Over 10'

Adams, John
- Chairman Dances; Foxtrot for Orchestra (2222-4221)

Alwyn, William
- Elizabethan Dances for Orchestra (2222-4330)

Asia, Daniel
- Symphony No.4 (2222-4220)

Atterberg, Kurt
- Symphony No.4 in G minor, op.14 (2222-4221)

Bäck, Sven-Erik
- Four Motets (2222-4220)

Bacon, Ernst
- Fables for Narrator and Orchestra; Or the Secretary Bird and Associates: Studies in the Ecology of Academic Democracy (2222-4331)

Bartók, Béla
- Dance Suite (2222-4221)
- Two Portraits, op.5 (2222-4221)

Bates, Mason
- Music from Underground Spaces (2222-4331)
- Rusty Air in Carolina (2222-4331)

Bernstein, Leonard
- Facsimile (2222-4321)

Blacher, Boris
- Studie im Pianissimo (2222-4331)

Carter, Elliott
- The Minotaur: Suite from the Ballet (2222-4220)

Copland, Aaron
- Rodeo (2222-4331)

Corigliano, John
- Gazebo Dances (2222-4331)

Cowell, Henry
- Symphony No.17; Lancaster (2222-4221)

Danielpour, Richard
- First Light (2222-4220)

Einem, Gottfried von
- Rondo vom goldenen Kalb; Three Nocturnes to scenes by Tatjana Gsovsky, op.13 (2222-4331)

Greenwood, Jonny
- Doghouse (2222-4331)

Harbison, John
- Partita (2222-4220)

Hesketh, Kenneth
- Danceries (2222-4331)

Lutosławski, Witold
- Little Suite (2222-4331)

MacMillan, James
- The Sacrifice: Three Interludes (2222-4331)

Magnard, Albéric
- Chant Funebre, op.9 (2222-4130)

Piazzolla, Astor
- Las Cuatro Estaciones Porteñas (2222-4331)

Rautavaara, Einojuhani
- Symphony No.1 (2222-4321)
- Symphony No.7; Angel of Light (2222-4331)

Rorem, Ned
- Design (2222-4220)

Sibelius, Jean
- Scenes Historique I, op.25 (2222-4330)

Takács, Jenö
- Eisenstädter Divertimento; Suite, op.75 (2222-4210)
- Ungarische Burgmusik; Antiqua hungarica, op.47 (2222-4330)

Tower, Joan
- Stepping Stones; Ballet (2222-4220)

Wilson, Ian
- Running, Thinking, Finding (2222-4220)

Zemlinsky, Alexander
- Sinfonietta, op.23 (2222-4330)

**3222 - 4331 - str
Maximum**

10' or Less

Bantock, Granville
- Pierrot of the Minute; Comedy Overture (3121-3210)

Bates, Mason
- White Lies For Lomax (3222-4331)

Blacher, Boris
- Rondo (3222-4231)

Bleyle, Karl
- Reineke Fuchs; Overture, op.23 (3222-3310)

Britten, Benjamin
- Men of Goodwill; Variations on a Christmas Carol (God rest ye merry, Gentlemen) (3222-4231)

Busoni, Ferruccio
- Lustspiel Overture, op.38 (Busoni Verz. 245) (3222-4200)

Copland, Aaron
- An Outdoor Overture (3222-4230)

Einem, Gottfried von
- Capriccio, op.2 (3222-4331)

Elgar, Edward
- Falstaff: Two Interludes (3222-2000)

Kodály, Zoltán
- Intermezzo: From "Háry János" (3222-4300)

Korngold, Erich Wolfgang
- Straussiana (3121-2220)

Morawetz, Oskar
- Carnival Overture (3222-4321)

Revueltas, Silvestre
- Janitzio (3222-4221)

Sierra, Roberto
- Alegría (3222-4331)

Toch, Ernst
- Epilogue (3222-2200)

Over 10'

Alexandrov, Anatoly
- Classic Suite in B-flat major, op.32 (3222-2100)

Bantock, Granville
- The Helena Variations (3222-4231)

Binkerd, Gordon
- Symphony No.3 (3222-3331)
Bjelinski, Bruno
- Mediterranian Sinfonietta (3222-2200)
Blacher, Boris
- Fürstin Tarakanowa: Suite (3222-4331)
- Lysistrata: Suite from the ballet (3222-4331)
- Symphony (3222-4231)
Brandmüller, Theo
- Reminiszenzen (3222-2230)
Britten, Benjamin
- The Young Person's Guide to the Orchestra, op.34; (Variations and Fugue on a Theme of Purcell) (3222-4231)
Bruns, Victor
- Symphony No.6; Sinfonia breve, op.67 (3222-4300)
Delius, Frederick
- Petite Suite No.1 (3222-4200)
Einem, Gottfried von
- Bruckner Dialog, op.39 (3222-4331)
- Concerto for Orchestra, op.4 (3222-4331)
- Medusa, op.24; Ballet in three scenes to a scenario by M. Gale Hoffman (3222-4331)
- Medusa, op.24a: Three movements for orchestra (3222-4331)
- Nachtstück, op.29 (3222-4331)
- Philadelphia Symphony, op.28 (3222-4331)
- Prinzessin Turandot, op.1; Ballet in two scenes to a scenario by Luigi Malipiero (3222-4331)
- Symphonische Szenen, op.22 (3222-4331)
- Tanz-Rondo, op.27 (3222-4331)
- Turandot, op.1a; Four episodes for orchestra (3222-4331)
- Wiener Symphonie, op.49 (3222-4331)
Kodály, Zoltán
- Concerto for Orchestra (3222-4331)
- Symphony in C (3222-4331)
- Variations on a Hungarian Folksong; The Peacock (3222-4330)
Leyendecker, Ulrich
- Verwandlung; Four Pieces for Chamber Orchestra (3020-2111)
Maasz, Gerhard
- Tripartita (3000-0000)
Rachmaninoff, Sergei
- Caprice bohémien, op.12 (3222-4231)

Rautavaara, Einojuhani
- Garden of Spaces (3000-3100)
Saint-Saëns, Camille
- Symphony in F; Urbs Roma (3222-4200)
Schmitt, Florent
- Reflets d'Allemagne: Suite for orchestra, op.28 (3222-4231)
Sibelius, Jean
- Scenes Historiques, op.66 (3222-4000)
Zimmermann, Udo
- Tänzerinnen; Choreographies based on E. Degas (3220-0200)

Other Combinations with Woodwinds in 3

10' or Less

Antheil, George
- Jazz Symphony (1030-0330)
Bavicchi, John
- Fantasia on Korean Folk Tunes, op.53 (2131-2231)
Bernstein, Leonard
- On the Town: Three Dance Episodes (1130-2331)
Bolcom, William
- A Seattle Overture (2232-2331)
Britten, Benjamin
- Overture Paul Bunyan (2131-2221)
- Peter Grimes: Passacaglia, op.33b (2223-4331)
Copland, Aaron
- Letter from Home (2232-2220)
Delius, Frederick
- Irmelin: Prelude (2332-2000)
Dohnanyi, Ernest von
- The Veil of Pierette: Jolly Funeral March, op.18, No.3 (1123-4230)
- The Veil of Pierette: Pierette's dance of madness, op.18, No.6 (2233-4231)
Foss, Lukas
- Symphonie de Rossi; Suite Salomon Rossi (1302-0220)
Gardner, John
- Overture "Half Holiday" (2131-2210)
Harbison, John
- Waltz-Passacaglia (2223-4230)
Le Grand, Robert
- Effets de Nuit (2332-2000)
Matsudaira, Yoritsune
- Pastorale (2332-2000)
Moncayo, José Pablo
- Huapango (3232-4331)

Prokofiev, Sergei
- Autumn; A symphonic sketch for small orchestra, op.8 (2232-4100)
Rachmaninoff, Sergei
- Vocalise, op.34 (2322-2000)
Shostakovich, Dmitri
- Five Fragments, op.42 (2232-2111)

Over 10'

Berio, Luciano
- Requies (2232-2210)
Bose, Hans-Jürgen von
- Musik für ein Haus voll Zeit (2131-1110)
Britten, Benjamin
- Peter Grimes: Four Sea Interludes, op.33a (2223-4331)
Chávez, Carlos
- Sinfonía (2223-4331)
- Sinfonía India (Symphony No.2) (2131-2210)
Copland, Aaron
- The City: Incidental music for the documentary film (1131-2210)
Cowell, Henry
- Symphonic Set, op.17 (2232-2221)
David, Johann Nepomuk
- Sinfonia breve, Wk47 (1131-4000)
Dittrich, Paul-Heinz
- Abwärts wend ich mich (2131-2220)
Ekström, Lars
- Järnnatten (The Lonely Night) (1213-1220)
Fómina, Silvia
- Permanenza; Für mikropolyphonisches, im Raum verteiltes Orchester (2030-1010)
Goehr, Alexander
- Little Symphony, op.15 (1230-2001)
Kirchner, Volker David
- Bildnisse I (2322-2220)
- Bildnisse II (2322-2220)
- Bildnisse III (1231-2000)
Krenek, Ernst
- Symphony No.3, op.16 (2223-2100)
Lutoslawski, Witold
- Jeux Venitiens (2131-1110)
Martinů, Bohuslav
- Concerto Grosso (1330-2000)
Nørgård, Per
- Aspects of Leaving (2132-2211)
Respighi, Ottorino
- Antiche Danze ed Arie: Suite 1 (2302-2100)
Saint-Saëns, Camille
- Suite in D major (2322-2200)

Schollum, Robert
- Sonate (2223-3221)
Stockhausen, Karlheinz
- Formel, Nr.1/6 (0333-3000)
Trexler, Georg
- Music for Orchestra (2223-2200)
Weingartner, Felix
- Symphony No.4 in F Major, op.61
  (2223-4230)

Larger Than All Previous

Berio, Luciano
- Kol od (Chemins VI) (3141-2211)
Erbse, Heimo
- Allegro - Lento - Allegro: No.3 from
  "Divertimento for Mozart" (2243-
  2200)
Górecki, Henryk Mikołaj
- Three Dances, op.34 (2222-3431)
Hamel, Peter Michael
- Semiramis; Music in three parts
  (0251-2000)
Lavista, Mario
- Lacrymosa (0212-0040)
León, Tania
- Bele (2000-0430)
Lobanov, Vasily
- Symphony No.1 for Chamber
  Orchestra (4000-0100)
Rautavaara, Einojuhani
- Praevariata (2222-4431)
Schuller, Gunther
- Journey to the Stars (1021-2222)
Xenakis, Iannis
- Alax; Pour 30 musiciens divises en
  3 ensembles (3030-6030)
Zimmermann, Udo
- Songerie Pour Orchestre de
  Chambre (4000-0300)

NO BRASS

1010 - 0000 - str
Exact

Aguila, Miguel del
- A Conga Line in Hell, op.40
Atterberg, Kurt
- Suite No.2
Balogh, Ernö
- Pastorale and Capriccio, op.21
Beynon, Jared
- Unicorn
Campos-Parsi, Héctor
- Divertimento del Sur
Debussy, Claude
- La plus que lente
Haubenstock-Ramati, Roman
- Ständchen sur le nom de Heinrich
  Strobel: 3. part of "Petite musique
  de nuit"
Holst, Gustav
- Morris Dance Tunes
Ishii, Maki
- Sieben Stücke (Seven Pieces)
Koch, Erland von
- Dalecarlia Suite
- Dance No.4
- Dance No.5
Larsson, Lars-Erik
- Pastoral for liten orkester
Maasz, Gerhard
- Musik (Nr.1)
Musto, John
- Divertimento
Schickele, Peter
- Broadway Boogie

1110 - 0000 - str
Exact

Benjamin, Arthur
- Sonatina for Chamber Orchestra
Bialas, Günter
- Sinfonia Piccola
Finnissy, Michael
- Câtana
Honegger, Arthur
- Napoleón: La romance de Violine
Horovitz, Joseph
- Adagio Cantabile
- Valse
Ives, Charles Edward
- The Rainbow

Keuning, Hans P.
- Remarkable Dances
Maler, Wilhelm
- Drei Festmusiken
Ponce, Manuel
- Instantáneas Mexicanas, No.7:
  Jugando
Redel, Martin Christoph
- Kammersinfonie II (Chamber
  Symphony II), op.17
Wiechowicz, Stanisław
- Nocturne

1111 - 0000 - str
Exact

Antoniou, Theodore
- Events III; Music for Orchestra,
  Tape and Slide-Projection
Barati, George
- Chamber Concerto
Edlund, Lars
- Tracce
Gillis, Don
- Four Scenes from Yesterday
Hindemith, Paul
- Sing- und Spielmusik für Liebhaber
  und Freunde; Ein Jäger aus
  Kurpfalz, der reitet durch den
  grünen Wald, op.45, No.3
Huë, Georges Adolphe
- Rêverie pour petit orchestre
- Sérénade pour orchestre
Kelly, Bryan
- Concertante Dances
Pierné, Gabriel
- Ballet de Cour, No.3: La Canarie
Schmitt, Florent
- Soirs, op.5
Schubert, Heino
- Concerto
Schwaen, Kurt
- Zwingerserenade
Vate, Nancy van de
- Variations for Chamber Orchestra
Wirth, Carl Anton
- Serenade

3332 - 0000 - str
Maximum

Avshalomov, Jacob
 - Cues from "The Little Clay Cart"
   (2120-0000)
Bantock, Granville
 - Four Landscapes from the Chinese
   (2121-0000)
Barclay, Robert Lenard
 - Nocturne and Scherzo (2222-0000)
Bedford, David
 - The Transfiguration: A Meditation
   (2200-0000)
Beyer, Frank Michael
 - Ricercare I (2030-0000)
Brant, Henry
 - A Requiem in Summer; In Memory
   of my Father (2222-0000)

Denhoff, Michael
 - Melancolia (2221-0000)
Diehl, Paula
 - Right of Way (0320-0000)
Donato, Anthony
 - Mission San José de Aguaya
   (2222-0000)
Gould, Morton
 - Serenade ("Orfeo") from "Audubon"
   (2232-0000)
Grosse, Erwin
 - Kammersinfonie (Chamber
   Symphony), op.48 (2030-0000)
Halvorsen, Johan
 - Sérénade, op.33 (3220-0000)
Holst, Gustav
 - Greeting (2121-0000)
Howells, Herbert
 - Puck's Minuet, op.20, No.1 (2031-
   0000)

Kreutz, Arthur
 - American Dances (2222-0000)
Maasz, Gerhard
 - Tripartita (3000-0000)
Rogers, Bernard
 - Elegy: From Symphony No.3 (0300-
   0000)
Schönherr, Max
 - Das trunkene Mücklein (2200-0000)
Sgrizzi, Luciano
 - Suite Belge, (2121-0000)
Tomlinson, Ernest
 - A Georgian Miniature (2121-0000)
 - Little Serenade (2121-0000)
Vinter, Gilbert
 - Dance of the Marionettes (2121-
   0000)

ENSEMBLE AND CHAMBER ORCHESTRA

The following categories list only Ensemble and Chamber Orchestra repertoire (no solo repertoire).
Entries are listed with the woodwinds and brass count in brackets, i.e.: (1111 - 1111)

Compositions That Use **NO PERCUSSION** (Maximum Instrumentation Listed)	1111 - 1111 - str page 290 2222 - 2221 - str page 294 larger than 2222 - 2221 - str page 298	
Compositions That Use **NO HARP or PIANO** (Maximum Instrumentation Listed)	1111 - 1111 - str page 299 2222 - 2221 - str page 302 larger than 2222 - 2221 - str page 310	
Compositions That Use **SAXOPHONE(S)**	page 313	
Compositions That Use **ELECTRONICS** (Tape, CD, Live-Electronics, etc.)	page 315	

EXACT & MAXIMUM INSTRUMENTATION
(for the Categories "Ensemble" and "Chamber Orchestra")

Exact (E): Will return pieces in exactly the given instrumentation

Maximum (M): Will return pieces in exactly the given instrumentation OR SMALLER
Example No.1: "1010 - 0110 - str" can also return a piece that uses 1010 - 0100 - str
Example No.2: "str with a maximum of [1.1.2.2.2]" can also return a piece that uses [1.0.2.1.2]
Maximum Searches will list the woodwind and brass count in brackets, i.e., (1111 - 1111)

NO PERCUSSION

1111 - 1111 - str
Maximum

5' or Less

Brant, Henry
- Lyric Piece (1111-1110)

Cowell, Henry
- Polyphonica (1111-1110)
- Teheran Movement (1111-0100)

De Brant, Cyr
- Song of Yesteryear (1111-1000)

Debussy, Claude
- La plus que lente (1010-0000)

Griffes, Charles Tomlinson
- Three Tone Pictures (1111-1000)

Gürsching, Albrecht
- Drei Plus Vier (0011-1000)

Hindemith, Paul
- Sing- und Spielmusik für Liebhaber und Freunde (1111-0000)

Honegger, Arthur
- Blues (1111-1100)
- Napoléon: Danse des Enfants (1011-0000)
- Napoléon: La romance de Violine (1110-0000)

Huë, Georges Adolphe
- Rêverie pour petit orchestre (1111-0000)
- Sérénade pour orchestre (1111-0000)

Hvidtfelt Nielsen, Svend
- Impromptu (1010-1000)

Ives, Charles Edward
- Adagio Sostenuto (1110-0000)
- Gyp the Blood or Hearst!? Which is Worst?! (1011-0100)
- The Rainbow (1110-0000)
- Tone Roads No.1 (1011-0000)

Koch, Erland von
- Dance No.4 (1010-0000)
- Dance No.5 (1010-0000)

Larsson, Lars-Erik
- Pastoral for liten orkester (1010-0000)

Martin, Frank
- Fox Trot (1111-1110)

Martinů, Bohuslav
- Nonet (1111-1000)

Matthews, Colin
- L; bent (1111-1000)

Maxwell Davies, Peter
- Canzona (1111-1000)
- A Welcome to Orkney (1111-1000)

Milhaud, Darius
- Chamber Symphony No.2 (1101-0000)
- Chamber Symphony No.3 (1011-0000)

Müller-Wieland, Jan
- Allegria (0110-1100)

Nørgård, Per
- Snip Snap (1111-1000)
- Without Jealousy (1011-0100)

Pierné, Gabriel
- Album Pour Mes Petites Amis (Album for My Little Friends) (1110-1000)
- Ballet de Cour (1111-0000)

Pilati, Mario
- Alla Culla (1111-1000)

Poulenc, Francis
- Esquisse d'une Fanfare (1111-1110)
- Mouvements perpétuels for nine instruments (1111-1000)

Rihm, Wolfgang
- Chiffre VIII (0011-1010)

Satie, Erik
- Les Pantins Dansent (1111-1100)

Schelling, Ernest
- Tarantella (1101-0000)

Schickele, Peter
- Broadway Boogie (1010-0000)

Schnittke, Alfred
- 3 X 7 (0010-1010)

Schönberg, Arnold
- Das Wappenschild (1111-1000)

Shulman, Alan
- Vodka Float (0010-0000)

Talbot, Joby
- Arbor Low (1111-1000)

Warlock, Peter
- An Old Song (1110-1000)

6' - 10'

Adams, John
- Christian Zeal and Activity (1011-0000)

Atterberg, Kurt
- Suite No.2 (1010-0000)

Babbitt, Milton
- Composition for 12 Instruments (1111-1100)

Balogh, Ernö
- Pastorale and Capriccio (1010-0000)

Banks, Don
- Elizabethan Miniatures (1000-0000)

Bauer, Marion
- Concertino (0110-0000)

Bavicchi, John
- Fantasy, op.36 (1111-1000)

Boccadoro, Carlo
- Adagio (1111-1000)

Brown, Earle
- Novara (1010-0100)

Bruun, Peter
- Bag Den Kan Fredens Ranker Gro (1111-1000)

Buck, Ole
- Chamber Music I (1111-1100)
- Chamber Music II (1111-1000)
- Landscapes IV (1011-0100)

Cheslock, Louis
- Theme and Variations (1000-1000)

Copland, Aaron
- Symphony No.1 (1111-1100)

Crawford, Ruth
- Music for Small Orchestra (1011-0000)

Dallapiccola, Luigi
- Piccola Musica Notturna (Ensemble Version) (1110-0000)

Davico, Vincenzo
- Poemetti Pastorali (1111-1000)

Debussy, Claude
- Deux Arabesques (1010-0000)

Dillon, James
- ...Once Upon A Time (1111-1110)
- Zone (...de azul) (0010-1110)

Earls, Paul
- And On The Seventh Day (1111-1000)

Eaton, John
- Adagio and Allegro (1100-0000)

Finzi, Gerald
- Love's Labour's Lost (1111-1000)
- A Severn Rhapsody (1110-1000)

Françaix, Jean
- Sérénade (1111-1110)

Fundal, Karsten
- Hoquetus (1111-1000)

Gordon, Michael
- Acid Rain (1010-0000)
- Love Bead (1111-1110)

Grainger, Percy Aldridge
- My Robin is to the Greenwood Gone (1100-0000)

Gyring, Elizabeth
- Scherzo No.2 for Orchestra (1010-0110)

Helfer, Walter
- A Water Idyll (1111-1000)

Hindemith, Paul
- Plöner Musiktag (1000-0100)

Holst, Gustav
- Morris Dance Tunes (1010-0000)

Honegger, Arthur
- Pastorale d'été (1111-1000)
Horovitz, Joseph
- Adagio Cantabile (1110-0000)
Hvidtfelt Nielsen, Svend
- Flowerfall (1010-0100)
Imbrie, Andrew
- Dandelion Wine (0110-0000)
Kelemen, Milko
- Konstellationen (1111-1110)
Killmayer, Wilhelm
- Sinfonia 2 (1101-0000)
Kirchner, Leon
- Music for Twelve (1111-1110)
Koch, Erland von
- Dalecarlia Suite (1010-0000)
Komarova, Tatjana
- Sonnenuntergänge auf B 612
  (Sunsets on B 612) (1111-0000)
Ledenjov, Roman
- Notturni (1111-1000)
LeFanu, Nicola
- Preludio I (1111-1000)
León, Tania
- The Beloved (1111-0000)
Luening, Otto
- Prelude to a Hymn Tune by William
  Billings (1111-1000)
Lutosławski, Witold
- Bucolics (1111-1000)
- Dance Preludes (1111-1000)
MacRae, Stuart
- The Broken Spectre (1111-1000)
Marthinsen, Niels
- A Bright Kind of High (1010-0100)
Martinů, Bohuslav
- Serenata No.1 (0110-1000)
- Serenata No.3 (0110-0000)
Matsushita, Shin-ichi
- Fresque Sonore (1110-1000)
Moeran, E. J.
- Whythorne's Shadow (1110-1000)
Muhly, Nico
- By All Means (1110-1110)
Muldowney, Dominic
- Variations on "Mein junges Leben
  hat ein End" (1010-0100)
Nordentoft, Anders
- The City of Threads (1111-1000)
Pärt, Arvo
- Pari Intervallo (0010-0010)
Payne, Anthony
- Hidden Music (1111-1000)
Pierné, Gabriel
- Giration (1011-0110)
Poulenc, Francis
- Deux Marches et un Intermède
  (1111-0100)

Primosch, James
- Five Miniatures (1110-1110)
Rapoport, Eda
- Israfel (1000-0000)
Rihm, Wolfgang
- abgewandt 1 (1111-1000)
- Chiffre IV (0010-0000)
- Chiffre VI (0011-1000)
Rota, Nino
- Canzona (1111-1100)
Schoeck, Othmar
- Serenade (1111-1000)
Schwaen, Kurt
- Zwingerserenade (1111-0000)
Sørensen, Bent
- Clairobscur (1111-1000)
Staud, Johannes Maria
- Configurations / Reflet (0111-1000)
Stock, David
- Capriccio (1111-1100)
Terzakis, Dimitri
- Hommage à Morse (1110-0010)
Thomas, Augusta Reed
- Capricious Angels (1110-1000)
Trantow, Herbert
- Kleine Tafelmusik (1100-0000)
Vate, Nancy van de
- Variations for Chamber Orchestra
  (1111-0000)
Webern, Anton
- Konzert (1110-1100)
Weiner, Leo
- Divertimento No.1 (1000-1100)
Williams, Graham
- Cerberus (1111-1000)
Wittinger, Róbert
- Compensazioni (1110-1110)
Wyner, Yehudi
- Passage (1010-0100)
Xenakis, Iannis
- Kaï (1011-0110)

11' - 15'

Ali-Zadeh, Franghiz
- Dilogie I for Nine Players (1111-
  1000)
Ballif, Claude
- Imaginaire No.1 (1010-0110)
- Le Taille-Lyre (1010-0010)
Bavicchi, John
- Concertante, op.44 (0101-0000)
Bawden, Rupert
- The Donkey Dances (1110-0000)
Bennett, Richard Rodney
- Nocturnes (1111-1000)
Bentzon, Niels Viggo
- Sonata for 12 Instruments (1111-
  1110)

Berners, Lord
- L'Uomo dai Baffi (1111-0000)
Bialas, Günter
- Sinfonia Piccola (1110-0000)
Birtwistle, Sir Harrison
- Tragoedia (1111-1000)
Bloch, Ernest
- Four Episodes (1111-1000)
Boccadoro, Carlo
- Ae Fond Kiss (1010-0000)
Bon, André
- Travelling (1111-1000)
Braun, Yehezkel
- Serenade for Chamber Orchestra
  (1111-1000)
Britten, Benjamin
- Sinfonietta (1111-1000)
Burgon, Geoffrey
- Suite from Bleak House (1011-
  1100)
Cordero, Roque
- Ocho Miniaturas (1111-1110)
Cowell, Henry
- Sinfonietta (1111-1110)
Dalby, Martin
- De Patre Ex Filio (0011-1000)
Denisov, Edison
- Femme et Oiseaux (1111-0000)
Döhl, Friedhelm
- Octet (1111-0000)
Einem, Gottfried von
- Steinbeis-Serenade (0111-1100)
Ekimovsky, Viktor
- Brandenburg Concerto for Flute,
  Oboe, Violin, Strings and
  Harpsichord (1100-0000)
Engelmann, Hans Ulrich
- Sinfonia da Camera (1111-1000)
Firsova, Elena
- Music for Twelve (1111-1100)
Fontyn, Jacqueline
- Nonetto (1111-1000)
Frackenpohl, Arthur
- Divertimento in F (1010-1110)
Frankel, Benjamin
- Bagatelles "Cinque Pezzi Notturni"
  (1111-1000)
Fuchs, Kenneth
- Out of the Dark (1111-1000)
Genzmer, Harald
- Capriccio für Kammerorchester
  (0111-1000)
Gürsching, Albrecht
- Piccola Sinfonia (0011-1000)
Guy, Barry
- Bitz! (1110-0000)
Halffter, Rodolfo
- Divertimento Para Nueve
  Instrumentos (1111-0100)

Hamilton, Iain
- Arias (1111-1110)
Harvey, Jonathan
- Tendril (1111-1000)
Hauer, Josef Matthias
- 1. Tanzsuite (1111-0000)
Helm, Everett
- Serenade (0111-0000)
Hidalgo, Manuel
- Nahezu Stilles Auge des
  Wirbelsturms (1111-1000)
Hindson, Matthew
- Technologic 145 (1111-1110)
Holt, Simon
- Capriccio Spettrale (1010-1100)
- Era Madrugada (1010-1000)
- Kites (1111-1000)
- Lilith (1010-1000)
James, Dorothy
- Suite for Small Orchestra (1111-
  1100)
Kahn, Erich Itor
- Actus Tragicus (1111-1000)
- Petite Suite Bretonne (1111-1000)
Kallstenius, Edvin
- Suite for 9 Instruments (1111-1000)
Knussen, Oliver
- Processionals (1111-1000)
Koch, Erland von
- Four Swedish Folk Melodies (1111-
  1000)
Lampersberg, Gerhard
- Symphony (1011-1110)
Larsson, Lars-Erik
- Divertimento (1111-1000)
- Gustaviansk Suite (1000-0000)
Linke, Norbert
- Profit tout Clair (0111-1000)
Lord, David
- Septet (1010-0000)
Lorentzen, Bent
- Paesaggio (1111-1000)
Lutyens, Elisabeth
- Six Tempi for 10 Instruments (1111-
  1100)
Maasz, Gerhard
- Musik (Nr.1) (1010-0000)
Malipiero, Gian Francesco
- Ritrovari (1111-1000)
Matsushita, Shin-ichi
- Haleines Astrals (1111-1110)
Matthews, Colin
- A Voice to Wake (1110-1000)
Matthus, Siegfried
- Ich komm einen Weg (0011-1000)
Maxwell Davies, Peter
- Ricercar and Doubles on "To many
  a well" (1111-1000)

McGlaughlin, William
- Aaron's Horizons (1011-0000)
Milhaud, Darius
- Concert de chambre (1111-1000)
- Musique pour Graz (1111-0100)
Moravec, Paul
- Northern Lights Electric (1010-
  0000)
Morris, Harold
- Variations on the American Negro
  Spiritual "I was Way Down A-
  Yonder" (1111-1000)
Morthenson, Jan Wilhelm
- Labor (1111-1010)
Müller-Siemens, Detlev
- Pavane (1111-0000)
- Phoenix 1 (1111-1110)
- Phoenix 3 (1111-1110)
- Refuge (1111-1000)
- Variationen über einen Ländler von
  Schubert (1111-1000)
Musgrave, Thea
- Chamber Concerto No.1 (0111-
  1110)
- Chamber Concerto No.2 (1010-
  0000)
Osborne, Nigel
- Fantasia (1111-1000)
Pape, Andy
- Min Fynske Barndom (1111-1000)
Patterson, Paul
- At the Still Point of the Turning
  World (1110-1000)
Payne, Anthony
- A Sea Change (1010-0000)
Piston, Walter
- Divertimento (1111-0000)
Primosch, James
- Septet (1110-0000)
Redel, Martin Christoph
- Kammersinfonie II (1110-0000)
Reimann, Aribert
- Metamorphosen über ein Menuett
  von Franz Schubert (1111-1000)
Rochberg, George
- Cheltenham Concerto (1111-1110)
Rosing-Schow, Niels
- Meeting (0111-1000)
Salviucci, Giovanni
- Sinfonia da Camera (1111-1100)
Samazeuilh, Gustave
- Divertissement et Musette (1111-
  1000)
Satie, Erik
- Sports et Divertissements (1111-
  1000)
Saxton, Robert
- Canzona (1110-1000)

Schubert, Manfred
- Septet in Two Movements (0011-
  1000)
Schuller, Gunther
- Chimeric Images (1011-1100)
Sekles, Bernhard
- Serenade for 11 Solo Instruments
  (1111-1000)
Sharp, Elliott
- Dark Matters (1010-0010)
Sjöblom, Heimer
- Liten Svit I Spelmanston (1111-
  1000)
Szalonek, Witold
- Connections (1110-1000)
Takemitsu, Tōru
- Eucalypts I (1100-0000)
Talbot, Joby
- Animisation (1111-1110)
Tavener, John
- Grandma's Footsteps (0101-1000)
Taylor, Deems
- The Portrait of a Lady (1111-1000)
Treibmann, Karl Ottomar
- Second Symphonic Essay (1111-
  1000)
Ullmann, Jakob
- Composition for 10 Instruments I-V
  (1010-1000)
Wilson, Ian
- ...and flowers fall... (0011-1000)
Xenakis, Iannis
- Anaktoria (0011-1000)
- Phlegra (1111-1110)

16' - 20'

Bawden, Rupert
- Wanderjahr (1010-0000)
Bennett, Richard Rodney
- A Book of Hours (1111-1000)
- Dream Dancing (1111-1100)
Berkeley, Lennox
- Diversions for Eight Instruments
  (0111-1000)
Blomdahl, Karl-Birger
- Concerto grosso (1011-1000)
Bolcom, William
- Octet (1011-0000)
Braun, Yehezkel
- Apartment To Let (1111-1000)
Brødsgaard, Anders
- Ghostorchestra (1100-0100)
Brown, James Francis
- Sinfonietta (1111-1000)
Buck, Ole
- Landscapes I (1010-0100)
- Landscapes II (1010-0100)

Burgon, Geoffrey
- Brideshead Variations (1101-1100)
Chapple, Brian
- Venus Fly Trap (1111-1110)
Dalby, Martin
- Man Walking (0101-1000)
Denhoff, Michael
- O Orpheus singt (0011-1000)
Diamond, David
- Elegies (1100-0000)
Dittrich, Paul-Heinz
- Concert Avec Plusieurs Instruments
  No.1 (1100-1000)
Erbse, Heimo
- For String and Wind Players (0111-
  1000)
Grosskopf, Erhard
- Sonata concertante 1 (1111-1000)
Gudmundsen-Holmgreen, Pelle
- Nær og Fjern (Near and Distant)
  (1111-1000)
Halffter, Cristóbal
- Antiphonismoi (1110-0000)
Hauer, Josef Matthias
- 2. Tanzsuite (1111-0000)
Heath, Dave
- Forest (1010-0000)
Herrmann, Peter
- Sonata for Chamber Orchestra
  (1100-0100)
Holloway, Robin
- Concertino No.1 (1111-1110)
Huber, Nicolaus A.
- Rose Selavy (1111-1110)
Hurd, Michael
- Captain Coram's Kids (1101-0000)
Imbrie, Andrew
- Chamber Symphony (1111-1110)
Jaroch, Jiří
- II. Nonet (1111-1000)
Kelemen, Milko
- Nonett (1111-0000)
Kelly, Bryan
- Concertante Dances (1111-0000)
Lendvai, Erwin
- Kammersuite (1111-1000)
Levi, Paul Alan
- Elegy and Recreations (0110-1000)
Losonczy, Andor
- Phonophobie (1011-0110)
Lumsdaine, David
- Salvation Creek with Eagle (1111-
  1110)
Malipiero, Gian Francesco
- Ricercari (1111-1000)
Martinů, Bohuslav
- Nonet No.2 (1111-1000)
Matthews, Colin
- Suns Dance (1111-1000)

Maxwell Davies, Peter
- Sinfonia (1111-1000)
Melby, John
- Wind, Sand and Stars (1110-1000)
Milhaud, Darius
- Jeux de Printemps (1011-0100)
Müller-Siemens, Detlev
- Phoenix 2 (1111-1110)
Musgrave, Thea
- Space Play (1111-1000)
Myaskovsky, Nikolai Yakovlevich
- Concertino Lyrico (1011-1000)
Neikrug, Marc
- Concertino (1110-0000)
Nordentoft, Anders
- Hymn (1010-1100)
Nørgård, Per
- Scintillation (1010-1000)
Nussio, Otmar
- Divertimento (0011-1000)
Osborne, Nigel
- In Camera (1111-1110)
Payne, Anthony
- The Stones and Lonely Places Sing
  (1010-1000)
Reimann, Aribert
- Invenzioni (1111-1110)
Rochberg, George
- Chamber Symphony for 9
  Instruments (0111-1110)
Roussel, Albert
- Le Marchand de Sable qui Passe
  (The Sandman Passing By) (1010-
  1000)
Saint-Saëns, Camille
- L'assassinat de Duc de Guise
  (1111-1000)
Schifrin, Lalo
- Variants on a Madrigal by Gesualdo
  (1111-1111)
Schubert, Heino
- Concerto (1111-0000)
Schubert, Manfred
- Nachtstück und Passacaglia (0011-
  1000)
Schumann, William
- Night Journey (1111-1000)
Searle, Humphrey
- Variations and Finale (1111-1000)
Smolka, Martin
- Octet (0011-1000)
Sørensen, Bent
- Shadowland (1111-1000)
Stürmer, Bruno
- Suite für Neun Solo-Instrumente
  (1111-0000)
Vinter, Gilbert
- The Poet Speaks (0010-0000)

Watkins, Michael Blake
- Sinfonietta (1111-1110)
Wolf-Ferrari, Ermanno
- Sinfonia da Camera in B-flat (1111-
  1000)
Wyner, Yehudi
- Serenade for Seven Instruments
  (1000-1110)
Xenakis, Iannis
- Waarg (1111-1111)
Yuasa, Joji
- Projection for Seven Players (1110-
  1100)

Over 20'

Ballif, Claude
- Imaginaire No.3 (0011-1000)
Barati, George
- Chamber Concerto (1111-0000)
Ben-Haim, Paul
- Kabbalat shabbat (1100-0100)
Braun, Yehezkel
- Serenade II (1111-1000)
Buck, Ole
- Landscapes III (1011-0100)
Burkhard, Willy
- Serenade (1011-1000)
Chávez, Carlos
- Suite for Double Quartet (1111-
  0000)
Copland, Aaron
- Appalachian Spring (1011-0000)
Davis, Anthony
- Litany of Sins (1111-1000)
Eberhard, Dennis
- Endgame (0011-1000)
Ferguson, Howard
- Serenade (0011-1000)
Geissler, Fritz
- Symphony No.6 (1111-1000)
Hamilton, Iain
- The Alexandrian Sequence (1111-
  1110)
Harrison, Lou
- Solstice (1100-1000)
Heiller, Anton
- Kammersymphonie (0111-0000)
Hindemith, Paul
- Der Dämon (1010-1100)
- Hérodiade (1111-1000)
Honegger, Arthur
- Symphony No.2 (0000-0100)
Jelinek, Hanns
- Prelude, Passacaglia and Fugue
  (1011-1000)
Joubert, John
- Octet (0011-1000)

Juon, Paul
- Kammersinfonie (Chamber Symphony) (0111-1000)
Kancheli, Giya
- Abii ne Viderem (1000-0000)
- Besuch In Der Kindheit (Childhood Revisited) (0100-0000)
- A Life Without Christmas (1000-0000)
Krenek, Ernst
- Symphonische Musik für 9 Soloinstrumente (1111-0000)
Marthinsen, Niels
- Shadow Figures (1010-1100)
Müller-Zürich, Paul
- Marienleben (1110-1000)
Nilsson, Bo
- Hemsoborna (1000-0000)
Platz, Robert H. P.
- CHLEBNICOV (1110-1110)
Reger, Max
- Suite in A minor (1111-1000)
Rota, Nino
- Cristallo di Rocca (1000-0000)
Sharp, Elliott
- Akadak (1010-0000)
Stöhr, Richard
- Kammersymphonie (0111-1000)
Wolf-Ferrari, Ermanno
- Chamber Symphony (1111-1000)

2222 - 2221 - str
Maximum

5' or Less

Alfvén, Hugo
- Elegi; För liten orkester, ur orkestersviten Gustav II Adolf (0121-0000)
Almand, Claude
- Chorale for Chamber Orchestra (1120-2000)
Aubert, Louis
- La Lettre (2222-2000)
Beck, Jeremy
- Sparks and Flame (Ash) (1011-2000)
Berio, Luciano
- Variazione sull'aria di Papageno: No.2 from "Divertimento for Mozart" (0020-0000)
Bittner, Julius
- Der Musikant; Serenade (1121-2000)
Brant, Henry
- Prelude and Fugue (0000-2221)

Chávez, Carlos
- Energia - for Nine Instruments (2001-1110)
Copland, Aaron
- Billy the Kid: Waltz (Billy and his Sweetheart) (1121-1210)
- Down a Country Lane (2121-2110)
Delius, Frederick
- Fennimore and Gerda: Intermezzo (2222-2100)
Dohnanyi, Ernest von
- The Veil of Pierette: Waltz, op.18, No.2 (2222-2000)
- The Veil of Pierette: Menuett, op.18, No.5 (1122-2000)
Donato, Anthony
- Mission San José de Aguaya (2222-0000)
Duparc, Henri
- Aux étoiles (2222-2000)
Elgar, Edward
- Chanson de Matin, op.15, No.2 (1121-2000)
- Chanson de Nuit, op.15, No.1 (1121-2000)
- Salut d'Amour, op.12 (1222-2000)
Etler, Alvin
- Elegy for Small Orchestra (1122-2000)
Gaubert, Philippe
- Madrigal (2222-2000)
Guarnieri, Camargo
- Ponteios No.1 (1010-2100)
Holliger, Heinz
- Choral à 8 (0020-2000)
- Sommerkanon IV (2210-0000)
Holst, Gustav
- Greeting (2121-0000)
Honegger, Arthur
- Interlude de "La Mort de Sainte Alméenne," H.20A (1122-2100)
- La Roue: Overture pour le film d'Abel Gance, H.44 (2022-0000)
- Toccata, H.207 (2222-2200)
Järnefelt, Armas
- Berceuse (0021-2000)
Kander, Susan
- She Never Lost A Passenger Overture (2020-0110)
Matthews, David
- From Sea to Sky; Overture, op.59 (0200-2000)
McCabe, John
- Shepherd's Dream (0201-0200)
Milhaud, Darius
- Chamber Symphony No.1; Le Printemps, op.43 (2110-0000)

Pepping, Ernst
- Invention für Kleines Orchester: From "Musiken für Orchester" (2222-2200)
Ponce, Manuel
- Instantáneas Mexicanas, No.3: Cielito lindo (1121-0000)
- Instantáneas Mexicanas, No.4: Si algún ser (1121-0000)
- Instantáneas Mexicanas, No.6: Mañanitas de los niños (1120-0000)
Read, Gardner
- Petite Pastorale, op.40a (1122-2000)
Revueltas, Silvestre
- Batik (1020-0000)
Rodríguez, Robert Xavier
- Adagio for Small Orchestra (1112-2000)
Saint-Saëns, Camille
- Une nuit à Lisbonne, op.63 (1111-2000)
Santórsola, Guido
- Prelúdio No.3 (1121-2000)
Saturen, David
- Expression; Lyric piece for small orchestra (1120-2220)
Stravinsky, Igor
- Tango (1211-2000)

6' - 10'

Aperghis, Georges
- Ascoltare stanca; Pour 18 Instrumentistes (1200-2000)
Arnell, Richard
- Sonata for Chamber Orchestra, op.18 (1111-2000)
Barnett, Carol
- Sumervar (2212-2000)
Bartók, Béla
- Rumanian Folk Dances (2022-2000)
- Suite, op.14 (2212-2000)
Bedford, David
- Trona For 12 (1111-0220)
Bentzon, Niels Viggo
- Prelude and Rondo, op.56 (2222-2000)
Blake, David
- Scherzo and Two Dances (1020-0000)
Blomdahl, Karl-Birger
- Adagio from "Vaknatten"; Incidental music from the play (1100-2000)
Brant, Henry
- A Requiem in Summer; In Memory of my Father (2222-0000)

Bräutigam, Helmut
- Festliche Musik (2200-0200)
Bridge, Frank
- There Is A Willow Grows Aslant A
  Brook (1121-1000)
Brown, Earle
- Modules 1 & 2 (2222-2221)
Cowell, Henry
- Carol (2222-2200)
Davison, John
- Symphony No.6 (0200-2000)
Delius, Frederick
- Petite Suite No.2 (2222-2000)
Fauré, Gabriel
- Romance, op.28 (2122-1000)
Faust, George
- Adagio for Small Orchestra (2222-
  2000)
Ficher, Jacobo
- Dos Poemas; De El Jardino de R.
  Tagore, op.10, No.16 (1111-2000)
Françaix, Jean
- Onze Variations sur un Thème de
  Haydn (0222-2100)
Fuleihan, Anis
- Divertimento (0211-1100)
Gilbert, Anthony
- Sinfonia for Chamber Orchestra
  (1211-2100)
Glazunov, Alexander
- Serenade for Small Orchestra No.2,
  op.11 (2122-2000)
Harrison, Lou
- Alleluia (2220-2000)
- Seven Pastorales (2101-0000)
Hauer, Josef Matthias
- Zwölftonspiel XVII (Twelve-tone
  game XVII) (1121-1110)
Hindemith, Paul
- Sonata for 10 Instruments (1021-
  1000)
Holliger, Heinz
- Ad Marginem (2020-0000)
- Engführung (1221-2000)
- Der Ferne Klang (2221-1000)
Holloway, Robin
- Inquietus, op.66 (1211-1000)
Honegger, Arthur
- Prélude pour Aglavaine et
  Sélysette; D'après la pièce de
  Maeterlinck, H.10 (1122-2100)
Jost, Christian
- Mascarade: Tableau from the opera
  "Vipern" (2121-2110)
Kaun, Hugo
- Elegie, op.70, No.5 (2121-2000)
- Fröhliches Wandern, op.70, No.1
  (2021-2000)
- Idyll, op.70, No.2 (2021-2000)

Kodály, Zoltán
- Hungarian Rondo (0022-0000)
Kolb, Barbara
- The Web Spinner (2222-2000)
Krása, Hans
- Overture for Small Orchestra (0020-
  0200)
Krenek, Ernst
- Von Vorn Herein, op.219 (1120-
  1100)
Laderman, Ezra
- Cadence (2000-0000)
LeFanu, Nicola
- Preludio II (1111-2000)
Liebermann, Rolf
- Suite on Six Swiss Folksongs
  (2222-2000)
MacKenzie, Sir Alexander C.
- Benedictus, op.37, No.3 (2022-
  2000)
Martinů, Bohuslav
- Jazz Suite, H.172 (0111-0220)
Milhaud, Darius
- Chamber Symphony No.5; Dixtuor
  d'Instruments à Vent, op.75 (2222-
  2000)
Moncayo, José Pablo
- Homenaje a Cervantes (0200-0000)
Muldowney, Dominic
- Double Helix (2010-0100)
Müller-Siemens, Detlev
- Zwei Stücke (Two Pieces) (2222-
  2000)
Pärt, Arvo
- Collage on B-A-C-H (0200-0000)
Paz, Juan Carlos
- Obertura Para Doce Instrumentos
  (Overture for 12 Instruments) (1111-
  2110)
Poot, Marcel
- Fantasia (1111-2110)
Porrino, Ennio
- Tre Canzoni Italiane (2121-2110)
Ravel, Maurice
- Pavane pour une infant défunte
  (2122-2000)
Revueltas, Silvestre
- Planos (Planes) (0021-0100)
Rodrigo, Joaquín
- Tres Viejos Aires de Danza (1111-
  2000)
Ruders, Poul
- Trapeze (0200-2000)
Sallinen, Aulis
- Sunrise Serenade (0000-0200)
Schoeck, Othmar
- Serenade (Interlude) (0200-0000)

Shchedrin, Rodion
- Shepherd's Pipes of Vologda
  (0200-1000)
Sibelius, Jean
- Suite Mignonne, op.98a (2000-
  0000)
Stern, Robert
- Ricordanza (2121-2100)
Strauss, Richard
- Ariadne auf Naxos: Overture and
  Dance Scene, op.60 (2222-2000)
Stravinsky, Igor
- Concertino for 12 Instruments
  (1212-0220)
- Eight Instrumental Miniatures
  (2222-1000)
Thiele, Siegfried
- Drei Orchestermotetten nach
  Machaut (1221-2120)
Walton, William
- Siesta (1121-2000)
Webern, Anton
- Symphony, op.21 (0020-2000)
Wolpe, Michael
- Chamber Piece No.1 (1211-1110)
Wyner, Yehudi
- Amadeus' Billiard (0002-2000)

11' - 15'

Adolphe, Bruce
- Three Pieces; For Kids in the
  Audience and Chamber Orchestra
  (2222-2200)
Ardevol, José
- Concerto Grosso No.1 (1101-0200)
Arnold, Malcolm
- Sinfonietta No.1, op.48 (0200-2000)
- Sinfonietta No.2, op.65 (2000-2000)
- Sinfonietta No.3 (2202-2000)
Bedford, David
- This One For You (2222-2200)
Benjamin, Arthur
- Sonatina for Chamber Orchestra
  (1110-0000)
Berkeley, Lennox
- Windsor Variations, op.75 (1202-
  2000)
Blake, David
- Sonata alla Marchia (0200-2000)
Brauel, Henning
- Les Fenêtres Simultanées (1111-
  2110)
Britten, Benjamin
- Sinfonietta, op.1 (1111-2000)
Castro, José Maria
- Concerto Grosso (2222-2100)
Cerha, Friedrich
- Sinfonie (2222-2111)

Chapple, Brian
- Little Symphony (1202-2000)
Conyngham, Barry
- Glimpses of Bennelong (1200-2000)
Delius, Frederick
- Two Pieces for Small Orchestra (1122-2000)
Druckman, Jacob
- Nor Spell, Nor Charm (1222-2000)
Erdmann, Dietrich
- Epitaph (0020-0000)
Firsova, Elena
- Autumn Music, op.39 (1202-2000)
Haieff, Alexei Vasilievich
- Divertimento (2110-0220)
Hallberg, Björn Wilho
- Novelletten (1121-1110)
Hamilton, Iain
- Sonata, op.34 (2111-1100)
Hartley, Walter Sinclair
- Chamber Symphony (1111-2110)
Helfer, Walter
- Prelude to a Midsummer Night's Dream (1112-1100)
Helm, Everett
- Italienische Suite (2111-2220)
Henze, Hans Werner
- Three Mozart Organ Sonatas for 14 Players (2211-0000)
Herrera de la Fuente, Luis
- Fronteras; Ballet (2222-2200)
Holloway, Robin
- First Idyll, op.42 (1222-2000)
- Ode, op.45 (0200-2000)
Honegger, Arthur
- Suite Archaïque, H.203 (2222-0220)
Indy, Vincent d'
- Suite dans le style ancient, op.24 (2000-0100)
Kelterborn, Rudolf
- Four Movements for Classical Orchestra (0200-2000)
- Vier Nachstücke für Kammerorchester (0020-2000)
Kisielewski, Stefan
- Concerto for Chamber Orchestra (1211-0000)
Kósa, György
- Chamber Music (1121-1100)
Krauze, Zygmunt
- Tableau Vivant (1121-1110)
Krol, Bernhard
- Concerto Grosso, op.15 (0201-0200)
Levy, Marvin David
- Trialogus II (1211-1110)

Linke, Norbert
- Divisioni (2222-2200)
Martinů, Bohuslav
- Sérénade; Pour orchestre de chambre (1212-2210)
- Tre Ricercari, op. H.267 (1202-0200)
Matthews, Colin
- Tosca Revisited (1121-2100)
McAlister, Clark
- A Christmas Pastorale (1201-2000)
McCabe, John
- Red Leaves (0200-2000)
McKay, George Frederick
- Fantasy on a Western Folk Song; O! Bury me not on the lone prairie (2120-0100)
- Variants on a Texas Tune, Mustang grey (2121-2000)
Milford, Robin
- Suite for Chamber Orchestra (2122-1000)
Milner, Anthony
- Chamber Symphony (1212-2000)
Moravec, Paul
- Sempre Diritto!; (Straight Ahead) (0200-2000)
Müller-Hornbach, Gerhard
- Passacaglia II (1111-1120)
Nono, Luigi
- Canti Per 13 (1121-1110)
Patterson, Paul
- Europhony, op.55 (0200-2000)
Pernes, Thomas
- Gesänge (0121-1000)
Porrino, Ennio
- Notturno e Danza (1121-2110)
Pousseur, Henri
- Symphonies à Quinze Solistes (1111-2110)
Rieti, Vittorio
- Due Pastorali (1112-2100)
Saxton, Robert
- Traumstadt (2222-2210)
Scherchen, Tona
- Khouang (1121-1110)
Schlee, Thomas Daniel
- Sonata da Camera, op.42 (0100-2000)
Schuller, Gunther
- Chamber Symphony (2222-1111)
Schweitzer, Benjamin
- flekkicht; For baroque orchestra (2201-2000)
Sgrizzi, Luciano
- Englische Suite nach Werken der Virginalisten (2121-2200)

- Suite Belge; D'après des œuvres de clavecinistes belges du 18ème siècle (2121-0000)
Standford, Patric
- Notte (1201-2000)
Stockhausen, Karlheinz
- Kontra-Punkte Nr.1 (1021-0110)
Stravinsky, Igor
- Concerto in E-flat "Dumbarton Oaks" (1011-2000)
Sutermeister, Heinrich
- Sérénade pour Montreux (0200-2000)
Thiele, Siegfried
- Wolkenbilder; Four Movements (1200-2000)
Tomlinson, Ernest
- A Georgian Miniature (2121-0000)
Vinter, Gilbert
- Dance of the Marionettes (2121-0000)
Weir, Judith
- Isti Mirant Stella (2222-2200)
Wilby, Philip
- The Wings of Morning (0200-2000)
Winters, Geoffrey
- Concertino, op.18 (0000-2000)
Xenakis, Iannis
- Jalons (1121-1111)

16' - 20'

Amy, Gilbert
- D'Après "Ecrits Sur Toiles"; Pour Orchestre de Chambre (2222-2000)
Ardevol, José
- Concerto Grosso No.2 (0222-0210)
Atterberg, Kurt
- Barocco-Suite No.5, op.23 (1210-0000)
Bawden, Rupert
- Ultima Scena (2010-0000)
Bedford, David
- With 100 Kazoos; For chamber ensemble and 100 kazoos (1120-1110)
Blake, David
- Seasonal Variants (1020-0000)
Dalby, Martin
- Cancionero Para Una Mariposa (1002-0020)
David, Johann Nepomuk
- Sinfonia preclassica super nomen H-A-S-E, Wk44 (2000-2000)
Feldman, Morton
- The Turfan Fragments (2222-2220)
Forst, Rudolf
- Divertimento for Chamber Orchestra (1121-1100)

Gill, Jeremy
- Chamber Symphony (1111-2110)
Glass, Philip
- Concerto Grosso (1111-2111)
Guenther, Felix
- Deutsches Rokoko; Eine Suite für
  Kleines Orchester nach Alten
  Meistern (1121-2000)
Heitzeg, Steve
- Flower of the Earth; Homage to
  Georgia O'Keeffe (1201-2000)
Holloway, Robin
- Second Idyll, op.54 (1202-2000)
Johnson, Hunter
- Concerto for Small Orchestra
  (2020-0000)
Joubert, John
- Sinfonietta, op.38 (0202-2000)
Klenau, Paul von
- Altdeutsche Liedersuite (Old
  German Song Suite) (2222-2210)
Kodály, Zoltán
- Summer Evening (1222-2000)
Kreutz, Arthur
- American Dances (2222-0000)
Lazarof, Henri
- Espaces (2020-0000)
Lees, Benjamin
- Concertante Breve (0100-2000)
Lumsdaine, David
- Sunflower (1222-2000)
MacRae, Stuart
- Portrait (1111-2110)
Martinů, Bohuslav
- The Amazing Flight; Ballet
  mécanique, H.159 (0021-0100)
Matthews, David
- Serenade, op.29 (1202-2000)
Maw, Nicholas
- Sonata for Strings and Two Horns
  (0000-2000)
Musgrave, Thea
- Night Music (1201-2000)
Olivier, François
- Suite Pour Petit Orchestre (1111-
  2100)
Piston, Walter
- Sinfonietta (2222-2000)
Platz, Robert H. P.
- PIECE NOIRE (2110-1110)
Raphael, Günter
- Variationen über eine Schottische
  Volksweise, op.23 (2112-2000)
Ravel, Maurice
- Le Tombeau de Couperin (2222-
  2100)
Reich, Steve
- Eight Lines (2020-0000)

Rorem, Ned
- A Quaker Reader; Suite (2222-
  2110)
Sawer, David
- Take Off (1020-0000)
Schurmann, Gerard
- Variants (1202-2000)
Searle, Humphrey
- Three Songs of Jocelyn Brooke,
  op.25b (2121-1100)
Shchedrin, Rodion
- Music for the Town of Koethen
  (0202-0000)
Spinner, Leopold
- Ricercata, op.21 (2220-1111)
Standford, Patric
- Suite for Small Orchestra (2121-
  2000)
Voss, Friedrich
- Résonances; 12 Poems (1111-
  2110)
Weir, Judith
- Winter Song (2222-2200)
Yun, Isang
- Konzertante Figuren (2211-2110)
Zilcher, Hermann
- Lustspielsuite; Der Widerspenstigen
  Zähmung, op.54b (1111-2100)

Over 20'

Amram, David
- Shakespearean Concerto (0100-
  2000)
Argento, Dominick
- Royal Invitation; (Homage to the
  Queen of Tonga) (1202-2000)
Arnold, Malcolm
- Concerto for 28 Players, op.105
  (1201-2000)
Beyer, Frank Michael
- Musikalisches Opfer; Ricercare a 3,
  Fuga canonica & 9 Kanons (1221-
  1100)
Bolcom, William
- Symphony No.3 (1212-2000)
Cage, John
- Quartets I-VIII; For an Orchestra of
  24 Instruments (1212-2000)
Cowie, Edward
- Leonardo (2222-2000)
Degen, Helmut
- Chamber Symphony; (Symphony
  No.2) (2101-2100)
Glass, Philip
- Glassworks (2020-2000)
Goehr, Alexander
- Sinfonia, op.42 (1220-2000)

Gregson, Edward
- Music for Chamber Orchestra
  (0202-2000)
Griffes, Charles Tomlinson
- The Kairn of Koridwen; A Druid
  Legend (1020-2000)
Hamilton, Iain
- Symphony No.3 (2222-2000)
Harneit, Johannes
- Triptychon (13X3), op.20 (1121-
  2100)
Holloway, Robin
- Concertino No.2, op.10 (1211-2000)
- Fourth Idyll (2222-2200)
Honegger, Arthur
- Symphony No.2 (0000-0100)
Kancheli, Giya
- Magnum Ignotum (1222-2000)
Karayev, Kara
- Symphony No.3 for Chamber
  Orchestra (2202-2000)
Kupferman, Meyer
- Little Symphony (1202-2000)
Ligeti, György
- Kammerkonzert (Chamber
  Concerto) (1120-1010)
Lloyd, Jonathan
- Symphony No.3 (1121-2000)
Matthews, David
- Symphony No.4, op.51 (1202-2000)
Maw, Nicholas
- Serenade (1202-2000)
- Sinfonia (1222-2000)
Maxwell Davies, Peter
- Sinfonietta Accademica (2222-
  2200)
Milhaud, Darius
- Musique pour Lisbonne, op.420
  (0200-2000)
Nilsson, Bo
- Bombi Bitt (2010-0000)
Nyman, Michael
- Concert Suite from Prospero's
  Books (2222-2210)
Panufnik, Andrzej
- Sinfonia Mistica; Symphony No.6
  (2222-2000)
Rodrigo, Joaquín
- Soleriana; Suite for chamber
  orchestra (2111-1100)
Roselius, Ludwig
- Friesische Musik, op.30 (1221-
  1000)
Rosenman, Leonard
- Chamber Music No.2 (1120-0000)
Sallinen, Aulis
- Concerto for Chamber Orchestra
  (1121-1000)

Sawer, David
- Cat's-eye (0020-0110)
Saxton, Robert
- Elijah's Violin (1202-2000)
Saygun, A. Adnan
- Symphony No.1 (1222-2000)
Schnittke, Alfred
- Suite in Old Style (0200-2000)
Schönberg, Arnold
- Kammersymphonie Nr.2 (Chamber Symphony No.2), op.38 (2222-2200)
Schwertsik, Kurt
- Compagnie Masquerade; Ein Divertissement für kleines Orchester, einer Idee & teilweise erhaltenen Violinstimme Mozarts folgend (2222-2110)
Swayne, Giles
- Symphony for Small Orchestra (1202-2000)
Tchaikovsky, Boris
- Chamber Symphony (0200-2000)
Tubin, Eduard
- Symphony No.7 (2222-2200)
Yun, Isang
- Kammersinfonie I (Chamber Symphony I) (0200-2000)

Larger Than 2222 - 2221 - str

10' or Less

Antheil, George
- Suite for Orchestra (2220-3001)
Arnold, Malcolm
- Trevelyan Suite, op.96 (3220-2000)
Berio, Luciano
- Re-Call (2141-2321)
Delius, Frederick
- Irmelin: Prelude (2332-2000)
Gould, Morton
- Serenade ("Orfeo") from "Audubon" (2232-0000)
Klebe, Giselher
- Con moto, op.2 (2222-4231)

Lang, David
- Open (2222-4000)
Le Grand, Robert
- Effets de Nuit (2332-2000)
Matsudaira, Yoritsune
- Pastorale (2332-2000)
Morthenson, Jan Wilhelm
- Antiphonia II (3020-0000)
Ponce, Manuel
- Suite en Estilo Antiguo (1111-4000)
Prokofiev, Sergei
- Autumn; A symphonic sketch for small orchestra, op.8 (2232-4100)
Rachmaninoff, Sergei
- Vocalise, op.34 (2322-2000)
Rogers, Bernard
- Elegy: From Symphony No.3 (0300-0000)
Satie, Erik
- Illusion [Tendrement] (1121-2230)

Over 10'

Atterberg, Kurt
- De Fåvitska Jungfrurna; The wise and the foolish virgins. Rhapsody on old Swedish folksongs (2222-3000)
Baggiani, Guido
- Double (2332-2000)
Barclay, Robert Lenard
- Symphony in One Movement (2222-4200)
Berio, Luciano
- Kol od (Chemins VI) (3141-2211)
Beyer, Frank Michael
- Ricercare I (2030-0000)
Blacher, Boris
- Studie im Pianissimo (2222-4331)
Fauré, Gabriel
- Symphony in F major (2222-4000)
Fómina, Silvia
- Permanenza; Für mikropolyphonisches, im Raum verteiltes Orchester (2030-1010)
Goehr, Alexander
- Little Symphony, op.15 (1230-2001)

Grosse, Erwin
- Kammersinfonie (Chamber Symphony), op.48 (2030-0000)
Hier, Ethel Glenn
- Carolina Christmas; Suite for Chamber Orchestra (2222-4000)
Hindemith, Paul
- Concert Music for Strings and Brass, op.50 (0000-4431)
Kirchner, Volker David
- Bildnisse I (2322-2220)
- Bildnisse II (2322-2220)
Klebe, Giselher
- Scene und Arie, op.54 (0000-0330)
Levy, Marvin David
- Trialogus I (0000-3000)
Maasz, Gerhard
- Tripartita (3000-0000)
Maros, Rudolf
- Gemma; In Memoriam Zoltán Kodály (2220-4200)
Martinů, Bohuslav
- Concerto Grosso (1330-2000)
Novák, Vítêzslav
- Serenade, op.36 (2222-4000)
Prokofiev, Sergei
- Sinfonietta, op.48 (2222-4200)
Respighi, Ottorino
- Antiche Danze ed Arie: Suite 1 (2302-2100)
Roslavets, Nikolai Andreyevich
- Chamber Symphony; For 18 solo instruments (2232-2100)
Schönberg, Arnold
- Kammersymphonie Nr.1 (Chamber Symphony No.1), op.9 (1232-2000)
Šulek, Stjepan
- Concerto Classique (2222-4200)
Vivier, Claude
- Deva et Asura (2222-2320)

NO HARP or PIANO

1111 - 1111 - str
Maximum

5' or Less

Bedford, Herbert
- The Lonely Dancer of Gedār (1101-1000)

Brant, Henry
- Lyric Piece (1111-1110)

Cowell, Henry
- Polyphonica (1111-1110)
- Teheran Movement (1111-0100)

De Brant, Cyr
- Song of Yesteryear (1111-1000)

Glass, Philip
- Interlude from "Orphée" (1011-1110)

Gürsching, Albrecht
- Drei Plus Vier (0011-1000)

Hindemith, Paul
- Sing- und Spielmusik für Liebhaber und Freunde (1111-0000)

Honegger, Arthur
- Blues (1111-1100)
- Napoléon: Danse des Enfants (1011-0000)
- Napoléon: La romance de Violine (1110-0000)

Horovitz, Joseph
- Horizon Overture (1111-1110)

Huë, Georges Adolphe
- Rêverie pour petit orchestre (1111-0000)
- Sérénade pour orchestre (1111-0000)

Indy, Vincent d'
- Sérénade (1111-0100)

Ives, Charles Edward
- Tone Roads No.1 (1011-0000)

Maxwell Davies, Peter
- Canzona (1111-1000)
- A Welcome to Orkney (1111-1000)

Milhaud, Darius
- Chamber Symphony No.2 (1101-0000)
- Chamber Symphony No.3 (1011-0000)

Pierné, Gabriel
- Album Pour Mes Petites Amis (Album for My Little Friends) (1110-1000)
- Ballet de Cour (1111-0000)

Poulenc, Francis
- Esquisse d'une Fanfare (1111-1110)
- Mouvements perpétuels for nine instruments (1111-1000)
- Valse (1111-1110)

Rodrigo, Joaquín
- Cyrano de Bergerac (1000-0100)

Satie, Erik
- Les Pantins Dansent (1111-1100)

Schelling, Ernest
- Tarantella (1101-0000)

Schmitt, Florent
- Hymne à Tanit (1111-1000)
- Reflets d'Allemagne (1111-1000)

Stravinsky, Igor
- Ragtime (1010-1110)

Surinach, Carlos
- Danza Andaluza (1111-1100)

Talbot, Joby
- Arbor Low (1111-1000)

Warlock, Peter
- An Old Song (1110-1000)

Wellesz, Egon
- Pastorale (1100-0110)

6' - 10'

Atterberg, Kurt
- Suite No.2 (1010-0000)

Banks, Don
- Elizabethan Miniatures (1000-0000)

Bauer, Marion
- Concertino (0110-0000)

Berlin, David
- Structures for Chamber Orchestra (1111-1120)

Boccadoro, Carlo
- Adagio (1111-1000)

Bolcom, William
- Session I (1101-0010)

Bruun, Peter
- Bag Den Kan Fredens Ranker Gro (1111-1000)

Buck, Ole
- Chamber Music I (1111-1100)
- Chamber Music II (1111-1000)

Cohn, James
- Homage (1111-1110)

Daniels, Mabel W.
- Deep Forest (1111-1100)

Dillon, James
- ...Once Upon A Time (1111-1110)

Dubois, Pierre-Max
- Trois Sérénades (0111-0000)

Earls, Paul
- And On The Seventh Day (1111-1000)

Eaton, John
- Adagio and Allegro (1100-0000)

Finzi, Gerald
- Love's Labour's Lost (1111-1000)
- A Severn Rhapsody (1110-1000)

Françaix, Jean
- Sérénade (1111-1110)

Franco, Johan
- Sinfonia (1111-1110)

Fundal, Karsten
- Hoquetus (1111-1000)

Glass, Philip
- Meetings along the Edge (1000-0000)

Górecki, Henryk Mikołaj
- Concerto (1010-0100)

Grainger, Percy Aldridge
- My Robin is to the Greenwood Gone (1100-0000)

Gyring, Elizabeth
- Scherzo No.2 for Orchestra (1010-0110)

Hansson, C.J. Gunnar
- Suite No.1 (1111-1000)

Hemberg, Eskil
- Migraine pour orchestre (1111-1000)

Hewitt, Harry
- Overture (1111-1100)

Hindemith, Paul
- Plöner Musiktag (1000-0100)

Holst, Gustav
- Morris Dance Tunes (1010-0000)

Honegger, Arthur
- Fantasio (1111-1110)
- Pastorale d'été (1111-1000)

Kelemen, Milko
- Konstellationen (1111-1110)

Koch, Erland von
- Dalecarlia Suite (1010-0000)

Komarova, Tatjana
- Sonnenuntergänge auf B 612 (Sunsets on B 612) (1111-0000)

Lang, David
- Spud (1110-1000)

Ledenjov, Roman
- Notturni (1111-1000)

LeFanu, Nicola
- Preludio I (1111-1000)

Lutosławski, Witold
- Bucolics (1111-1000)
- Dance Preludes (1111-1000)

MacRae, Stuart
- The Broken Spectre (1111-1000)

Martinů, Bohuslav
- Serenata No.1 (0110-1000)
- Serenata No.3 (0110-0000)

Moeran, E. J.
- Whythorne's Shadow (1110-1000)

Nordentoft, Anders
- The City of Threads (1111-1000)
Osborne, Nigel
- Eulogy (1111-1110)
Pärt, Arvo
- Fratres (1111-1000)
- Pari Intervallo (0010-0010)
Payne, Anthony
- Hidden Music (1111-1000)
Pierné, Gabriel
- Ballet de Cour (1111-1000)
Poulenc, Francis
- Deux Marches et un Intermède
  (1111-0100)
Primosch, James
- Five Miniatures (1110-1110)
Revueltas, Silvestre
- Ocho Por Radio (0011-0100)
Riegger, Wallingford
- Scherzo (1111-1100)
Rihm, Wolfgang
- Chiffre VI (0011-1000)
Rota, Nino
- Canzona (1111-1100)
Schoeck, Othmar
- Serenade (1111-1000)
Schwaen, Kurt
- Zwingerserenade (1111-0000)
Searle, Humphrey
- Night Music (1111-1110)
Sørensen, Bent
- Clairobscur (1111-1000)
Staud, Johannes Maria
- Configurations / Reflet (0111-1000)
Stock, David
- Capriccio (1111-1100)
Stroman, Scott
- Clown Dances (0011-0110)
Talbot, Joby
- Minus 1500 (0001-0000)
Tanaka, Karen
- Echo Canyon (1111-1110)
Terzakis, Dimitri
- Hommage à Morse (1110-0010)
Thomas, Augusta Reed
- Capricious Angels (1110-1000)
Vate, Nancy van de
- Variations for Chamber Orchestra
  (1111-0000)
Vostřák, Zbyněk
- Tao (1111-0000)
Weiner, Leo
- Divertimento No.1 (1000-1100)
Wilson, Richard
- Fantasy and Variations (1011-0110)
Wittinger, Róbert
- Compensazioni (1110-1110)
Xenakis, Iannis
- Kaï (1011-0110)

11' - 15'

Alizade, Akshin
- Symphony No.4 (1111-1000)
Ali-Zadeh, Franghiz
- Dilogie I for Nine Players (1111-1000)
- Sturm und Drang for Chamber
  Orchestra (1111-1000)
Bäck, Sven-Erik
- Chamber Symphony (1011-1110)
Bavicchi, John
- Concertante, op.44 (0101-0000)
Bialas, Günter
- Sinfonia Piccola (1110-0000)
Braun, Yehezkel
- Serenade for Chamber Orchestra
  (1111-1000)
Britten, Benjamin
- Sinfonietta (1111-1000)
Burgon, Geoffrey
- The Chronicles of Narnia Suite
  (1101-1100)
Cohn, James
- Variations on The Wayfaring
  Stranger (1111-1110)
Cordero, Roque
- Ocho Miniaturas (1111-1110)
Cowell, Henry
- Sinfonietta (1111-1110)
Dalby, Martin
- De Patre Ex Filio (0011-1000)
Dazzi, Gualtiero
- Sable (1010-1000)
Delás, José Luis de
- Denkbild - Kurze Schatten (1010-1000)
Döhl, Friedhelm
- Octet (1111-0000)
Eisler, Hanns
- Five Pieces for Orchestra (1111-1110)
- Three Pieces for Orchestra (1111-1110)
Erdmann, Dietrich
- Musica Multicolore (0111-1000)
- Nuancen (1010-0000)
Fontyn, Jacqueline
- Nonetto (1111-1000)
Frackenpohl, Arthur
- Divertimento in F (1010-1110)
Fuchs, Kenneth
- Out of the Dark (1111-1000)
Genzmer, Harald
- Capriccio für Kammerorchester
  (0111-1000)
Godfrey, Daniel Strong
- Concentus (1111-1110)

Gubaidulina, Sofia
- Concordanza (1111-1000)
Gürsching, Albrecht
- Piccola Sinfonia (0011-1000)
Haas, Georg Friedrich
- "...aus freier Lust...verbunden..."
  (1010-0000)
- "...Einkland freier Wesen..." (1010-0111)
Halffter, Rodolfo
- Divertimento Para Nueve
  Instrumentos (1111-0100)
Hamilton, Iain
- Arias (1111-1110)
Hidalgo, Manuel
- Nahezu Stilles Auge des
  Wirbelsturms (1111-1000)
Holt, Simon
- Capriccio Spettrale (1010-1100)
- Kites (1111-1000)
Horne, David
- Persistence (1111-1110)
James, Dorothy
- Suite for Small Orchestra (1111-1100)
Kahn, Erich Itor
- Actus Tragicus (1111-1000)
Kallstenius, Edvin
- Suite for 9 Instruments (1111-1000)
Kisielewski, Stefan
- Rencontres dans un désert (1011-0110)
Klebe, Giselher
- Divertissement joyeux (0011-1110)
Knussen, Oliver
- Processionals (1111-1000)
Koch, Erland von
- Ballet Suite: Peter Tailless, the Cat
  (1111-1110)
- Four Swedish Folk Melodies (1111-1000)
Koppel, Anders
- Concertino for Chamber Ensemble
  (1111-1000)
Larsson, Lars-Erik
- Divertimento (1111-1000)
Linke, Norbert
- Profit tout Clair (0111-1000)
Lorentzen, Bent
- Paesaggio (1111-1000)
Maasz, Gerhard
- Musik (Nr.1) (1010-0000)
Malipiero, Gian Francesco
- Ritrovari (1111-1000)
Marsh, Roger
- Dying for It (1111-0000)
Matthus, Siegfried
- Ich komm einen Weg (0011-1000)

Milhaud, Darius
- Musique pour Graz (1111-0100)
Müller-Siemens, Detlev
- Variationen über einen Ländler von Schubert (1111-1000)
Mundry, Isabel
- Le Silence (1110-1110)
Musgrave, Thea
- Chamber Concerto No.1 (0111-1110)
Nørgård, Per
- Prelude and Fugue (With a Crab Canon) (1010-0000)
Pape, Andy
- Min Fynske Barndom (1111-1000)
Patterson, Paul
- At the Still Point of the Turning World (1110-1000)
Piston, Walter
- Divertimento (1111-0000)
Quinet, Marcel
- Sinfonietta (1111-1000)
Read, Gardner
- Partita for Small Orchestra (1111-1110)
Redel, Martin Christoph
- Kammersinfonie II (1110-0000)
Reimann, Aribert
- Metamorphosen über ein Menuett von Franz Schubert (1111-1000)
Rochberg, George
- Cheltenham Concerto (1111-1110)
Rosing-Schow, Niels
- Meeting (0111-1000)
Salviucci, Giovanni
- Sinfonia da Camera (1111-1100)
Samazeuilh, Gustave
- Divertissement et Musette (1111-1000)
Schubert, Manfred
- Septet in Two Movements (0011-1000)
Schwartz, Francis
- Flaming June (1110-1001)
Silverman, Stanley
- Planh (1010-0000)
Sjöblom, Heimer
- Liten Svit I Spelmanston (1111-1000)
Smirnov, Dmitri
- The River of Life (1111-1110)
Spratlan, Lewis
- Diary Music I (1111-0100)
Szymanski, Pawel
- Sixty-Odd Pages (1111-1110)
Talbot, Joby
- Animisation (1111-1110)
Tavener, John
- Grandma's Footsteps (0101-1000)

Treibmann, Karl Ottomar
- Second Symphonic Essay (1111-1000)
Turnage, Mark-Anthony
- On All Fours (1111-1011)
Ullmann, Jakob
- Composition for 10 Instruments I-V (1010-1000)
Xenakis, Iannis
- Anaktoria (0011-1000)
- Atrées (1010-1110)
- Phlegra (1111-1110)

16' - 20'

Aa, Michel van der
- Above (1111-0100)
- Here [enclosed] (0011-0110)
Abendroth, Walter
- Divertimento für Kammerorchester (1111-1110)
Blomdahl, Karl-Birger
- Concerto grosso (1011-1000)
Boucourechliev, André
- Le Chevelure de Bérénice (1111-1110)
Braun, Yehezkel
- Apartment To Let (1111-1000)
Brown, James Francis
- Sinfonietta (1111-1000)
Cohn, James
- Symphony No.4 in A (1111-1100)
Dalby, Martin
- Man Walking (0101-1000)
Denhoff, Michael
- O Orpheus singt (0011-1000)
Diamond, David
- Elegies (1100-0000)
Erbse, Heimo
- For String and Wind Players (0111-1000)
Essl, Karl-Heinz
- O Tiempo Tus Piramides (1111-1110)
Ferrari, Luc
- Flashes (1111-1110)
Geissler, Fritz
- Chamber Symphony (1111-1000)
Giefer, Willy
- Pro - Kontra (1111-1000)
Gudmundsen-Holmgreen, Pelle
- Nær og Fjern (Near and Distant) (1111-1000)
Hindemith, Paul
- Tuttifäntchen (1111-1100)
Holloway, Robin
- Concertino No.1 (1111-1110)

Holmboe, Vagn
- Chamber Symphony No.1 (1111-1100)
- Symphony No.1 (1111-1110)
Honegger, Arthur
- Le Dit des Jeux du Monde (1000-0100)
Hurd, Michael
- Captain Coram's Kids (1101-0000)
Jaroch, Jiri
- II. Nonet (1111-1000)
Kelemen, Milko
- Nonett (1111-0000)
Kelly, Bryan
- Concertante Dances (1111-0000)
Lobanov, Vasily
- Sinfonietta for Chamber Orchestra (1111-1110)
Malipiero, Gian Francesco
- Ricercari (1111-1000)
Martinů, Bohuslav
- Nonet No.2 (1111-1000)
Matthews, Colin
- Suns Dance (1111-1000)
Maxwell Davies, Peter
- Sinfonia (1111-1000)
Melby, John
- Wind, Sand and Stars (1110-1000)
Milhaud, Darius
- Jeux de Printemps (1011-0100)
Musgrave, Thea
- Space Play (1111-1000)
Nelson, Larry
- Catena (1110-1110)
Nørgård, Per
- Amled (1111-1100)
Nussio, Otmar
- Divertimento (0011-1000)
Osborne, Nigel
- In Camera (1111-1110)
Reimann, Aribert
- Invenzioni (1111-1110)
Rochberg, George
- Chamber Symphony for 9 Instruments (0111-1110)
Schubert, Heino
- Concerto (1111-0000)
Schubert, Manfred
- Nachtstück und Passacaglia (0011-1000)
Schulhoff, Erwin
- Suite for Chamber Orchestra (0011-0110)
Search, Frederick
- Sinfonietta (1111-1110)
Searle, Humphrey
- Variations and Finale (1111-1000)
Smolka, Martin
- Octet (0011-1000)

Sørensen, Bent
- Shadowland (1111-1000)
Stenhammar, Wilhelm
- Lodolezzi Sjunger (1000-0000)
Stürmer, Bruno
- Suite für Neun Solo-Instrumente
  (1111-0000)
Swayne, Giles
- Into the Light (0011-0110)
Thomas, Kurt
- Serenade (1111-1110)
Trapp, Max
- Divertimento für Kammerorchester
  (1111-1111)
Trojan, Václav
- Sinfonietta Armoniosa (1010-0110)
Watkins, Michael Blake
- Sinfonietta (1111-1110)
Xenakis, Iannis
- Waarg (1111-1111)

Over 20'

Apostel, Hans Erich
- Kammersymphonie (Chamber
  Symphony) (1111-1000)
Ballif, Claude
- Imaginaire No.3 (0011-1000)
Barati, George
- Chamber Concerto (1111-0000)
Bergman, Erik
- Tutti e soli (1011-0000)
Braun, Yehezkel
- Serenade II (1111-1000)
Burgon, Geoffrey
- Suite from Martin Chuzzlewit (1111-
  1000)
Burkhard, Willy
- Toccata for Chamber Orchestra
  (1011-0100)
Cage, John
- Thirteen (1111-0110)
Chávez, Carlos
- Suite for Double Quartet (1111-
  0000)
Cohn, James
- Symphony No.3 in G (1111-1110)
- Symphony No.5 (1111-1110)
Cordero, Roque
- Dodecaconcerto (1111-1110)
Donovan, Richard
- Symphony for Chamber Orchestra
  (1111-0100)
Eberhard, Dennis
- Endgame (0011-1000)
Einfeldt, Dieter
- Apokalypse (0011-0110)
Ferguson, Howard
- Serenade (0011-1000)

Geissler, Fritz
- Symphony No.6 (1111-1000)
Hamilton, Iain
- The Alexandrian Sequence (1111-
  1110)
Heiller, Anton
- Kammersymphonie (0111-0000)
Hiller, Lejaren
- Divertimento (1111-1110)
Honegger, Arthur
- Le Dit des Jeux du Monde (1000-
  0100)
- Symphony No.2 (0000-0100)
Imbrie, Andrew
- From Time to Time (1111-0000)
Jelinek, Hanns
- Prelude, Passacaglia and Fugue
  (1011-1000)
Joubert, John
- Octet (0011-1000)
Krenek, Ernst
- Symphonische Musik für 9
  Soloinstrumente (1111-0000)
Martin, Frank
- Concerto (1111-1110)
Muldowney, Dominic
- The Earl of Essex Galliard (0011-
  0110)
Müller-Zürich, Paul
- Marienleben (1110-1000)
Nørgård, Per
- Amled (1111-1100)
Ostendorf, Jens-Peter
- Septett "Geschichte Vom..." (0011-
  0110)
Platz, Robert H. P.
- CHLEBNICOV (1110-1110)
Reger, Max
- Suite in A minor (1111-1000)
Rózsa, Miklós
- Hungarian Serenade (1111-1100)
Satie, Erik
- Le Piège de Méduse (0010-0110)
Schmitt, Florent
- Soirs (1111-0000)
Stravinsky, Igor
- L'Histoire du Soldat (The Soldier's
  Tale) (0011-0110)

**2222 - 2221 - str
Maximum**

5' or Less

Adamo, Mark
- Overture to Lysistrata (2222-2200)
Adler, Samuel
- Show An Affirming Flame; A Poem
  for Orchestra ("September 1, 1939"
  by W. H. Auden) (2222-2200)
Alfvén, Hugo
- Elegi; För liten orkester, ur
  orkestersviten Gustav II Adolf
  (0121-0000)
Almand, Claude
- Chorale for Chamber Orchestra
  (1120-2000)
Bales, Richard
- Primavera (1121-2210)
Berio, Luciano
- Variazione sull'aria di Papageno:
  No.2 from "Divertimento for Mozart"
  (0020-0000)
Berners, Lord
- For a Statesman: No.1 of "Three
  Small Funeral Marches" (1121-
  2210)
Bittner, Julius
- Der Musikant; Serenade (1121-
  2000)
Black, Stanley
- A Costume Comedy Overture
  (2222-2200)
Blumer, Theodor
- Vagabund; Scherzo for Orchestra
  (2222-2210)
Brant, Henry
- Prelude and Fugue (0000-2221)
Cerha, Friedrich
- Scherzino (2121-1110)
Chávez, Carlos
- Energia; For Nine Instruments
  (2001-1110)
Copland, Aaron
- Down a Country Lane (2121-2110)
Cowell, Henry
- Saturday Night at the Firehouse
  (1121-2200)
Crawford, Ruth
- Rissolty-Rossolty (1121-2210)
Delius, Frederick
- Fennimore and Gerda: Intermezzo
  (2222-2100)
Dohnanyi, Ernest von
- The Veil of Pierette: Menuett (1122-
  2000)
- The Veil of Pierette: Waltz (2222-
  2000)

Donato, Anthony
- Mission San José de Aguaya
  (2222-0000)
Duparc, Henri
- Aux étoiles (2222-2000)
Elgar, Edward
- May Song (1121-2210)
- Minuet, op.21 (1121-2000)
- Salut d'Amour, op.12 (1222-2000)
Etler, Alvin
- Elegy for Small Orchestra (1122-
  2000)
Françaix, Jean
- 85 Measures et un Da Capo (2001-
  0210)
Fricker, Peter Racine
- Fantasie: No.4 from "Divertimento
  for Mozart" (2222-2200)
Granados, Enrique
- Danzas Espanolas, No.6: Jota
  (1121-2210)
- Goyescas: Intermezzo (1121-2210)
Guarnieri, Camargo
- Ponteios No.1 (1010-2100)
Henze, Hans Werner
- Finale - Vivace assai: Nr.12 from
  "Divertimento for Mozart" (2222-
  2200)
Holliger, Heinz
- Choral à 8 (0020-2000)
- Sommerkanon IV (2210-0000)
Holst, Gustav
- Greeting (2121-0000)
Honegger, Arthur
- Deux Pièces pour "La Rédemption
  de François Villon," H.209 (1111-
  1200)
- Interlude de "La Mort de Sainte
  Alméene," H.20A (1122-2100)
- La Roue: Overture pour le film
  d'Abel Gance, H.44 (2022-0000)
- Toccata, H.207 (2222-2200)
- Vivace, H.220 (1122-2000)
Humperdinck, Engelbert
- Humoreske in E Dur (2222-2200)
Ibert, Jacques
- Hommage à Mozart (2222-2200)
Järnefelt, Armas
- Berceuse (0021-2000)
- Präludium (1121-2200)
Kander, Susan
- She Never Lost A Passenger
  Overture (2020-0110)
Koch, Erland von
- Dance No.2 (2222-2200)
- Kleine Lustspiel Ouvertüre (2222-
  2210)
- Sicilienne (1010-2210)

Koechlin, Charles
- Sur Les Flots Lointains (2122-2200)
Lecocq, Charles
- Fricassée (2222-2210)
MacMillan, James
- Memoire imperiale; A variation on
  General John Reid's March "Garb of
  Gaul" (2222-2200)
Matthews, David
- From Sea to Sky; Overture, op.59
  (0200-2000)
Maxwell Davies, Peter
- Threnody on a Plainsong for
  Michael Vyner (0202-2200)
McCabe, John
- Shepherd's Dream (0201-0200)
- Sam (2020-0100)
Myaskovsky, Nikolai Yakovlevich
- Military March No.1 (1121-2210)
Nielsen, Carl
- Festival Prelude (2222-2220)
Pepping, Ernst
- Invention für Kleines Orchester:
  From "Musiken für Orchester"
  (2222-2200)
Pierné, Gabriel
- Ballet de Cour, No.1: Rigaudon
  (1112-1100)
Ponce, Manuel
- Gavota (2111-2000)
- Instantáneas Mexicanas, No.3:
  Cielito lindo (1121-0000)
- Instantáneas Mexicanas, No.4: Si
  algún ser (1121-0000)
- Instantáneas Mexicanas, No.6:
  Mañanitas de los niños (1120-0000)
Poot, Marcel
- Ouverture Joyeuse (2222-2220)
Poulenc, Francis
- Bucolique (2222-2000)
- Matelote Provençale (2222-2200)
- Overture (2121-2210)
Ravel, Maurice
- Fanfare (2222-2100)
Read, Gardner
- Petite Pastorale, op.40a (1122-
  2000)
Reizenstein, Franz
- Capriccio (1121-2200)
Revueltas, Silvestre
- Batik (1020-0000)
Rodríguez, Robert Xavier
- Adagio for Small Orchestra (1112-
  2000)
Roux, Maurice le
- Allegro Moderato: No.9 from
  "Divertimento for Mozart" (2222-
  2200)

Saint-Saëns, Camille
- Rigaudon, op.93, No.2 (2222-2020)
Satie, Erik
- Carnet de croquis et d'esquisses
  (2222-0000)
- La Diva de l'Empire (2011-1110)
- Trois Mélodies de 1916 (2222-
  1111)
- Trois petites pièces montées (1111-
  1210)
Saturen, David
- Expression, Lyric piece for small
  orchestra (1120-2220)
Scharwenka, Franz Xaver
- À la Hongroise, op.43, No.6 (1121-
  2210)
- A Polish Dance Theme (1121-2210)
Schuller, Gunther
- Little Fantasy (1111-2110)
Schwertsik, Kurt
- Schrumpf-Symphonie, op.80 (2222-
  2200)
Sibelius, Jean
- Valse Romantique, op.62b (2020-
  2000)
- Valse Triste: From "Kuolema,"
  op.44, No.1 (1010-2000)
Tower, Joan
- Paganini Trills (2222-2220)
Weir, Judith
- Still, Glowing (2020-0000)
Wellejus, Henning
- Postvognen Ruller (The Mailcoach
  is Rolling), op.16 (2222-2210)
Wilson, Ian
- What We Can See of the Sky Has
  Fallen (2122-2100)
Wimberger, Gerhard
- Allegro Giocoso: No.8 from
  "Divertimento for Mozart" (2222-
  2200)

6' - 10'

Albéniz, Isaac
- Iberia: Evocatión (2222-2200)
- Iberia: Lavapiés (2222-2200)
- Iberia: Triana (2222-2200)
Arnell, Richard
- Sonata for Chamber Orchestra,
  op.18 (1111-2000)
Bacri, Nicolas
- Folia; Chaconne symphonique pour
  orchestre, op.30 (2222-2200)
Baird, Tadeusz
- Overture in Old Style (2202-2000)
Barnett, Carol
- Sumervar (2212-2000)

Bartók, Béla
- Bartók Suite (1121-2210)
- Rumanian Folk Dances (2022-2000)

Bavicchi, John
- Music for Small Orchestra, op.81 (2222-2200)

Becker, Günther
- Game for Nine (1020-0000)

Bedford, David
- Trona For 12 (1111-0220)

Bentzon, Niels Viggo
- Prelude and Rondo, op.56 (2222-2000)

Berlin, David
- Structures for Chamber Orchestra (1111-1120)

Blacher, Boris
- Hommage à Mozart; Metamorphoses on a group of Mozart themes for orchestra (1202-2200)
- Kleine Marschmusik (2222-2220)
- Orchester-Capriccio über ein Volkslied (2222-2220)

Black, Stanley
- Percussion Fantasy (2222-2200)

Blomdahl, Karl-Birger
- Adagio from "Vaknatten": Incidental music from the play (1100-2000)

Bond, Victoria
- Concertino (1212-2000)
- Journal (1212-2200)

Bossi, Marco Enrico
- Siciliana e Giga (stile antico) per Orchestra, op.73 (2111-1000)

Brandmüller, Theo
- Venezianische Schatten (1111-2100)

Brant, Henry
- A Requiem in Summer; In Memory of my Father (2222-0000)

Bräutigam, Helmut
- Festliche Musik (2200-0200)

Bridge, Frank
- Two Intermezzi: From the incidental music to the play "Threads" (1121-2210)

Brown, Earle
- Modules 1 & 2 (2222-2210)

Buck, Ole
- Overture (2222-2200)

Cohn, James
- The Little Circus, op.51 (1021-2221)

Csonka, Paul
- Prisma Sinfonico (Symphonic Prism) (2222-2210)

Davison, John
- Symphony No.6 (0200-2000)

Delius, Frederick
- Five Little Pieces (1121-2100)
- Petite Suite No.2 (2222-2000)
- A Song Before Sunrise (2122-2000)

Döhl, Friedhelm
- Ikaros; Ballet nach einem Gedicht von E. Lindgren (2222-2220)

Einem, Gottfried von
- Introduktion - Wandlungen: No.1 from "Divertimento for Mozart," op.21 (2222-2200)

Engelmann, Hans Ulrich
- Ezra Pound Music (1201-0010)

Erdmann, Dietrich
- Concert Piece (0000-2000)

Fenby, Eric
- Rossini on Ilkla Moor; Overture (2222-2210)

Ficher, Jacobo
- Dos Poemas; De El Jardino de R. Tagore, op.10, No.16 (1111-2000)

Finke, Fidelio
- Festliche Musik (2112-1220)

Françaix, Jean
- Onze Variations sur un Thème de Haydn (0222-2100)

Freyhan, Michael
- Toy Symphony (2020-0200)

Fujiie, Keiko
- Beber, op.31 (2222-2200)

Fuleihan, Anis
- Divertimento (0211-1100)

Gianneo, Luis
- Variaciones Sobre Tema de Tango (2222-2200)

Girnatis, Walter
- Scherzo Fantastique (2222-2210)

Glazunov, Alexander
- Serenade for Small Orchestra No.2, op.11 (2122-2000)

Granados, Enrique
- À la Cubana; Marche militaire (1121-2210)

Gutchë, Gene
- Rondo capriccioso, op.21 (2222-0000)

Hahn, Reynaldo
- La Fête Chez Thérèse: Suite No.1 (1121-2210)

Halffter, Rodolfo
- Obertura Festiva (Festive Overture) (2222-2200)

Hartley, Walter Sinclair
- Sinfonia No.7 (2121-2211)

Harvey, Jonathan
- Hidden Voice 1 (1111-2000)

Hindemith, Paul
- Sonata for 10 Instruments (1021-1000)

Holliger, Heinz
- Ad Marginem (2020-0000)
- Engführung (1221-2000)
- Der Ferne Klang (2221-1000)

Holloway, Robin
- Overture on a Nursery Rhyme, op.75a (2222-2211)

Holmboe, Vagn
- Prelude to a Maple Tree, op.168 (1111-2100)
- Prelude to the Pollution of Nature (1111-2100)
- Prelude to the Seagulls and Cormorants, op.174 (1111-2100)
- Prelude to the Unsettled Weather, op.188 (1111-2100)

Holst, Gustav
- Two Songs Without Words, op.22 / H88 (2122-2210)

Honegger, Arthur
- Prélude pour Aglavaine et Sélysette; D'après la pièce de Maeterlinck, H.10 (1122-2100)

Horne, David
- Flicker (2222-2200)

Horovitz, Joseph
- Concertino Classico (0000-0200)

Hutcheson, Jere
- Transitions for Orchestra (2222-2221)

Janáček, Leoš
- Adagio (2222-2220)

Jost, Christian
- Mascarade: Tableau from the opera "Vipern" (2121-2110)

Kallstenius, Edvin
- Dalsland-Rhapsodie, op.22 (2222-2210)

Kaun, Hugo
- Elegie, op.70, No.5 (2121-2000)
- Fröhliches Wandern, op.70, No.1 (2021-2000)
- Idyll, op.70, No.2 (2021-2000)

Kelterborn, Rudolf
- Musica luminosa per orchestra (2222-2200)

Kingman, Daniel
- A Revolutionary Garland (2222-2200)

Kodály, Zoltán
- Hungarian Rondo (0022-0000)

Kolb, Barbara
- The Web Spinner (2222-2000)

Korngold, Erich Wolfgang
- Dance in the Old Style (2222-2200)

Kósa, György
- Suite; Three ironic portraits (1122-2201)

La Violette, Wesley
- Nocturne for Orchestra (1221-2110)
Laderman, Ezra
- Cadence (2000-0000)
LeFanu, Nicola
- Preludio II (1111-2000)
Lewis, Harold Merrills
- Two Preludes on Southern Folk
  Hymn Tunes (1111-2000)
MacKenzie, Sir Alexander C.
- Benedictus, op.37, No.3 (2022-2000)
Maros, Rudolf
- Sinfonietta No.1 (2000-0200)
Matthus, Siegfried
- Sonata by G. Gabrieli (2202-2220)
Maxwell Davies, Peter
- Chat Moss (2111-2000)
- Jimmack the Postie (2222-2220)
- Ojai Festival Overture (2222-2200)
Milhaud, Darius
- Actualités; Musik zu einer
  Filmwochenschau, op.104 (0020-0210)
- Chamber Symphony No.5; Dixtuor
  d'Instruments à Vent, op.75 (2222-2000)
- Trois Rag-Caprices (1111-2110)
Moncayo, José Pablo
- Homenaje a Cervantes (0200-0000)
Moravec, Paul
- Adelphony (2222-2210)
Muldowney, Dominic
- Three-Part Motet (1020-1110)
Müller-Siemens, Detlev
- Zwei Stücke (Two Pieces) (2222-2000)
Naylor, Bernard
- Variations (1111-2200)
Nono, Luigi
- Incontri (2222-2110)
Nørgård, Per
- Bright Dances, op.24 (1111-2100)
Palau Boix, Manuel
- Homenaje a Debussy (2222-2200)
Paz, Juan Carlos
- Obertura Para Doce Instrumentos
  (Overture for 12 Instruments) (1111-2110)
Pompey, Angel Martin
- Serenata madrilena (2222-2200)
Poot, Marcel
- Fantasia (1111-2110)
- Fête à Thélème (1121-2210)
- Musique Legère (2121-2210)
Porrino, Ennio
- Tre Canzoni Italiane (2121-2110)
Powell, Mel
- Stanzas (2121-2210)

Revueltas, Silvestre
- Alcancias (1120-1210)
- Colorines (1122-1110)
- El Renacuajo Paseador (1020-0210)
- Troka (1121-1211)
Rodrigo, Joaquín
- Dos Danzas Españolas; Suite for
  castanets and orchestra (2222-2200)
- Tres Viejos Aires de Danza (1111-2000)
Rogers, Bernard
- Elegy; To the Memory of Franklin D.
  Roosevelt (1000-2000)
Rorem, Ned
- Triptych; Three Pieces for Chamber
  Orchestra (2222-2200)
Ruders, Poul
- Trapeze (0200-2000)
Satie, Erik
- Jack in the Box, op.post (2222-2200)
Schickele, Peter
- Songs from Shakespeare (2222-2210)
Schoeck, Othmar
- Serenade (Interlude) (0200-0000)
Schönherr, Max
- Tänze aus Salzburg (1121-2000)
Schwertsik, Kurt
- Mozart, auf und davon, op.94 (2222-2110)
Shchedrin, Rodion
- Shepherd's Pipes of Vologda (0200-1000)
Sibelius, Jean
- Suite Mignonne, op.98a (2000-0000)
Smit, Andre-Jean
- Suite Pittoresque (1121-2000)
Stern, Robert
- Ricordanza (2121-2100)
Stevens, Bernard
- Eclogue (1111-2000)
Stiller, Andrew
- A Periodic Table of the Elements (1111-1210)
Strauss, Richard
- Ariadne auf Naxos: Overture and
  Dance Scene, op.60 (2222-2000)
Stravinsky, Igor
- Concertino for 12 Instruments (1212-0220)
- Eight Instrumental Miniatures (2222-1000)
- Suite No.1; For Small Orchestra (2122-1111)

Swafford, Jan
- Late August (1222-2200)
Szymanski, Pawel
- Intermezzo (2000-0000)
Takács, Jenö
- Volkstänze aus dem Burgenland,
  op.57 (2121-2110)
Tanaka, Karen
- Wave Mechanics (2121-2200)
Tcherepnin, Alexander
- Suite populaire russe (1111-2110)
Terzakis, Dimitri
- Ichochronos II (2010-1001)
Thiele, Siegfried
- Drei Orchestermotetten nach
  Machaut (1221-2120)
Tower, Joan
- Island Rhythms (2222-2210)
Vaughan Williams, Ralph
- English Folk Song Suite (2121-2220)
Walton, William
- Siesta (1121-2000)
Weigl, Karl
- Music for the Young (2222-2100)
Weiner, Leo
- Fasching; Carnival Humoresque,
  op.5 (2121-2210)
- Serenade for Small Orchestra in F
  minor, op.3 (2222-2200)
Wyner, Yehudi
- Amadeus' Billiard (0002-2000)

11' - 15'

Absil, Jean
- Petite Suite, op.20 (1111-2000)
Adolphe, Bruce
- Three Pieces; For Kids in the
  Audience and Chamber Orchestra (2222-2200)
Alnar, Hasan Ferit
- Zwei Türkische Orchesterstücke;
  Improvisation und zwei Tänze (2222-2200)
Alwyn, William
- Concerto Grosso No.1 in Bb (1100-2100)
Apostel, Hans Erich
- Five Austrian Miniatures (2222-2210)
- Variations on Three Folksongs,
  op.23 (1122-2100)
Arnold, Malcolm
- Serenade for Small Orchestra (2222-2200)
- Sinfonietta No.1, op.48 (0200-2000)
- Sinfonietta No.2, op.65 (2000-2000)
- Sinfonietta No.3 (2202-2000)

Bacri, Nicolas
- Symphony No.4; Symphonie
  Classique Sturm und Drang, op.49
  (2222-2000)

Baur, Jürg
- Triton-Sinfonietta; Drei Grotesken
  (1111-2110)

Bedford, David
- This One For You (2222-2200)

Bentzon, Niels Viggo
- Mini-Symphony, op.231 (2222-
  2110)

Berkeley, Lennox
- Partita, op.66 (1121-2110)
- Windsor Variations, op.75 (1202-
  2000)
- Sinfonietta, op.34 (2222-2000)

Besch, Otto
- Divertimento (2122-2200)

Binkerd, Gordon
- Movement for Orchestra (2222-
  2200)

Blake, David
- Sonata alla Marchia (0200-2000)

Bon, André
- Ode; Pour orchestre "Mozart"
  (2222-2000)
- Ode II; Pour orchestre de chambre
  (2201-2000)

Brauel, Henning
- Les Fenêtres Simultanées (1111-
  2110)

Britten, Benjamin
- Sinfonietta, op.1 (1111-2000)

Bush, Alan
- Partita Concertante, op.63 (2121-
  2210)

Campo, Frank
- Partita for Two Chamber
  Orchestras, op.45 (1121-1000)

Castro, José Maria
- Concerto Grosso (2222-2100)

Cerha, Friedrich
- Sinfonie (2222-2111)

Chapple, Brian
- Little Symphony (1202-2000)

Cohn, James
- Sinfonietta in F (1121-2000)

Coleman, Linda Robbins
- For A Beautiful Land (2222-2000)

Conyngham, Barry
- Glimpses of Bennelong (1200-
  2000)

Coolidge, Peggy Stuart
- Pioneer Dances (1121-1210)

Cowell, Henry
- Old American Country Set (2222-
  2211)

Cruft, Adrian
- Partita, op.7 (2222-2100)

Dalby, Martin
- Nozze di Primavera (2222-2200)

Danielpour, Richard
- Souvenirs (2222-2220)

Dean, Brett
- Testament; Music for orchestra,
  after "Testament: Music for twelve
  violas" (2222-2200)

Delius, Frederick
- Two Pieces for Small Orchestra
  (1122-2000)

Diamond, David
- Concerto for Small Orchestra
  (1111-2100)
- Heroic Piece (1211-2111)

Dubois, Pierre-Max
- Analogie; Suite for Orchestra (2111-
  2111)

Erdmann, Dietrich
- Epitaph (0020-0000)

Etler, Alvin
- Music for Chamber Orchestra
  (1111-2110)

Ettinger, Max
- An den Wassern Babylons; Songs
  of Babylonian Jews for Small
  Orchestra (1110-0210)

Firsova, Elena
- Autumn Music, op.39 (1202-2000)

Fletcher, Horace Grant
- Two Orchestral Pieces for Small
  Orchestra (2222-2210)

Frank, Gabriela Lena
- Elegía Andina (2222-2200)

Frazelle, Kenneth
- Laconic Variations (2222-2200)

Geissler, Fritz
- Five Miniatures (2111-2210)

Gerster, Ottmar
- Oberhessische Bauerntänze für
  Kleines Orchester (1121-2210)

Gilbert, Anthony
- Tree of Singing Names (1111-2100)

Girnatis, Walter
- Festmusik der Schiffergilde (2121-
  2200)

Goeb, Roger
- Prairie Songs (2222-2210)

Goehr, Alexander
- Still Lands (2121-2110)

Hagen, Daron
- Chimera; A song cycle for speaker
  and seven players (1010-2010)

Hahn, Reynaldo
- La Fête Chez Thérèse: Suite No.2
  (1121-2210)

Haieff, Alexei Vasilievich
- Divertimento (2110-0220)

Hallberg, Björn Wilho
- Novelletten (1121-1110)

Hallén, Andreas
- In Autumn (Om hösten) (2022-
  2000)

Helm, Everett
- Italienische Suite (2111-2220)

Herrera de la Fuente, Luis
- Fronteras; Ballet (2222-2200)

Hidalgo, Manuel
- L'Obvio (1020-0000)

Holloway, Robin
- First Idyll, op.42 (1222-2000)
- Ode, op.45 (0200-2000)
- Third Idyll; Frost at Midnight, op.78
  (2202-0200)

Holmboe, Vagn
- Prelude to a Dolphin, op.166 (1111-
  2100)
- Prelude to a Living Stone, op.172
  (1111-2100)
- Prelude to the Victoria
  Embankment, op.184 (1111-2100)

Honegger, Arthur
- Suite Archaïque, H.203 (2222-
  0220)

Hutcheson, Jere
- Taj Mahal (2222-2200)

Ifukube, Akira
- Triptyque aborigène; Trois tableaux
  pour orchestre de chambre (1111-
  2100)

Indy, Vincent d'
- Suite dans le style ancien, op.24
  (2000-0100)

Kallstenius, Edvin
- Suite for 14 Instruments, op.23c
  (1121-2100)

Kelterborn, Rudolf
- Four Movements for Classical
  Orchestra (0200-2000)
- Vier Nachtstücke für
  Kammerorchester (0020-2000)

Kisielewski, Stefan
- Concerto for Chamber Orchestra
  (1211-0000)
- Symphony for 15 Performers (2111-
  1110)

Koc, Marcelo
- Tres Piezas Para Orquesta (1111-
  2100)

Koch, Erland von
- Three Miniatures for Orchestra
  (2222-2210)

Krätzschmar, Wilfried
- Ballets imaginaires (1101-2000)

Krol, Bernhard
- Concerto Grosso, op.15 (0201-0200)

Kurz, Siegfried
- Sonatina for Orchestra, op.34 (2222-2200)

Lehmann, Hans Ulrich
- Chamber Music II (2221-2200)

León, Tania
- Hechizos (1120-1110)

Leplin, Emanuel
- Three Dances for Small Orchestra (2222-2200)

Linke, Norbert
- Divisioni (2222-2200)
- Konkretionen V (1121-1110)

Lutosławski, Witold
- Little Suite (1121-1000)
- Ten Polish Dances (1121-1100)

Manén, Joan
- Divertimento, op.A-32 (2222-2000)

Martinů, Bohuslav
- Sérénade; Pour orchestre de chambre (1212-2210)

Maxwell Davies, Peter
- An Orkney Wedding, with Sunrise; Version for Chamber Orchestra (2222-2220)

McAlister, Clark
- A Christmas Pastorale (1201-2000)

McCabe, John
- Concerto for Chamber Orchestra (1222-2000)
- Red Leaves (0200-2000)

McKay, George Frederick
- Fantasy on a Western Folk Song; O! Bury me not on the lone prairie (2120-0100)
- Variants on a Texas Tune; Mustang grey (2121-2000)

Meale, Richard
- Variations (2222-2220)

Milford, Robin
- Suite for Chamber Orchestra (2122-1000)

Milhaud, Darius
- Le boeuf sur le toit, Ballet, op.58 (2121-2210)
- Musique pour San Francisco, op.436 (2222-2220)
- Sérénade, op.62 (2222-2200)

Milner, Anthony
- Chamber Symphony (1212-2000)

Mochizuki, Misato
- La Chambre Claire (1121-1110)

Moore, Douglas
- Village Music (2121-2210)

Moravec, Paul
- Ancient Lights (2222-2210)
- Sempre Diritto! (Straight Ahead) (0200-2000)
- Streamline (2222-2210)

Müller-Hornbach, Gerhard
- Passacaglia II (1111-1120)

Neikrug, Marc
- Chetro Ketl (1222-2200)

Neubert, Günter
- Music for Orchestra on a Theme by Robert Schumann (2112-2110)

Nono, Luigi
- Canti Per 13 (1121-1110)

Nussio, Otmar
- Boccaccio-Suite; Novelle dal Decamerone (2222-2210)

Paccagnini, Angelo
- Dialoghi (2220-2200)

Patterson, Paul
- Europhony, op.55 (0200-2000)

Payne, Anthony
- Spring's Shining Wake (1121-2000)
- Symphonies of Wind and Rain (1121-1000)

Pernes, Thomas
- Gesänge (0121-1000)

Polovinkin, Leonid
- Tänze der Rätsel (1112-2100)

Prokofiev, Sergei
- Classical Symphony in D, Symphony No.1, op.25 (2222-2200)
- A Summer Day, op.65a (2222-2200)

Riege, Ernst
- Rondo Giocoso (2222-2200)

Rieti, Vittorio
- Due Pastorali (1112-2100)
- Sinfonietta per Piccola Orchestra (1112-2220)

Rodrigo, Joaquín
- Palillos y Panderetas; Música para una tonadilla imaginaria (2222-2200)

Rogers, Bernard
- The Plains (1121-2100)

Ropartz, Joseph Guy Marie
- Cinq pièces brèves (1111-2000)

Rosenberg, Hilding Constantin
- Dance Suite from the Grand Opera "The Marionettes" (2222-2200)

Roussel, Albert
- Concert pour petit orchestre, op.34 (2222-2100)

Rueda, Jesús
- Elephant Skin (2222-2200)

Satie, Erik
- Cinéma: Entr'acte symphonique du ballet "Relâche" (1111-2210)

Schafer, Robert Murray
- Cortège (2222-2200)

Schlee, Thomas Daniel
- Sonata da Camera, op.42 (0100-2000)

Schmitt, Florent
- Enfants, op.94 (2111-1100)

Sgrizzi, Luciano
- Suite Belge; D'après des œuvres de clavecinistes belges du 18ème siècle (2121-0000)

Sibelius, Jean
- Belsazars Gaestabud (Belshazzar's Feast); Incidental Music, op.51 (2120-2000)

Sørensen, Bent
- Minnewater; Thousands of Canons (2110-2110)

Staempfli, Edward
- Präludium und Variationen (1111-2110)

Standford, Patric
- Notte (1201-2000)

Stanford, Charles Villiers
- Suite of Ancient Dances, op.58 (2222-2200)

Stevens, Bernard
- Introduction, Variations & Fugue on a Theme of Giles Farnaby (2222-2200)

Sutermeister, Heinrich
- Sérénade pour Montreux (0200-2000)

Swanson, Howard
- Short Symphony (2222-2210)

Thiele, Siegfried
- Intrada, Cantus, Toccata (2222-2210)
- Wolkenbilder; Four Movements (1200-2000)

Tomlinson, Ernest
- A Georgian Miniature (2121-0000)

Tower, Joan
- The Last Dance (2222-2210)
- Made in America (2222-2210)

Trexler, Georg
- Small Suite (1111-2000)

Vincent, John
- Suite from the Ballet "Three Jacks" (2222-2110)

Vinci, Albert
- Dance Suite (1111-1210)

Vinter, Gilbert
- Dance of the Marionettes (2121-0000)

Wagner, Joseph
- Four Miniatures (2222-2200)

Weir, Judith
- Isti Mirant Stella (2222-2200)

Wellejus, Henning
- Vor Barndoms Venner (Our
  Childhood Friends), op.15 (2222-
  2210)
Wilby, Philip
- The Wings of Morning (0200-2000)
Wunsch, Hermann
- Fest auf Monbijo; Suite in fünf
  Sätzen, op.50 (2222-2200)

16' - 20'

Aa, Michel van der
- Attach; for ensemble and
  soundtrack (0121-0100)
Abendroth, Walter
- Sinfonietta, op.32 (1212-1220)
Aitken, Robert
- Spiral (2222-2200)
Amy, Gilbert
- D'Après "Ecrits Sur Toiles"; Pour
  Orchestre de Chambre (2222-2000)
Arnold, Malcolm
- Concerto for Clarinet and
  Orchestra, op.115 (2202-2000)
Atterberg, Kurt
- Barocco-Suite No.5, op.23 (1210-
  0000)
Bedford, David
- The Valley Sleeper, the Children,
  the Snakes and the Giant (2222-
  2200)
- With 100 Kazoos; For chamber
  ensemble and 100 kazoos (1120-
  1110)
Bentzon, Niels Viggo
- Symphony No.11, op.158 (2222-
  2000)
Berkeley, Lennox
- Divertimento in Bb, op.18 (2222-
  2210)
Bialas, Günter
- Der Weg nach Eisenstadt; Haydn
  Phantasies for Small Orchestra
  (1202-2000)
Biersack, Anton
- Bagatellen (2222-0100)
Bondon, Jacques
- Symphonie latine (2222-2210)
Buck, Ole
- Pastorals (2221-1200)
Busch, Adolf
- Divertimento, op.30 (1111-2100)
Chávez, Carlos
- Discovery (1211-2100)
Cowell, Henry
- American Melting Pot Set (1111-
  2111)

Dalby, Martin
- Aleph (2000-1110)
- Cancionero Para Una Mariposa
  (1002-0020)
David, Johann Nepomuk
- Sinfonia preclassica super nomen
  H-A-S-E, Wk44 (2000-2000)
- Symphonic Variations on a Theme
  by H. Schütz, Wk29b (2222-0220)
- Variations on a Theme by J. S.
  Bach, Wk29a (1201-2000)
Essl, Karl-Heinz
- Et Consumimur Igni (0000-2220)
Feldman, Morton
- The Turfan Fragments (2222-2220)
Ficher, Jacobo
- Seis Fabulas (Six Fables) (2222-
  2200)
Forst, Rudolf
- Divertimento for Chamber
  Orchestra (1121-1100)
Fortner, Wolfgang
- Suite for Orchestra; After music by
  Jan Pieters Sweelinck (0002-0200)
Gebhard-Elsass, Hans
- Ländliche Suite, op.23 (1110-0210)
Gill, Jeremy
- Chamber Symphony (1111-2110)
Glass, Philip
- Concerto Grosso (1111-2111)
Goehr, Alexander
- Concerto for Eleven, op.32 (1020-
  0201)
Guenther, Felix
- Deutsches Rokoko; Eine Suite für
  Kleines Orchester nach alten
  Meistern (1121-2000)
Halffter, Cristóbal
- Dalíniana; Three pieces on three
  paintings by Salvador Dalí (2222-
  2200)
Harneit, Johannes
- Triptychon (13X3), op.20 (1121-
  2100)
Heitzeg, Steve
- Flower of the Earth; Homage to
  Georgia O'Keeffe (1201-2000)
Holloway, Robin
- Second Idyll, op.54 (1202-2000)
Holmboe, Vagn
- Concerto for Orchestra, op.38
  (2222-2200)
Ives, Charles Edward
- Symphony No.3; The Camp
  Meeting, S.3 (1111-2010)
Jacob, Gordon
- Sinfonietta No.1 for Small Orchestra
  (2222-2210)

Jelinek, Hanns
- Parergon, op.15B (2222-2100)
Jerger, Wilhelm
- Symphony No.1; Classical
  Symphony (2222-2220)
Joubert, John
- Sinfonietta, op.38 (0202-2000)
Knipper, Lew
- Wantsch; Turkmenische Suite,
  op.29 (1111-2110)
Koch, Erland von
- Oxberg Variations; On a Theme
  from Dalekarlien (2222-2220)
- Schwedische Tanz-Rhapsodie
  (2222-2220)
Kodály, Zoltán
- Summer Evening (1222-2000)
Kreutz, Arthur
- American Dances (2222-0000)
Lees, Benjamin
- Concerto for Chamber Orchestra
  (2222-2200)
Lumsdaine, David
- Sunflower (1222-2000)
MacRae, Stuart
- Portrait (1111-2110)
Magnard, Albéric
- Suite in Ancient Style, op.2 (2222-
  2100)
Matthews, Colin
- Night Music, op.10 (2222-2100)
Matthews, David
- Serenade, op.29 (1202-2000)
Maw, Nicholas
- Sonata for Strings and Two Horns
  (0000-2000)
Maxwell Davies, Peter
- Carolisima; Serenade for Chamber
  Orchestra (1120-1110)
Meester, Louis de
- Sinfonietta Buffa (0000-0200)
Moore, Douglas
- Farm Journal; Suite for Chamber
  Orchestra (2222-2100)
Musgrave, Thea
- Night Music (1201-2000)
Nelson, Larry
- Loose Leaves (1120-0000)
Nyman, Michael
- Strong on Oaks; Strong on the
  Causes of Oaks (2222-2200)
Olivier, François
- Suite Pour Petit Orchestre (1111-
  2100)
Pärt, Arvo
- Symphony No.1; "Polyphonic," op.9
  (1111-2110)

Payne, Anthony
- Orchestral Variations; "The Seeds Long Hidden" (2222-2200)
Piston, Walter
- Sinfonietta (2222-2000)
Rorem, Ned
- A Quaker Reader; Suite (2222-2110)
Satie, Erik
- Mercure; Poses plastiques, op.post (2121-2211)
Schollum, Robert
- Serenade, Werk 39a (2222-2110)
Schurmann, Gerard
- Variants (1202-2000)
Sessions, Roger
- Concertino (1111-2110)
Shostakovich, Dmitri
- Chamber Symphony, op.83a (1211-2100)
Standford, Patric
- Suite for Small Orchestra (2121-2000)
Stanford, Charles Villiers
- Songs of the Sea, op.91 (2121-2220)
Stravinsky, Igor
- Concerto in E-flat "Dumbarton Oaks" (1011-2000)
- Danses Concertantes (1111-2110)
Thiele, Siegfried
- Concerto for Orchestra (2222-2110)
- Sonatina (2222-2100)
Toch, Ernst
- Fünf Stücke (Five Pieces), op.33 (2020-0000)
Tower, Joan
- Chamber Dance (2222-2200)
- Duets (2222-2200)
Villa-Lobos, Heitor
- Sinfonietta No.1 (2222-2220)
Vincent, John
- The House that Jack Built: From the ballet "Three Jacks" (2222-2110)
Weir, Judith
- Winter Song (2222-2200)
Wimberger, Gerhard
- Partita Giocosa (1121-1110)
Wolpe, Michael
- Caprisma 2 (2110-0000)
Woolrich, John
- Suite from Bitter Fruit (1111-1121)
Yun, Isang
- Konzertante Figuren (2211-2110)
Zbinden, Julien-François
- Symphony No.1, op.18 (2221-2100)
Zilcher, Hermann
- Lustspielsuite; Der Widerspenstigen Zähmung, op.54b (1111-2100)

Over 20'

Amram, David
- Shakespearean Concerto (0100-2000)
Argento, Dominick
- Royal Invitation (Homage to the Queen of Tonga) (1202-2000)
Arnold, Malcolm
- Concerto for 28 Players, op.105 (1201-2000)
Bedford, David
- Symphony for 12 Musicians (1201-1000)
Bentzon, Niels Viggo
- Sinfonia, op.402 (2222-2210)
- Symphony No.6, op.66 (2222-2000)
Blacher, Boris
- Feste im Süden: Suite (2222-2220)
Blake, David
- Chamber Symphony (1111-2100)
Bräutigam, Helmut
- Tänzerische Suite (2222-2200)
Britten, Benjamin
- Plymouth Town (1122-2110)
Cage, John
- Quartets I-VIII; For an Orchestra of 24 Instruments (1212-2000)
Carter, Elliott
- Symphony No.1 (2222-2210)
Casella, Alfredo
- Serenata, op.46b (2122-2110)
Consoli, Marc-Antonio
- Odefonia (2222-2210)
Copland, Aaron
- Dance Panels; Ballet in Seven Sections (2121-2210)
Cowell, Henry
- Symphony No.10 (2222-2200)
Cowie, Edward
- Leonardo (2222-2000)
David, Johann Nepomuk
- Partita No.2, Wk27 (2222-2220)
Degen, Helmut
- Chamber Symphony (Symphony No.2) (2101-2100)
Dillon, James
- Windows and Canopies (2201-2000)
Einem, Gottfried von
- Münchner Symphonie, op.70 (2222-2220)
Finzi, Gerald
- Love's Labour's Lost: Suite, op.28b (2121-2100)
Frazelle, Kenneth
- Concerto for Chamber Orchestra (2222-2200)

Gál, Hans
- Ballet Suite "Scaramussio," op.36 (2222-2210)
- Idyllikon; Four movements for small orchestra, op.79 (2222-2000)
Genzmer, Harald
- Sinfonia da Camera (2111-1000)
Goehr, Alexander
- Sinfonia, op.42 (1220-2000)
Goldstein, Mikhail
- Ukranian Symphony in Old Style (2222-2200)
Grabner, Hermann
- Divertimento für Kleines Orchester, op.56 (1121-2210)
Gregson, Edward
- Music for Chamber Orchestra (0202-2000)
Haas, Joseph
- Variationen-Suite; Über ein altes Rokoko-Thema, op.64 (1022-2100)
Halffter, Ernesto
- El Cojo Enamorado: Ballet Suite (2121-2210)
Hamilton, Iain
- Symphony No.3 (2222-2000)
Hanuš, Jan
- Prazská Nokturna (Prague Nocturne), op.75 (2222-2100)
Harneit, Johannes
- Triptychon (13X3) (1121-2100)
Hasquenoph, Pierre
- Symphony No.1, op.10 (2222-2220)
Holloway, Robin
- Concertino No.2, op.10 (1211-2000)
- Fourth Idyll (2222-2200)
Holmboe, Vagn
- Chamber Symphony No.2, op.100 (1111-2100)
- Chamber Symphony No.3 (1111-2200)
Jenner, Gustav
- Serenade for Orchestra (2222-2200)
Juon, Paul
- Serenade, op.40 (2122-2000)
Kaipainen, Jouni
- Accende Lumen Sensibus, op.52 (1212-2100)
Kancheli, Giya
- Magnum Ignotum (1222-2000)
Koch, Erland von
- Skandinavische Tänze (2222-2210)
Kupferman, Meyer
- Little Symphony (1202-2000)
Lazar, Filip
- Concerto Grosso No.1, op.17 (0202-2100)

Lloyd, Jonathan
- Symphony No.1 (2222-2200)
- Symphony No.3 (1121-2000)
MacMillan, James
- Tryst (2222-2200)
Matthews, Colin
- Pursuit; Ballet (1120-1000)
Matthews, David
- Symphony No.4, op.51 (1202-2000)
Maw, Nicholas
- Serenade (1202-2000)
- Sinfonia (1222-2000)
Maxwell Davies, Peter
- Sinfonietta Accademica (2222-2200)
- Strathclyde Concerto No.10, Concerto for Orchestra (2222-2200)
- Symphony No.4 (2222-2200)
Milhaud, Darius
- Musique pour Lisbonne, op.420 (0200-2000)
Moeschinger, Albert
- Symphony No.2, op.73 (1111-2000)
Mundry, Isabel
- Le Voyage (2110-1110)
Panufnik, Andrzej
- Sinfonia Mistica; Symphony No.6 (2222-2000)
Rautavaara, Einojuhani
- Autumn Gardens (2222-2000)
- Symphony No.2 (2222-2110)
Reizenstein, Franz
- Serenade in F, op.29a (2222-2000)
Rodrigo, Joaquín
- Soleriana; Suite for chamber orchestra (2111-1100)
Rogers, Bernard
- The Musicians of Bremen (2111-1100)
Roselius, Ludwig
- Friesische Musik, op.30 (1221-1000)
Saint-Saëns, Camille
- Symphony in A (2222-2200)
Sallinen, Aulis
- Concerto for Chamber Orchestra (1121-1000)
Satie, Erik
- Relâche; Ballet (1111-2210)
Saxton, Robert
- Elijah's Violin (1202-2000)
Saygun, A. Adnan
- Symphony No.1 (1222-2000)
Schenker, Friedrich
- Hades di Orfeo; Dramma per musica (0200-0010)
Schickele, Peter
- Concerto for Chamber Orchestra (2222-2200)

Schiske, Karl
- Chamber Concerto, op.28 (1111-2100)
Schönberg, Arnold
- Kammersymphonie Nr.2 (Chamber Symphony No.2), op.38 (2222-2200)
Schwertsik, Kurt
- Compagnie Masquerade; Ein Divertissement für kleines Orchester, einer Idee & teilweise erhaltenen Violinstimme Mozarts folgend (2222-2110)
Shostakovich, Dmitri
- Hamlet: Suite from the Theatre Music, op.32a (1111-2211)
Sibelius, Jean
- Pelleas & Melisande, op.46 (1122-2000)
Swayne, Giles
- Symphony for Small Orchestra (1202-2000)
Thomson, Virgil
- Suite from "The River" (1221-2220)
Trexler, Georg
- Concerto for Orchestra (2222-2200)
Tubin, Eduard
- Symphony No.7 (2222-2200)
Weill, Kurt
- Quodlibet: Suite aus "Zaubernacht." Eine Unterhaltungsmusik, op.9 (2222-2220)
Widmann, Jörg
- Freie Stücke (2121-1110)
Yun, Isang
- Kammersinfonie I (Chamber Symphony I) (0200-2000)

Larger Than 2222 - 2221 - str

5' or Less

Berio, Luciano
- Re-Call (2141-2321)
Daugherty, Michael
- Pachelbel's Key (2222-4221)
Dohnanyi, Ernest von
- The Veil of Pierette: Jolly Funeral March, op.18, No.3 (1123-4230)
Erbse, Heimo
- Allegro - Lento - Allegro (2243-2200)
Gardner, John
- Overture "Half-Holiday" (2131-2210)
Harbison, John
- Waltz-Passacaglia (2223-4230)
Kodály, Zoltán
- Intermezzo (3222-4300)

Krenek, Ernst
- Ouvertüre "Triumph der Empfindsamkeit" (2222-0230)
Lang, David
- Open (2222-4000)
Le Grand, Robert
- Effets de Nuit (2332-2000)
Morthenson, Jan Wilhelm
- Antiphonia II (3020-0000)
Nørgård, Per
- Towards Freedom? (2222-4220)
Pierné, Gabriel
- Ballet de Cour (2222-2230)
Rachmaninoff, Sergei
- Vocalise (2322-2000)
Rogers, Bernard
- Elegy: From Symphony No.3 (0300-0000)
Satie, Erik
- Illusion [Tendrement] (1121-2230)
- Je te veux (2121-2230)
- Poudre d'or (2121-2230)
Sibelius, Jean
- Valse Chevaleresque (2222-4230)
Sierra, Roberto
- Sonatina (2222-4221)
Stravinsky, Igor
- Circus Polka (2222-4231)
Toch, Ernst
- Epilogue (3222-2200)
Weiner, Leo
- Soldatenspiel (2222-4230)

6' - 10'

Adès, Thomas
- The Origin of the Harp (0030-0000)
Antheil, George
- Suite for Orchestra (2220-3001)
Arnold, Malcolm
- Symphonic Study "Machines" (0000-4331)
- Trevelyan Suite (3220-2000)
Bavicchi, John
- Fantasia on Korean Folk Tunes, op.53 (2131-2231)
Blacher, Boris
- Alla Marcia (2222-4331)
- Musica giocosa (2222-4231)
- Rondo (3222-4231)
Bresgen, Cesar
- Intrada (2222-4230)
Britten, Benjamin
- Gloriana (2222-4231)
Busoni, Ferruccio
- Lustspiel Overture (3222-4200)
Cowell, Henry
- Hymn and Fuguing Tune No.3 (2222-4221)

Daugherty, Michael
- Ghost Ranch (0000-4000)
Dohnanyi, Ernest von
- The Veil of Pierette: Wedding
  Waltz, op.18, No.4 (2222-4230)
Duparc, Henri
- Danse Lente (2222-4200)
Einem, Gottfried von
- Capriccio (3222-4331)
Engelmann, Hans Ulrich
- Kaleidoskop (1111-0330)
Ferguson, Howard
- Overture for an Occasion (2222-
  4230)
Foss, Lukas
- Symphonie de Rossi (1302-0220)
German, Sir Edward
- Coronation March (2222-2230)
Holliger, Heinz
- Ostinato Funebre (2232-2110)
Klebe, Giselher
- Con moto (2222-4231)
Kodály, Zoltán
- Minuetto Serio (2222-4200)
Kurz, Siegfried
- Music for Brass, Kettledrums and
  Strings (0000-0230)
Martinů, Bohuslav
- Ouverture (2222-4200)
Matthews, Colin
- Little Suite No.2 (1131-1100)
Ponce, Manuel
- Suite en Estilo Antiguo (1111-4000)
Quilter, Roger
- Three English Dances (2222-2231)
Rautavaara, Einojuhani
- Praevariata (2222-4431)
Reger, Max
- Suite (2222-3200)
Revueltas, Silvestre
- Janitzio (3222-4221)
- Toccata Without a Fugue (1030-
  1100)
Rihm, Wolfgang
- Form / 2 Formen (2020-2332)
Sierra, Roberto
- Alegría (3222-4331)
Trojahn, Manfred
- Mit durchscheinender Melancholie
  (2222-4220)
Uhl, Alfred
- Wiener Waltzer (2222-4220)
Weigl, Karl
- Comedy Overture (2222-4200)

11' - 15'

Baggiani, Guido
- Double (2332-2000)
Barclay, Robert Lenard
- Symphony in One Movement
  (2222-4200)
Binkerd, Gordon
- Symphony No.3 (3222-3331)
Blacher, Boris
- Concertante Musik (2222-4231)
- Lysistrata (3222-4331)
- Studie im Pianissimo (2222-4331)
- Two Inventions (2222-4200)
Brandmüller, Theo
- Reminiszenzen (3222-2230)
Busoni, Ferruccio
- Concertante Suite from W. A.
  Mozart's Opera "Idomeneo" (2222-
  2230)
- Tanzwalzer (2222-4230)
Cowell, Henry
- Symphonic Set (2232-2221)
David, Johann Nepomuk
- Chaconne (2222-4230)
Einem, Gottfried von
- Bruckner Dialog (3222-4331)
- Nachtstück (3222-4331)
Engelmann, Hans Ulrich
- Partita (0000-0300)
Falla, Manuel de
- Seven Popular Spanish Songs
  (2233-2221)
Fauré, Gabriel
- Symphony in F major (2222-4000)
Ferguson, Howard
- Four Diversions on Ulster Airs
  (2212-4230)
Finke, Fidelio
- Eight Bagatelles (2222-2230)
Fómina, Silvia
- Permanenza (2030-1010)
Górecki, Henryk Mikołaj
- Three Dances (2222-3431)
Hasquenoph, Pierre
- Variations en Trois Mouvements
  (2222-2320)
Hier, Ethel Glenn
- Carolina Christmas (2222-4000)
Holmboe, Vagn
- Vinter (2222-4200)
Horovitz, Joseph
- Sinfonietta for Light Orchestra
  (2121-2230)
Kirchner, Volker David
- Bildnisse III (1231-2000)
Kodály, Zoltán
- Dances of Galanta (2222-4200)
- Marosszéker Tänze (2222-4200)

Lavista, Mario
- Lacrymosa (0212-0040)
Lutosławski, Witold
- Little Suite (2222-4331)
Maros, Rudolf
- Gemma (2220-4200)
Morawetz, Oskar
- Overture to a Fairy Tale (2222-
  4200)
Nørgård, Per
- Aspects of Leaving (2132-2211)
Prokofiev, Sergei
- Divertimento (2222-4231)
Revueltas, Silvestre
- Le Noche de los Mayas: Suite
  (2121-4111)
Schollum, Robert
- Sonate (2223-3221)
Sibelius, Jean
- Scenes Historique I (2222-4330)
Šulek, Stjepan
- Concerto Classique (2222-4200)
Suter, Robert
- Epitaffio (0000-3300)
Vines, Nicholas
- Firestick (0030-2000)
Vivier, Claude
- Deva et Asura (2222-2320)
Weiss, Manfred
- Abendmusik (2222-3220)

16' - 20'

Abendroth, Walter
- Concerto for Orchestra (2222-4200)
Alexandrov, Anatoly
- Classic Suite in B-flat major (3222-
  2100)
Angerer, Paul
- Musica Fera (2222-3321)
Atterberg, Kurt
- De Fåvitska Jungfrurna (2222-
  3000)
Bantock, Granville
- Helena (3222-4231)
Bjelinski, Bruno
- Mediterranian Sinfonietta (3222-
  2200)
Blacher, Boris
- Fürstin Tarakanowa (3222-4300)
Busch, Adolf
- Variations on a Theme by W. A.
  Mozart (2222-3200)
Butting, Max
- Sinfonietta mit Banjo (2123-1220)
David, Johann Nepomuk
- Sinfonia breve (1131-4000)
Diehl, Paula
- Right of Way (0320-0000)

Döhl, Friedhelm
- Passion (2122-2320)
Einem, Gottfried von
- Philadelphia Symphony (3222-4331)
Grosse, Erwin
- Kammersinfonie (Chamber Symphony) (2030-0000)
Harbison, John
- Partita (2222-4220)
Herrmann, Peter
- Three Pieces for Orchestra (2222-4230)
Hindemith, Paul
- Concert Music for Strings and Brass (0000-4431)
Honegger, Arthur
- Tête d'Or (1111-0330)
Jirák, K. B.
- Serenade for Small Orchestra (2222-4200)
Kirchner, Volker David
- Bildnisse I (2322-2220)
LeFanu, Nicola
- Farne (2222-2331)
Reger, Max
- Eine Balletstuite (2222-4200)
Riisager, Knudåge
- Variations on a Theme by Mezangeau (2222-4200)
Villa-Lobos, Heitor
- Sinfonietta No.2 (1111-3221)

Over 20'

Atterberg, Kurt
- Symphony No.4 in G minor (2222-4221)
Blacher, Boris
- Symphony (3222-4231)
Bräutigam, Helmut
- Music for Orchestra (2222-4200)
Bruns, Victor
- Sinfonietta (2121-3200)
- Symphony No.6 (3222-4300)
Chávez, Carlos
- Sinfonía (2223-4331)
Cowell, Henry
- Symphony No.17 (2222-4221)
David, Johann Nepomuk
- Symphony No.3 (2222-4200)
- Symphony No.7 (2222-4200)
Einem, Gottfried von
- Concerto for Orchestra (3222-4331)
- Rondo vom goldenen Kalb (2222-4331)
- Symphonische Szenen (3222-4331)
- Wiener Symphonie (3222-4331)
Goehr, Alexander
- Little Symphony (1230-2001)
Grinberg, Alexander
- Carillon (3121-1111)
Kajanus, Robert
- Sinfonietta in Bb major (2222-3000)
Kodály, Zoltán
- Symphony in C (3222-4331)
Krek, Uroš
- Simfonietta (2222-4230)
Krenek, Ernst
- Symphony No.3 (2223-2100)

Magnard, Albéric
- Symphony No.3 in B minor (2222-4230)
Milhaud, Darius
- Protée (1200-4220)
Piazzolla, Astor
- Las Cuatro Estaciones Porteñas (2222-4331)
Prokofiev, Sergei
- Peter and the Wolf (1111-3110)
- Sinfonietta (2222-4200)
Rautavaara, Einojuhani
- Symphony No.1 (2222-4321)
Reznicek, Emil Nikolaus von
- Symphony in the Old Style (2222-4200)
Rosenberg, Hilding Constantin
- Sinfonia da Chiesa No.2 (2222-4200)
Saint-Saëns, Camille
- Suite in D major (2322-2200)
- Symphony in F (3222-4200)
Schickele, Peter
- Legend (2222-3221)
Schmidt, Franz
- Concerto for Piano in E-flat Major (2222-4200)
Schönberg, Arnold
- Kammersymphonie Nr.1 (1232-2000)
Schreker, Franz
- Symphony in A minor (2222-4231)
Sibelius, Jean
- Scaramouche (2002-4000)
Trexler, Georg
- Music for Orchestra (2223-2200)
Zemlinsky, Alexander
- Symphony No.2 (2222-4231)

SAXOPHONE(S)

10' or Less

Babbitt, Milton
- All Set (0000-0110)

Benjamin, Arthur
- From San Domingo (1121-2100)
- Two Jamaican Pieces (1121-2100)

Bermel, Derek
- Hot Zone (1111-1110)
- Tag Rag (2222-2221)

Bernstein, Leonard
- On the Town: Three Dance Episodes (1130-2331)

Cohn, James
- Homage (1111-1110)

Dubois, Pierre-Max
- Trois Sérénades (0111-0000)

Engelmann, Hans Ulrich
- Kaleidoskop (1111-0330)

Erdmann, Dietrich
- Concert Piece (0000-2000)

Françaix, Jean
- 85 Measures et un Da Capo (2001-0210)

Franco, Johan
- Sinfonia (1111-1110)

Glass, Philip
- Façades (0000-0000)
- Meetings along the Edge: From "Passages" (1000-0000)
- Offering: From "Passages" (1000-0000)

Grainger, Percy Aldridge
- Green Bushes (2112-2100)

Gudmundsen-Holmgreen, Pelle
- Caravanfanfan-farefare No.1 (0000-0210)
- Caravanfanfan-farefare No.3 (0000-0110)

Halffter, Ernesto
- Cavatina (2211-1110)

Harle, John
- Cinéma (René Clair's "Entr'acte") (0110-0000)

Honegger, Arthur
- Sérénade à Angélique; H.182 (1111-2110)

Hrabovsky, Leonid
- Four Inventions for Chamber Orchestra (1111-1111)

Ince, Kamran
- Evil Eye Deflector (1111-1110)
- Turquoise (1111-0100)

Kander, Susan
- She Never Lost A Passenger Overture (2020-0110)

Koppel, Anders
- Pogo (0100-0000)

Nancarrow, Conlon
- Study No.1 (1111-1110)
- Study No.2 (1121-1110)
- Study No.3c (1131-0100)

Prokofiev, Sergei
- Lieutenant Kije: Troika, op.60 (2121-2230)

Quilter, Roger
- Three English Dances, op.11 (2222-2231)

Rihm, Wolfgang
- Music-Hall Suite (0010-0100)

Rosenberg, Hilding Constantin
- Ouvertura Piccola (2102-2210)

Staud, Johannes Maria
- Bernice: Suite 2 (1010-1211)

Talbot, Joby
- Compound Fracture (2000-0000)

Wellesz, Egon
- Pastorale (1100-0110)

Woolrich, John
- Caprichos (1010-1110)
- Darlington Doubles (1000-1100)
- From the Shadow (1010-1100)

11' - 20'

Asia, Daniel
- Rivalries (1111-1110)

Ballif, Claude
- Suite Dracoula (1100-1010)

Banks, Don
- Equation I and II (0000-0000)

Berio, Luciano
- Chemins IIb (2122-2321)
- Kod od (Chemins VI) (3141-2211)

Braunfels, Walter
- Divertimento, op.42 (2222-1200)

Butting, Max
- Sinfonietta mit Banjo; 1. Rundfunkmusik, op.37 (2123-1220)

Cerha, Friedrich
- Quellen (0010-1010)

Cohn, James
- Symphony No.4 in A, op.29 (1111-1100)
- Variations on The Wayfaring Stranger (1111-1110)

Copland, Aaron
- Prairie Journal (2221-2321)

Dubois, Pierre-Max
- Sérieux s'absenir (1121-1111)

Eisler, Hanns
- Suite for Orchestra No.2: From the music to the film *Niemandsland*, op.24 (0030-0211)
- Suite for Orchestra No.3: From the music to the film *Kuhle Wampe*, op.26 (0030-0211)
- Suite for Orchestra No.5: From the music to the film *Dans les Rules*, op.34 (0030-0311)
- Suite for Orchestra No.6: From the music to the film *Le Grand Jeu*, op.40 (0030-0311)
- Suite No.1: From the movie *Opus III*, op.23 (2121-0211)

Fortner, Wolfgang
- Suite for Orchestra; After music by Jan Pieters Sweelinck (0002-0200)

Furrer, Beat
- Studie 2; A un moment de terre perdue (1020-0121)

Grainger, Percy Aldridge
- Hill Song (2402-1101)

Harbison, John
- Confinement (1110-0110)

Harvey, Jonathan
- Valley of Aosta (1100-0100)

Hesketh, Kenneth
- Theatrum (1120-0000)
- Three Movements from "Theatrum" (1120-0000)

Honegger, Arthur
- Les Misérables: Suite pour orchestre tirée de la musique du film de Raymond Bernard, H.88A (1121-1110)
- Regain: Suite d'orchestre tirée de la musique du film de Jean Giono et Marcel Pagnol, H.117A (1111-0220)

Ives, Charles Edward
- Four Ragtime Dances (1111-1111)

Knipper, Lew
- Wantsch; Turkmenische Suite, op.29 (1111-2110)

Kopelent, Marek
- Intimissimo (0110-0110)

Koppel, Anders
- Seven Scenes from Everyday Cow Life (0100-0000)

Leyendecker, Ulrich
- Jiddische Rumba (0010-0010)
- Verwandlung; Four Pieces for Chamber Orchestra (3020-2111)

Lindberg, Magnus
- Tendenza (1132-1111)

Loevendie, Theo
- Laps (1011-0110)

MacMillan, James
- Sinfonietta (1111-1111)

Marquez, Arturo
- Danzón No.4 (2222-4231)
Maxwell Davies, Peter
- Crossing Kings Reach (1111-1110)
Milhaud, Darius
- La creation du monde; Ballet, op.81a (2121-1210)
Mochizuki, Misato
- Chimera (0010-0110)
Morthenson, Jan Wilhelm
- Antiphonia I (2222-2002)
Müller-Wieland, Jan
- Amtsantritt von Leonce und Lena; Zweite imaginäre Theaterszene nach dem Schluss von Georg Büchner (0000-0000)
Nono, Luigi
- Canti Per 13 (1121-1110)
Riedel, Georg
- Nursery Rhymes (0000-1211)
Saariaho, Kaija
- Verblendungen (2111-4111)
Sharp, Elliott
- Ripples & Heats (0010-0110)
Shchetinsky, Alexander
- Glossolalie (2121-1110)
Sierra, Roberto
- Cuentos (1111-1110)
Sotelo, Mauricio
- De Imaginum, Signorum, et Idearum Compositione I (1010-0000)
Staud, Johannes Maria
- Bernice: Suite 1 (1010-1220)

Turnage, Mark-Anthony
- Dark Crossing (2121-2110)
- On All Fours (1111-1011)
Villa-Lobos, Heitor
- Sinfonietta No.2 (1111-3221)
Weill, Kurt
- Aufstieg und Fall der Stadt Mahagonny (Rise and Fall of the City of Mahagonny): Suite (2112-2221)
Woolrich, John
- Suite from Bitter Fruit (1111-1121)

Over 20'

Bose, Hans-Jürgen von
- Scene (1111-1111)
Brødsgaard, Anders
- Procession II (1120-1110)
Bryars, Gavin
- Four Elements (0010-1111)
Cage, John
- Cheap Imitation; Version for 24 Players (3221-1111)
Cohn, James
- Symphony No.3 in G, op.27 (1111-1110)
- Symphony No.5 (1111-1110)
Cordero, Roque
- Dodecaconcerto (1111-1110)
David, Johann Nepomuk
- Magische Quadrate; Symphonische Phantasie, Wk52 (2111-2110)

Glass, Philip
- Glassworks (2020-2000)
Grinberg, Alexander
- Carillon (1221-1111)
Haas, Georg Friedrich
- in vain (2121-2020)
Hesketh, Kenneth
- The Circling Canopy of Night (1120-1000)
Hovhaness, Alan
- Saint Vartan Symphony (0000-1410)
Kats-Chernin, Elena
- Clocks; For ensemble and tape (1111-1110)
Koppel, Anders
- Partita (0100-0000)
Matsushita, Shin-ichi
- Correlaziono per 3 Gruppi (2020-0000)
Matthews, Colin
- Pursuit; Ballet (1111-1000)
Milhaud, Darius
- La Carnaval de Londres: Suite sur les airs de "l' Opéra du Gueux," op.172 (1111-0110)
Rosenman, Leonard
- Chamber Music No.2 (1120-0000)
Saygun, A. Adnan
- Bir Orman Masali; A Forest Tale (1111-1110)
Zimmermann, Bernd Alois
- Metamorphose; Music for the film of the same title by Michael Wolgensinger (1111-1100)

ELECTRONICS

15' or Less

Adams, John
- Christian Zeal and Activity (1011-0000)

Antoniou, Theodore
- Events III; Music for Orchestra, Tape and Slide-Projection (1111-0000)
- Op Ouvertüre für Orchester und drei Lautsprechergruppen (Tonband) (1120-2221)

Babbitt, Milton
- Composition for String Orchestra and Tape (0000-0000)
- Correspondences for String Orchestra and Tape (0000-0000)

Baggiani, Guido
- Memoria (1121-1121)

Bates, Mason
- Music from Underground Spaces (2222-4331)
- Rusty Air in Carolina (2222-4331)
- White Lies For Lomax (3222-4331)

Bolcom, William
- Session IV (0010-0010)

Boulez, Pierre
- Originel (2232-2221)
- Transitoire V (2232-2221)
- Transitoire VII (2232-2221)

Delás, José Luis de
- Cinco Sellos (1020-0100)
- Conjuntos (1110-1000)
- Eilanden (0010-0000)

Felder, David
- Gone Grey (0000-0000)

Fómina, Silvia
- Permanenza; Für mikropolyphonisches, im Raum verteiltes Orchester (2030-1010)

Gaslini, Giorgio
- Canto Dalla Città Inquieta: From "Totale" (2110-1100)

Harvey, Jonathan
- Soleil Noir / Chitra (1000-0011)
- Valley of Aosta (1100-0100)

Holliger, Heinz
- Ad Marginem (2020-0000)
- Der Ferne Klang (2221-1000)

Komorous, Rudolf
- Düstere Anmut (1110-1110)

Malec, Ivo
- Tutti; Concert collectif (2121-2210)

Muldowney, Dominic
- Entr'acte (1010-0100)

Nilsson, Bo
- Taqsim-Caprice-Maqam (2022-2201)

Saariaho, Kaija
- Verblendungen (2111-4111)

Schaathun, Asbjørn
- "S" (1110-1100)

Sierra, Roberto
- Concertino (1111-1110)

Stahmer, Klaus Hinrich
- Dans Une Lumière Eclatante (1010-0000)

Over 15'

Aa, Michel van der
- Above; For ensemble and soundtrack (1111-0100)
- Attach; For ensemble and soundtrack (0121-0100)
- Here [enclosed] (0011-0110)

Amy, Gilbert
- La Variation Ajoutée; Pour 17 Instruments & Bande Électroacoustique (2121-1011)

Anderson, Julian
- Book of Hours; In two parts (2121-1110)

André, Mark
- ...Das O... (0022-0020)

Bates, Mason
- Omnivorous Furniture (1111-1110)

Brødsgaard, Anders
- Ghostorchestra (1100-0100)

Bryars, Gavin
- Four Elements (0010-1111)

Dean, Brett
- Carlo; Music for strings and sampler (0000-0000)

Harvey, Jonathan
- Bhakti (1120-1110)
- Inner Light 1 (1010-0000)
- Smiling Immortal (1110-1100)
- Two Interludes for an Opera (1121-1111)

Haubenstock-Ramati, Roman
- Polyphonien; For 2, 3 or 4 chamber orchestras (2000-0020)

Hiller, Lejaren
- Algorithms I; For 9 Instruments and Tape (1011-0100)
- Algorithms II (With Ravi Kumra); For 9 Instruments and Tape (1011-2000)

Höller, York
- Arcus (1122-1110)
- Mythos (1010-2121)
- Résonance (2222-2221)

Hölszky, Adriana
- Tragoedia (Der unsichtbare Raum) (1110-0121)

Huber, Nicolaus A.
- Eröffnung und Zertrümmerung (0110-0110)
- Music on Canvas (1111-1110)
- Rose Selavy (1111-1110)
- Six Bagatelles (1111-0000)

Kancheli, Giya
- A Life Without Christmas: The Morning Prayers. For Chamber Orchestra and Tape (1000-0000)
- Magnum Ignotum (1222-2000)

Kats-Chernin, Elena
- Clocks (1111-1110)

Kopelent, Marek
- Intimissimo (0110-0110)

Korndorf, Nikolai
- Confessiones; Chamber Symphony for 14 Instruments (2110-1110)

Melby, John
- Wind, Sand and Stars (1110-1000)

Obst, Michael
- Kristallwelt (1121-1210)
- Nachtstücke (1010-0010)

Osborne, Nigel
- Wildlife (1010-1100)

Platz, Robert H. P.
- CHLEBNICOV (1110-1110)
- PIECE NOIRE (2110-1110)

Rautavaara, Einojuhani
- Cantus Arcticus; Concerto for Birds and Orchestra (2222-2210)

Rosenman, Leonard
- Chamber Music No.2 (1120-0000)

Roumain, Daniel Bernard
- Call Them All (1111-1111)

Saariaho, Kaija
- Aer: Part 7 of "Maa" (1000-0000)
- Io (3000-2011)
- Lichtbogen (1000-0000)
- Solar (1110-0100)

Schenker, Friedrich
- Jessenin-Majakowski-Recital (0200-0010)

Schwehr, Cornelius
- Aber die Schönheit des Gitters (1010-0000)

Sharp, Elliott
- Akadak (1010-0000)

Staud, Johannes Maria
- Berenice: Suite 1 (1010-1220

TWENTY-FIRST-CENTURY REPERTOIRE

The following pieces were composed in the year 2000 or later.
Chamber Orchestra, Ensemble *and* Solo Repertoire are included, listed according to duration.
Entries are listed with the year of composition in brackets.

10' or Less

Adamo, Mark
- Overture to Lysistrata (2005)

Adler, Samuel
- Show An Affirming Flame; A Poem for Orchestra ("September 1, 1939" by W. H. Auden) (2001)

Aperghis, Georges
- Heysel, Pour 18 Instrumentistes (2002)

Auerbach, Lera
- Serenade for a Melancholic Sea (2002)

Baltakas, Vykintas
- about to drink dense clouds (2003)

Bates, Mason
- White Lies For Lomax (2008)

Benjamin, Arthur
- Olicantus (2002)

Bermel, Derek
- Tag Rag (2003)

Bolcom, William
- A Seattle Overture (2005)

Brødsgaard, Anders
- Magam (2002)

Bruun, Peter
- Tre Små Stykker (2004)

Carter, Elliott
- Réflexions (2004)
- Sound Fields (2007)

Cerha, Friedrich
- Scherzino (2000)

Danielpour, Richard
- Adagietto for String Orchestra (2005)
- Nocturne (2000)
- Swan Song (2003)
- Washington Speaks (2005)

Daugherty, Michael
- Ghost Ranch; Above Clouds (2005)
- Pachelbel's Key; For Youth Orchestra (2002)

Dean, Brett
- Etüdenfest (2000)

Frazelle, Kenneth
- The Four Winds (After Mozart) (2000)

Golijov, Osvaldo
- ZZ's Dream (2008)

Greenwood, Jonny
- smear (2004)

Gudmundsen-Holmgreen, Pelle
- Caravanfanfan-farefare No.1 (2001)
- Caravanfanfan-farefare No.3 (2001)

Harvey, Jonathan
- Moving Trees (2002)

Henze, Hans Werner
- L'heure bleu (2001)

Hesketh, Kenneth
- Notte Oscura (2002)

Hindson, Matthew
- Auto-Electric (2003)
- Comin' Right Atcha (2006)
- Flash Madness (2006)
- Ictalurus Punctatus; For amplified cello and orchestra (2008)
- Lament (2006)
- Lullaby (2003)
- Song and Dance (2006)

Höller, York
- Feuerwerk (2004)

Jost, Christian
- Mascarade: Tableau from the opera "Vipern" (2003)

Kolb, Barbara
- The Web Spinner (2003)

Lang, David
- Open (2008)

Lindberg, Magnus
- Counter Phrases (2003)

Locklair, Dan
- In Memory H. H. L. (2005)

Matthews, Colin
- Flourish with Fireflies (2002)

McCabe, John
- Shepherd's Dream (2002)

Muhly, Nico
- By All Means (2004)

Nieder, Fabio
- "das ewig liecht"; Canon cancrizans per augmentationem in contrario motu (from J. S. Bach's "Kunst der Fuge") (2001)

Nørgård, Per
- Lysning (2006)
- Shaking Hands (2000)

- Snip Snap (2006)

Pärt, Arvo
- Orient & Occident (2000)

Rautavaara, Einojuhani
- Adagio Celeste (2000)

Rihm, Wolfgang
- Nach-Schrift; Eine Chiffre (2004)

Roumain, Daniel Bernard
- Harvest (2004)

Saariaho, Kaija
- Message Pour Gérard (2000)

Schwertsik, Kurt
- Mozart, auf und davon, op.94 (2005)

Sharp, Elliot
- No Time Like The Stranger (2004)

Smolka, Martin
- Oh, My Admired C minor (2002)

Sørensen, Bent
- The Weeping White Room (2002)

Staud, Johannes Maria
- Berenice: Suite No.2 (2003)
- Configurations / Reflet (2002)

Talbot, Joby
- Minus 1500 (2001)

Tavener, John
- Remembering Lennox through Michael (2004)

Thomas, Augusta Read
- Capricious Angels (2009)

Weir, Judith
- Still, Glowing (2008)

Woolrich, John
- Stealing a March (2000)

Yanov-Yanovsky, Dmitri
- Message (2001)

Yuasa, Joji
- Projection (2008)

11' - 20'

Aa, Michel van der
- Here [in circles] (2002)
- Here [enclosed] (2003)
- Here [to be found] (2001)
- Imprint; For baroque orchestra (2005)

Abels, Michael
- Delights & Dances (2007)
Adamo, Mark
- Alcott Music: Suite from "Little Women" (2007)
Adler, Samuel
- Beyond the Pale; A Portrait of a Klezmer for Clarinet and String Orchestra (2007)
- Concerto for Horn and Orchestra (2002)
Aguila, Miguel del
- Concerto for Clarinet (2003)
Amrhein, Karen Amanda
- Event Horizon; For Clarinet and Orchestra (2002)
Anderson, Julian
- Alhambra Fantasy (2000)
Aperghis, Georges
- Le Reste du temps (2003)
Auerbach, Lera
- Concerto for Violin No.2 (2004)
Bates, Mason
- Icarian Rhapsody (2001)
- Music from Underground Spaces (2008)
- Omnivorous Furniture (2004)
- Rusty Air in Carolina (2006)
Bennett, Richard Rodney
- Country Dances; Book 1 (2001)
Bermel, Derek
- Natural Selection (2000)
- Three Rivers (2001)
- Turning Variations (2006)
Beyer, Frank Michael
- Meridian; Concerto for flute and string ensemble (2004)
- Passionato con Arietta (2005)
Boelter, Karl
- Dharma (2001)
- Images from Goldsmith (2001)
Brown, James Francis
- Sinfonietta (2002)
Bruun, Peter
- Twelve to Remember, Twelve to Come (2001)
Buck, Ole
- Flower Ornament Music (2002)
Carter, Elliott
- Concerto for Flute (2008)
- Dialogues; For piano and large ensemble (2003)
Danielpour, Richard
- Souvenirs (2008)
Dean, Brett
- Short Stories; Five Interludes for String Orchestra (2005)

- Testament; Music for orchestra, after "Testament: Music for twelve violas" (2008)
Duddell, Joe
- Alberti Addict (2000)
Felder, David
- Gone Grey (2004)
Fennelly, Brian
- Sigol for Strings (2007)
Frank, Gabriela Lena
- Elegía Andina (2000)
- Manchay Tiempo (Time of Fear) (2005)
Fundal, Karsten
- Oscillation (2000)
Gill, Jeremy
- Chamber Symphony (2005)
Gordon, Michael
- Who by Water (2004)
Greenbaum, Matthew
- Castelnau; For String Orchestra (2008)
Greenwood, Jonny
- Popcorn Superhet Receiver (2005)
Harbison, John
- Canonical American Songbook (2005)
- Partita (2001)
Harvey, Jonathan
- Jubilus (2003)
- Two Interludes for an Opera (2003)
Henze, Hans Werner
- Chamber Concerto 05 (2005)
Hesketh, Kenneth
- After Verdi!; Divertimento in five sections (2001)
- Detail from the Record (2001)
- Netsuke (2004)
Hidalgo, Manuel
- Introduction and Fugue (2004)
- Variations on the Variations op.30 by Webern (2001)
Hindson, Matthew
- Balkan Connection (2003)
- Whitewater; For 12 solo strings (2000)
Holt, Simon
- Capriccio Spettrale (2008)
Huber, Nicolaus A.
- Music on Canvas (2003)
- Rose Selavy (2000)
Hutcheson, Jere
- The Four Temperaments; Concerto for Trombone and Small Orchestra (2009)
- Taj Mahal (2004)
- Wild Nights; Concertino for Bassoon and Mixed Ensemble (2008)

Kats-Chernin, Elena
- Torque (2002)
Katz, Gil S.
- Tribal (2010)
Knussen, Oliver
- Requiem; Songs for Sue, op.33 (2006)
Lang, David
- increase (2002)
Lindberg, Magnus
- Corrente - China Version (2000)
- Jubilees (2002)
MacMillan, James
- The Sacrifice: Three Interludes (2006)
MacRae, Stuart
- Portrait II (2000)
Matthews, Colin
- A Voice to Wake (2004)
Matthus, Siegfried
- Concerto for Trumpet and String Orchestra (2001)
Maxwell Davies, Peter
- Crossing Kings Reach (2001)
Mochizuki, Misato
- 4 D (2003)
- Chimera (2000)
- Wise Water (2002)
Mundry, Isabel
- Panorama ciego (2001)
- Schwankende Zeit (2008)
Panufnik, Roxanna
- The Frog and the Nightingale (2003)
- Powers & Dominions; Concertino for Harp (2001)
Pape, Andy
- Min Fynske Barndom: Suite (2004)
Pärt, Arvo
- These Words... (2008)
Rihm, Wolfgang
- In Frage (2000)
- Sotto Voce 2; Capriccio (2007)
- Eine Stimme 1-3 (2005)
- Die Stücke des Sängers (2001)
Rosing-Schow, Niels
- Equinoxe (2003)
Roumain, Daniel Bernard
- Call Them All (2006)
Rueda, Jesús
- Elephant Skin (2002)
Saariaho, Kaija
- Aile Du Songe (2001)
- Leino Songs (2007)
Schultz, Wolfgang-Andreas
- Was mir die Aeolsharfe erzählt... (2004)
Schwantner, Joseph
- Angelfire (2002)

Schweitzer, Benjamin
- unplugged. unperfumed (2001)
- flekkicht; For baroque orchestra (2004)
Schwertsik, Kurt
- Now you hear me, now you don't (2008)
Sharp, Elliot
- Dark Matters (2008)
- Evolute (2007)
- On Corlear's Hook (2007)
- Points & Fields (2009)
- Racing Hearts (2001)
- Ripples & Heats (2004)
Sierra, Roberto
- Danzas Concertantes (Guitar Concerto) (2007)
- Doce Bagatelas (2000)
- Folias (Guitar Concerto) (2002)
- The Güell Concerto (2006)
- Serenata (2005)
- Sinfonia No.1 (2002)
Smolka, Martin
- Octet (2001)
- Solitudo (2003)
Sotelo, Mauricio
- Chalan (2003)
- Wall of Light Black (2006)
- Wall of Light Red (2004)
Staud, Johannes Maria
- Berenice: Lied vom Verschwinden (2003)
- Berenice: Suite 1 (2003)
- A Map is not the Territory (2001)
Stranz, Ulrich
- Anstieg - Ausblick für Orchester (2002)
Thomas, Augusta Read
- Murmurs in the Mist of Memory (2001)
Tower, Joan
- Chamber Dance (2006)
- The Last Dance (2000)
- In Memory (2002)
- Made in America (2004)
Turnage, Mark-Anthony
- Dark Crossing (2000)
Vir, Param
- Hayagriva (2005)
Volans, Kevin
- Joining Up The Dots (2006)
Watkins, Huw
- Rondo (2005)
Weir, Judith
- Tiger under the Table (2002)
- Winter Song (2006)

Widmann, Jörg
- ad absurdum; Concerto for Trumpet (2002)
- …umdüstert… (2000)
Wilson, Ian
- Inquieto; Concerto for Marimba (2001)
- Mutazione; Concerto for Piano (2003)
Woolrich, John
- After the Clock (2005)
- Cutting a Caper (2001)
- Suite from Bitter Fruit (2002)
Yanov-Yanovsky, Dmitri
- Night Music: Voice in the Leaves (2000)
Yu, Julian
- Not a Stream but an Ocean (2000)

Over 20'

Aa, Michel van der
- Here trilogy; For soprano, chamber orchestra and soundtrack (2001-2003)
Aguila, Miguel del
- Salon Buenos Aires (2010)
Anderson, Julian
- Book of Hours; In two parts (2004)
André, Mark
- …Das O…: From …22,1… (2003)
Aperghis, Georges
- Dark Side (2003)
Auerbach, Lera
- Concerto for Violin No.1 (2000)
- Dialogues on Stabat Mater (2005)
- Fragile Solitudes (2008)
- Suite Concertante (2001)
Beyer, Frank Michael
- Concerto for Viola and Orchestra (2003)
Bolcom, William
- Medusa; A Monodrama for dramatic soprano and string orchestra (2003)
Corigliano, John
- Conjurer; Concerto for Percussionist and String Orchestra (2007)
- Symphony No.2 for String Orchestra (2000)
Cotton, Jeffery
- Concerto for Clarinet, Strings and Harp (2003)
- Symphony for Strings (2004)
Danielpour, Richard
- Apparitions (2003)
Daugherty, Michael
- Tell My Fortune (2004)

Frazelle, Kenneth
- Concerto for Chamber Orchestra (2002)
- The Four Winds; (After Mozart) (2000)
Glass, Philip
- Book of Longing (2007)
Greenwood, Jonny
- Doghouse (2010)
Gruber, HK
- Zeitfluren; Timescapes (2001)
Haas, Georg Friedrich
- in vain (2000)
Harneit, Johannes
- Ohne Leben Tod (Without Life Death), op.23 (2004)
- Triptychon (13X3), op.20 (2003)
Hindson, Matthew
- Dangerous Creatures (2008)
Holloway, Robin
- Fourth Idyll (2007)
Imbrie, Andrew
- From Time to Time (2000)
Kancheli, Giya
- Kápote (2006)
Laderman, Ezra
- Nonet of the Night (2004)
Lang, David
- Child (2001)
MacMillan, James
- A Deep but Dazzling Darkness (2002)
Marquez, Arturo
- Espejos en la Arena (2000)
Matthews, Colin
- Continuum (2000)
Maxwell Davies, Peter
- De Assumtione Beatae Mariae Virginis (2001)
Neikrug, Marc
- Concerto for Clarinet (2004)
Nørgård, Per
- Concerto for Violin No.2; Borderlines (2002)
Obst, Michael
- Nosferatu (2002)
Pärt, Arvo
- Lamentate; Homage to Anish Kapoor and his sculpture "Marsyas" (2002)
- Symphony No.4 (2008)
Rautavaara, Einojuhani
- Incantations (2008)
Rihm, Wolfgang
- Aria / Ariadne; "Szenarie" (2001)
- Frage (Question) (2000)
- Jagden und Formen (2001)
- Sphäre um Sphäre (2003)

Rodríguez, Robert Xavier
 - A Midsummer Night's Dream;
   Incidental Music (2001)
Roumain, Daniel Bernard
 - Voodoo Violin Concerto No.1
   (2002)
Ruders, Poul
 - Abysm (2000)
Saariaho, Kaija
 - Nymphéa Reflection (2001)
 - Quatre Instants (2002)
 - The Tempest Songbook (2004)
Schickele, Peter
 - Concerto for Cello and Orchestra;
   In Memoriam F.D.R. (2000)

Schurmann, Gerard
 - Sonata for String Orchestra (2004)
Schwantner, Joseph
 - Chasing Light (2008)
 - New Morning for the World (2004)
Schwertsik, Kurt
 - Compagnie Masquerade; Ein
   Divertissement für kleines
   Orchester, einer Idee & teilweise
   erhaltenen Violinstimme Mozarts
   folgend (2005)
Sharp, Elliot
 - Akadak (2004)
 - Calling (2002)
 - Polymerae (2008)

 - Proof Of Erdös (2005)
Vir, Param
 - The Theatre of Magical Beings
   (2003)
Wallin, Rolf
 - Appearances (2002)
Widmann, Jörg
 - Freie Stücke (2002)
Zender, Hans
 - Bardo (2000)
Zwilich, Ellen Taaffe
 - Concerto for Clarinet (2002)

REPERTOIRE LISTED BY DURATION

**The sections are divided in String Orchestra, Ensemble and Chamber Orchestra.
Only orchestral and ensemble compositions are listed (no solo repertoire).**

5' or Less

STRING ORCHESTRA

Antheil, George
- Lithuanian Night

Argento, Dominick
- Valse Triste

Berners, Lord
- Adagio, Variations and Hornpipe from "The Triumph of Neptune"

Binkerd, Gordon
- Two Meditations for Strings

Bridge, Frank
- Rosemary

Carter, Elliott
- Sound Fields

Chávez, Carlos
- Sarabande: From "The Daughter of Colchis"

Cowell, Henry
- Hymn and Fuguing Tune No.2
- Movement

Danielpour, Richard
- Nocturne

Finzi, Gerald
- Prelude, op.25

Hartley, Walter Sinclair
- Psalm for Strings

Hindson, Matthew
- Lullaby

Honegger, Arthur
- Largo, H.105

Ives, Charles Edward
- Hymn: Largo Cantabile

Järnefelt, Armas
- Die Verlassene; Stimmungsbild nach einem finnischen Volkslied

Jenkins, Karl
- Passacaglia

Lloyd, Jonathan
- Keir's Kick

Locklair, Dan
- In Memory H. H. L.

Lutosławski, Witold
- Overture for Strings

Maxwell Davies, Peter
- Farewell to Stromness
- Vanitas, Arrangement of a fragment by Johan Ban for string orchestra

Nielsen, Carl
- At the Bier of a Young Artist, F.58

Nørgård, Per
- Adagio Di Preludio
- Four Observations - From an Infinite Rapport; Hommage a Béla Bartók
- Voyage into the Broken Screen; Hommage a Sibelius

Pierné, Gabriel
- Album Pour Mes Petites Amis (Album for My Little Friends): La Veillee de l'Ange Gardien, op.14, No.3
- Album Pour Mes Petites Amis (Album for My Little Friends): Chanson d'Autrefois, op.14, No.5
- Ballet de Cour, No.2: Passepied
- Ballet de Cour, No.5: Menuet de Roy
- Serenade, op.7

Rachmaninoff, Sergei
- Vocalise, op.34

Rihm, Wolfgang
- Kolchis

Schickele, Peter
- Requiem

Schönberg, Arnold
- Notturno in A-flat Major

Sibelius, Jean
- Canzonetta, op.62a
- Romance in C major, op.42

Tavener, John
- Remembering Lennox through Michael

Thomson, Virgil
- Thoughts for Strings

ENSEMBLE

Abrahamsen, Hans
- Aarhus Ragtime

Aperghis, Georges
- Heysel, Pour 18 Instrumentistes

Argento, Dominick
- Valse Triste

Benjamin, George
- Fanfare for Aquarius
- Olicantus

Berio, Luciano
- Re-Call

Bonnet, Antoine
- La terre habitable III; Les hautes terres du Sertalejo

Bose, Hans-Jürgen von
- Concertino Per Il H. W. H.

Cerha, Friedrich
- Scherzino

Chávez, Carlos
- Cantos de México
- Energia; For Nine Instruments

Chou, Wen-Chung
- Yu ko

Cowell, Henry
- Polyphonica; For 12 Instruments or Chamber Orchestra

Del Tredici, David
- Acrostic Song

Felder, David
- Passageways IIA

Feldman, Morton
- Madame Press Died Last Week at Ninety

Françaix, Jean
- 85 Measures et un Da Capo

Fundal, Karsten
- Zoom; Figure and Ground Study III

Goehr, Alexander
- …kein Gedanke, nur ruhiger Schlaf; In memoriam Olivier Messiaen, op.65

Gudmundsen-Holmgreen, Pelle
- Caravanfanfan-farefare No.1

Gürsching, Albrecht
- Drei Plus Vier

Harbison, John
- Exequien for Calvin Simmons

Holliger, Heinz
- Choral à 8
- Sommerkanon IV

Hvidtfelt Nielsen, Svend
- Impromptu

Ives, Charles Edward
- Adagio Sostenuto; At Sea

Knussen, Oliver
- Notre Dame des Jouets; Organum from a Music Box, op.27, No.1
- Organum, op.27, No.2
Komorous, Rudolf
- York
Kozinski, Stefan
- The Maloney Rag
Lang, David
- Open
Laufer, Kenneth
- The Twelve-Note Rag
Lutosławski, Witold
- Slides; For 11 Soloists
Martinů, Bohuslav
- Nonet, H.144
Matthews, Colin
- Flourish with Fireflies
- L, bent
- Little Continuum: No.1 of "Two Tributes"
Maxwell Davies, Peter
- A Welcome to Orkney
Milhaud, Darius
- Chamber Symphony No.1; Le Printemps, op.43
- Chamber Symphony No.2; Pastorale, op.49
- Chamber Symphony No.3; Sérénade, op.71
Morthenson, Jan Wilhelm
- Antiphonia II
Müller-Wieland, Jan
- Allegria
Nancarrow, Conlon
- Study No.2
- Study No.3c
- Study No.5
- Study No.6
- Study No.9
- Study No.16
Nørgård, Per
- Snip Snap
- Without Jealousy
Poulenc, Francis
- Mouvements perpétuels for nine instruments
Prokofiev, Sergei
- March in B-flat Major, op.99
Revueltas, Silvestre
- Batik
Rihm, Wolfgang
- Cantus Firmus; Musik in Memoriam Luigi Nono (1. Versuch)
- Chiffre VIII
- Fusées
- Kolchis
Satie, Erik
- Carnet de croquis et d'esquisses

Saxton, Robert
- Birthday Music for Sir William Glock
Schaathun, Asbjørn
- "S"
Schnittke, Alfred
- 3 X 7
- Hymn IV
- Polyphonic Tango
Schönberg, Arnold
- Das Wappenschild, op.8/2
Stravinsky, Igor
- Ragtime
Swayne, Giles
- PP, op.46
Talbot, Joby
- Arbor Low
- Compound Fracture
Wellesz, Egon
- Pastorale
Wolpe, Stefan
- Chamber Piece No.2
Wood, Hugh
- Comus Quadrilles
Woolrich, John
- Darlington Doubles

CHAMBER ORCHESTRA

Adamo, Mark
- Overture to Lysistrata
Adler, Samuel
- Show An Affirming Flame; A Poem for Orchestra ("September 1, 1939" by W. H. Auden)
Alfvén, Hugo
- Elegi; För liten orkester, ur orkestersviten Gustav II Adolf
Almand, Claude
- Chorale for Chamber Orchestra
Alonso-Crespo, Eduardo
- Yubarta: Overture
Asia, Daniel
- B for J
Aubert, Louis
- La Lettre
Bales, Richard
- Primavera
Barlow, Fred
- Cinq Enfantines
Beck, Jeremy
- Sparks and Flame (Ash)
Bedford, Herbert
- The Lonely Dancer of Gedār; Oriental Dance for Small Orchestra, op.36
Ben-Haim, Paul
- Chorale Prelude by J. S. Bach

Benjamin, Arthur
- Caribbean Dance; A New Jamaican Rumba
- From San Domingo
- Two Jamaican Pieces
Bentzon, Jørgen
- Sinfonia Buffo, op.35
Berio, Luciano
- Variazione sull'aria di Papageno: No.2 from "Divertimento for Mozart"
Bermel, Derek
- Tag Rag
Berners, Lord
- For a Statesman: No.1 of "Three Small Funeral Marches"
Beydts, Louis
- Hue!; Croquis parisien pour petit orchestre
Bittner, Julius
- Der Musikant; Serenade
Black, Stanley
- A Costume Comedy Overture
Bleyle, Karl
- Bacchanten-Overture, op.52
Blumer, Theodor
- Vagabund; Scherzo for Orchestra
Brant, Henry
- Lyric Piece
- Prelude and Fugue
Bridge, Frank
- Norse Legend
Britten, Benjamin
- Irish Reel
- Overture Paul Bunyan
Chou, Wen-Chung
- Two Miniatures from T'ang
Copland, Aaron
- Billy the Kid: Prairie Night & Celebration Dance
- Billy the Kid: Waltz (Billy and his Sweetheart)
- Down a Country Lane
- John Henry
Cowell, Henry
- Saturday Night at the Firehouse
- Teheran Movement
Crawford, Ruth
- Rissolty-Rossolty
Daugherty, Michael
- Pachelbel's Key; For Youth Orchestra
- Oh Lois!: From "Metropolis Symphony"
De Brant, Cyr
- A Song of Yesteryear; Sarabande
Debussy, Claude
- La plus que lente

Delius, Frederick
- Fennimore and Gerda: Intermezzo
- Hassan: Intermezzo and Serenade
- Irmelin, Prelude

Dohnanyi, Ernest von
- The Veil of Pierette: Waltz, op.18, No.2
- The Veil of Pierette: Jolly Funeral March, op.18, No.3
- The Veil of Pierette: Menuett, op.18, No.5

Donato, Anthony
- Mission San José de Aguaya

Duparc, Henri
- Aux étoiles

Elgar, Edward
- Chanson de Matin, op.15, No.2
- Chanson de Nuit, op.15, No.1
- May Song
- Minuet, op.21
- Salut d'Amour, op.12
- Serenade Lyrique

Erbse, Heimo
- Allegro - Lento - Allegro: No.3 from "Divertimento for Mozart"

Etler, Alvin
- Elegy for Small Orchestra

Falla, Manuel de
- El Amor Brujo: Ritual Fire Dance

Filippi, Amedeo De
- Raftsman's Dance

Franze, Juan Pedro
- Lamento quechua, op.6

Fricker, Peter Racine
- Fantasie: No.4 from "Divertimento for Mozart"

Gardner, John
- Overture "Half Holiday"

Gaubert, Philippe
- Madrigal

Gillis, Don
- Four Scenes from Yesterday: Courthouse Square

Glass, Philip
- Interlude from "Orphée"

Granados, Enrique
- Danzas Espanolas, No.6: Jota
- Goyescas: Intermezzo

Guarnieri, Camargo
- Ponteios No.1

Halffter, Ernesto
- Cavatina

Harbison, John
- David's Fascinating Rhythm Method
- Waltz-Passacaglia

Hartley, Walter Sinclair
- Three Patterns for Small Orchestra

Haubenstock-Ramati, Roman
- Ständchen sur le nom de Heinrich Strobel: 3rd part of "Petite musique de nuit"

Henze, Hans Werner
- Finale - Vivace assai: Nr.12 from "Divertimento for Mozart"

Herbert, Victor
- Al Fresco, Intermezzo

Hindemith, Paul
- Sing- und Spielmusik für Liebhaber und Freunde; Ein Jäger aus Kurpfalz, der reitet durch den grünen Wald, op.45, No.3

Hindson, Matthew
- Auto-Electric
- Boom-Box
- Flash Madness
- RPM

Holst, Gustav
- Greeting

Honegger, Arthur
- Allegretto, H.221
- Blues, H.66a
- Deux Pièces pour "La Rédemption de François Villon," H.209
- Interlude de "La Mort de Sainte Alméene," H.20A
- Napoleón: Danse des Enfants
- Napoleón: La romance de Violine
- La Roue: Overture pour le film d'Abel Gance, H.44
- Toccata, H.207
- Vivace, H.220

Horovitz, Joseph
- Horizon Overture
- Valse

Howells, Herbert
- Puck's Minuet, op.20, No.1

Hrabovsky, Leonid
- Four Inventions for Chamber Orchestra

Huë, Georges Adolphe
- Rêverie pour petit orchestre
- Sérénade pour orchestre

Humperdinck, Engelbert
- Humoreske in E Dur

Ibert, Jacques
- Hommage à Mozart

Indy, Vincent d'
- Sérénade, op.16: Valse

Ives, Charles Edward
- The Gong on the Hook and Ladder; Firemen's Parade on Main Street
- Gyp the Blood or Hearst!? Which is Worst?!
- The Rainbow
- Tone Roads No.1, S.49
- Tone Roads No.3, S.49

Järnefelt, Armas
- Berceuse
- Präludium

Kallstenius, Edvin
- Berceuse

Kander, Susan
- She Never Lost A Passenger Overture

Kelly, Bryan
- Cookham Rondo

King, Alastair
- Master Irpy

Klebe, Giselher
- Moments musicaux, op.19

Koch, Erland von
- Dance No.2
- Dance No.4
- Dance No.5
- Kleine Lustspiel Ouvertüre
- Sicilienne

Kodály, Zoltán
- Intermezzo: From "Háry János"

Koechlin, Charles
- Sur Les Flots Lointains

Korngold, Erich Wolfgang
- Der Schneemann: Overture

Krenek, Ernst
- Campo Marzio, op.80
- Ouvertüre "Triumph der Empfindsamkeit" (Triumph of Sensitivity), op.43a

Larsson, Lars-Erik
- Pastoral for liten orkester

Le Grand, Robert
- Effets de Nuit

Lecocq, Charles
- Fricassée

Lincke, Paul
- Träume vom Lido

Linke, Paul
- Hanako; Japanese Intermezzo

Lutosławski, Witold
- Prelude for Guildhall School of Music: Worldes Blis Ne Last No Throwe

MacMillan, James
- Memoire imperiale; A variation on General John Reid's March "Garb of Gaul"

Martin, Frank
- Fox Trot

Matsudaira, Yoritsune
- Pastorale

Matthews, David
- From Sea to Sky; Overture, op.59

Maxwell Davies, Peter
- Canzona (After Giovanni Gabrieli)
- Threnody on a Plainsong for Michael Vyner

McCabe, John
- Sam
- Shepherd's Dream
Milhaud, Darius
- Trois Valses
Moross, Jerome
- Paeans
Myaskovsky, Nikolai Yakovlevich
- Military March No.1
Nancarrow, Conlon
- Study No.1
Nielsen, Carl
- Festival Prelude
Nørgård, Per
- Towards Freedom?
Pepping, Ernst
- Invention für Kleines Orchester: From "Musiken für Orchester"
Piazzolla, Astor
- Danza Criolla
Pierné, Gabriel
- Album Pour Mes Petites Amis (Album for My Little Friends): Farandole, op.14, No.2
- Album Pour Mes Petites Amis (Album for My Little Friends): Petite Gavotte, op.14, No.4
- Album Pour Mes Petites Amis (Album for My Little Friends): Marche des Petits Soldats de Plomb (March of the Little Lead Soldiers), op.14, No.6
- Ballet de Cour, No.1: Rigaudon
- Ballet de Cour, No.3: La Canarie
- Ballet de Cour, No.6: Passamezzo
Pilati, Mario
- Alla Culla; Ninna-nanna per piccola orchestra
Ponce, Manuel
- Gavota
- Instantáneas Mexicanas, No.3: Cielito lindo
- Instantáneas Mexicanas, No.4: Si algún ser
- Instantáneas Mexicanas, No.6: Mañanitas de los niños
Poot, Marcel
- Ouverture Joyeuse
Poulenc, Francis
- Bucolique
- L'embarquement pour Cythère
- Esquisse d'une Fanfare: Ouverture pour le Vᵉ acte de "Romeo et Juliette"
- Matelote Provençale
- Mouvements perpétuels; Nos. 1 & 2
- Overture
- Pièce brève; On the name of Albert Roussel

- Valse
Prokofiev, Sergei
- Lieutenant Kije: Troika, op.60
Rachmaninoff, Sergei
- Vocalise, op.34
Ravel, Maurice
- Fanfare
Read, Gardner
- Petite Pastorale, op.40a
Reizenstein, Franz
- Capriccio
Rodrigo, Joaquín
- Cyrano de Bergerac; Music for Edmond Rostand's play of the same name
- Homenaje a la Tempranica
Rodríguez, Robert Xavier
- Adagio for Small Orchestra
Rogers, Bernard
- Elegy: From Symphony No.3
Rorem, Ned
- Waiting
Rosenberg, Hilding Constantin
- Ouvertura Piccola
Roux, Maurice le
- Allegro Moderato: No.9 from "Divertimento for Mozart"
Saariaho, Kaija
- Forty Heartbeats
Saint-Saëns, Camille
- Rigaudon, op.93, No.2
- Une nuit à Lisbonne, op.63
Santórsola, Guido
- Prelúdio No.3
Satie, Erik
- La Diva de l'Empire
- Illusion [Tendrement]
- Je te veux
- Les Pantins Dansent
- Poudre d'or
- Trois Mélodies de 1916
- Trois petites pièces montées
Saturen, David
- Expression; Lyric piece for small orchestra
Scharwenka, Franz Xaver
- À la Hongroise, op.43, No.6
- A Polish Dance Theme
Schelling, Ernest
- Tarantella
Schickele, Peter
- Broadway Boogie
- What Did You Do Today at Jeffey's House?
Schmitt, Florent
- Cançunik: Suite No.1, op.79
- Hymne à Tanit
- Reflets d'Allemagne: Heidelberg, op.28

Schreker, Franz
- Valse Lente; Weißer Tanz
Schuller, Gunther
- Little Fantasy
Schwertsik, Kurt
- Schrumpf-Symphonie, op.80
Shulman, Alan
- Vodka Float
Sibelius, Jean
- Dance Intermezzo, op.45, No.2
- Valse Chevaleresque, op.96c
- Valse Romantique, op.62b
- Valse Triste: From "Kuolema," op.44, No.1
Sierra, Roberto
- Sonatina: From "Let's Make a Symphony"
Slonimsky, Nicolas
- Little March for the Big Bowl; Marche grotesque
Stravinsky, Igor
- Circus Polka; Composed for a Young Elephant
- Tango
Surinach, Carlos
- Danza Andaluza
Tavener, John
- Variations on "Three Blind Mice"
Toch, Ernst
- Epilogue
- Intermezzo
Tomlinson, Ernest
- Little Serenade
Tower, Joan
- Paganini Trills
Tubin, Eduard
- Valse Triste
Villa-Lobos, Heitor
- Ouverture de l'homme tel...
Warlock, Peter
- An Old Song
Weiner, Leo
- Soldatenspiel, op.16
Weir, Judith
- Still, Glowing
Wellejus, Henning
- Postvognen Ruller (The Mailcoach is Rolling), op.16
Wilson, Ian
- What We Can See of the Sky Has Fallen
Wimberger, Gerhard
- Allegro Giocoso: No.8 from "Divertimento for Mozart"
Winkler, Gerhard
- Wolken über Samland

6' - 10'

STRING ORCHESTRA

Adler, Samuel
- Concertino for Strings
Alonso-Crespo, Eduardo
- Sinfonietta for Strings
Bacewicz, Grażyna
- Symphoniette
Barber, Samuel
- Adagio for Strings
- Serenade, op.1
Bartók, Béla
- Rumanian Folk Dances
Baumann, Herbert
- Nordic Impressions; Suite for String Orchestra
Bayoras, Feliksas
- Präludium und Toccata für Streichorchester
Bedford, David
- Piece for Mo
Bernstein, Leonard
- Mass: Two Meditations
Blacher, Boris
- Divertimento
Blackford, Richard
- Music for Carlow
Blomdahl, Karl-Birger
- Preludio and Allegro
Boyle, Rory
- Moel Bryn Divisions
Brandmüller, Theo
- Carillon joyeux
Bridge, Frank
- Two Old English Songs
Britten, Benjamin
- Prelude and Fugue, op.29
Chávez, Carlos
- Sonante
Corigliano, John
- Voyage (for String Orchestra)
Cowell, Henry
- Hymn and Fuguing Tune No.5
- Hymn, Chorale and Fuguing Tune No.8
Danielpour, Richard
- Adagietto for String Orchestra
- Swan Song
Daugherty, Michael
- Strut
Denisov, Edison
- Aquarell
Elgar, Edward
- Sospiri, op.70

Fine, Irving
- Serious Song; A Lament for String Orchestra
Finzi, Gerald
- Romance, op.11
Foulds, John
- Music-Pictures (Group IV), op.55
Geissler, Fritz
- Regiser Festmusik
Gillis, Don
- Three Sketches
Glass, Philip
- Company
- Façades
- Runaway Horses: From "Mishima"
Goossens, Eugene
- Miniature Fantasy for String Orchestra, op.2
- Pastorale, op.59
Górecki, Henryk Mikołaj
- Three Pieces in Old Style
Haas, Pavel
- Study for Strings
Harrison, Lou
- Suite No.2
Hasquenoph, Pierre
- Concertino for Strings
Herrmann, Peter
- Sonatina for String Orchestra
Hewitt, Harry
- Spoon River: Prelude and Elegy, op.26, No.3&4
Heyn, Volker
- Phryh
Hindson, Matthew
- Song and Dance
- Technologic 1-2
Hummel, Bertold
- Drei Kleine Stücke, op.19b
Knight, Edward
- Cadillac Ranch
Koch, Erland von
- Sechs Schwedische Bauernmelodien; Aus Dalekarlien
Kühnl, Claus
- Vision; For 20 String Soloists
Lees, Benjamin
- Intermezzo
Lutosławski, Witold
- Five Folk Melodies
Menotti, Gian Carlo
- Pastorale
Milhaud, Darius
- Chamber Symphony No.4; Dixtuor à Cordes, op.74
Moeschinger, Albert
- Quatre pièces brèves
Nielsen, Carl
- Bohemian Danish Folksong, F.130

Nørgård, Per
- Fugitive Summer
- Lysning
- Out Of This World - Parting
- Pastorale: From Babette's Feast
Orbón, Julián
- Partita No.2
Panufnik, Andrzej
- Jagiellonian Triptych
- Landscape
- Lullaby
Pärt, Arvo
- Cantus in Memory of Benjamin Britten
- Festina Lente
- Fratres; For strings and percussion
- Mein Weg; For 14 strings and percussion
- Orient & Occident
- Psalom
- Silouans Song; "My soul yearns after the Lord…"
- Summa
Poot, Marcel
- Musique pour cordes
Prokofiev, Sergei
- Andante, op.50a
Rathaus, Karol
- Music for Strings; Adagio for Strings, op.49
Rautavaara, Einojuhani
- Epitaph for Béla Bartók
- Pelimannit (The Fiddlers)
Reger, Max
- Christmas, op.145, No.3
Rihm, Wolfgang
- Segmente, op.12
Rorem, Ned
- Pilgrims
Rosenberg, Hilding Constantin
- Bianca-Nera; Overture
Schickele, Peter
- Elegy for String Orchestra
Schreker, Franz
- Scherzo
Schuman, William
- Amaryllis; Variants on an Old English Round
Schwertsik, Kurt
- Mond-Lichtung; Eine Nacht-partie für Streichorchester, op.75
Sibelius, Jean
- Impromptu; On the Impromptus op.5/5 and 5/6
Smirnov, Dmitri
- Two Ricercares
Stranz, Ulrich
- Contrasubjekte; Passacaglia über B-A-C-H für Streicher

Theodorakis, Mikis
 - Oedipus Tyrannos; Ode for String
   Orchestra
Thiele, Siegfried
 - Trauermusik
Thomson, Virgil
 - Autumn; Concertino for Harp,
   Percussion and Strings
Toovey, Andrew
 - Mozart
Turina, Joaquin
 - Oración del Torero, op.34
Vaughan Williams, Ralph
 - English Folk Song Suite
Vir, Param
 - Before Krishna
Voss, Friedrich
 - Epitaph
 - Tragic Overture; In Memoriam D.
   Hammarskjoeld
Weiss, Manfred
 - Five Pieces
Yanov-Yanovsky, Dmitri
 - Message

ENSEMBLE

Anderson, Julian
 - Tiramisu
Arnold, Malcolm
 - Trevelyan Suite, op.96
Auric, Georges
 - La fontaine de jouvence
Babbitt, Milton
 - All Set
 - Composition for 12 Instruments
Baltakas, Vykintas
 - about to drink dense clouds
Becker, Günther
 - Game for Nine
Bedford, David
 - Piece for Mo
 - Trona For 12
Bennett, Richard Rodney
 - Calendar; For Chamber Ensemble
Bentzon, Niels Viggo
 - Two Monkton-Blues, op.127
Bermel, Derek
 - Continental Divide
 - Hot Zone
Blake, David
 - Scherzo and Two Dances
Boccadoro, Carlo
 - Adagio
Bolcom, William
 - Session I
 - Session IV

Bonnet, Antoine
 - La terre habitable II; Aubrac
 - La terre habitable V; Liberté grande
Brødsgaard, Anders
 - Magam
Brown, Earle
 - Available Forms I
 - Novara
Bruun, Peter
 - Bag Den Kan Fredens Ranker Gro
   (Behind it grow the branches of
   peace)
 - Himmel og Jord (Heaven and Earth)
Buck, Ole
 - Aquarelles
 - Chamber Music I
 - Chamber Music II
 - Landscapes IV
Burt, Francis
 - Echoes
Carter, Elliott
 - Réflexions
Chen, Yi
 - Sparkle, Octet
Cordero, Roque
 - Permutaciones 7
Crawford, Ruth
 - Music for Small Orchestra
Czernowin, Chaya
 - Afatsim
Dallapiccola, Luigi
 - Piccola Musica Notturna
Daugherty, Michael
 - Jackie's Song
 - Snap!
Davico, Vincenzo
 - Poemetti Pastorali
Davis, Anthony
 - Wayang II
Debussy, Claude
 - Deux Arabesques
Delás, José Luis de
 - Cinco Sellos
Denisov, Edison
 - Epitaph
Dessau, Paul
 - Alice the Firefighter
 - Alice's Monkey Business
Dillon, James
 - ...Once Upon A Time
 - Zone (...de azul)
Döhl, Friedhelm
 - Medeas Lied
Françaix, Jean
 - Onze Variations sur un Thème de
   Haydn
 - Sérénade
Frounberg, Ivar
 - En Vue de Roesnaes

Fundal, Karsten
 - Hoquetus
Glass, Philip
 - Façades
 - Runaway Horses: From "Mishima"
Gordon, Michael
 - Acid Rain
 - Love Bead
Górecki, Henryk Mikołaj
 - Concerto
Grainger, Percy Aldridge
 - Green Bushes; Passacaglia on an
   English folksong: British folkmusic
   settings No.12
 - My Robin is to the Greenwood
   Gone; Old English Popular Music
   No.2
Grantham, Donald
 - Fantasy on Mr. Hyde's Song
 - Slobberin' Goblins
Gudmundsen-Holmgreen, Pelle
 - Mester Jacob (Frère Jacques)
Gutchë, Gene
 - Rondo capriccioso, op.21
Harle, John
 - Cinéma (René Clair's "Entr'acte")
Harvey, Jonathan
 - Hidden Voice 1
 - Moving Trees
Henze, Hans Werner
 - L'heure bleu
Heyn, Volker
 - Phryh
Hibbard, William
 - Stabiles for 13 Instruments
Hindemith, Paul
 - Sonata for 10 Instruments
Hindson, Matthew
 - Comin' Right Atcha
Höller, York
 - Feuerwerk
Holliger, Heinz
 - Ad Marginem
 - Engführung
 - Der Ferne Klang
 - Ostinato Funebre
Holmboe, Vagn
 - Prelude to a Maple Tree, op.168
 - Prelude to a Pine Tree
 - Prelude to a Willow Tree
 - Prelude to the Calm Sea, op.187
 - Prelude to the Pollution of Nature
Homs, Joaquim
 - Nonet; Obra encàrrec Festival
   Internacional de Música de
   Barcelona 1979
Hosokawa, Toshio
 - Medea Fragments I

Hübler, Klaus K.
- Kryptogramm
Hvidtfelt Nielsen, Svend
- Flowerfall
Imbrie, Andrew
- Dandelion Wine
Ince, Kamran
- Turquoise
Ishii, Maki
- Präludium und Variationen (Prelude and Variations); For Nine Players
Jekimowski, Viktor
- Chamber Variations for 13 Players, op.15
Killmayer, Wilhelm
- Führe mich, Alter, nur immer in deinen geschnörkelten Frühlings-Garten! Noch duftet und taut frisch und gewürzig sein Flor
Kirchner, Leon
- Music for Twelve
Knussen, Oliver
- Two Organa, op.27
Komarova, Tatjana
- Sonnenuntergänge auf B 612 (Sunsets on B 612)
Komorous, Rudolf
- Düstere Anmut
Koppel, Anders
- Pogo
Laderman, Ezra
- Cadence
Lang, David
- Spud
Lehmann, Hans Ulrich
- Composition for 19
León, Tania
- The Beloved
- Indigena
Lieberson, Peter
- Free and Easy Wanderer
- Raising the Gaze
Lindberg, Magnus
- Counter Phrases
Lutosławski, Witold
- Bucolics
- Chain 1 [Launch 1]
- Dance Preludes
- Dance Preludes; 3rd Version
- Interlude
MacRae, Stuart
- The Broken Spectre
- The Broken Spectre (revisited)
- The Witch's Kiss
Mansurian, Tigran
- Da Ich Nicht Hoffe für 14 Instrumentalisten (In Memoriam Igor Stravinsky)
- Tovem for 15 Instruments

Maros, Rudolf
- Musica da Camera per 11
Marthinsen, Niels
- A Bright Kind of High
- A Miniature
- Outland
Martinů, Bohuslav
- Jazz Suite, H.172
- Serenata No.1
- Serenata No.3
Matsushita, Shin-ichi
- Composizione da Camera
- Fresque Sonore
Matthews, Colin
- Elegia: No.2 of "Two Tributes"
- Little Suite No.2, op.18b
Milhaud, Darius
- Actualités; Musik zu einer Filmwochenschau, op.104
- Chamber Symphony No.4; Dixtuor à Cordes, op.74
Muhly, Nico
- By All Means
Muldowney, Dominic
- Double Helix
- Three-Part Motet
- Variations on "Mein junges Leben hat ein End"
Müller-Siemens, Detlev
- Zwei Stücke (Two Pieces)
Nancarrow, Conlon
- Study No.7
- Study No.12
Nono, Luigi
- Incontri
Nordentoft, Anders
- The City of Threads
- Zenerva Sesio
Nørgård, Per
- Surf
Orbón, Julián
- Partita No.2
Osborne, Nigel
- Eulogy
Pärt, Arvo
- Fratres; For chamber ensemble
Paz, Juan Carlos
- Obertura Para Doce Instrumentos (Overture for 12 Instruments)
Petyrek, Felix
- Arabian Suite
Picker, Tobias
- The Blue Hula
Pokorný, Petr
- Hommage a "Brundibár"; Overture for small orchestra
Primosch, James
- Five Miniatures

Revueltas, Silvestre
- Homenaje a Federico Garccía Lorca
- Ocho Por Radio; Eight Musicians Broadcasting
- Sensemayá (for chamber ensemble)
- Colorines
Rihm, Wolfgang
- abgewandt 1
- Bild (eine Chiffre)
- Chiffre III
- Chiffre IV
- Chiffre V
- Chiffre VI
- Form / 2 Formen; For 20 instrumentalists in 4 groups of 5 players
- Gedrängte Form
- Music-Hall Suite
- Nach-Schrift; Eine Chiffre
- Nucleus
- Pol
- Ricercare; Musik In Memoriam Luigi Nono (2.Versuch)
Rosing-Schow, Niels
- Canon and Corale
Ruders, Poul
- Diferencias
- Greeting Concertino
- Nightshade
Schleiermacher, Steffen
- Trotz Reaktion I
- Trotz Reaktion II
- Trotz Reaktion III
- Trotz Reaktion IV
Schnittke, Alfred
- Pantomime; Suite for Chamber Orchestra
Schönberg, Arnold
- Four Pieces
- Six Little Piano Pieces, op.19
Schuller, Gunther
- Automation (Music for a real or imagined film score)
Smirnov, Dmitri
- Elegie In Memoriam Edison Denissow for 16 Players, op.97b
Smolka, Martin
- Oh, My Admired C minor
Sørensen, Bent
- Clairobscur
- The Weeping White Room
Staud, Johannes Maria
- Configurations / Reflet
Stravinsky, Igor
- Concertino for 12 Instruments
- Eight Instrumental Miniatures

Stroman, Scott
- Clown Dances
Takemitsu, Tōru
- Rain Coming
Talbot, Joby
- Minus 1500
Tanaka, Karen
- Echo Canyon
- Water and Stone
- Wave Mechanics
Terzakis, Dimitri
- Hommage à Morse
- Ichochronos II
Thomas, Augusta Read
- Capricious Angels
Vir, Param
- Contrapulse
Vostřák, Zbyněk
- Tao, op.41
Vries, Klaas de
- Bewegingen (Movements)
Webern, Anton
- Fünf Stücke, op.10
- Konzert; Anton Schönberg zum 60.
  Geburtstag, op.24
Weir, Judith
- Sederunt Principes
Williams, Graham
- Cerberus
Wilson, Richard
- Fantasy and Variations
Wittinger, Róbert
- Compensazioni, op.9
Wolpe, Stefan
- Chamber Piece No.1
Woolrich, John
- Caprichos
- From the Shadow
- Music from the House of Crossed
  Desires
- Stealing a March
Wyner, Yehudi
- Amadeus' Billiard
- Passage
Xenakis, Iannis
- Kaï
Ye, Xiaogang
- Nine Horses, op.19
Yuasa, Joji
- Projection
Zimmermann, Bernd Alois
- Un "Petit Rien"

CHAMBER ORCHESTRA

Abrahamsen, Hans
- Stratifications
Absil, Jean
- Deux Danses Rituelles
- Triptique
Adams, John
- Christian Zeal and Activity
Adès, Thomas
- The Origin of the Harp, op.13
Adler, Samuel
- City By The Lake: A Portrait of
  Rochester, NY
Aguila, Miguel del
- Toccata, op.28
Albéniz, Isaac
- Iberia: Lavapiés
- Iberia: Triana
Antheil, George
- Archipelago "Rhumba"
- Jazz Symphony
- Suite for Orchestra
Aperghis, Georges
- Ascoltare stanca, Pour 18
  Instrumentistes
- The Boor: Overture to the opera
- The Dream of Valentino: Dances
  from Valentino
Arnell, Richard
- Sonata for Chamber Orchestra,
  op.18
Arnold, Malcolm
- Symphonic Study "Machines,"
  op.30
Atterberg, Kurt
- Eine Värmlandsrhapsodie, op.36
- Suite No.2
Bacri, Nicolas
- Folia; Chaconne symphonique pour
  orchestre, op.30
Baird, Tadeusz
- Overture in Old Style
Balogh, Ernö
- Pastorale and Capriccio, op.21
Banks, Don
- Elizabethan Miniatures
Bantock, Granville
- Four Landscapes from the Chinese
- Pierrot of the Minute; Comedy
  Overture
Barber, Samuel
- Essay No.1, op.12
Barnett, Carol
- Sumervar
Bartók, Béla
- Bartók Suite
- Hungarian Folksongs
- Rumanian Folk Dances

- Suite, op.14
Bates, Mason
- White Lies For Lomax
Bauer, Marion
- Concertino
Bavicchi, John
- Fantasia on Korean Folk Tunes,
  op.53
- Fantasy, op.36
- Music for Small Orchestra, op.81
Benjamin, Arthur
- Overture to an Italian Comedy
- Waltz and Hyde Park Gallop: From
  the film *An Ideal Husband*
Bennett, Richard Rodney
- Sinfonietta
- Suite Française for Small Orchestra
Bentzon, Niels Viggo
- Overture for Chamber Orchestra,
  op.14
- Prelude and Rondo, op.56
Berlin, David
- Structures for Chamber Orchestra
Bernstein, Leonard
- Fancy Free: Three Dance
  Variations
- On the Town: Three Dance
  Episodes
Beyer, Johanna
- Fragment for Chamber Orchestra
Blacher, Boris
- Alla Marcia
- Hommage à Mozart,
  Metamorphoses on a group of
  Mozart themes for orchestra
- Kleine Marschmusik
- Musica giocosa
- Orchester-Capriccio über ein
  Volkslied
- Rondo
Black, Stanley
- Percussion Fantasy
Bleyle, Karl
- Reineke Fuchs, Overture, op.23
Blomdahl, Karl-Birger
- Adagio from "Vaknatten": Incidental
  music from the play
Blumer, Theodor
- Lyrisches Intermezzo
Boccadoro, Carlo
- Mouvement for Orchestra
Bolcom, William
- A Seattle Overture
Bond, Victoria
- Concertino
- Journal
Bossi, Marco Enrico
- Siciliana e Giga (stile antico) per
  Orchestra, op.73

Brandmüller, Theo
- Venezianische Schatten
Brant, Henry
- A Requiem in Summer; In Memory
  of my Father
Bräutigam, Helmut
- Festliche Musik
Bresgen, Cesar
- Intrada
Bridge, Frank
- There Is A Willow Grows Aslant A
  Brook
- Two Entr'actes
- Two Intermezzi: From the incidental
  music to the play "Threads"
- Vignettes de danse
Britten, Benjamin
- Gloriana: The Courtly Dances
- Men of Goodwill; Variations on a
  Christmas Carol (God rest ye merry,
  Gentlemen)
- Peter Grimes: Passacaglia, op.33b
Brown, Earle
- Modules 1 & 2
- Module 3
Bruns, Victor
- Minna von Barnhelm: Overture,
  op.39
Bruun, Peter
- Tre Små Stykker
Buck, Ole
- Preludes I - V
- Overture
Busoni, Ferruccio
- Berceuse elegiaque
- Lustspiel Overture, op.38 (Busoni
  Verz. 245)
Cheslock, Louis
- Theme and Variations
Chou, Wen-Chung
- Landscapes
Cohn, James
- Homage
- The Little Circus, op.51
Copland, Aaron
- Letter from Home
- An Outdoor Overture
- Symphony No.1: Prelude
Corigliano, John
- Elegy
Cowell, Henry
- Carol
- Hymn and Fuguing Tune No.3
Csonka, Paul
- Prisma Sinfonico (Symphonic
  Prism)
Daniels, Mabel W.
- Deep Forest; Prelude for Little
  Symphony Orchestra, op.34, No.1

Daugherty, Michael
- Ghost Ranch; Above Clouds
Davis, Anthony
- Notes from the Underground
Davison, John
- Symphony No.6
Debussy, Claude
- Lindaraja
Delius, Frederick
- Five Little Pieces
- Petite Suite No.2
- A Song Before Sunrise
Denisov, Edison
- Hommage à Pierre
Dessau, Paul
- Alice Helps the Romance
- Alice in the Wooly West
- Sonatine; For small orchestra and
  obbligato piano
Diamond, David
- Hommage à Satie; À mémoire for
  chamber orchestra
Diehl, Paula
- Insiders
Döhl, Friedhelm
- Ikaros; Ballet nach einem Gedicht
  von E. Lindgren
Dohnanyi, Ernest von
- The Veil of Pierette: Pierrot's
  complaint of love, op.18, No.1
- The Veil of Pierette: Wedding
  March, op.18, No.4
- The Veil of Pierette: Pierette's
  dance of madness, op.18, No.6
Dubois, Pierre-Max
- Trois Sérénades
Duparc, Henri
- Danse Lente
Earls, Paul
- And On The Seventh Day
Eaton, John
- Adagio and Allegro
Einem, Gottfried von
- Capriccio, op.2
- Introduktion - Wandlungen: No.1
  from "Divertimento for Mozart,"
  op.21
Elgar, Edward
- Dream Children, op.43
- Falstaff, Two Interludes
Engelmann, Hans Ulrich
- Capricciosi
- Ezra Pound Music
- Impromptu
- Kaleidoskop
Erdmann, Dietrich
- Concert Piece

Farago, Marcel
- Divertimento for Chamber
  Orchestra, op.18
Farkas, Ferenc
- Two Hungarian Dances
Faust, George
- Adagio for Small Orchestra
Felder, David
- Three Lines from Twenty Poems
Fenby, Eric
- Rossini on Ilkla Moor; Overture
Ferguson, Howard
- Overture for an Occasion, op.16
Ficher, Jacobo
- Dos Poemas; De El Jardino de R.
  Tagore, op.10, No.16
Finke, Fidelio
- Festliche Musik
Finzi, Gerald
- Love's Labour's Lost; Three
  Soliloquies, op.28
- A Severn Rhapsody, op.3
Foss, Lukas
- Symphonie de Rossi; Suite
  Salomon Rossi
Franco, Johan
- Sinfonia
Freyhan, Michael
- Toy Symphony
Fujiie, Keiko
- Beber, op.31
Fuleihan, Anis
- Divertimento
Geissler, Fritz
- Italienische Lustspiel-Ouvertüre
German, Sir Edward
- The Conquerer; Incidental music:
  Romance and two Dances
- Coronation March
Gianneo, Luis
- Variaciones Sobre Tema de Tango
Gilbert, Anthony
- Sinfonia for Chamber Orchestra
Girnatis, Walter
- Scherzo Fantastique
Glass, Philip
- Meetings along the Edge: From
  "Passages"
- Offering: From "Passages"
Glazunov, Alexander
- Serenade for Small Orchestra No.2,
  op.11
Górecki, Henryk Mikołaj
- Genesis II: Canti Strumentali,
  op.19/2
Gould, Morton
- Serenade ("Orfeo") from "Audubon"
Granados, Enrique
- À la Cubana; Marche militaire

Gudmundsen-Holmgreen, Pelle
- Variationer til Moster Rix (Variations for Aunt Rix)
Gyring, Elizabeth
- Scherzo No.2 for Orchestra
Haas, Joseph
- Lyrisches Intermezzo
Hahn, Reynaldo
- La Fête Chez Thérèse: Suite No.1
Hansson, C.J. Gunnar
- Suite No.1
Harbison, John
- Remembering Gatsby; Foxtrot for Orchestra
Harrison, Lou
- Alleluia
- Seven Pastorales
Hartley, Walter Sinclair
- Sinfonia No.7
Hauer, Josef Matthias
- Zwölftonspiel XVII (Twelve-tone game XVII)
Helfer, Walter
- A Water Idyll
Hemberg, Eskil
- Migraine pour orchestre, op.19b
Hesketh, Kenneth
- Notte Oscura
Hewitt, Harry
- Overture: Taming of the Shrew
Hill, Mabel Wood
- Reactions to "Prose Rhythms" of Fiona Macleod
Hindemith, Paul
- Plöner Musiktag: Tafelmusik
Hindson, Matthew
- Lament
- LiteSPEED
Holloway, Robin
- Inquietus, op.66
- Overture on a Nursery Rhyme, op.75a
Holmboe, Vagn
- Prelude to the Unsettled Weather, op.188
- Prelude to the Seagulls and Cormorants, op.174
Holst, Gustav
- Morris Dance Tunes
- Two Songs Without Words, op.22 / H88
Honegger, Arthur
- Fantasio, Ballet pantomime de Georges Wague, H.46
- Pastorale d'été, Poème symphonique, H.31

- Prélude pour Aglavaine et Sélysette; D'après la pièce de Maeterlinck, H.10
- Sérénade à Angélique, H.182
- Sous-marine, Ballet, H.58
Horne, David
- Flicker
Horovitz, Joseph
- Adagio Cantabile
- Concertino Classico
Hudec, Jiri
- Drei Stilisierte Polkas im Volkston
Hutcheson, Jere
- Transitions for Orchestra
Ince, Kamran
- Evil Eye Deflector
Ives, Charles Edward
- Central Park in the Dark
Janáček, Leoš
- Adagio
- Mährische Volkstänze (Moravian Folk Dances)
Jost, Christian
- Mascarade: Tableau from the opera "Vipern"
Kallstenius, Edvin
- Dalsland-Rhapsodie, op.22
Kaun, Hugo
- Elegie, op.70, No.5
- Fröhliches Wandern, op.70, No.1
- Idyll, op.70, No.2
Kelemen, Milko
- Konstellationen
Kelterborn, Rudolf
- Musica luminosa per orchestra
Kennan, Kent
- Dance Divertimento
Killmayer, Wilhelm
- Sinfonia 2
Kingman, Daniel
- A Revolutionary Garland
Kirk, Theron
- Adagietto
Klebe, Giselher
- Con moto, op.2
Knussen, Oliver
- Music for a Puppet Court; Puzzle pieces for 2 Chamber Orchestras, op.11
Koch, Erland von
- Dalecarlia Suite
Kodály, Zoltán
- Hungarian Rondo
- Minuetto Serio
Kolb, Barbara
- The Web Spinner
Kopelent, Marek
- Still-Leben

Korngold, Erich Wolfgang
- Dance in the Old Style
- Straussiana
Kósa, György
- Suite; Three ironic portraits
Krása, Hans
- Overture for Small Orchestra
Krenek, Ernst
- Von Vorn Herein, op.219
Kubik, Gail
- Folk Song Suite
- Music for Dancing
Kühnl, Claus
- Monodie; Music of the silence, op.12
Kulenty, Hanna
- Passacaglia
Kurz, Siegfried
- Music for Brass, Kettledrums and Strings, op.36
La Violette, Wesley
- Nocturne for Orchestra
Lazar, Filip
- Suite Valaque
Ledenjov, Roman
- Notturni
LeFanu, Nicola
- Preludio I
- Preludio II
Lewis, Harold Merrills
- Two Preludes on Southern Folk Hymn Tunes
Liebermann, Rolf
- Suite on Six Swiss Folksongs
Luening, Otto
- Prelude to a Hymn Tune by William Billings
MacKenzie, Sir Alexander C.
- Benedictus, op.37, No.3
Malec, Ivo
- Tutti; Concert collectif
Malipiero, Gian Francesco
- Grottesco
Maros, Rudolf
- Sinfonietta No.1
Marquez, Arturo
- Paisajes Bajo el Signo de Cosmos
Martin, Frank
- Overture to Racine's "Athalie"
Martinů, Bohuslav
- Comedy on the Bridge: Little Suite from the opera
- Ouverture, H.345
Matthus, Siegfried
- Drei Sommerbilder
- Small Concerto for Orchestra
- Sonata by G. Gabrieli

Maxwell Davies, Peter
- Chat Moss
- Five Klee Pictures; For school, amateur or professional orchestra
- Jimmack the Postie
- Ojai Festival Overture

Menotti, Gian Carlo
- Introduction, March and Shepherd's Dance: From "Amahl and the Night Visitors"

Milhaud, Darius
- Chamber Symphony No.5; Dixtuor d'Instruments à Vent, op.75
- Trois Rag-Caprices

Moeran, E. J.
- Whythorne's Shadow

Moncayo, José Pablo
- Cumbres
- Homenaje a Cervantes
- Huapango

Montsalvatge, Xavier
- Serenade a Lydia de Cadaques

Moravec, Paul
- Adelphony

Morawetz, Oskar
- Carnival Overture

Müller-Wieland, Jan
- Two Pieces for Chamber Orchestra

Muñoz Molleda, José
- Circo, Suite

Nabokoff, Nicholas
- Le Fiance, op.9

Naylor, Bernard
- Variations

Nørgård, Per
- Bright Dances, op.24
- Dream Play

Oldham, Arthur
- Variations on a Carol Tune

Palau Boix, Manuel
- Homenaje a Debussy

Pärt, Arvo
- Collage on B-A-C-H
- Pari Intervallo
- Wenn Bach Bienen gezüchtet hätte…

Payne, Anthony
- Hidden Music

Pergament, Moses
- Vision: Ballet

Pfundt, Reinhard
- Bartók-Reflexionen

Piazzolla, Astor
- Milonga del Ángel

Pierné, Gabriel
- Ballet de Cour, No.4: Pavane et Saltarello
- Giration, Divertissement choréographique

Pompey, Angel Martin
- Serenata madrilena

Ponce, Manuel
- Suite en Estilo Antiguo

Poot, Marcel
- Fantasia
- Fête à Thélème
- Musique Legère

Porrino, Ennio
- Tre Canzoni Italiane

Poulenc, Francis
- Deux Marches et un Intermède

Powell, Mel
- Stanzas

Prokofiev, Sergei
- Autumn; A symphonic sketch for small orchestra, op.8
- Overture; American, op.42
- Overture on Hebrew Themes, op.34a

Quilter, Roger
- As you like it: Suite, op.21
- Three English Dances, op.11

Rapoport, Eda
- Israfel; Tone Picture after Edgar Allan Poe

Rautavaara, Einojuhani
- Lintukoto (Isle of Bliss)

Ravel, Maurice
- Cinq Mélodies populaires grecques (Five Greek Folk Melodies)
- Ma Mère l'Oye (Mother Goose): Prelude et Danse du Rouet
- Pavane pour une infante défunte

Reger, Max
- Suite, op.44

Revueltas, Silvestre
- Alcancias
- El Renacuajo Paseador
- Janitzio
- Planos (Planes)
- Troka

Riegger, Wallingford
- Scherzo

Rodrigo, Joaquín
- Dos Danzas Españolas; Suite for castanets and orchestra
- Tres Viejos Aires de Danza

Roentgen, Julius
- Old Netherlands Dances, op.46

Rogers, Bernard
- Elegy; To the Memory of Franklin D. Roosevelt

Rorem, Ned
- Triptych; Three Pieces for Chamber Orchestra

Rota, Nino
- Canzona

Rózsa, Miklós
- Kaleidoscope; Six short pieces for small orchestra, op.19a
- Notturno ungherese, op.28

Ruders, Poul
- Trapeze

Sallinen, Aulis
- Sunrise Serenade

Sandström, Sven-David
- In the Meantime

Santander, Manuel
- Ritmos de Cadiz

Satie, Erik
- Jack in the Box, op.post
- La belle excentrique; Fantasie sérieuse pour orchestra de music-hall

Saxton, Robert
- Variation on "Sumer is Icumen In"

Schickele, Peter
- Songs from Shakespeare

Schlemm, Gustav Adolf
- Polka-Fughetta

Schnittke, Alfred
- Four Aphorisms

Schoeck, Othmar
- Serenade (Interlude)
- Serenade, op.1

Schönherr, Max
- Tänze aus Salzburg
- Das trunkene Mücklein

Schwaen, Kurt
- Zwingerserenade

Schwertsik, Kurt
- Mozart, auf und davon, op.94

Scott, Cyril
- Summer Gardens

Searle, Humphrey
- Night Music

Shchedrin, Rodion
- Shepherd's Pipes of Vologda

Shostakovich, Dmitri
- Five Fragments, op.42

Sibelius, Jean
- Suite Mignonne, op.98a

Sierra, Roberto
- Alegría

Smit, Andre-Jean
- Suite Pittoresque

Stern, Robert
- Ricordanza

Stevens, Bernard
- Eclogue

Stiller, Andrew
- A Periodic Table of the Elements

Stock, David
- Capriccio

Strauss, Richard
- Ariadne auf Naxos: Overture and Dance Scene, op.60

Stravinsky, Igor
- Suite No.1; For Small Orchestra
- Bluebird Pas de Deux
- Suite No.2; For Small Orchestra

Stürmer, Bruno
- Tanzsuite (Dance Suite), op.24

Swafford, Jan
- Late August

Szabelski, Bolesław
- Preludes

Szymanski, Pawel
- Intermezzo

Takács, Jenö
- Overtura Semiseria, op.69
- Volkstänze aus dem Burgenland, op.57

Tcherepnin, Alexander
- Suite populaire russe

Thiele, Siegfried
- Drei Orchestermotetten nach Machaut

Toch, Ernst
- Circus Overture

Tower, Joan
- Island Rhythms

Trantow, Herbert
- Kleine Tafelmusik

Treibmann, Karl Ottomar
- Capriccio 71

Trojahn, Manfred
- Mit durchscheinender Melancholie

Tull, Fisher
- Capriccio

Uhl, Alfred
- Wiener Walzer

Vate, Nancy van de
- Variations for Chamber Orchestra

Vaughan Williams, Ralph
- English Folk Song Suite

Vercoe, Elizabeth
- Changes; A little music for Mozart

Vinter, Gilbert
- Christmas Sinfonietta

Vir, Param
- The Field of Opportunity

Wagenaar, Bernard
- Song of Mourning; A reflection upon the slain Dutch patriots

Wagner, Joseph
- Pastoral costarricense; Un recuerdo sentimental

Walton, William
- Siesta

Webern, Anton
- Symphony, op.21
- Variations, op.30

Weigl, Karl
- Comedy Overture, op.32
- Music for the Young

Weinberger, Jaromir
- Overture to a Knightly Play

Weiner, Leo
- Divertimento No.1, On old Hungarian folk dances, op.20
- Fasching; Carnival Humoresque, op.5
- Serenade for Small Orchestra in F minor, op.3

Westergaard, Peter
- Fünf Sätze

Wielecki, Tadeusz
- Melody with Accompaniment

Wiener, Karl
- Kammerstück für 12 Soloinstrumente, op.7

Yu, Julian
- Great Ornamented Fuga Canonica, op.17

Zbinden, Julien-François
- Orchalau Concerto, op.38

Zender, Hans
- Kalligraphie II

11' - 15'

STRING ORCHESTRA

Antheil, George
- Serenade

Antoniou, Theodore
- Kinesis ABCD for two String
  Groups, op.31

Armstrong, Craig
- Slow Movement

Arnell, Richard
- Classical Variations in C

Arnold, Malcolm
- Variations on a Ukranian Folk Song,
  op.9a

Babbitt, Milton
- Composition for String Orchestra
  and Tape
- Correspondences for String
  Orchestra and Tape

Bacewicz, Grażyna
- Simfonietta

Bäck, Sven-Erik
- A Game Around A Game
- Sumerkei

Banks, Don
- Equation I and II

Bates, Mason
- Icarian Rhapsody

Baur, Jürg
- Abbreviaturen
- Fresken

Bavicchi, John
- Canto I, op.96

Becker, Günther
- Correspondences II

Benjamin, Arthur
- Ballade

Bennett, Richard Rodney
- Metamorphoses
- Reflections on a 16th-Century Tune
- Reflections on a Theme of William
  Walton; For 11 solo strings

Bentzon, Jørgen
- Sinfonietta, op.41

Bentzon, Niels Viggo
- Copenhagen Concerto No.3,
  op.169

Berkeley, Lennox
- Antiphon
- Serenade for Strings
- Suite for Strings

Beyer, Frank Michael
- Passionato con Arietta
- Streicherfantasien; On a motif by
  Johann Sebastian Bach

- Versi

Blake, David
- Nocturne

Bliss, Arthur
- Two Contrasts for String Orchestra

Britten, Benjamin
- Variations on "Sellenger's Round";
  Aldeburgh Variations

Burkhard, Willy
- Toccata, op.55

Copland, Aaron
- Two Pieces

D'Alessandro, Raffaele
- Concerto Grosso, op.57

David, Johann Nepomuk
- Concerto No.2, Wk40/2

Dean, Brett
- Short Stories; Five Interludes for
  String Orchestra

Dessau, Paul
- Musik für 15 Streichinstrumente

Diamond, David
- Rounds for String Orchestra

Einem, Gottfried von
- Concertino Carintico, op.86

Elgar, Edward
- Serenade in E minor, op.20

Erbse, Heimo
- Capriccio, op.4

Erdmann, Dietrich
- Serenità notturna

Felder, David
- Gone Grey

Fennelly, Brian
- Sigol for Strings

Frank, Gabriela Lena
- Manchay Tiempo (Time of Fear)

Geiser, Walther
- Fantasie III für Streichorchester,
  op.39

Giefer, Willy
- Concerto per archi

Glass, Philip
- Phaedra

Gould, Morton
- Harvest

Greenbaum, Matthew
- Castelnau; For String Orchestra

Harbison, John
- Incidental Music to Shakespeare's
  "The Merchant of Venice"

Hidalgo, Manuel
- Einfache Musik

Hindson, Matthew
- Balkan Connection

Holloway, Robin
- Serenade in G, op.64a

Holmboe, Vagn
- Sinfonia 1, op.73
- Sinfonia 2, op.73
- Sinfonia 3, op.73

Holst, Gustav
- St. Paul's Suite, op.29, No.2

Juon, Paul
- Five Pieces for String Orchestra

Kancheli, Giya
- Largo and Allegro

Kats-Chernin, Elena
- Zoom and Zip

Kelterborn, Rudolf
- Kammersinfonie II
- Lamentationes
- Passions

Krek, Uroš
- Sinfonia per archi

Kulenty, Hanna
- Breathe

Laks, Simon
- Sinfonietta for Strings

Lees, Benjamin
- Interlude for String Orchestra

Lutosławski, Witold
- Musique funèbre

Maayani, Ami
- Songs of King Solomon

Maros, Rudolf
- Eufonia No.1

Martin, Frank
- Passacaille

Matthus, Siegfried
- Visionen

Milner, Anthony
- Concerto for String Orchestra

Moeschinger, Albert
- Fantasie, op.64
- Le Voyage

Moravec, Paul
- Aubade

Neubert, Günter
- Music for Strings in Three Parts

Nielsen, Carl
- Suite for Strings (Little Suite), op.1 /
  F.6

Nørgård, Per
- Metamorphose, op.4

Oldham, Arthur
- Divertimento

Panufnik, Andrzej
- Divertimento for Strings
- Old Polish Suite

Pärt, Arvo
- These Words...
- Trisagion

Rautavaara, Einojuhani
- Divertimento

Redel, Martin Christoph
- Traumtanz
Rosenberg, Hilding Constantin
- Suite on Popular Swedish Folk
  Melodies
Schauss, Ernst
- Serenade
Schenker, Friedrich
- Little Symphony
Schultz, Wolfgang-Andreas
- Was mir die Aeolsharfe erzählt...
Schwarz-Schilling, Reinhard
- Introduction and Fugue
Schwertsik, Kurt
- Möbelmusik-Klassisch, op.68
Sheinkman, Mordechai
- Serenade
Shostakovich, Dmitri
- Two Pieces; Prelude and Scherzo,
  op.11
Sibelius, Jean
- Rakastava, op.14
Stranz, Ulrich
- Sieben Feld-, Wald- und
  Wiesenstücke
Stravinsky, Igor
- Concerto in D
Strohbach, Siegfried
- Serenade in D major
Thärichen, Werner
- Divertimento, op.57
Thomas, Augusta Read
- Murmurs in the Mist of Memory
Tower, Joan
- In Memory
Treibmann, Karl Ottomar
- Symphony for 15 Strings
Volans, Kevin
- Joining Up The Dots
Voss, Friedrich
- Concerto da camera
- Fantasia
Webern, Anton
- Fünf Sätze, op.5
Weiner, Leo
- Divertimento No.2 in A minor;
  Hungarian Folk Melodies, op.24
Weiss, Manfred
- Music for Strings
Wittinger, Róbert
- Sinfonia, op.18
Wolschina, Reinhard
- Vier Aphorismen
Zimmermann, Udo
- Music for Strings
Zwilich, Ellen Taaffe
- Prologue and Variations

ENSEMBLE

Abrahamsen, Hans
- Märchenbilder
Adès, Thomas
- Chamber Symphony, op.2
Aguila, Miguel del
- A Conga Line in Hell, op.43
Ali-Zadeh, Franghiz
- Crossing II
- Dilogie II for Nine Players
Anderson, Allen
- Charrette
Anderson, Julian
- Alhambra Fantasy
- Khorovod
Anderson, T.J.
- Chamber Symphony
Aperghis, Georges
- In extremis; Pour 8 Instrumentistes
- Pièce pour douze, op.99
- Variations pour quatorze
  instruments
Baggiani, Guido
- Double
- Memoria
Baird, Tadeusz
- Four Novelettes
Ballif, Claude
- Imaginaire No.1, op.41, No.1
- La musique d'Erich Zahn
- Le Taille-Lyre, op.64, No.1
Banks, Don
- Equation I and II
- Sonata da Camera; In Memoriam
  Matyas Seiber
Bawden, Rupert
- The Donkey Dances
Becker, Günther
- Correspondences II
Beltrami, Marco
- Iskios; City of Shadows
Benjamin, George
- Three Inventions for Chamber
  Orchestra
Bennett, Richard Rodney
- Metamorphoses
Bentzon, Niels Viggo
- Sonata for 12 Instruments, op.257
Berio, Luciano
- Chemins II (su Sequenza VI)
Bermel, Derek
- Natural Selection
- Three Rivers
Berners, Lord
- L'Uomo dai Baffi
Birkenkötter, Jörg
- Four Pieces for Ensemble

Birtwistle, Sir Harrison
- Carmen Arcadiae Perpetuum
- Silbury Air
- Tragoedia
Boccadoro, Carlo
- Ae Fond Kiss; For 7 instruments
Bon, André
- Travelling
Bonnet, Antoine
- La terre habitable I; Les eaux
  étroites
- La terre habitable IV; La presqu'île
Boone, Charles
- Second Landscape
Bose, Hans-Jürgen von
- Prozess
- Travesties in a Sad Landscape
Boyle, Rory
- Night Pictures
Britten, Benjamin
- Sinfonietta, op.1
Brown, Earle
- Sign Sounds
Bryars, Gavin
- Aus den Letzten Tagen
Buck, Ole
- A Tree
Cassuto, Alvaro
- Song of Loneliness
Cerha, Friedrich
- Quellen
Chen, Qigang
- Luminères de Guang-Ling
Cowell, Henry
- Sinfonietta
Dalby, Martin
- De Patre Ex Filio
Dazzi, Gualtiero
- Sable; In Memoriam Edmond Jabès
Debussy, Claude
- Petite suite
Delás, José Luis de
- Concetti; Musica para Gesualdo di
  Venosa
- Denkbild - Kurze Schatten
- Imago
Denhoff, Michael
- Einsamkeit; In Memoriam W.
  Buchebner
Denisov, Edison
- Femme et Oiseaux
Dickinson, Peter
- Juilliard Dances
Dobbins, Lori
- Music for Chamber Orchestra
Döhl, Friedhelm
- Octet (Varianti)
Duddell, Joe
- Alberti Addict

334

Einem, Gottfried von
 - Steinbeis-Serenade; Variations, op.61
Eisler, Hanns
 - Suite for Orchestra No.2: From the music to the film *Niemandsland*, op.24
 - Suite for Orchestra No.3: From the music to the film *Kuhle Wampe*, op.26
 - Suite for Orchestra No.6: From the music to the film *Le Grand Jeu*, op.40
Engelmann, Hans Ulrich
 - Ciacona
 - Sinfonia da Camera
Erdmann, Dietrich
 - Epitaph
 - Musica Multicolore
 - Nuancen
Feldman, Morton
 - For Frank O'Hara
Firsova, Elena
 - Music for Twelve
Fontyn, Jacqueline
 - Nonetto
Franke, Bernd
 - Konform - Kontraform
Frankel, Benjamin
 - Bagatelles "Cinque Pezzi Notturni"
Fuchs, Kenneth
 - Out of the Dark (After Three Paintings by Helen Frankenthaler)
Furrer, Beat
 - In der Stille des Hauses wohnt ein Ton (In the silence of the house there lives a sound)
Genzmer, Harald
 - Capriccio für Kammerorchester (Nonett)
Goehr, Alexander
 - ...a musical offering (J. S. B. 1985)
Grainger, Percy Aldridge
 - Hill Song
Gubaidulina, Sofia
 - Concordanza
Gürsching, Albrecht
 - Piccola Sinfonia; Septett Nr.2
Guy, Barry
 - Bitz!
Haas, Georg Friedrich
 - "...aus freier Lust...verbunden..."
 - "...Einklang freier Wesen..."
 - Monodie
Hagen, Daron
 - Chimera; A song cycle for speaker and seven players

Halffter, Rodolfo
 - Divertimento Para Nueve Instrumentos
Harbison, John
 - Confinement
Harvey, Jonathan
 - Soleil Noir / Chitra
 - Tendril
 - Valley of Aosta
Haubenstock-Ramati, Roman
 - Séquences 2
Hauer, Josef Matthias
 - 1. Tanzsuite, op.70
Hayden, Sam
 - Collateral Damage
Henze, Hans Werner
 - Three Mozart Organ Sonatas for 14 Players
Hesketh, Kenneth
 - Netsuke
 - Three Movements from "Theatrum"
 - Torturous Instruments
Hidalgo, Manuel
 - Nahezu Stilles Auge des Wirbelsturms
 - L'Obvio
Hindemith, Paul
 - Kammermusik No.1 (with Finale 1921), op.24, No.1
Hindson, Matthew
 - Technologic 145
Holmboe, Vagn
 - Prelude to a Dolphin, op.166
 - Prelude to a Living Stone, op.172
Holt, Simon
 - Capriccio Spettrale
 - Era Madrugada
 - Kites
 - Lilith
Horváth, Josef Maria
 - Origines
Hosokawa, Toshio
 - Garten Lieder (Garden Songs)
Huggler, John
 - Sinfonia for 13 Players, op.78
Indy, Vincent d'
 - Suite dans le style ancien, op.24
Kahn, Erich Itor
 - Actus Tragicus
Kahowez, Günther
 - Bardo-Puls; Musik nach dem tibetanischen Totenbuch
Kallstenius, Edvin
 - Suite for 9 Instruments, op.23b
 - Suite for 14 Instruments, op.23c
Kisielewski, Stefan
 - Rencontres dans un désert
 - Symphony for 15 Performers

Kitzke, Jerome
 - Present Music
Knussen, Oliver
 - Processionals, op.2
 - Requiem, Songs for Sue, op.33
Komorous, Rudolf
 - Rossi
Koppel, Anders
 - Concertino for Chamber Ensemble
 - Seven Scenes from Everyday Cow Life
Krása, Hans
 - Brundibár: Suite from the opera
Krauze, Zygmunt
 - Tableau Vivant
Krenek, Ernst
 - Small Symphony, op.58
Lampersberg, Gerhard
 - Symphony
Lang, David
 - increase
Layton, Billy Jim
 - Divertimento, op.6
Lehmann, Hans Ulrich
 - Chamber Music II
León, Tania
 - Hechizos
 - sin normas ajenas
Leyendecker, Ulrich
 - Jiddische Rumba
Lieberson, Peter
 - Accordance for 8 Instruments
Ligeti, György
 - Melodien
Lindberg, Magnus
 - Arena II
 - Corrente
 - Corrente - China Version
 - Coyote Blue
 - Duo Concertante
 - Jubilees
 - Tendenza
Loevendie, Theo
 - Back Bay Bicinium
 - Laps
Lord, David
 - Septet
Lorentzen, Bent
 - Paesaggio
 - Paradiesvogel
 - Wunderblumen
 - Zauberspiegel
Lutyens, Elisabeth
 - Six Tempi for 10 Instruments
Malipiero, Gian Francesco
 - Endecatode; For 14 instruments and percussion
Marsh, Roger
 - Dying for It

Martinů, Bohuslav
- Tre Ricercari, H.267
Martland, Steve
- Remembering Lennon
Mason, Benedict
- The Hinterstoisser Traverse
- Imposing a Regular Pattern in
  Chaos and Heterophony
Matsushita, Shin-ichi
- Haleines Astrals
Matthews, Colin
- Contraflow
- Hidden Variables
- Tosca Revisited
- Two Tributes
- A Voice to Wake
Matthus, Siegfried
- Ich komm einen Weg
- Octet on an Octet
Maxwell Davies, Peter
- Ricercar and Doubles on "To many
  a well"
McKinley, William Thomas
- Paintings No.6 (To hear the light
  dancing)
Milhaud, Darius
- Concert de chambre, op.389
- La creation du monde; Ballet,
  op.81a
- Musique pour Ars Nova, op.432
- Musique pour Graz, op.429
Mochizuki, Misato
- 4 D
- La Chambre Claire
- Chimera
Moravec, Paul
- Northern Lights Electric
Morthenson, Jan Wilhelm
- Labor
Muldowney, Dominic
- Entr'acte
- Solo / Ensemble
Müller-Hornbach, Gerhard
- Passacaglia II
Müller-Siemens, Detlev
- Pavane
- Phoenix 1
- Phoenix 3
- Refuge
- Variationen über einen Ländler von
  Schubert (Variations on a Landler
  by Schubert)
Müller-Wieland, Jan
- Narrativo e Sonnambulo
- Der Revolutionsplatz
Mundry, Isabel
- Schwankende Zeit
- Le Silence; Tystnaden

Musgrave, Thea
- Chamber Concerto No.1
- Chamber Concerto No.2
Mykietyn, Paweł
- Eine Kleine Herbstmusik (A Little
  Autumn Music)
Nancarrow, Conlon
- Three Movements
Nono, Luigi
- Canti Per 13
Nordentoft, Anders
- Entgegen
Nordheim, Arne
- Tractatus
Nørgård, Per
- Prelude and Fugue (With a Crab
  Canon)
Nørholm, Ib
- The Garden With The Paths That
  Part, op.86
Osborne, Nigel
- Fantasia
- Stone Garden
Paccagnini, Angelo
- Musica da Camera
Pape, Andy
- Min Fynske Barndom: Suite
Patterson, Paul
- At the Still Point of the Turning
  World, op.41
Pauels, Heinz
- Capriccio; For piano, five solo
  instruments and percussion, op.92b
Paumgartner, Bernhard
- Divertimento; 5 old-english dances
Pavlenko, Sergei
- Symphony No.3 for Chamber
  Orchestra (For the Centenary of
  Igor Stravinsky)
Payne, Anthony
- A Sea Change
- Symphonies of Wind and Rain
Pernes, Thomas
- Gesänge
Phibbs, Joseph
- Cayuga
Piston, Walter
- Divertimento
Platz, Robert H. P.
- From Fear of Thunder, Dreams…
Pousseur, Henri
- Symphonies à Quinze Solistes
Powell, Mel
- Modules, An Intermezzo for
  Chamber Orchestra
Primosch, James
- Septet
Qu, Xiao-song
- Ji No.1

Rasmussen, Karl Aage
- Berio Mask
- Italian Concerto
Redel, Martin Christoph
- Dispersion, op.16
Reimann, Aribert
- Metamorphosen über ein Menuett
  von Franz Schubert
Rihm, Wolfgang
- Chiffre II; Silence to be beaten
- Chiffre VII
- Verborgene Formen
Rodríguez, Robert Xavier
- Five Études
Rosing-Schow, Niels
- Equinoxe
- Meeting
Roslavets, Nikolai Andreyevich
- Chamber Symphony
- Chamber Symphony; For 18 solo
  instruments
Rushton, Edward
- Lost City Life
Samazeuilh, Gustave
- Divertissement et Musette
Satie, Erik
- Sports et Divertissements
Sawer, David
- Tiroirs
Saxton, Robert
- Canzona; In Memoriam Igor
  Stravinsky
- Processions and Dances
- Traumstadt
Scherchen, Tona
- Tjao-Houen
Schnittke, Alfred
- Little Tragedies: Suite from the
  music to the film
Schubert, Manfred
- Septet in Two Movements
Schuller, Gunther
- Chimeric Images
Schweitzer, Benjamin
- unplugged. unperfumed
Sekles, Bernhard
- Serenade for 11 Solo Instruments,
  op.14
Shchedrin, Rodion
- The Frescoes of Dionysus for Nine
  Instruments
- The Geometry of Sound
Sierra, Roberto
- Concertino
- Cuentos
Silverman, Stanley
- Planh; For chamber ensemble

Smirnov, Dmitri
- Jacob's Ladder, op.58
- The River of Life, op.66
Smolka, Martin
- Solitudo
Sørensen, Bent
- Minnewater; Thousands of Canons
- Minnelieder - Zweites Minnewater
- Sirenengesang
Sotelo, Mauricio
- De Imaginum, Signorum, et
  Idearum Compositione I
Spratlan, Lewis
- Diary Music I
Stahmer, Klaus Hinrich
- Dans Une Lumière Eclatante
Staud, Johannes Maria
- Berenice: Suite 2
Stockhausen, Karlheinz
- Kontra-Punkte Nr.1
Szalonek, Witold
- Connections
Szymanski, Pawel
- Through the Looking Glass I
Takemitsu, Tōru
- Archipelago S.
- Tree Line
- Water Ways
Talbot, Joby
- Animisation
Tavener, John
- Grandma's Footsteps
Taylor, Deems
- The Portrait of a Lady, op.14
Torke, Michael
- Adjustable Wrench
Treibmann, Karl Ottomar
- Second Symphonic Essay; For ten
  instruments
Ullmann, Jakob
- Composition for 10 Instruments I-V
Vines, Nicholas
- Firestick
Vir, Param
- Hayagriva
Vivier, Claude
- Deva et Asura
Volans, Kevin
- Joining Up The Dots
Wallin, Rolf
- Solve et Coagula
Webern, Anton
- Passacaglia, op.1
- Sechs Stücke, op.6
Weir, Judith
- Musicians Wrestle Everywhere
- Tiger under the Table
Wilby, Philip
- An Imagined Fable

Wilson, Ian
- ...and flowers fall...
Wilson, Richard
- Contentions
Wolpe, Stefan
- Piece for Two Instrumental Units
Woolrich, John
- After the Clock
- Lending Wings
Xenakis, Iannis
- Anaktoria
- Atrées
- Jalons
- Palimpsest
- Phlegra
Ye, Xiaogang
- Strophe
Yu, Julian
- Philopentatonia, op.32
Yun, Isang
- Impression
- Kammerkonzert II (Chamber
  Concerto II)
Zender, Hans
- 4 Enso (LO-SHU VII)

CHAMBER ORCHESTRA

Abels, Michael
- More Seasons
Absil, Jean
- Introduction et Valses
- Petite Suite, op.20
Adams, John
- Chairman Dances, Foxtrot for
  Orchestra
Aguila, Miguel del
- Conga for Orchestra, op.44
- A Conga Line in Hell, op.40
Alizade, Akshin
- Symphony No.4
Ali-Zadeh, Franghiz
- Sturm und Drang for Chamber
  Orchestra
Alnar, Hasan Ferit
- Zwei Türkische Orchesterstücke;
  Improvisation und zwei Tänze
Alwyn, William
- Concerto Grosso No.1 in Bb
Antheil, George
- Music to a World's Fair Film
Antoniou, Theodore
- Events III; Music for Orchestra,
  Tape and Slide-Projection
- Op Ouvertüre für Orchester und
  drei Lautsprechergruppen
  (Tonband)

Apostel, Hans Erich
- Five Austrian Miniatures
- Variations on Three Folksongs,
  op.23
Ardevol, José
- Concerto Grosso No.1
Arnold, Malcolm
- Serenade for Small Orchestra
- Sinfonietta No.1, op.48
- Sinfonietta No.2, op.65
- Sinfonietta No.3
Asia, Daniel
- Rivalries
Auric, Georges
- La Peintre et son Modèle; Ballet in
  one act
Avshalomov, Jacob
- Cues from "The Little Clay Cart"
Bäck, Sven-Erik
- Chamber Symphony
- Fantasia on "Dies Sind Die Heiligen
  Zehn Gebot"
Bacri, Nicolas
- Symphony No.4; Symphonie
  Classique Sturm und Drang, op.49
Barclay, Robert Lenard
- Nocturne and Scherzo
- Symphony in One Movement
Bartók, Béla
- Two Portraits, op.5
Bates, Mason
- Music from Underground Spaces
- Rusty Air in Carolina
Baur, Jürg
- Triton-Sinfonietta; Drei Grotesken
Bavicchi, John
- Concertante, op.44
Becker, John J.
- When the Willow Nods: Second
  Suite in one Movement from Stage
  Work No.5-b
Bedford, David
- This One For You
- The Transfiguration: A Meditation
Benjamin, Arthur
- Light Music Suite
- Sonatina for Chamber Orchestra
Bennett, Richard Rodney
- Country Dances; Book 1
- Nocturnes
- Serenade for Small Orchestra
Bentzon, Niels Viggo
- Mini-Symphony, op.231
- Pupitre 14, op.339
Bergsma, William
- Symphony for Chamber Orchestra
Berio, Luciano
- Chemins IIb

337

Berkeley, Lennox
- Nocturne, op.25
- Partita, op.66
- Sinfonietta, op.34
- Windsor Variations, op.75
Besch, Otto
- Divertimento
Beynon, Jared
- Unicorn
Bialas, Günter
- Sinfonia Piccola
Binkerd, Gordon
- Movement for Orchestra
- Symphony No.3
Birtwistle, Sir Harrison
- Three Movements with Fanfares
Blacher, Boris
- Concertante Musik
- Lysistrata: Suite from the ballet
- Studie im Pianissimo
- Two Inventions
Blake, David
- Sonata alla Marchia
Bleyle, Karl
- Schneewittchensuite, op.50
Bloch, Ernest
- Four Episodes
Boelter, Karl
- Dharma
Bon, André
- Ode; Pour orchestre "Mozart"
- Ode II; Pour orchestre de chambre
Bond, Victoria
- Journal
Bose, Hans-Jürgen von
- Musik für ein Haus voll Zeit
Brandmüller, Theo
- Reminiszenzen
Brauel, Henning
- Les Fenêtres Simultanées
Braun, Yehezkel
- Serenade for Chamber Orchestra
Britten, Benjamin
- Sinfonietta, op.1
- Soirées musicales, op.9; Suite of Five Movements from Rossini
- Suite on English Folk Tunes, op.90
Brust, Herbert
- Kurische Nehrung, op.36
- Ostpreußische Fischertänze, op.34
Burgon, Geoffrey
- The Chronicles of Narnia Suite
- Suite from Bleak House
Bush, Alan
- Partita Concertante, op.63
Busoni, Ferruccio
- Concertante Suite from W. A. Mozart's Opera "Idomeneo" (Busoni Verz. B85)

- Tanzwalzer, op.53 (Busoni Verz. 288)
Cage, John
- The Seasons; Ballet in One Act
Campo, Frank
- Partita for Two Chamber Orchestras, op.45
Casella, Alfredo
- Divertimento Per Fulvia: Suite from "La camera dei diseegni," op.64
Castro, José Maria
- Concerto Grosso
Cerha, Friedrich
- Sinfonie
Chapple, Brian
- Little Symphony
Chávez, Carlos
- Sinfonía de Antígona (Symphony No.1)
- Sinfonía India (Symphony No.2)
Cohn, James
- Sinfonietta in F
- Variations on The Wayfaring Stranger
Coleman, Linda Robbins
- For A Beautiful Land
Conyngham, Barry
- Glimpses of Bennelong
Coolidge, Peggy Stuart
- Pioneer Dances
Cooper, Paul
- Love Songs and Dances; Concertante for 21 Players
Copland, Aaron
- Orchestral Variations
- Prairie Journal
- Three Latin American Sketches
Cordero, Roque
- Ocho Miniaturas
Cowell, Henry
- Old American Country Set
- Ongaku
- Symphonic Set, op.17
Creston, Paul
- Out of the Cradle Endlessly Rocking; After the poem by Walt Whitman
Cruft, Adrian
- Partita, op.7
Dalby, Martin
- Nozze di Primavera
Danielpour, Richard
- First Light
- Souvenirs
Daugherty, Michael
- Sunset Strip
David, Johann Nepomuk
- Chaconne, Wk71

Dean, Brett
- Testament; Music for orchestra, after "Testament: Music for twelve violas"
Delius, Frederick
- Petite Suite No.1
- Two Pieces for Small Orchestra
Diamond, David
- Concerto for Small Orchestra
- Heroic Piece
Donato, Anthony
- Serenade for Small Orchestra
Druckman, Jacob
- Nor Spell, Nor Charm
Dubois, Pierre-Max
- Analogie; Suite for Orchestra
- Sérieux s'abstenir
Einem, Gottfried von
- Bruckner Dialog, op.39
- Nachtstück, op.29
- Tanz-Rondo, op.27
Eisler, Hanns
- Five Pieces for Orchestra: From the music to the film The 400 Million
- Suite No.1: From the movie Opus III, op.23
- Three Pieces for Orchestra: From the music to the film The 400 Million
Ekström, Lars
- Järnnatten (The Lonely Night)
Engelmann, Hans Ulrich
- Partita
- Shadows; Scenes for Orchestra
- Strukturen; Den Taten der neuen Bildhauer
Erdmann, Eduard
- Ständchen, op.16
Etler, Alvin
- Music for Chamber Orchestra
Ettinger, Max
- An den Wassern Babylons; Songs of Babylonian Jews for Small Orchestra
Falla, Manuel de
- El Sombrero des Tres Picos: Suite No.1
Fauré, Gabriel
- Masques et Bergamasques, op.112
- Symphony in F major
Felder, David
- Journal
Ferguson, Howard
- Four Diversions on Ulster Airs, op.7
Finke, Fidelio
- Eight Bagatelles
Firsova, Elena
- Autumn Music, op.39

Fletcher, Horace Grant
- Two Orchestral Pieces for Small Orchestra

Fómina, Silvia
- Permanenza; Für mikropolyphonisches, im Raum verteiltes Orchester

Foulds, John
- Keltic Suite, op.29

Frackenpohl, Arthur
- Divertimento in F

Frank, Gabriela Lena
- Elegía Andina

Frazelle, Kenneth
- Laconic Variations

Fundal, Karsten
- Oscillation

Gaslini, Giorgio
- Canto Dalla Città Inquieta: From "Totale"

Gaubert, Philippe
- Rhapsodie sur des thèmes populaires

Gauldin, Robert
- Diverse Dances

Geissler, Fritz
- Chamber Symphony (1954)
- Five Miniatures

German, Sir Edward
- Gipsy Suite; Four characteristic dances
- Tom Jones: Three Dances

Gerster, Ottmar
- Oberhessische Bauerntänze für Kleines Orchester

Gilbert, Anthony
- Tree of Singing Names

Ginastera, Alberto
- Estancia: Four Dances from Estancia, op.8a

Girnatis, Walter
- Festmusik der Schiffergilde

Glass, Philip
- The Secret Agent: Three Pieces

Gnessin, Mikhail
- Jewish Orchestra at the Burgermaster's Ball

Godfrey, Daniel Strong
- Concentus

Goeb, Roger
- Prairie Songs

Goehr, Alexander
- Still Lands

Górecki, Henryk Mikołaj
- Three Dances, op.34

Gruber, HK
- Manhattan Broadcast

Hahn, Reynaldo
- La Fête Chez Thérèse: Suite No.2

Haieff, Alexei Vasilievich
- Divertimento

Halffter, Ernesto
- Las Doncellas

Halffter, Rodolfo
- La Madrugada del Panadero: Suite del Ballet

Hallberg, Björn Wilho
- Novelletten

Hallén, Andreas
- In Autumn (Om hösten)

Hamilton, Iain
- Arias
- Sonata, op.34

Harbison, John
- Canonical American Songbook

Hartley, Walter Sinclair
- Chamber Symphony
- Concertino for Chamber Ensemble

Harty, Hamilton
- Fantasy Scenes: From an Eastern Romance

Hasquenoph, Pierre
- Variations en Trois Mouvements

Helfer, Walter
- A Fantasy on Children's Tunes
- Prelude to a Midsummer Night's Dream

Helm, Everett
- Italienische Suite
- Serenade

Herrera de la Fuente, Luis
- Fronteras, Ballet

Hesketh, Kenneth
- After Verdi!; Divertimento in five sections
- Danceries

Hier, Ethel Glenn
- Carolina Christmas; Suite for Chamber Orchestra

Holloway, Robin
- First Idyll, op.42
- Ode, op.45
- Third Idyll, Frost at Midnight, op.78

Holmboe, Vagn
- Prelude to the Victoria Embankment, op.184
- Vinter, op.194

Honegger, Arthur
- Suite Archaïque, H.203

Horne, David
- Persistence

Horovitz, Joseph
- Sinfonietta for Light Orchestra

Hovhaness, Alan
- Zartik Parkim (Awake my Glory)

Hutcheson, Jere
- Taj Mahal

Ifukube, Akira
- Triptyque aborigène; Trois tableaux pour orchestre de chambre

Inghelbrecht, D.E.
- La Métamorphose d'Ève, Ballet

Ishii, Maki
- Sieben Stücke (Seven Pieces)

Ives, Charles Edward
- Four Ragtime Dances

Jacob, Gordon
- Divertimento
- Suite in F for Small Orchestra

James, Dorothy
- Suite for Small Orchestra

Kahn, Erich Itor
- Petite Suite Bretonne

Kelly, Bryan
- Cookham Concertino

Kelterborn, Rudolf
- Four Movements for Classical Orchestra
- Traummusik; 6 Stücke für kleines Orchester
- Vier Nachtstücke für Kammerorchester

Kirchner, Volker David
- Bildnisse II
- Bildnisse III

Kisielewski, Stefan
- Concerto for Chamber Orchestra

Klebe, Giselher
- Divertissement joyeux, op.5
- Scene und Arie, op.54

Koc, Marcelo
- Tres Piezas Para Orquesta

Koch, Erland von
- Ballet Suite: Peter Tailless, the Cat
- Four Swedish Folk Melodies
- Three Miniatures for Orchestra

Kodály, Zoltán
- Dances of Galanta
- Marosszéker Tänze

Kolb, Barbara
- Yet That Things Go Round

Kósa, György
- Chamber Music

Krätzschmar, Wilfried
- Ballets imaginaires

Krol, Bernhard
- Concerto Grosso, op.15

Kulenty, Hanna
- Trigon

Kurz, Siegfried
- Sonatina for Orchestra, op.34

Lambert, Constant
- Comus: Suite from the Ballet to Purcell's music

Lampersberg, Gerhard
- Verwirrung; Concerto for Cello

Larsson, Lars-Erik
- Divertimento, op.15
- Gustaviansk Suite, op.28
Lavista, Mario
- Lacrymosa
Leigh, Walter
- Suite from Shakespeare's "A
  Midsummer Night's Dream"
Leplin, Emanuel
- Three Dances for Small Orchestra
Levy, Marvin David
- Trialogus II
Leyendecker, Ulrich
- Verwandlung; Four Pieces for
  Chamber Orchestra
Lindberg, Magnus
- Marea
Linke, Norbert
- Divisioni
- Konkretionen V
Locklair, Dan
- In the Autumn Days
Ludewig, Wolfgang
- Fantasia; On a Theme by W. A.
  Mozart
Lutosławski, Witold
- Little Suite
- Ten Polish Dances
Maasz, Gerhard
- Musik (Nr.1)
- Tripartita
MacMillan, James
- The Sacrifice: Three Interludes
MacRae, Stuart
- Portrait II
Maganini, Quinto
- An Ornithological Suite, op.23
Magnard, Albéric
- Chant Funebre, op.9
Malipiero, Gian Francesco
- Oriente Immaginario; Tre stui per
  piccola orchestra
- Ritrovari
Manén, Joan
- Divertimento, op.A-32
Maros, Rudolf
- Gemma; In Memoriam Zoltán
  Kodály
Marquez, Arturo
- Danzón No.2
- Danzón No.4
Martinů, Bohuslav
- Concerto Grosso
- Sérénade; Pour orchestre de
  chambre
Matthews, Colin
- Dowlandia
Matthews, David
- Burnham Wick, op.73

Maxwell Davies, Peter
- An Orkney Wedding, with Sunrise;
  Version for Chamber Orchestra
McAlister, Clark
- A Christmas Pastorale
McCabe, John
- Concerto for Chamber Orchestra
- Red Leaves
- The Lion, the Witch and the
  Wardrobe: Suite
McGlaughlin, William
- Aaron's Horizons
McKay, George Frederick
- Fantasy on a Western Folk Song;
  O! Bury me not on the lone prairie
- Variants on a Texas Tune; Mustang
  grey
Meale, Richard
- Variations
Milford, Robin
- Suite for Chamber Orchestra
Milhaud, Darius
- Le boeuf sur le toit; Ballet, op.58
- Musique pour San Francisco,
  op.436
- Sérénade, op.62
Milner, Anthony
- Chamber Symphony
Mitsukuri, Shukichi
- Sinfonietta in D Major
Moore, Douglas
- Village Music
Moravec, Paul
- Ancient Lights
- Sempre Diritto! (Straight Ahead)
- Streamline
Morawetz, Oskar
- Overture to a Fairy Tale
Morris, Harold
- Variations on the American Negro
  Spiritual "I was Way Down A-
  Yonder"
Morthenson, Jan Wilhelm
- Antiphonia I
Moyzes, Alexander
- Slowakische Volkslieder, op.15
Neikrug, Marc
- Chetro Ketl
Neubert, Günter
- Music for Orchestra on a Theme by
  Robert Schumann
Nilsson, Bo
- Taqsim-Caprice-Maqam
Nørgård, Per
- Aspects of Leaving
- Tango Chikane (reduced version)
Nussio, Otmar
- Boccaccio-Suite; Novelle dal
  Decamerone

Paccagnini, Angelo
- Dialoghi
Patterson, Paul
- Europhony, op.55
Paumgartner, Bernhard
- Suite in G minor
Payne, Anthony
- Spring's Shining Wake
Pfitzner, Hans
- Das Christ-Elflein, op.20
Piazzolla, Astor
- Tangazo; Variations on Buenos
  Aires
Polovinkin, Leonid
- Tänze der Rätsel
Porrino, Ennio
- Notturno e Danza
Prokofiev, Sergei
- Classical Symphony in D,
  Symphony No.1, op.25
- Divertimento, op.43
- Festive Poem "Thirty Years"
- A Summer Day, op.65a
Quilter, Roger
- A Children's Overture, op.17
- Where the Rainbow Ends: Suite
Quinet, Marcel
- Sinfonietta
Rasmussen, Karl Aage
- Symphonie Classique
Read, Gardner
- Partita for Small Orchestra, op.70
Redel, Martin Christoph
- Kammersinfonie II (Chamber
  Symphony II), op.17
Revueltas, Silvestre
- Le Noche de los Mayas
Riege, Ernst
- Rondo Giocoso
Riegger, Wallingford
- Dichotomy, op.12
Rieti, Vittorio
- Due Pastorali
- Sinfonietta per Piccola Orchestra
Rihm, Wolfgang
- Dunkles Spiel
Rochberg, George
- Cheltenham Concerto
Rodrigo, Joaquín
- Musica para un Jardín
- Palillos y Panderetas; Música para
  una tonadilla imaginaria
Rogers, Bernard
- Five Fairy Tales (Once Upon a
  Time)
- The Plains
Ropartz, Joseph Guy Marie
- Cinq pièces brèves
- Sons de Cloches

Rorem, Ned
- Ideas; For easy orchestra
Rosenberg, Hilding Constantin
- Dance Suite from the Grand Opera
  "The Marionettes"
Rouse, Christopher
- Iscariot
Roussel, Albert
- Concert pour petit orchestre, op.34
Rueda, Jesús
- Elephant Skin
Saariaho, Kaija
- Verblendungen
Salmhofer, Franz
- Overture
Salviucci, Giovanni
- Sinfonia da Camera
Satie, Erik
- Cinéma: Entr'acte symphonique du
  ballet "Relâche"
Saxton, Robert
- The Ring of Eternity
Schafer, Robert Murray
- Cortège
Scherchen, Tona
- Khouang
Schlee, Thomas Daniel
- Sonata da Camera, op.42
Schmitt, Florent
- Enfants, op.94
- Pupazzi, op.36
- Reflets d'Allemagne, op.28
Schnittke, Alfred
- Suite in Old Style
Schollum, Robert
- Sonate
- Tanzsuite, Werk 21
Schuller, Gunther
- Chamber Symphony
- Journey to the Stars
Schweitzer, Benjamin
- flekkicht; For baroque orchestra
Scott, Cyril
- Suite Phantastique
Sgrizzi, Luciano
- Englische Suite nach Werken der
  Virginalisten
- Suite Belge; D'après des œuvres
  de clavecinistes belges du 18ème
  siècle
Shchetinsky, Alexander
- Glossolalie
Sheng, Bright
- Postcards
Sibelius, Jean
- Belsazars Gaestabud (Belshazzar's
  Feast); Incidental Music, op.51
- Scenes Historique I, op.25

Sierra, Roberto
- Descarga
- The Güell Concerto (2006)
- Serenata
Sjöblom, Heimer
- Liten Svit I Spelmanston
Slonimsky, Sergei
- Concerto Buffo
Staempfli, Edward
- Präludium und Variationen
Standford, Patric
- Notte
Stanford, Charles Villiers
- Suite of Ancient Dances, op.58
Steffen, Wolfgang
- Kammerkonzert, op.48
Stevens, Bernard
- Introduction, Variations & Fugue on
  a Theme of Giles Farnaby
Stockhausen, Karlheinz
- Formel, Nr.1/6
Stranz, Ulrich
- Anstieg - Ausblick für Orchester
Stravinsky, Igor
- Concerto in E-flat "Dumbarton
  Oaks"
Šulek, Stjepan
- Concerto Classique
Suter, Robert
- Epitaffio
Sutermeister, Heinrich
- Sérénade pour Montreux
Swafford, Jan
- Chamber Sinfonietta
Swanson, Howard
- Short Symphony
Szymanski, Pawel
- Sixty-Odd Pages
Takács, Jenö
- Eisenstädter Divertimento; Suite,
  op.75
Takemitsu, Tōru
- Eucalypts I
Tansman, Alexandre
- Suite Baroque
Tcherepnin, Alexander
- La Femme et son Ombre: Ballet
  Suite
Terzakis, Dimitri
- Hommage à Dionysos
- Tropi
Thiele, Siegfried
- Intrada, Cantus, Toccata
- Wolkenbilder; Four Movements
Tomlinson, Ernest
- A Georgian Miniature
Tower, Joan
- The Last Dance
- Made in America

Trexler, Georg
- Introduzione e Scherzo
- Small Suite
Turnage, Mark-Anthony
- On All Fours
Vincent, John
- Suite from the Ballet "Three Jacks"
Vinci, Albert
- Dance Suite
Vinter, Gilbert
- Dance of the Marionettes
Vuataz, Roger
- Petit Concert, op.39
Wagenaar, Bernard
- Sinfonietta
Wagner, Joseph
- Four Miniatures
Weigl, Karl
- Pictures and Tales; Suite for small
  orchestra, op.2
Weingartner, Felix
- Overture to Shakespeare's "The
  Tempest," op.65
Weir, Judith
- Isti Mirant Stella
Weiss, Manfred
- Abendmusik
Wellejus, Henning
- Vor Barndoms Venner (Our
  Childhood Friends), op.15
Westerman, Gerhart von
- Kleine Suite, op.3
Wilby, Philip
- The Wings of Morning
Willi, Herbert
- Für 16; Kleines Kammerkonzert
  (For 16; Small Chamber Concerto)
Wimberger, Gerhard
- Concertino per orchestra
- Multiplay; Kanonische Reflexionen
  für 23 Spieler (Kammerorchester)
Winters, Geoffrey
- Concertino, op.18
Wunsch, Hermann
- Fest auf Monbijou, op.50
Yu, Julian
- First Australian Suite, op.22
- Not a Stream but an Ocean
Zimmermann, Udo
- Tänzerinnen; Choreographies
  based on E. Degas

16' - 20'

STRING ORCHESTRA

Adamo, Mark
 - Alcott Music: Suite from "Little
   Women"
Arutiunian, Alexander
 - Sinfonietta
Bäck, Sven-Erik
 - Four Motets for Strings
 - Sinfonia per archi
Baird, Tadeusz
 - String Quartet (Arranged for String
   Orchestra)
Bantock, Granville
 - Celtic Symphony
Bennett, Richard Rodney
 - Music for Strings
Bentzon, Niels Viggo
 - Concerto per archi, op.114
 - Copenhagen Concerto, op.167
 - Copenhagen Concerto No.2,
   op.168
 - Divertimento, op.19
 - Lille Suite, op.60
Beyer, Frank Michael
 - Liturgia
Blacher, Boris
 - Concerto for String Orchestra
 - Partita
Braun, Peter Michael
 - Problems and Solutions
Britten, Benjamin
 - Simple Symphony, op.4
Cooper, Paul
 - Symphony No.3; "Lamentations"
Cowell, Henry
 - Ensemble; Revised Version of
   String Quintet and Thundersticks
David, Johann Nepomuk
 - Concerto No.3
 - Sinfonia per archi, Wk54
Gál, Hans
 - Musik, op.73
Ginastera, Alberto
 - Glosses sobre temes de Pau
   Casals, op.46; For string orchestra
   and string quintet "in lontano"
Glass, Philip
 - Mishima (Music from the Film)
Gough, Orlando
 - Mungo Dances
Helm, Everett
 - Concerto for Strings
Henze, Hans Werner
 - Arien des Orpheus

Hindson, Matthew
 - Whitewater; For 12 solo strings
Holmboe, Vagn
 - Sinfonia 4, op.73
Hvidtfelt Nielsen, Svend
 - Singing the Dreams
Ireland, John
 - Concertino Pastorale
Jenkins, Karl
 - Palladio
Kalsons, Romualds
 - Symphony for Chamber Orchestra
Kancheli, Giya
 - Sio
Koch, Erland von
 - Musica intima
Kunad, Rainer
 - Concerto per Archi; conatum 36
Larsson, Lars-Erik
 - Sinfonietta, op.10
MacMillan, James
 - Í; A Meditation on Iona
Manicke, Dietrich
 - Musica serena
Mieg, Peter
 - Concerto Veneziano
Müller-Wieland, Jan
 - Amtsantritt von Leonce und Lena;
   Zweite imaginäre Theaterszene
   nach dem Schluss von Georg
   Büchner
Nørgård, Per
 - Tributes; Album for Strings
Ohse, Reinhard
 - Serenade
Payne, Anthony
 - Songs and Seascapes
Prokofiev, Sergei
 - Visions fugitives, op.22
Ratner, Leonard
 - Suite for Strings
Röttger, Heinz
 - Sinfonietta per archi
Shostakovich, Dmitri
 - Chamber Symphony, op.110a
Sierra, Roberto
 - Doce Bagatelas
Smirnov, Dmitri
 - Between Scylla and Charybdis,
   op.104
Vivier, Claude
 - Zipangu
Wolschina, Reinhard
 - Wandlungen
Yun, Isang
 - Colloides sonores

ENSEMBLE

Aa, Michel van der
 - Above; For ensemble and
   soundtrack
 - Attach; For ensemble and
   soundtrack
Adès, Thomas
 - Living Toys, op.9
Amy, Gilbert
 - 7 Sites; For 14 players
 - La Variation Ajoutée; Pour 17
   Instruments & Bande
   Électroacoustique
Aperghis, Georges
 - Von Zeit zu Zeit; Pour 16
   Instrumentistes
Ardevol, José
 - Concerto Grosso No.2
Atterberg, Kurt
 - Barocco-Suite No.5, op.23
Bacewicz, Grażyna
 - Contradizione
Bainbridge, Simon
 - Landscape and Memory
Ballif, Claude
 - Suite Dracoula
Barreau, Gisèle
 - Piano-piano
Bartholomée, Pierre
 - Fancy as a Ground
Bates, Mason
 - Omnivorous Furniture
Bawden, Rupert
 - The Angel and the Ship of Souls
 - Ultima Scena
 - Wanderjahr
Benjamin, George
 - At First Light
Bennett, Richard Rodney
 - A Book of Hours
 - Commedia III
 - Dream Dancing
Benson, Warren
 - Shadow Wood; Six Poems of
   Tennessee Williams
Bentzon, Niels Viggo
 - Chamber Concerto for 11
   Instruments, op.52
 - Sinfonia da Camera, op.139
Berkeley, Lennox
 - Diversions for Eight Instruments,
   op.63
Beyer, Frank Michael
 - Architettura per musica
Birkenkötter, Jörg
 - Halt!
 - Schwebende Form

Blake, David
- Seasonal Variants
Bolcom, William
- Octet
Bousch, François
- Spirales Insolites
Brandmüller, Theo
- Missa Morgenstern
Braun, Peter Michael
- Terms
Brødsgaard, Anders
- Ghostorchestra
Brown, Earle
- Centering
Brown, James Francis
- Sinfonietta
Buck, Ole
- Flower Ornament Music
- Landscapes I
- Landscapes II
Burgon, Geoffrey
- Goldberg's Dream (Running
  Figures)
Butting, Max
- Sinfonietta mit Banjo; 1.
  Rundfunkmusik, op.37
Carter, Elliott
- Penthode; For five groups of four
  instrumentalists
Casken, John
- Amarantos
Chapple, Brian
- Venus Fly Trap
Dalby, Martin
- Aleph
- Cancionero Para Una Mariposa
- Man Walking; Serenade for Octet
Davis, Anthony
- Undine
- Wayang IV
Denhoff, Michael
- O Orpheus singt
Denisov, Edison
- Chamber Symphony No.2
Dittrich, Paul-Heinz
- Concert Avec Plusieurs Instruments
  No.1
Einfeldt, Dieter
- Mobiles
- Sinfonia da Camera
Eisler, Hanns
- Suite for Orchestra No.5: From the
  music to the film *Dans les Rules*,
  op.34
Erbse, Heimo
- For String and Wind Players
Ferrari, Luc
- Flashes; For 14 instruments

Frankel, Benjamin
- Catalogue of Incidents
Furrer, Beat
- Gaspra
- Studie 2; A un moment de terre
  perdue
Giefer, Willy
- Pro - Kontra
Gilbert, Anthony
- Crow-Cry
Glass, Philip
- Mishima (Music from the Film)
Goehr, Alexander
- Concerto for Eleven, op.32
- Idées Fixes; Sonata for 13, op.63
Gordon, Michael
- Who by Water
Gudmundsen-Holmgreen, Pelle
- Nær og Fjern (Near and Distant)
Halffter, Cristóbal
- Antiphonismoi
Harneit, Johannes
- Triptychon (13X3), op.20
Harvey, Jonathan
- Smiling Immortal
- Two Interludes for an Opera
- Wheel of Emptiness
Haubenstock-Ramati, Roman
- Beaubourg Musique
- Invocations
Hauer, Josef Matthias
- 2. Tanzsuite, op.71
Heath, Dave
- Forest
Henze, Hans Werner
- Chamber Concerto 05
Hesketh, Kenneth
- Theatrum
Hiller, Lejaren
- Algorithms II (With Ravi Kumra) for
  9 Instruments and Tape
Höller, York
- Arcus
- Résonance
Honegger, Arthur
- Le Dit des Jeux du Monde: Suite
  d'orchestre en 4 mouvements
Hosokawa, Toshio
- Landscape VI
- Seascapes - Daybreak
Hoyland, Vic
- Andacht zum Kleinen
- Fox
Huber, Nicolaus A.
- Air mit Sphinxes
- Hölderlin in Darkness: A Dedication
- Music on Canvas
- Rose Selavy

Hurd, Michael
- Captain Coram's Kids
Hvidtfelt Nielsen, Svend
- Movements
- Singing the Dreams
Ibert, Jacques
- Divertissement
Ichiyanagi, Toshi
- Symphony No.1; Time Current
Jaroch, Jirí
- II. Nonet
Kelemen, Milko
- Nonett
Kernis, Aaron Jay
- Invisible Mosaic II
Kopelent, Marek
- Intimissimo
Korngold, Erich Wolfgang
- Suite from the Music to
  Shakespeare's "Much Ado About
  Nothing," op.11
Kubo, Mayako
- Miniatur I
Lieberson, Peter
- Lalita; Chamber Variations
Lazarof, Henri
- Espaces
Levi, Paul Alan
- Elegy and Recreations
Lindberg, Magnus
- Engine
Lobanov, Vasily
- Sinfonietta for Chamber Orchestra,
  op.47
Losonczy, Andor
- Phonophobie
Markevitch, Igor
- Petite Suite d'après Schumann
Marthinsen, Niels
- Chimes at Midnight
- Cupid and Death
Martinů, Bohuslav
- The Amazing Flight; Ballet
  mécanique, H.159
- Nonet No.2
Matthews, Colin
- Suns Dance
- ...through the glass
- Two Part Invention
Maxwell Davies, Peter
- Carolísima; Serenade for Chamber
  Orchestra
- Crossing Kings Reach
McCabe, John
- Rainforest I
Melby, John
- Wind, Sand and Stars

Milhaud, Darius
- L'Homme et son Désir, op.48
- Jeux de Printemps, op.243
Mochizuki, Misato
- Wise Water
Muldowney, Dominic
- Sinfonietta
Müller-Siemens, Detlev
- Phoenix 2
Müller-Wieland, Jan
- Amtsantritt von Leonce und Lena;
  Zweite imaginäre Theaterszene
  nach dem Schluss von Georg
  Büchner
Musgrave, Thea
- Lamenting with Ariadne
- Space Play
Musto, John
- Divertimento
Neikrug, Marc
- Mobile
- Concertino
Nelson, Larry
- Loose Leaves
Nordentoft, Anders
- Hymne
Nørgård, Per
- Night-Symphonies; Day Breaks
- Scintillation
Obst, Michael
- Kristallwelt
Osborne, Nigel
- In Camera
- Prelude and Fugue
- Wildlife
- Zansa
Pade, Steen
- Sinfonietta
Payne, Anthony
- The Stones and Lonely Places Sing
Platz, Robert H. P.
- PIECE NOIRE
Provazník, Anatol
- Ländliche Suite, op.53
Rasmussen, Karl Aage
- A Ballad of Game and Dream
- Movements on a Moving Line
Reich, Steve
- Eight Lines
Reimann, Aribert
- Invenzioni
Riedel, Georg
- Nursery Rhymes
Rihm, Wolfgang
- abgewandt 2; Musik in memoriam
  Luigi Nono (3. Versuch)
- Cuts and Dissolves;
  Orchesterskizzen
- In Frage

- Pol - Kolchis - Nucleus
Rochberg, George
- Chamber Symphony for 9
  Instruments
Ruders, Poul
- Corpus Cum Figuris
- Four Dances in One Movement
Runswick, Daryl
- Songs of Love and Farewell
Saariaho, Kaija
- Aer: Part 7 of "Maa"
- Lichtbogen
- Io
- Solar
Sackman, Nicholas
- Corranach
Satie, Erik
- Mercure; Poses plastiques, op.post
Sawer, David
- Take Off
Saxton, Robert
- Chamber Symphony: The Circles of
  Light
Scherchen, Tona
- Bien
Schifrin, Lalo
- Variants on a Madrigal by Gesualdo
Schleiermacher, Steffen
- Zeit Verschiebung
Schubert, Manfred
- Nachtstück und Passacaglia
Schulhoff, Erwin
- Suite for Chamber Orchestra
Schuman, William
- Night Journey
Schwehr, Cornelius
- Aber die Schönheit des Gitters
Searle, Humphrey
- Three Songs of Jocelyn Brooke,
  op.25b
- Variations and Finale, op.34
Smolka, Martin
- Octet
- Rain, A Window, Roofs, Chimneys,
  Pigeons And So
Sørensen, Bent
- Shadowland
Sotelo, Mauricio
- Wall of Light Black
Staud, Johannes Maria
- A Map is not the Territory
Stürmer, Bruno
- Suite für Neun Solo-Instrumente,
  op.9
Swayne, Giles
- Into the Light
Szymanski, Pawel
- Quasi una Sinfonietta

Toch, Ernst
- Fünf Stücke (Five Pieces), op.33
Turnage, Mark-Anthony
- Dark Crossing
Wallin, Rolf
- Boyl
Watkins, Huw
- Rondo
Watkins, Michael Blake
- Sinfonietta
Widmann, Jörg
- ...umdüstert...
Wiegold, Peter
- The Flowers Appear on the Earth
Wolpe, Michael
- Caprisma 2
Woolrich, John
- Suite from Bitter Fruit
Wyner, Yehudi
- Serenade for Seven Instruments
Xenakis, Iannis
- Thalleïn
- Waarg
Yanov-Yanovsky, Dmitri
- Chamber Music for Twelve
  Musicians
Yuasa, Joji
- Projection for Seven Players

CHAMBER ORCHESTRA

Abendroth, Walter
- Concerto for Orchestra, op.14
- Divertimento für Kammerorchester,
  op.24
- Konzertante Phantasie für
  Orchester, op.23
- Sinfonietta, op.32
Aitken, Robert
- Spiral
Alexandrov, Anatoly
- Classic Suite in B-flat major, op.32
Alwyn, William
- Elizabethan Dances for Orchestra
Amy, Gilbert
- D'Après "Ecrits Sur Toiles"; Pour
  Orchestre de Chambre
Angerer, Paul
- Musica Fera
- Sinfonia
Antoniou, Theodore
- Events I
Arnold, Malcolm
- Concerto for Clarinet and
  Orchestra, op.115

Atterberg, Kurt
- De Fåvitska Jungfrurna; The wise
  and the foolish virgins. Rhapsody on
  old Swedish folksongs.

Bäck, Sven-Erik
- Movimento I

Bantock, Granville
- The Helena Variations

Barraud, Henry
- Concerto da Camera
- Images pour un Poète Maudit; Pour
  25 musiciens

Bartók, Béla
- Dance Suite

Baur, Jürg
- Carmen Variations; Theme,
  Variations and Finale on a Theme
  from Bizet's "Carmen"
- Sentieri musicali; Auf Mozarts
  Spuren. Sinfonietta

Bavicchi, John
- Fireworks, op.48

Bedford, David
- The Valley Sleeper, the Children,
  the Snakes and the Giant
- With 100 Kazoos; For chamber
  ensemble and 100 kazoos

Bentzon, Niels Viggo
- Symphony No.11, op.158

Berio, Luciano
- Kol od (Chemins VI)
- Requies

Berkeley, Lennox
- Divertimento in Bb, op.18

Bermel, Derek
- Turning Variations

Bernstein, Leonard
- 1600 Pennsylvania Avenue: Suite
  for Orchestra
- Facsimile

Beyer, Frank Michael
- Ricercare I

Bialas, Günter
- Der Weg nach Eisenstadt; Haydn
  Phantasies for Small Orchestra

Biersack, Anton
- Bagatellen

Bjelinski, Bruno
- Mediterranian Sinfonietta
- Serenade

Blacher, Boris
- Collage
- Fürstin Tarakanowa

Blomdahl, Karl-Birger
- Concerto grosso

Bolcom, William
- Symphony No.1

Bondon, Jacques
- Symphonie latine

Boucourechliev, André
- Le Chevelure de Bérénice

Braun, Yehezkel
- Apartment To Let
- Illuminations to the Book of Ruth

Braunfels, Walter
- Divertimento, op.42

Britten, Benjamin
- Johnson Over Jordan: Suite
- Matinées musicales, op.24; Second
  Suite of Five Movements from
  Rossini
- Peter Grimes: Four Sea Interludes,
  op.33a
- The Young Person's Guide to the
  Orchestra, op.34, (Variations and
  Fugue on a Theme of Purcell)

Bruns, Victor
- Das Edelfräulein als Bäuerin:
  Orchestersuite, op.69

Buck, Ole
- Pastorals

Burgon, Geoffrey
- Brideshead Variations

Burkhard, Willy
- Kleine konzertante Suite
  (Kaleidoskop) für Orchester, op.79

Busch, Adolf
- Divertimento, op.30
- Variations on a Theme by W. A.
  Mozart

Chávez, Carlos
- Discovery

Cohn, James
- Symphony No.4 in A, op.29

Copland, Aaron
- Music for Movies

Corigliano, John
- Gazebo Dances

Cowell, Henry
- American Melting Pot Set

David, Johann Nepomuk
- Kume, kum, Geselle min;
  Divertimento nach alten
  Volksliedern, Wk24
- Sinfonia breve, Wk47
- Sinfonia preclassica super nomen
  H-A-S-E, Wk44
- Symphonic Variations on a Theme
  by H. Schütz, Wk29b
- Variations on a Theme by J. S.
  Bach, Wk29a

Diamond, David
- Elegies
- Music for Chamber Orchestra

Diehl, Paula
- Right of Way

Döhl, Friedhelm
- Passion

Dubois, Pierre-Max
- Queue Leu Leu; File de Danses

Einem, Gottfried von
- Medusa, op.24a; Three movements
  for orchestra
- Philadelphia Symphony, op.28
- Turandot, op.1a; Four episodes for
  orchestra

Eppert, Carl
- A Little Symphony; Symphony No.2

Essl, Karl-Heinz
- Et Consumimur Igni
- O Tiempo Tus Piramides

Feldman, Morton
- The Turfan Fragments

Ficher, Jacobo
- Seis Fabulas (Six Fables)

Finnissy, Michael
- Câtana

Forst, Rudolf
- Divertimento for Chamber
  Orchestra

Fortner, Wolfgang
- Suite for Orchestra; After music by
  Jan Pieters Sweelinck

Gál, Hans
- Zauberspiegel-Suite;
  Weihnachtsmusik. Musik zu einem
  Märchenspiel, op.38

Gebhard-Elsass, Hans
- Ländliche Suite, op.23

Geissler, Fritz
- Chamber Symphony (1970)

Gill, Jeremy
- Chamber Symphony

Gillis, Don
- Four Scenes from Yesterday

Glass, Philip
- Concerto Grosso

Grosse, Erwin
- Kammersinfonie (Chamber
  Symphony), op.48

Grosskopf, Erhard
- Sonata concertante 1

Guenther, Felix
- Deutsches Rokoko; Eine Suite für
  Kleines Orchester nach alten
  Meistern

Hagen, Daron
- Night Music; Five Scenes for
  Chamber Orchestra

Halffter, Cristóbal
- Dalíniana; Three pieces on three
  paintings by Salvador Dalí

Harbison, John
- The Most Often Used Chords (Gli
  Accordi Piu Usati)
- Partita

Harty, Hamilton
- A John Field Suite

Hauer, Josef Matthias
- Romantische Phantasie, op.37

Heitzeg, Steve
- Flower of the Earth; Homage to Georgia O'Keeffe

Henze, Hans Werner
- Drei Dithyramben; In Memoriam Willy Strecker
- Katharina Blum: Concerto suite
- Symphony No.1

Herrmann, Peter
- Sonata for Chamber Orchestra
- Three Pieces for Orchestra

Hesketh, Kenneth
- Detail from the Record

Hidalgo, Manuel
- Variations on the Variations op.30 by Webern

Hindemith, Paul
- Concert Music for Strings and Brass, op.50
- Tuttifäntchen: Suite

Hindson, Matthew
- Speed

Holloway, Robin
- Concertino No.1, op.2
- Second Idyll, op.54

Holmboe, Vagn
- Chamber Symphony No.1, op.53
- Concerto for Orchestra, op.38
- Symphony No.1, op.4

Honegger, Arthur
- Concerto da Camera, H.196
- Les Misérables: Suite pour orchestre tirée de la musique du film de Raymond Bernard, H.88A
- Regain: Suite d'orchestre tirée de la musique du film de Jean Giono et Marcel Pagnol, H.117A
- Tête d'Or; Musique pour une pièce de Paul Claudel, H.199

Imbrie, Andrew
- Chamber Symphony

Ives, Charles Edward
- Symphony No.3; The Camp Meeting, S.3

Jacob, Gordon
- Sinfonietta No.1 for Small Orchestra

Janáček, Leoš
- Suite, op.3

Jelinek, Hanns
- Parergon, op.15B

Jerger, Wilhelm
- Symphony No.1; Classical Symphony

Jirák, K. B.
- Serenade for Small Orchestra, op.69

Johnson, Hunter
- Concerto for Small Orchestra

Joubert, John
- Sinfonietta, op.38

Kelly, Bryan
- Concertante Dances

Kirchner, Volker David
- Bildnisse I

Klenau, Paul von
- Altdeutsche Liedersuite (Old German Song Suite)

Knipper, Lew
- Wantsch; Turkmenische Suite, op.29

Koch, Erland von
- Oxberg Variations; On a Theme from Dalekarlien
- Schwedische Tanz-Rhapsodie

Kodály, Zoltán
- Concerto for Orchestra
- Summer Evening

Kreutz, Arthur
- American Dances

Kunad, Rainer
- Dialog, conatum 40

Lam, Bun-Ching
- Saudades de Macau

Lazar, Filip
- Concerto No.4; Concerto di Camera, op.24

Lees, Benjamin
- Concertante Breve
- Concerto for Chamber Orchestra

LeFanu, Nicola
- Farne

Lendvai, Erwin
- Kammersuite, op.32

León, Tania
- Tones

Levy, Marvin David
- Trialogus I

Lopatnikoff, Nikolai
- Symphonietta, op.27

Lumsdaine, David
- Salvation Creek with Eagle
- Sunflower

MacMillan, James
- Sinfonietta

MacRae, Stuart
- Portrait

Magnard, Albéric
- Suite in Ancient Style, op.2

Malipiero, Gian Francesco
- Ricercari

Martinů, Bohuslav
- Sinfonietta la Jolla, H.328

Matthews, Colin
- Night Music, op.10

Matthews, David
- Serenade, op.29

Maw, Nicholas
- Sonata for Strings and Two Horns

Maxwell Davies, Peter
- Sinfonia

Meester, Louis de
- Sinfonietta Buffa

Milhaud, Darius
- Le Bal Martiniquais
- Opus Americanum No.2 (Moïse)

Moore, Douglas
- Farm Journal; Suite for Chamber Orchestra

Morris, Harold
- Suite for Small Orchestra

Musgrave, Thea
- Night Music

Myaskovsky, Nikolai Yakovlevich
- Concertino Lyrico, op.32

Nelson, Larry
- Catena

Nørgård, Per
- Amled: Suite
- Voyage into the Golden Screen

Nussio, Otmar
- Divertimento
- Suite from the Tessin

Nyman, Michael
- Strong on Oaks; Strong on the Causes of Oaks

Olivier, François
- Suite Pour Petit Orchestre

Pärt, Arvo
- Symphony No.1; "Polyphonic," op.9

Payne, Anthony
- Orchestral Variations; "The Seeds Long Hidden"

Pfundt, Reinhard
- Musique Pour Sanssouci

Piston, Walter
- Sinfonietta

Poulenc, Francis
- Hoops, Ballet

Rachmaninoff, Sergei
- Caprice bohémien, op.12

Raphael, Günter
- Variationen über eine Schottische Volksweise, op.23

Rautavaara, Einojuhani
- Cantus Arcticus; Concerto for Birds and Orchestra

Ravel, Maurice
- Ma Mère l'Oye (Mother Goose): Cinq pièces enfantines (Suite)
- Le Tombeau de Couperin

Reger, Max
- Eine Balletsuite, op.130
Respighi, Ottorino
- Antiche Danze ed Arie: Suite 1
Revueltas, Silvestre
- Paisajes
Riisager, Knudåge
- Variations on a Theme by
  Mezangeau, op.12
Rodríguez, Robert Xavier
- Estampie; Ballet for Small
  Orchestra
Rorem, Ned
- Design
- A Quaker Reader; Suite
- Symphony No.2
Roselius, Ludwig
- Lilofee Suite, op.16
Rosenberg, Hilding Constantin
- Sinfonia da Chiesa No.1
Roters, Ernst
- Tanzsuite, op.23
Röttger, Heinz
- Sinfonische Meditationen
Roumain, Daniel Bernard
- Call Them All
Roussel, Albert
- Le Marchand de Sable qui Passe
  (The Sandman Passing By), op.13
Saint-Saëns, Camille
- L'assassinat de Duc de Guise;
  Tableux d'histoire, op.128
Satie, Erik
- Mercure; Poses plastiques, op.post
Schickele, Peter
- Thurber's Dogs
Schlemm, Gustav Adolf
- Serenade
Schollum, Robert
- Serenade, Werk 39a
Schubert, Heino
- Concerto
Schulhoff, Erwin
- Suite
Schurmann, Gerard
- Variants
Search, Frederick
- Sinfonietta
Sessions, Roger
- Concertino
Shchedrin, Rodion
- Music for the City of Köthen

Shostakovich, Dmitri
- Chamber Symphony, op.83a
Sibelius, Jean
- Scenes Historiques, op.66
Siegl, Otto
- Lyrische Tanzmusik, op.82
Spinner, Leopold
- Ricercata, op.21
Standford, Patric
- Suite for Small Orchestra
Stanford, Charles Villiers
- Songs of the Sea, op.91
Stenhammar, Wilhelm
- Lodolezzi Sjunger: Suite, op.39
Stravinsky, Igor
- Danses Concertantes
- Scenes de Ballet
Takács, Jenö
- Ländliches Barock; Suite, op.48
- Ungarische Burgmusik; Antiqua
  hungarica, op.47
- Von fremden Ländern und
  Menschen, op.37
Tansman, Alexandre
- Des Kaisers neue Kleider; Musik zu
  einem Andersen-Ballett
- Sinfonia Piccola
- Sinfonietta
Thiele, Siegfried
- Concerto for Orchestra
- Sonatina
Thomas, Kurt
- Serenade, op.10
Torke, Michael
- Ash
Tower, Joan
- Chamber Dance
- Duets
Trapp, Max
- Divertimento für Kammerorchester,
  op.27
Treibmann, Karl Ottomar
- First Symphonic Essay
Trojan, Václav
- Sinfonietta Armoniosa
Turina, Joaquin
- Cinq Danzas Gitanas, op.55
Turok, Paul
- Antoniana; Suite for Small
  Orchestra after Vivaldi, op.47

Uhl, Alfred
- Vergnügliche Musik aus einer
  deutschen Kleinstadt
Vactor, David van
- Divertimento
Villa-Lobos, Heitor
- Sinfonietta No.1
- Sinfonietta No.2
Vincent, John
- The House that Jack Built: From the
  ballet "Three Jacks"
Vinter, Gilbert
- The Poet Speaks; Suite from pieces
  by Robert Schumann
Vlad, Roman
- In Memoriam di Valentino Bucchi
Voss, Friedrich
- Résonances; 12 Poems
Weill, Kurt
- Aufstieg und Fall der Stadt
  Mahagonny (Rise and Fall of the
  City of Mahagonny): Suite
Weingartner, Felix
- Symphony No.4 in F Major, op.61
Weir, Judith
- Winter Song
Westergaard, Peter
- L'Homme Armé, op.22a
Westerman, Gerhart von
- Serenade, op.7
Wilson, Ian
- Running, Thinking, Finding
Wimberger, Gerhard
- Partita Giocosa
Wolf-Ferrari, Ermanno
- Sinfonia da Camera in B-flat, op.8
Yun, Isang
- Konzertante Figuren
Zbinden, Julien-François
- Symphony No.1, op.18
Zilcher, Hermann
- Lustspielsuite; Der Widerspenstigen
  Zähmung, op.54b
Zimmermann, Udo
- Songerie Pour Orchestre de
  Chambre

21' - 25'

STRING ORCHESTRA

Adams, John
- Shaker Loops
Apostel, Hans Erich
- Adagio, op.11
Arnold, Malcolm
- Symphony for Strings
Beyer, Frank Michael
- Griechenland; For three groups of
  strings
Blacher, Boris
- Pentagramm
Bliss, Arthur
- Music for Strings
Borges, Joaquin
- Suite Sofia
Britten, Benjamin
- Variations on a Theme of Frank
  Bridge, op.10
Cage, John
- Twenty Three
Chávez, Carlos
- Sinfonía No.5
David, Johann Nepomuk
- Concerto No.1, Wk40/1
Dean, Brett
- Carlo; Music for strings and sampler
Erdmann, Dietrich
- Divertimento
Füssl, Karl Heinz
- Szenen, op.6
Ginastera, Alberto
- Concerto per Corde, op.33
Harvey, Jonathan
- Gong-Ring
Herrmann, Peter
- Sinfonietta
Hummel, Bertold
- Symphony for Strings, op.20
Jolivet, André
- Symphonie pour cordes
Laks, Simon
- Symphony for Strings
Mommer, Hans Günter
- Concerto for Strings
Myaskovsky, Nikolai Yakovlevich
- Sinfonietta, op.32
Nørgård, Per
- Constellations, op.22
Qu, Xiao-song
- String Symphony
Rorem, Ned
- String Symphony

Rosenberg, Hilding Constantin
- Concerto No.1 for String Orchestra
Schnittke, Alfred
- Trio-Sonata
Schurmann, Gerard
- Sonata for String Orchestra
Strauss, Richard
- Metamorphosen; For 23 solo strings
Thiele, Siegfried
- Übungen im Verwandeln
Zemlinsky, Alexander
- String Quartet No.4, op.25

ENSEMBLE

Adolphe, Bruce
- Marita and Her Heart's Desire; A
  Chamber Music Fairy Tale for
  Family Audiences
Anderson, Julian
- Book of Hours
André, Mark
- ...Das O...: From ...22,1...
Bedford, David
- Symphony for 12 Musicians
Bergman, Erik
- Silence and Eruptions, op.91
Birkenkötter, Jörg
- Klaenge Schatten
Blomdahl, Karl-Birger
- Game for Eight
Bolcom, William
- Summer Divertimento
Bose, Hans-Jürgen von
- Scene
Boulez, Pierre
- Dérive 2 (Work in progress)
Braun, Yehezkel
- Emek Hayarden (The Yordan
  Valley): Ballet Suite
Buck, Ole
- Landscapes III
Burkhard, Willy
- Serenade, op.77
Chávez, Carlos
- Suite for Double Quartet
Conyngham, Barry
- Dwellings
Copland, Aaron
- Appalachian Spring: Suite (original
  version)
Dalby, Martin
- Chamber Symphony (O Bella e
  Vaga Aurora)
Denisov, Edison
- Chamber Symphony
Dillon, James
- Überschreiten

Einfeldt, Dieter
- Apokalypse
Ferrari, Luc
- Entrée; For 15 instruments
Fuchs, Kenneth
- Face of the Night (After a Painting
  by Robert Motherwell)
Górecki, Henryk Mikołaj
- Kleines Requiem für eine Polka,
  op.66
Gruber, HK
- Zeitfluren; Timescapes
Guy, Barry
- Play
Hamilton, Iain
- The Alexandrian Sequence
Harneit, Johannes
- Ohne Leben Tod (Without Life
  Death), op.23
Hasquenoph, Pierre
- Variations Pour 14
Hesketh, Kenneth
- The Circling Canopy of Night
Hindemith, Paul
- Der Dämon: Konzertsuite aus der
  Tanzpantomime
Höller, York
- Mythos
Huber, Nicolaus A.
- Eröffnung und Zertrümmerung
- Six Bagatelles
Husa, Karel
- Cayuga Lake (Memories)
Imbrie, Andrew
- From Time to Time
- Spring Fever
Jelinek, Hanns
- Prelude, Passacaglia and Fugue,
  op.4
Joubert, John
- Octet, op.33
Kagel, Mauricio
- Finale mit Kammerensemble
Kancheli, Giya
- Magnum Ignotum
Kats-Chernin, Elena
- Clocks; For ensemble and tape
Korndorf, Nikolai
- Confessiones; Chamber Symphony
  for 14 Instruments
Krebs, Joachim
- Slow-Mobile
Kyburz, Hanspeter
- Parts
Laderman, Ezra
- Nonet of the Night
Levinson, Gerald
- Light Dances / Stones Sing

Ligeti, György
- Kammerkonzert (Chamber Concerto)

Marthinsen, Niels
- Shadow Figures

Martland, Steve
- American Invention

Matsushita, Shin-ichi
- Correlaziono per 3 Gruppi

Matthews, Colin
- Pursuit; Ballet

Montsalvatge, Xavier
- Cinco Invocaciones al Crucificado

Mundry, Isabel
- Le Voyage

Prokofiev, Sergei
- Peter and the Wolf, op.67

Reich, Steve
- City Life

Rosenman, Leonard
- Chamber Music No.2

Rota, Nino
- Cristallo di Rocca

Ruders, Poul
- Abysm

Satie, Erik
- Le Piège de Méduse; Sept toutes petites danses

Sawer, David
- Cat's-eye

Schenker, Friedrich
- Hades di Orfeo; Dramma per musica

Scherchen, Tona
- L'Invitation au voyage

Schnittke, Alfred
- Music for Piano and Chamber Orchestra

Schönberg, Arnold
- Kammersymphonie Nr.1 (Chamber Symphony No.1), op.9

Stravinsky, Igor
- L'Histoire du Soldat (The Soldier's Tale): Suite

Wallin, Rolf
- Appearances

Widmann, Jörg
- Freie Stücke

Zimmermann, Bernd Alois
- Metamorphose; Music for the film of the same title by Michael Wolgensinger

CHAMBER ORCHESTRA

Amram, David
- Shakespearean Concerto

Antheil, George
- Dreams
- Serenade II

Ardevol, José
- Musica para Pequena Orquesta. Himno (Music for small orchestra. Hymn)

Argento, Dominick
- Royal Invitation (Homage to the Queen of Tonga)

Arnold, Malcolm
- Concerto for 28 Players, op.105

Asia, Daniel
- Symphony No.4

Atterberg, Kurt
- Symphony No.4 in G minor, op.14

Bäck, Sven-Erik
- Four Motets

Bacon, Ernst
- Fables for Narrator and Orchestra; Or the Secretary Bird and Associates: Studies in the Ecology of Academic Democracy

Barati, George
- Chamber Concerto

Bartel, Hans-Christian
- Concerto

Bartók, Béla
- Concerto for Piano No.1

Baur, Jürg
- Frammenti; Erinnerungen an Schubert

Bentzon, Niels Viggo
- Sinfonia, op.402

Bergman, Erik
- Tutti e soli, op.113

Blacher, Boris
- Demeter: Suite
- Feste im Süden: Suite
- Symphony

Blake, David
- Chamber Symphony

Borkovec, Pavel
- Sinfonietta da Camera

Braun, Yehezkel
- Serenade II

Bräutigam, Helmut
- Music for Orchestra, Wk.8

Britten, Benjamin
- Plymouth Town

Bruns, Victor
- Symphony No.6; Sinfonia breve, op.67

Burgon, Geoffrey
- Suite from Martin Chuzzlewit

Burkhard, Willy
- Toccata for Chamber Orchestra, op.86

Carter, Elliott
- The Minotaur: Suite from the Ballet
- Symphony No.1
- Variations for Orchestra

Casella, Alfredo
- Serenata, op.46b

Cohn, James
- Symphony No.3 in G, op.27
- Symphony No.5

Consoli, Marc-Antonio
- Odefonia

Copland, Aaron
- The City: Incidental music for the documentary film
- Music for the Theatre
- Rodeo
- Appalachian Spring: Suite

Cowell, Henry
- Symphony No.7
- Symphony No.9
- Symphony No.10
- Symphony No.16; Icelandic
- Symphony No.17; Lancaster

Cowie, Edward
- Leonardo

David, Johann Nepomuk
- Symphony No.8, Wk59

Degen, Helmut
- Chamber Symphony (Symphony No.2)

Delás, José Luis de
- Conjuntos

Denhoff, Michael
- Melancolia

Dillon, James
- Windows and Canopies

Donovan, Richard
- Symphony for Chamber Orchestra

Edlund, Lars
- Tracce

Einem, Gottfried von
- Concerto for Orchestra, op.4
- Münchner Symphonie, op.70

Ferguson, Howard
- Serenade

Finzi, Gerald
- Love's Labour's Lost: Suite, op.28b

Fitelberg, Jerzy
- Suite No.3

Gál, Hans
- Ballet Suite "Scaramussio," op.36

Geissler, Fritz
- Symphony No.6, Concertante Symphony

Genzmer, Harald
- Sinfonia da Camera

Ginastera, Alberto
- Variationes Concertantes, op.23
Goehr, Alexander
- Sinfonia, op.42
Goldstein, Mikhail
- Ukranian Symphony in Old Style
Grabner, Hermann
- Divertimento für Kleines Orchester, op.56
Gregson, Edward
- Music for Chamber Orchestra
Halffter, Ernesto
- El Cojo Enamorado; Ballet Suite
Hamel, Peter Michael
- Semiramis; Music in three parts
Hanuš, Jan
- Prazská Nokturna (Prague Nocturne), op.75
Hasquenoph, Pierre
- Symphony No.1, op.10
Haubenstock-Ramati, Roman
- Polyphonien; For 2, 3 or 4 chamber orchestras
Heiller, Anton
- Kammersymphonie (Chamber Symphony)
Henze, Hans Werner
- Aria de la Folia Española
Hindemith, Paul
- Hérodiade
Hindson, Matthew
- Dangerous Creatures
Holloway, Robin
- Concertino No.2, op.10
- Fourth Idyll
Holmboe, Vagn
- Chamber Symphony No.3
Honegger, Arthur
- Symphony No.2, H.153
Ibert, Jacques
- Tropismes pour les Amours Imaginaires
Janáček, Leoš
- Jenufa-Rhapsodie
Kaipainen, Jouni
- Accende Lumen Sensibus, op.52
Kajanus, Robert
- Sinfonietta in Bb major, op.16
Kancheli, Giya
- Abii ne Viderem
- A Life Without Christmas: The Morning Prayers. For Chamber Orchestra and Tape
Karayev, Kara
- Symphony No.3 for Chamber Orchestra
Kasilag, Lucrecia
- Legend of the Sarimanok

Kodály, Zoltán
- Variations on a Hungarian Folksong; The Peacock
Korngold, Erich Wolfgang
- Much Ado About Nothing: Suite, op.11
Krebs, Joachim
- Musik für Kleines Orchester (Music for Small Orchestra)
Kupferman, Meyer
- Little Symphony
Lazar, Filip
- Concerto Grosso No.1, op.17
Lees, Benjamin
- Divertimento-Burlesca
Lobanov, Vasily
- Symphony No.1 for Chamber Orchestra
MacMillan, James
- Symphony No.2
Martin, Frank
- Concerto
Martinů, Bohuslav
- Toccata e due canzoni, H.311
Matthews, David
- Symphony No.4, op.51
Matthus, Siegfried
- Divertimento for Orchestra; Triangle Concerto
Maxwell Davies, Peter
- Caroline Mathilde: Concert Suite from Act I of the ballet
- Caroline Mathilde: Concert Suite from Act II of the ballet
Milhaud, Darius
- Musique pour Lisbonne, op.420
- La Rose des Vents; Ballet, op.367
Moeschinger, Albert
- Symphony No.2, op.73
Müller-Zürich, Paul
- Marienleben, op.8
Musgrave, Thea
- The Seasons
Nyman, Michael
- Concert Suite from Prospero's Books
Panufnik, Andrzej
- Sinfonia Mistica; Symphony No.6
Poulenc, Francis
- L'histoire de Babar, le petit éléphant
- Sinfonietta
Prokofiev, Sergei
- Peter and the Wolf, op.67
- Sinfonietta, op.48
Rautavaara, Einojuhani
- Symphony No.1
- Symphony No.2

Reger, Max
- Suite in A minor, op.103a
Rihm, Wolfgang
- Gesungene Zeit
Rogers, Bernard
- The Musicians of Bremen
Roselius, Ludwig
- Friesische Musik, op.30
Rosenberg, Hilding Constantin
- Sinfonia da Chiesa No.2
Rózsa, Miklós
- Hungarian Serenade, op.25
Saint-Saëns, Camille
- Suite in D major
- Symphony in A
Sallinen, Aulis
- Concerto for Chamber Orchestra
Satie, Erik
- Relâche, Ballet
Saxton, Robert
- Elijah's Violin
Saygun, A. Adnan
- Symphony No.1
Schickele, Peter
- Legend
- Symphony No.2; The Sweet Season
- Three Girls, Three Women
Schiske, Karl
- Chamber Concerto, op.28
Schmitt, Florent
- Soirs, op.5
Schnittke, Alfred
- Suite in Old Style
Schönberg, Arnold
- Kammersymphonie Nr.2 (Chamber Symphony No.2), op.38
Schuller, Gunther
- Contours
Schwertsik, Kurt
- Compagnie Masquerade; Ein Divertissement für kleines Orchester, einer Idee & teilweise erhaltenen Violinstimme Mozarts folgend
Sheng, Bright
- H'un (Lacerations): In Memoriam 1966-76
Shostakovich, Dmitri
- Hamlet: Suite from the Theatre Music, op.32a
- The Human Comedy: Suite, op.37
Silvestrov, Valentin
- Symphony No.2
Spitzmüller, Alexander
- 40. Mai; Suite, op.25

Surinach, Carlos
 - Acrobats of God; Ballet for chamber
 orchestra
 - Embattled Garden; Ballet for
 chamber orchestra
Swayne, Giles
 - Symphony for Small Orchestra
Thomson, Virgil
 - Suite from "The River"
Tower, Joan
 - Stepping Stones; Ballet
Trexler, Georg
 - Concerto for Orchestra
 - Music for Orchestra

Tubin, Eduard
 - Symphony No.7
Villa-Lobos, Heitor
 - Francette et Pia
Walker, Robert
 - Chamber Symphony No.1
Weill, Kurt
 - Quodlibet: Suite aus "Zaubernacht."
 Eine Unterhaltungsmusik, op.9
 - Der Silbersee: Suite aus dem
 Wintermärchen

Xenakis, Iannis
 - Alax, Pour 30 musiciens divises en
 3 ensembles
Yun, Isang
 - Kammersinfonie I (Chamber
 Symphony I)
Zemlinsky, Alexander
 - Sinfonietta, op.23

26' - 30'

STRING ORCHESTRA

Adler, Samuel
- Elegy for String Orchestra

Alwyn, William
- Sinfonietta for String Orchestra

Atterberg, Kurt
- Suite No.7, op.29

Bacewicz, Grażyna
- Symphony for String Orchestra

Bäck, Sven-Erik
- String Symphony

Bartók, Béla
- Divertimento
- Music for Strings, Percussion and Celesta

Brott, Alexander
- Three Astral Visions

Cotton, Jeffery
- Symphony for Strings

Danielpour, Richard
- Apparitions

Geissler, Fritz
- String Symphony; Symphony No.4

Glass, Philip
- Symphony No.3

Klengel, Julius
- Serenade in F major, op.24

Rouse, Christopher
- Concerto per Corde

Rózsa, Miklós
- Concerto, op.17

Saariaho, Kaija
- Nymphéa Reflection

Schönberg, Arnold
- Verklärte Nacht, op.4

Shostakovich, Dmitri
- Symphony for Strings, op.118a

ENSEMBLE

André, Mark
- Fatal

Apostel, Hans Erich
- Kammersymphonie (Chamber Symphony), op.41

Ballif, Claude
- Imaginaire No.3, op.41, No.3

Birtwistle, Sir Harrison
- Secret Theatre

Bryars, Gavin
- Four Elements

Cage, John
- Thirteen
- Ten

Casken, John
- Vaganza

Cerha, Friedrich
- Jahrlang ins Ungewisse Hinab

Cordero, Roque
- Dodecaconcerto

Davis, Anthony
- Litany of Sins

Eberhard, Dennis
- Endgame

Haas, Georg Friedrich
- Quasi Una Tânpûrâ

Harrison, Lou
- Solstice

Harvey, Jonathan
- Inner Light 1

Koppel, Anders
- Partita

Krenek, Ernst
- Symphonische Musik für 9 Soloinstrumente, op.11

Lindberg, Magnus
- Joy

Maxwell Davies, Peter
- De Assumtione Beatae Mariae Virginis

McGuire, John
- Cadence Music

Milhaud, Darius
- Protée, op.17

Ostendorf, Jens-Peter
- Septett "Geschichte Vom…"

Platz, Robert H. P.
- CHLEBNICOV

Rihm, Wolfgang
- Sphäre um Sphäre

Staud, Johannes Maria
- Berenice: Suite 1

Watkins, Michael Blake
- Concertante

Wood, Hugh
- Chamber Concerto, op.15

CHAMBER ORCHESTRA

Bacri, Nicolas
- Symphony No.5; Concerto pour orchestre, op.55

Bantock, Granville
- Russian Scenes

Barber, Samuel
- Medea: Ballet Suite, op.23

Bentzon, Niels Viggo
- Symphony No.6, op.66

Bräutigam, Helmut
- Tänzerische Suite

Britten, Benjamin
- Death in Venice: Suite, op.88a

Bruns, Victor
- Sinfonietta, op.23

Chávez, Carlos
- Sinfonía

Copland, Aaron
- Dance Panels; Ballet in Seven Sections

Corigliano, John
- Creations: Two Scenes from Genesis

David, Johann Nepomuk
- Symphony No.7, Wk49
- Partita No.2, Wk27

Einem, Gottfried von
- Medusa, op.24; Ballet in three scenes to a scenario by M. Gale Hoffman
- Symphonische Szenen, op.22

Frazelle, Kenneth
- Concerto for Chamber Orchestra

Gál, Hans
- Idyllikon; Four movements for small orchestra, op.79

Gerhard, Roberto
- Pandora: Orchestral suite from the ballet

Goehr, Alexander
- Little Symphony, op.15

Grinberg, Alexander
- Carillon

Hamilton, Iain
- Symphony No.3

Holmboe, Vagn
- Chamber Symphony No.2, op.100

Ibert, Jacques
- La Licorne, or The Triumph of Chastity; Ballet

Juon, Paul
- Serenade, op.40

Kancheli, Giya
- Besuch In Der Kindheit (Childhood Revisited)

Kodály, Zoltán
- Symphony in C

Krek, Uroš
- Simfonietta

Krenek, Ernst
- Symphony No.3, op.16

León, Tania
- The Golden Windows

Lloyd, Jonathan
- Symphony No.1

Lobanov, Vasily
- Symphony No.2 for Chamber Orchestra; "Intermezzo," op.36

MacMillan, James
- Tryst
Magnard, Albéric
- Symphony No.3 in B minor, op.11
Maw, Nicholas
- Sinfonia
Maxwell Davies, Peter
- Sinfonietta Accademica
Milhaud, Darius
- La Carnaval de Londres: Suite sur les airs de "l' Opéra du Gueux," op.172
- Les Songes; Ballet, op.124
Novák, Vítêzslav
- Serenade, op.36
Piazzolla, Astor
- Las Cuatro Estaciones Porteñas

Pillney, Karl Hermann
- Eskapaden eines Gassenhauers; Für Hörer mit Sinn für musikalische Eulenspiegeleien
Pisk, Paul Amadeus
- Partita, op.10
Raasted, N.O.
- Sinfonia da Chiesa, op.76
Ravel, Maurice
- Ma Mère l'Oye (Mother Goose); Ballet en un acte, cinq tableaux et un apothéose
Reizenstein, Franz
- Serenade in F, op.29a
Revueltas, Silvestre
- Musica Para Charlar
Riege, Ernst
- Serenade

Rogers, Bernard
- A Letter from Pete
Saygun, A. Adnan
- Bir Orman Masali; A Forest Tale
Schickele, Peter
- Concerto for Chamber Orchestra
Schreker, Franz
- Symphony in A minor, op.1
Schuman, William
- The Witch of Endor; Ballet
Sibelius, Jean
- Pelleas & Melisande, op.46
- Svanevit Suite, op.54
Strauss, Richard
- Tanzsuite nach Couperin
Vir, Param
- The Theatre of Magical Beings

31' - 40'

STRING ORCHESTRA

Corigliano, John
 - Symphony No.2 for String
   Orchestra
Lutosławski, Witold
 - Preludes and Fugue
Maw, Nicholas
 - Life Studies; Eight studies for 15
   solo strings
Mirzoyan, Edvard
 - Symphony for Strings and Timpani
Schnittke, Alfred
 - Labyrinths, Ballet Suite

ENSEMBLE

Ben-Haim, Paul
 - Kabbalat shabbat (Friday Evening
   Service)
Beyer, Frank Michael
 - Musikalisches Opfer; Ricercare a 3,
   Fuga canonica & 9 Kanons
Braun, Peter Michael
 - Quanta
Cage, John
 - Cheap Imitation; Version for 24
   Players
Eötvös, Peter
 - Chinese Opera
Glass, Philip
 - Glassworks
Hiller, Lejaren
 - Algorithms I; For 9 Instruments and
   Tape
 - Divertimento

Muldowney, Dominic
 - The Earl of Essex Galliard
Nørgård, Per
 - Amled, Prince of Jutland
Obst, Michael
 - Nachtstücke
Rihm, Wolfgang
 - Kein Firmament
Schenker, Friedrich
 - Gute Behandlung der Pferde
Stöhr, Richard
 - Kammersymphonie, op.32
Surinach, Carlos
 - Apasionada, Ballet for chamber
   orchestra
Wolf-Ferrari, Ermanno
 - Chamber Symphony, op.8

CHAMBER ORCHESTRA

Adolphe, Bruce
 - Three Pieces; For Kids in the
   Audience and Chamber Orchestra
Bartók, Béla
 - Suite No.2, op.4
Bolcom, William
 - Symphony No.3
Cage, John
 - Quartets I-VIII; For an Orchestra of
   24 Instruments
David, Johann Nepomuk
 - Magische Quadrate; Symphonische
   Phantasie, Wk52
 - Symphony No.1 in A minor, Wk18
 - Symphony No.3, Wk28
Einem, Gottfried von
 - Symphony No.4, op.80
 - Wiener Symphonie, op.49
Hovhaness, Alan
 - Saint Vartan Symphony

Jenner, Gustav
 - Serenade for Orchestra
Juon, Paul
 - Kammersinfonie (Chamber
   Symphony), op.27
Lloyd, Jonathan
 - Symphony No.3
Maw, Nicholas
 - Serenade
Maxwell Davies, Peter
 - Strathclyde Concerto No.10;
   Concerto for Orchestra
 - Symphony No.4
Mozart, Wolfgang Amadeus
 - Divertimento for Mozart; 12 aspects
   of the aria "Ein Mädchen oder
   Weibchen wünscht Papageno sich"
Rautavaara, Einojuhani
 - Symphony No.7; Angel of Light
Reznicek, Emil Nikolaus von
 - Symphony in the Old Style
Roussel, Albert
 - Le festin de l'araignée; Ballet-
   pantomime en un acte, op.17
Saint-Saëns, Camille
 - Symphony in F; Urbs Roma
Schwarz-Schilling, Reinhard
 - Partita
Shostakovich, Dmitri
 - Chamber Symphony, op.73a
Strauss, Richard
 - Le Bourgeois Gentilhomme (Der
   Bürger als Edelmann): Suite, op.60
Treibmann, Karl Ottomar
 - Symphony No.2
Yun, Isang
 - Kammersinfonie II (Chamber
   Symphony II)
Zemlinsky, Alexander
 - Symphony No.2 in Bb major

Over 40'

ENSEMBLE

Cage, John
- Sixteen Dances

Feldman, Morton
- For Samuel Beckett; For 23 players
- Samuel Beckett; Words & Music

Glass, Philip
- Book of Longing

Harvey, Jonathan
- Bhakti

Hindemith, Paul
- In Sturm und Eis; Music to Arnold Fanck's film *Im Kampf mit dem Berge*

Hölszky, Adriana
- Tragoedia (Der unsichtbare Raum)

Honegger, Arthur
- Le Dit des Jeux du Monde, 10 Danses; 2 interludes et 1 épilogue pour orchestre de chambre, pour le poème de Paul Méral, H.19

Lang, David
- Child

Obst, Michael
- Nosferatu

Oliver, Stephen
- Nicholas Nickelby (incidental music)

Rihm, Wolfgang
- Jagden und Formen

Rodríguez, Robert Xavier
- A Midsummer Night's Dream; Incidental Music

Schenker, Friedrich
- Jessenin-Majakowski-Recital

Sibelius, Jean
- Scaramouche; Tragic Pantomime, op.71

CHAMBER ORCHESTRA

Bonnet, Antoine
- Trajectoires

Dittrich, Paul-Heinz
- Abwärts wend ich mich

Einem, Gottfried von
- Prinzessin Turandot, op.1; Ballet in two scenes to a scenario by Luigi Malipiero
- Rondo vom goldenen Kalb; Three Nocturnes to scenes by Tatjana Gsovsky, op.13

Falla, Manuel de
- Fuego Fatuo

Gál, Hans
- Symphony No.2, op.53

Haas, Georg Friedrich
- in vain

Haas, Joseph
- Variationen-Suite; Über ein altes Rokoko-Thema, op.64

Koch, Erland von
- Skandinavische Tänze

Milhaud, Darius
- Vendanges; Ballet, op.317

Nilsson, Bo
- Hemsoborna
- Bombi Bitt

Prokofiev, Sergei
- Cinderella; Ballet in three acts. Op.87
- Eugene Onegin; For narrator, actors and orchestra, op.71

Rodrigo, Joaquín
- Soleriana; Suite for chamber orchestra

Schmidt, Franz
- Concerto for Piano in E-flat Major

Shostakovich, Dmitri
- New Babylon, op.1

REPERTOIRE LISTED BY TITLE

The following is a complete listing of all compositions by title. Chamber Orchestra, Ensemble *and* Solo Repertoire are included. If known, the year of composition in listed in brackets.

"..."; Double Concerto for Accordion and Viola - Haas, Georg Friedrich (1994)

1600 Pennsylvania Avenue: Suite for Orchestra - Bernstein, Leonard (1976)

3 X 7 - Schnittke, Alfred (1989)

4 D - Mochizuki, Misato (2003)

4 Enso (LO-SHU VII) - Zender, Hans (1997)

40. Mai; Suite, op.25 - Spitzmüller, Alexander (1941)

7 Sites; For 14 players - Amy, Gilbert (1975)

85 Measures et un Da Capo - Françaix, Jean (1991)

A

À l'île de Gorée - Xenakis, Iannis (1986)

A la Cubana, Marche militaire - Granados, Enrique (1884)

A la Hongroise, op.43, No.6 - Scharwenka, Franz Xaver

À travers Paris, Images symphoniques - Beydts, Louis (1958)

A un Jeune Gentilhomme - Roussel, Albert (1908)

Aarhus Ragtime - Abrahamsen, Hans (1990)

Aaron's Horizons - McGlaughlin, William (1998)

Abbreviaturen - Baur, Jürg (1969)

Abendmusik - Weiss, Manfred (1989)

Abendstimmung, op.120 - Sinding, Christian

Aber die Schönheit des Gitters - Schwehr, Cornelius (1992)

abgewandt 1 - Rihm, Wolfgang (1989)

abgewandt 2; Musik in memoriam Luigi Nono (3. Versuch) - Rihm, Wolfgang (1990)

Abii ne Viderem - Kancheli, Giya (1992)

about to drink dense clouds - Baltakas, Vykintas (2003)

Above; For ensemble and sountrack - Aa, Michel van der (1999)

Abschied vom Walde - Braunfels, Walter (1913)

Abschiedsstücke - Rihm, Wolfgang (1993)

Abwärts wend ich mich - Dittrich, Paul-Heinz (1989)

Abysm - Ruders, Poul (2000)

Accende Lumen Sensibus, op.52 - Kaipainen, Jouni (1996)

Accordance for 8 Instruments - Lieberson, Peter (1975)

Ach, trauriger Mond; Klage um Federico Garcia Lorca - Brandmüller, Theo (1977)

Acid Rain - Gordon, Michael (1986)

Aconcagua (Concierto para Bandoneón) - Piazzolla, Astor

Acrobats of God; Ballet for chamber orchestra - Surinach, Carlos (1960)

Acrostic Song - Del Tredici, David (1987)

Actualités; Musik zu einer Filmwochenschau, op.104 - Milhaud, Darius (1928)

Actuelles 1968 - Paccagnini, Angelo (1968)

Actus Tragicus - Kahn, Erich Itor (1955)

ad absurdum; Concerto for Trumpet - Widmann, Jörg

Ad Marginem - Holliger, Heinz (1983)

Adages, op.120c - Milhaud, Darius (1932)

Adagietto - Kirk, Theron

Adagietto for String Orchestra - Danielpour, Richard (2005)

Adagio, op.11 - Apostel, Hans Erich (1937)

Adagio - Boccadoro, Carlo

Adagio - Janácek, Leoš (1891)

Adagio and Allegro - Eaton, John (1960)

Adagio Cantabile - Horovitz, Joseph (1973)

Adagio Di Preludio - Nørgård, Per (1951)

Adagio for Small Orchestra - Faust, George (1966)

Adagio for Small Orchestra - Rodríguez, Robert Xavier (1967)

Adagio for Solo Horn and Chamber Symphony - Dennison, Sam

Adagio for Strings - Barber, Samuel (1938)

Adagio from "Vaknatten": Incidental music from the play - Blomdahl, Karl-Birger (1945)

Adagio Sostenuto; At Sea - Ives, Charles Edward

Adagio: Variations and Hornpipe from "The Triumph of Neptune" - Berners, Lord (1926)

Adelphony - Moravec, Paul (1997)

Adjustable Wrench - Torke, Michael (1987)

Ae Fond Kiss; For 7 instruments - Boccadoro, Carlo

Aeolian Song - Benson, Warren

Aer: Part 7 of "Maa" - Saariaho, Kaija (1991)

Afatsim - Czernowin, Chaya (1996)

Africa, op.89 - Saint-Saëns, Camille (1891)

After the Clock - Woolrich, John (2005)

After Verdi!; Divertimento in five sections - Hesketh, Kenneth (2001)

Ahnung - Lampersberg, Gerhard (1980)

Aile Du Songe - Saariaho, Kaija (2001)

Air: From "Opera" - Berio, Luciano (1969)

Air and Dance - Delius, Frederick (1915)

Air and Scherzo - Cowell, Henry (1963)

Air mit Sphinxes - Huber, Nicolaus A. (1987)

Airs chantés - Poulenc, Francis (1928)

Akanthos; Phonèmes de Iannis Xenakis - Xenakis, Iannis (1977)

Al Fresco; Intermezzo - Herbert, Victor (1904)

Alax; Pour 30 musiciens divises en 3 ensembles - Xenakis, Iannis (1985)

Alba - Osborne, Nigel (1984)

Alberti Addict - Duddell, Joe (2000)

Album Pour Mes Petites Amis (Album for My Little Friends): Farandole, op.14, No.2 - Pierné, Gabriel

Album Pour Mes Petites Amis (Album for My Little Friends): La Veillee de l'Ange Gardien, op.14, No.3 - Pierné, Gabriel

Album Pour Mes Petites Amis (Album for My Little Friends): Chanson d'Autrefois, op.14, No.5 - Pierné, Gabriel

Album Pour Mes Petites Amis (Album for My Little Friends): Marche des Petits Soldats de Plomb (March of the Little Lead Soldiers), op.14, No.6 - Pierné, Gabriel

Album Pour Mes Petites Amis (Album for My Little Friends): Petite Gavotte, op.14, No.4 - Pierné, Gabriel

Alcancias - Revueltas, Silvestre

Alcott Music: Suite from "Little Women" - Adamo, Mark (2007)

Alegría - Sierra, Roberto (1996)

Aleph - Dalby, Martin (1975)

The Alexandrian Sequence - Hamilton, Iain

Algorithms I; For 9 Instruments and Tape - Hiller, Lejaren

Algorithms II (With Ravi Kumra) for 9 Instruments and Tape - Hiller, Lejaren

Alhambra Fantasy - Anderson, Julian (2000)

Alice Helps the Romance - Dessau, Paul (1929)

Alice in the Wooly West - Dessau, Paul (1926)

Alice the Firefighter - Dessau, Paul (1926)

Alice's Monkey Business - Dessau, Paul (1928)

Aliquant - Wilkinson, Marc (1959)

All Set - Babbitt, Milton (1957)

Alla Culla; Ninna-nanna per piccola orchestra - Pilati, Mario (1940)

Alla Marcia - Blacher, Boris (1934)

Allegretto - Guilmant, Felix-Alexandre (1964)

Allegretto, H.221 - Honegger, Arthur (1938)

Allegretto Sombreoso; Incantation - Ives, Charles Edward

Allegria - Müller-Wieland, Jan (1991)

Allegro - Lento - Allegro: No.3 from "Divertimento for Mozart" - Erbse, Heimo (1956)

Allegro appassionato, op.43 - Saint-Saëns, Camille (1875)

Allegro appassionato, op.70 - Saint-Saëns, Camille (1884)

Allegro Giocoso: No.8 from "Divertimento for Mozart" - Wimberger, Gerhard (1956)

Allegro Moderato: No.9 from "Divertimento for Mozart" - Roux, Maurice le (1956)

Alleluia - Harrison, Lou

Alma redemptoris mater, op.7, No.1 - Ballif, Claude

Altdeutsche Liedersuite (Old German Song Suite) - Klenau, Paul von (1934)

Amadeus' Billiard - Wyner, Yehudi (1991)

Amarantos - Casken, John (1978)

Amaryllis; Variants on an Old English Round - Schuman, William

The Amazing Flight; Ballet mécanique, H.159 - Martinů, Bohuslav (1927)

American Dances - Kreutz, Arthur (1941)

American Invention - Martland, Steve (1985)

American Melting Pot Set - Cowell, Henry (1940)

Amled; Prince of Jutland - Nørgård, Per (1993)

Amled: Suite - Nørgård, Per (1993)

El Amor Brujo (First Version) - Falla, Manuel de (1915)

El Amor Brujo (Second Version) - Falla, Manuel de (1925)

El Amor Brujo: Chanson du Feu Follet - Falla, Manuel de

El Amor Brujo: Récit du Pécheur et Pantomime - Falla, Manuel de

El Amor Brujo: Ritual Fire Dance - Falla, Manuel de

Amor Timido, op.50 - Wellesz, Egon (1933)

Amtsantritt von Leonce und Lena; Zweite imaginäre Theaterszene nach dem Schluss von Georg Büchner - Müller-Wieland, Jan (1998)

An den Wassern Babylons; Songs of Babylonian Jews for Small Orchestra - Ettinger, Max

An den Wassern zu Babel saßen wir und weinten; Psalm 137 - Pärt, Arvo (1976)

An die Musik - Birtwistle, Sir Harrison (1988)

Anaktoria - Xenakis, Iannis (1969)

Analogie; Suite for Orchestra - Dubois, Pierre-Max

Ancient Lights - Moravec, Paul (1990)

...and flowers fall... - Wilson, Ian (1990)

And On The Seventh Day - Earls, Paul (1958)

Andacht zum Kleinen - Hoyland, Vic (1980)

Andante - Indy, Vincent d'

Andante, op.50a - Prokofiev, Sergei (1930)

Andante sostenuto, op.51 - Klengel, Julius

An Angel Serves a Small Breakfast; 2. Concerto - Wilson, Ian (1999)

Animisation - Talbot, Joby (1995)

The Angel and the Ship of Souls - Bawden, Rupert (1983)

Anstieg - Ausblick für Orchester - Stranz, Ulrich (2002)

Antiche Danze ed Arie: Suite 1 - Respighi, Ottorino (1917)

Antiphon - Berkeley, Lennox (1973)

Antiphonia I - Morthenson, Jan Wilhelm (1963)

Antiphonia II - Morthenson, Jan Wilhelm (1965)

Antiphonismoi - Halffter, Cristóbal (1967)

Antoniana; Suite for Small Orchestra after Vivaldi, op.47 - Turok, Paul (1977)

Apartment To Let - Braun, Yehezkel

Apasionada; Ballet for chamber orchestra - Surinach, Carlos (1960)

Apokalypse - Einfeldt, Dieter

Appalachian Spring: Suite (original version) - Copland, Aaron (1944)

Appalachian Spring: Suite (full orchestra version) - Copland, Aaron (1944)

Apparitions - Danielpour, Richard (2003)

Appearances - Wallin, Rolf (2002)

Aqua - Heitzeg, Steve (1999)

Aquarell - Denisov, Edison (1975)

Aquarelles - Buck, Ole (1983)

Arabesque; For piano and chamber ensemble - Krauze, Zygmunt (1983)

Arabian Suite - Petyrek, Felix (1925)

Arbor Low - Talbot, Joby (1994)

Arcana - Schafer, Robert Murray (1972)

Archaische Tänze; Neun sinfonische Reigen für kleines Orchester, op.30 - Lendvai, Erwin (1922)

Archipelago "Rhumba" - Antheil, George (1935)

Archipelago S. - Takemitsu, Tōru (1993)

Architettura per musica - Beyer, Frank
Michael (1989)

Arcus - Höller, York (1978)

Arena II - Lindberg, Magnus (1996)

Aria, op.112 - Bazelaire, Paul

Aria; For Orchestra, or Divers Soli and
Orchestra - Roussel, Albert

Aria / Ariadne; "Szenarie" - Rihm,
Wolfgang (2001)

Aria de la Folia Española - Henze,
Hans Werner (1977)

Aria of the Blessed Virgin after Henry
Purcell - Fussell, Charles (1968)

Ariadne auf Naxos: Overture and
Dance Scene, op.60 - Strauss,
Richard (1916)

Arias - Hamilton, Iain (1962)

Arias and Barcarolles - Bernstein,
Leonard (1988)

Arien des Orpheus - Henze, Hans
Werner (1981)

The Art of the Fugue - Osborne, Nigel
(1993)

As you like it: Suite, op.21 - Quilter,
Roger (1920)

Ascoltare stanca; Pour 18
Instrumentistes - Aperghis, Georges
(1972)

Ash - Torke, Michael (1988)

Aspects of Leaving - Nørgård, Per
(1997)

L'assassinat de Duc de Guise;
Tableux d'histoire, op.128 - Saint-
Saëns, Camille (1908)

At First Light - Benjamin, George
(1982)

At the Bier of a Young Artist, F.58 -
Nielsen, Carl (1910)

At the Still Point of the Turning World,
op.41 - Patterson, Paul (1980)

Atemkristal - Pasquet, Yves-Marie

Atrées - Xenakis, Iannis (1960)

Attach; For ensemble and soundtrack
- Aa, Michel van der (1999)

Aubade - Moravec, Paul (1990)

Aufstieg und Fall der Stadt
Mahagonny (Rise and Fall of the
City of Mahagonny): Alabama Song
- Weill, Kurt (1927)

Aufstieg und Fall der Stadt
Mahagonny (Rise and Fall of the
City of Mahagonny): Suite - Weill,
Kurt (1929)

Aus den Letzten Tagen - Bryars,
Gavin (1991)

"...aus freier Lust...verbunden..." -
Haas, Georg Friedrich (1996)

Auto-Electric - Hindson, Matthew
(2003)

Automation (Music for a real or
imagined film score) - Schuller,
Gunther (1962)

Automne malade - Halffter, Ernesto

Autumn; A symphonic sketch for small
orchestra, op.8 - Prokofiev, Sergei
(1910)

Autumn; Concertino for Harp,
Percussion and Strings - Thomson,
Virgil (1964)

Autumn Music, op.39 - Firsova, Elena
(1988)

Aux étoiles - Duparc, Henri (1910)

Available Forms I - Brown, Earle
(1961)

Away - Lindberg, Magnus (1994)

B

B for J - Asia, Daniel

B.W.V. - Aperghis, Georges (1973)

Babil - Aperghis, Georges (1996)

Bacchanten-Overture, op.52 - Bleyle,
Karl

Le bachelier de Salamanque, op.20,
No.1 - Roussel, Albert (1919)

Bach to the Future - Nørgård, Per
(1996)

Das Bächlein, op.88/1 - Strauss,
Richard (1933)

Back Bay Bicinium - Loevendie, Theo

Bag Den Kan Fredens Ranker Gro
(Behind it grow the branches of
peace) - Bruun, Peter (1999)

Bagatellen - Biersack, Anton

Bagatelles "Cinque Pezzi Notturni" -
Frankel, Benjamin (1959)

La Bal masqué; Cantate profane sur
un texte de Max Jacob - Poulenc,
Francis (1932)

La Bal Martiniquais - Milhaud, Darius

Balkan Connection - Hindson,
Matthew (2003)

Ballad, op.33 - Zbinden, Julien-
François (1961)

A Ballad of Game and Dream -
Rasmussen, Karl Aage (1974)

Ballade - Benjamin, Arthur (1947)

Ballade, op.19 - Fauré, Gabriel

Ballade - Goldmark, Carl (1913)

Ballade - Poot, Marcel (1952)

Ballade Concertante; For Zheng and
String Orchestra - Yu, Julian (1999)

Ballade von der sexuellen Hörigkeit:
From "Die Dreigroschenoper" - Weill,
Kurt (1928)

Ballata, op.92 - Foerster, Josef
Bohuslav (1911)

Ballet de Cour, No.1: Rigaudon -
Pierné, Gabriel (1901)

Ballet de Cour, No.2: Passepied -
Pierné, Gabriel (1901)

Ballet de Cour, No.3: La Canarie -
Pierné, Gabriel (1901)

Ballet de Cour, No.4: Pavane et
Saltarello - Pierné, Gabriel (1901)

Ballet de Cour, No.5: Menuet de Roy -
Pierné, Gabriel (1901)

Ballet de Cour, No.6: Passamezzo -
Pierné, Gabriel (1901)

Ballet Suite "Scaramussio," op.36 -
Gál, Hans (1929)

Ballet Suite: Peter Tailless, the Cat -
Koch, Erland von (1948)

Ballets imaginaires - Krätzschmar,
Wilfried

Balletsuite - Rasch, Kurt

Eine Balletsuite, op.130 - Reger, Max
(1913)

Bardo - Zender, Hans (2000)

Bardo-Puls; Musik nach dem
tibetanischen Totenbuch - Kahowez,
Günther (1974)

Barocco-Suite No.5, op.23 - Atterberg,
Kurt

Bartók Suite - Bartók, Béla

Bartók-Reflexionen - Pfundt, Reinhard
(1983)

Batik - Revueltas, Silvestre

Beaubourg Musique - Haubenstock-
Ramati, Roman (1988)

Beber, op.31 - Fujiie, Keiko (1994)

Before Krishna - Vir, Param (1987)

Bele - León, Tania

La belle excentrique; Fantasie
sérieuse pour orchestra de music-
hall - Satie, Erik (1920)

The Beloved - León, Tania

Belsazars Gaestabud (Belshazzar's
Feast); Incidental Music, op.51 -
Sibelius, Jean (1906)

Benedictus, op.37, No.3 - MacKenzie,
Sir Alexander C.

Berceuse - Järnefelt, Armas (1904)

Berceuse - Kallstenius, Edvin (1939)

Berceuse elegiaque - Busoni,
Ferruccio (1907)

Berenice: Lied vom Verschwinden -
Staud, Johannes Maria (2003)

Berenice: Suite 1 - Staud, Johannes
Maria (2003)

Berenice: Suite 2 - Staud, Johannes
Maria (2003)

Berio Mask - Rasmussen, Karl Aage
(1977)

Berlin im Licht-Song - Weill, Kurt (1928)

Besuch In Der Kindheit (Childhood Revisited) - Kancheli, Giya (1998)

Besuch in Urach, op.62/40 - Schoeck, Othmar (1950)

Between Scylla and Charybdis, op.104 - Smirnov, Dmitri (1998)

Bewegingen (Movements) - Vries, Klaas de

Beyond the Pale; A Portrait of a Klezmer for Clarinet and String Orchestra - Adler, Samuel (2007)

Bhakti - Harvey, Jonathan (1982)

Bianca-Nera; Overture - Rosenberg, Hilding Constantin (1946)

Bien - Scherchen, Tona (1973)

Bild (eine Chiffre) - Rihm, Wolfgang (1984)

Bildnisse I - Kirchner, Volker David (1982)

Bildnisse II - Kirchner, Volker David (1984)

Bildnisse III - Kirchner, Volker David (1991)

Billy the Kid: Prairie Night & Celebration Dance - Copland, Aaron (1938)

Billy the Kid: Waltz (Billy and his Sweetheart) - Copland, Aaron (1938)

Bir Orman Masali, A Forest Tale - Saygun, A. Adnan

Birthday Music for Sir William Glock - Saxton, Robert (1988)

Bitz! - Guy, Barry (1979)

Black Riddle; Five Songs for Soprano and Large Chamber Ensemble - Woolrich, John (1984)

Blind Visions - Burt, Francis (1995)

The Blue Hula - Picker, Tobias (1981)

Bluebird Pas de Deux - Stravinsky, Igor (1941)

Blues, H.66a - Honegger, Arthur (1928)

Boccaccio-Suite; Novelle dal Decamerone - Nussio, Otmar

Le boeuf sur le toit; Ballet, op.58 - Milhaud, Darius (1919)

Bohemian Danish Folksong, F.130 - Nielsen, Carl (1928)

Bombi Bitt - Nilsson, Bo (1966)

A Book of Hours - Bennett, Richard Rodney (1991)

Book of Hours; In two parts - Anderson, Julian (2004)

Book of Longing - Glass, Philip (2007)

Boom-Box - Hindson, Matthew (1999)

The Boor: Overture to the opera - Argento, Dominick (1957)

Le Bourgeois Gentilhomme (Der Bürger als Edelmann): Suite, op.60 - Strauss, Richard (1918)

Boyl - Wallin, Rolf (1995)

Brandenburg Concerto for Flute, Oboe, Violin, Strings and Harpsichord - Ekimovsky, Viktor (1979)

Brautlied: "Wo du hingehst..." (Bride's Song: Where you are going...) - Kaminski, Heinrich (1911)

Breathe - Kulenty, Hanna (1987)

Brideshead Variations - Burgon, Geoffrey (1981)

Bright Dances, op.24 - Nørgård, Per (1959)

A Bright Kind of High - Marthinsen, Niels (1996)

Brillantes Concertino: No.5 from "Divertimento for Mozart" - Bentzon, Niels Viggo (1956)

Broadway Boogie - Schickele, Peter

The Broken Spectre - MacRae, Stuart (1996)

Bruckner Dialog, op.39 - Einem, Gottfried von (1971)

Brundibár: Suite from the opera - Krása, Hans (1943)

Bucolics - Lutosławski, Witold (1952)

Bucolique - Poulenc, Francis (1954)

Burleske, AV 85 - Strauss, Richard (1886)

Burnham Wick, op.73 - Matthews, David (1997)

By All Means - Muhly, Nico (2004)

C

Cadence - Laderman, Ezra (1978)

Cadence Music - McGuire, John (1982)

Cadillac Ranch - Knight, Edward (1998)

The Cage - Osborne, Nigel (1981)

Calendar; For Chamber Ensemble - Bennett, Richard Rodney (1960)

Call Them All - Roumain, Daniel Bernard (2006)

Calmo - Berio, Luciano (1989)

Campo Marzio, op.80 - Krenek, Ernst (1937)

Cancionero Para Una Mariposa - Dalby, Martin (1971)

Canções típicas brasileiras - Villa-Lobos, Heitor (1935)

Cançunik: Suite No.1, op.79 - Schmitt, Florent (1929)

Canon and Corale - Rosing-Schow, Niels (1984)

Canonical American Songbook - Harbison, John (2005)

Cantate de Psaumes, op.425 - Milhaud, Darius (1967)

Canti Per 13 - Nono, Luigi (1955)

Cántico de la Esposa - Rodrigo, Joaquín (1934)

Canto Dalla Città Inquieta: From "Totale" - Gaslini, Giorgio (1965)

Canto di giorno; For cello and orchestra - Beyer, Frank Michael (1998/99)

Canto I, op.96 - Bavicchi, John (1987)

Cantos de México - Chávez, Carlos (1933)

Cantus Arcticus; Concerto for Birds and Orchestra - Rautavaara, Einojuhani (1972)

Cantus Firmus; Musik in memoriam Luigi Nono (1. Versuch) - Rihm, Wolfgang (1990)

Cantus in Memory of Benjamin Britten - Pärt, Arvo (1977)

Canzona (After Giovanni Gabrieli) - Maxwell Davies, Peter (1969)

Canzona - Rota, Nino (1935)

Canzona di Ombra; For solo oboe and strings - Beyer, Frank Michael (1986)

Canzona; In Memoriam Igor Stravinsky - Saxton, Robert (1978)

Canzona for Chamber Orchestra - Hunt, Frederick

Canzona, op.76 - Burkhard, Willy (1945)

Canzonetta, op.62a - Sibelius, Jean (1911)

Canzonetta for Clarinet and Orchestra - Pierné, Gabriel

Capriccio, op.2 - Einem, Gottfried von (1943)

Capriccio, op.4 - Erbse, Heimo (1952)

Capriccio; For piano, five solo instruments and percussion, op.92b - Pauels, Heinz (1960)

Capriccio - Reizenstein, Franz (1957)

Capriccio - Stock, David (1963)

Capriccio - Tull, Fisher (1980)

Capriccio "Kraft-Variations"; On a Theme by Paganini - Matthus, Siegfried (1999)

Capriccio 71 - Treibmann, Karl Ottomar

Capriccio for Cello and Chamber Orchestra, op.145 - Krenek, Ernst (1955)

Capriccio für Kammerorchester (Nonett) - Genzmer, Harald

Capriccio notturno; In Memoriam Carl Nielsen, op.20 - Bacri, Nicolas (1987)

Capriccio Spettrale - Holt, Simon

Capricciosi - Engelmann, Hans Ulrich (1968)

Caprice - Aubert, Louis (1924)

Caprice bohémien, op.12 - Rachmaninoff, Sergei (1894)

Caprice Nr. I, op.A-14 - Manén, Joan

Caprice Nr. II, op.A-15 - Manén, Joan

Caprichos - Woolrich, John (1997)

Capricious Angels - Thomas, Augusta Read (2009)

Capricorn Concerto - Barber, Samuel (1944)

Caprisma 2 - Wolpe, Michael

Captain Coram's Kids - Hurd, Michael (1988)

Caravanfanfan-farefare No.1 - Gudmundsen-Holmgreen, Pelle (2001)

Caravanfanfan-farefare No.3 - Gudmundsen-Holmgreen, Pelle (2001)

Caribbean Dance; A New Jamaican Rumba - Benjamin, Arthur (1946)

Carillon - Grinberg, Alexander (1988)

Carillon joyeux - Brandmüller, Theo (1994)

Carlo; Music for strings and sampler - Dean, Brett (1997)

Carmen Arcadiae Perpetuum - Birtwistle, Sir Harrison (1978)

Carmen Variations; Theme, Variations and Finale on a Theme from Bizet's "Carmen" - Baur, Jürg (1947)

La Carnaval de Londres: Suite sur les airs de "l' Opéra du Gueux," op.172 - Milhaud, Darius (1937)

Le carnaval des animaux; Grande fantasie zoologique - Saint-Saëns, Camille (1886)

Carnet de croquis et d'esquisses - Satie, Erik (1914)

Carnival Overture - Morawetz, Oskar (1946)

Carol - Cowell, Henry (1965)

Carolina Christmas; Suite for Chamber Orchestra - Hier, Ethel Glenn

Caroline Mathilde: Concert Suite from Act I of the ballet - Maxwell Davies, Peter (1991)

Caroline Mathilde: Concert Suite from Act II of the ballet - Maxwell Davies, Peter (1991)

Carolísima; Serenade for Chamber Orchestra - Maxwell Davies, Peter (1994)

Castelnau; For String Orchestra - Greenbaum, Matthew (2008)

Catalogue de fleurs, op.60 - Milhaud, Darius (1920)

Catalogue of Incidents - Frankel, Benjamin (1965)

Câtana - Finnissy, Michael

Catena - Nelson, Larry (1986)

Cat's-eye - Sawer, David (1986)

Cavatina - Halffter, Ernesto (1934)

Cayuga - Phibbs, Joseph (1999)

Cayuga Lake (Memories) - Husa, Karel (1992)

Celtic Symphony - Bantock, Granville (1940)

Centering - Brown, Earle (1973)

Central Park in the Dark - Ives, Charles Edward (1906)

Cerberus - Williams, Graham (1977)

Chaconne, Wk71 - David, Johann Nepomuk (1972)

Chain 1 [Launch 1] - Lutosławski, Witold (1983)

Chain 2 [Launch 2]; Dialogue for Violin and Orchestra - Lutosławski, Witold (1985)

Chairman Dances; Foxtrot for Orchestra - Adams, John (1985)

Chalan - Sotelo, Mauricio (2003)

Chamber Concerto - Barati, George (1952)

Chamber Concerto - Erb, Donald

Chamber Concerto - Geissler, Fritz

Chamber Concerto, op.31 - Kurz, Siegfried

Chamber Concerto, op.28 - Schiske, Karl (1949)

Chamber Concerto - Studer, Hans (1947)

Chamber Concerto, op.15 - Wood, Hugh (1971)

Chamber Concerto 05 - Henze, Hans Werner (2005)

Chamber Concerto for 11 Instruments, op.52 - Bentzon, Niels Viggo (1948)

Chamber Concerto in D minor, op.24 - Raphael, Günter

Chamber Concerto No.1; For flute and strings, op.19 - Firsova, Elena (1978)

Chamber Concerto No.1 - Musgrave, Thea (1962)

Chamber Concerto No.2 - Holmboe, Vagn (1952)

Chamber Concerto No.2 - Musgrave, Thea (1966)

Chamber Concerto No.2, op.26; Concerto for Cello No.2 - Firsova, Elena (1982)

Chamber Concerto No.3; For piano and orchestra, op.33 - Firsova, Elena (1985)

Chamber Concerto No.4; For horn and 13 performers, op.37 - Firsova, Elena (1987)

Chamber Concerto No.5; For cello and small orchestra - Firsova, Elena (1996)

Chamber Concerto No.6; The Temple of Mnemosyne, op.80 - Firsova, Elena (1996)

Chamber Dance - Tower, Joan (2006)

Chamber Music - Kósa, György (1928)

Chamber Music for Twelve Musicians - Yanov-Yanovsky, Dmitri (1993)

Chamber Music I - Buck, Ole (1979)

Chamber Music II - Buck, Ole (1982)

Chamber Music II - Lehmann, Hans Ulrich (1979)

Chamber Music IV - Schmidt, Christfried (1972)

Chamber Music No.1 - Rosenman, Leonard

Chamber Music No.2 - Rosenman, Leonard

Chamber Piece No.1 - Wolpe, Stefan

Chamber Piece No.2 - Wolpe, Stefan

Chamber Sinfonietta - Swafford, Jan

Chamber Symphony - Adams, John (1992)

Chamber Symphony, op.2 - Adès, Thomas (1990)

Chamber Symphony - Anderson, T.J. (1968)

Chamber Symphony - Bäck, Sven-Erik (1955)

Chamber Symphony - Blake, David (1966)

Chamber Symphony (O Bella e Vaga Aurora) - Dalby, Martin (1982)

Chamber Symphony (Symphony No.2) - Degen, Helmut (1947)

Chamber Symphony - Denisov, Edison (1982)

Chamber Symphony (1954) - Geissler, Fritz (1954)

Chamber Symphony (1970) - Geissler, Fritz (1970)

Chamber Symphony - Gill, Jeremy (2005)

Chamber Symphony - Hartley, Walter Sinclair (1954)

Chamber Symphony - Imbrie, Andrew (1968)

Chamber Symphony - Milner, Anthony (1968)

Chamber Symphony - Roslavets, Nikolai Andreyevich (1926)

Chamber Symphony; For 18 solo instruments - Roslavets, Nikolai Andreyevich (1935)

Chamber Symphony - Schuller, Gunther (1989)

Chamber Symphony, op.73a - Shostakovich, Dmitri (1946)

Chamber Symphony, op.110a - Shostakovich, Dmitri (1960)

Chamber Symphony, op.83a - Shostakovich, Dmitri (1949)

Chamber Symphony, op.8 - Wolf-Ferrari, Ermanno (1901)

Chamber Symphony for 9 Instruments - Rochberg, George (1953)

Chamber Symphony No.1, op.53 - Holmboe, Vagn (1951)

Chamber Symphony No.1; Le Printemps, op.43 - Milhaud, Darius (1917)

Chamber Symphony No.1 - Walker, Robert (1981)

Chamber Symphony No.2 - Denisov, Edison (1994)

Chamber Symphony No.2, op.100 - Holmboe, Vagn (1968)

Chamber Symphony No.2; Pastorale, op.49 - Milhaud, Darius (1918)

Chamber Symphony No.3 - Holmboe, Vagn (1969)

Chamber Symphony No.3; Sérénade, op.71 - Milhaud, Darius (1921)

Chamber Symphony No.4; Dixtuor à Cordes, op.74 - Milhaud, Darius (1921)

Chamber Symphony No.5; Dixtuor d'Instruments à Vent, op.75 - Milhaud, Darius (1922)

Chamber Symphony: The Circles of Light - Saxton, Robert (1986)

Chamber Variations for 13 Players, op.15 - Jekimowski, Viktor (1974)

La Chambre Claire - Mochizuki, Misato (1998)

Changes; A little music for Mozart - Vercoe, Elizabeth (1991)

Chanson à Bercer, op.19, No.1 - Schmitt, Florent (1898)

Chanson de Matin, op.15, No.2 - Elgar, Edward (1899)

Chanson de Nuit, op.15, No.1 - Elgar, Edward (1899)

Chanson et Étude, op.A-8 - Manén, Joan

Chanson hébraïque - Ravel, Maurice (1910)

Chansons pour les oiseaux - Beydts, Louis

Chansons villageoises - Poulenc, Francis (1942)

Chant et Danse - Bondon, Jacques (1974)

Chant Funebre, op.9 - Magnard, Albéric (1895)

Chantefables pour les enfants sages; Pour Soprano et 20 musiciens - Albin, Roger

Chantefleur et Chantefables - Lutosławski, Witold (1990)

Le chapeau de paille d'Italie - Ibert, Jacques (1929)

Charlie Rutlage - Ives, Charles Edward (1920)

Charrette - Anderson, Allen (1984)

Chat Moss - Maxwell Davies, Peter (1994)

Château de l'âme - Saariaho, Kaija (1996)

Cheap Imitation, Version for 24 Players - Cage, John

Cheironomiës - Gesten; Conductor's Improvisation, Klangskizze in Modellen für variable Besetzung - Antoniou, Theodore (1971)

Cheltenham Concerto - Rochberg, George (1960)

Chemins II (su Sequenza VI) - Berio, Luciano (1967)

Chemins IIb - Berio, Luciano (1970)

Chemins IV (su Sequenza VII) - Berio, Luciano (1975)

Chemins V (su Sequenza XI) - Berio, Luciano (1992)

Chetro Ketl - Neikrug, Marc (1986)

Le Chevelure de Bérénice - Boucourechliev, André (1988)

Chiffre I - Rihm, Wolfgang (1982)

Chiffre II; Silence to be beaten - Rihm, Wolfgang (1983)

Chiffre III - Rihm, Wolfgang (1983)

Chiffre IV - Rihm, Wolfgang (1984)

Chiffre V - Rihm, Wolfgang (1984)

Chiffre VI - Rihm, Wolfgang (1985)

Chiffre VII - Rihm, Wolfgang (1985)

Chiffre VIII - Rihm, Wolfgang (1988)

Chiffre-Cycle - Rihm, Wolfgang (1982-1988)

Child - Lang, David (2001)

A Children's Overture, op.17 - Quilter, Roger

Chimera; A song cycle for speaker and seven players - Hagen, Daron (1981)

Chimera - Mochizuki, Misato (2000)

Chimeric Images - Schuller, Gunther (1988)

Chimes at Midnight - Marthinsen, Niels (1993)

Chinese Opera - Eötvös, Peter (1986)

CHLEBNICOV - Platz, Robert H. P. (1979)

Choral à 8 - Holliger, Heinz (1983)

Chorale for Chamber Orchestra - Almand, Claude

Chorale Prelude by J. S. Bach - Ben-Haim, Paul

Das Christ-Elflein, op.20 - Pfitzner, Hans (1906)

Christian Zeal and Activity - Adams, John (1973)

Christmas, op.145, No.3 - Reger, Max (1916)

A Christmas Pastorale - McAlister, Clark

Christmas Sinfonietta - Vinter, Gilbert (1956)

The Chronicles of Narnia Suite - Burgon, Geoffrey (1991)

Ciacona - Engelmann, Hans Ulrich (1993)

Cinco Invocaciones al Crucificado - Montsalvatge, Xavier (1969)

Cinco Sellos - Delás, José Luis de (1972)

Cinderella; Ballet in three acts, op.87 - Prokofiev, Sergei (1944)

Cinéma: Entr'acte symphonique du ballet "Relâche" - Satie, Erik (1924)

Cinéma (René Clair's "Entr'acte") - Harle, John (1995)

Cinq Chansons de Charles Vildrac, op.167 - Milhaud, Darius (1937)

Cinq Danzas Gitanas, op.55 - Turina, Joaquin (1931)

Cinq Enfantines - Barlow, Fred

Cinq Études pour Piano et Orchestre, op.63 - Milhaud, Darius (1920)

Cinq Melodies (sans paroles), op.35 - Prokofiev, Sergei (1920)

Cinq Mélodies populaires grecques (Five Greek Folk Melodies) - Ravel, Maurice (1906)

Cinq pièces brèves - Ropartz, Joseph Guy Marie

Circle with Four Trios; Conductor and Audience - Tan, Dun (1992)

The Circling Canopy of Night -
Hesketh, Kenneth (1999)

Circo; Suite - Muñoz Molleda, José
(1964)

Circus Overture - Toch, Ernst (1953)

Circus Polka; Composed for a Young
Elephant - Stravinsky, Igor (1942)

The City: Incidental music for the
documentary film - Copland, Aaron
(1939)

City By The Lake: A Portrait of
Rochester, NY - Adler, Samuel
(1968)

City Life - Reich, Steve (1995)

The City of Threads - Nordentoft,
Anders (1994)

Clairobscur - Sørensen, Bent (1987)

Clarinet Sonata - Bernstein, Leonard
(1942)

Clarino Concerto - Pape, Andy (1990)

Classic Suite in B-flat major, op.32 -
Alexandrov, Anatoly (1926)

Classical Symphony in D; Symphony
No.1, op.25 - Prokofiev, Sergei
(1917)

Classical Variations in C - Arnell,
Richard (1939)

Clocks; For ensemble and tape - Kats-
Chernin, Elena (1993)

The Cloisters - Corigliano, John
(1965)

Clown Dances - Stroman, Scott (1984)

El Cojo Enamorado: Ballet Suite -
Halffter, Ernesto (1955)

Coleccion Nocturna - Felder, David
(1984)

Collage - Blacher, Boris (1968)

Collage on B-A-C-H - Pärt, Arvo
(1964)

Collateral Damage - Hayden, Sam
(1999)

Colloïdes sonores - Yun, Isang (1961)

Colorines - Revueltas, Silvestre

Comedy on the Bridge: Little Suite
from the opera - Martinů, Bohuslav
(1935)

Comedy Overture, op.32 - Weigl, Karl
(1933)

Comin' Right Atcha - Hindson,
Matthew (2006)

Commedia for (Almost) 18th Century
Orchestra - Bolcom, William (1971)

Commedia III - Bennett, Richard
Rodney (1973)

Compagnie Masquerade; Ein
Divertissement für kleines
Orchester, einer Idee & teilweise
erhaltenen Violinstimme Mozarts
folgend - Schwertsik, Kurt (2005)

Company - Glass, Philip (1983)

Compensazioni, op.9 - Wittinger,
Róbert (1967)

Composition for 10 Instruments I-V -
Ullmann, Jakob (1982)

Composition for 12 Instruments -
Babbitt, Milton (1948)

Composition for 19 - Lehmann, Hans
Ulrich (1965)

Composition for String Orchestra and
Tape - Babbitt, Milton (1967)

Composizione da Camera -
Matsushita, Shin-ichi

Compound Fracture - Talbot, Joby
(1995)

Comus: Suite from the Ballet to
Purcell's music - Lambert, Constant

Comus Quadrilles - Wood, Hugh
(1988)

Con moto, op.2 - Klebe, Giselher
(1953)

Concentus - Godfrey, Daniel Strong
(1985)

Concert Avec Plusieurs Instruments
No.1 - Dittrich, Paul-Heinz (1976)

Concert de chambre, op.389 -
Milhaud, Darius (1961)

Concert Music for Strings and Brass,
op.50 - Hindemith, Paul (1930)

Concert Piece - Erdmann, Dietrich

Concert Piece, op.26 - Goehr,
Alexander (1969)

Concert Piece for Organ and Chamber
Orchestra, op.30 - Geiser, Walther
(1944)

Concert Piece in D, op.12 - Dohnanyi,
Ernest von (1904)

Concert Piece in D major; Concertino
Part I, op.31a (Busoni Verz. 236) -
Busoni, Ferruccio

Concert Piece in G-flat, op.39 -
Pierné, Gabriel (1903)

Concert Piece in One Movement,
op.21 - Zilcher, Hermann

Concert pour petit orchestre, op.34 -
Roussel, Albert (1927)

Concert Suite from Prospero's Books -
Nyman, Michael (1994)

Concertante - Watkins, Michael Blake
(1973)

Concertante Breve - Lees, Benjamin
(1959)

Concertante Dances - Kelly, Bryan
(1980)

Concertante for Violin, Flute and Oboe
- Bolcom, William (1961)

Concertante Musik - Blacher, Boris
(1937)

Concertante Suite - Neubert, Günter
(1971)

Concertante Suite from W. A. Mozart's
Opera "Idomeneo" (Busoni Verz.
B85) - Busoni, Ferruccio

Concertante, op.44 - Bavicchi, John
(1961)

Concertino - Bauer, Marion (1940)

Concertino - Baur, Jürg (1959)

Concertino - Berio, Luciano (1949)

Concertino - Bond, Victoria (1981)

Concertino; For violin, accordion and
chamber orchestra - Cerha,
Friedrich (1994)

Concertino: No.11 from "Divertimento
for Mozart" - Jarre, Maurice (1956)

Concertino - Krek, Uroš (1967)

Concertino, op.79 - Lothar, Mark
(1972)

Concertino - Neikrug, Marc (1977)

Concertino, op.71 - Raphael, Günter

Concertino, op.82 - Raphael, Günter

Concertino, op.57 - Roussel, Albert
(1936)

Concertino - Ryden, William (1999)

Concertino - Schönherr, Max

Concertino, op.42 - Schroeder,
Hermann

Concertino - Sessions, Roger

Concertino - Sierra, Roberto (1995)

Concertino, op.15 - Weiner, Leo
(1923)

Concertino, op.18 - Winters, Geoffrey
(1959)

Concertino - Zechlin, Ruth

Concertino Carintico, op.86 - Einem,
Gottfried von (1989)

Concertino Classico - Horovitz,
Joseph (1985)

Concertino da Camera - Ibert,
Jacques (1936)

Concertino de Printemps, op.135 -
Milhaud, Darius (1934)

Concertino Dedicato, op.248 - Lukáš,
Zdenek

Concertino for 12 Instruments -
Stravinsky, Igor (1952)

Concertino for Cello in G minor,
op.132 - Prokofiev, Sergei (1952)

Concertino for Chamber Ensemble -
Hartley, Walter Sinclair (1952)

Concertino for Chamber Ensemble -
Koppel, Anders (1999)

Concertino for Double Bass -
Kauffmann, Leo Justinus (1942)

Concertino for Harp and Orchestra -
Farkas, Ferenc (1937)

Concertino for Harpsichord and String
Orchestra - Farkas, Ferenc (1949)

Concertino for Piano and Orchestra, H.55 - Honegger, Arthur (1924)

Concertino for Piano, Strings and Percussion - Antoniou, Theodore (1962)

Concertino for Strings - Adler, Samuel (1956)

Concertino for Strings - Hasquenoph, Pierre

Concertino in D - Raphael, Günter

Concertino Lyrico, op.32 - Myaskovsky, Nikolai Yakovlevich (1929)

Concertino No.1, op.2 - Holloway, Robin (1964)

Concertino No.2, op.10 - Holloway, Robin (1967)

Concertino Pastorale - Ireland, John (1939)

Concertino pastorale, op.35 - Koch, Erland von (1947)

Concertino Per II H. W. H. - Bose, Hans-Jürgen von (1991)

Concertino per orchestra - Wimberger, Gerhard (1981)

Concertino, op.36 - Schlee, Thomas Daniel

Concertino, op.94 - Burkhard, Willy (1954)

Concerto; Épisodes pour trompette et orchestre, op.39 - Bacri, Nicolas (1992)

Concerto - Bartel, Hans-Christian (1967)

Concerto - Becker, Günther (1974)

Concerto, op.61 - Bruns, Victor

Concerto - Erdmann, Dietrich (1986)

Concerto - Erdmann, Dietrich (1988)

Concerto - Górecki, Henryk Mikołaj (1957)

Concerto; Recitativo ed Aria for Harpsichord and Orchestra - Haubenstock-Ramati, Roman (1954)

Concerto - Martin, Frank (1949)

Concerto, op.17 - Rózsa, Miklós (1943)

Concerto - Schubert, Heino (1975)

Concerto; For Marimba and Small Orchestra, op.38 - Yu, Julian (1996)

Concerto for Flute, Loshu 5 - Zender, Hans (1987)

Concerto breve, op.36 - Zbinden, Julien-François (1962)

Concerto Breve for Bass Trombone - Hartley, Walter Sinclair

Concerto Buffo - Slonimsky, Sergei

Concerto Classique - Šulek, Stjepan (1952)

Concerto Conciso, op.18 - Adès, Thomas (1997)

Concerto da Camera - Barraud, Henry (1934)

Concerto da camera; Auf der Suche nach der verlorenen Zeit - Baur, Jürg (1975)

Concerto da Camera - Hasquenoph, Pierre

Concerto da Camera, H.196 - Honegger, Arthur (1948)

Concerto da Camera, op.11 - Papandopulo, Boris (1928)

Concerto da camera - Voss, Friedrich (1953)

Concerto da Camera Nr.2, op.A-24 - Manén, Joan

Concerto Espagnol, op.A-7 - Manén, Joan

Concerto for 2 Guitars and Orchestra, op.201 - Castelnuovo-Tedesco, Mario

Concerto for 2 Violins and Orchestra - Martinů, Bohuslav (1950)

Concerto for 2 Violins, Viola, Violoncello and Orchestra - Neikrug, Marc

Concerto for 28 Players, op.105 - Arnold, Malcolm (1970)

Concerto for Alto and Orchestra - Boivin, Philippe (1986)

Concerto for Alto Saxophone and Orchestra - Martino, Donald (1987)

Concerto for Bass Trombone - Zwilich, Ellen Taaffe

Concerto for Bassoon - Alonso-Crespo, Eduardo (1996)

Concerto for Bassoon, op.41 - Bruns, Victor

Concerto for Bassoon - Schenker, Friedrich (1970)

Concerto for Bassoon and Low Strings - Gubaidulina, Sofia (1975)

Concerto for Bassoon and Orchestra - Zwilich, Ellen Taaffe (1992)

Concerto for Cello - Baker, David (1975)

Concerto for Cello - Blacher, Boris (1964)

Concerto for Cello, op.29 - Bruns, Victor

Concerto for Cello - Cassadó, Gaspar

Concerto for Cello - Engelmann, Hans Ulrich (1948)

Concerto for Cello, op.10 - Firsova, Elena (1973)

Concerto for Cello, op.67 - Gál, Hans

Concerto for Cello - Hochstetter, Armin Caspar (1935)

Concerto for Cello - Jacobi, Frederick (1930)

Concerto for Cello - Martin, Frank (1966)

Concerto for Cello, op.41 - Rautavaara, Einojuhani (1968)

Concerto for Cello (After G. M. Monn) - Schönberg, Arnold (1933)

Concerto for Cello - Trexler, Georg (1952)

Concerto for Cello - Volans, Kevin (1997)

Concerto for Cello - Weiss, Manfred

Concerto for Cello and Chamber Orchestra - Biggs, John (1996)

Concerto for Cello and Orchestra, H.72 - Honegger, Arthur (1929)

Concerto for Cello and Orchestra; In Memoriam F.D.R. - Schickele, Peter (2000)

Concerto for Cello in A minor - Klengel, Julius

Concerto for Cello in B minor - Klengel, Julius

Concerto for Cello in C minor, op.21 - Atterberg, Kurt

Concerto for Cello in E minor, op.58 - Prokofiev, Sergei (1938)

Concerto for Cello No.2, op.119 - Saint-Saëns, Camille (1902)

Concerto for Chamber Orchestra - Capanna, Robert (1974)

Concerto for Chamber Orchestra - Frazelle, Kenneth (2002)

Concerto for Chamber Orchestra - Kisielewski, Stefan (1943)

Concerto for Chamber Orchestra - Lees, Benjamin (1966)

Concerto for Chamber Orchestra - McCabe, John (1962)

Concerto for Chamber Orchestra - Sallinen, Aulis (1960)

Concerto for Chamber Orchestra - Schickele, Peter (1998)

Concerto for Clarinet - Aguila, Miguel del (2003)

Concerto for Clarinet, op.76 - Bruns, Victor

Concerto for Clarinet - Carter, Elliott (1996)

Concerto for Clarinet - Copland, Aaron (1948)

Concerto for Clarinet - Knight, Edward (1992)

Concerto for Clarinet - Neikrug, Marc

Concerto for Clarinet, op.47 - Schroeder, Hermann

Concerto for Clarinet - Zwilich, Ellen Taaffe (2002)

Concerto for Clarinet, Strings and
Harp - Cotton, Jeffery (2003)

Concerto for Clarinet and Chamber
Orchestra - Braun, Yehezkel

Concerto for Clarinet and Orchestra,
op.115 - Arnold, Malcolm (1974)

Concerto for Clarinet and Orchestra -
Milhaud, Darius

Concerto for Clarinet and String
Orchestra, op.11 - Bavicchi, John
(1954)

Concerto for Double Bass, Shadows
of Noh - Conyngham, Barry (1979)

Concerto for Double Bass and
Orchestra No.3; Four scenes after
Picasso - Proto, Frank

Concerto for Doublebass, op.73 -
Bruns, Victor

Concerto for Doublebass -
Papandopulo, Boris (1968)

Concerto for Eleven, op.32 - Goehr,
Alexander (1970)

Concerto for Flute and Orchestra -
Ibert, Jacques (1934)

Concerto for Flute, op.51 - Bruns,
Victor

Concerto for Flute - Carter, Elliott
(2008)

Concerto for Flute - David, Johann
Nepomuk (1936)

Concerto for Flute - Osborne, Nigel
(1980)

Concerto for Flute; Dances with the
winds, op.69 - Rautavaara,
Einojuhani

Concerto for Flute and Chamber
Orchestra - Dubois, Pierre-Max

Concerto for Flute and English Horn,
op.74 - Bruns, Victor

Concerto for Flute and Harp -
Denisov, Edison

Concerto for Flute and Orchestra,
op.63 - Bacri, Nicolas (1999)

Concerto for Flute and Orchestra -
Schickele, Peter

Concerto for Flute and Orchestra -
Zwilich, Ellen Taaffe

Concerto for Flute and Strings -
Bjelinski, Bruno (1955)

Concerto for Flute, Oboe and Bassoon
- Bräutigam, Helmut

Concerto for Guitar and Chamber
Ensemble - Bennett, Richard
Rodney (1970)

Concerto for Guitar and Chamber
Orchestra - Arnold, Malcolm (1959)

Concerto for Guitar and Orchestra -
Adler, Samuel (1994)

Concerto for Guitar and Small
Orchestra - Villa-Lobos, Heitor
(1951)

Concerto for Guitar No.1 - Brouwer,
Léo (1972)

Concerto for Guitar No.4; Concierto de
Toronto - Brouwer, Léo (1987)

Concerto for Harp and Chamber
Orchestra, op.126 - Krenek, Ernst
(1951)

Concerto for Harp and Small
Orchestra - Hamilton, Iain (1995)

Concerto for Harp and Strings -
Schmitt, Meinrad (1983)

Concerto for Harpsichord - Martin,
Frank (1952)

Concerto for Harpsichord -
Papandopulo, Boris

Concerto for Harpsichord (or piano),
op.40 - Górecki, Henryk Mikołaj
(1980)

Concerto for Harpsichord and
Orchestra, op.407 - Milhaud, Darius
(1964)

Concerto for Harpsichord and Small
Orchestra - Martinů, Bohuslav
(1935)

Concerto for High Trumpet and String
Orchestra - Blacher, Boris (1970)

Concerto for Horn - Bresgen, Cesar
(1963)

Concerto for Horn, op.63 - Bruns,
Victor

Concerto for Horn - Krek, Uroš (1961)

Concerto for Horn and Chamber
Orchestra - Dubois, Pierre-Max

Concerto for Horn and Orchestra -
Adler, Samuel (2002)

Concerto for Horn and String
Orchestra - Zwilich, Ellen Taaffe

Concerto for Horn in A minor, op.28 -
Atterberg, Kurt

Concerto for Mandolin - Erdmann,
Dietrich (1979)

Concerto for Oboe; For oboe,
concertino group and orchestra -
Carter, Elliott (1987)

Concerto for Oboe - Dittrich, Paul-
Heinz (1976)

Concerto for Oboe - Matthus,
Siegfried (1985)

Concerto for Oboe - Schenker,
Friedrich (1969)

Concerto for Oboe and Orchestra,
op.35 - Eder, Helmut (1962)

Concerto for Oboe and Small
Orchestra, H.353 - Martinů,
Bohuslav (1955)

Concerto for Oboe and String
Orchestra - Beyer, Frank Michael
(1986)

Concerto for Orchestra, op.14 -
Abendroth, Walter (1935)

Concerto for Orchestra, op.4 - Einem,
Gottfried von (1943)

Concerto for Orchestra, op.38 -
Holmboe, Vagn (1945)

Concerto for Orchestra - Kodály,
Zoltán (1940)

Concerto for Orchestra - Thiele,
Siegfried (1997)

Concerto for Orchestra - Trexler,
Georg (1962)

Concerto for Organ - Brandmüller,
Theo (1981)

Concerto for Organ, Wk61 - David,
Johann Nepomuk (1965)

Concerto for Organ, op.62 - Einem,
Gottfried von (1981)

Concerto for Organ - Weiss, Manfred
(1977)

Concerto for Organ and Orchestra -
Arnold, Malcolm (1954)

Concerto for Organ and Strings,
op.230 - Krenek, Ernst (1979)

Concerto for Organ No.2 - Eben, Petr

Concerto for Percussion and Chamber
Orchestra - Foss, Lukas (1974)

Concerto for Percussion and Chamber
Orchestra - Foss, Lukas (1974)

Concerto for Piano - Aguila, Miguel del
(1997)

Concerto for Piano No.1; Original
version, op.13 - Britten, Benjamin
(1938)

Concerto for Piano, op.22 - Erbse,
Heimo (1965)

Concerto for Piano - Erdmann,
Dietrich (1950)

Concerto for Piano, op.57 - Gál, Hans

Concerto for Piano - Ligeti, György
(1988)

Concerto for Piano; Based on the
Piano Quartet op.25 by J. Brahms -
Matthus, Siegfried (1992)

Concerto for Piano, op.14 - Mossolow,
Alexander (1927)

Concerto for Piano - Neikrug, Marc
(1995)

Concerto for Piano - Pasatieri,
Thomas (1994)

Concerto for Piano, op.45 -
Rautavaara, Einojuhani

Concerto for Piano - Rihm, Wolfgang
(1969)

Concerto for Piano - Röttger, Heinz
(1951)

Concerto for Piano, op.36 - Roussel, Albert (1927)

Concerto for Piano, op.35 - Schroeder, Hermann

Concerto for Piano, op.30 - Thomas, Kurt

Concerto for Piano, op.49 - Wellesz, Egon (1934)

Concerto for Piano - Wolschina, Reinhard (1988)

Concerto for Piano 4 hands and Chamber Orchestra - Schnittke, Alfred (1988)

Concerto for Piano and 7 Instruments - Erickson, Robert

Concerto No.2 for Piano and Orchestra - Adler, Samuel (1997)

Concerto for Piano and Orchestra - Boucourechliev, André (1975)

Concerto for Piano and String Orchestra, op.12 - Ferguson, Howard (1951)

Concerto for Piano in E-flat Major - Schmidt, Franz (1934)

Concerto for Piano in G Major, op.46 - Castelnuovo-Tedesco, Mario (1927)

Concerto for Piano No.1 - Bartók, Béla (1926)

Concerto for Piano No.1, op.28 - Blacher, Boris (1947)

Concerto for Piano No.1, op.18 - Krenek, Ernst (1923)

Concerto for Piano No.2; In variable Metres - Blacher, Boris (1952)

Concerto for Piano No.2, op.81 - Krenek, Ernst (1937)

Concerto for Piano No.2 - Wimberger, Gerhard (1980/81)

Concerto for Piano No.3, op.258 - Lukáš, Zdenek (1993)

Concerto for Piano, Violin and Cello; Triple Concerto - Zwilich, Ellen Taaffe

Concerto for Prepared Piano and Chamber Orchestra - Cage, John

Concerto for Saxophone - Muldowney, Dominic (1984)

Concerto for Small Orchestra - Diamond, David

Concerto for Small Orchestra - Johnson, Hunter

Concerto for Small Orchestra and Solo Viola - Bartel, Hans-Christian (1963)

Concerto for String Orchestra - Blacher, Boris (1940)

Concerto for String Orchestra - Milner, Anthony (1982)

Concerto for String Quartet (After G. F. Händel's Concerto Grosso, op.6, No.7) - Schönberg, Arnold (1933)

Concerto for Strings - Helm, Everett

Concerto for Strings - Mommer, Hans Günter (1958)

Concerto for Three Trumpets and String Orchestra; O namenlose Freude - Matthus, Siegfried (1990)

Concerto for Trombone - Bresgen, Cesar (1980)

Concerto for Trumpet, op.50 - Bruns, Victor

Concerto for Trumpet, op.23 - Kurz, Siegfried

Concerto for Trumpet and Orchestra - Herrmann, Peter

Concerto for Trumpet and String Orchestra - Matthus, Siegfried (2001)

Concerto for Trumpet and Strings - Addison, John

Concerto for Two Celli in E minor - Klengel, Julius

Concerto for Two Pianos and Orchestra - Milhaud, Darius

Concerto for Viola - Baur, Jürg (1952)

Concerto for Viola - Blacher, Boris (1954)

Concerto for Viola, op.69 - Bruns, Victor

Concerto for Viola, op.108 - Milhaud, Darius (1929)

Concerto for Viola, op.108 - Milhaud, Darius (1929)

Concerto for Viola - Rosenberg, Hilding Constantin (1942)

Concerto for Viola - Schenker, Friedrich (1975)

Concerto for Viola, op.45 - Schroeder, Hermann (1973)

Concerto for Viola and Orchestra - Beyer, Frank Michael (2003)

Concerto for Viola and Orchestra, op.93 - Burkhard, Willy (1953)

Concerto for Viola No.1, Remembering Child - Nørgård, Per (1986)

Concerto for Violin, op.14 - Barber, Samuel (1939)

Concerto for Violin - Blacher, Boris (1948)

Concerto for Violin No.1, op.15 - Britten, Benjamin (1939)

Concerto for Violin, op.36 - Bruns, Victor

Concerto for Violin, op.53 - Bruns, Victor

Concerto for Violin, op.69 - Burkhard, Willy (1943)

Concerto for Violin - Busch, Adolf

Concerto for Violin, op.39 - Gál, Hans

Concerto for Violin - Martin, Frank (1951)

Concerto for Violin - Matthus, Siegfried (1968)

Concerto for Violin - Menotti, Gian Carlo (1952)

Concerto for Violin, op.33 - Schiske, Karl (1952)

Concerto for Violin, op.37 - Zbinden, Julien-François (1965)

Concerto for Violin and Cello, Wk68 - David, Johann Nepomuk (1969)

Concerto for Violin and Cello, op.61 - Klengel, Julius

Concerto for Violin and Orchestra - Ben-Haim, Paul

Concerto for Violin and Orchestra - Boelter, Karl (1999)

Concerto for Violin and Orchestra - Herrmann, Peter

Concerto for Violin and Orchestra - Zwilich, Ellen Taaffe (1997)

Concerto for Violin and Orchestra in D - Bolcom, William (1983)

Concerto for Violin and Orchestra No.1 in E - Martinů, Bohuslav (1932/33)

Concerto for Violin and Orchestra No.2 - Neikrug, Marc (1998)

Concerto for Violin and Orchestra, op.28 - Antoniou, Theodore (1965)

Concerto for Violin and Small Orchestra - Hutcheson, Jere (1989)

Concerto for Violin and Viola, Double Concerto - Britten, Benjamin (1932)

Concerto for Violin and Violoncello, Double Concerto - Zwilich, Ellen Taaffe

Concerto for Violin in A major, op.20 - Sinigaglia, Leone

Concerto for Violin in B minor, op.11 - Zilcher, Hermann

Concerto for Violin in C major, op.21 - Raphael, Günter

Concerto for Violin in D minor - Fauré, Gabriel

Concerto for Violin in D minor - Harty, Hamilton

Concerto for Violin in E minor, op.7 - Atterberg, Kurt

Concerto for Violin in G major, op.52 - Weingartner, Felix

Concerto for Violin in Two Movements - Hamel, Peter Michael (1986/1989)

Concerto for Violin No.1, Wk45 - David, Johann Nepomuk (1952)

Concerto for Violin No.2; In form of a ballad - Baur, Jürg (1978)

Concerto for Violin No.2, Wk50 - David, Johann Nepomuk (1957)

Concerto for Violin No.2, op.87 - Raphael, Günter

Concerto for Violin No.2 - Schnittke, Alfred (1966)

Concerto for Violin No.2; Borderlines - Nørgård, Per (2002)

Concerto for Violin No.3, Wk56 - David, Johann Nepomuk (1961)

Concerto for Violin No.3 - Schnittke, Alfred (1978)

Concerto for Violoncello and Orchestra - Bialas, Günter (1960)

Concerto for Violoncello and Orchestra No.2 - Bialas, Günter (1992)

Concerto Grosso No.3 - Schnittke, Alfred (1985)

Concerto Grosso; Pour Trois Chanteurs, Actrice, 19 Instrumentistes et band magnétique - Aperghis, Georges (1972)

Concerto grosso - Blomdahl, Karl-Birger (1944)

Concerto Grosso - Castro, José Maria

Concerto Grosso, op.57 - D'Alessandro, Raffaele (1947)

Concerto Grosso - Glass, Philip (1992)

Concerto Grosso, op.15 - Krol, Bernhard (1956)

Concerto Grosso - Martinů, Bohuslav (1937)

Concerto Grosso, Werk 34 - Schollum, Robert (1948)

Concerto Grosso No.1 - Ardevol, José

Concerto Grosso No.1, op.17 - Lazar, Filip (1930)

Concerto Grosso No.1 - Schnittke, Alfred (1977)

Concerto Grosso No.1 in Bb - Alwyn, William (1943)

Concerto Grosso No.2 - Ardevol, José

Concerto Grosso No.2, op.25 - Krenek, Ernst (1924)

Concerto in A minor, op.60 - Weingartner, Felix (1916)

Concerto in B-flat Major; For Flute and Chamber Orchestra, op.62 - Müller, Sigfrid Walther (1940)

Concerto in D - Stravinsky, Igor (1946)

Concerto in E-flat "Dumbarton Oaks" - Stravinsky, Igor (1938)

Concerto in F Major; For Bassoon and Orchestra, op.56 - Müller, Sigfrid Walther (1938)

Concerto lirico for Piano and Orchestra - Bialas, Günter (1967)

Concerto No.1, Wk40/1 - David, Johann Nepomuk (1950)

Concerto No.1 for Koto and Orchestra - Cowell, Henry (1961)

Concerto No.1 for String Orchestra - Rosenberg, Hilding Constantin (1946)

Concerto No.2, Wk40/2 - David, Johann Nepomuk (1951)

Concerto No.3 - David, Johann Nepomuk (1974)

Concerto No.4, Concerto di Camera, op.24 - Lazar, Filip (1935)

Concerto per archi, op.114 - Bentzon, Niels Viggo (1957)

Concerto per archi - Giefer, Willy (1970)

Concerto per Archi; conatum 36 - Kunad, Rainer

Concerto per Corde, op.33 - Ginastera, Alberto (1964)

Concerto per Corde - Rouse, Christopher (1990)

Concerto piccolo - Koch, Erland von (1962)

Concerto Piccolo after B-A-C-H - Pärt, Arvo (1994)

Concerto Piece on a Theme by W. A. Mozart (K.251), op.81 - Zilcher, Hermann

Concerto Rapsodico - Füssl, Karl Heinz (1957)

Concerto Romano, op.43 - Casella, Alfredo (1926)

Concerto Serenade for Violin and String Orchestra - Bolcom, William (1964)

Concerto Veneziano - Mieg, Peter (1955)

Concetti; Musica para Gesualdo di Venosa - Delás, José Luis de (1974)

Concierto Barroco (Guitar Concerto) - Sierra, Roberto (1996)

Concierto Caribe - Sierra, Roberto (1993)

Concierto Como Un Divertimento - Rodrigo, Joaquín (1981)

Concierto heroico - Rodrigo, Joaquín (1942)

Concierto In Modo Galante - Rodrigo, Joaquín (1949)

Concierto Pastoral - Rodrigo, Joaquín (1977)

Concierto Serenata - Rodrigo, Joaquín (1952)

Concordanza - Gubaidulina, Sofia (1971)

Confessiones; Chamber Symphony for 14 Instruments - Korndorf, Nikolai (1979)

Configurations / Reflet - Staud, Johannes Maria (2002)

Confinement - Harbison, John (1965)

Conga for Orchestra, op.44 - Aguila, Miguel del (1994)

A Conga Line in Hell, op.40 - Aguila, Miguel del (1993)

A Conga Line in Hell, op.43 - Aguila, Miguel del (1994)

Conjuntos - Delás, José Luis de (1975)

Conjurer; Concerto for Percussionist and String Orchestra - Corigliano, John (2007)

Connections - Szalonek, Witold (1972)

The Conquerer; Incidental music: Romance and two Dances - German, Sir Edward (1905)

Consort Music 1 - Rechberger, Herman (1976)

Consort Music 2 - Rechberger, Herman (1977)

The Consul: Lullaby - Menotti, Gian Carlo (1950)

The Consul: Magda's Aria (To this we've come) - Menotti, Gian Carlo (1950)

Constellations, op.22 - Nørgård, Per (1958)

Contentions - Wilson, Richard

Continental Divide - Bermel, Derek (1996)

Continuum - Matthews, Colin (2000)

Contours - Schuller, Gunther (1958)

Contradizione - Bacewicz, Grażyna (1966)

Contraflow - Matthews, Colin (1992)

Contrapulse - Vir, Param (1985)

Contrasubjekte; Passacaglia über B-A-C-H für Streicher - Stranz, Ulrich (1980)

Cookham Concertino - Kelly, Bryan (1969)

Cookham Rondo - Kelly, Bryan (1969)

Copenhagen Concerto, op.167 - Bentzon, Niels Viggo (1964)

Copenhagen Concerto No.2, op.168 - Bentzon, Niels Viggo (1964)

Copenhagen Concerto No.3, op.169 - Bentzon, Niels Viggo (1964)

Coquetterie Posthume - Debussy, Claude

Corale (su Sequenza VIII) - Berio, Luciano (1981)

Coronation March - German, Sir Edward (1911)

Corpus Cum Figuris - Ruders, Poul (1985)

Corranach - Sackman, Nicholas (1985)

El Corregidor y la Molinera - Falla, Manuel de (1917)

Correlaziono per 3 Gruppi - Matsushita, Shin-ichi

Corrente - Lindberg, Magnus (1992)

Corrente - China Version - Lindberg, Magnus (2000)

Correspondences I - Becker, Günther (1966)

Correspondences II - Becker, Günther (1968)

Correspondences for String Orchestra and Tape - Babbitt, Milton (1967)

Cortège - Schafer, Robert Murray (1977)

A Costume Comedy Overture - Black, Stanley (1955)

Counter Phrases - Lindberg, Magnus (2003)

Country Dances; Book 1 - Bennett, Richard Rodney (2001)

Couronne de Gloire; Cantata for Baritone and Small Orchestra - Milhaud, Darius

Coyote Blue - Lindberg, Magnus (1993)

Crazy Rosa - La Madre - Hoyland, Vic (1988)

La creation du monde; Ballet, op.81a - Milhaud, Darius (1923)

Creations: Two Scenes from Genesis - Corigliano, John (1972)

Cristallo di Rocca - Rota, Nino (1950)

Cromos Nacionales; Rapsodia guatemalteca Nr.2 - Molina Pinillos, José (1939)

Crossing II - Ali-Zadeh, Franghiz (1993)

Crossing Kings Reach - Maxwell Davies, Peter (2001)

Crow-Cry - Gilbert, Anthony (1976)

Cuatre Cançons En llengua Catalana - Rodrigo, Joaquín (1946)

Las Cuatro Estaciones Porteñas - Piazzolla, Astor

Cuatro Madrigales Amatorios - Rodrigo, Joaquín

Cuatro Versos (Cello Concerto) - Sierra, Roberto (1999)

Cuentos - Sierra, Roberto (1997)

Cues from "The Little Clay Cart" - Avshalomov, Jacob (1954)

Cumbres - Moncayo, José Pablo

Cumnock Fair - MacMillan, James (1999)

Cupid and Death - Marthinsen, Niels (1994)

Cuts and Dissolves, Orchesterskizzen - Rihm, Wolfgang (1976)

Cutting a Caper - Woolrich, John (2001)

Cyrano de Bergerac; Music for Edmond Rostand's play of the same name - Rodrigo, Joaquín (1955)

D

D'une Source Oubliée I - Bonnet, Antoine (1987)

Da Ich Nicht Hoffe für 14 Instrumentalisten (In memoriam Igor Stravinsky) - Mansurian, Tigran (1983)

Dalecarlia Suite - Koch, Erland von (1957)

Dalíniana; Three pieces on three paintings by Salvador Dalí - Halffter, Cristóbal (1994)

Dalsland-Rhapsodie, op.22 - Kallstenius, Edvin (1936)

Der Dämon: Konzertsuite aus der Tanzpantomime - Hindemith, Paul (1923)

Dance Divertimento - Kennan, Kent

Dance in the Old Style - Korngold, Erich Wolfgang (1919)

Dance Intermezzo, op.45, No.2 - Sibelius, Jean (1904)

Dance Marathon ($1000 stake) - King, Alastair

Dance No.2 - Koch, Erland von (1938)

Dance No.4 - Koch, Erland von (1956)

Dance No.5 - Koch, Erland von (1957)

Dance of the Marionettes - Vinter, Gilbert (1956)

Dance Panels; Ballet in Seven Sections - Copland, Aaron (1959)

Dance Preludes - Lutosławski, Witold (1959)

Dance Preludes; 2nd Version - Lutosławski, Witold (1955)

Dance Preludes; 3rd Version - Lutosławski, Witold (1959)

Dance Suite - Bartók, Béla (1923)

Dance Suite - Vinci, Albert

Dance Suite from the Grand Opera "The Marionettes" - Rosenberg, Hilding Constantin (1938)

Danceries - Hesketh, Kenneth

Dances of Galanta - Kodály, Zoltán (1933)

Dandelion Wine - Imbrie, Andrew (1967)

Dangerous Creatures - Hindson, Matthew (2008)

The Daniel Jazz, op.21 - Gruenberg, Louis (1924)

D'Anne jouant de l'espinette - Ravel, Maurice (1898)

Dans Une Lumière Eclatante - Stahmer, Klaus Hinrich (1989)

Danse de la Peur - Martin, Frank (1936)

Danse Lente - Duparc, Henri (1910)

Danses Concertantes - Stravinsky, Igor (1942)

Danza Andaluza - Surinach, Carlos

Danza Criolla - Piazzolla, Astor

Danzas Concertantes (Guitar Concerto) - Sierra, Roberto (2997)

Danzas Espanolas, No.6: Jota - Granados, Enrique (1890)

Danzón No.2 - Marquez, Arturo (1994)

Danzón No.3 - Marquez, Arturo

Danzón No.4 - Marquez, Arturo

D'Après "Ecrits Sur Toiles"; Pour Orchestre de Chambre - Amy, Gilbert (1984)

Darf ich... - Pärt, Arvo (1995)

Dark Crossing - Turnage, Mark-Anthony (2000)

Dark Side - Aperghis, Georges (2003)

Darlington Doubles - Woolrich, John (1988)

David's Fascinating Rhythm Method - Harbison, John (1991)

Dayspring; Fanfare/Concertino for solo guitar and orchestra - Locklair, Dan (1988)

De Assumtione Beatae Mariae Virginis - Maxwell Davies, Peter (2001)

A Deep but Dazzling Darkness - MacMillan, James (2002)

De Fåvitska Jungfrurna; The wise and the foolish virgins. Rhapsody on old Swedish folksongs. - Atterberg, Kurt (1947)

De Imaginum, Signorum, et Idearum Compositione I - Sotelo, Mauricio (1996)

De Patre Ex Filio - Dalby, Martin (1988)

Dead Elvis - Daugherty, Michael (1993)

Death in Venice: Suite, op.88a - Britten, Benjamin (1973)

Deep Forest; Prelude for Little Symphony Orchestra, op.34, No.1 - Daniels, Mabel W. (1932)

Déjà vu - Stranz, Ulrich (1973)

Delights & Dances - Abels, Michael (2007)

Demeter: Suite - Blacher, Boris (1963)

Denkbild - Kurze Schatten - Delás, José Luis de (1977)

Der 129. Psalm, op.53 - Milhaud, Darius (1919)

Der die Gesänge Zerschlug - Ruzicka, Peter (1985)

Dérive 2 - Boulez, Pierre (1988/2001)

Des Kaisers neue Kleider; Musik zu einem Andersen-Ballett - Tansman, Alexandre (1959)

Descarga - Sierra, Roberto (1988)

Design - Rorem, Ned (1953)

Detail from the Record - Hesketh, Kenneth (2001)

Detto II; Concerto for cello and 13 instruments - Gubaidulina, Sofia (1972)

Deutsche Tänze; For cello and double bass with chamber orchestra - Beyer, Frank Michael (1982)

Deutsches Rokoko; Eine Suite für Kleines Orchester nach alten Meistern - Guenther, Felix (1931)

Deux Airs de Ballet: Pasquinade - Ganne, Louis (1897)

Deux Arabesques - Debussy, Claude

Deux Chansons Populaires - Grandjany, Marcel

Deux Danses Rituelles - Absil, Jean

Deux Marches et un Intermède - Poulenc, Francis (1938)

Deux Mélodies hébraïques - Ravel, Maurice (1919)

Deux Pièces pour "La Rédemption de François Villon," H.209 - Honegger, Arthur (1951)

Deuxième concert symphonique "Haut les Rêves!"; En homage à Gaston Bachelard, op.49, No.2 - Ballif, Claude (1984)

Deva et Asura - Vivier, Claude (1972)

Dharma - Boelter, Karl (2001)

Dialog - Blacher, Boris (1950)

Dialog, conatum 40 - Kunad, Rainer

Dialoghi - Paccagnini, Angelo (1963)

Dialogue in Praise of the Owl and the Cuckoo - Füssl, Karl Heinz (1947)

Dialogues; For piano and large ensemble - Carter, Elliott (2003)

Diary Music I - Spratlan, Lewis (1972)

Dichotomy, op.12 - Riegger, Wallingford (1932)

Diferencias - Ruders, Poul (1980)

Dilogie II for Nine Player - Ali-Zadeh, Franghiz (1989)

Dimanche d'été - Le Grand, Robert

Diplipito - Kancheli, Giya (1997)

Discovery - Chávez, Carlos (1969)

Dispersion, op.16 - Redel, Martin Christoph (1972)

Distant Hills; Chamber Version - Albert, Stephen (1989)

Distant Runes and Incantations - Schwantner, Joseph (1983)

Le Dit des Jeux du Monde; 10 Danses, 2 interludes et 1 épilogue pour orchestre de chambre, pour le poème de Paul Méral, H.19 - Honegger, Arthur (1918)

Le Dit des Jeux du Monde: Suite d'orchestre en 4 mouvements - Honegger, Arthur (1918)

La Diva de l'Empire - Satie, Erik (1904)

Diverse Dances - Gauldin, Robert (1957)

Diversions for Eight Instruments, op.63 - Berkeley, Lennox (1964)

Divertimento - Bartók, Béla (1940)

Divertimento, op.19 - Bentzon, Niels Viggo (1942)

Divertimento - Besch, Otto (1941)

Divertimento - Blacher, Boris (1935)

Divertimento, op.42 - Braunfels, Walter (1929)

Divertimento, op.30 - Busch, Adolf

Divertimento - Erdmann, Dietrich (1953)

Divertimento - Fuleihan, Anis

Divertimento - Haieff, Alexei Vasilievich (1953)

Divertimento - Hiller, Lejaren

Divertimento - Jacob, Gordon (1938)

Divertimento, op.15 - Larsson, Lars-Erik (1935)

Divertimento, op.6 - Layton, Billy Jim (1958)

Divertimento, op.A-32 - Manén, Joan (1937)

Divertimento; Serenata No.4 - Martinů, Bohuslav (1932)

Divertimento - Musto, John

Divertimento - Nussio, Otmar (1951)

Divertimento - Oldham, Arthur (1951)

Divertimento; 5 old-english dances - Paumgartner, Bernhard

Divertimento - Piston, Walter (1946)

Divertimento, op.43 - Prokofiev, Sergei (1929)

Divertimento - Rautavaara, Einojuhani (1953)

Divertimento, op.57 - Thärichen, Werner

Divertimento - Vactor, David van

Divertimento del Sur - Campos-Parsi, Héctor

Divertimento for Chamber Orchestra - Forst, Rudolf

Divertimento for Mozart; 12 aspects of the aria "Ein Mädchen oder Weibchen wünscht Papageno sich" - Mozart, Wolfgang Amadeus (1956)

Divertimento for Orchestra; Triangle Concerto - Matthus, Siegfried (1985)

Divertimento for Chamber Orchestra, op.18 - Farago, Marcel

Divertimento for Strings - Panufnik, Andrzej (1947)

Divertimento für Kammerorchester, op.24 - Abendroth, Walter (1949)

Divertimento für Kammerorchester, op.27 - Trapp, Max (1931)

Divertimento für Kleines Orchester, op.56 - Grabner, Hermann (1941)

Divertimento in Bb, op.18 - Berkeley, Lennox (1943)

Divertimento in F - Frackenpohl, Arthur (1952)

Divertimento No.1, On old Hungarian folk dances, op.20 - Weiner, Leo (1934)

Divertimento No.2 - Fuleihan, Anis (1941)

Divertimento No.2 in A minor; Hungarian Folk Melodies, op.24 - Weiner, Leo (1938)

Divertimento Para Nueve Instrumentos - Halffter, Rodolfo

Divertimento Per Fulvia: Suite from "La camera dei diseegni," op.64 - Casella, Alfredo (1940)

Divertimento-Burlesca - Lees, Benjamin (1957)

Divertimento 1950 - Eitler, Esteban (1950)

Divertissement - Ibert, Jacques (1930)

Divertissement et Musette - Samazeuilh, Gustave (1912)

Divertissement joyeux, op.5 - Klebe, Giselher (1949)

Divisioni - Linke, Norbert

Doce Bagatelas - Sierra, Roberto (2000)

Dodecaconcerto - Cordero, Roque

Domaines - Boulez, Pierre (1969)

Las Doncellas - Halffter, Ernesto

Don Quichotte à Dulcinée - Ravel, Maurice (1933)

The Donkey Dances - Bawden, Rupert (1995)

Dorische Musik (Dorian Music) - Kaminski, Heinrich (1933)

Dors là-bas petit Baya; Berceuse d'Afrique - Büsser, Henri

Dos canciones - Halffter, Ernesto (1927)

Dos Danzas Españolas; Suite for castanets and orchestra - Rodrigo, Joaquín (1969)

Dos Poemas; De El Jardino de R. Tagore, op.10, No.16 - Ficher, Jacobo

Double - Baggiani, Guido (1984)

Double Concerto - Bresgen, Cesar (1979)

Double Concerto - Cooper, Paul (1985)

Double Concerto; For Violin, Piano and Chamber Orchestra, op.124 - Krenek, Ernst (1950)

Double Concerto, op.41 - Schroeder, Hermann

Double Concerto for Violin and Viola - Halffter, Cristóbal (1984)

Double Helix - Muldowney, Dominic (1977)

Dowlandia - Matthews, Colin (1997)

Down a Country Lane - Copland, Aaron (1962)

Dream Children, op.43 - Elgar, Edward (1902)

Dream Dancing - Bennett, Richard Rodney (1986)

The Dream of Valentino: Dances from Valentino - Argento, Dominick

Dream Play - Nørgård, Per (1975)

Dreams - Antheil, George (1934)

Drei Dithyramben; In Memoriam Willy Strecker - Henze, Hans Werner (1958)

Drei Festmusiken - Maler, Wilhelm

Drei Kleine Stücke, op.19b - Hummel, Bertold (1960)

Drei Lieder (Three Songs), Nr.1/10 - Stockhausen, Karlheinz (1950)

Drei Lieder nach Eichendorff (Three Songs after Eichendorff) - Hruby, Viktor (1940)

Drei Orchestermotetten nach Machaut - Thiele, Siegfried (1972)

Drei Plus Vier - Gürsching, Albrecht

Drei Sommerbilder - Matthus, Siegfried (1975)

Drei Stilisierte Polkas im Volkston - Hudec, Jiri (1969)

Drowning by Numbers for Chamber Orchestra - Nyman, Michael (1998)

Due Pastorali - Rieti, Vittorio (1925)

Duérmete; Niño - Rodrigo, Joaquín (1952)

Duet - Reich, Steve (1993)

Duet from "Háry János," No.8: Tiszán innen, Dunán túl (Far away from the Danube) - Kodály, Zoltán (1926)

Duets - Tower, Joan (1994)

Dunkles Spiel - Rihm, Wolfgang (1990)

Duo concertant - Martinů, Bohuslav (1937)

Duo Concertante - Lindberg, Magnus (1992)

Duo-Konzert - Heiß, Hermann (1948)

The Duration of Exile - Muldowney, Dominic (1983)

Durch die Nacht (Through the Night), op.67a - Krenek, Ernst (1931)

Düstere Anmut - Komorous, Rudolf (1968)

Dwellings - Conyngham, Barry (1982)

Dying for It - Marsh, Roger (1988)

E

E vó: Sicilian Lullaby from "Opera" - Berio, Luciano (1972)

The Earl of Essex Galliard - Muldowney, Dominic (1976)

Die Ebene - Staud, Johannes Maria (1997)

Échange - Xenakis, Iannis (1989)

Échec au roi; Ballet en 1 acte - Martinů, Bohuslav (1930)

Echo Canyon - Tanaka, Karen (1995)

Echoes - Burt, Francis (1989)

Echos 13; For Horn, Trombone, Harp, Piano and 9 instruments - Amy, Gilbert (1976)

Eclogue - Stevens, Bernard (1946)

Ecossaise - Auric, Georges (1952)

Écrits Sur Toiles; Pour Ensemble de Chambre & Voix récitée - Amy, Gilbert (1983)

Das Edelfräulein als Bäuerin: Orchestersuite, op.69 - Bruns, Victor

Effets de Nuit - Le Grand, Robert

Eight Bagatelles - Finke, Fidelio

Eight Instrumental Miniatures - Stravinsky, Igor (1962)

Eight Lines - Reich, Steve (1983)

Eight Poems of Emily Dickinson - Copland, Aaron (1958-70)

Eilanden - Delás, José Luis de (1967)

Einfache Musik - Hidalgo, Manuel (1989)

"…Einklang freier Wesen…" - Haas, Georg Friedrich (1996)

Einsamkeit; In Memoriam W. Buchebner - Denhoff, Michael (1982)

Eisenstädter - Takács, Jenö (19662)

Elegi; För liten orkester, ur orkestersviten Gustav II Adolf - Alfvén, Hugo (1938)

Elegia; No.2 of "Two Tributes" - Matthews, Colin (1998)

Elegía Andina - Frank, Gabriela Lena (2000)

Elegie, op.70, No.5 - Kaun, Hugo (1907)

Elegie In Memoriam Edison Denissow for 16 Players, op.97b - Smirnov, Dmitri (1997)

Elegies - Diamond, David

Elegy - Corigliano, John (1965)

Elegy - Kennan, Kent

Elegy; To the Memory of Franklin D. Roosevelt - Rogers, Bernard

Elegy: From Symphony No.3 - Rogers, Bernard

Elegy and Recreations - Levi, Paul Alan (1981)

Elegy for Small Orchestra - Etler, Alvin (1959)

Elegy for Small Orchestra - Etler, Alvin (1959)

Elegy for String Orchestra - Adler, Samuel (1962)

Elegy for String Orchestra - Schickele, Peter

Elenka - Bresgen, Cesar (1980)

Elephant Skin - Rueda, Jesús (2002)

Elijah's Violin - Saxton, Robert (1988)

Elizabethan Dances for Orchestra - Alwyn, William (1958)

Elizabethan Miniatures - Banks, Don (1962)

L'embarquement pour Cythère - Poulenc, Francis

Embattled Garden; Ballet for chamber orchestra - Surinach, Carlos (1957)

The Embroidered Pannier; An Old Dance - Davis, John David (1934)

Emek Hayarden (The Yordan Valley), Ballet Suite - Braun, Yehezkel

Emilie vor ihrem Brauttag (Emilie before her wedding day); Cantata, op.58 - Hauer, Josef Matthias (1928)

En Vue de Roesnaes - Frounberg, Ivar (1981)

Ende September, op.103/1 - Hubay, Jenö (1910)

Endecatode; For 14 instruments and percussion - Malipiero, Gian Francesco (1966)

Endgame - Eberhard, Dennis (1987)

Endless Parade - Birtwistle, Sir Harrison (1987)

Energia - for Nine Instruments - Chávez, Carlos (1925)

Enfants, op.94 - Schmitt, Florent (1941)

Engführung - Holliger, Heinz (1984)

Engine - Lindberg, Magnus (1996)

Englische Suite nach Werken der Virginalisten - Sgrizzi, Luciano (1952)

English Folk Song Suite - Vaughan Williams, Ralph (1923)

English Folk Song Suite - Vaughan Williams, Ralph (1923)

Ensemble; Revised Version of String Quintet and Thundersticks - Cowell, Henry (1956)

Entgegen - Nordentoft, Anders (1985)

Entr'acte - Muldowney, Dominic (1976)

Entrée; For 15 instruments - Ferrari, Luc

Epicycle - Xenakis, Iannis (1989)

Epilogue - Toch, Ernst (1959)

Epiphyt - Hübler, Klaus K. (1988)

Epitaffio - Suter, Robert (1968)

Epitaph - Denisov, Edison (1983)

Epitaph - Erdmann, Dietrich (1987)

Epitaph - Voss, Friedrich (1960)

Epitaph for Béla Bartók - Rautavaara, Einojuhani (1956)

Equation I and II - Banks, Don (1969)

Equinoxe - Rosing-Schow, Niels (2003)

Era Madrugada - Holt, Simon (1984)

Le Erbe Nella Thule - Brizzi, Aldo (1985)

Erinnerung: From "Lieder und Gesänge" (2.Folge Nr.2) - Marx, Joseph (1911)

Eröffnung und Zertrümmerung - Huber, Nicolaus A. (1991)

Es ist alles wie ein wunderbarer Garten - Ast, Max

Es ist genug; Variations on a Theme by J. S. Bach - Denisov, Edison (1986)

Eskapaden eines Gassenhauers; Für Hörer mit Sinn für musikalische Eulenspiegeleien - Pillney, Karl Hermann (1968)

Espaces - Lazarof, Henri (1966)

Espejos en la Arena - Marquez, Arturo

La Espera - Rodrigo, Joaquín (1952)

Espressioni liriche: No.7 from "Divertimento for Mozart" - Klebe, Giselher (1956)

Esquisse d'une Fanfare: Ouverture pour le Ve acte de "Romeo et Juliette" - Poulenc, Francis

Essay No.1, op.12 - Barber, Samuel (1937)

Estampie; Ballet for Small Orchestra - Rodríguez, Robert Xavier (1981)

Estancia: Four Dances from Estancia, op.8a - Ginastera, Alberto (1941)

Et Consumimur Igni - Essl, Karl-Heinz (1960)

Et Laetitia Cordis - Braun, Yehezkel

Etüdenfest - Dean, Brett (2000)

Eucalypts I - Takemitsu, Tōru (1970)

Eufonia No.1 - Maros, Rudolf

Eugene Onegin; For narrator, actors and orchestra, op.71 - Prokofiev, Sergei (1936)

Eulogy - Osborne, Nigel (1990)

Europhony, op.55 - Patterson, Paul (1985)

Evening Piece - Harris, Roy

Event Horizon; For Clarinet and Orchestra - Amrhein, Karen Amanda (2002)

Event: Synergy II; For instrumental ensemble and two conductors - Brown, Earle (1968)

Events I - Antoniou, Theodore (1967/68)

Events III; Music for Orchestra, Tape and Slide-Projection - Antoniou, Theodore (1969)

Evil Eye Deflector - Ince, Kamran (1996)

Evocación: From "Iberia" - Albéniz, Isaac

Evocations for Clarinet and Chamber Orchestra - Avshalomov, Jacob

"das ewig liecht"; Canon cancrizans per augmentationem in contrario motu (from J. S. Bach's "Kunst der Fuge") - Nieder, Fabio (2001)

Exequien for Calvin Simmons - Harbison, John (1982)

Expression; Lyric piece for small orchestra - Saturen, David

Extase - Chen, Qigang

Extase II - Chen, Qigang

Exultation - Cowell, Henry

Ezra Pound Music - Engelmann, Hans Ulrich (1959)

F

Fables for Narrator and Orchestra; Or the Secretary Bird and Associates: Studies in the Ecology of Academic Democracy - Bacon, Ernst

Façades - Glass, Philip (1981)

Face of the Night (After a Painting by Robert Motherwell) - Fuchs, Kenneth

Facsimile - Bernstein, Leonard (1946)

Falstaff: Two Interludes - Elgar, Edward (1913)

Fancy as a Ground - Bartholomée, Pierre (1980)

Fancy Free: Three Dance Variations - Bernstein, Leonard (1944)

Fanfare - Ravel, Maurice

Fanfare for Aquarius - Benjamin, George (1983)

Fantaisie - Gnessin, Mikhail (1919)

Fantasia, On a Theme by W. A. Mozart - Ludewig, Wolfgang (1977)

Fantasia - Osborne, Nigel (1983)

Fantasia - Poot, Marcel (1942)

Fantasia - Voss, Friedrich (1956)

Fantasia, op.22 - Zbinden, Julien-François (1954)

Fantasia on "Dies Sind Die Heiligen Zehn Gebot" - Bäck, Sven-Erik (1957)

Fantasia on Korean Folk Tunes, op.53 - Bavicchi, John (1966)

Fantasie, op.111 - Fauré, Gabriel (1919)

Fantasie: No.4 from "Divertimento for Mozart" - Fricker, Peter Racine (1956)

Fantasie - Huë, Georges Adolphe

Fantasie, op.64 - Moeschinger, Albert (1944)

Fantasie I, op.31 - Geiser, Walther (1948)

Fantasie III für Streichorchester, op.39 - Geiser, Walther (1949)

Fantasie Pastorale, op.188 - Milhaud, Darius (1938)

Fantasio; Ballet pantomime de Georges Wague, H.46 - Honegger, Arthur (1922)

Fantasy and Variations - Wilson, Richard

Fantasy for Double Bass and Orchestra - Proto, Frank

Fantasy on a Western Folk Song; O! Bury me not on the lone prairie - McKay, George Frederick

A Fantasy on Children's Tunes -
Helfer, Walter
Fantasy on Mr. Hyde's Song -
Grantham, Donald
Fantasy Scenes; From an Eastern
Romance - Harty, Hamilton
Fantasy, op.36 - Bavicchi, John (1959)
Farewell & Hail, op.28 - Bavicchi, John
(1957)
Farewell to Stromness - Maxwell
Davies, Peter (1980)
Farm Journal; Suite for Chamber
Orchestra - Moore, Douglas (1950)
Farne - LeFanu, Nicola (1980)
Fasching; Carnival Humoresque, op.5
- Weiner, Leo (1907)
Fatal - André, Mark (1995)
Les fées - Saint-Saëns, Camille
(1892)
Femme et Oiseaux - Denisov, Edison
(1996)
La Femme et son Ombre: Ballet Suite
- Tcherepnin, Alexander (1948)
Les Fenêtres Simultanées - Brauel,
Henning (1975)
Fennimore and Gerda: Intermezzo -
Delius, Frederick (1910)
Der Ferne Klang - Holliger, Heinz
(1984)
Fest auf Monbijou; Suite in fünf
Sätzen, op.50 - Wunsch, Hermann
Festa Musicale - Schönherr, Max
Feste im Süden: Suite - Blacher, Boris
(1935)
Le festin de l'araignée; Ballet-
pantomime en un acte, op.17 -
Roussel, Albert (1912)
Festina Lente - Pärt, Arvo (1988)
Festival Prelude - Nielsen, Carl (1900)
Festive Poem "Thirty Years," op.113 -
Prokofiev, Sergei (1947)
Festliche Musik - Bräutigam, Helmut
(1939)
Festliche Musik - Finke, Fidelio
Festmusik der Schiffergilde - Girnatis,
Walter
Fête à Thélème - Poot, Marcel (1957)
La Fête Chez Thérèse: Suite No.1 -
Hahn, Reynaldo (1910)
La Fête Chez Thérèse: Suite No.2 -
Hahn, Reynaldo (1910)
Feuerwerk - Höller, York (2004)
Le Fiance, op.9 - Nabokoff, Nicholas
(1934)
The Field of Opportunity - Vir, Param
(1994)
Fields / Singing - Boone, Charles
(1976)
Figures - Castelnuovo-Tedesco, Mario

Finale - Vivace assai: Nr.12 from
"Divertimento for Mozart" - Henze,
Hans Werner (1956)
Finale mit Kammerensemble - Kagel,
Mauricio
Firestick - Vines, Nicholas (1999)
Fireworks, op.48 - Bavicchi, John
(1962)
First Australian Suite, op.22 - Yu,
Julian (1990)
First Idyll, op.42 - Holloway, Robin
(1980)
First Light; Concerto for Chamber
Orchestra in One Movement -
Danielpour, Richard (1988)
First Symphonic Essay - Treibmann,
Karl Ottomar
Five Austrian Miniatures - Apostel,
Hans Erich (1959)
Five Études - Rodríguez, Robert
Xavier (1983)
Five Fairy Tales (Once Upon a Time) -
Rogers, Bernard (1936)
Five Folk Melodies - Lutosławski,
Witold (1952)
Five Fragments, op.42 - Shostakovich,
Dmitri (1935)
Five Klee Pictures; For school,
amateur or professional orchestra -
Maxwell Davies, Peter (1959)
Five Little Pieces - Delius, Frederick
(1923)
Five Miniatures - Geissler, Fritz
Five Miniatures - Primosch, James
(1982)
Five Orchestra Songs, op.4 - Berg,
Alban (1912)
Five Orchestra Songs - Reger, Max
(1901)
Five Pieces - Weiss, Manfred
Five Pieces for Orchestra: From the
music to the film The 400 Million -
Eisler, Hanns (1938)
Five Pieces for String Orchestra -
Juon, Paul (1901)
Five Songs, op.15 - Bartók, Béla
(1916)
Five Songs - Ives, Charles Edward
Five Songs: From "Hungarian
Folkmusic" - Kodály, Zoltán
Five Songs, op.60 - Schoeck, Othmar
(1946)
Flash Madness - Hindson, Matthew
(2006)
Flashes; For 14 instruments - Ferrari,
Luc
flekkicht; For baroque orchestra -
Schweitzer, Benjamin (2004)
Flicker - Horne, David (1997)

Flourish with Fireflies - Matthews,
Colin (2002)
Flower of the Earth; Homage to
Georgia O'Keeffe - Heitzeg, Steve
(1987)
Flower of the Mountain: From "Distant
Hills" - Albert, Stephen (1985)
Flower of the Mountain: From "Distant
Hills." Version for full orchestra -
Albert, Stephen (1985)
Flower Ornament Music - Buck, Ole
(2002)
Flowerfall - Hvidtfelt Nielsen, Svend
(1993)
The Flowers Appear on the Earth -
Wiegold, Peter (1978)
Flute Sonata - Poulenc, Francis
(1957)
Foam - Abrahamsen, Hans (1970)
Folia; Chaconne symphonique pour
orchestre, op.30 - Bacri, Nicolas
(1990)
Folias (Guitar Concerto) - Sierra,
Roberto (2002)
Folk Song Suite - Kubik, Gail
Folk Songs - Berio, Luciano (1964)
Folk Songs - Berio, Luciano (1964)
Folk-Song Set - Finnissy, Michael
(1970)
La fontaine de jouvence - Auric,
Georges
For A Beautiful Land - Coleman, Linda
Robbins (1996)
For a Change - Nørgård, Per (1982)
For a Statesman: No.1 of "Three
Small Funeral Marches" - Berners,
Lord (1916)
For Frank O'Hara - Feldman, Morton
(1973)
For Miles - Bainbridge, Simon (1994)
For Samuel Beckett; For 23 players -
Feldman, Morton (1987)
For String and Wind Players - Erbse,
Heimo (1970)
Forest - Heath, Dave (1988)
Form / 2 Formen; For 20
instrumentalists in 4 groups of 5
players - Rihm, Wolfgang (1994)
Formel, Nr.1/6 - Stockhausen,
Karlheinz (195)
Forty Heartbeats - Saariaho, Kaija
(1998)
Foster Suite - Janssen, Werner (1937)
Four Aphorisms - Schnittke, Alfred
(1988)
Four Capriccios, op.9 - Kurtág, György
(1971)
Four Dances in One Movement -
Ruders, Poul (1983)

Gesungene Zeit - Rihm, Wolfgang (1992)

Ghost Ranch; Above Clouds - Daugherty, Michael (2005)

Ghostorchestra - Brødsgaard, Anders (1993)

Il Gigante Golia; Texte d'un petit motet sarde pour Soprano et orchestre de 16 musiciens - Aperghis, Georges (1975)

Gigue - Huë, Georges Adolphe

Gipsy Suite; Four characteristic dances - German, Sir Edward (1892)

Giration; Divertissement choréographique - Pierné, Gabriel (1935)

Glassworks - Glass, Philip (1981)

Glimpses of Bennelong - Conyngham, Barry (1987)

Gloriana: The Courtly Dances - Britten, Benjamin (1953)

Glosses sobre temes de Pau Casals, op.46; For string orchestra and string quintet "in lontano" - Ginastera, Alberto (1976)

Glossolalie - Shchetinsky, Alexander (1989)

Goldberg's Dream (Running Figures) - Burgon, Geoffrey (1975)

The Golden Bird, op.77 - Russo, William (1984)

The Golden Windows - León, Tania

The Gong on the Hook and Ladder; Firemen's Parade on Main Street, S.38 - Ives, Charles Edward

Gone Grey - Felder, David (2004)

Gong-Ring - Harvey, Jonathan (1984)

Gothic Suite; For organ, strings and percussion - Albright, William Hugh (1973)

Gottvertrauen, op.55/1 - Weingartner, Felix (1914)

Goyescas: Intermezzo - Granados, Enrique (1915)

Graal Théâtre - Saariaho, Kaija (1997)

Gran Nada - Hidalgo, Manuel (1997)

Le Grand Lustucru: From "Marie Galante" - Weill, Kurt (1934)

Grandma's Footsteps - Tavener, John (1968)

Grania and Diarmid: There are seven that pull the thread, op.42 - Elgar, Edward (1901)

Grapes of Wrath - Death, Alternative music to the film of the same name - Eisler, Hanns (1942)

Grave; Metamorphosis - Lutosławski, Witold (1981)

Great Ornamented Fuga Canonica, op.17 - Yu, Julian (1988)

Green Bushes; Passacaglia on an English folksong. British folkmusic settings No.12 - Grainger, Percy Aldridge (1906)

Greeting - Holst, Gustav

Greeting Concertino - Ruders, Poul (1982)

Griechenland; For three groups of strings - Beyer, Frank Michael (1981)

Grottesco - Malipiero, Gian Francesco (1918)

The Güell Concerto - Sierra, Roberto (2006)

Gustaviansk Suite, op.28 - Larsson, Lars-Erik

Gute Behandlung der Pferde - Schenker, Friedrich (1986)

Gyp the Blood or Hearst!? Which is Worst?! - Ives, Charles Edward

H

Haddock's Eyes - Del Tredici, David (1985)

Hades di Orfeo; Dramma per musica - Schenker, Friedrich (1977)

Haleines Astrals - Matsushita, Shin-ichi

Halil; Nocturne for solo flute and small orchestra - Bernstein, Leonard (1981)

Halt! - Birkenkötter, Jörg (1995)

Hamabdil; Hebrew melody for Violoncello with Accompaniment of Strings, Kettledrum and Harp - Bantock, Granville (1919)

Hamlet, op.77 - Prokofiev, Sergei (1938)

Hamlet; Incidental music to Shakespeare's tragedy, op.32 - Shostakovich, Dmitri (1932)

Hamlet: Suite from the Theatre Music, op.32a - Shostakovich, Dmitri (1932)

Hanako; Japanese Intermezzo - Linke, Paul (1939)

Happy End - Denisov, Edison (1985)

Harvest - Gould, Morton (1945)

Harvest - Roumain, Daniel Bernard (2004)

Hassan: Intermezzo and Serenade - Delius, Frederick (1923)

Havanaise, op.83 - Saint-Saëns, Camille (1887)

Hayagriva - Vir, Param (2005)

Hechizos - León, Tania

The Helena Variations - Bantock, Granville

Hemsoborna - Nilsson, Bo (1964)

Here trilogy; For soprano, chamber orchestra and soundtrack - Aa, Michel van der (2001-2003)

Hérodiade - Hindemith, Paul (1944)

Heroic Piece - Diamond, David

L'heure bleu - Henze, Hans Werner (2001)

Hexen - Aguila, Miguel del (1987)

Heysel; Pour 18 Instrumentistes - Aperghis, Georges (2002)

Hidden Music - Payne, Anthony (1992)

Hidden Variables - Matthews, Colin (1989)

Hidden Voice 1 - Harvey, Jonathan (1995)

Hidden Voice 2 - Harvey, Jonathan (1999)

Hill Song - Grainger, Percy Aldridge (1921)

Himmel og Jord (Heaven and Earth) - Bruun, Peter (1996)

The Hinterstoisser Traverse - Mason, Benedict (1986)

L'histoire de Babar, le petit éléphant - Poulenc, Francis (1940)

L'Histoire du Soldat (The Soldier's Tale): Suite - Stravinsky, Igor (1920)

Histoires naturelles - Ravel, Maurice (1906)

Hölderlin in Darkness: A Dedication - Huber, Nicolaus A. (1992)

A Holiday Tune - Dale, Benjamin (1925)

Homage - Cohn, James (1959)

Homage to T. S. Eliot - Gubaidulina, Sofia (1987)

Home on the Range - Guion, David (1930)

Homenaje a Cervantes - Moncayo, José Pablo

Homenaje a Debussy - Palau Boix, Manuel (1929)

Homenaje a Federico Garccía Lorca - Revueltas, Silvestre

Homenaje a la Tempranica - Rodrigo, Joaquín (1939)

Hommage a "Brundibár"; Overture for small orchestra - Pokorný, Petr (1999)

Hommage à Dionysos - Terzakis, Dimitri (1980)

Hommage à Morse - Terzakis, Dimitri (1970)

Hommage à Mozart; Metamorphoses on a group of Mozart themes for orchestra - Blacher, Boris (1956)

Hommage à Mozart - Ibert, Jacques (1956)

Hommage à Pierre - Denisov, Edison (1985)

Hommage à Satie; À mémoire for chamber orchestra - Diamond, David (1934)

L'Homme Armé, op.22a - Westergaard, Peter

L'Homme et son Désir, op.48 - Milhaud, Darius (1918)

Hoops; Ballet - Poulenc, Francis (1963)

Hoquetus - Fundal, Karsten (1984)

Hora de Junio - Revueltas, Silvestre

L'Horizon chimérique, op.118 - Fauré, Gabriel (1921)

Horizon Overture - Horovitz, Joseph (1972)

Hot Zone - Bermel, Derek (1996)

Hot-Sonate - Schulhoff, Erwin (1930)

The House that Jack Built: From the ballet "Three Jacks" - Vincent, John (1942)

Huapango - Moncayo, José Pablo

Hue!; Croquis parisien pour petit orchestre - Beydts, Louis (1958)

The Human Comedy: Suite, op.37 - Shostakovich, Dmitri (1934)

Humoreske in E Dur - Humperdinck, Engelbert

H'un (Lacerations): In Memoriam 1966-76 - Sheng, Bright (1988)

Hungarian Folksongs - Bartók, Béla (1917)

Hungarian Rondo - Kodály, Zoltán (1917)

Hungarian Serenade - Rózsa, Miklós

Hymn and Fuguing Tune No.2 - Cowell, Henry (1944)

Hymn and Fuguing Tune No.3 - Cowell, Henry (1944)

Hymn and Fuguing Tune No.5 - Cowell, Henry (1945)

Hymn and Fuguing Tune No.10 - Cowell, Henry (1955)

Hymn IV - Schnittke, Alfred (1979)

Hymn to the Night - Schafer, Robert Murray (1976)

Hymn, Chorale and Fuguing Tune No.8 - Cowell, Henry (1947)

Hymn: Largo Cantabile - Ives, Charles Edward

Hymne - Nordentoft, Anders (1996)

Hymne à Tanit - Schmitt, Florent (1925)

I

Í; A Meditation on Iona - MacMillan, James (1996)

I Am A Donut; Dialectic II. Concerto Grosso for Flute, Trumpet, Bass Clarinet and 11 Players - Runswick, Daryl (1993)

...Ibant Obscuri Sola sub Nocte per Umbras... - Vries, Klaas de

Icarian Rhapsody - Bates, Mason (2001)

Ich komm einen Weg - Matthus, Siegfried (1989)

Ichochronos II - Terzakis, Dimitri (1972)

Ictalurus Punctatus; For amplified cello and orchestra - Hindson, Matthew (2008)

Ideas; For easy orchestra - Rorem, Ned (1961)

Idées Fixes; Sonata for 13, op.63 - Goehr, Alexander (1997)

Idyll, op.70, No.2 - Kaun, Hugo (1907)

Idyllikon; Four movements for small orchestra, op.79 - Gál, Hans (1959)

If Love Is Real - Schickele, Peter (1991)

Ikarische Klage - Widmann, Jörg (1999)

Ikaros; Ballet nach einem Gedicht von E. Lindgren - Döhl, Friedhelm (1978)

Illuminations - Furrer, Beat (1985)

Illuminations to the Book of Ruth - Braun, Yehezkel

Illusion [Tendrement] - Satie, Erik (1902)

Imágenes (Double Concerto) - Sierra, Roberto (1993)

Images - Zwilich, Ellen Taaffe

Images from Goldsmith - Boelter, Karl (2001)

Images pour un Poète Maudit; Pour 25 musiciens - Barraud, Henry (1954)

Imaginaire No.1, op.41, No.1 - Ballif, Claude (1963)

Imaginaire No.3, op.41, No.3 - Ballif, Claude (1969)

An Imagined Fable - Wilby, Philip (1993)

Imaginées VI - Auric, Georges (1976)

Imago - Delás, José Luis de (1965)

Immer Wieder... - Vlad, Roman (1965)

Imposing a Regular Pattern in Chaos and Heterophony - Mason, Benedict (1990)

Impresiones de Estio I-IV - Mendoza, Vicente

Impression - Yun, Isang (1986)

Imprint; For baroque orchestra - Aa, Michel van der (2005)

Impromptu - Engelmann, Hans Ulrich (1949)

Impromptu - Gubaidulina, Sofia (1997)

Impromptu - Hvidtfelt Nielsen, Svend (1995)

Impromptu; On the Impromptus op.5/5 and 5/6 - Sibelius, Jean

In Autumn (Om hösten) - Hallén, Andreas (1895)

In Camera - Osborne, Nigel (1979)

In der Stille des Hauses wohnt ein Ton (In the silence of the house there lives a sound) - Furrer, Beat (1987)

In extremis; Pour 8 Instrumentistes - Aperghis, Georges (1998)

In Frage - Rihm, Wolfgang (2000)

In Memoriam di Valentino Bucchi - Vlad, Roman

In Memoriam Ernst Klein - Cerha, Friedrich (1985)

In Memory - Tower, Joan (2002)

In Memory H. H. L. - Locklair, Dan (2005)

In Silence, In Memory - Nelson, Larry (1994)

In Sturm und Eis; Music to Arnold Fanck's film *Im Kampf mit dem Berge* - Hindemith, Paul (1921)

In the Autumn Days - Locklair, Dan (1884)

In the Meantime - Sandström, Sven-David (1970)

in vain - Haas, Georg Friedrich (2000)

Incantations - Rautavaara, Einojuhani (2008)

Incidental Music to Shakespeare's "The Merchant of Venice" - Harbison, John (1971)

Incontri - Nono, Luigi (1955)

increase - Lang, David (2002)

Indian Fantasia, op.44 (Busoni Verz. 264) - Busoni, Ferruccio

Indigena - León, Tania

Indina Serenade, op.14, No.2 - Converse, Frederick Shepherd

Inner Light 1 - Harvey, Jonathan (1973)

Inquieto; Concerto for Marimba - Wilson, Ian (2001)

Inquietus, op.66 - Holloway, Robin (1986)

Insiders - Diehl, Paula (1992)

Instantáneas Mexicanas, No.3: Cielito lindo - Ponce, Manuel (1938)

J

K

Kammermusik No.1 (with Finale 1921), op.24, No.1 - Hindemith, Paul (1922)

Kammersinfonie, op.48 - Grosse, Erwin (1961)

Kammersinfonie, op.27 - Juon, Paul (1905)

Kammersinfonie I (Chamber Symphony I) - Yun, Isang (1987)

Kammersinfonie II - Kelterborn, Rudolf (1964)

Kammersinfonie II (Chamber Symphony II), op.17 - Redel, Martin Christoph (1972)

Kammersinfonie II (Chamber Symphony II) - Yun, Isang (1989)

Kammerstück für 12 Soloinstrumente, op.7 - Wiener, Karl (1932)

Kammersuite, op.32 - Lendvai, Erwin (1923)

Kammersymphonie (Chamber Symphony) - Heiller, Anton (1946)

Kammersymphonie (Chamber Symphony) - Schreker, Franz (1916)

Kammersymphonie, op.32 - Stöhr, Richard (1921)

Kammersymphonie (Chamber Symphony), op.41 - Apostel, Hans Erich (1968)

Kammersymphonie Nr.1 (Chamber Symphony No.1), op.9 - Schönberg, Arnold (1906)

Kammersymphonie Nr.2 (Chamber Symphony No.2), op.38 - Schönberg, Arnold (1940)

Kápote - Kancheli, Giya (2006)

Katharina Blum: Concerto suite - Henze, Hans Werner (1975)

Katharsis; After the poem by Toula S. Tolia with illustrations by Kostas Andreou - Antoniou, Theodore

Keil - Schleiermacher, Steffen (1998)

Kein Firmament - Rihm, Wolfgang (1988)

...kein Gedanke, nur ruhiger Schlaf; In Memoriam Olivier Messiaen, op.65 - Goehr, Alexander (1998)

1. Keintate - Cerha, Friedrich (1982)

2. Keintate - Cerha, Friedrich (1985)

Keir's Kick - Lloyd, Jonathan (1982)

Keltic Suite, op.29 - Foulds, John (1911)

Kerob-shal, op.67 - Schmitt, Florent (1924)

Khorovod - Anderson, Julian (1994)

Khouang - Scherchen, Tona (1968)

Kinesis ABCD for two String Groups, op.31 - Antoniou, Theodore (1966)

Kiss on Wood - MacMillan, James (1993)

Kites - Holt, Simon (1983)

Klage, op.22 - Zilcher, Hermann

Klangspiele I - Wolschina, Reinhard (1987)

Klangspiele II - Wolschina, Reinhard (1989)

Klangspiele III - Wolschina, Reinhard (1990)

Eine Kleine Herbstmusik (A Little Autumn Music) - Mykietyn, Paweł (1995)

Kleine konzertante Suite (Kaleidoskop) für Orchester, op.79 - Burkhard, Willy (1946)

Kleine Lustspiel Ouvertüre - Koch, Erland von (1952)

Kleine Marschmusik - Blacher, Boris (1932)

Kleine Suite, op.3 - Westerman, Gerhart von (1940)

Kleine Tafelmusik - Trantow, Herbert (1958)

Kleine Weihnachtsmusik - Degen, Helmut (1942)

Kleines Konzert - Uhl, Alfred (1963)

Kleines Requiem für eine Polka, op.66 - Górecki, Henryk Mikołaj (1993)

Knoxville: Summer of 1915, op.24 - Barber, Samuel (1947)

Kol od (Chemins VI) - Berio, Luciano (1996)

Kolchis - Rihm, Wolfgang (1991)

Konform - Kontraform - Franke, Bernd (1988)

Konkretionen V - Linke, Norbert (1969)

Konstellationen - Kelemen, Milko (1959)

Kontra-Punkte Nr.1 - Stockhausen, Karlheinz (1953)

Konzert; Anton Schönberg zum 60. Geburtstag, op.24 - Webern, Anton (1934)

Konzertante Figuren - Yun, Isang (1972)

Konzertante Phantasie für Orchester, op.23 - Abendroth, Walter (1948)

Kristallwelt - Obst, Michael (1983)

Kryptogramm - Hübler, Klaus K. (1989)

Kume, kum, Geselle min; Divertimento nach alten Volksliedern, Wk24 - David, Johann Nepomuk (1939)

Kurische Nehrung, op.36 - Brust, Herbert

L

L; bent - Matthews, Colin (1993)

Labor - Morthenson, Jan Wilhelm (1974)

Labyrinths: Ballet Suite - Schnittke, Alfred (1971)

Lachrymae, op.48a - Britten, Benjamin (1948)

Laconic Variations - Frazelle, Kenneth (1997)

Lacrymosa - Lavista, Mario

Laetare Anima Mea, op.77a - Sibelius, Jean (1914)

Lalinia electra; Part 1 - Brouk, Joanna

Lalita; Chamber Variations - Lieberson, Peter (1984)

Lament - Hindson, Matthew (2006)

Lamentate; Homage to Anish Kapoor and his sculpture "Marsyas" - Pärt, Arvo (2002)

Lamentationes - Kelterborn, Rudolf (1961)

Lamenting with Ariadne - Musgrave, Thea (1999)

Lamento quechua, op.6 - Franze, Juan Pedro (1952)

Ländliche Suite, op.23 - Gebhard-Elsass, Hans (1935)

Ländliche Suite, op.53 - Provazník, Anatol (1935)

Ländliches Barock, Suite, op.48 - Takács, Jenö (1941)

Landscape - Panufnik, Andrzej (1962)

Landscape and Memory - Bainbridge, Simon (1995)

Landscape VI - Hosokawa, Toshio (1994)

Landscapes - Chou, Wen-Chung

Landscapes I - Buck, Ole (1992)

Landscapes II - Buck, Ole (1994)

Landscapes III - Buck, Ole

Landscapes IV - Buck, Ole (1995)

Laps - Loevendie, Theo

Largo - Mule, Giuseppe (1931)

Largo, H.105 - Honegger, Arthur (1936)

Largo and Allegro - Kancheli, Giya (1963)

The Last Dance - Tower, Joan (2000)

Late August - Swafford, Jan

Lavapiés: From "Iberia" - Albéniz, Isaac (1908)

Legend - Schickele, Peter

Legend of the Sarimanok - Kasilag, Lucrecia

Leino Songs - Saariaho, Kaija (2007)

Lending Wings - Woolrich, John (1989)

Leonardo - Cowie, Edward (1982)

Letter from Home - Copland, Aaron (1944)

A Letter from Pete - Rogers, Bernard

La Lettre - Aubert, Louis (1900)

La Libellule - Saint-Saëns, Camille (1894)

Lichtbogen - Saariaho, Kaija (1986)

Lichtenberg-Splitter - Cerha, Friedrich (1997)

La Licorne, or The Triumph of Chastity; Ballet - Ibert, Jacques (1950)

Liebeslied (Love Song) - Banfield, Raffaello de (1968)

Liebestoto: No.10 from "Divertimento for Mozart" - Wildberger, Jacques (1956)

Lied der Waldtaube: From "Gurre-Lieder" - Schönberg, Arnold (1922)

Lied der Yvette: From the opera "Leonore 40/45" - Liebermann, Rolf (1952)

Lieder der Mädchen (Songs of the Girls) - Gelbrun, Arthur (1945)

Lieder des verliebten Muezzin, op.42 - Szymanowski, Karol (1934)

Lieutenant Kije: Troika, op.60 - Prokofiev, Sergei (1934)

Life Studies; Eight studies for 15 solo strings - Maw, Nicholas (1976)

A Life Without Christmas: The Morning Prayers. For Chamber Orchestra and Tape - Kancheli, Giya (1990)

A Life Without Christmas: Midday Prayers. Concerto for clarinet, boy soprano and chamber ensemble - Kancheli, Giya (1990)

A Life Without Christmas: The Evening Prayers. For Chamber Orchestra and 8 Alto Singers - Kancheli, Giya (1991)

A Life Without Christmas: The Night Prayers. For Soprano Saxophone, Strings and Tape - Kancheli, Giya (1994)

Lift Up Your Heads; Motet - Ben-Haim, Paul

Light Dances / Stones Sing - Levinson, Gerald (1978)

Light Music Suite - Benjamin, Arthur (1935)

Lilith - Holt, Simon (1990)

Lille Suite, op.60 - Bentzon, Niels Viggo (1950)

Lilofee Suite, op.16 - Roselius, Ludwig (1937)

Lindaraja - Debussy, Claude (1901)

Linea Meridiana - Boone, Charles (1975)

Lintukoto (Isle of Bliss) - Rautavaara, Einojuhani (1995)

The Lion, the Witch and the Wardrobe: Suite - McCabe, John (1971)

L'Invitation au voyage - Scherchen, Tona (1977)

Lit de Neige - Boucourechliev, André (1984)

Litany of Sins - Davis, Anthony (1991)

Liten Svit I Spelmanston - Sjöblom, Heimer (1973)

LiteSPEED - Hindson, Matthew (1997)

Lithuanian Night - Antheil, George (1919)

The Little Circus, op.51 - Cohn, James (1974)

Little Continuum: No.1 of "Two Tributes" - Matthews, Colin (1999)

Little Fantasy - Schuller, Gunther (1957)

Little March for the Big Bowl, Marche grotesque - Slonimsky, Nicolas (1943)

Little Serenade - Tomlinson, Ernest

Little Suite - Lutosławski, Witold (1951)

Little Suite - Lutosławski, Witold (1951)

Little Suite No.2, op.18b - Matthews, Colin (1979)

Little Symphony - Chapple, Brian (1982)

A Little Symphony; Symphony No.2 - Eppert, Carl (1933)

Little Symphony, op.15 - Goehr, Alexander (1963)

Little Symphony - Kupferman, Meyer (1952)

Little Symphony - Schenker, Friedrich (1966)

Little Tragedies, Suite from the music to the film - Schnittke, Alfred (1994)

Liturgia - Beyer, Frank Michael (1996)

Living Toys, op.9 - Adès, Thomas (1993)

L'Obvio - Hidalgo, Manuel (1982)

Lodolezzi Sjunger: Suite, op.39 - Stenhammar, Wilhelm (1941)

The Lonely Dancer of Gedār; Oriental Dance for Small Orchestra, op.36 - Bedford, Herbert (1926)

Lonely Hearts; Song Cycle for Mezzo Soprano, 14 Players, Two Conductors and Click-Track Tape - Muldowney, Dominic (1988)

Loose Leaves - Nelson, Larry (1989)

Lost City Life - Rushton, Edward (1998)

Love Bead - Gordon, Michael (1997)

Love Songs and Dances; Concertante for 21 Players - Cooper, Paul (1987)

Love's Labour's Lost: Suite, op.28b - Finzi, Gerald (1955)

Love's Labour's Lost: Three Soliloquies, op.28 - Finzi, Gerald (1955)

Lullaby - Hindson, Matthew (2003)

Lullaby - Panufnik, Andrzej (1947)

Luminères de Guang-Ling - Chen, Qigang

Lune de miel - Barlow, Fred

Lustspiel Overture, op.38 (Busoni Verz. 245) - Busoni, Ferruccio

Lustspielsuite; Der Widerspenstigen Zähmung, op.54b - Zilcher, Hermann

Lyric Piece - Brant, Henry (1933)

Lyrical Concerto, op.39 - Yu, Julian (1997)

Lyrische Tanzmusik, op.82 - Siegl, Otto (1934)

Lyrisches Intermezzo - Blumer, Theodor (1939)

Lyrisches Intermezzo - Haas, Joseph (1938)

Lysistrata: Suite from the ballet - Blacher, Boris (1950)

Lysning - Nørgård, Per (2006)

M

Das Mädchen mit den verbundenen Augen: From "Sechs Gesänge," op.13/2 - Zemlinsky, Alexander (1914)

Ma Mère l'Oye (Mother Goose); Ballet en un acte, cinq tableaux et un apothéose - Ravel, Maurice (1912)

Ma Mère l'Oye (Mother Goose): Cinq pièces enfantines (Suite) - Ravel, Maurice (1912)

Ma Mère l'Oye (Mother Goose): Prelude et Danse du Rouet - Ravel, Maurice (1912)

Machines Agricoles; 6 pastoral songs, op.56 - Milhaud, Darius (1919)

Madame Press Died Last Week at Ninety - Feldman, Morton (1970)

Made in America - Tower, Joan (2004)

Madrigal - Gaubert, Philippe

La Madrugada del Panadero: Suite del Ballet - Halffter, Rodolfo

Magam - Brødsgaard, Anders (2002)

Magische Quadrate; Symphonische Phantasie, Wk52 - David, Johann Nepomuk (1959)

Magnum Ignotum - Kancheli, Giya (1994)

Mährische Volkstänze (Moravian Folk Dances) - Janáček, Leoš (1892)

The Maiden on the Moor - Schickele, Peter

Maienblüten: From "Lieder und Gesänge" (1.Folge Nr.16) - Marx, Joseph (1909)

The Maloney Rag - Kozinski, Stefan (1976)

Man Walking; Serenade for Octet - Dalby, Martin (1981)

Manchay Tiempo (Time of Fear) - Frank, Gabriela Lena (2005)

Manhattan Broadcast - Gruber, HK (1964)

A Map is not the Territory - Staud, Johannes Maria (2001)

March for Violin and Orchestra - Kupkovic, Ladislav (1978)

March in B-flat Major, op.99 - Prokofiev, Sergei (1944)

Le Marchand de Sable qui Passe (The Sandman Passing By), op.13 - Roussel, Albert (1908)

Märchenbilder - Abrahamsen, Hans (1984)

Marea - Lindberg, Magnus (1990)

Marienleben, op.8 - Müller-Zürich, Paul

Marienlied: From "Lieder und Gesänge" (1.Folge Nr.17) - Marx, Joseph (1910)

Marita and Her Heart's Desire; A Chamber Music Fairy Tale for Family Audiences. - Adolphe, Bruce (1993)

Marosszéker Tänze - Kodály, Zoltán (1927)

Mascarade: Tableau from the opera "Vipern" - Jost, Christian (2003)

Masques et Bergamasques, op.112 - Fauré, Gabriel (1919)

Mass: Meditation No.1 - Bernstein, Leonard (1971)

Mass: Two Meditations - Bernstein, Leonard (1971)

Master Irpy - King, Alastair (1999)

Matelote Provençale - Poulenc, Francis (1952)

Matinées musicales, op.24; Second Suite of Five Movements from Rossini - Britten, Benjamin (1941)

La Mauvaise Prière - Aubert, Louis (1932)

Maxim's - Muldowney, Dominic (1986)

May Song - Elgar, Edward (1901)

Measure for Measure - Foss, Lukas (1984)

Medea Fragments I - Hosokawa, Toshio (1996)

Medea: Ballet Suite, op.23 - Barber, Samuel (1947)

Medeas Lied - Döhl, Friedhelm (1991)

Mediterranian Sinfonietta - Bjelinski, Bruno

The Medium: Baba's Aria (Afraid, am I afraid?) - Menotti, Gian Carlo (1946)

The Medium: The Black Swan - Menotti, Gian Carlo (1946)

The Medium: Monica's Waltz - Menotti, Gian Carlo (1946)

Medusa; A Monodrama for dramatic soprano and string orchestra - Bolcom, William (2003)

Medusa, op.24; Ballet in three scenes to a scenario by M. Gale Hoffman - Einem, Gottfried von (1957)

Medusa, op.24a: Three movements for orchestra - Einem, Gottfried von (1957)

Meeting - Rosing-Schow, Niels (1985)

Meetings along the Edge: From "Passages" - Glass, Philip (1990)

Mein Weg; For 14 strings and percussion - Pärt, Arvo (1999)

Meinem Kinde, op.37/3 - Strauss, Richard (1897)

Melancolia - Denhoff, Michael (1980)

Melodien - Ligeti, György (1971)

Melodies from the East - Ben-Haim, Paul

Melody with Accompaniment - Wielecki, Tadeusz (1981)

Memoire imperiale; A variation on General John Reid's March "Garb of Gaul" - MacMillan, James (1993)

Memoria - Baggiani, Guido (1983)

Memorial Music - Palmer, Robert

Mémoriale (…explosante-fixe…Originel) - Boulez, Pierre (1985)

Men of Goodwill; Variations on a Christmas Carol (God rest ye merry, Gentlemen) - Britten, Benjamin (1947)

Mercure; Poses plastiques, op.post - Satie, Erik (1924)

Meridian; Concerto for flute and string ensemble - Beyer, Frank Michael (2004)

Message - Yanov-Yanovsky, Dmitri (2001)

Message Pour Gérard - Saariaho, Kaija (2000)

Mester Jacob (Frère Jacques) - Gudmundsen-Holmgreen, Pelle (1964)

La Metamorfosi di Narciso; Allegoria sonora per un violoncello principale e gruppo strumentale - Pintscher, Matthias (1992)

Metamorphose, op.4 - Nørgård, Per (1953)

Metamorphose; Music for the film of the same title by Michael Wolgensinger - Zimmermann, Bernd Alois (1954)

La Métamorphose d'Ève; Ballet - Inghelbrecht, D.E. (1928)

Metamorphosen - Boßler, Kurt (1973/74)

Metamorphosen; For 23 solo strings - Strauss, Richard (1945)

Metamorphosen über ein Menuett von Franz Schubert - Reimann, Aribert (1997)

Metamorphoses - Bennett, Richard Rodney (1980)

Metamorphosis; Piano Concerto No.1 - Danielpour, Richard (1990)

Metasinfonia; Symphony No.7 - Panufnik, Andrzej (1978)

A Midsummer Night's Dream; Incidental Music - Rodríguez, Robert Xavier (2001)

Migraine pour orchestre, op.19b - Hemberg, Eskil (1973)

Military March No.1 - Myaskovsky, Nikolai Yakovlevich

Millennium Fantasy - Zwilich, Ellen Taaffe

Milonga del Ángel - Piazzolla, Astor

Mimaamaquim; Psaume 130, H.192 - Honegger, Arthur (1947)

Min Fynske Barndom: Suite - Pape, Andy (2004)

Minha mäe me deu um lenço - Halffter, Ernesto (1940)

Miniatur I - Kubo, Mayako (1981)

Miniaturas Medievales - Muñoz Molleda, José (1974)

A Miniature - Marthinsen, Niels (1995)

Miniature Fantasy for String Orchestra, op.2 - Goossens, Eugene (1911)

Mini-Symphony, op.231 - Bentzon, Niels Viggo (1968)

Minna von Barnhelm: Overture, op.39 - Bruns, Victor

Minnelieder - Zweites Minnewater - Sørensen, Bent (1994)

Minnewater; Thousands of Canons - Sørensen, Bent (1988)

The Minotaur: Suite from the Ballet - Carter, Elliott (1047)

Minuet, op.21 - Elgar, Edward (1897)

Minuetto Serio - Kodály, Zoltán (1953)

Minus 1500 - Talbot, Joby (2001)

Mirage for Ud and Chamber Ensemble - Ali-Zadeh, Franghiz (1998)

A Mirror on Which to Dwell; For Soprano and Ensemble - Carter, Elliott (1975)

Les Misérables: Suite pour orchestre tirée de la musique du film de Raymond Bernard, H.88A - Honegger, Arthur (1934)

Mishima (Music from the Film) - Glass, Philip (1985)

Missa Morgenstern - Brandmüller, Theo (1978)

Missa Parodia II - Smalley, Roger (1967)

Mission San José de Aguaya - Donato, Anthony

Mit durchscheinender Melancholie - Trojahn, Manfred (1995)

Mnemosyne - Firsova, Elena (1995)

Möbelmusik-Klassisch, op.68 - Schwertsik, Kurt (1994)

Mobile - Neikrug, Marc (1981)

Mobiles - Einfeldt, Dieter

Module 3 - Brown, Earle (1969)

Modules; An Intermezzo for Chamber Orchestra - Powell, Mel (1985)

Modules 1 & 2 - Brown, Earle (1966)

Moel Bryn Divisions - Boyle, Rory (1985)

Moments musicaux, op.19 - Klebe, Giselher (1955)

Mónár Anna; Székler Ballade - Kodály, Zoltán (1936)

Mond-Lichtung; Eine Nacht-partie für Streichorchester, op.75 - Schwertsik, Kurt (1997)

Monodie - Haas, Georg Friedrich (1999)

Monodie; Music of the silence, op.12 - Kühnl, Claus (1981)

Monolog der Stella (Stella's Monologue); Concert Aria, op.57a - Krenek, Ernst (1928)

Monologue - Schnittke, Alfred (1989)

Morceau de concert, op.62 - Saint-Saëns, Camille (1880)

Morceau de concert, op.94 - Saint-Saëns, Camille (1887)

Morceau de concert, op.154 - Saint-Saëns, Camille

More Seasons - Abels, Michael (1999)

Morgen - Strauss, Richard (1894)

Morgen, op.27/4 - Strauss, Richard (1894)

Morris Dance Tunes - Holst, Gustav

Mort de Socrate - Satie, Erik (1918)

The Most Often Used Chords (Gli Accordi Piu Usati) - Harbison, John (1993)

Mouvement for Orchestra - Boccadoro, Carlo

Mouvements perpétuels for nine instruments - Poulenc, Francis (1918)

Mouvements perpétuels; Nos. 1 & 2 - Poulenc, Francis (1918)

Movement - Cowell, Henry (1934)

Movement for Orchestra - Binkerd, Gordon (1964)

Movements - Hvidtfelt Nielsen, Svend (1999)

Movements on a Moving Line - Rasmussen, Karl Aage (1987)

Movimento I - Bäck, Sven-Erik (1965)

Moving Trees - Harvey, Jonathan (2002)

Mozart - Toovey, Andrew (1991)

Moz-Art à la Haydn; Play on music for 2 violins, 2 small string orchestras, double bass and conductor - Schnittke, Alfred (1977)

Mozart, auf und davon, op.94 - Schwertsik, Kurt (2005)

Much Ado About Nothing: Suite, op.11 - Korngold, Erich Wolfgang (1919)

La Muerte Alegre - Roldán, Amadeo

Multiplay; Kanonische Reflexionen für 23 Spieler (Kammerorchester) - Wimberger, Gerhard (1973)

Münchner Symphonie, op.70 - Einem, Gottfried von (1983)

Mungo Dances - Gough, Orlando (1998)

Murmurs in the Mist of Memory - Thomas, Augusta Read (2001)

Music - Trexler, Georg

Music for a Puppet Court; Puzzle pieces for 2 Chamber Orchestras, op.11 - Knussen, Oliver (1983)

Music for Boston - Milhaud, Darius

Music for Brass, Kettledrums and Strings, op.36 - Kurz, Siegfried

Music for Carlow - Blackford, Richard (1987)

Music for Chamber Orchestra - Diamond, David

Music for Chamber Orchestra - Dobbins, Lori (1987)

Music for Chamber Orchestra - Etler, Alvin

Music for Chamber Orchestra - Gregson, Edward (1968)

Music for Dancing - Kubik, Gail

Music for Movies - Copland, Aaron (1942)

Music for Orchestra, Wk.8 - Bräutigam, Helmut

Music for Orchestra - Trexler, Georg

Music for Orchestra on a Theme by Robert Schumann - Neubert, Günter (1969)

Music for Piano and Chamber Orchestra - Schnittke, Alfred (1964)

Music for Small Orchestra, op.81 - Bavicchi, John (1981)

Music for Small Orchestra - Crawford, Ruth (1926)

Music for Strings - Bennett, Richard Rodney (1977)

Music for Strings - Bliss, Arthur (1935)

Music for Strings; Adagio for Strings, op.49 - Rathaus, Karol (1941)

Music for Strings - Weiss, Manfred

Music for Strings - Zimmermann, Udo (1968)

Music for Strings in Three Parts - Neubert, Günter (1967)

Music for Strings, Percussion and Celesta - Bartók, Béla (1936)

Music for the City of Köthen - Shchedrin, Rodion (1984)

Music for the Theatre - Copland, Aaron (1925)

Music for the Young - Weigl, Karl (1939)

Music for Twelve - Firsova, Elena (1986)

Music for Twelve - Kirchner, Leon (1985)

Music for two violins and string orchestra, op.18 - Schaeuble, Hans (1959)

Music from the House of Crossed Desires - Woolrich, John (1996)

Music from Underground Spaces - Bates, Mason (2008)

Music in Two Movements for Harp and String Orchestra - Bialas, Günter (1966)

Music on Canvas - Huber, Nicolaus A. (2003)

Music to a World's Fair Film - Antheil, George (1939)

Musica - Gielen, Michael (1954)

Musica da Camera - Paccagnini, Angelo (1960)

Musica da Camera per 11 - Maros, Rudolf

Musica Fera - Angerer, Paul (1956)

Musica giocosa - Blacher, Boris (1959)

Musica intima - Koch, Erland von (1965)

Musica luminosa per orchestra - Kelterborn, Rudolf (1983/84)

Musica Multicolore - Erdmann, Dietrich (1981)

Musica Para Charlar - Revueltas, Silvestre

Musica para Pequena Orquesta. Himno (Music for small orchestra. Hymn) - Ardevol, José

Musica para un Jardín - Rodrigo, Joaquín (1957)

Musica serena - Manicke, Dietrich (1981)

...a musical offering (J. S. B. 1985) - Goehr, Alexander (1985)

Music-Hall Suite - Rihm, Wolfgang (1979)

The Musicians of Bremen - Rogers, Bernard

Musicians Wrestle Everywhere - Weir, Judith (1994)

Music-Pictures (Group IV), op.55 - Foulds, John (1917)

Music; For oboe and 13 instruments - Lampersberg, Gerhard (1956)

Musik (Nr.1) - Maasz, Gerhard

Musik, op.73 - Gál, Hans

Musik der Frühe; Concerto for violin and orchestra - Beyer, Frank Michael (1993)

Musik für 15 Streichinstrumente - Dessau, Paul (1979)

Musik für ein Haus voll Zeit - Bose, Hans-Jürgen von (1978)

Musik für Kleines Orchester (Music for Small Orchestra) - Krebs, Joachim

Musikalisches Opfer; Ricercare a 3, Fuga canonica & 9 Kanons - Beyer, Frank Michael (1985)

Der Musikant: Serenade - Bittner, Julius (1911)

Musique - Debussy, Claude

Musique de Cour; D'après les themes de Robert de la Visée - Tansman, Alexandre (1960)

La musique d'Erich Zahn - Ballif, Claude (1964)

Musique funèbre - Lutosławski, Witold (1958)

Musique Legère - Poot, Marcel (1943)

Musique pour Ars Nova, op.432 - Milhaud, Darius (1969)

Musique pour cordes - Poot, Marcel (1963)

Musique pour Graz, op.429 - Milhaud, Darius (1969)

Musique pour Lisbonne, op.420 - Milhaud, Darius (1966)

Musique pour San Francisco, op.436 - Milhaud, Darius (1971)

Musique Pour Sanssouci - Pfundt, Reinhard

Musiquette - Poot, Marcel (1930)

Mutazione; Concerto for Piano - Wilson, Ian (2003)

Muttertändelei, op.43, No.2 - Strauss, Richard (1899)

Mxyzptlk: From "Metropolis Symphony" - Daugherty, Michael (1989)

My Lady Brocade - Ketèlbey, Albert W. (1933)

My Robin is to the Greenwood Gone: Old English Popular Music No.2 - Grainger, Percy Aldridge (1911)

Myrtle Blossoms from Eden - Ben-Haim, Paul

Mythos - Höller, York (1979)

N

Nachhall, op.70 - Schoeck, Othmar (1956)

Nach-Schrift; Eine Chiffre - Rihm, Wolfgang (2004)

Die Nachtigall (The Nightingale), op.68 - Krenek, Ernst (1931)

Nachtstück, op.29 - Einem, Gottfried von (1960)

Nachtstück und Passacaglia - Schubert, Manfred (1967)

Nachtstücke - Obst, Michael (1990)

Nær og Fjern (Near and Distant) - Gudmundsen-Holmgreen, Pelle (1987)

Nahezu Stilles Auge des Wirbelsturms - Hidalgo, Manuel (1996)

Napoleón: Danse des Enfants - Honegger, Arthur (1927)

Napoleón: La romance de Violine - Honegger, Arthur (1927)

Narcissus-Fragment; For 2 narrators and 26 players - Furrer, Beat (1993)

Narrativo e Sonnambulo - Müller-Wieland, Jan (1989)

Natural Selection - Bermel, Derek (2000)

Nature, op.8/1 - Schönberg, Arnold (1904)

Near the Western Necropolis - Wilson, Ian (1998)

Netsuke - Hesketh, Kenneth (2004)

Der neue Orpheus; Cantata for Soprano, Violin and Orchestra, op.16 - Weill, Kurt (1925)

New Babylon, op.18 - Shostakovich, Dmitri (1929)

New Morning for the World; "Daybreak of Freedom" - Schwantner, Joseph (2004)

Le Nez de Martin - Aubert, Louis (1943)

Nicholas Nickelby (incidental music) - Oliver, Stephen (1980)

Nie Ward Ich, Herrin, Müd', op.8/4 - Schönberg, Arnold (1904)

Night Journey - Schuman, William

Night Music; Five Scenes for Chamber Orchestra - Hagen, Daron (1984)

Night Music, op.10 - Matthews, Colin (1977)

Night Music - Musgrave, Thea (1969)

Night Music - Searle, Humphrey (1947)

Night Music: Voice in the Leaves - Yanov-Yanovsky, Dmitri (2000)

Night Pictures - Boyle, Rory (1986)

Nightshade - Ruders, Poul (1987)

Night-Symphonies; Day Breaks - Nørgård, Per (1992)

Nine Horses, op.19 - Ye, Xiaogang (1993)

Nine Variations on Paganini; For Double Bass and orchestra - Proto, Frank

Le Noche de los Mayas - Revueltas, Silvestre

Noches en los Jardines de España (Nights in the Gardens of Spain) - Falla, Manuel de (1915)

Nocturne, op.25 - Berkeley, Lennox (1946)

Nocturne - Blake, David (1994)

Nocturne - Danielpour, Richard (2000)

Nocturne - Huë, Georges Adolphe

Nocturne - Standford, Patric (1968)

Nocturne - Wiechowicz, Stanisław (1960)

Nocturne and Scherzo - Barclay, Robert Lenard (1947)

Nocturne for Orchestra - La Violette, Wesley

Nocturnes - Bennett, Richard Rodney (1963)

Nocturnes, Fragment VII - Nørgård, Per (1961)

Nocturnos - Engelmann, Hans Ulrich (1958)

Nonet; Obra encàrrec Festival Internacional de Música de Barcelona 1979 - Homs, Joaquim (1979)

II. Nonet - Jaroch, Jirí (1965)

Nonet, H.144 - Martinů, Bohuslav (1925)

Nonet No.2 - Martinů, Bohuslav (1959)

Nonet of the Night - Laderman, Ezra (2004)

Nonett - Kelemen, Milko (1990)

Nonette "Zeitgeist" - Jahn, Thomas

Nonetto - Fontyn, Jacqueline (1969)

Nor Spell, Nor Charm - Druckman, Jacob (1990)

Nordic Impressions; Suite for String Orchestra - Baumann, Herbert (1959)

Nordungarische Bauernlieder und Tänze; Kleine Suite, op.5 - Rózsa, Miklós (1929)

Norse Legend - Bridge, Frank (1905)

Northern Lights Electric - Moravec, Paul (1994)

The Nose: Suite, op.15a - Shostakovich, Dmitri (1928)

Nosferatu - Obst, Michael (2002)

Not a Stream but an Ocean - Yu, Julian (2000)

Notes from the Underground - Davis, Anthony (1988)

Notre Dame des Jouets; Organum from a Music Box, op.27, No.1 - Knussen, Oliver (1995)

Notte - Standford, Patric (1968)

Notte Oscura - Hesketh, Kenneth (2002)

Notturni; Concerto da camera quasi una sinfonia piccola, op.14 - Bacri, Nicolas (1986)

Notturni - Ledenjov, Roman (1968)

Notturni trasognati - Trojahn, Manfred (1977)

Notturno; Music for Julia - Lachenmann, Helmut (1968)

Notturno e Danza - Porrino, Ennio (1936)

Notturno in A-flat Major - Schönberg, Arnold (1896)

Notturno ungherese, op.28 - Rózsa, Miklós

Nouveaux Divertissements - Zimmermann, Udo (1987)

Novara - Brown, Earle (1962)

Novelletten - Hallberg, Björn Wilho (1973)

Now you hear me, now you don't - Schwertsik, Kurt (2008)

Nozze di Primavera - Dalby, Martin (1984)

Nuancen - Erdmann, Dietrich (1978)

Nucleus - Rihm, Wolfgang (1996)

Une nuit à Lisbonne, op.63 - Saint-Saëns, Camille (1880)

Nursery Rhymes - Riedel, Georg (1986)

Nuun - Furrer, Beat (1996)

Nuut - Hidalgo, Manuel (1992)

Nymphéa Reflection - Saariaho, Kaija (2001)

O

...Das O...: From ...22,1... - André, Mark (2003)

Ô beaux rêves évanouis: "Air de Béatrix" - Saint-Saëns, Camille

O Notte - Rihm, Wolfgang (1975)

O Orpheus singt - Denhoff, Michael (1977)

O Tiempo Tus Piramides - Essl, Karl-Heinz (1989)

Oberhessische Bauerntänze für Kleines Orchester - Gerster, Ottmar (1937)

Obertura Festiva (Festive Overture) - Halffter, Rodolfo

Obertura Para Doce Instrumentos (Overture for 12 Instruments) - Paz, Juan Carlos

Oblivion - Piazzolla, Astor

Océan de Terre, op.10 - Knussen, Oliver (1976)

Ocho Miniaturas - Cordero, Roque

Ocho Por Radio; Eight Musicians Broadcasting - Revueltas, Silvestre

Octet - Bolcom, William

Octet (Varianti) - Döhl, Friedhelm (1961)

Octet, op.33 - Joubert, John (1961)

Octet - Smolka, Martin (2001)

Octet on an Octet - Matthus, Siegfried (1976)

Ode; Pour orchestre "Mozart" - Bon, André (1979)

Ode, op.45 - Holloway, Robin (1980)

Ode II; Pour orchestre de chambre - Bon, André (1985)

Ode Super "Chrysea Phorminx" - Vlad, Roman (1964)

Ode to Napoleon - Schönberg, Arnold (1942)

Odefonia - Consoli, Marc-Antonio (1978)

Odelette, op.162 - Saint-Saëns, Camille (1920)

Oedipus Tyrannos; Ode for String Orchestra - Theodorakis, Mikis (1964)

Of Discoveries - Sierra, Roberto (1992)

Offering: From "Passages" - Glass, Philip (1990)

Oh Lois!: From "Metropolis Symphony" - Daugherty, Michael (1989)

Oh, My Admired C minor - Smolka, Martin (2002)

Ohne Leben Tod (Without Life Death), op.23 - Harneit, Johannes (2004)

Oiseau d'éternité; Five Poems for Soprano, Mezzo-Soprano and Baritone - Burgan, Patrick

Ojai Festival Overture - Maxwell Davies, Peter (1991)

Old American Country Set - Cowell, Henry (1939)

Old American Songs; First Set - Copland, Aaron (1950)

Old American Songs; Second Set - Copland, Aaron (1952)

Old Netherlands Dances, op.46 - Roentgen, Julius

Old Polish Suite - Panufnik, Andrzej (1950)

An Old Song - Warlock, Peter (1923)

Olicantus - Benjamin, George (2002)

O-Mega - Xenakis, Iannis (1997)

Omnivorous Furniture - Bates, Mason (2004)

On All Fours - Turnage, Mark-Anthony (1985)

On the Town: Three Dance Episodes - Bernstein, Leonard (1945)

...Once Upon A Time - Dillon, James

Ongaku - Cowell, Henry (1957)

Onze Variations sur un Thème de Haydn - Françaix, Jean (1982)

Op Ouvertüre für Orchester und drei Lautsprechergruppen (Tonband) - Antoniou, Theodore (1966)

Open - Lang, David (2008)

Open House - Bolcom, William

Opus Americanum No.2 (Moïse) - Milhaud, Darius

Oración del Torero, op.34 - Turina, Joaquin (1926)

Orchalau Concerto, op.38 - Zbinden, Julien-François

Orchester-Capriccio über ein Volkslied - Blacher, Boris (1933)

Orchestral Variations - Copland, Aaron (1957)

Orchestral Variations; "The Seeds Long Hidden" - Payne, Anthony (1994)

Organum, op.27, No.2 - Knussen, Oliver (1994)

Orient & Occident - Pärt, Arvo (2000)

Oriente Immaginario; Tre stui per piccola orchestra - Malipiero, Gian Francesco (1920)

The Origin of the Harp, op.13 - Adès, Thomas (1994)

Originel: From "…explosante-fixe…" - Boulez, Pierre (1993)

Origines - Horváth, Josef Maria (1975)

An Orkney Wedding, with Sunrise; Version for Chamber Orchestra - Maxwell Davies, Peter (1985)

An Ornithological Suite, op.23 - Maganini, Quinto (1931)

Orphée Sérénade - Bolcom, William (1984)

Orpheus - Foss, Lukas (1974)

Oscillation - Fundal, Karsten (2000)

Ostinato Funebre - Holliger, Heinz (1991)

Ostpreußische Fischertänze, op.34 - Brust, Herbert

Où nous avons aimé - Saint-Saëns, Camille

Out of the Cradle Endlessly Rocking; After the poem by Walt Whitman - Creston, Paul (1934)

Out of the Dark (After Three Paintings by Helen Frankenthaler) - Fuchs, Kenneth

Out Of This World - Parting - Nørgård, Per (1994)

An Outdoor Overture - Copland, Aaron (1938)

Outland - Marthinsen, Niels (1999)

Ouvertura Piccola - Rosenberg, Hilding Constantin (1934)

Ouverture, H.345 - Martinů, Bohuslav (1953)

Ouverture de l'homme tel… - Villa-Lobos, Heitor (1952)

Ouverture Joyeuse - Poot, Marcel (1934)

Ouvertüre "Triumph der Empfindsamkeit" (Triumph of Sensitivity), op.43a - Krenek, Ernst (1926)

Overtura Semiseria, op.69 - Takács, Jenö (1959)

Overture - Buck, Ole (1966)

Overture: Taming of the Shrew - Hewitt, Harry

Overture - Poulenc, Francis (1939)

Overture - Poulenc, Francis (1965)

Overture; American, op.42 - Prokofiev, Sergei (1926)

Overture - Salmhofer, Franz (1922)

Overture for an Occasion, op.16 - Ferguson, Howard (1953)

Overture for Chamber Orchestra, op.14 - Bentzon, Niels Viggo (1942)

Overture for Small Orchestra - Krása, Hans (1944)

Overture for Strings - Lutosławski, Witold (1949)

Overture "Half Holiday" - Gardner, John (1962)

Overture in Old Style - Baird, Tadeusz (1950)

Overture on a Nursery Rhyme, op.75a - Holloway, Robin (1995)

Overture on Hebrew Themes, op.34a - Prokofiev, Sergei (1919)

Overture Paul Bunyan - Britten, Benjamin (1978)

Overture to a Fairy Tale - Morawetz, Oskar (1956)

Overture to a Knightly Play - Weinberger, Jaromir (1931)

Overture to an Italian Comedy - Benjamin, Arthur (1937)

Overture to Lysistrata - Adamo, Mark (2005)

Overture to Racine's "Athalie" - Martin, Frank (1946)

Overture to Shakespeare's "The Tempest," op.65 - Weingartner, Felix (1919)

Oxberg Variations, On a Theme from Dalekarlien - Koch, Erland von (1956)

P

Pachelbel's Key; For Youth Orchestra - Daugherty, Michael (2002)

Paeans - Moross, Jerome (1933)

Paesaggio - Lorentzen, Bent (1983)

Paganini Trills - Tower, Joan (1996)

Paintings No.6 (To hear the light dancing) - McKinley, William Thomas (1981)

Paisajes - Revueltas, Silvestre

Paisajes Bajo el Signo de Cosmos - Marquez, Arturo

Palillos y Panderetas; Música para una tonadilla imaginaria - Rodrigo, Joaquín (1982)

Palimpsest - Xenakis, Iannis (1979)

Palladio - Jenkins, Karl (1995)

Pandora: Orchestral suite from the ballet - Gerhard, Roberto (1943)

Panorama ciego - Mundry, Isabel (2001)

Les Pantins Dansent - Satie, Erik (1913)

Pantomime; Suite for Chamber Orchestra - Schnittke, Alfred (1975)

Papageno's Pocket-Size Concerto: No.6 from "Divertimento for Mozart" - Haubenstock-Ramati, Roman (1956)

Papillons - Saint-Saëns, Camille

Paradiesvogel - Lorentzen, Bent (1983)

Parenthèses; Pour Percussion Solo et 16 Instrumentistes - Aperghis, Georges (1977)

Parergon, op.15B - Jelinek, Hanns (1957)

Parergon zum "Eugen Onegin" - Blacher, Boris (1966)

Pari Intervallo - Pärt, Arvo (1995)

Paroles tissées (Woven words) - Lutosławski, Witold (1965)

Partita, op.66 - Berkeley, Lennox (1965)

Partita - Blacher, Boris (1945)

Partita, op.7 - Cruft, Adrian (1951)

Partita - Engelmann, Hans Ulrich (1953)

Partita - Harbison, John (2001)

Partita - Koppel, Anders (1996)

Partita - Lutosławski, Witold (1988)

Partita, op.10 - Pisk, Paul Amadeus (1924)

Partita - Rangström, Ture (1933)

Partita - Schwarz-Schilling, Reinhard (1934/35)

Partita - Zwilich, Ellen Taaffe

Partita Concertante, op.63 - Bush, Alan (1965)

Partita for Piano and Orchestra - Brunner, Adolf (1938/39)

Partita for Small Orchestra, op.70 - Read, Gardner (1946)

Partita for Two Chamber Orchestras, op.45 - Campo, Frank

Partita Giocosa - Wimberger, Gerhard (1961)

Partita No.2, Wk27 - David, Johann Nepomuk (1940)

Partita No.2 - Orbón, Julián

Parts - Kyburz, Hanspeter (1994)

Passacaglia - Jenkins, Karl (1995)

Passacaglia - Kulenty, Hanna (1992)

Passacaglia, op.1 - Webern, Anton (1908)

Passacaglia II - Müller-Hornbach, Gerhard (1981)

Passacaille - Martin, Frank (1944)

Passage - Wyner, Yehudi (1983)

Passageways IIA - Felder, David (1991)

Passion - Döhl, Friedhelm (1984)

Passion Prayers - Thomas, Augusta Read (1999)

Passionato con Arietta - Beyer, Frank Michael (2005)

Passions - Kelterborn, Rudolf (1998)

Pastoral - Carter, Elliott

Pastoral costarricense; Un recuerdo sentimental - Wagner, Joseph

Pastoral for liten orkester - Larsson, Lars-Erik (1941)

Pastorale, op.59 - Goossens, Eugene (1942)

Pastorale - Matsudaira, Yoritsune (1935)

Pastorale - Menotti, Gian Carlo (1933)

Pastorale: From Babette's Feast - Nørgård, Per (1988)

Pastorale - Wellesz, Egon (1935)

Pastorale and Capriccio, op.21 - Balogh, Ernö

Pastorale d'été; Poème symphonique, H.31 - Honegger, Arthur (1920)

Pastorale et Danses - Ropartz, Joseph Guy Marie

Pastorals - Buck, Ole (1975)

Pavana Real; Ballet in three acts - Rodrigo, Joaquín (1955)

Pavane - Müller-Siemens, Detlev (1985)

Pavane pour une infante défunte - Ravel, Maurice (1910)

Paysage d'Auvergne; Danse paysanne pour orchestre - Arbeau, Pierre

Peanuts® Gallery - Zwilich, Ellen Taaffe (1996)

La Peintre et son Modèle; Ballet in one act - Auric, Georges (1950)

Pelimannit (The Fiddlers) - Rautavaara, Einojuhani (1952)

Pelleas & Melisande, op.46 - Sibelius, Jean (1905)

Pentagramm - Blacher, Boris (1974)

Penthode; For five groups of four instrumentalists - Carter, Elliott (1985)

Percussion Fantasy - Black, Stanley

A Periodic Table of the Elements - Stiller, Andrew (1988)

Permanenza; Für mikropolyphonisches, im Raum verteiltes Orchester - Fómina, Silvia (1994)

Permutaciones 7 - Cordero, Roque

Persistence - Horne, David (1995)

Un Pétale de Lumière - Chen, Qigang

Peter and the Wolf, op.67 - Prokofiev, Sergei (1936)

Peter Grimes: Four Sea Interludes, op.33a - Britten, Benjamin (1945)

Peter Grimes: Passacaglia, op.33b - Britten, Benjamin (1945)

Petit Concert, op.39 - Vuataz, Roger (1939)

Un petit peu d'exercice - Milhaud, Darius (1934)

Un "Petit Rien" - Zimmermann, Bernd Alois (1964)

Petite Pastorale, op.40a - Read, Gardner

Petite Suite, op.20 - Absil, Jean (1936)

Petite suite - Debussy, Claude

Petite Suite; D'après la musique écrite pour "Un torero hermosisimo" - Pittaluga, Gustavo (1934)

Petite Suite Bretonne - Kahn, Erich Itor (1936)

Petite Suite d'après Schumann - Markevitch, Igor (1933)

Petite Suite No.1 - Delius, Frederick (1889)

Petite Suite No.2 - Delius, Frederick (1890)

Pfeffer und Salz (Pepper and Salt) - Lampersberg, Gerhard (1981)

Phaedra; Cantata for Mezzo-Soprano and Small Orchestra, op.93 - Britten, Benjamin (1975)

Phaedra - Glass, Philip (1986)

Phantasiestück in C.'s Manier - Cerha, Friedrich (1989)

Philadelphia Symphony, op.28 - Einem, Gottfried von (1961)

Philopentatonia, op.32 - Yu, Julian (1994)

Phlegra - Xenakis, Iannis (1975)

Phoenix 1 - Müller-Siemens, Detlev (1993)

Phoenix 2 - Müller-Siemens, Detlev (1994)

Phoenix 3 - Müller-Siemens, Detlev (1995)

Phonophobie - Losonczy, Andor (1975)

Phryh - Heyn, Volker (1982)

Piano-piano - Barreau, Gisèle (1981)

Piccola Musica Notturna - Dallapiccola, Luigi (1954)

Piccola Sinfonia; Septett Nr.2 - Gürsching, Albrecht

Pictures and Tales; Suite for small orchestra, op.2 - Weigl, Karl

Pictures from Lake Arre - Nørgård, Per

Pièce brève; On the name of Albert Roussel - Poulenc, Francis

Piece for Mo - Bedford, David (1963)

Piece for Two Instrumental Units - Wolpe, Stefan

PIECE NOIRE - Platz, Robert H. P. (1989)

Pièce pour douze, op.99 - Aperghis, Georges (1991)

Le Piège de Méduse; Sept toutes petites danses - Satie, Erik (1913)

Pierrot lunaire, op.21; Three times seven poems from Albert Giraud's "Pierrot lunaire" - Schönberg, Arnold (1912)

Pierrot of the Minute; Comedy Overture - Bantock, Granville

Pilgrims - Rorem, Ned (1958)

Pinocchio; Ballet in 4 acts - Bjelinski, Bruno (1960)

Pioneer Dances - Coolidge, Peggy Stuart

The Plains - Rogers, Bernard

Les Plaintes de Chtchaza - Volkonsky, André (1962)

Planh; For chamber ensemble - Silverman, Stanley (1955)

Planos (Planes) - Revueltas, Silvestre

Play - Guy, Barry (1976)

Plöner Musiktag: Tafelmusik - Hindemith, Paul (1932)

La plus que lente - Debussy, Claude (1912)

Plymouth Town - Britten, Benjamin (1931)

Un poco giocoso; Concertante Scenes - Becker, Günther (1983)

Poem in October - Corigliano, John (1970)
Poème - Bachelet, Alfred
Poème slave - Arbeau, Pierre
Poemetti Pastorali - Davico, Vincenzo (1924)
The Poet Speaks; Suite from pieces by Robert Schumann - Vinter, Gilbert (1959)
Pogo - Koppel, Anders (1997)
"points on the curve to find..." - Berio, Luciano (1974)
Pol - Rihm, Wolfgang (1996)
Pol - Kolchis - Nucleus - Rihm, Wolfgang (1996)
Polichinelle - Arbeau, Pierre
A Polish Dance Theme - Scharwenka, Franz Xaver
Polka-Fughetta - Schlemm, Gustav Adolf
Polyphonic Tango - Schnittke, Alfred (1979)
Polyphonica; For 12 Instruments or Chamber Orchestra - Cowell, Henry (1930)
Polyphonien; For 2, 3 or 4 chamber orchestras - Haubenstock-Ramati, Roman (1993)
Ponteios No.1 - Guarnieri, Camargo (1955)
Ponteios No.3 - Guarnieri, Camargo (1955)
Ponteios No.5 - Guarnieri, Camargo (1955)
Pornography - Osborne, Nigel (1985)
Portrait - MacRae, Stuart (1999)
Portrait II - MacRae, Stuart (2000)
The Portrait of a Lady, op.14 - Taylor, Deems (1932)
Postcards - Sheng, Bright (1997)
Postlude; For harp and orchestra, op.18 - Firsova, Elena (1977)
Postvognen Ruller (The Mailcoach is Rolling), op.16 - Wellejus, Henning (1959)
Poudre d'or - Satie, Erik (1902)
Powers & Dominions, Concertino for Harp - Panufnik, Roxanna (2001)
PP, op.46 - Swayne, Giles (1987)
Praeludium - Stravinsky, Igor (1937)
Prairie Journal - Copland, Aaron (1937)
Prairie Songs - Goeb, Roger
Präludium - Järnefelt, Armas (1905)
Präludium und Toccata für Streichorchester - Bayoras, Feliksas (1966)
Präludium und Variationen - Staempfli, Edward (1945)

Präludium und Variationen (Prelude and Variations); For Nine Players - Ishii, Maki
Prazská Nokturna (Prague Nocturne), op.75 - Hanuš, Jan (1973)
Prelude, op.25 - Finzi, Gerald (1920s)
Prelude and Fugue - Brant, Henry (1935)
Prelude and Fugue, op.29 - Britten, Benjamin (1943)
Prelude and Fugue - Osborne, Nigel (1975)
Prelude and Fugue (With a Crab Canon) - Nørgård, Per (1982)
Prelude and Rondo, op.56 - Bentzon, Niels Viggo (1949)
Prelude for Guildhall School of Music: Worldes Blis Ne Last No Throwe - Lutosławski, Witold (1989)
Prelude to a Dolphin, op.166 - Holmboe, Vagn (1986)
Prelude to a Hymn Tune by William Billings - Luening, Otto (1943)
Prelude to a Living Stone, op.172 - Holmboe, Vagn (1989)
Prelude to a Maple Tree, op.168 - Holmboe, Vagn (1986)
Prelude to a Midsummer Night's Dream - Helfer, Walter
Prelude to a Pine Tree - Holmboe, Vagn (1986)
Prelude to a Willow Tree - Holmboe, Vagn (1987)
Prelude to the Calm Sea, op.187 - Holmboe, Vagn (1991)
Prelude to the Pollution of Nature - Holmboe, Vagn (1989)
Prelude to the Seagulls and Cormorants, op.174 - Holmboe, Vagn (1989)
Prelude to the Unsettled Weather, op.188 - Holmboe, Vagn (1991)
Prelude to the Victoria Embankment, op.184 - Holmboe, Vagn (1990)
Prelude, Fugue and Riffs; For solo clarinet and orchestra - Bernstein, Leonard (1949)
Prelude, Passacaglia and Fugue, op.4 - Jelinek, Hanns (1922)
Preludes - Szabelski, Bolesław (1963)
Preludes and Fugue - Lutosławski, Witold (1972)
Preludes I - V - Buck, Ole (1967)
Preludio and Allegro - Blomdahl, Karl-Birger (1948)
Preludio Classico - Szeryng, Henryk
Preludio Classico - Szeryng, Henryk
Preludio I - LeFanu, Nicola (1967)
Preludio II - LeFanu, Nicola (1976)

Prelúdio No.3 - Santórsola, Guido (1936)
Prélude pour Aglavaine et Sélysette, D'après la pièce de Maeterlinck, H.10 - Honegger, Arthur (1917)
Present Music - Kitzke, Jerome (1982)
Prière - Honegger, Arthur (1925)
Primavera - Bales, Richard
Prinz Chocolat; Musical fairytale in 5 episodes, op.66 - Einem, Gottfried von (1983)
Prinzessin Turandot, op.1; Ballet in two scenes to a scenario by Luigi Malipiero - Einem, Gottfried von (1943)
Prisma Sinfonico (Symphonic Prism) - Csonka, Paul
Pro - Kontra - Giefer, Willy (1970)
Pro Et Contra, Concerto for Cello - Pärt, Arvo (1966)
Problems and Solutions - Braun, Peter Michael (1974)
Procession II - Brødsgaard, Anders (1986)
Processionals, op.2 - Knussen, Oliver (1978)
Processions and Dances - Saxton, Robert (1981)
Profit tout Clair - Linke, Norbert (1967)
Projection - Yuasa, Joji (2008)
Projection for Seven Players - Yuasa, Joji (1955)
Prologue - Birtwistle, Sir Harrison (1971)
Prologue and Variations - Zwilich, Ellen Taaffe
Protée, op.17 - Milhaud, Darius (1919)
Prozess - Bose, Hans-Jürgen von (1988)
Prunella - Dale, Benjamin (1923)
Psalm for Strings - Hartley, Walter Sinclair
Psalom - Pärt, Arvo (1995)
Puck's Minuet, op.20, No.1 - Howells, Herbert
Pulcinella: Suite - Stravinsky, Igor (1920)
Pupazzi, op.36 - Schmitt, Florent (1907)
Pupitre 14, op.339 - Bentzon, Niels Viggo (1974)
Pursuit; Ballet - Matthews, Colin (1987)

Q

A Quaker Reader; Suite - Rorem, Ned (1976)
Quanta - Braun, Peter Michael (1958)
Quartets I-VIII; For an Orchestra of 24 Instruments - Cage, John
Quasi una Sinfonietta - Szymanski, Pawel (1990)
Quasi una Sonata - Schnittke, Alfred (1987)
Quasi Una Tânpûrâ - Haas, Georg Friedrich (1991)
Quatre antiennes à la Sainte Vierge, op.7 - Ballif, Claude (1952)
Quatre Chansons Françaises - Britten, Benjamin (1928)
Quatre Instants - Saariaho, Kaija (2002)
Quatre pièces brèves - Moeschinger, Albert (1953)
Quatre poèmes de Ronsard, op.100 - Schmitt, Florent (1941)
Quellen - Cerha, Friedrich (1992)
Queue Leu Leu; File de Danses - Dubois, Pierre-Max
Quiet City - Copland, Aaron (1940)
Quodlibet: Suite aus "Zaubernacht." Eine Unterhaltungsmusik, op.9 - Weill, Kurt (1922)

R

Raftsman's Dance - Filippi, Amedeo De (1939)
Ragtime - Stravinsky, Igor (1918)
The Rainbow - Ives, Charles Edward
Rain Coming - Takemitsu, Tōru (1982)
Rain, A Window, Roofs, Chimneys, Pigeons And So - Smolka, Martin (1991)
Rainforest I - McCabe, John (1984)
Raising the Gaze - Lieberson, Peter (1988)
Rakastava, op.14 - Sibelius, Jean (1911)
Ranas - Revueltas, Silvestre
Reactions to "Prose Rhythms" of Fiona Macleod - Hill, Mabel Wood (1933)
Recall - Nørgård, Per (1968)
Re-Call - Berio, Luciano (1995)

Recit and Aria - Hesketh, Kenneth (1994)
Red Leaves - McCabe, John (1991)
The Red Violin: Suite for Violin and Orchestra - Corigliano, John (1999)
Reflections on a 16th-Century Tune - Bennett, Richard Rodney (1999)
Reflections on a Theme of William Walton; For 11 solo strings - Bennett, Richard Rodney (1985)
Reflets d'Allemagne: Heidelberg, op.28 - Schmitt, Florent (1905)
Reflets d'Allemagne: Suite for orchestra, op.28 - Schmitt, Florent (1905)
Réflexions - Carter, Elliott (2004)
Refrains, op.13 - Füssl, Karl Heinz (1972)
Refrains - Vries, Klaas de
Refuge - Müller-Siemens, Detlev (1998)
Regain: Suite d'orchestre tirée de la musique du film de Jean Giono et Marcel Pagnol, H.117A - Honegger, Arthur (1937)
Regiser Festmusik - Geissler, Fritz
Reineke Fuchs, Overture, op.23 - Bleyle, Karl
Relâche; Ballet - Satie, Erik (1924)
Remarkable Dances - Keuning, Hans P. (1974)
Remembering Ansel Adams - Bacon, Ernst
Remembering Gatsby; Foxtrot for Orchestra - Harbison, John (1985)
Remembering Lennon - Martland, Steve (1985)
Remembering Lennox through Michael - Tavener, John (2004)
Reminiszenzen - Brandmüller, Theo (1976)
El Renacuajo Paseador - Revueltas, Silvestre
Rencontres dans un désert - Kisielewski, Stefan (1969)
Requiem; Songs for Sue, op.33 - Knussen, Oliver (2006)
Requiem - Matsudaira, Yoritsune (1992)
Requiem - Schickele, Peter (1968)
A Requiem in Summer; In Memory of my Father - Brant, Henry
Requies - Berio, Luciano (1984)
Résonance - Höller, York (1981)
Résonances; 12 Poems - Voss, Friedrich (1957)
Le Reste du temps - Aperghis, Georges (2003)

Retablo de Navidad - Rodrigo, Joaquín (1952)
Retrats catalans - Brouwer, Léo (1983)
Rêverie pour petit orchestre - Huë, Georges Adolphe
A Revolutionary Garland - Kingman, Daniel
Der Revolutionsplatz - Müller-Wieland, Jan (1989)
Rhapsodia piemontese, op.26 - Sinigaglia, Leone
Rhapsodic Fantasy - Colgrass, Michael (1964)
Rhapsodie - Grandjany, Marcel
Rhapsodie sur des thèmes populaires - Gaubert, Philippe (1925)
Rhapsody - Nørgård, Per (1952)
Rhapsody, op.3 - Rózsa, Miklós (1929)
Rhapsody, op.25 - Zbinden, Julien-François
Rhapsody for Harp - Coolidge, Peggy Stuart
Rhapsody No.1 - Bartók, Béla (1928)
Rhapsody No.2 - Bartók, Béla (1928)
Rhapsody-Concerto; Concerto for Viola and Orchestra - Martinů, Bohuslav (1952)
Ricercar and Doubles on "To many a well" - Maxwell Davies, Peter (1959)
Ricercare; Musik in memoriam Luigi Nono (2.Versuch) - Rihm, Wolfgang (1990)
Ricercare I - Beyer, Frank Michael (1957)
Ricercari - Malipiero, Gian Francesco (1925)
Ricercata, op.21 - Spinner, Leopold (1965)
Ricordanza - Stern, Robert (1955)
Rigaudon, op.93, No.2 - Saint-Saëns, Camille (1892)
Right of Way - Diehl, Paula (1994)
The Ring of Eternity - Saxton, Robert (1983)
Rissolty-Rossolty - Crawford, Ruth
Ritmos de Cadiz - Santander, Manuel (1963)
Ritorno Degli Snovidenia (The return of the dreams) - Berio, Luciano (1977)
Ritournelles - Aperghis, Georges (1992)
Ritrovari - Malipiero, Gian Francesco (1926)
Rivalries - Asia, Daniel
The River of Life, op.66 - Smirnov, Dmitri (1992)

Rodeo - Copland, Aaron (1942)
Romance, op.28 - Fauré, Gabriel
Romance, op.11 - Finzi, Gerald (1928)
Romance - Zwilich, Ellen Taaffe
Romance in C major, op.42 - Sibelius,
  Jean (1903)
Romance in D major, op.100 -
  Sinding, Christian
Romance in Early Spring - Fenney,
  William
Romantic Concerto - Sobanski, Hans
  Joachim
Romantische Phantasie, op.37 -
  Hauer, Josef Matthias (1925)
Romanze, op.2, No.1 - Nielsen, Carl
  (1889)
Romanza e Scherzoso in F minor;
  Concertino Part II, op.54 (Busoni
  Verz. 290) - Busoni, Ferruccio
Romanze, Werk 25 - Schollum, Robert
  (1942)
Romanze in Es Dur, op.61 - Strauss,
  Richard (1879)
A Rome Dairy - Kennan, Kent
Romualdo's Song from "The Black
  Maskers" - Sessions, Roger
Rondo - Blacher, Boris (1938)
Rondo - Poot, Marcel (1928)
Rondo - Watkins, Huw (2005)
Rondo capriccioso, op.21 - Gutchë,
  Gene
Rondo concertante (Busoni Verz. B87)
  - Busoni, Ferruccio
Rondo Giocoso - Riege, Ernst (1934)
Rondo vom goldenen Kalb; Three
  Nocturnes to scenes by Tatjana
  Gsovsky, op.13 - Einem, Gottfried
  von (1950)
Ronsard à son âme - Ravel, Maurice
  (1935)
Rosaliana - Rodrigo, Joaquín (1965)
La Rose des Vents; Ballet, op.367 -
  Milhaud, Darius (1957)
Rose Selavy - Huber, Nicolaus A.
  (2000)
Rosemary - Bridge, Frank (1906)
Das Rosenband, op.31/1 - Strauss,
  Richard (1897)
Rossi - Komorous, Rudolf (1975)
Rossini on Ilkla Moor; Overture -
  Fenby, Eric (1946)
La Roue: Overture pour le film d'Abel
  Gance, H.44 - Honegger, Arthur
  (1922)
Rounds for String Orchestra -
  Diamond, David (1944)
Royal Invitation (Homage to the
  Queen of Tonga) - Argento,
  Dominick (1964)

RPM - Hindson, Matthew (1997)
Rumanian Folk Dances - Bartók, Béla
  (1915)
Rumanian Folk Dances - Bartók, Béla
  (1915)
Runaway Horses: From "Mishima" -
  Glass, Philip (1985)
Running, Thinking, Finding - Wilson,
  Ian (1989)
Russian Scenes - Bantock, Granville
  (1902)
Rusty Air in Carolina - Bates, Mason
  (2006)

S

"S" - Schaathun, Asbjørn (1992)
Sable; In Memoriam Edmond Jabès -
  Dazzi, Gualtiero (1991)
The Sacrifice: Three Interludes -
  MacMillan, James (2006)
Saint Vartan Symphony - Hovhaness,
  Alan
Salut d'Amour, op.12 - Elgar, Edward
  (1889)
Salvation Creek with Eagle -
  Lumsdaine, David (1974)
Sam - McCabe, John (1973)
Samuel Beckett; Words & Music -
  Feldman, Morton (1987)
San Zeno / Verona - Boone, Charles
  (1976)
Sancta Maria - Mercurio, Steven
  (1998)
Sapphic Poem - Bantock, Granville
  (1908)
Saraband for the Golden Goose -
  Clarke, Henry (1957)
Sarabande from "The Daughter of
  Colchis" - Chávez, Carlos
Sarabande Triste, op.58 - Jongen,
  Joseph (1925)
Saturday Night at the Firehouse -
  Cowell, Henry (1948)
Saudades de Macau - Lam, Bun-
  Ching (1989)
Scaramouche: Tragic Pantomime,
  op.71 - Sibelius, Jean (1913)
Scene - Bose, Hans-Jürgen von
  (1991)
Scene und Arie, op.54 - Klebe,
  Giselher (1968)
Scenes de Ballet - Stravinsky, Igor
  (1944)
Scenes Historique I, op.25 - Sibelius,
  Jean (1911)

Scenes Historiques, op.66 - Sibelius,
  Jean (1912)
Scherzino - Cerha, Friedrich (2000)
Scherzo - Leschetitzky, Theodor
Scherzo - Riegger, Wallingford
Scherzo - Schreker, Franz (1900)
Scherzo and Two Dances - Blake,
  David (1981)
Scherzo Fantastique - Girnatis, Walter
  (1956)
Scherzo No.2 for Orchestra - Gyring,
  Elizabeth (1948)
Schicksalslieder von Hölderlin, op.28 -
  Rovsing Olsen, Poul (1953)
Der Schneemann: Overture -
  Korngold, Erich Wolfgang (1910)
Schneewittchensuite, op.50 - Bleyle,
  Karl
Schrumpf-Symphonie, op.80 -
  Schwertsik, Kurt (1999)
Der Schwanendreher; Concerto for
  Viola and Chamber Orchestra after
  old Folksongs - Hindemith, Paul
  (1936)
Schwankende Zeit - Mundry, Isabel
  (2008)
Schwebende Form - Birkenkötter, Jörg
  (1999)
Schwedische Tanz-Rhapsodie - Koch,
  Erland von (1957)
Scintillation - Nørgård, Per (1993)
A Sea Change - Payne, Anthony
  (1988)
Seascapes - Daybreak - Hosokawa,
  Toshio (1998)
Seasonal Variants - Blake, David
  (1985)
The Seasons; Ballet in One Act -
  Cage, John
The Seasons - Musgrave, Thea
  (1988)
A Seattle Overture - Bolcom, William
  (2005)
Sechs Gesänge, op.13 - Zemlinsky,
  Alexander (1913)
Sechs Orchesterlieder, op.8 -
  Schönberg, Arnold (1904)
Sechs Schwedische Bauernmelodien;
  Aus Dalekarlien - Koch, Erland von
  (1971)
Sechs Stücke, op.6 - Webern, Anton
  (1909)
Second Idyll, op.54 - Holloway, Robin
  (1983)
Second Landscape - Boone, Charles
  (1973)
Second Symphonic Essay; For ten
  instruments - Treibmann, Karl
  Ottomar

The Secret Agent: Three Pieces - Glass, Philip (1996)

Secret Theatre - Birtwistle, Sir Harrison (1984)

Sederunt Principes - Weir, Judith (1987)

Der See; Concerto for Harp - Matthus, Siegfried (1989)

Session I - Bolcom, William

Segmente, op.12 - Rihm, Wolfgang

Sehnsucht, op.8/3 - Schönberg, Arnold (1904)

Seis Fabulas (Six Fables) - Ficher, Jacobo

Self Portrait - Clarke, James (1991)

Selige Nacht: From "Lieder und Gesänge" (3.Folge Nr.9) - Marx, Joseph (1914)

Semiramis; Music in three parts - Hamel, Peter Michael (1983)

Sempre Diritto! (Straight Ahead) - Moravec, Paul (1991)

Sensemayá (for chamber ensemble) - Revueltas, Silvestre (1937)

Sentieri musicali; Auf Mozarts Spuren. Sinfonietta - Baur, Jürg (1990)

Sentimento del tempo - Baur, Jürg (1980)

Sept Chansons populaires espagnoles - Falla, Manuel de (1915)

Sept Haïkaï; Esquisses japonaises for Piano Solo, Xylophone and Marimba - Messiaen, Olivier

Septet - Lord, David (1967)

Septet - Primosch, James (1985)

Septet in Two Movements - Schubert, Manfred (1967)

Septett "Geschichte Vom…" - Ostendorf, Jens-Peter (1990)

Séquences - Haubenstock-Ramati, Roman (1958)

Séquences 2 - Haubenstock-Ramati, Roman (1958)

Serale - Banfield, Raffaello de (1968)

Serenade - Antheil, George (1948)

Serenade, op.1 - Barber, Samuel (1928)

Serenade; After Plato's "Symposium" - Bernstein, Leonard (1954)

Serenade - Bjelinski, Bruno (1957)

Serenade, op.77 - Burkhard, Willy (1945)

Serenade - Ferguson, Howard (1933)

Serenade - Helm, Everett (1957)

Serenade, op.40 - Juon, Paul (1909)

Serenade, op.29 - Matthews, David (1982)

Serenade - Maw, Nicholas (1973)

Serenade, op.36 - Novák, Vítêzslav (1905)

Serenade - Ohse, Reinhard

Serenade, op.7 - Pierné, Gabriel (1883)

Serenade - Riege, Ernst (1963)

Serenade - Schauss, Ernst

Serenade - Schlemm, Gustav Adolf

Serenade, op.1 - Schoeck, Othmar (1907)

Serenade, Werk 39a - Schollum, Robert (1952)

Serenade - Sheinkman, Mordechai (1957)

Serenade, op.10 - Thomas, Kurt

Serenade, op.7 - Westerman, Gerhart von (1937)

Serenade - Wirth, Carl Anton (1962)

Sérénade - Absil, Jean (1965)

Sérénade - Aubert, Louis (1906)

Sérénade - Boutry, Roger

Sérénade - Français, Jean (1934)

Sérénade, op.33 - Halvorsen, Johan (1913)

Sérénade, op.16: Valse - Indy, Vincent d'

Sérénade; Pour orchestre de chambre - Martinů, Bohuslav (1931)

Sérénade, op.62 - Milhaud, Darius (1921)

Serenade ("Orfeo") from "Audubon" - Gould, Morton (1970)

Serenade (Interlude) - Schoeck, Othmar (1917)

Sérénade à Angélique, H.182 - Honegger, Arthur (1945)

Serenade a Lydia de Cadaques - Montsalvatge, Xavier (1972)

Serenade for 11 Solo Instruments, op.14 - Sekles, Bernhard (1913)

Serenade for Chamber Orchestra - Braun, Yehezkel

Serenade for Orchestra - Jenner, Gustav (1911/12)

Serenade for Seven Instruments - Wyner, Yehudi (1958)

Serenade for Small Orchestra - Arnold, Malcolm (1950)

Serenade for Small Orchestra - Bennett, Richard Rodney (1977)

Serenade for Small Orchestra - Donato, Anthony (1961)

Serenade for Small Orchestra, op.69 - Jirák, K. B. (1954)

Serenade for Small Orchestra in F minor, op.3 - Weiner, Leo (1906)

Serenade for Small Orchestra No.2, op.11 - Glazunov, Alexander (1888)

Serenade for Strings - Berkeley, Lennox (1939)

Serenade for Strings in E-flat - Wolf-Ferrari, Ermanno (1896)

Serenade for Violin and Orchestra - Pasatieri, Thomas (1994)

Serenade II - Antheil, George (1949)

Serenade II - Braun, Yehezkel

Serenade in D major - Strohbach, Siegfried

Serenade in E minor, op.20 - Elgar, Edward (1892)

Serenade in F, op.29a - Reizenstein, Franz (1951)

Serenade in F major, op.24 - Klengel, Julius

Serenade in G, op.64a - Holloway, Robin (1986)

Serenade Lyrique - Elgar, Edward (1899)

Sérénade mélancolique - Aubert, Louis (1923)

Sérénade pour Montreux - Sutermeister, Heinrich (1970)

Sérénade pour orchestre - Huë, Georges Adolphe

Serenata, op.46b - Casella, Alfredo (1930)

Serenata - Sierra, Roberto (2005)

Serenata madrilena - Pompey, Angel Martin (1949)

Serenata No.1 - Martinů, Bohuslav (1932)

Serenata No.1 in D major, op.69a - Sibelius, Jean (1913)

Serenata No.2 in G minor, op.69b - Sibelius, Jean (1913)

Serenata No.3 - Martinů, Bohuslav (1932)

Serenità notturna - Erdmann, Dietrich (1984)

Sérieux s'abstenir - Dubois, Pierre-Max

Serious Song; A Lament for String Orchestra - Fine, Irving (1955)

Serranilla - Rodrigo, Joaquín (1928)

Session IV - Bolcom, William

Sette Canzonette Veneziane - Malipiero, Gian Francesco (1961)

Seven Pastorales - Harrison, Lou

Seven Popular Spanish Songs - Falla, Manuel de

Seven Scenes from Everyday Cow Life - Koppel, Anders (1998)

Seven Words; For cello, bayan and strings in 7 movements - Gubaidulina, Sofia (1982)

A Severn Rhapsody, op.3 - Finzi, Gerald (1923)

Shadow (...of a doubt) - Obst, Michael (1997)

Shadow Figures - Marthinsen, Niels (1992)

Shadow Wood; Six Poems of Tennessee Williams - Benson, Warren (1992)

Shadowland - Sørensen, Bent

Shadows; Scenes for Orchestra - Engelmann, Hans Ulrich (1964)

Shaker Loops - Adams, John (1978)

Shakespearean Concerto - Amram, David

Shaking Hands - Nørgård, Per (2000)

She Never Lost A Passenger Overture - Kander, Susan (1996)

Shepherd's Dream - McCabe, John (2002)

Shepherd's Hey; British Folk Music Settings, No.3 - Grainger, Percy Aldridge (1908)

Shepherd's Pipes of Vologda - Shchedrin, Rodion (1995)

Shin'anim Sha'ananim - Amy, Gilbert (1979)

Shining Forth; Concerto for Cello - Wilson, Ian (1998)

Short Stories; Five Interludes for String Orchestra - Dean, Brett (2005)

Short Symphony - Swanson, Howard (1948)

Show An Affirming Flame; A Poem for Orchestra ("September 1, 1939" by W. H. Auden) - Adler, Samuel (2001)

Si j'etais Domenico...; Phantasmagorie für Streicher mit konzertierendem Cembalo - Brandmüller, Theo (1984)

Siciliana e Giga (stile antico) per Orchestra, op.73 - Bossi, Marco Enrico

Sicilienne - Koch, Erland von (1942)

Sicut Cervus Desiderat ad Fontes Aquarum, op.7 - Rihm, Wolfgang (1970)

Sieben Feld-, Wald- und Wiesenstücke - Stranz, Ulrich (1983)

Sieben Stücke (Seven Pieces) - Ishii, Maki

Siesta - Walton, William (1929)

Sign Sounds - Brown, Earle (1972)

Sigol for Strings - Fennelly, Brian (2007)

Der Silbersee: Suite aus dem Wintermärchen - Weill, Kurt (1933)

Silbury Air - Birtwistle, Sir Harrison (1977)

Silence - Aubert, Louis (1908)

Le Silence; Tystnaden - Mundry, Isabel (1993)

Silence and Eruptions, op.91 - Bergman, Erik (1979)

Silk Road; Concerto for Percussion and Chamber Orchestra - Ali-Zadeh, Franghiz (1999)

Silouans Song; "My soul yearns after the Lord..." - Pärt, Arvo (1991)

Simfonietta - Bacewicz, Grażyna (1935)

Simfonietta - Krek, Uroš (1951)

Simple Symphony, op.4 - Britten, Benjamin (1934)

sin normas ajenas - León, Tania

Sinfonia - Angerer, Paul (1945)

Sinfonia, op.402 - Bentzon, Niels Viggo (1977)

Sinfonia - Franco, Johan (1932)

Sinfonia, op.42 - Goehr, Alexander (1979)

Sinfonia - Maw, Nicholas (1966)

Sinfonia - Maxwell Davies, Peter (1962)

Sinfonia, op.18 - Wittinger, Róbert (1964)

Sinfonía - Chávez, Carlos (1915)

Sinfonia 1, op.73 - Holmboe, Vagn

Sinfonia 2, op.73 - Holmboe, Vagn

Sinfonia 2 - Killmayer, Wilhelm (1969)

Sinfonia 3, op.73 - Holmboe, Vagn

Sinfonia 4, op.73 - Holmboe, Vagn

Sinfonia breve, Wk47 - David, Johann Nepomuk (1955)

Sinfonia Buffo, op.35 - Bentzon, Jørgen (1939)

Sinfonia Concertante - Hamilton, Iain

Sinfonia Concertante, op.125 - Prokofiev, Sergei (1952)

Sinfonia da Camera, op.139 - Bentzon, Niels Viggo (1962)

Sinfonia da Camera - Einfeldt, Dieter

Sinfonia da Camera - Engelmann, Hans Ulrich (1981)

Sinfonia da Camera - Genzmer, Harald

Sinfonia da Camera - Salviucci, Giovanni (1936)

Sinfonia da Camera in B-flat, op.8 - Wolf-Ferrari, Ermanno (1901)

Sinfonia da Chiesa, op.76 - Raasted, N. O. (1947)

Sinfonia da Chiesa No.1 - Rosenberg, Hilding Constantin (1923)

Sinfonia da Chiesa No.2 - Rosenberg, Hilding Constantin (1924)

Sinfonía de Antígona (Symphony No.1) - Chávez, Carlos (1933)

Sinfonia for 13 Players, op.78 - Huggler, John (1974)

Sinfonia for Chamber Orchestra - Gilbert, Anthony (1965)

Sinfonía India (Symphony No.2) - Chávez, Carlos (1935)

Sinfonia Mistica; Symphony No.6 - Panufnik, Andrzej (1977)

Sinfonía No.5 - Chávez, Carlos (1953)

Sinfonia No.7 - Hartley, Walter Sinclair

Sinfonia per archi - Bäck, Sven-Erik (1951)

Sinfonia per archi, Wk54 - David, Johann Nepomuk (1959)

Sinfonia per archi - Krek, Uroš (1973)

Sinfonia Piccola - Bialas, Günter (1960)

Sinfonia Piccola - Tansman, Alexandre (1952)

Sinfonia preclassica super nomen H-A-S-E, Wk44 - David, Johann Nepomuk (1953)

Sinfonie - Cerha, Friedrich (1975)

Sinfonietta, op.32 - Abendroth, Walter (1959)

Sinfonietta - Arutiunian, Alexander (1966)

Sinfonietta - Bennett, Richard Rodney (1984)

Sinfonietta, op.41 - Bentzon, Jørgen (1941)

Sinfonietta, op.34 - Berkeley, Lennox (1950)

Sinfonietta, op.1 - Britten, Benjamin (1932)

Sinfonietta - Brown, James Francis (2002)

Sinfonietta, op.23 - Bruns, Victor

Sinfonietta - Cowell, Henry (1928)

Sinfonietta - Halffter, Ernesto (1927)

Sinfonietta - Herrmann, Peter

Sinfonietta, op.38 - Joubert, John (1962)

Sinfonietta, op.10 - Larsson, Lars-Erik (1932)

Sinfonietta - MacMillan, James (1991)

Sinfonietta - Muldowney, Dominic (1986)

Sinfonietta, op.32 - Myaskovsky, Nikolai Yakovlevich (1929)

Sinfonietta - Pade, Steen (1998)

Sinfonietta - Piston, Walter (1941)

Sinfonietta - Poulenc, Francis (1947)

Sinfonietta, op.48 - Prokofiev, Sergei (1909)

Sinfonietta - Quinet, Marcel (1953)

Sinfonietta - Search, Frederick

Sinfonietta - Tansman, Alexandre (1924)

Sinfonietta - Wagenaar, Bernard (1930)

Sinfonietta - Watkins, Michael Blake (1982)

Sinfonietta, op.83 - Weingartner, Felix (1935)

Sinfonietta, op.23 - Zemlinsky, Alexander (1934)

Sinfonietta Accademica - Maxwell Davies, Peter (1983)

Sinfonietta Armoniosa - Trojan, Václav (1970)

Sinfonietta Buffa - Meester, Louis de (1949)

Sinfonietta da Camera - Borkovec, Pavel (1947)

Sinfonietta for Chamber Orchestra, op.47 - Lobanov, Vasily (1986)

Sinfonietta for Light Orchestra - Horovitz, Joseph (1971)

Sinfonietta for String Orchestra - Alwyn, William (1970)

Sinfonietta for Strings - Alonso-Crespo, Eduardo (1996)

Sinfonietta for Strings - Laks, Simon (1936)

Sinfonietta in Bb major, op.16 - Kajanus, Robert

Sinfonietta in D Major - Mitsukuri, Shukichi (1934)

Sinfonietta in F - Cohn, James (1955)

Sinfonietta la Jolla, H.328 - Martinů, Bohuslav (1950)

Sinfonietta mit Banjo; 1. Rundfunkmusik, op.37 - Butting, Max (1929)

Sinfonietta No.1, op.48 - Arnold, Malcolm (1954)

Sinfonietta No.1 - Maros, Rudolf

Sinfonietta No.1 - Villa-Lobos, Heitor

Sinfonietta No.1 for Small Orchestra - Jacob, Gordon

Sinfonietta No.2, op.65 - Arnold, Malcolm (1958)

Sinfonietta No.2 - Villa-Lobos, Heitor

Sinfonietta No.3 - Arnold, Malcolm (1964)

Sinfonietta per archi - Röttger, Heinz (1968)

Sinfonietta per Piccola Orchestra - Rieti, Vittorio (1934)

Sinfonische Meditationen - Röttger, Heinz

Sing- und Spielmusik für Liebhaber und Freunde: Ein Jäger aus Kurpfalz, der reitet durch den grünen Wald, op.45, No.3 - Hindemith, Paul (1928)

Singing the Dreams - Hvidtfelt Nielsen, Svend (1991)

Sio - Kancheli, Giya (1998)

Sirenengesang - Sørensen, Bent (1994)

Six Bagatelles - Huber, Nicolaus A. (1981)

Six Children's Songs - Blech, Leo

Six Children's Songs - Lutosławski, Witold (1947)

Six Little Piano Pieces, op.19 - Schönberg, Arnold (1911)

Six Poèmes d'Apollinaire, H.12, No.1: À la Santé - Honegger, Arthur (1916)

Six Poèmes d'Apollinaire, H.12, No.3: Automne - Honegger, Arthur (1915)

Six Poèmes d'Apollinaire, H.12, No.4: Saltimbanques - Honegger, Arthur (1917)

Six Poèmes d'Apollinaire, H.12, No.5: L'Adieu - Honegger, Arthur (1917)

Six Poèmes d'Apollinaire, H.12, No.6: Les Cloches - Honegger, Arthur (1917)

Six Tempi for 10 Instruments - Lutyens, Elisabeth (1957)

Sixteen Dances - Cage, John

Sixty-Odd Pages - Szymanski, Pawel (1987)

Skandinavische Tänze - Koch, Erland von

Skolen på Hovedet - Christensen, Bernhard (1933)

The Skull; Cantata for Tenor and Orchestra - Burt, Francis (1955)

Slides; For 11 Soloists - Lutosławski, Witold (1988)

Slobberin' Goblins - Grantham, Donald

Slow Movement - Armstrong, Craig (1994)

Slowakische Volkslieder, op.15 - Moyzes, Alexander (1933)

Slow-Mobile - Krebs, Joachim

Small Concerto for Orchestra - Matthus, Siegfried (1963)

Small Suite - Trexler, Georg (1954)

Small Symphony, op.58 - Krenek, Ernst (1928)

Smiling Immortal - Harvey, Jonathan (1977)

Snap! - Daugherty, Michael (1987)

Snip Snap - Nørgård, Per (2006)

Socrate; Drame symphonique en 3 parties - Satie, Erik (1918)

Soirées musicales, op.9; Suite of Five Movements from Rossini - Britten, Benjamin (1936)

Soirs, op.5 - Schmitt, Florent (1896)

Solar - Saariaho, Kaija (1993)

Soldatenspiel, op.16 - Weiner, Leo (1924)

Soleil Noir / Chitra - Harvey, Jonathan (1995)

Soleriana; Suite for chamber orchestra - Rodrigo, Joaquín (1953)

Solitudo - Smolka, Martin (2003)

Solo / Ensemble - Muldowney, Dominic (1974)

Solo for a Percussionist with Small Orchestra - Schenker, Friedrich (1997)

Solstice - Harrison, Lou

Solve et Coagula - Wallin, Rolf (1992)

El Sombrero de Tres Picos (The Three Cornered Hat): Scenes and Dances from Part 1 - Falla, Manuel de (1919)

El Sombrero des Tres Picos: Suite No.1 - Falla, Manuel de (1919)

Le sommeil de colombes - Aubert, Louis

Sommerkanon IV - Holliger, Heinz (1978)

Sommerlied: From "Lieder und Gesänge" (1.Folge Nr.22) - Marx, Joseph (1909)

Sonante - Chávez, Carlos (1974)

Sonata, op.34 - Hamilton, Iain (1957)

Sonata alla Marchia - Blake, David (1978)

Sonata by G. Gabrieli - Matthus, Siegfried (1988)

Sonata concertante 1 - Grosskopf, Erhard (1966)

Sonata concertante 2 - Grosskopf, Erhard (1967)

Sonata da Camera; In Memoriam Matyas Seiber - Banks, Don (1961)

Sonata da camera for Violoncello and Chamber Orchestra - Martinů, Bohuslav (1940)

Sonata da Camera, op.42 - Schlee, Thomas Daniel

Sonata for 10 Instruments - Hindemith, Paul (1917)

Sonata for 12 Instruments, op.257 - Bentzon, Niels Viggo (1970)

Sonata for Cello and Eight Instruments - Watkins, Huw (1998)

Sonata for Chamber Orchestra, op.18 - Arnell, Richard

Sonata for Chamber Orchestra - Herrmann, Peter

Sonata for String Orchestra - Schurmann, Gerard (2004)

Sonata for Strings and Two Horns - Maw, Nicholas (1967)

Sonata for Violin and Chamber Orchestra - Schnittke, Alfred (1968)

Sonata pian' e forte; For Soprano, Mezzo and 12 Instrumentalists - Amy, Gilbert (1974)

Sonate - Schollum, Robert (1952)

Sonatina - Garcia Leoz, Jesus (1945)

Sonatina: From "Let's Make a Symphony" - Sierra, Roberto (1997)

Sonatina - Thiele, Siegfried (1974)

Sonatina for Chamber Orchestra - Benjamin, Arthur (1940)

Sonatina for Orchestra, op.34 - Kurz, Siegfried

Sonatina for String Orchestra - Herrmann, Peter

Sonatine; For small orchestra and obbligato piano - Dessau, Paul (1975)

Song and Dance - Hindson, Matthew (2006)

A Song Before Sunrise - Delius, Frederick (1918)

Song of Loneliness - Cassuto, Alvaro (1972)

Song of Mourning; A reflection upon the slain Dutch patriots - Wagenaar, Bernard (1944)

A Song of Orpheus; Fantasy for Cello - Schuman, William

A Song of Yesteryear: Sarabande - De Brant, Cyr

Songerie Pour Orchestre de Chambre - Zimmermann, Udo (1982)

Les Songes; Ballet, op.124 - Milhaud, Darius (1933)

Songs and Seascapes - Payne, Anthony (1984)

Songs by Myself - Birtwistle, Sir Harrison (1984)

Songs from Shakespeare - Schickele, Peter

Songs from the Page of Swords - Asia, Daniel

Songs of Joy and Rhythm, op.7 - Górecki, Henryk Mikołaj (1956)

Songs of King Solomon - Maayani, Ami (1962)

Songs of Love and Farewell - Runswick, Daryl (1987)

Songs of the Sea, op.91 - Stanford, Charles Villiers (1904)

Sonne der Gerechtigkeit; Choralkonzert für Blechbläser und Streicher - Zipp, Friedrich

Die Sonne der Inkas; Cantata - Denisov, Edison (1964)

Sonnenuntergänge auf B 612 (Sunsets on B 612) - Komarova, Tatjana (1998)

Sonnets to Orpheus; Book 1 - Danielpour, Richard (1992)

Sonnets to Orpheus; Book 2 - Danielpour, Richard (1994)

Sons de Cloches - Ropartz, Joseph Guy Marie

Sospiri, op.70 - Elgar, Edward (1914)

Sotto Voce 2; Capriccio - Rihm, Wolfgang (2007)

Sound Fields - Carter, Elliott (2007)

Sounds for His Animation; Concerto for Synthesizer and Chamber Orchestra - Bates, Mason (1998)

Soupir, op.109, No.3 - Büsser, Henri

Sous-marine; Ballet, H.58 - Honegger, Arthur (1925)

Souvenirs - Danielpour, Richard (2008)

Space Play - Musgrave, Thea (1974)

Sparkle; Octet - Chen, Yi

Sparks and Flame (Ash) - Beck, Jeremy (1997)

Sparrows - Schwantner, Joseph (1962)

Speed - Hindson, Matthew (1997)

Sphäre um Sphäre - Rihm, Wolfgang (2003)

Spijze, spij (Sleep, sleep) - Lutosławski, Witold (1954)

Spiral - Aitken, Robert

Spirales Insolites - Bousch, François (1982)

Spoon River: Prelude and Elegy, op.26, No.3&4 - Hewitt, Harry (1959)

Sports et Divertissements - Satie, Erik (1914)

Spring Concertino - Bolcom, William (1987)

Spring Fever - Imbrie, Andrew (1996)

Spring Yearning - Lam, Bun-Ching (1976)

Spring's Shining Wake - Payne, Anthony (1982)

Spud - Lang, David (1986)

St. Paul's Suite, op.29, No.2 - Holst, Gustav (1913)

Stabiles for 13 Instruments - Hibbard, William (1969)

Ständchen, op.16 - Erdmann, Eduard (1930)

Ständchen sur le nom de Heinrich Strobel: 3rd part of "Petite musique de nuit" - Haubenstock-Ramati, Roman (1958)

Stanford Serenade, op.430 - Milhaud, Darius (1969)

Stanzas - Powell, Mel (1965)

Stealing a March - Woolrich, John (2000)

Steinbeis-Serenade; Variations, op.61 - Einem, Gottfried von (1981)

Stepping Stones; Ballet - Tower, Joan (1993)

Still, Glowing - Weir, Judith (2008)

Still Lands - Goehr, Alexander (1990)

Still-Leben - Kopelent, Marek (1968)

Eine Stimme 1-3 - Rihm, Wolfgang (2005)

Stone Garden - Osborne, Nigel (1988)

The Stones and Lonely Places Sing - Payne, Anthony (1979)

Strathclyde Concerto No.10; Concerto for Orchestra - Maxwell Davies, Peter (1996)

Stratifications - Abrahamsen, Hans (1975)

Straussiana - Korngold, Erich Wolfgang (1920)

Streamline - Moravec, Paul (1988)

Streicherfantasien; On a motif by Johann Sebastian Bach - Beyer, Frank Michael (1977)

String Quartet (Arranged for String Orchestra) - Baird, Tadeusz (1957)

String Quartet No.2 in F-sharp minor; For Soprano and String Orchestra, op.10 - Schönberg, Arnold (1908/1929)

String Quartet No.4, op.25 - Zemlinsky, Alexander (1936)

String Symphony - Bäck, Sven-Erik (1986)

String Symphony; Symphony No.4 - Geissler, Fritz

String Symphony - Qu, Xiao-song

String Symphony - Rorem, Ned (1985)

Strong on Oaks; Strong on the Causes of Oaks - Nyman, Michael (1997)

Strophe - Ye, Xiaogang (1985)

Structures for Chamber Orchestra - Berlin, David (1975)

Strukturen; Den Taten der neuen Bildhauer - Engelmann, Hans Ulrich (1954)

Strut - Daugherty, Michael (1989-94)

Die Stücke des Sängers - Rihm, Wolfgang (2001)

Studie 2; A un moment de terre perdue - Furrer, Beat (1990)

Studie im Pianissimo - Blacher, Boris (1953)

Study for Strings - Haas, Pavel (1943)

Study No.1 - Nancarrow, Conlon (1995)

Study No.2 - Nancarrow, Conlon
(1995)
Study No.3c - Nancarrow, Conlon
(1995)
Study No.5 - Nancarrow, Conlon
(1995)
Study No.6 - Nancarrow, Conlon
(1995)
Study No.7 - Nancarrow, Conlon
(1995)
Study No.9 - Nancarrow, Conlon
(1995)
Study No.12 - Nancarrow, Conlon
(1995)
Study No.16 - Nancarrow, Conlon
(1995)
Sturm und Drang for Chamber
Orchestra - Ali-Zadeh, Franghiz
(1998)
Suaire de Sons - Pasquet, Yves-Marie
Suíte Sugestiva; Cinémas - Villa-
Lobos, Heitor (1929)
Suite, op.14 - Bartók, Béla (1916)
Suite: From "The Aviary" and from
"The Insect World" - Bennett,
Richard Rodney (1965)
Suite, op.3 - Janáček, Leoš (1891)
Suite; Three ironic portraits - Kósa,
György (1915)
Suite; For Ondes Martenot (or Piano)
and String Orchestra - Milhaud,
Darius
Suite, op.27 - Rathaus, Karol (1929)
Suite, op.44 - Reger, Max (1900)
Suite, op.129 - Schmitt, Florent (1954)
Suite - Schönberg, Arnold (1934)
Suite - Schulhoff, Erwin (1921)
Suite Archaïque, H.203 - Honegger,
Arthur (1951)
Suite Baroque - Tansman, Alexandre
(1958)
Suite Belge; D'après des œuvres de
clavecinistes belges du 18ème
siècle - Sgrizzi, Luciano (1953)
Suite dans le style ancien, op.24 -
Indy, Vincent d' (1886)
Suite Dracoula - Ballif, Claude (1990)
Suite en Estilo Antiguo - Ponce,
Manuel
Suite for 14 Instruments, op.23c -
Kallstenius, Edvin (1949)
Suite for 9 Instruments, op.23b -
Kallstenius, Edvin (1949)
Suite for Chamber Orchestra - Milford,
Robin (1925)
Suite for Chamber Orchestra -
Schulhoff, Erwin (1921)
Suite for Double Quartet - Chávez,
Carlos

Suite for Orchestra - Antheil, George
(1926)
Suite for Orchestra; After music by
Jan Pieters Sweelinck - Fortner,
Wolfgang (1930)
Suite for Orchestra No.2: From the
music to the film *Niemandsland*,
op.24 - Eisler, Hanns (1931)
Suite for Orchestra No.3: From the
music to the film *Kuhle Wampe*,
op.26 - Eisler, Hanns (1931)
Suite for Orchestra No.5: From the
music to the film *Dans les Rules*,
op.34 - Eisler, Hanns (1933)
Suite for Orchestra No.6: From the
music to the film *Le Grand Jeu*,
op.40 - Eisler, Hanns (1933)
Suite for Small Orchestra - James,
Dorothy (1952)
Suite for Small Orchestra - Jones,
Charles
Suite for Small Orchestra - Morris,
Harold
Suite for Small Orchestra - Naginski,
Charles
Suite for Small Orchestra - Standford,
Patric (1966)
Suite for Strings - Berkeley, Lennox
(1974)
Suite for Strings - Ratner, Leonard
Suite for Strings (Little Suite), op.1 /
F.6 - Nielsen, Carl (1888)
Suite for Violin and Orchestra -
Rosenberg, Hilding Constantin
Suite Française for Small Orchestra -
Bennett, Richard Rodney (1970)
Suite from Bitter Fruit - Woolrich, John
(2002)
Suite from Bleak House - Burgon,
Geoffrey (1991)
Suite from Los Alamos - Neikrug,
Marc (1998)
Suite from Martin Chuzzlewit - Burgon,
Geoffrey (1994)
Suite from Shakespeare's "A
Midsummer Night's Dream" - Leigh,
Walter (1937)
Suite from the Ballet "Three Jacks" -
Vincent, John (1942)
Suite from the Music to Shakespeare's
"Much Ado About Nothing", op.11 -
Korngold, Erich Wolfgang (1920)
Suite from "The River" - Thomson,
Virgil
Suite from the Tessin - Nussio, Otmar

Suite from "Triumph der
Empfindsamkeit" (Triumph of
Sensitivity), op.43a - Krenek, Ernst
(1926)
Suite für Neun Solo-Instrumente, op.9
- Stürmer, Bruno (1923)
Suite in A minor, op.103a - Reger,
Max
Suite in Ancient Style, op.2 - Magnard,
Albéric (1889)
Suite in D major - Saint-Saëns,
Camille
Suite in F for Small Orchestra - Jacob,
Gordon
Suite in G minor - Paumgartner,
Bernhard
Suite in Old Style - Schnittke, Alfred
(1972)
Suite Mignonne, op.98a - Sibelius,
Jean (1921)
Suite No.1: From the movie *Opus III*,
op.23 - Eisler, Hanns (1930)
Suite No.1 - Hansson, C.J. Gunnar
Suite No.1; For Small Orchestra -
Stravinsky, Igor (1925)
Suite No.2 - Atterberg, Kurt (1915)
Suite No.2 - Harrison, Lou
Suite No.2; For Small Orchestra -
Stravinsky, Igor (1921)
Suite No.2, op.4 - Bartók, Béla (1907)
Suite No.3 - Fitelberg, Jerzy (1930)
Suite No.7, op.29 - Atterberg, Kurt
Suite of Ancient Dances, op.58 -
Stanford, Charles Villiers (1895)
Suite of Dances - Price, Florence
Suite on English Folk Tunes, op.90 -
Britten, Benjamin (1974)
Suite on Popular Swedish Folk
Melodies - Rosenberg, Hilding
Constantin (1927)
Suite on Six Swiss Folksongs -
Liebermann, Rolf (1947)
Suite para orquesta de cámara - Elias,
Alfonso de
Suite pastorale in modo antico -
Atterberg, Kurt
Suite Paysanne Hongroise - Bartók,
Béla (1917)
Suite Phantastique - Scott, Cyril
Suite Pittoresque - Smit, Andre-Jean
Suite populaire russe - Tcherepnin,
Alexander
Suite Pour Petit Orchestre - Olivier,
François
Suite Sofia - Borges, Joaquin (1993)
Suite Valaque - Lazar, Filip (1925)
Sumerkei - Bäck, Sven-Erik
Sumervar - Barnett, Carol (1988)
Summa - Pärt, Arvo (1991)

A Summer Day, op.65a - Prokofiev, Sergei (1941)

Summer Divertimento - Bolcom, William (1973)

Summer Evening - Kodály, Zoltán (1906)

Summer Gardens - Scott, Cyril

Sunflower - Lumsdaine, David (1975)

Sunrise Serenade - Sallinen, Aulis (1989)

Suns Dance - Matthews, Colin (1985)

Sunset Strip - Daugherty, Michael (1999)

Sur Les Flots Lointains - Koechlin, Charles (1933)

Surabaya Johnny: From "Happy End" - Weill, Kurt (1929)

Surf - Nørgård, Per (1983)

Svanevit Suite, op.54 - Sibelius, Jean (1909)

Swan of Tuonela: From Lemminkäinen Suite, op.22 - Sibelius, Jean (1893)

Swan Song - Danielpour, Richard (2003)

Symphonic Rhapsody, op.147 - Reger, Max

Symphonic Set, op.17 - Cowell, Henry (1939)

Symphonic Study "Machines," op.30 - Arnold, Malcolm (1951)

Symphonic Variations on a Theme by H. Schütz, Wk29b - David, Johann Nepomuk (1942)

Symphonie Classique - Rasmussen, Karl Aage (1969)

Symphonie de Rossi; Suite Salomon Rossi - Foss, Lukas (1975)

Symphonie latine - Bondon, Jacques (1973)

Symphonie pour cordes - Jolivet, André (1961)

Symphonies à Quinze Solistes - Pousseur, Henri (1954)

Symphonies of Wind and Rain - Payne, Anthony (1992)

Symphoniette - Bacewicz, Grażyna (1929)

Symphonietta, op.27 - Lopatnikoff, Nikolai (1942)

Symphonische Musik für 9 Soloinstrumente, op.11 - Krenek, Ernst (1923)

Symphonische Szenen, op.22 - Einem, Gottfried von (1956)

Symphony - Blacher, Boris (1938)

Symphony - Lampersberg, Gerhard (1956)

Symphony, op.21 - Webern, Anton (1928)

Symphony for 12 Musicians - Bedford, David (1981)

Symphony for 15 Performers - Kisielewski, Stefan (1961)

Symphony for 15 Strings - Treibmann, Karl Ottomar (1979)

Symphony for Cello and Orchestra, op.68 - Britten, Benjamin (1963)

Symphony for Chamber Orchestra - Bergsma, William (1942)

Symphony for Chamber Orchestra - Donovan, Richard (1937)

Symphony for Chamber Orchestra - Kalsons, Romualds (1981)

Symphony for Small Orchestra - Krása, Hans (1923)

Symphony for Small Orchestra - Swayne, Giles (1984)

Symphony for String Orchestra - Bacewicz, Grażyna (1946)

Symphony for Strings - Arnold, Malcolm (1946)

Symphony for Strings - Cotton, Jeffery (2004)

Symphony for Strings, op.20 - Hummel, Bertold (1964)

Symphony for Strings - Laks, Simon (1964)

Symphony for Strings, op.118a - Shostakovich, Dmitri (1964)

Symphony for Strings and Timpani - Mirzoyan, Edvard (1962)

Symphony III for String Orchestra, op.29 - Eder, Helmut (1959)

Symphony in A - Saint-Saëns, Camille

Symphony in A minor, op.1 - Schreker, Franz (1899)

Symphony in C - Kodály, Zoltán (1930s)

Symphony in F; Urbs Roma - Saint-Saëns, Camille

Symphony in F major - Fauré, Gabriel

Symphony in One Movement - Barclay, Robert Lenard (1950)

Symphony in the Old Style - Reznicek, Emil Nikolaus von

Symphony No.1 - Bolcom, William (1957)

Symphony No.1 - Carter, Elliott (1942)

Symphony No.1: Prelude - Copland, Aaron (1924)

Symphony No.1, op.10 - Hasquenoph, Pierre

Symphony No.1 - Henze, Hans Werner (1947/1991)

Symphony No.1, op.4 - Holmboe, Vagn (1935)

Symphony No.1; Time Current - Ichiyanagi, Toshi (1986)

Symphony No.1; Classical Symphony - Jerger, Wilhelm

Symphony No.1 - Lloyd, Jonathan (1983)

Symphony No.1; "Polyphonic," op.9 - Pärt, Arvo (1963)

Symphony No.1 - Rautavaara, Einojuhani (1956)

Symphony No.1 - Saygun, A. Adnan

Symphony No.1, op.18 - Zbinden, Julien-François

Symphony No.1 for Chamber Orchestra - Lobanov, Vasily (1977)

Symphony No.1 in A minor, Wk18 - David, Johann Nepomuk (1937)

Symphony No.2, op.53 - Gál, Hans

Symphony No.2, H.153 - Honegger, Arthur (1941)

Symphony No.2 - MacMillan, James (1999)

Symphony No.2, op.73 - Moeschinger, Albert (1948)

Symphony No.2 - Rautavaara, Einojuhani (1957)

Symphony No.2 - Rorem, Ned (1956)

Symphony No.2; The Sweet Season - Schickele, Peter

Symphony No.2 - Silvestrov, Valentin (1965)

Symphony No.2 - Treibmann, Karl Ottomar (1981)

Symphony No.2 in Bb major - Zemlinsky, Alexander (1897)

Symphony No.2 for Chamber Orchestra; "Intermezzo," op.36 - Lobanov, Vasily (1981)

Symphony No.2 for String Orchestra - Corigliano, John (2000)

Symphony No.3 - Binkerd, Gordon (1959)

Symphony No.3 - Bolcom, William (1979)

Symphony No.3; "Lamentations" - Cooper, Paul (1971)

Symphony No.3, Wk28 - David, Johann Nepomuk (1941)

Symphony No.3 - Glass, Philip (1995)

Symphony No.3 - Hamilton, Iain

Symphony No.3; The Camp Meeting, S.3 - Ives, Charles Edward (1904)

Symphony No.3, op.16 - Krenek, Ernst (1922)

Symphony No.3 - Lloyd, Jonathan (1987)

Symphony No.3; For soprano and baritone (or tape) and chamber orchestra - Tishchenko, Boris

Symphony No.3 for Chamber Orchestra - Karayev, Kara (1964)

Symphony No.3 for Chamber Orchestra (For the Centenary of Igor Stravinsky) - Pavlenko, Sergei (1982)

Symphony No.3 in B minor, op.11 - Magnard, Albéric (1896)

Symphony No.3 in G, op.27 - Cohn, James (1955)

Symphony No.4 - Alizade, Akshin (1998)

Symphony No.4 - Asia, Daniel

Symphony No.4; Symphonie Classique Sturm und Drang, op.49 - Bacri, Nicolas (1995)

Symphony No.4, op.80 - Einem, Gottfried von (1986)

Symphony No.4, op.51 - Matthews, David (1990)

Symphony No.4 - Maxwell Davies, Peter (1989)

Symphony No.4 in A, op.29 - Cohn, James (1956)

Symphony No.4 in F Major, op.61 - Weingartner, Felix (1917)

Symphony No.4 in G minor, op.14 - Atterberg, Kurt

Symphony No.5; Concerto pour orchestre, op.55 - Bacri, Nicolas (1997)

Symphony No.5 - Cohn, James (1959)

Symphony No.6, op.66 - Bentzon, Niels Viggo (1950)

Symphony No.6; Sinfonia breve, op.67 - Bruns, Victor

Symphony No.6 - Davison, John

Symphony No.6; Concertante Symphony - Geissler, Fritz

Symphony No.7 - Cowell, Henry (1952)

Symphony No.7, Wk49 - David, Johann Nepomuk (1957)

Symphony No.7; Angel of Light - Rautavaara, Einojuhani (1994)

Symphony No.7 - Tubin, Eduard (1958)

Symphony No.8, Wk 59 - David, Johann Nepomuk (1964)

Symphony No.8, Wk59 - David, Johann Nepomuk (1965)

Symphony No.9 - Cowell, Henry (1953)

Symphony No.10 - Cowell, Henry (1953)

Symphony No.11, op.158 - Bentzon, Niels Viggo (1964)

Symphony No.16; Icelandic - Cowell, Henry (1962)

Symphony No.17; Lancaster - Cowell, Henry (1962)

Synthese; For 4X4 instruments, op.47 - Schiske, Karl (1958)

Syringa - Carter, Elliott (1978)

Syzygy - Del Tredici, David (1966)

Szenen, op.6 - Füssl, Karl Heinz (1964)

T

Tableau Vivant - Krauze, Zygmunt (1982)

Tabula Rasa; Double Concerto - Pärt, Arvo (1977)

Tafelmusik: From op.48 - Lendvai, Erwin (1932)

Tag Rag - Bermel, Derek (2003)

Le Taille-Lyre, op.64, No.1 - Ballif, Claude (1990)

Taj Mahal - Hutcheson, Jere (2004)

Take Off - Sawer, David (1987)

Tangazo; Variations on Buenos Aires - Piazzolla, Astor

Tango - Stravinsky, Igor (1953)

Tango Chikane (reduced version) - Nørgård, Per

Tänze aus Salzburg - Schönherr, Max

Tänze der Rätsel - Polovinkin, Leonid (1930)

Tänzerinnen; Choreographies based on E. Degas - Zimmermann, Udo (1973)

Tänzerische Suite - Bräutigam, Helmut

Tanz-Rondo, op.27 - Einem, Gottfried von (1959)

Tanzsuite, op.23 - Roters, Ernst

Tanzsuite, Werk 21 - Schollum, Robert

Tanzsuite (Dance Suite), op.24 - Stürmer, Bruno

Tanzsuite nach Couperin - Strauss, Richard (1923)

Tanzsuite No.1, op.70 - Hauer, Josef Matthias (1936)

Tanzsuite No.2, op.71 - Hauer, Josef Matthias (1936)

Tanzwalzer, op.53 (Busoni Verz. 288) - Busoni, Ferruccio

Tao, op.41 - Vostřák, Zbyněk (1967)

Taqsim-Caprice-Maqam - Nilsson, Bo (1973)

Tarantella - Schelling, Ernest

Tarantella, op.39 - Takács, Jenö (1937)

Tartini-Variations; Introduction, Andante et Variazioni, op.A-2 - Manén, Joan

Technologic 1-2 - Hindson, Matthew (1998)

Technologic 145 - Hindson, Matthew (1998)

El Tecolote (The Owl) - Revueltas, Silvestre

Teheran Movement - Cowell, Henry (1957)

The Telephone: Lucy's Aria (Hello! Oh, Margaret it's you) - Menotti, Gian Carlo (1947)

Tell My Fortune - Daugherty, Michael (2004)

Tema con variazioni, op.29a - Rózsa, Miklós

Tempi Concertati - Berio, Luciano (1959)

The Tempest Songbook - Saariaho, Kaija (2004)

Temporal Variations - Britten, Benjamin (1936)

Ten - Cage, John

Ten Polish Dances - Lutosławski, Witold (1951)

Tendenza - Lindberg, Magnus (1982)

Tendril - Harvey, Jonathan (1987)

Terms - Braun, Peter Michael (1963)

La terre habitable I; Les eaux étroites - Bonnet, Antoine (1998)

La terre habitable II; Aubrac - Bonnet, Antoine (1995)

La terre habitable III; Les hautes terres du Sertalejo - Bonnet, Antoine (1996)

La terre habitable IV; La presqu'île - Bonnet, Antoine (1996)

La terre habitable V; Liberté grande - Bonnet, Antoine (1997)

Testament; Music for orchestra, after "Testament: Music for twelve violas" - Dean, Brett (2008)

Tête d'Or; Musique pour une pièce de Paul Claudel, H.199 - Honegger, Arthur (1950)

Texturae II - Acker, Dieter (1972)

Thalleïn - Xenakis, Iannis (1984)

That White and Radiant Legend - Bedford, David (1966)

The Theatre of Magical Beings - Vir, Param (2003)

Theatrum - Hesketh, Kenneth (1996)

Theme and Variations - Cheslock, Louis (1934)

There Is A Willow Grows Aslant A Brook - Bridge, Frank (1928)

There is sweet music here, op.93 - Bavicchi, John (1985)

These Words... - Pärt, Arvo (2008)

Third Idyll; Frost at Midnight, op.78 - Holloway, Robin (1993)

Thirteen - Cage, John

This One For You - Bedford, David (1965)

Thoughts for Strings - Thomson, Virgil (1982)

Three Astral Visions - Brott, Alexander (1959)

Three Berceuses, op.48 - Szymanowski, Karol (1922)

Three Dances, op.34 - Górecki, Henryk Mikołaj (1973)

Three Dances for Small Orchestra - Leplin, Emanuel (1942)

Three Dialogues - Wolschina, Reinhard (1975)

Three English Dances, op.11 - Quilter, Roger (1910)

Three Girls, Three Women - Schickele, Peter

Three Inventions for Chamber Orchestra - Benjamin, George (1995)

Three Latin American Sketches - Copland, Aaron (1959-72)

Three Lines from Twenty Poems - Felder, David (1987)

Three Miniatures for Orchestra - Koch, Erland von (1951)

Three Movements - Nancarrow, Conlon (1993)

Three Movements for Trumpet and Orchestra - Asia, Daniel

Three Movements from "Theatrum" - Hesketh, Kenneth (1998)

Three Movements with Fanfares - Birtwistle, Sir Harrison (1964)

Three Mozart Organ Sonatas for 14 Players - Henze, Hans Werner (1991)

Three Novels - Wolschina, Reinhard (1980)

Three Old Fashioned Dances for Chamber Orchestra, op.102 - Converse, Frederick Shepherd (1938)

Three Patterns for Small Orchestra - Hartley, Walter Sinclair (1951)

Three Pieces; For Kids in the Audience and Chamber Orchestra - Adolphe, Bruce (1988)

Three Pieces for Chamber Orchestra, op.37 - Tcherepnin, Alexander (1927)

Three Pieces for Orchestra: From the music to the film *The 400 Million* - Eisler, Hanns (1938)

Three Pieces for Orchestra - Herrmann, Peter (1973)

Three Pieces in Old Style - Górecki, Henryk Mikołaj (1963)

Three Poems of Robert Frost - Carter, Elliott (1975)

Three Rivers - Bermel, Derek (2001)

Three Sephardic Songs - Castelnuovo-Tedesco, Mario

Three Sketches - Gillis, Don (1942)

Three Songs - Crawford, Ruth

Three Songs of Jocelyn Brooke, op.25b - Searle, Humphrey (1954)

Three Strange Cases - Schickele, Peter

Three Village Scenes - Bartók, Béla (1926)

Three-Part Motet - Muldowney, Dominic (1976)

Threnody on a Plainsong for Michael Vyner - Maxwell Davies, Peter (1989)

...through the glass - Matthews, Colin (1994)

Through the Looking Glass I - Szymanski, Pawel (1987)

Thurber's Dogs - Schickele, Peter

Tiger under the Table - Weir, Judith (2002)

Time In Tempest Everywhere; For Soprano, Oboe and Chamber Orchestra - Adler, Samuel (1993)

Tiramisu - Anderson, Julian (1994)

Tiroirs - Sawer, David (1996)

Tjao-Houen - Scherchen, Tona (1973)

Toccata; Chamber Orchestra version, op.28 - Aguila, Miguel del (1988)

Toccata, op.55 - Burkhard, Willy (1939)

Toccata, H.207 - Honegger, Arthur (1951)

Toccata e due canzoni, H.311 - Martinů, Bohuslav (1946)

Toccata for Chamber Orchestra, op.86 - Burkhard, Willy (1951)

Toccata sin Fuga - Revueltas, Silvestre (1933)

Der Tod der Geliebten (The Death of the Beloved) - Banfield, Raffaello de (1969)

Tom Jones: Three Dances - German, Sir Edward (1907)

Le Tombeau de Couperin - Ravel, Maurice (1917)

Tone Roads No.1, S.49 - Ives, Charles Edward (1911)

Tone Roads No.3, S.49 - Ives, Charles Edward (1911)

Tones - León, Tania

Torque - Kats-Chernin, Elena (2002)

Torturous Instruments - Hesketh, Kenneth (1998)

Tosca Revisited - Matthews, Colin (1978)

Tovem for 15 Instruments - Mansurian, Tigran (1979)

Towards Freedom? - Nørgård, Per (1977)

Toy Symphony - Freyhan, Michael (1962)

Tracce - Edlund, Lars (1972)

Trace - Boone, Charles (1983)

Tractatus - Nordheim, Arne (1986)

Tragic Overture; In Memoriam D. Hammarskjoeld - Voss, Friedrich (1961)

Tragoedia - Birtwistle, Sir Harrison (1965)

Tragoedia (Der unsichtbare Raum) - Hölszky, Adriana (1996)

Trajectoires - Bonnet, Antoine (1988)

The Transfiguration: A Meditation - Bedford, David (1988)

Transitions for Orchestra - Hutcheson, Jere (1973)

Transitoire V: From "...explosante-fixe..." - Boulez, Pierre (1993)

Transitoire VII - Boulez, Pierre (1991)

Trapeze - Ruders, Poul (1992)

Trauermusik - Bialas, Günter (1994)

Trauermusik - Thiele, Siegfried (1966)

Traum durch die Dämmerung, op.29/1 - Strauss, Richard (1895)

Träume vom Lido - Lincke, Paul (1939)

Traummusik; 6 Stücke für kleines Orchester - Kelterborn, Rudolf (1971)

Traumstadt - Saxton, Robert (1980)

Traumtanz - Redel, Martin Christoph (1981)

Travelling - Bon, André (1989)

Travesties in a Sad Landscape - Bose, Hans-Jürgen von (1978)

Tre Canzoni Italiane - Porrino, Ennio (1939)

Tre Ricercari, H.267 - Martinů, Bohuslav (1938)

Tre Små Stykker - Bruun, Peter (2004)

A Tree - Buck, Ole (1996)

Tree Line - Takemitsu, Tōru (1988)

Tree of Singing Names - Gilbert, Anthony (1989)

TreeStone - Albert, Stephen (1983)

Tres Piezas Para Orquesta - Koc, Marcelo (1958)

Tres Viejos Aires de Danza - Rodrigo, Joaquín (1929)

Trevelyan Suite, op.96 - Arnold, Malcolm (1967)

Trialogus I - Levy, Marvin David (1972)

Trialogus II - Levy, Marvin David (1972)

Triana: From "Iberia" - Albéniz, Isaac (1907)

Trias - Engelmann, Hans Ulrich (1962)

Tributes; Album for Strings - Nørgård, Per (1994-1995)

Trigon - Kulenty, Hanna (1989)

Trio-Sonata - Schnittke, Alfred (1987)

Tripartita - Maasz, Gerhard (1967)

Triple Concerto - Eckhardt-Gramatté, Sophie Carmen (1949)

Triple Concerto - Martino, Donald (1977)

Triple Concerto; Overture, Variations and Finale on Rocco's Aria from Beethoven's "Fidelio" - Schenker, Friedrich (1969)

Tríptic de Mossén Cinto - Rodrigo, Joaquín (1935)

Triptique - Absil, Jean

Triptych; Three Pieces for Chamber Orchestra - Rorem, Ned (1992)

Triptychon (13X3), op.20 - Harneit, Johannes (2003)

Triptyque aborigène; Trois tableaux pour orchestre de chambre - Ifukube, Akira (1939)

Trisagion - Pärt, Arvo (1994)

Triton-Sinfonietta; Drei Grotesken - Baur, Jürg (1974)

Trois Chansons sur des Poèmes de Charles Vildrac - Ibert, Jacques

Trois images concertantes - Bondon, Jacques (1982)

Trois Mélodies de 1916 - Satie, Erik

Trois petites pièces montées - Satie, Erik (1919)

Trois Poèmes de Stéphane Mallarmé - Debussy, Claude

Trois poèmes de Stéphane Mallarmé - Ravel, Maurice (1913)

Trois Rag-Caprices - Milhaud, Darius (1930)

Trois Sérénades - Dubois, Pierre-Max

Trois Valses - Milhaud, Darius (1945)

Troka - Revueltas, Silvestre

Trona For 12 - Bedford, David (1967)

Tropi - Terzakis, Dimitri (1978)

Tropismes pour les Amours Imaginaires - Ibert, Jacques

Trotz Reaktion I - Schleiermacher, Steffen (1994)

Trotz Reaktion II - Schleiermacher, Steffen (1996)

Trotz Reaktion III - Schleiermacher, Steffen (1997)

Trotz Reaktion IV - Schleiermacher, Steffen (1997)

Troubadours (Variations for Guitar and Chamber Orchestra) - Corigliano, John (1993)

Das trunkene Mücklein - Schönherr, Max

Tryst - MacMillan, James (1989)

Turandot, op.1a; Four episodes for orchestra - Einem, Gottfried von (1954)

The Turfan Fragments - Feldman, Morton (1980)

Turning Variations - Bermel, Derek (2006)

Turquoise - Ince, Kamran (1996)

Tutti; Concert collectif - Malec, Ivo (1962)

Tutti e soli, op.113 - Bergman, Erik (1990)

Tuttifäntchen: Suite - Hindemith, Paul (1925)

The Twelve-Note Rag - Laufer, Kenneth (1977)

Twelve to Remember, Twelve to Come - Bruun, Peter (2001)

Twenty Three - Cage, John

Two Contrasts for String Orchestra - Bliss, Arthur (1970)

Two Entr'actes - Bridge, Frank (1926)

Two Hungarian Dances - Farkas, Ferenc (1949)

Two Interludes for an Opera - Harvey, Jonathan (2003)

Two Intermezzi: From the incidental music to the play "Threads" - Bridge, Frank (1921)

Two Inventions - Blacher, Boris (1954)

Two Jamaican Pieces - Benjamin, Arthur (1938)

Two Meditations for Strings - Binkerd, Gordon (1981)

Two Miniatures from T'ang - Chou, Wen-Chung (1957)

Two Monkton-Blues, op.127 - Bentzon, Niels Viggo (1960)

Two Old English Songs - Bridge, Frank (1916)

Two Orchestral Pieces for Small Orchestra - Fletcher, Horace Grant (1956)

Two Organa, op.27 - Knussen, Oliver (1995)

Two Part Invention - Matthews, Colin (1988)

Two Pieces - Copland, Aaron (1928)

Two Pieces; Prelude and Scherzo, op.11 - Shostakovich, Dmitri (1925)

Two Pieces for Chamber Orchestra - Müller-Wieland, Jan (1986)

Two Pieces for Small Orchestra - Delius, Frederick (1912)

Two Portraits, op.5 - Bartók, Béla (1910)

Two Preludes on Southern Folk Hymn Tunes - Lewis, Harold Merrills

Two Ricercares - Smirnov, Dmitri (1983)

Two Romances - Reger, Max (1900)

Two Songs Without Words, op.22 / H88 - Holst, Gustav (1906)

Two Tributes - Matthews, Colin (1999)

Two Village Scenes (Slovak Folksongs) - Bartók, Béla (1924)

U

Überschreiten - Dillon, James

Übungen im Verwandeln - Thiele, Siegfried (1978)

The Ugly Duckling, op.18 - Prokofiev, Sergei (1914)

Ukranian Symphony in Old Style - Goldstein, Mikhail (1948)

Ultima Scena - Bawden, Rupert (1989)

Umbrellas & Sewing Machines - Schneid, Tobias P.M.

...umdüstert... - Widmann, Jörg (2000)

Umsungen - Rihm, Wolfgang (1984)

Und gestern hat er mir Rosen gebracht: From "Lieder und Gesänge" (1.Folge Nr.24) - Marx, Joseph (1908)

Und kehrt er einst Heim: From "Sechs Gesänge," op.13/5 - Zemlinsky, Alexander (1914)

Undine - Davis, Anthony (1986)

Ungarische Burgmusik; Antiqua hungarica, op.47 - Takács, Jenö (1941)

Unicorn - Beynon, Jared (1974)

unplugged. unperfumed - Schweitzer, Benjamin (2001)

L'Uomo dai Baffi - Berners, Lord (1918)

V

Vagabund; Scherzo for Orchestra - Blumer, Theodor (1955)

Vaganza - Casken, John (1985)

Valley of Aosta - Harvey, Jonathan (1988)

The Valley Sleeper, the Children, the Snakes and the Giant - Bedford, David (1982)

Valse - Horovitz, Joseph (1973)

Valse - Poulenc, Francis (1932)

Valse Chevaleresque, op.96c - Sibelius, Jean (1920)

Valse Lente - Riisager, Knudåge (1935)

Valse Lente; Weißer Tanz - Schreker, Franz (1908)

Valse Romantique, op.62b - Sibelius, Jean (1911)

Valse Triste - Argento, Dominick (1996)

Valse Triste: From "Kuolema," op.44, No.1 - Sibelius, Jean (1904)

Valse Triste - Tubin, Eduard (1939)

Vanitas; Arrangement of a fragment by Johan Ban for string orchestra - Maxwell Davies, Peter (1991)

Variaciones Sobre Tema de Tango - Gianneo, Luis

Variants - Schurmann, Gerard (1970)

Variants on a Madrigal by Gesualdo - Schifrin, Lalo (1969)

Variants on a Texas Tune; Mustang grey - McKay, George Frederick

La Variation Ajoutée; Pour 17 Instruments & Bande Électroacoustique - Amy, Gilbert (1984)

Variation on "Sumer is Icumen In" - Saxton, Robert (1987)

Variationen über eine Schottische Volksweise, op.23 - Raphael, Günter

Variationen über einen Ländler von Schubert (Variations on a Landler by Schubert) - Müller-Siemens, Detlev (1978)

Variationen-Suite; Über ein altes Rokoko-Thema, op.64 - Haas, Joseph (1924)

Variationer til Moster Rix (Variations for Aunt Rix) - Gudmundsen-Holmgreen, Pelle (1968)

Variationes Concertantes, op.23 - Ginastera, Alberto (1953)

Variations - Crumb, David

Variations - Meale, Richard (1970)

Variations - Naylor, Bernard (1960)

Variations, op.30 - Webern, Anton (1941)

Variations and Finale, op.34 - Searle, Humphrey (1958)

Variations en Trois Mouvements - Hasquenoph, Pierre

Variations for Chamber Orchestra - Vate, Nancy van de (1959)

Variations for Orchestra - Carter, Elliott (1955)

Variations on "Mein junges Leben hat ein End" - Muldowney, Dominic (1976)

Variations on "Sellenger's Round"; Aldeburgh Variations - Britten, Benjamin (1953)

Variations on a Carol Tune - Oldham, Arthur (1949)

Variations on a Hungarian Folksong, The Peacock - Kodály, Zoltán (1939)

Variations on a Hungarian Peasant Song, op.4 - Rózsa, Miklós (1929)

Variations on a Theme by J. S. Bach, Wk29a - David, Johann Nepomuk (1942)

Variations on a Theme by Mezangeau, op.12 - Riisager, Knudåge (1926)

Variations on a Theme by W. A. Mozart - Busch, Adolf

Variations on a Theme by W. A. Mozart, op.95 - Zilcher, Hermann

Variations on a Theme of Frank Bridge, op.10 - Britten, Benjamin (1937)

Variations on a Theme of Muzio Clementi - Blacher, Boris (1961)

Variations on a Ukranian Folk Song, op.9a - Arnold, Malcolm (1993)

Variations on an Elizabethan Theme (Sellinger's Round) - Berkeley, Lennox (1953)

Variations on the American Negro Spiritual "I was Way Down A-Yonder" - Morris, Harold

Variations on the Variations op.30 by Webern - Hidalgo, Manuel (2001)

Variations on The Wayfaring Stranger - Cohn, James (1960)

Variations on "Three Blind Mice" - Tavener, John (1972)

Variations on Three Folksongs, op.23 - Apostel, Hans Erich (1956)

Variations Pour 14 - Hasquenoph, Pierre

Variations pour quatorze instruments - Aperghis, Georges (1973)

Variazione sull'aria di Papageno: No.2 from "Divertimento for Mozart" - Berio, Luciano (1956)

Eine Värmlandsrhapsodie, op.36 - Atterberg, Kurt (1934)

The Veil of Pierette: Wedding March, op.18, No.4 - Dohnanyi, Ernest von (1910)

The Veil of Pierette: Pierrot's complaint of love, op.18, No.1 - Dohnanyi, Ernest von (1910)

The Veil of Pierette: Waltz, op.18, No.2 - Dohnanyi, Ernest von (1910)

The Veil of Pierette: Jolly Funeral March, op.18, No.3 - Dohnanyi, Ernest von (1910)

The Veil of Pierette: Menuett, op.18, No.5 - Dohnanyi, Ernest von (1910)

The Veil of Pierette: Pierette's dance of madness, op.18, No.6 - Dohnanyi, Ernest von (1910)

Vendanges, Ballet, op.317 - Milhaud, Darius (1952)

Venetianisches Wiegenlied: From "Italienisches Liederbuch" (No.17) - Marx, Joseph (1912)

Venezianische Schatten - Brandmüller, Theo (1981)

Venus Fly Trap - Chapple, Brian (1979)

Verblendungen - Saariaho, Kaija (1984)

Verborgene Formen - Rihm, Wolfgang (1997)

Vergnügliche Musik aus einer deutschen Kleinstadt - Uhl, Alfred (1944)

Verklärte Nacht, op.4; Version for String Orchestra - Schönberg, Arnold (1899/1916)

Verklärte Nacht, op.4; Revised version 1943 - Schönberg, Arnold (1899/1943)

Die Verlassene; Stimmungsbild nach einem finnischen Volkslied - Järnefelt, Armas

Vernal Showers - Dillon, James

Versi - Beyer, Frank Michael (1968)

Verwandlung; Four Pieces for Chamber Orchestra - Leyendecker, Ulrich (1980)

Verwirrung; Concerto for Cello - Lampersberg, Gerhard (1984)

Vier Aphorismen - Wolschina, Reinhard (1981)

Vier Bet- und Bussgesänge - Reznicek, Emil Nikolaus von (1915)

Vier Lieder, op.13 - Webern, Anton (1918)

Vier Nachtstücke für Kammerorchester - Kelterborn, Rudolf (1963)

Vignettes de danse - Bridge, Frank (1925)

Village Music - Moore, Douglas (1942)

Villanelle - Dukas, Paul (1906)

Vintage Alice; Fantascene on a Mad-Tea-Party for soprano solo, folk group and chamber orchestra - Del Tredici, David (1972)

Vinter, op.194 - Holmboe, Vagn (1994)

Visage penché - Aubert, Louis (1907)

Vision; For 20 String Soloists - Kühnl, Claus (1983)

Vision: Ballet - Pergament, Moses (1923)

Visionen - Matthus, Siegfried (1978)

Visions fugitives, op.22 - Prokofiev, Sergei (1917)

Vivace, H.220 - Honegger, Arthur

Vocalise, op.34 - Rachmaninoff, Sergei (1912)

Vodka Float - Shulman, Alan (1947)

Voice and Instruments 1 - Feldman, Morton (1972)

A Voice to Wake - Matthews, Colin (2004)

Volkstänze aus dem Burgenland, op.57 - Takács, Jenö (1952)

Voll jener Süße, op.8/5 - Schönberg, Arnold (1904)

Vom Ewigen Leben - Schreker, Franz (1923)

Von fremden Ländern und Menschen, op.37 - Takács, Jenö (1937)

Von Vorn Herein, op.219 - Krenek, Ernst (1974)

Von Zeit zu Zeit; Pour 16 Instrumentistes - Aperghis, Georges (1971)

Voodoo Violin Concerto No.1 - Roumain, Daniel Bernard (2002)

Vor Barndoms Venner (Our Childhood Friends), op.15 - Wellejus, Henning (1950)

Vox Cordis Mei, op.293 - Lukáš, Zdenek (1997)

Voyage; For flute and string orchestra - Corigliano, John (1983)

Voyage (for String Orchestra) - Corigliano, John (1976)

Voyage - Hamilton, Iain

Le Voyage - Moeschinger, Albert (1958)

Le Voyage - Mundry, Isabel (1996)

Le Voyage de Tchong-Li - Beydts, Louis (1932)

Voyage into the Broken Screen; Hommage a Sibelius - Nørgård, Per (1995)

Voyage into the Golden Screen - Nørgård, Per (1968)

Voyants; For piano and chamber orchestra - Kolb, Barbara (1991)

V'shamru; For Baritone (Cantor) and Chamber Orchestra - Asia, Daniel

W

Waarg - Xenakis, Iannis (1988)

Waiting - Rorem, Ned (1996)

Waldseligkeit, op.49, No.1 - Strauss, Richard (1901)

Wall of Light Black - Sotelo, Mauricio (2006)

Wall of Light Red - Sotelo, Mauricio (2004)

Waltz and Hyde Park Gallop: From the film *An Ideal Husband* - Benjamin, Arthur (1947)

Waltz-Passacaglia - Harbison, John

Wanderjahr - Bawden, Rupert (1990)

Wandlungen - Wolschina, Reinhard (1985)

Wantsch; Turkmenische Suite, op.29 - Knipper, Lew (1932)

Das Wappenschild, op.8/2 - Schönberg, Arnold (1904)

Was mir die Aeolsharfe erzählt... - Schultz, Wolfgang-Andreas (2004)

Washington Speaks - Danielpour, Richard (2005)

Water and Stone - Tanaka, Karen (1999)

A Water Idyll - Helfer, Walter (1937)

Water Music for 4th of July Evening - Antheil, George (1942)

Water Ways - Takemitsu, Tōru (1978)

Wave Mechanics - Tanaka, Karen (1994)

Wayang II - Davis, Anthony (1982)

Wayang IV - Davis, Anthony (1981)

The Web Spinner - Kolb, Barbara (2003)

The Weeping White Room - Sørensen, Bent (2002)

Der Weg nach Eisenstadt; Haydn Phantasies for Small Orchestra - Bialas, Günter (1980)

A Welcome to Orkney - Maxwell Davies, Peter (1980)

Die Weise von Liebe und Tod des Cornets Christoph Rilke - Martin, Frank (1943)

Wenn Bach Bienen gezüchtet hätte... - Pärt, Arvo (1976/2001)

Wenn Vöglein klagen, op.8/6 - Schönberg, Arnold (1904)

Wer, wenn ich schriee, hörte mich... (Who, if I screamed, would hear me...) - Haas, Georg Friedrich (1999)

What Did You Do Today at Jeffey's House? - Schickele, Peter (1994)

What We Can See of the Sky Has Fallen - Wilson, Ian (1999)

Wheel of Emptiness - Harvey, Jonathan (1997)

When the Willow Nods; Second Suite in one Movement from Stage Work No.5-b - Becker, John J.

Where the Rainbow Ends: Suite - Quilter, Roger

White Lies For Lomax - Bates, Mason (2008)

White Spirituals - Franceschini, Romulus

Whitewater; For 12 solo strings - Hindson, Matthew (2000)

Who by Water - Gordon, Michael (2004)

Who's Afraid of Red, Yellow and Blue?; Concerto for Alto Saxophone - Wilson, Ian (1998)

Whythorne's Shadow - Moeran, E. J. (1932)

Wiener Symphonie, op.49 - Einem, Gottfried von (1976)

Wiener Walzer - Uhl, Alfred (1942)

Wild Nights; Concertino for Bassoon and Mixed Ensemble - Hutcheson, Jere (2008)

Wildlife - Osborne, Nigel (1984)

Wind, Sand and Stars - Melby, John (1983)

Windows and Canopies - Dillon, James

Windsor Variations, op.75 - Berkeley, Lennox (1969)

The Wings of Morning - Wilby, Philip (1988)

Winter Song - Weir, Judith (2006)

Winter Songs I-III - Czernowin, Chaya (2003)

The Winter's Passed - Barlow, Wayne (1940)

Wise Water - Mochizuki, Misato (2002)

The Witch of Endor; Ballet - Schuman, William

The Witch's Kiss - MacRae, Stuart (1997)

With 100 Kazoos; For chamber ensemble and 100 kazoos - Bedford, David (1971)

Without Jealousy - Nørgård, Per (1984)

Wolken über Samland - Winkler, Gerhard (1941)

Wolkenbilder; Four Movements - Thiele, Siegfried (1977)

Wonne der Wehmut - Salmhofer, Franz

Words Overheard - Birtwistle, Sir Harrison (1985)

Wunderblumen - Lorentzen, Bent (1982)

Y

Yarrageh; Nocturne - Edwards, Ross (1989)

Yet That Things Go Round - Kolb, Barbara (1987)

York - Komorous, Rudolf (1967)

The Young Person's Guide to the Orchestra, op.34; Variations and Fugue on a Theme of Purcell - Britten, Benjamin (1946)

Youthful Rapture - Grainger, Percy Aldridge (1901)

Youth's Dream and Time's Truths - Watkins, Michael Blake (1973)

Yu ko - Chou, Wen-Chung

Yubarta: Overture - Alonso-Crespo, Eduardo (1989)

Z

Zansa - Osborne, Nigel (1985)

Zartik Parkim (Awake my Glory) - Hovhaness, Alan

Zauberspiegel - Lorentzen, Bent (1998)

Zauberspiegel-Suite; Weihnachtsmusik. Musik zu einem Märchenspiel, op.38 - Gál, Hans (1930)

Zeit Verschiebung - Schleiermacher, Steffen (1997)

Zeitfluren; Timescapes - Gruber, HK (2001)

Zenerva Sesio - Nordentoft, Anders (1992)

Zigeuner: From "Lieder und Gesänge" (3.Folge Nr.8) - Marx, Joseph (1911)

Zipangu - Vivier, Claude (1980)

Zone (...de azul) - Dillon, James Zoom and Zip - Kats-Chernin, Elena (1997)

Zoom; Figure and Ground Study III - Fundal, Karsten (1997)

Zwei Lieder, op.8 - Webern, Anton (1910)

Zwei Stücke (Two Pieces) - Müller-Siemens, Detlev (1977)

Zwei Türkische Orchesterstücke; Improvisation und zwei Tänze - Alnar, Hasan Ferit (1935)

Zwingerserenade - Schwaen, Kurt

Zwölftonspiel XVII (Twelve-tone game XVII) - Hauer, Josef Matthias

Arrangements by the
Verein für Musikalische Privataufführungen

In 1918, Arnold Schönberg and some fellow composers founded the *Verein für Musikalische Privat-aufführungen* (Society for Private Musical Performances) in Vienna, Austria. This circle included musicians like Hanns Eisler, Erwin Stein, and Schönberg's pupil Anton Webern.

Between 1918 and 1921, the *Verein* organized a number of concerts, mainly with the focus of performing the new compositions of its own members, but also including arrangements of other works that were created by its members. This way a large number of arrangements, mostly for piano solo or piano trio, were created.[1] Besides those soloistic or chamber music arrangements, a total of twenty-two arrangements for larger chamber ensembles were created.

The following is a listing of these arrangements created by the members of the *Verein*. Since many of these pieces would usually not be included in this catalog (because of the size of the ensemble or the date of composition), they are listed here in the appendix. These extraordinary arrangements will make a wonderful addition to any chamber orchestra concert and therefore deserve a place in this catalog. Surprisingly, these arrangements are largely unknown. I hope that their inclusion in this catalog will help to promote these works.

---

[1] See Metzger & Riehn, *Schönberg's Verein für Musikalische Privataufführungen. Musik Konzepte Heft 36* (München: Edition Text & Kritik, 1984).

Bruckner, Anton   (1824-1896)

Symphony No.7 (1883)   64'
  0 0 1 0 — 1 0 0 0 — 3kybd[pf 4hand.harm] —
  str[1.1.1.1.1]
  Arranged by Hanns Eisler (1st and 3rd movement),
  Erwin Stein (2nd movement) and Karl Rankl
  (4th movement).
  mvt durations: 20' 22' 10' 12'
  Breitkopf

Busoni, Ferruccio   (1866-1924)

Berceuse élégiaque, op.42 (1909)   10'
  1 0 1 0 — 0 0 0 0 — 2kybd[pf.harm] — str
  Arranged by Erwin Stein.
  Breitkopf

Debussy, Claude   (1862-1918)

Prélude à L'après-midi d'un faune   10'
(1894)
  1 1 1 0 — 0 0 0 0 — 1perc — 2kybd[pf.harm] —
  str[1.1.1.1.1]
  Arranged by Benno Sachs.
  Belmont
  Score and parts for sale available through UE.

Denza, Luigi   (1846-1922)

Funiculi, Funicula (1880)   3'
  0 0 1 0 — 0 0 0 0 — gtr, mand — str[1.0.1.1.0]
  Arranged by Arnold Schönberg.
  Belmont
  Score and parts for sale available through UE.

Mahler, Gustav   (1860-1911)

Das Lied von der Erde (1909)   63'
  solo A and T
  1[1/pic] 1[1/eh] 1[1/Ebcl/bcl] 1 — 1 0 0 0 —
  2perc — 2kybd[pf.harm/cel] — str[1.1.1.1.1]
  perc: glsp, tri, cym, tam-tam, tambn, sd, bd
  Arranged by Arnold Schönberg and Anton Webern (1921).
  Completed by Rainer Riehn (1983).
  UE

Lieder eines fahrenden Gesellen (1896)   16'
  solo medium voice
  1 0 1 0 — 0 0 0 0 — 1perc — 2kybd[pf.harm] —
  str[1.1.1.1.1]
  Arranged by Arnold Schönberg and Erwin Stein.
  UE

Symphony No.4 (1901)   54'
  solo S
  1 1 2[1.bcl] 0 — 0 0 0 0 — 2perc —
  2kybd[harm/pf 4hand.pf/pf 4hand] — str[1.1.1.1.1]
  Arranged by Erwin Stein.
  Weinberger

Reger, Max   (1873-1916)

Concerto for Violin, op.101 (1908)   58'
  solo vl
  1 0 1 0 — 1 0 0 0 — 2kybd[pf.harm] —
  str[1.1.1.1.1]
  Arranged by Rudolf Kolisch and Hanns Eisler.
  mvt durations: 28' 16' 14'
  Kolisch

Eine Romantische Suite, op.125 (1912)   29'
  1 1 0 0 — 0 0 0 0 — 2kybd[pf.harm] —
  str[1.1.1.1.1]
  Arranged by Arnold Schönberg and Rudolf Kolisch.
  ASC

Schönberg, Arnold   (1874-1951)

Fünf Orchesterstücke, op.16 (1909)   16'
  1[1/pic] 1 1 1 — 1 0 0 0 — 2kybd[cel.harm] —
  str[1.1.1.1.1]
  Arranged by Felix Greissle.
  mvt durations: 2' 5' 3' 2' 4'
  Peters

Sechs Orchesterlieder, op.8 (1905)   23'
  solo high or medium voice
  1 1 1 1[opt] — 1[opt] 0 0 0 — 2kybd[pf.harm] —
  str[1.1.1.1.1]
  Arranged by Erwin Stein, Hanns Eisler and Klaus Simon.
  Contents - 1. Natur (Eisler); 2. Das Wappenschild (Stein);
  3. Sehnsucht (Simon); 4. Nie ward ich, Herrin, müd'
  (Simon); 5. Voll jener Süße (Stein); 6. Wenn Vöglein
  klagen (Simon)
  mvt durations: 4' 3' 2' 4' 5' 5'
  UE

Schubert, Franz   (1797-1828)

Ständchen, op.957, No.4 (1828)   3'
  0 0 1 1 — 0 0 0 0 — gtr, mand — str[1.1.1.1.0]
  Arranged by Arnold Schönberg.
  Belmont
  Score and parts for sale available through UE.

Sioly, Johann (1843-1911)

Weil I A Alter Drahrer Bin 1'

0 0 1 0 — 0 0 0 0 — gtr, mand — str[1.0.1.1.0]
Arranged by Arnold Schönberg in 1921.
Belmont
Score and parts for sale available through UE.

Strauß (Jr), Johann (1825-1899)

Kaiser Walzer, op.437 (1889) 10'

1 0 1 0 — 0 0 0 0 — pf — str[1.0.1.1.0]
Arranged by Arnold Schönberg.
Schott

Lagunenwalzer, op.411 (1883) 8'

2kybd[pf.harm] — str[1.1.1.1.0]
Arranged by Arnold Schönberg in 1921.
Belmont
Score and parts for sale available through UE.

Rosen aus dem Süden, op.338 7'
(1880)

2kybd[pf.harm] — str[1.1.1.1.0]
Arranged by Arnold Schönberg.
Belmont
Score and parts for sale available through UE.

Schatzwalzer, op.418 (1885) 9'

2kybd[pf.harm] — str[1.1.1.1.0]
Arranged by Anton Webern.
Staatsbibliothek

Wein, Weib und Gesang, op.333 7'
(1869)

2kybd[pf.harm] — str[1.1.1.1.0]
Arranged by Alban Berg.
Staatsbibilothek

Webern, Anton (1883-1945)

Orchesterstücke, op.6 (1909) 13'

1 1 1 0 — 0 0 0 0 — 3perc — 2kybd[pf.harm] —
str[1.1.1.1.1]
Arranged by the composer.
mvt durations: 1' 2' 1' 4' 3' 2'
UE

Zemlinsky, Alexander (1871-1942)

23. Psalm, op.14 (1910) 10'
solo 2 S, 2 A, 2 T, 2 B
1 1 1 1 — 1 0 0 0 — 1perc — 2kybd[pf.harm] —
str[1.1.1.1.1]
Arranged by Erwin Stein.
UE

Das Mädchen mit den verbundenen 3'
Augen, From "Maeterlincklieder"
op.13, No.2 (1910)
solo medium voice
1 0 1 0 — 0 0 0 0 — 2kybd[pf.harm] —
str[1.1.1.1.1]
Arranged by Erwin Stein.
UE

Und kehrt er einst heim, From 3'
"Maeterlincklieder" op.13, No.5 (1914)
solo medium voice
1 0 1 0 — 0 0 0 0 — 2kybd[pf.harm] —
str[1.1.1.1.1]
Arranged by Erwin Stein.
UE

PUBLISHERS

The shortened version of the name on the left is used throughout the main part of this book to indicate the publisher. On the right you will find the available contact information. Since the publishing business moves extremely fast and company changes appear very frequently, some of this information will change continuously. For the latest information I recommend contacting one of the following two organizations:

Major Orchestra Librarians' Association (MOLA)
A constantly updated list of publishers can
be found on: www.mola-inc.org
Click on *Resources*, then on *PAD*
(Publishers, Agencies and Dealers)

Music Publishers' Association
243 5th Avenue, Suite 236
New York, NY 10016
www.mpa.org
admin@mpa.org

ACA
American Composers Alliance
802 W. 109th Street, 1st Floor
New York, NY 10040
USA
Tel: 212-925-0458
Fax: 212-925-6798
www.composers.com
info@composers.com

Alfred
Alfred Publishing Company
P. O. Box 10003
Van Nuys, CA 91410
USA
Tel: 818-891-5999
Fax: 800-632-1928
www.alfred.com
sales@alfred.com

Alhambra
Alhambra RXR
see: Schirmer

AME
American Music Edition
see: Presser

AMP
Associated Music Publishers
see: Schirmer (rentals) or Hal Leonard (sales)

Amphion
see: Ricordi

A-R Editions	A-R Editions, Inc. 8551 Research Way, Suite 180 Middleton, WI 53562 USA Tel: 608-836-9000 Fax: 608-831-8200 www.areditions.com info@areditions.com
ASC	Arnold Schönberg Center Palais Fanto Schwarzenbergplatz 6 Vienna, 1030 Austria Tel: +43 (0) 1 712 18 88 88 Fax: +43 (0) 1 712 18 88 88 www.schoenberg.at office@schoenberg.at
Augener	Augener, Ltd. see: ECS
B&S	Boccaccini e Spada Edizioni Musicali Via Arezzo 17 Rome, 00040 Italy Tel: +39 (0) 6 9310 217 Fax: +39 (0) 6 9311 903 www.boccacciniespada.com
Bärenreiter	Bärenreiter Verlag Heinrich Schütz Allee 35 Kassel, 34131 Germany Tel: +49 (0) 561 3105-0 Fax: +49 (0) 561 3105-240 www.baerenreiter.com info@baerenreiter.com
Barry	Barry Editorial Talcahuano 638 Planta Baja H Buenos Aires, C1013AAN Argentina Tel: +54 (0)11 4371 1313 Fax: +54 (0)11 4383 0745 www.barryeditorial.com.ar contacto@barryeditorial.com.ar U.S. Agent: Boosey & Hawkes

Belaieff	M. P. Belaieff see: Peters
Belmont	Belmont Music Publishers P. O. Box 231 1221 Bienveneda Avenue Pacific Palisades, CA 90272 USA Tel: 310-454-1867 Fax: 310-573-1925 www.schoenbergmusic.com office@schoenbergmusic.com Music of Arnold Schönberg.
Belwin	CPP / Belwin see: Alfred U.S. Agent: EAM (rentals), Alfred (sales)
Bèrben	Bèrben Edizioni Musicali Via Redipuglia 65 Ancona, 60122 Italy Tel: +33 (0) 71 2044 28 Fax: +33 (0) 71 57414 www.berben.it info@berben.it
Billaudot	Editions Gerard Billaudot 14 Rue de l'Echiquier Paris, 75010 France Tel: +33 (1) 4770 1446 Fax: +33 (0) 1 4523 2254 www.billaudot.com info@billaudot.com U.S. Agent: Presser
Birchard	C. C. Birchard see: EAM (rentals), Alfred (sales)
BKJ	BKJ Publications P. O. Box 610377 Newton Highlands, MA 02161 USA Tel: 617-965-9788 www.gasilvis.net/jb.htm Music of John Bavicchi.

Boelke	Boelke-Bomart / Mobart Music Publishers c/o Music Associates of America 224 King Street Englewood, NJ 07631 USA Tel: 201-569-2898 Fax: 201-569-7023 www.musicassociatesofamerica.com maasturm@sprynet.com
Boelter	Karl Boelter School of Music SUNY Fredonia Fredonia, NY 14163 USA Tel: 716-673-3151 Fax: 716-673-3154 Karl.Boelter@fredonia.edu U.S. Agent: Fleisher
Boosey & Hawkes	Boosey & Hawkes, Inc. 35 E. 21st Street New York, NY 10010 USA Tel: 212-358-5300 Fax: 212-358-5307 www.boosey.com usrental@boosey.com
Bosworth	Bosworth see: Shawnee
Bote & Bock	Bote & Bock, GmbH & Co. Lützowufer 26 Berlin, 10787 Germany Tel: +49 (0) 30 2500 1300 Fax: +49 (0) 30 2500 1399 www.boosey.com musikverlag@boosey.com U.S. Agent: Boosey & Hawkes
Breitkopf	Breitkopf & Härtel Walkmühlstrasse 52 Wiesbaden, 65195 Germany Tel: +49 (0) 611 45008-0 Fax: +49 (0) 611 45008-5961 www.breitkopf.com info@breitkopf.com U.S. Agent: Schirmer (rentals)

Broude Bros.	Broude Bros., Ltd. 141 White Oaks Road Williamstown, MA 01267 USA Tel: 800-225-3197 www.broude.us broude@broude.us
Carlanita	Carlanita Music Company U.S. Agent: Schirmer (rentals), Hal Leonard (sales) Music of Carlos Chavez.
CFE	Composers Facsimile Edition see: ACA
Chester Novello	Chester Novello 14-15 Berners Street London, W1T 3LJ England Tel: +44 (0) 20 7612 7400 Fax: +44 (0) 20 7612 7545 www.chesternovello.com promotion@musicsales.co.uk U.S. Agent: Schirmer (rentals), Hal Leonard (sales)
Coleman	Coleman Creative Services 1220 31st Street, Suite 1 Des Moines, IA 50311 USA Tel: 515-255-4543 Fax: 515-277-6814 www.lindarobbinscoleman.com lindarobbinscoleman@mac.com Music of Linda Robbins Coleman.
Consort	Consort Press 1225 S. Rice Road #41 Ojai, CA 93023 USA Tel: 805-646-4779 www.consortpress.com office@consortpress.com Music by John Biggs.
Cotton	Jeffrey Cotton Music Wired Musician, Inc. 1329 Tasker Street Philadelphia, PA 19148 USA Tel: 215-589-3191 www.wiredmusician.net OR www.jefferycotton.com library@jefferycotton.net Music by Jeffery Cotton.

Dantalian	Dantalian, Inc. 11 Pembroke Street Newton, MA 02458 USA Tel: 617-244-7230 Fax: 617-244-7230 www.dantalia.com dantinfo@dantalian.com Music of Donald Martino.
De Haske	De Haske GmbH P. O. Box 60 Hagendorn, 6332 Switzerland Tel: +41 (0)41 7843 084 Fax: +41 (0)41 7843 080 www.dehaske.com sales@dehaske.com
Donemus	Donemus Music Center The Netherlands Rokin 111 Amsterdam, 1012 KN Netherlands Tel: +31 (0)20 344 6000 Fax: +31 (0)20 673 3588 www.donemus.nl info@mcn.nl U.S. Agent: Presser
Dunvagen	Dunvagen Music Publishers, Inc. 632 Broadway, Suite 802 New York, NY 10012 USA Tel: 212-979-2080 www.dunvagen.com info@dunvagen.com U.S. Agent: Schirmer Music of Philip Glass.
Durand	Durand Editions Musicales, Inc. 16 Rue des Fossés Saint-Jacques Paris, 75005 France Tel: +33 (0)1 4441 5090 Fax: +33 (0)1 4441 5091 www.durand-salabert-eschig.com U.S. Agent: Boosey & Hawkes (rentals), Hal Leonard (sales)

EAM	European American Music Distributors LLC 254 West 31st Street, Floor 15 New York, NY 10001 USA Tel: 212-461-6940 Fax: 212-810-4565 www.eamdllc.com info@eamdllc.com U.S. Agent: EAM (rentals), Alfred (sales)
ECFAM	Edward Collins Fund for American Music c/o Jon Becker P. O. Box 3292 Madison, WI 53704 USA Tel: 877-223-8068 www.ecfam.com consultant@ecfam.com Music of Edward Collins.
ECS	ECS Publishing 138 Ipswich Street Boston, MA 02215 USA Tel: 617-236-1935 Fax: 617-236-0261 www.ecspublishing.com office@ecspub.com
Edition Dania	Edition Dania see: Fleisher
EDY	Editions Doberman Yppan C. P. 2021 Saint-Nicolas, Québec, G7A 4X5 Canada Tel: 418-831-1304 Fax: 418-836-3645 www.dobermaneditions.com doberman.yppan@videotron.ca
Elkan-Vogel	Elkan-Vogel, Inc. see: Presser
EMI	EMI Music Publishing 810 Seventh Avenue, 36th Floor New York, NY 10019 USA Tel: 212-830-2000 Fax: 212-830-5196 www.emimusicpub.com U.S. Agent: Schirmer

EMT	Editions Musicales Transatlantiques 2 Passage de Crimee Paris, 75019 France Tel: +33 (0)1 4209 9770 Fax: +33 1 4209 9335 www.editions-transatlantiques.com U.S. Agent: Schirmer
Engstrøm	Engstrøm & Sodering Musikforlag Borgergade 17 Copenhagen, 1300 Denmark
Enoch & Cie	Enoch & Cie 193 Boulevard Pereire Paris, 75017 France Tel: +33 (0)1 4574 0172 Fax: +33 (0)1 4572 5753 www.editions-enoch.com contact@editions-enoch.com U.S. Agent: Schirmer
Eschig	Editions Max Eschig see: Durand
Eulenburg	Edition Eulenburg see: Schott
Faber	Faber Music, Ltd. 74-77 Great Russell Street London, WC1B 3DA England Tel: +44 (0)20 7908 5310 Fax: +44 (0)20 7908 5339 www.fabermusic.com information@fabermusic.com U.S. Agent: Schott/EAM
Fennica Gehrman	Fennica Gehrman P. O. Box 158 Helsinki, 00121 Finland Tel: +358 (0)10 387 1222 Fax: +358 (0)10 387 1221 www.fennicagehrman.fi info@fennicagehrman.fi U.S. Agent: Boosey & Hawkes

Fischer (C.)

Carl Fischer, Inc.
65 Bleecker Street, 8th Floor
New York, NY 10012
USA
Tel: 212-777-0900
Fax: 212-477-6996
www.carlfischer.com
cf-info@carlfischer.com
U.S. Agent: Presser

Fischer (J.)

J. Fischer
see: Alfred

Fleisher

Edwin A. Fleisher Collection
FreeLibrary of Philadelphia
1901 Vine Street
Philadelphia, PA 19103
USA
Tel: 215-686-5322
www.library.phila.gov

Gehrmans

Carl Gehrmans Musikförlag
Box 42026
Stockholm, 12612
Sweden
Tel: +46 (0)8 6100 610
Fax: +46 (0)8 6100 J49627
www.gehrmans.se
info@gehrmans.se
U.S. Agent: Boosey & Hawkes

GunMar

Margun Music / GunMar Music
see: Shawnee

Hal Leonard

Hal Leonard Publishing Corp.
P. O. Box 13819
7777 W. Bluemound Road
Milwaukee, WI 53213
USA
Tel: 646-562-5880
www.halleonard.com
halinfo@halleonard.com

Hamelle

Hamelle & Cie
see: Leduc
U.S. Agent: King

Hansen	Edition Wilhelm Hansen
	Bornholmsgade 1
	Copenhagen, 1266
	Denmark
	Tel: +45 33 1178 88
	Fax: +45 33 1481 78
	www.ewh.dk
	ewh@ewh.dk
	U.S. Agent: Schirmer
Happy Lemon	Happy Lemon Music Publishing
	6808 Old Harford Road
	Baltimore, MD 21234
	USA
	www.happylemonmusicpublishing.com
	info@karenamrhein.com
	Music of Karen Amrhein.
Harmonia	Harmonia BV
	see: De Haske
Hendon	Hendon Music, Inc.
	see: Boosey & Hawkes
Heugel	Heugel & Cie.
	see: King
Hildegard	Hildegard Publishing Company
	P. O. Box 18860
	Mount Airy, PA 19119
	USA
	Tel: 610-667-8634
	Fax: 215-359-0654
	www.hildegard.com
	mail@hildegard.com
	U.S. Agent: Presser
Holab	Bill Holab Music
	377 Sterling Place, No.4
	Brooklyn, NY 11238
	USA
	Tel: 718-499-3946
	Fax: 718-228-8085
	www.billholabmusic.com
	bill@holabmusic.com

Hug   Hug & Co. Musikverlage
                                 Limmatquai 28-30
                                 Zürich, 8001
                                 Switzerland
                                 Tel: +41 (0)44 269 4141
                                 Fax: +41 (0)44 269 4101
                                 www.hug-musikverlage.ch
                                 info.zuerich@musikhug.ch
                                 U.S. Agent: EAM

IMI   Israel Music Institute
                                 P. O. Box 51197
                                 Tel Aviv, 67138
                                 Israel
                                 Tel: +972 (0)3 624 7095
                                 Fax: +972 (0)3 561 2826
                                 www.imi.org.il
                                 musicinst@bezeqint.net
                                 U.S. Agent: Presser

Jobert   Editions Jobert
                                 see: Lemoine

Kahnt   C. F. Kahnt Musikverlag
                                 see: Peters

Kallisti   Kallisti Music Press
                                 810 S. Saint Bernard Street
                                 Philadelphia, PA 19143
                                 USA
                                 Tel: 215-724-6511
                                 www.kallistimusic.com

Kalmus   Edwin F. Kalmus & Co., Inc.
                                 P. O. Box 5011
                                 Boca Raton, FL 33431
                                 USA
                                 Tel: 800-434-6340
                                 Fax: 561-241-6347
                                 www.kalmus-music.com
                                 info@kalmus-music.com

King   Robert King Music Co.
                                 140 Main Street
                                 North Easton, MA 02356
                                 USA
                                 Fax: 508-238-2571
                                 www.rkingmusic.com
                                 commerce@rkingmusic.com

Kistner & Siegel	Kistner & Siegel Musikverlag Uhlstrasse 82-84 Brühl, 50321 Germany Tel: +49 (0)2232 9494 240 Fax: +49 (0)2232 9494 219 www.kistnerundsiegel.de info@kistnerundsiegel.de
Leduc	Alphonse Leduc 175 Rue St. Honore Paris, 75040 France Tel: +33 (0)1 4296 8911 Fax: +33 (0)1 4286 0283 www.alphonseleduc.com alphonseleduc@wanadoo.fr U.S. Agent: King
Lemoine	Editions Henry Lemoine 27 Boulevard Beaumarchais Paris, 75004 France Tel: +33 (0)1 5668 8665 Fax: +33 (0)1 5668 9066 www.henry-lemoine.com info@henry-lemoine.com
Lengnick	Alfred Lengnick & Co. see: Ricordi (UK)
Liben	Liben Music Publishers 1191 Eversole Road Cincinnati, OH 45230 USA Tel: 513-232-6920 Fax: 513-232-1866 www.liben.com info@liben.com Music of Frank Proto
LKMP	Lauren Keiser Music Publishing 12685 Dorsett Rd., #331 Maryland Heights, MO 63043 USA Tel: 203-560-9436 Fax: 314-270-5305 www.laurenkeisermusic.com info@laurenkeisermusic.com

Luck's

Luck's Music Library
32300 Edward
P. O. Box 71397
Madison Heights, MI 48071
USA
Tel: 800-348-8749
Fax: 248-583-1114
www.lucksmusic.com
sales@lucksmusic.com

Malcolm

Malcolm Music, Ltd.
see: Shawnee

Margun

Margun Music / GunMar Music
see: Hal Leonard

Marks

Edward B. Marks Music Co.
126 East 38th Street
New York, NY 10016
USA
Tel: 212-779-7977
Fax: 212-779-7920
www.ebmarks.com
ehause@carlinamerica.com
U.S. Agent: Presser (rentals), Hal Leonard (sales)

MCA

MCA Music Publishing
1755 Broadway, 8th Floor
New York, NY 10019
USA
Tel: 212-841-8000
Fax: 212-582-7340
U.S. Agent: EAM (rentals), Hal Leonard (sales)

Mercury

Mercury Music
see: Presser

Merion

Merion Music, Inc.
see: Presser

MMB

MMB Music
see: LKMP

Moeck

Moeck Musik
P. O. Box 3131
Celle, 29231
Germany
Tel: +49 (0)5141 8853 0
Fax: +49 (0)5141 8853 42
www.moeck.com
info@moeck.com
U.S. Agent: EAM

MPH	Musikproduktion Jürgen Höflich Enhuberstrasse 6-8 München, 80333 Germany Tel: +49 (0)89 5220 81 Fax: +49 (0)89 5254 11 www.musikmph.de hoeflich@musikmph.de
Nona Music	Nona Music 310 Gershwin Dr. Sarasota, FL 34237 USA www.nonamusic.com nona@nonamusic.com Music of Gil Katz.
Nordiska	Nordiska Musikförlaget St. Eriksgatan 58 Stockholm, 11234 Sweden Tel: +46 (0)8 650 1313 Fax: +46 (0)8 650 1919 U.S. Agent: Schirmer
Norsk	Norsk Musikforlag A/S P. O. Box 1499 Vika Oslo, 0116 Norway Tel: +47 (0) 2300 2010 Fax: +47 (0) 2300 2011 www.norskmusikforlag.no order@musikforlaget.no
Novello	Novello & Co. see: Chester Novello
Oxford	Oxford University Press 198 Madison Avenue New York, NY 10016 USA Tel: 212-726-6000 Fax: 212-726-6441 www.oup.com musicrental.us@oup.com

Paterson	Paterson's Publications see: Chester Novello
Peer	Peermusic Classical 250 West 57th Street, Suite 820 New York, NY 10107 USA Tel: 212-265-3910 ex.17 Fax: 212-489-2465 www.peermusicclassical.com peerclassical@peermusic.com U.S. Agent: Presser
Peters	Edition Peters 70-30 80th Street Glendale, NY 11385 USA Tel: 718-416-7800 Fax: 718-416-7805 www.edition-peters.com info@edition-peters.com
Piedmont	Piedmont Music Co. see: Presser
Presser	Theodore Presser Company 588 North Gulph Road King of Prussia, PA 19406 USA Tel: 610-592-1222 Fax: 610-592-1229 www.presser.com sales@presser.com
Pro Musica	Pro Musica Musikverlag Riebeckstrasse 26 Leipzig, 04317 Germany Tel: +49 (0)341 2615 066
PWM	Polskie Wydawnictwo Muzyczne Al. Krasinskiego 11A Krakow, 31-111 Poland Tel: +48 (0)12 422 7044 Fax: +48 (0)12 422 0174 www.pwm.com.pl pwm@pwm.com.pl U.S. Agent: Presser, Boosey & Hawkes

Red Poppy	Red Poppy see: Schirmer
Ricordi	G. Ricordi & Co. Via Liguria 4, fr. Sesta Ulteriano S. Giuliano Milanese, 20098 Italy Tel: +39 (0)2 98813 4220 Fax: +39 (0)2 98813 4258 www.ricordi.it rental.ricordi@umusic.com U.S. Agent: Boosey & Hawkes (rentals), Hal Leonard (sales)
Ricordi (UK)	G. Ricordi & Co. (London) Ltd. 20 Fulham Broadway London, SW6 1AH England Tel: +44 (0)20 7835 5380 Fax: +44 (0)20 7835 5384 www.ricordi.co.uk promotion.ricordi.london@umusic.com U.S. Agent: Hal Leonard
Rideau Rouge	Editions Rideau Rouge see: Hal Leonard
Ries & Erler	Ries & Erler Musikverlag Wandalenallee 8 Berlin, 14052 Germany Tel: +49 (0)30 825 1049 Fax: +49 (0)30 825 9721 www.rieserler.de verlag@rieserler.de U.S. Agent: Fischer (C.)
Russian	Russian Author's Society Bolshaya Bronnaya Str. 6a Moscow, 123995 Russia Tel: +495 697 45 99 Fax: +495 609 93 63 www.rao.ru rao@rao.ru U.S. Agent: Schirmer
Salabert	Editions Salabert see: Durand

Schirmer	G. Schirmer, Inc. 257 Park Avenue South, 20th Floor New York, NY 10010 USA Tel: 212-254-2100 Fax: 212-254-2013 www.schirmer.com rental@schirmer.com
Schirmer (E.C.)	E. C. Schirmer Music Co. see: ECS
Schott	Schott Music GmbH & Co KG Weihergarten 5 Mainz, 55116 Germany Tel: +49 (0)6131 2460 Fax: +49 (0)6131 246 211 www.schott-music.com info@schott-music.com U.S. Agent: EAM
SchwartzWorks	SchwartzWorks Inc. 435 South Gulfstream Ave. Apt., 1008 Sarasota, FL 34236 USA
Seesaw	Seesaw see: Subito
Senart	Senart see: Durand
Shawnee	Shawnee Press, Inc. 421 E. Iris, Suite 202 Nashville, TN 37204 USA Tel: 800-962-8584 Fax: 800-971-4310 www.shawneepress.com info@shawneepress.com U.S. Agent: Schirmer
Sikorski	Hans Sikorski Internationale Musikverlage Johnsallee 23 Hamburg, 20148 Germany Tel: +49 (0)40 4141 000 Fax: +49 (0)40 4141 0041 www.sikorski.de contact@sikorski.de U.S. Agent: Schirmer (rentals), Hal Leonard (sales)

Simrock	Ahn & Simrock Deichstrasse 9 Hamburg, 20459 Germany Tel: +49 (0)40 300 66 780 Fax: +49 (0)40 300 66 789 www.ahnundsimrockverlag.de lv@ahnundsimrockverlag.de U.S. Agent: Boosey & Hawkes (rentals), Hal Leonard (sales)
Sonzogno	Casa Musicale Sonzogno Via Bigli 11 Milano, 20121 Italy Tel: +39 (0)2 7600 0065 Fax: +39 (0)2 7601 4512 www.sonzogno.it sonzogno@sonzogno.it U.S. Agent: Presser
Staatsbibliothek	Staatsbibliothek zu Berlin - Preußischer Kulturbesitz Unter den Linden 8 Berlin, 10117 Germany Tel: +49 (0)30 266 435201 Fax: +49 (0)30 266 335201 www.staatsbibliothek-berlin.de musikabt@sbb.sbk-berlin.de
Stainer & Bell	Stainer & Bell, Ltd. P. O. Box 110 Victoria House 23 Gruneisen Road London, N3 1DZ England Tel: +44 (0)20 8343 2535 Fax: +44 (0)20 8343 3024 www.stainer.co.uk post@stainer.co.uk U.S. Agent: ECS
Stone Circle Music	Stone Circle Music 1693 Ashland Avenue Saint Paul, MN 55104 USA Tel: 651-644-4700 www.steveheitzeg.com steve@steveheitzeg.com Music of Steve Heitzeg.

Subito	Subito Music Corp. 60 Depot Street Verona, NJ 07044 USA Tel: 973-857-3440 Fax: 973-857-3442 www.subitomusic.com mail@subitomusic.com
Tonger	P. J. Tonger Musikverlag Hald-und-Neu-Strasse 18 Karlsruhe, 76131 Germany Tel: +49 (0)721 6268 566 Fax: +49 (0)221 9355 650 www.tonger.de info@tonger.de
Tonos	Tonos Musik GmbH Bertholdstraße 6 Baden-Baden, 76530 Germany Tel: +49 (0)7221 97370 0 Fax: +49 (0)7221 97370 27 www.tonosmusic.com mail@tonosmusic.com
Tritó	Tritó Av. de la Catedral 3 Barcelona, 08002 Spain Tel: +34 (0)93 342 6175 Fax: +34 (0)93 302 2670 www.trito.es info@trito.es
UE	Universal Edition AG Karlsplatz 6 Wien, 1010 Austria Tel: +43 (0)1 33723 0 Fax: +43 (0)1 33723 400 www.universaledition.com office@universaledition.com U.S. Agent: EAM (rentals), Presser (sales)
Unión	Unión Musical Ediciones Marques de la Ensenada 4, 3 Madrid, 28004 Spain U.S. Agent: Schirmer

United	United Music Publishers, Ltd. 33 Lea Road Waltham Abbey Essex, EN9 1ES England Tel: +44 (0)1992 703110 Fax: +44 (0)1992 703189 www.ump.co.uk info@ump.co.uk
VAAP	VAAP see: Russian
Vieweg	Chr. Friedrich Vieweg Musikverlag Nibelungenstrasse 48 München, 80639 Germany U.S. Agent: Schirmer
Warner	Warner / Chappell Music, Inc. 105858 Santa Monica Boulevard Los Angeles, CA 90025 USA Tel: 310-441-8600 Fax: 310-441-8780 www.warnerchappell.com U.S. Agent: EAM (rentals), Alfred (sales)
Weinberger	Josef Weinberger Musikverlag Neulerchenfelderstrasse 3-7 Wien, 1160 Austria Tel: +43 (0)1 403 5991 Fax: +43 (0)1 403 5991 13 www.weinberger.co.at office@weinberger.co.at
Weintraub	Weintraub Music Co. see: Schirmer
Witmark	Tams-Witmark Music Library, Inc. 560 Lexington Avenue New York, NY 10022 USA Tel: 212-688-9191 Fax: 212-688-5656 www.tams-witmark.com

Zerboni   Edizioni Suvini Zerboni
                               Galleria del Corso 4
                               20122 Milano
                               Italy
                               Tel: +39 (0)2 7707 01
                               Fax: +39 (0)2 7707 0261
                               www.esz.it
                               suvini.zerboni@sugarmusic.com

Zimmermann   Musikverlag Zimmermann
                               Strubbergstrasse 80
                               Frankfurt, 60459
                               Germany
                               Tel: +49 (0)69 9782 866
                               Fax: +49 (0) 69 9782 8679
                               www.zimmermann-frankfurt.de
                               info@zimmermann-frankfurt.de

zOaR   zOaR Music
                               206 East 7th Street, No.14
                               New York, NY 10009
                               USA
                               info@elliotsharp.com
                               Music of Elliot Sharp.

RESOURCES

BOOKS

Daniels, David
Orchestral Music: A Handbook. Fourth Edition
Lanham, MD: Scarecrow Press, 2005

Metzger, Heinz Klaus (Ed.) & Riehn, Rainer (Ed.)
Schönberg's Verein für Musikalische Privataufführungen. Musik Konzepte Heft 36
München: Edition Text & Kritik, 1984

Saltonstall, Cecilia Drinker
Catalog of Music for Small Orchestra
Washington, DC: Music Library Assn., 1947

Saltonstall, Cecilia Drinker
A New Catalogue of Music for Small Orchestra
Stratham, 1981

Scott, William
A Conductor's Repertory of Chamber Music for Nine to Fifteen Solo Instruments
Westport, CT: Greenwood Press, 1993

WEBSITES

www.artofthestates.org
The Art of the States website features American composers and performers. It offers a wealth of information about modern American music and also gives access to full length recordings of several compositions.

http://brahms.ircam.fr
Base de Documentation sur la Musique Contemporaine. Huge database of modern composers. (French only)

www.compositiontoday.com
A website for new music and contemporary composers.

www.cs.vu.nl/~rutger/vuko/nl/lijst_van_ooit/
A list of chamber orchestra repertoire provided by the Dutch VU-Kamerorkest.

www.ircam.fr
Website of the Institut de Recherche et Coordination Acoustique/Musique at the Centre Pompidou in Paris.

www.musikrat.de/index.php?id=5543
Offers information and recordings of a large number of contemporary German composers. (German only)

www.musiquecontemporaine.fr
The French gateway to contemporary music. Offers access to a wealth of documents, videos and audio files, all about contemporary music.

www.modern-sounds.com
Links to audio files and audio excerpts of contemporary music.

www.wnyc.org
New York City Public Radio. In the *Listen* box click on Q2 to listen to an all New Music radio station.

www.pytheasmusic.org
Pytheas Center for Contemporary Music. A great resource to research modern composers and their works.

www.schoenberg.at
Website of the Arnold Schönberg Center in Vienna. An amazing resource for Schönberg's music and the music of his time.

www.sequenza21.com
A blog devoted to new music.

ABOUT THE AUTHOR

German conductor **Dirk Meyer** moved to the United States in 2002. He acquired both a Masters of Music degree and a Doctor of Musical Arts degree in orchestral conducting from Michigan State University. He expanded his studies with teachers like Jorma Panula and Neeme Järvi.

Meyer currently holds conducting positions with the Sarasota Orchestra and the Sarasota Youth Orchestras in Florida. In addition, he has guest conducted numerous orchestras throughout the country, including the Florida Orchestra, the philharmonic orchestras of Orlando and Naples, as well as the Missouri and Traverse Symphony orchestras. Outside of the United States Meyer has appeared with orchestras in many countries, including Germany, Bulgaria, Estonia, the Czech Republic and South Africa.

He earned his Bachelor degrees in Music and Philosophy from the Folkwang Conservatory in Essen and the University Duisburg-Essen (Germany). He lives in Sarasota, Florida, with his wife, Jennifer, and their little Schnauzers, Nugget and Cosmo.

You can visit him on the web at www.dirkmeyer.eu

CPSIA information can be obtained at www.ICGtesting.com
Printed in the USA
BVOW09*0728030616

450530BV00002B/3/P